MW00559303

Financial Modeling
of the Equity
Market

THE FRANK J. FABOZZI SERIES

Financial Modeling
of the Equity Market

From CAPM to Cointegration

FRANK J. FABOZZI

SERGIO M. FOCARDI

PETTER N. KOLM

WILEY

John Wiley & Sons, Inc.

Published by John Wiley & Sons, Inc., Hoboken, New Jersey
Published simultaneously in Canada

For general information on our other products and services or for technical support, please contact our Customer Care Department within the United States at (800) 762-2974, outside the United States at (317) 572-3993 or fax (317) 572-4002.

Wiley also publishes its books in a variety of electronic formats. Some content that appears in print may not be available in electronic books. For more information about Wiley products, visit our web site at www.wiley.com.

ISBN-13 978-0-471-69900-2
ISBN-10 0-471-69900-4

Printed in the United States of America

10 9 8 7 6 5 4 3 2 1

FJF
*To my wife Donna and my children,
Francesco, Patricia, and Karly*

SMF
*To the memory of Bertrand Russell to whom I owe
the foundation of my intellectual development*

PNK
To my best friend, my wife, and my love—Carmen

Contents

Preface

This book is about financial modeling for equity asset management. We take a broad view of financial modeling, encompassing pure modeling as well as model engineering and financial optimization. Our perspective is that of an asset management firm. When reasoning and making decisions about modeling, a firm needs to grasp all the aspects related to modeling. This includes not only the mathematical models per se but also methods for model estimation, the optimization process that translates model forecasts into active strategies, and methods that help mitigate eventual inadequacies of the models being used.

Our perspective is similar to that of physical engineering, where the knowledge of a few abstract laws of physics is a far cry from building an automobile or an airplane. We broadly define financial modeling as theoretical financial and mathematical principles as well as statistical methods that allow for representing and forecasting financial data, procedures for estimating and testing these representations, and methods for engineering and optimizing financial strategies. Without a methodology for engineering, estimating, and testing financial strategies, a financial model is of little use.

In this book we offer an up-to-date treatment of financial modeling for asset management, presenting and discussing a number of developments at the forefront of equity modeling technology: robust estimation, robust optimization, the analysis of transaction costs, linear and nonlinear dynamic models, and model risk mitigation techniques.

Since the downturn in the U.S. equity market in 2002, there has been an increased use of financial modeling and optimization in equity portfolio management. Under pressure to boost returns and reduce costs, asset management firms have begun to look with increasing attention at quantitative techniques. Not only has the diffusion of quantitative methods in equity portfolio management broadened since the turn of the century, but the variety of models and depth of use have also increased.

Three trends are worth pointing out. First, there is a greater use of predictive models. Predictive models assume that it is possible to make conditional forecasts of expected returns, an objective that was previously considered not achievable by classical financial theory. Second, in order to exploit forecasts, optimization techniques are now being used. Previously, optimization technologies were considered too brittle for safe deployment in asset management. Third, as a consequence of a greater use of predictive models and optimization, there is a growing interest in "robust" methods—particularly methods for robust estimation and robust optimization—as well as a heightened attention to the analysis of transaction costs.

Two technology trends have also facilitated the deployment of modeling in equity asset management. First, the continuous decrease in the cost of computers coupled with a parallel increase in computational power makes the necessary computing power affordable even to small firms. Second, statistical software packages now offer a broad variety of general and specialized econometric building blocks. The availability of these software packages proved to be a powerful enabler for the deployment of modeling.

The book is divided into four parts. In Part One we cover modern portfolio theory, numerical optimization methods, the analysis of transaction costs, and the handling of nonnormal distributions in portfolio allocation applications through the consideration of higher moments. We present important recent theoretical advances as well as the basic modeling techniques. In Part One these methods are applied in the classical one-period mean-variance and utility-maximization frameworks. This allows us to give an up-to-date treatment of modern portfolio theory and to explain new methods of analysis of transaction costs, numerical optimization, and the handling of higher moments in a unified and concrete framework.

In Part Two we introduce robust methodologies. As mentioned above, robust techniques have become fundamental in the practical deployment of modern portfolio theory. We discuss both the classical and more recent methods for forecasting expected return and risk. In particular, we address topics including dimensionality reduction and the robust estimation of the covariance matrix of returns. Part Two provides a comprehensive presentation of robust methodologies for estimation and optimization.

In Part Three we discuss the motivation for adopting predictive models and present several families of models. We begin with an analysis of the empirical evidence of feedbacks in financial markets. We then describe the statistical properties of models that allow to capture these feedbacks, including regressive and autoregressive models, state-space models, and nonlinear hidden variable, regime-switching models. We discuss cointegration and its many different representations, including dynamic factor analysis. We also elaborate on the process and the pitfalls of the model selection process.

In Part Four we discuss current methods for estimating dynamic models. We close with a discussion on how to mitigate model risk in a dynamic framework.

Two appendices provide complementary mathematical details for the interested reader. Appendix A discusses solutions of difference equations. Appendix B presents a number of mathematical facts on regressions, correlations, and copulas. In several chapters throughout the book we make use of the MSCI World Index and its individual constituents (country indices) in various illustrations. Appendix C provides some basic statistics and properties of this data set.

The purpose of this book is to serve as a working tool for practitioners who use financial modeling in their work and for students who are pursuing careers in finance. Since most of the subjects are advanced in nature, we have tried to offer an intuitive and simplified treatment of most mathematical topics, although at no time have we compromised mathematical rigor. When we feel the subject is too technical, we offer references to the original work. In summary, we feel the book should be of interest to practitioners, students, and researchers who need an updated and integrated view of equity modeling.

Frank J. Fabozzi
Sergio M. Focardi
Petter N. Kolm

Acknowledgments

In writing a book that covers a wide range of technical topics in financial modeling drawing from a wide range of fields in applied mathematics and financial econometrics, we were fortunate to have received comments from the following individuals:

- Rustam Ibragimov at Harvard University, Department of Economics, reviewed Chapters 2, 4, 5, 8, 9, 10, 11, 12, 14, 16, and Appendix B.
- Bernd Hanke of Goldman Sachs Asset Management reviewed Chapters 2, 3, 4, 5, and 7.
- Russell Fogler of Fogler Research and Management reviewed Chapter 3, 9, 12, 13, 16, and 17.
- Harry Farrell of TRG Management reviewed Chapters 2, 3, 4, 7, and 9.
- Dessislava Pachamanova of Babson College reviewed Chapters 6 and 9.
- Stan Beckers of KULeuven reviewed Chapters 5 and 7.
- Volker Ziemann of Edhec Risk and Asset Management Research Center reviewed Chapters 11 and 12.
- Yu Zhu of China Europe International Business School reviewed Chapters 2 and 4.
- Thomas Philips of OTA Asset Management reviewed Chapters 2 and 7.
- Donald Goldfarb and Garud Iyengar of Columbia University reviewed Chapter 9 and allowed us to use their illustration in that chapter.
- Eric Sorensen, Eddie Qian, and Ronald Hua of Panagora reviewed Chapters 4, 6, and 9.
- Jarrod Wilcox of Wilcox Investments reviewed Chapters 2 and 7.
- Jeff Miller of Millennium Partners reviewed Chapters 4 and 8.
- Massimo Guidolin, Senior Economist at the Federal Reserve Bank of St. Louis, reviewed Chapter 16.
- Sadayuki Ono of the University of York reviewed Chapter 16.
- Milan Borkovec and Ian Domowitz of ITG Inc. reviewed Chapter 3.
- John M. Manoyan of CYMALEX Advisors reviewed Chapter 6.
- Sebastian Ceria and Robert Stubbs of Axioma reviewed Chapter 9.
- Da-shan Huang of Kyoto University reviewed Chapters 6 and 9.

Reviews and editorial comments on the entire manuscript were made by Caroline Jonas of The Intertek Group and Carmen Manoyan.

We thank Morgan Stanley Capital International, Inc., http://www.msci.com, for providing us with the MSCI World Index dataset used in some of the examples throughout the book. In particular, we are indebted to Nicholas G. Keyes for preparing and for answering all our questions in regards to the dataset.

Our thanks go to Deepti Bathula for her assistance in preparing various computational illustrations in Parts One and Two of the book.

Megan Orem typeset the book and provided editorial assistance. We appreciate her patience and understanding in working through several revisions of the chapters and several reorganizations of the table of contents.

About the Authors

Frank J. Fabozzi is the Frederick Frank Adjunct Professor of Finance in the School of Management at Yale University. Prior to joining the Yale faculty, he was a Visiting Professor of Finance in the Sloan School at MIT. Frank is a Fellow of the International Center for Finance at Yale University and on the Advisory Council for the Department of Operations Research and Financial Engineering at Princeton University. He is the editor of *The Journal of Portfolio Management* and an associate editor of the *The Journal of Fixed Income*. He earned a doctorate in economics from the City University of New York in 1972. In 2002 Frank was inducted into the Fixed Income Analysts Society's Hall of Fame. He earned the designation of Chartered Financial Analyst and Certified Public Accountant. He has authored and edited numerous books in finance.

Sergio M. Focardi is a founding partner of the Paris-based consulting firm The Intertek Group. Sergio lectures at CINEF (Center for Interdisciplinary Research in Economics and Finance) at the University of Genoa and is a member of the Editorial Board of the *The Journal of Portfolio Management*. He has written numerous articles on econophysics and coauthored three books (*Modeling the Markets: New Theories and Techniques*; *Risk Management: Framework, Methods and Practice*; and, *The Mathematics of Financial Modeling and Investment Management*). Sergio holds a degree in Electronic Engineering from the University of Genoa and a postgraduate degree in Communications from the Galileo Ferraris Electrotechnical Institute (Turin).

Petter N. Kolm is a doctoral student in Finance at the School of Management, Yale University, and a financial consultant in New York City. Previously, he worked in the Quantitative Strategies Group at Goldman Sachs Asset Management where his responsibilities included researching and developing new quantitative investment strategies for the group's hedge fund. His current research interests include various topics in finance, such as equity and fixed income modeling, financial econometrics, risk management, and optimal portfolio strategies. Petter received a doctorate in mathematics from Yale University in 2000. He also holds an M.Phil. in applied mathematics from the Royal Institute of Technology in Stockholm and an M.S. in mathematics from ETH in Zürich.

CHAPTER 1

Introduction

Since the sharp stock market downturn in the United States in 2000, we have witnessed a progressive increase of the depth and breadth of financial modeling at many asset management firms. The need to reduce costs and to rely on a more predictable and repeatable business model were behind this change. This book discusses some of the major trends and innovations that characterize the modeling and selection of equity portfolios. It addresses the two major issues of modeling today: (1) the need to adopt increasingly sophisticated models to capture profit opportunities and (2) the need for robust and reliable solutions and methodologies, at the same time.

HISTORICAL PERSPECTIVE ON THE FINANCIAL MODELING OF THE EQUITY MARKET

Investment management as we know it today is a relatively recent discipline. Until the 18th century, wealth was essentially physical wealth associated with land ownership or privileges, such as the right to impose tariffs or exploit natural resources. Throughout the Middle Ages in Western Europe, lending money to realize a return was considered usury and condemned by the Church. Nevertheless, the same period saw the development of important international banks, such the Peruzzi and Bardi banks based in Florence. Interestingly enough, these banks were brought down when the English king Edward III defaulted completely on 1 million gold florins in loans in 1339.

The first exchange for trading financial contracts opened in Antwerp in the 16th century, but it was the opening of the stock exchange in Paris in 1720, followed by that in London in 1792, and New York in 1801 that ushered in the era of financial trading and investment as we know it today. Social, economic, and political developments were behind the change. The Industrial Revolution greatly accelerated the pace of the creation and destruction of capital and brought with it the need for continuous investment. While land was quite a permanent form of wealth, factories had to be built from scratch, required the continuous replacement of machinery, and lasted only a comparatively short period of time. The creation of a relatively stable and independent legal and social order, a development that took place in the 18th and 19th centuries, was also a powerful enabler of the creation of financial wealth.

Financial markets and their ability to create and destroy wealth fascinated people and created two opposing views of financial trading. On one hand, investing in financial assets was associated with gambling and speculation. Even a profoundly rational economic thinker like John Maynard Keynes had an essentially speculative view of financial markets, dominated, he believed, by the "animal spirit." Keynes himself was a successful investor. This view of investment as a form of gambling was reflected in the language. As recently as the 1970s, the French and Italian expressions for investing in stocks were respectively "jouer à la Bourse" and "giocare in Borsa," that is, "gambling in the Exchanges."

On the other hand, there was the view that markets are perfectly rational, transparent vehicles that serve to channel savings to the most productive destinations. People were truly fascinated by the fact that the independent action of myriads of individual investors led to the discovery of the "true value" of a financial contract. This view led to concentrating analytical efforts on analyzing the financial status of companies. The monumental treatise of Graham and Dodd[1] on financial analysis is perhaps the most complete expression of this view; published in 1934, it has remained mandatory reading for financial analysts to this day.

In a sense, the development of modern investment management is the progressive blending of these two initially irreconcilable views. There are explanations for why it took so long to arrive at a reasonably comprehensive understanding of financial markets. It is perhaps useful to briefly follow this development as it will give us the opportunity to discuss the key components of financial modeling and quantitative techniques that were to progressively become a part of the investment management process.

We will briefly outline the technical and scientific aspects of this development, but it should be noted that broad cultural and social

---

[1] Benjamin Graham (1894–1976) is often called "the father of value investing." His book *Security Analysis*, written together with David Dodd and published in 1934 by McGraw-Hill, has been considered a bible for serious investors ever since its appearance.

issues were also at work. The latter profoundly influenced economic thinking. The 18th and 19th centuries witnessed the development of the concept of free markets. Markets are as old as civilization itself. Trade routes, such as the long-distance trade route connecting ancient Egypt to Afghanistan, were established as earlier as 2250 BCE. However, such exchanges did not give rise to a merchant class; they were fixed price affairs with the price regulated by temple or palace.[2] Following the collapse of the Roman Empire in the West, it was only toward the end of the Middle Ages that economic activity and trading resumed in full earnest in Europe. And it was only at the end of the 18th century in, for example, England and post-Revolutionary France, that the concept of a modern state with an independent and stable legal system began to develop.

This development brought rules that encouraged economic and entrepreneurial activity and with it, the creation of a new wealth, less dependent on privileges. In the 19th century these developments were associated with the idea of individual freedom. As a consequence, the virtues of free markets became an article of faith. This is reflected in the language of economics that opposes the idea of *perfect* markets to markets with *defects* and *imperfections*. To draw a parallel in physics, the notion of an idealized *perfect* gas was developed about at the same time but it would have been considered ludicrous to consider real gases as gases with defects and imperfections!

From the scientific point of view, the major obstacles to a better understanding of financial markets were:

- A need for the concepts and mathematics of probability and statistics and, more in general, of uncertainty (these developed only much later)
- A need to perform onerous computations, made possible only by the relatively recent development of high-performance computers

Any phenomenon related to human behavior is essentially uncertain. Because finance and economics are deeply influenced by human behavior and human decision-making processes, the development of a quantitative theory of finance depended critically on the development of a quantitative theory of uncertainty. This task was achieved in full earnest only with the recent development of probability theory. A logically rigorous formulation was first developed in the first three decades of the 20th century. Before this time, probability theory was plagued by internal contradictions that made its application problematic.

---

[2] For a snapshot of trading routes in Antiquity, see Colin McEvedy, *Penguin Atlas of Ancient History* (New York: Penguin Books, 1967).

When Louis Bachelier discussed his now famous thesis on the theory of speculation in Paris in 1900, he was in advance of his times. Bachelier introduced a number of concepts that were not understood in his time, such as Brownian motion to describe stock price behavior or arbitrage arguments to price options. Unfortunately for Bachelier, his reasoning was too economic to satisfy mathematicians and too mathematical to satisfy economists.[3] When Albert Einstein introduced Brownian motion in physics in 1905, five years after Bachelier had introduced the same concept in economics, Einstein's theory was hailed as a major scientific advance.

Economics had to wait until the second half of the 20th century to see probability theory accepted as a mainstream tool in financial analysis. Acceptance went through a slow process that progressively introduced probabilistic notions in the logical structure of economic theory. Only when probability theory was blended with the key economic concepts of supply and demand and with the theory of financial decision-making through the work of Arrow and Debreu did probabilistic reasoning become a mainstream tool for economists.[4] Despite this major step forward, the path to modern financial econometrics was still long and arduous.

Between 1950 and 1960, three major developments took place. First, in 1952 Harry Markowitz outlined the theory of investment as the maximization of a risk-return trade-off.[5] Second, assuming that investors behave as theorized by Markowitz, between 1962 and 1964, William Sharpe, John Lintner, and Jan Mossin introduced the first asset pricing theory, the *capital asset pricing model* (CAPM).[6] Third, in 1965 Fama and Samuelson introduced the concept of efficient financial markets together with the notion that "properly anticipated prices fluctuate randomly."[7] This idea had been introduced by Bachelier 65 years earlier,

---

[3] Despite his genial intuitions, Bachelier did not enjoy a successful academic career.

[4] Kenneth Arrow, "The Role of Securities in the Optimal Allocation of Risk Bearing," *Review of Economic Studies*, 31 (1963), pp. 91–96 and Gerard Debreu, *Theory of Value* (New Haven: Yale University Press, 1959).

[5] Harry M. Markowitz, "Portfolio Selection," *Journal of Finance* (March 1952), pp. 77–91. The principles in Markowitz's article were then expanded in his book *Portfolio Selection*, Cowles Foundation Monograph 16 (New York: John Wiley & Sons, 1959).

[6] William F. Sharpe, "Capital Asset Prices," *Journal of Finance* (September 1964), pp. 425–442, John Lintner, "The Valuation of Risk Assets and the Selection of Risky Investments in Stock Portfolio and Capital Budgets," *Review of Economics and Statistics* (February 1965), pp. 13–37, and Jan Mossin, "Equilibrium in a Capital Asset Market," *Econometrica* (October 1966), pp. 768–783.

[7] Paul A. Samuelson, "Proof that Properly Anticipated Prices Fluctuate Randomly," *Industrial Management Review* (Spring 1965), pp. 41–50, and Eugene F. Fama, "The Behavior of Stock Market Prices," *Journal of Business* (1965), pp. 34–105.

but Fama and Samuelson put the concept into a more general framework of how financial markets process information.

It was believed that the above major milestones in the development of modern asset management and financial econometrics entailed the following three key conclusions:

- Logarithms of prices can be represented as unpredictable multivariate random walks.
- Markets exhibit a risk-return trade-off, where risk has to be computed taking into account correlations between stocks.
- There is no possibility of earning an excess returns in the sense that any return in excess of the risk-free rate offered by a risky security is determined by the risk-return relationship of the market for that risk.

These conclusions were enormously important for the asset management community. The ensuing debate focused on two issues:

- The predictability versus the nonpredictability of asset prices
- The paradox introduced by the concepts that (1) markets are efficient because investors can anticipate prices, but (2) investing resources in acquiring the ability to anticipate prices is futile as it does not bring any reward.

It was argued that if prices are not predictable, it was difficult to justify the asset management industry: it would simply not make sense to pay manager fees to obtain returns that could be obtained through a simple buy-and-hold strategy. For 14 years, between 1988 and 2002, the *Wall Street Journal* was to run a competition between experienced asset managers and pure random stock picking, personified by the random throwing of a dart. On average, professional managers realized an average 10.2% investment gain, while the darts managed just a 3.5% gain.[8]

The asset management community was split between those who claimed that regardless of the theory of efficient markets, a good manager could bring excess returns using intuition, judgment or information not available to other market participants, and those who maintained that because markets are efficient the best investment policy was buy-and-hold (i.e., passive). In hindsight we can say that the debate was ill-conceived. It was to slow down the development of a more scientific approach to asset management. Let us see why.

---

[8] Georgette Jasen, "Journal's Dartboard Retires After 14 Years of Stock Picks," *Wall Street Journal*, April 18, 2002.

Consider predictability. Technically, we call a process *predictable* if there is some dependence of future distributions (and therefore expected values) on past data. For example, a multivariate Gaussian random walk (see Chapter 7) is not predictable because conditional expected values of drifts and correlations are identical to the unconditional constant drifts and correlations. A lot of research was devoted to proving that, without overturning the notion of market efficiency, there might be subtle patterns that allow predictability. The theory of martingales was thus introduced in asset pricing theory.

All the reasoning about martingales and market efficiency is logically correct but misses one fundamental point: Any random walk model is an approximate model that is to this day very difficult to estimate. If we look at a random walk from the point of view of information, we see that a multivariate random walk conveys *a lot* of information in drifts and correlations. The random walk model of stock prices is, therefore, far from being uninformative.

The idea that no analysis was required to arrive at this model was a misconception, to say the least. Anyone who takes seriously the notion that markets reward risk cannot be indifferent to finding the optimal risk-return combination. This was the essential pragmatic teaching of Markowitz. But in the 1960s, approximate but robust estimates of drifts and correlation matrices were extremely difficult (not to say impossible) to obtain. The dispute over subtle patterns of predictability delayed the widespread acceptance of a much more fundamental paradigm of stable structures of risk and returns.

A 2000/2001 report on quantitative methods in investment management found that major asset management firms still believed that the key benefit of modeling was the discipline it brought to the investment process.[9] That is to say, the major benefit of quantitative methods was that it persuaded asset managers that the idea of risk-return optimization was real. This is more than half a century after Markowitz!

A preoccupation for logical details—even in the absence of insufficient empirical data—is a major difference between economics and the physical sciences. Physics and engineering never use more mathematics than strictly needed and make extensive use of data. The opposition of these views is illustrated by an anecdote reported at the beginning of Chapter 13 on model selection. When physicists of the Santa Fe Institute asked the economist Kenneth Arrow why economists use such sophisticated mathematics, Arrow reportedly answered that economists needed to use sophisticated mathematics precisely because of the scarcity of

---

[9] The Intertek Group four-part survey *Quantitative Methods in Asset Management*, September 2000/July 2001.

data. The assumption was that sophisticated mathematics would allow the absolute certainty of logical coherence.

Another, and perhaps even more important, point is that the theoretical assumption that logarithms of prices behave as multivariate random walks subject to risk-return constraints is a very strong assumption. Not only is the random walk hypothesis very far from being uninformative, it is actually a strong hypothesis on the structure of financial markets. In fact, the random walk hypothesis entails that drifts and volatility are time-invariant—a strong hypothesis. Should drifts and volatility vary with time, the random walk hypothesis would be at best an approximation. As we will see in Chapter 10, a simple econometric analysis shows that, over long time horizons, prices do not behave as time-invariant random walks.

Yet the debate on asset pricing continued to focus on the complicated details of martingale asset pricing, efficient versus inefficient markets, and so on, when it should have been clear that any time-invariant model of prices was untenable. At most, the random walk model could be only a temporarily valid approximation. Though the assumption of random walk behavior is difficult to reject for individual stock price processes, the assumption of multivariate random walk behavior is easy to reject.

The real problem is how to glean information from very noisy time series date. It was not fully realized that the assumption of absence of predictability cannot lead per se to a tenable theory of asset pricing. When combined with the assumption that risk is remunerated, these theoretical assumptions would imply the ability to capture a stable structure of drifts and volatilities that do not change with time. Such permanent structures do not exist in reality.

The last decade has witnessed a significant shift in financial econometrics. Academics have abandoned the preoccupation of staying within the basic paradigms of the nonpredictability of asset prices. It is clear by now that random walks are at best an approximation. If we estimate the parameters of a multivariate random walk from realistic price data, we obtain randomly varying quantities. Financial econometrics has abandoned the efforts to prove that they are meaningless and is now trying to extract information from these distributions. The aim of financial modeling is to provide the tools to extract this information and use it in a sound decision-making process. Our objective in this book is to explain and illustrate how this is done for the equity market.

CENTRAL THEMES OF THE BOOK

Three major lines of development have shaped modern financial econometrics and asset management theory. First, robust optimization and estimation. This line of development includes many advanced methods to optimize in a single- and multiperiod framework, estimate the correlation matrix, and mitigate model risk.

A second line of development is embodied in the quest for predictors. Predictors are variables of various natures such as economic quantities, financial ratios, or the lagged values of the same prices. These developments lead to the use of *Vector Autoregressive* (VAR) models and to strategies based on dynamic factorization and cointegration.

The third line of development attempts to represent states of the market using hidden variables. This approach leads to models such as Markov-switching models and GARCH models, whose interest resides essentially on their explanatory power. However, these techniques are data hungry and therefore difficult to deploy in practice.

The adoption of modeling techniques by asset management firms has greatly increased over the last five years. Models to predict expected returns are routinely used at major firms. In most cases, it is a question of relatively simple models based on factors or predictor variables. However, autoregressive models, cointegration and state-space models are also being used and experimented with. Nonlinear models such as neural networks and genetic algorithms are also being deployed, but a lack of transparency continues to hold back their wider diffusion in the industry.

In trying to address the question as to what techniques are actually being used in financial modeling, we will restrict our analysis to models of stock prices and returns, which is the subject of the book. We can reasonably state that financial modeling is presently characterized by three major challenges:

- The need to extract meaningful information from very noisy time series
- The need to make more robust both estimation and optimization
- The need to arrive at a sound decision-making process, possibly through formal optimization

As mentioned, today's financial econometrics is no longer deeply influenced by the debate on market efficiency and forecastability: it is now widely accepted that there is some forecastability in the market but that extracting this forecasting information is difficult. Forecastability is no longer considered a *market imperfection* but the natural result of the interaction of multiple interacting agents with different capabilities and motivations. At the same time it is clear that markets do not offer any easy profit opportunity; extracting profitability from markets requires hard work.

Modelers know that models can capture some true information, but they also know that models are only approximations of whatever true *data generation process* (DGP) might exist. In addition, models are subject to model risk. This means that models can lose their forecasting power if market conditions change. Gone are the heady days when techniques such as neural networks and genetic algorithms were expected to produce large excess returns. We are now moving towards a more industrial view of investment management with models as the industrial machine tools. Model risk mitigation techniques have become important.

On the technical side, we are seeing the diffusion of VAR and cointegration-based models. Factor analysis has been complemented by *dynamic* factor analysis. State-space models and regime switching models are also used with the aim of predicting expected return more faithfully than just taking the average of past returns. The reality of nonnormal distributions of asset returns is no longer questioned. The assumption of non-Gaussian distributions is particularly important for optimization and risk management. Non-Gaussian distributions enter modeling in different ways. A number of linear models assume nonnormal innovations while nonnormal models generate nonnormal variables from normal innovations.

The field of optimization has undergone important changes. The availability of low-cost high-performance computers makes optimization affordable to many organizations, while better forecasting models provide more reliable inputs. At the same time, progress in optimization techniques themselves has rendered the deployment of optimization techniques more reliable and more robust to use.

The aim of this book is to explain state-of-the-art techniques in equity modeling and asset management. Most techniques described herein are implemented in standard software packages either as finished applications or components. Portfolio managers and quantitative analysts do not have to code applications, but they do need to select models and set parameters, and interpret the results of simulations. This book provides the key tools and techniques.

ORGANIZATION OF THE BOOK

The book is organized as follows.

In Part One, we discuss the process of financial decision-making. In Chapter 2 we describe the classical mean-variance analysis and discuss the concepts of diversification and nondiversifiable risk. We describe the classical framework of mean-variance optimization, introduce the concepts of efficient sets and efficient frontiers, and discuss how to handle constraints such as long-only constraints.

In Chapter 3 we deal with the analysis of trading costs and optimization in executing trades—an important subject given that the diffusion of modeling techniques often results in increased trading volumes. In the chapter we introduce a taxonomy of trading costs and then discuss the market impact of trades. Different theories of market microstructure are introduced and quantitative models to evaluate the size of the market impact of trades are analyzed. We conclude the chapter with a discussion of how to incorporate trading costs in a portfolio management system.

In Chapter 4 we deal with the practical implementation of mean-variance portfolio optimization, beginning with a discussion of the question of portfolio rebalancing. Different approaches are discussed and illustrated with examples. We then analyze the various constraints that can be imposed in practice.

Chapter 5 discusses how to deal with nonnormal distributions, incorporating higher moments in portfolio management. We analyze in this chapter the behavior of a number of risk measures under different distributional assumptions. In particular, we discuss a coherent measure of risk known as *Conditional Value-at-Risk* (*CVaR*). We then go on to discuss the optimization framework with the expansion of utility functions. The mathematics of portfolio optimization with higher moments is introduced and polynomial goal programming discussed. A new approach to portfolio selection with higher moments proposed by Malevergne and Sornette is discussed and illustrated with examples.

The techniques of numerical optimization are the subject of Chapter 6. We discuss linear and quadratic programming and present the concepts of convex programming, conic optimization, and integer programming. We also explain how optimization algorithms work, illustrating the various techniques, from the simplex method to barrier and interior-point-methods. We close the chapter with a description of commercially available optimization software.

In Part Two, we present the classical framework of portfolio management and its practical application. Starting with Chapter 7, we introduce a number of price and return models that are used in portfolio management. In particular, we illustrate the different concepts of random walks and present their key properties. Random walks and trend-stationary processes are compared and a number of theoretical models of returns used within the classical framework are introduced.

The classical framework for portfolio management is based on the multivariate random walk model of logprices. The estimation of the vectors of drifts and of the covariance matrix are pivotal to this framework In Chapter 8 we illustrate methods for estimating expected returns and the covariance matrix. We introduce dimensionality reduction techniques such as factor models. Random matrix theory is used to illustrate just how noisy the covariance matrix really is.

In Chapter 9 we discuss methods for robust estimation and optimization. In addition to presenting averaging/shrinkage methods and the Black-Litterman approach, we discuss the portfolio resampling approach and the recently developed robust optimization techniques. Several of these approaches are illustrated with examples from portfolio management applications.

In Part Three, we cover linear dynamic models, cointegration, and Markov-switching models. In Chapter 10 we explain the need to introduce dynamic feedbacks in financial modeling. A number of tests of the random walk hypothesis are discussed. We argue that the hypothesis that stock prices evolve as a multivariate random walk together with the existence of risk premia lead to stock price models is not tenable in the long run. We discuss mean reversion and the concept of time diversification. We conclude that there are dynamic feedbacks in price processes and discuss the existence of return predictors.

Univariate models for stock prices and, in particular, ARMA models, are the topics we cover in Chapter 11. We begin by reviewing basic concepts in time series analysis, the condition of stationarity, the distinction between innovation and white noise. Using the results from difference equations in Appendix A, explicit solutions of autoregressive processes are presented. We end the chapter with a discussion of the concept of integrated processes.

Chapter 12 is devoted to multivariate models of stock prices. We present different forms of VAR models: stable VAR models, integrated VAR models, and *error-correction models* (ECM). We discuss the concepts of cointegration from different perspectives, including the existence of common trends, stationary linear combinations of integrated variables, and regression between integrated variables. ARDL models, hidden variable models—particularly state-space models—dynamic factor models, and Markov-switching models are all introduced. In the final section of the chapter we discuss explicit solutions of VAR models and their stochastic properties.

Model selection issues is the subject of Chapter 13. We make a distinction between the machine-learning and theoretical approaches to model selection, and present criteria for selecting model complexity. The relationship between model complexity and the size of data sample are discussed. We also address the problems of overfitting and data snooping. We conclude the chapter by outlining a methodology for model selection.

In Part Four we cover methods for estimating models and mitigating model risk. The concepts and techniques of estimation critical for estimating dynamic models are introduced in Chapter 14. In that chapter we discuss the basic concepts of estimators and their properties, the notion of sampling distribution, critical values, and confidence intervals. We then present the *Maximum Likelihood* (ML) and *Least Squares* (LS) estimation methods as well as the *Fisher Information matrix* and the *Cramer-Rao bound*. Finally, we go on to apply these concepts to linear regressions, showing the equivalence of ML and LS estimates for regressions, computing asymptotic distributions for estimators, and establishing key estimation formulas.

Methods for estimating linear dynamic models are the subject of Chapter 15. We begin by introducing estimation methods for stable VARs. These methods are a simple extension of estimation of regressions. We then discuss state-of-the-art methods for the estimation of cointegrated systems and conclude with a discussion of tests for determining the number of cointegrated relationships and common trends.

In Chapter 16 we introduce hidden variables models, beginning with a presentation of methods for linear state-space systems. We cover the Kalman filter and estimation methods based on ML estimates and the Subspace algorithms. We provide an illustration of estimation techniques for nonlinear Markov-switching models at the end of the chapter.

In the last chapter of the book, Chapter 17, we deal with model risk mitigation techniques. We start with by presenting Bayesian statistics and their application to the estimation of VAR models. Then we discuss successively averaging/shrinkage techniques and random coefficient model techniques. Before closing, we introduce the concepts of information theory, Shannon information, and symbolic dynamics, as well as various dynamic entropies used to gauge the predictability of time series in a model-free context.

There are three appendices to the book that handle certain mathematical concepts in more detail. In Appendix A we introduce the mathematics of difference equations and their explicit solutions. In Appendix B we introduce the concepts of correlation, regression, and copula functions. A description of the data used in illustrations in several of the chapters is provided in Appendix C.

Portfolio Allocation: Classical Theory and Modern Extensions

Mean-Variance Analysis and Modern Portfolio Theory

A major step in the direction of the quantitative management of portfolios was made by Harry Markowitz in his paper "Portfolio Selection" published in 1952 in the *Journal of Finance*. The ideas introduced in this article have come to build the foundations of what is now popularly referred to as *mean-variance analysis, mean-variance optimization,* and *Modern Portfolio Theory* (MPT). Initially, mean-variance analysis generated relatively little interest, but with time, the financial community adopted the thesis. Today, more than 50 years later, financial models based on those very same principles are constantly being reinvented to incorporate new findings that result from that seminal work. In 1990, Harry Markowitz, Merton Miller, and William Sharpe were awarded the Nobel prize for their pioneering work in the theory of financial economics.[1]

Though widely applicable, mean-variance analysis has had the most influence in the practice of portfolio management. In its simplest form, mean-variance analysis provides a framework to construct and select portfolios, based on the expected performance of the investments and the risk appetite of the investor. Mean-variance analysis also introduced a whole new terminology, which now has become the norm in the area of investment management. However, more than 50 years after Markowitz's seminal work, it appears that mean-variance portfolio optimization is utilized only at the more quantitative firms, where pro-

---

[1] Markowitz was awarded the prize for having developed the theory of portfolio choice, Sharpe for his contributions to the theory of price formation for financial assets and the development of the Capital Asset Pricing Model, and Miller for his work in the theory of corporate finance.

cesses for automated forecast generation and risk control are already in place. Today, in many firms, portfolio management remains a purely judgmental process based on qualitative, not quantitative, assessments. The first quantitative efforts at most firms appear to be focused on providing risk measures to portfolio managers. These measures offer asset managers a view of the level of risk in a particular portfolio, where risk is defined as underperformance relative to a mandate.

It may be useful to note here that the theory of portfolio selection is a normative theory. A *normative theory* is one that describes a standard or norm of behavior that investors should pursue in constructing a portfolio, in contrast to a theory that is actually followed. Asset pricing theory goes on to formalize the relationship that should exist between asset returns and risk if investors construct and select portfolios according to mean-variance analysis. In contrast to a normative theory, asset pricing theory is a *positive theory*—a theory that derives the implications of hypothesized investor behavior. An example of a positive theory is the *capital asset pricing model* (CAPM), discussed in more detail in Chapter 7. It seeks to explain and measure the excess return of an asset relative to the market. Specifically, as we will see, the CAPM states that an asset's excess return is proportional to the market's excess return, where the constant of proportionality is the covariance between the asset return and the market return divided by the variance of the market return. It is important to bear in mind that, like other financial theories, CAPM is a *model*. A model relies on a number of basic assumptions. Therefore, a model should be viewed as only an idealized description of the phenomenon or phenomena under study.

In this chapter, we begin with a general discussion of the benefits of diversification before we introduce the classical mean-variance framework. We derive the mean-variance portfolio for equality constraints and then illustrate some of its basic properties through practical examples. In particular, we show how the shape of the so-called efficient frontier changes with the addition of other assets (risky as well as risk-free) and with the introduction of short-selling constraints. In the presence of only risky assets, the mean-variance efficient frontier has a parabolic shape. However, with the inclusion of a risk-free asset, the efficient frontier becomes linear forming the so called Capital Market Line. We close the chapter with a discussion of utility functions and a general framework for portfolio choice.

THE BENEFITS OF DIVERSIFICATION

Conventional wisdom has always dictated "not putting all your eggs into one basket." In more technical terms, this old adage is addressing the benefits of diversification. Markowitz quantified the concept of diversification through the statistical notion of covariance between individual securities, and the overall standard deviation of a portfolio. In essence, the old adage is saying that investing all your money in assets that may all perform poorly at the same time—that is, whose returns are highly correlated—is not a very prudent investment strategy no matter how small the chance that any one asset will perform poorly. This is because if any one single asset performs poorly, it is likely, due to its high correlation with the other assets, that these other assets are also going to perform poorly, leading to the poor performance of the portfolio.

Diversification is related to the *Central Limit Theorem*, which states that the sum of identical and independent random variables with bounded variance is asymptotically Gaussian.[2] In its simplest form, we can formally state this as follows: if X_1, X_2, ..., X_N are N independent random variables, each X_i with an arbitrary probability distribution, with finite mean μ and variance σ^2, then

$$\lim_{N \to \infty} P\left(\frac{1}{\sigma\sqrt{N}} \sum_{i=1}^{N} (X_i - \mu) \leq y\right) = \frac{1}{\sqrt{2\pi}} \int_{-\infty}^{y} e^{-\frac{1}{2}s^2} ds$$

For a portfolio of N identically and independently distributed assets with returns R_1, R_2, ..., R_N, each in which we invest an equal amount, the portfolio return

$$R_p = \frac{1}{N} \sum_{i=1}^{N} R_i$$

is a random variable that will be distributed approximately Gaussian when N is sufficiently large. The Central Limit Theorem implies that the variance of this portfolio is

---

[2] This notion of diversification can be extended to more general random variables by the concept of *mixing*. Mixing is a weaker form of independence that can be defined for quite general stochastic processes. Under certain so-called *mixing conditions* a Central Limit Theorem can be shown to hold for quite general random variables and processes. See for example, James Davidson, *Stochastic Limit Theory* (Oxford: Oxford University Press, 1995).

$$\begin{aligned}
\operatorname{var}(R_p) &= \frac{1}{N^2} \sum_{i=1}^{N} \operatorname{var}(R_i) \\
&= \frac{1}{N^2} N \cdot \sigma^2 \\
&= \frac{\sigma^2}{N} \xrightarrow[N \to \infty]{} 0
\end{aligned}$$

where σ^2 is the variance of the assets. In particular, we conclude that in this setting as the number of assets increase the portfolio variance decreases towards zero. This is, of course, a rather idealistic situation. For real-world portfolios—even with a large number of assets—we cannot expect a portfolio variance of zero due to nonvanishing correlations.

It is well known that asset returns are not normal, but often do exhibit fat tails. There is also certain evidence that the variances of some asset returns are not bounded (i.e., they are infinite and therefore do not exist). This calls to question the principle of diversification. In particular, it can be shown that if asset returns behave like certain so-called stable Paretian distributions, diversification may no longer be a meaningful economic activity.[3] In general, however, most practitioners agree that a certain level of diversification is achievable in the markets.

The first study of its kind performed by Evans and Archer in 1968, suggests that the major benefits of diversification can be obtained with as few as 10 to 20 individual equities.[4] More recent studies by Campbell *et al.*[5] and Malkiel,[6] show that the volatility of individual stocks has increased over the period from the 1960s to the 1990s. On the other hand, the correlation between individual stocks has decreased over the same time period. Together, these two effects have canceled each other out, leaving the overall market volatility unchanged. However, Malkiel's study suggests that due to a general increase in idiosyncratic risk (firm specific) it now takes almost 200 individual equities to obtain the same amount of diversification that historically was possible with as few as 20 individual equities.

---

[3] Eugene F. Fama, "Portfolio Analysis In a Stable Paretian Market," *Management Science* 11, no. 3 (1965), pp. 404–419.

[4] John L. Evans, and Stephen H. Archer, "Diversification and the Reduction of Dispersion: An Empirical Analysis," *Journal of Finance* 23 (1968), pp. 761–767.

[5] John Y. Campbell, Martin Lettau, Burton G. Malkiel, and Yexiao Xu, "Have Individual Stocks Become More Volatile? An Empirical Exploration of Idiosyncratic Risk," *Journal of Finance* 56 (2001), pp. 1–43.

[6] Burton G. Malkiel, "How Much Diversification Is Enough?" Proceedings of the AIMR seminar "The Future of Equity Portfolio Construction," March 2002, pp. 26–27.

In these studies, the standard deviation of the portfolio was used to measure portfolio risk. With a different measure of risk the results will be different. For example, Vardharaj, Fabozzi, and Jones show that if portfolio risk is measured by the tracking error of the portfolio to a benchmark, more than 300 assets may be necessary in order to provide for sufficient diversification.[7]

The concept of diversification is so intuitive and so powerful that it has been continuously applied to different areas within finance. Indeed, a vast number of the innovations surrounding finance have either been in the application of the concept of diversification, or the introduction of new methods for obtaining improved estimates of the variances and covariances, thereby allowing for a more precise measure of diversification and consequently, for a more precise measure of risk. However, overall portfolio risk goes beyond just the standard deviation of a portfolio. Unfortunately, a portfolio with low expected standard deviation can still perform very poorly. There are many other dimensions to risk that are important to consider when devising an investment policy. Chapter 8 is dedicated to a more detailed discussion of different risk models, their measurement, and forecasting.

MEAN-VARIANCE ANALYSIS: OVERVIEW

Markowitz's starting point is that of a rational investor who, at time t, decides what portfolio of investments to hold for a time horizon of Δt. The investor makes decisions on the gains and losses he will make at time $t + \Delta t$, without considering eventual gains and losses either during or after the period Δt. At time $t + \Delta t$, the investor will reconsider the situation and decide anew. This one-period framework is often referred to as *myopic* (or "short-sighted") behavior. In general, a myopic investor's behavior is suboptimal in comparison to an investor who takes a broader approach and makes investment decisions based upon a multiperiod framework. For example, nonmyopic investment strategies are adopted when it is necessary to make trade-offs at future dates between consumption and investment or when significant trading costs related to specific subsets of investments are incurred throughout the holding period.

Markowitz reasoned that investors should decide on the basis of a trade-off between risk and expected return. Expected return of a security is defined as the expected price change plus any additional income over the time horizon considered, such as dividend payments, divided by [*Expected return*]

---

[7] Raman Vardharaj, Frank J. Fabozzi, and Frank J. Jones, "Determinants of Tracking Error for Equity Portfolios," *Journal of Investing* 13 (2004), pp. 37–47.

the beginning price of the security. He suggested that risk should be measured by the variance of returns—the average squared deviation around the expected return.

We note that it is a common misunderstanding that Markowitz's mean-variance framework relies on joint normality of security returns. Markowitz's mean-variance framework does not assume joint normality of security returns. However, later in this chapter we show that the mean-variance approach is consistent with two different frameworks: (1) expected utility maximization under certain assumptions, or (2) the assumption that security returns are jointly normally distributed.

Moreover, Markowitz argued that for any given level of expected return, a rational investor would choose the portfolio with minimum variance from amongst the set of all possible portfolios. The set of all possible portfolios that can be constructed is called the *feasible set*. *Minimum variance portfolios* are called *mean-variance efficient portfolios*. The set of all mean-variance efficient portfolios, for different desired levels of expected return, is called the *efficient frontier*. Exhibit 2.1 provides

EXHIBIT 2.1   Feasible and Markowitz Efficient Portfolios[a]

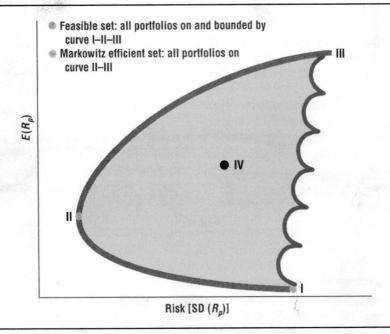

[a] The picture is for illustrative purposes only. The actual shape of the feasible region depends on the returns and risks of the assets chosen and the correlation among them.

a graphical illustration of the efficient frontier of risky assets. In particular, notice that the feasible set is bounded by the curve I-II-III. All portfolios on the curve II-III are efficient portfolios for different levels of risk. These portfolios offer the lowest level of standard deviation for a given level of expected return. Or equivalently, they constitute the portfolios that maximize expected return for a given level of risk. Therefore, the efficient frontier provides the best possible trade-off between expected return and risk—portfolios below it, such as portfolio IV, are inefficient and portfolios above it are unobtainable. The portfolio at point II is often referred to as the *global minimum variance portfolio* (GMV), as it is the portfolio on the efficient frontier with the smallest variance.

Exhibit 2.2 shows a schematic view of the investment process as seen from the perspective of modern portfolio theory. This process is often also referred to as *mean-variance optimization* or *theory of portfolio selection*. The inputs to the process are estimates of the expected returns, volatilities and correlations of all the assets together with various portfolio constraints. For example, constraints can be as straightforward as not allowing the short-selling of any assets, or as complicated as limiting assets to be traded only in round lots. An optimization software package is then used to solve a series of optimization problems in order to generate the efficient frontier. Depending upon the complexity of the portfolio, the optimizations can be solved either with a spreadsheet or with more specialized optimization software. After the efficient frontier has been calculated, an optimal portfolio is chosen based on the investor's objectives such as his degree of aversion to various kinds of risk. Later in this chapter, we describe what is meant by an investor's optimal portfolio.

EXHIBIT 2.2   The MPT Investment Process

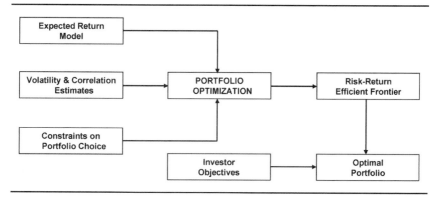

Source: Exhibit 2 in Frank J. Fabozzi, Francis Gupta, and Harry M. Markowitz, "The Legacy of Modern Portfolio Theory," *Journal of Investing* 11 (Fall 2002), p. 8.

Though the implementation of this process can get quite involved, the theory is relatively straightforward. In the next section we will begin by presenting Markowitz's classical framework. Our focus is on providing an intuitive and practical approach to modern portfolio theory as opposed to giving a complete theoretical treatment. In Chapter 4, we discuss some natural generalizations and extensions to this framework used by practitioners in the financial markets today. Furthermore, the incorporation of higher moments, alternative risk measures, and estimation/model risk are covered in Chapters 5 and 9.

CLASSICAL FRAMEWORK FOR MEAN-VARIANCE OPTIMIZATION

In this section we place the intuitive discussion thus far into a more formal mathematical context and develop the theory of mean-variance optimization. Suppose first that an investor has to choose a portfolio comprised of N risky assets.[8] The investor's choice is embodied in an N-vector $\mathbf{w} = (w_1, w_2, ..., w_N)'$ of weights, where each weight i represents the percentage of the i-th asset held in the portfolio, and

$$\sum_{i=1}^{N} w_i = 1$$

For now, we permit short selling, which means that weights can be negative. Later on in this chapter we will discuss no short-selling and in Chapter 4 we consider more general constraints.

Suppose the assets' returns $\mathbf{R} = (R_1, R_2, ..., R_N)'$ have expected returns $\boldsymbol{\mu} = (\mu_1, \mu_2, ..., \mu_N)'$ and an $N \times N$ covariance matrix given by

$$\Sigma = \begin{bmatrix} \sigma_{11} & \cdots & \sigma_{1N} \\ \vdots & & \vdots \\ \sigma_{N1} & \cdots & \sigma_{NN} \end{bmatrix}$$

where σ_{ij} denotes the covariance between asset i and asset j such that $\sigma_{ii} = \sigma_i^2$, $\sigma_{ij} = \rho_{ij}\sigma_i\sigma_j$ and ρ_{ij} is the correlation between asset i and asset j. Under these assumptions, the return of a portfolio with weights $\mathbf{w} = (w_1, w_2, ..., w_N)'$ is a random variable $R_p = \mathbf{w}'\mathbf{R}$ with expected return and variance given by[9]

---

[8] Throughout this book we denote by $\mathbf{x}'$ the transpose of a vector $\mathbf{x}$.

[9] Subsequently, we will use $E(R_p)$, where R_p is the return on a portfolio, and μ_p interchangeably.

$$\mu_p = \mathbf{w}'\mathbf{\mu}$$

$$\sigma_p^2 = \mathbf{w}'\mathbf{\Sigma}\mathbf{w}$$

For instance, if there are only two assets with weights $\mathbf{w} = (w_1, w_2)'$, then the portfolio's expected return is

$$\mu_p = w_1\mu_1 + w_2\mu_2$$

[handwritten: mean of portfolio = Sum of weighted Averages]

and its variance is

$$\sigma_p^2 = \begin{bmatrix} w_1 & w_2 \end{bmatrix} \begin{bmatrix} \sigma_{11} & \sigma_{12} \\ \sigma_{21} & \sigma_{22} \end{bmatrix} \begin{bmatrix} w_1 \\ w_2 \end{bmatrix}$$

$$= \begin{bmatrix} w_1\sigma_{11} + w_2\sigma_{21} & w_1\sigma_{12} + w_2\sigma_{22} \end{bmatrix} \begin{bmatrix} w_1 \\ w_2 \end{bmatrix}$$

$$= w_1^2\sigma_{11} + w_2^2\sigma_{22} + 2w_1w_2\sigma_{12}$$

In this chapter, we simply assume that expected returns, $\mathbf{\mu}$, and their covariance matrix, $\mathbf{\Sigma}$, are given. Naturally, in practice these quantities have to be estimated. We describe different techniques for this purpose in Chapters 8 and 9.

By choosing the portfolio's weights, an investor chooses among the available mean-variance pairs. To calculate the weights for one possible pair, we choose a target mean return, μ_0. Following Markowitz, the investor's problem is a constrained minimization problem in the sense that the investor must seek

$$\min_{\mathbf{w}} \mathbf{w}'\mathbf{\Sigma}\mathbf{w} \quad \leftarrow \text{ *risk*}$$

subject to the constraints[10]

$$\mu_0 = \mathbf{w}'\mathbf{\mu} \quad \leftarrow \text{ *return*}$$

$$\mathbf{w}'\mathbf{\iota} = 1, \mathbf{\iota}' = [1, 1, ..., 1]$$

---

[10] It is common in many practical applications to replace the targeted expected portfolio return constraint with $\mu_0 \leq \mathbf{w}'\mathbf{\mu}$, expressing the fact that the expected return should not be below a minimum value. However, with the introduction of inequality constraints, the portfolio optimization problem no longer becomes analytically tractable, but has to be solved by numerical optimization techniques.

We will refer to this version of the classical mean-variance optimization problem as the *risk minimization formulation*. This problem is a quadratic optimization problem with equality constraints, with the solution given by[11]

$$\mathbf{w} = \mathbf{g} + \mathbf{h}\mu_0$$

where $\mathbf{g}$ and $\mathbf{h}$ are the two vectors

$$\mathbf{g} = \frac{1}{ac - b^2} \cdot \Sigma^{-1}[c\iota - b\mu]$$

$$\mathbf{h} = \frac{1}{ac - b^2} \cdot \Sigma^{-1}[a\mu - b\iota]$$

and

$$a = \iota'\Sigma^{-1}\iota$$
$$b = \iota'\Sigma^{-1}\mu$$
$$c = \mu'\Sigma^{-1}\mu$$

Consider a two-dimensional Cartesian plane whose x and y coordinates are the portfolio standard deviation and expected return, respectively. In this plane, each feasible portfolio is represented by a point. Consider now the set of all efficient portfolios with all possible efficient portfolio pairs. This set is what we referred to earlier as the *efficient frontier*. Each portfolio on the efficient frontier is obtained by solving the optimization problem above for different choices of μ_0.

In this section we have described the classical formulation of the mean-variance optimization problem as one of minimizing portfolio risk subject to a targeted expected portfolio return. However, there are many other possible and equivalent formulations to this problem. For example, for a particular level of risk we can find a combination of assets that is going to give the highest expected return. We will discuss this and other alternatives later in this chapter.

Mathematically, the mean-variance problem as described above is an optimization problem referred to as a *quadratic program*. In the simple form presented, the problem can be solved analytically. In extensions

---

[11] This problem can be solved by the method of Lagrange multipliers. See Chapter 7 in Sergio M. Focardi and Frank J. Fabozzi, *The Mathematics of Financial Modeling and Investment Management* (Hoboken, NJ: John Wiley & Sons, 2004).

involving only so-called equality constraints,[12] finding the optimum portfolio reduces to solving a set of linear equations. However, in more complex cases, analytical solutions are often not available and numerical optimization techniques must be used. Chapter 6 provides an introduction to different optimization techniques for solving the mean-variance optimization problem and its generalizations.

Now that we know how to calculate the optimal portfolio weights for a targeted level of expected portfolio return, we will take a look at an example. First, we will use only four assets and later we will see how these results change as more assets are included. For this purpose, we will use the four country equity indices in the MSCI World Index for Australia, Austria, Belgium, and Canada.[13]

Let us assume that we are given the annualized expected returns, standard deviations, and correlations between these countries according to Exhibit 2.3. The expected returns vary from 7.1% to 9%, whereas the standard deviations range from 16.5% to 19.5%. Furthermore, we observe that the four country indices are not highly correlated with each other—the highest correlation, 0.47, is between Austria and Belgium. Therefore, we expect to see some benefits of portfolio diversification in this case.

Next, we compute the efficient frontier using the formulas presented above. By varying the targeted expected portfolio return over the window [5%, 12%], and for each increment solving the portfolio optimization problem described above, we calculate the weights. In Exhibit 2.4 we can now see explicitly what we derived theoretically: the weights vary linearly as we change the targeted expected return. Substituting the weights into the formulas of the portfolio expected return and standard deviation above, we can trace out the resulting efficient frontier as in Exhibit 2.5.

EXHIBIT 2.3   Annualized Expected Returns, Standard Deviations, and Correlations between the Four Country Equity Indices: Australia, Austria, Belgium, and Canada

Expected Returns	Standard Deviation	Correlations		1	2	3	4
7.9%	19.5%	Australia	1	1			
7.9%	18.2%	Austria	2	0.24	1		
9.0%	18.3%	Belgium	3	0.25	0.47	1	
7.1%	16.5%	Canada	4	0.22	0.14	0.25	1

---

[12] Constraints of the form $\mathbf{Aw} = \mathbf{b}$ and $\mathbf{Aw} \leq \mathbf{b}$ are referred to as equality and inequality constraints, respectively.

[13] For details on the MSCI World Index and its individual constituents, refer to Appendix C.

EXHIBIT 2.4   Weights of the Efficient Portfolios of Australia, Austria, Belgium, and Canada for Different Levels of Expected Return

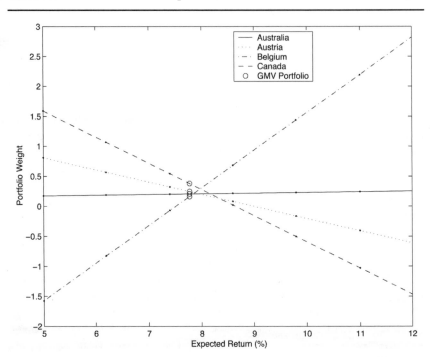

Note: The weights of the *global minimum variance portfolio* (GMV) are marked with circles.

We observe that the four assets in Exhibit 2.5 (represented by the diamond-shaped marks) are all below the efficient frontier. This means that for a targeted expected portfolio return, the mean-variance portfolio has a lower standard deviation. A utility maximizing investor, measuring utility as the trade-off between expected return and standard deviation, will prefer a portfolio over any of the individual assets. As a matter of fact, by construction, we know that the portfolios along the efficient frontier minimize the standard deviation of the portfolio for a given expected portfolio return.

The portfolio at the leftmost end of the efficient frontier (marked with a circle in Exhibit 2.5) is the portfolio with the smallest obtainable standard deviation. This portfolio is the global minimum variance portfolio (GMV). It can be computed directly by solving the optimization problem

$$\min_{\mathbf{w}} \mathbf{w}'\Sigma\mathbf{w}$$

EXHIBIT 2.5 The Mean-Variance Efficient Frontier of Country Equity Indices of Australia, Austria, Belgium, and Canada

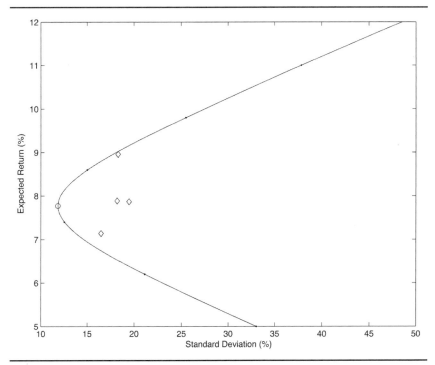

Note: Constructed from the data in Exhibit 2.3. The expected return and standard deviation combination of each country index is represented by a diamond-shaped mark. The GMV is represented by a circle.

subject to

$$w'\iota = 1, \iota' = [1, 1, ..., 1]$$

which has the solution[14]

$$w = \frac{1}{\iota'\Sigma^{-1}\iota} \cdot \Sigma^{-1}\iota$$

---

[14] This problem can also be solved by the method of Lagrange multipliers. See Chapter 7 in Focardi and Fabozzi, *The Mathematics of Financial Modeling and Investment Management.*

Increasing the Asset Universe

From theory we know that by introducing more (low-correlating) assets, for a targeted expected portfolio return, we should be able to decrease the standard deviation of the portfolio. In Exhibit 2.6 the assumed expected returns, standard deviations, and correlations of 18 countries in the MSCI World Index are presented.

Exhibit 2.7 illustrates how the efficient frontier widens as we go from 4 to 12 assets and then to 18 assets. By increasing the number of investment opportunities we increase our level of possible diversification.

We now ask whether it is possible in general to decrease portfolio risk (and keeping the expected portfolio return constant) by increasing the asset universe. To answer this question, we first observe that the portfolio variance can be bounded by

$$
\begin{aligned}
\text{var}(R_p) &= \mathbf{w}'\Sigma\mathbf{w} \\
&= \frac{1}{N^2}\sum_{i=1}^{N}\text{var}(R_i) + \frac{1}{N^2}\sum_{i \neq j}\text{cov}(R_i, R_j) \\
&\leq \frac{1}{N^2}N\sigma_{\text{max}}^2 + \frac{1}{N^2}(N-1)N \cdot A \\
&= \frac{\sigma_{\text{max}}^2}{N} + \frac{N-1}{N} \cdot A
\end{aligned}
$$

where σ_{max}^2 is the largest variance of all individual assets and A is the average pairwise asset covariance,

$$
A = \frac{1}{(N-1)N}\sum_{i \neq j}\text{cov}(R_i, R_j)
$$

If the average pairwise covariance A and all variances are bounded, then we conclude that

$$
\text{var}(R_p)\xrightarrow[N \to \infty]{}A
$$

This implies that the portfolio variance approaches A as the number of assets becomes large. Therefore we see that, in general, the benefits of diversification are limited up to a point and that we cannot expect to be able to completely eliminate portfolio risk.

EXHIBIT 2.6 Annualized Expected Returns, Standard Deviations, and Correlations between 18 Countries in the MSCI World Index

Expected Returns	Standard Deviation	Correlations		1	2	3	4	5	6	7	8	9	10	11	12	13	14	15	16	17	18
7.9%	19.5%	Australia	1	1																	
7.9%	18.2%	Austria	2	0.24	1																
9.0%	18.3%	Belgium	3	0.25	0.47	1															
7.1%	16.5%	Canada	4	0.22	0.14	0.25	1														
12.0%	18.4%	Denmark	5	0.24	0.44	0.48	0.21	1													
10.3%	20.4%	France	6	0.22	0.41	0.56	0.35	0.45	1												
9.5%	21.8%	Germany	7	0.26	0.48	0.57	0.35	0.48	0.65	1											
12.0%	28.9%	Hong Kong	8	0.31	0.17	0.17	0.19	0.18	0.22	0.24	1										
11.6%	23.3%	Italy	9	0.20	0.36	0.42	0.22	0.38	0.47	0.47	0.16	1									
9.5%	22.1%	Japan	10	0.32	0.28	0.28	0.18	0.28	0.27	0.29	0.24	0.21	1								
10.9%	19.7%	Netherlands	11	0.26	0.38	0.57	0.39	0.45	0.67	0.67	0.24	0.44	0.28	1							
7.9%	22.7%	Norway	12	0.33	0.37	0.41	0.27	0.41	0.45	0.47	0.21	0.32	0.28	0.50	1						
7.6%	21.5%	Singapore	13	0.34	0.22	0.23	0.20	0.22	0.22	0.26	0.44	0.19	0.34	0.24	0.28	1					
9.9%	20.8%	Spain	14	0.26	0.42	0.50	0.27	0.43	0.57	0.54	0.20	0.48	0.25	0.51	0.39	0.25	1				
16.2%	23.5%	Sweden	15	0.27	0.34	0.42	0.31	0.42	0.53	0.53	0.23	0.41	0.27	0.51	0.43	0.27	0.49	1			
10.7%	17.9%	Switzerland	16	0.26	0.47	0.59	0.32	0.49	0.64	0.69	0.23	0.45	0.32	0.67	0.48	0.25	0.53	0.51	1		
9.8%	18.5%	United Kingdom	17	0.25	0.34	0.47	0.38	0.40	0.58	0.53	0.22	0.40	0.28	0.68	0.43	0.24	0.46	0.45	0.57	1	
10.5%	16.5%	United States	18	0.05	0.05	0.21	0.62	0.11	0.29	0.29	0.13	0.17	0.08	0.32	0.15	0.12	0.21	0.22	0.26	0.31	1

EXHIBIT 2.7   The Efficient Frontier Widens as the Number of Low-Correlated Assets Increases

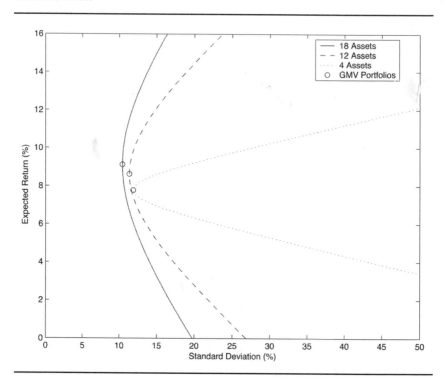

Note: The efficient frontiers have been constructed with 4, 12, and 18 countries (from the innermost to the outermost frontier) from the MSCI World Index.

At this point, we note that the results of modern portfolio theory are consistent with the assumptions that either returns are jointly normally distributed, or that all investors only care about the mean and the variance of their portfolios. We will make this statement more precise later on in this chapter, when we discuss the concept of utility functions. In practice, it is well known that asset returns are not normal and that many investors have preferences that go beyond that of the mean and the variance. The earliest studies showing nonnormality of asset returns date back to Benoit Mandelbrot[15] and Eugene Fama[16] in the early

---

[15] Benoit Mandelbrot, "The Variation in Certain Speculative Prices," *Journal of Business* 36 (1963), pp. 394–419.
[16] Eugene F. Fama, "The Behavior of Stock Market Prices," *Journal of Business* 38 (1965), pp. 34–105.

1960s. The movement sometimes referred to as *econophysics*[17] has developed methods for the accurate empirical analysis of the distribution of asset returns that show significant deviations from the normal distribution.[18,19] In particular, there is evidence that the variances of some asset returns are not bounded, but rather that they are infinite. Moreover, one can show that in specific cases where variances are unbounded and asset returns behave like certain stable Paretian distributions, diversification may no longer be possible.[20]

Adding Short-Selling Constraints

In our theoretical derivations above, we imposed no restrictions on the portfolio weights other than having them add up to one. In particular, we allowed the portfolio weights to take on both positive and negative values; that is, we did not restrict short selling. In practice, many portfolio managers cannot sell assets short. This could be for investment policy or legal reasons, or sometimes just because particular asset classes are difficult to sell short, such as real estate. In Exhibit 2.8 we see the effect of not allowing for short selling. Since we are restricting the opportunity set by constraining all the weights to be positive, the resulting efficient frontier is inside the unconstrained efficient frontier.

Alternative Formulations of Classical Mean-Variance Optimization

The mean-variance optimization problem has several alternative but equivalent formulations that are very useful in practical applications. These formulations are equivalent in the sense that they all lead to the same efficient frontier as they trade expected portfolio return versus portfolio risk in a similar way. We review two of these formulations here.

---

[17] Rosario N. Mantegna and H. Eugene Stanley, *An Introduction to Econophysics* (Cambridge: Cambridge University Press, 2000).

[18] Ulrich A. Mueller, Michel M. Dacorogna, and Olivier V. Pictet, "Heavy Tails in High-Frequency Financial Data, in Robert J. Adler, Raya E. Feldman, and Murad S. Taqqu (eds.), *A Practical Guide to Heavy Tails* (Boston, MA: Birkhaeuser, 1998), pp. 55–77.

[19] For recent empirical evidence on the distribution of asset returns and portfolio selection when distributions are nonnormal, see Svetlozar T. Rachev, and Stefan Mittnik, *Stable Paretian Models in Finance* (Chichester: John Wiley & Sons, 2000); and Svetlozar T. Rachev (ed.), *Handbook of Heavy Tailed Distributions in Finance* (New York: Elsevier/North Holland, 2001).

[20] Eugene F. Fama, "Portfolio Analysis In a Stable Paretian Market," *Management Science* 11, no. 3 (1965), pp. 404–419.

EXHIBIT 2.8　　The Effect of Restricting Short Selling: Constrained versus Unconstrained Efficient Frontiers Constructed from 18 Countries from the MSCI World Index

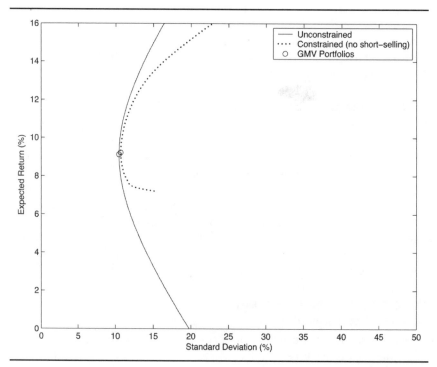

Expected Return Maximization Formulation

We previously formulated the mean-variance optimization problem as one of minimizing the risk of the portfolio for a certain level of targeted expected return μ_0. However, we could also begin by choosing a certain level of targeted portfolio risk, say σ_0, and then maximize the expected return of the portfolio:

$$\max_{\mathbf{w}} \mathbf{w}'\boldsymbol{\mu}$$

subject to the constraints[21]

---

[21] It is common in many practical applications that the equal sign in the risk constraint is replaced by a weak inequality, that is, $\mathbf{w}'\boldsymbol{\Sigma}\mathbf{w} \leq \sigma_0^2$, expressing the fact that the risk is not allowed to be above a maximum value.

$$w'\Sigma w = \sigma_0^2$$

$$w'\iota = 1 , \iota' = [1, 1, ..., 1]$$

This formulation, which we will refer to as the *expected return maximization formulation* of the classical mean-variance optimization problem, is often used by portfolio managers that are required to not take more risk, as measured by the standard deviation of the portfolio return, than a certain prespecified volatility. For example, portfolios managed relative to a benchmark can be modeled in this fashion. Here the objective is to maximize the excess return of the portfolio over the benchmark and at the same time make sure that the risks in so doing do not exceed a given tracking error over the benchmark. We come back to this particular problem later in Chapter 4 when we discuss index tracking.

Risk Aversion Formulation

Another alternative is to explicitly model the trade-off between risk and return in the objective function using a risk-aversion coefficient λ. We refer to the following formulation as the *risk aversion formulation* of the classical mean-variance optimization problem:

$$\max_{w} (w'\mu - \lambda w'\Sigma w)$$

subject to

$$w'\iota = 1 , \iota' = [1, 1, ..., 1]$$

The risk aversion coefficient is also referred to as the *Arrow-Pratt risk aversion index*. When λ is small (i.e., the aversion to risk is low), the penalty from the contribution of the portfolio risk is also small, leading to more risky portfolios. Conversely, when λ is large, portfolios with more exposures to risk become more highly penalized. If we gradually increase λ from zero and for each instance solve the optimization problem, we end up calculating each portfolio along the efficient frontier. It is a common practice to calibrate λ such that a particular portfolio has the desired risk profile. The calibration is often performed via backtests with historical data. For most portfolio allocation decisions in investment management applications, the risk aversion is somewhere between 2 and 4.

THE CAPITAL MARKET LINE

As demonstrated by William Sharpe,[22] James Tobin,[23] and John Lintner[24] the efficient set of portfolios available to investors who employ mean-variance analysis in the absence of a risk-free asset is inferior to that available when there is a risk-free asset. We present this formulation in this section.[25]

Assume that there is a risk-free asset, with a risk-free return denoted by R_f and that the investor is able to borrow and lend at this rate.[26] The investor has to choose a combination of the N risky assets plus the risk-free asset. The weights $\mathbf{w}'_R = (w_{R1}, w_{R2}, ..., w_{RN})$ do not have to sum to 1 as the remaining part $(1 - \mathbf{w}'_R \iota)$ can be invested in the risk-free asset. Note also that this portion of the investment can be positive or negative if we allow risk-free borrowing and lending. In this case, the portfolio's expected return and variance are

$$\mu_p = \mathbf{w}'_R \mu + (1 - \mathbf{w}'_R \iota) R_f$$

$$\sigma_p^2 = \mathbf{w}'_R \Sigma \mathbf{w}_R$$

because the risk-free asset has zero variance and is uncorrelated with the risky assets.

---

[22] William F. Sharpe, "Capital Asset Prices: A Theory of Market Equilibrium Under Conditions of Risk," *Journal of Finance* (September 1964), pp. 425–442.

[23] James Tobin, "Liquidity Preference as a Behavior Towards Risk," *Review of Economic Studies* (February 1958), pp. 65–86.

[24] John Lintner, "The Valuation of Risk Assets and the Selection of Risky Investments in Stock Portfolios and Capital Budgets," *Review of Economics and Statistics* (February 1965), pp. 13–37.

[25] For a comprehensive discussion of these models and computational issues, see Harry M. Markowitz (with a chapter and program by Peter Todd), *Mean-Variance Analysis in Portfolio Choice and Capital Markets* (Hoboken, NJ: John Wiley & Sons, 2000).

[26] We remark that, in practice, this assumption is not valid for most investors. Specifically, an investor may not be able to borrow and lend at the *same* interest rate, or may *only* be permitted to lend. If there are no short-selling restrictions on the risky assets, similar theoretical results to the ones presented in this section are obtained also for these cases. See, Fischer Black, "Capital Market Equilibrium with Restricted Borrowings," *Journal of Business* (July 1972) pp. 444–455; and Jonathan E. Ingersoll, Jr., *Theory of Financial Decision Making* (Savage, MD: Rowan & Littlefield Publishers, Inc., 1987).

The investor's objective is again for a targeted level of expected portfolio return, μ_o, to choose allocations by solving a quadratic optimization problem

$$\min_{\mathbf{w}_R} \mathbf{w}'_R \Sigma \mathbf{w}_R$$

subject to the constraint

$$\mu_0 = \mathbf{w}'_R \mu + (1 - \mathbf{w}'_R \iota) R_f$$

The optimal portfolio weights are given by

$$w_R = C\Sigma^{-1}(\mu - R_f \iota)$$

where

$$C = \frac{\mu_0 - R_f}{(\mu - R_f \iota)' \Sigma^{-1}(\mu - R_f \iota)}$$

The above formula shows that the weights of the risky assets of any minimum variance portfolio are proportional to the vector $\Sigma^{-1}(\mu - R_f \iota)$, with the proportionality constant C, defined above. Therefore, with a risk-free asset, all minimum variance portfolios are a combination of the risk-free asset and a given risky portfolio. This risky portfolio is called the *tangency portfolio*. Fama demonstrated that under certain assumptions the tangency portfolio must consist of all assets available to investors, and each asset must be held in proportion to its market value relative to the total market value of all assets.[27] Therefore, the tangency portfolio is often referred to as the "market portfolio," or simply the "market."[28]

We know that for a particular choice of weights, $\mathbf{w}_R^0$, such that $(\mathbf{w}_R^0)'\iota$ = 0, the portfolio only consists of the risk-free asset. On the other hand, for the choice of weights, $\mathbf{w}_R^M$, such that $(\mathbf{w}_R^M)'\iota = 1$, the portfolio consists of only risky assets and must therefore be the market portfolio. Because

---

[27] Eugene F. Fama, "Efficient Capital Markets: A Review of Theory and Empirical Work," *Journal of Finance* (May 1970), pp. 383–417.
[28] Although strictly speaking it is not fully correct, we will use the terms "market portfolio" and "tangency portfolio" interchangeably throughout this book.

$$\mathbf{w}_R^M = C^M \boldsymbol{\Sigma}^{-1}(\boldsymbol{\mu} - R_f \boldsymbol{\iota})$$

for some C^M, we have by using $(\mathbf{w}_R^M)'\boldsymbol{\iota} = 1$ that the weights of the market portfolio are given by

$$\mathbf{w}_R^M = \frac{1}{\boldsymbol{\iota}'\boldsymbol{\Sigma}(\boldsymbol{\mu} - R_f \boldsymbol{\iota})} \cdot \boldsymbol{\Sigma}^{-1}(\boldsymbol{\mu} - R_f \boldsymbol{\iota})$$

It is also easy to verify that the market portfolio can be calculated directly from the *maximal Sharpe ratio optimization problem*:

$$\max_{\mathbf{w}} \frac{\mathbf{w}'\boldsymbol{\mu} - R_f}{\sqrt{\mathbf{w}'\boldsymbol{\Sigma}\mathbf{w}}}$$

subject to $\mathbf{w}'\boldsymbol{\iota} = 1$.

In Exhibit 2.9 every combination of the risk-free asset and the market portfolio M is shown on the line drawn from the vertical axis at the risk-free rate tangent to the Markowitz efficient frontier. All the portfolios on the line are feasible for the investor to construct. The line from the risk-free rate that is tangent to the efficient frontier of risky assets is called the *Capital Market Line* (CML).

We observe that with the exception of the market portfolio, the minimum variance portfolios that are a combination of the market portfolio and the risk-free asset are superior to the portfolio on the Markowitz efficient frontier for the same level of risk. For example, compare portfolio P_A, which is on the Markowitz efficient frontier, with portfolio P_B, which is on the CML and therefore some combination of the risk-free asset and the market portfolio M. Notice that for the same level of risk, the expected return is greater for P_B than for P_A. A risk-averse investor will prefer P_B to P_A.

With the introduction of the risk-free asset, we can now say that an investor will select a portfolio on the CML that represents a combination of borrowing or lending at the risk-free rate and the market portfolio.[29] This important property is called *separation*. Portfolios to the left of the market portfolio represent combinations of risky assets and the risk-free asset. Portfolios to the right of the market portfolio include purchases of risky assets made with funds borrowed at the risk-free

---

[29] Today it is normal practice to use standard deviation rather than variance as the risk measure because with the inclusion of a risk-free asset the efficient frontier in the expected return/standard deviation coordinate system is linear.

EXHIBIT 2.9   Capital Market Line and the Markowitz Efficient Frontier

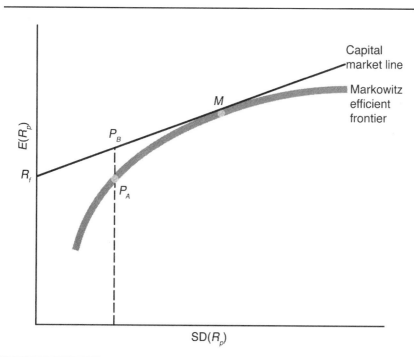

rate. Such a portfolio is called a *leveraged portfolio* because it involves the use of borrowed funds.

The separation property also has important implications in practice. Specifically, practical portfolio construction is normally broken down into at least the following two steps:

1. Asset allocation: Decide how to allocate the investor's wealth between the risk-free security and the set of risky securities.
2. Risky portfolio construction: Decide how to distribute the risky portion of the investment among the set of risky securities.

The first point is an integral part in devising an investment plan and policy for a particular investor. This is closely linked to an investor's strategic goals and general risk profile as well as his liquidity requirements. In this book the focus is more on the second point. In later chapters we will discuss various kinds of forecasting techniques that can be used in order to maximize different investment objectives and controlling the risk of the risky portion of the portfolio.

Deriving the Capital Market Line

To derive the CML, we begin with the efficient frontier. As we have seen above, in the absence of a risk-free asset, Markowitz efficient portfolios can be constructed by solving a constrained optimization problem that finds an optimal trade-off between return and variance, with the optimal portfolio being the one portfolio selected based on the investor's preference (which later we will see is quantified by the investor's utility function). However, the efficient frontier changes once a risk-free asset is introduced and we assume that investors can borrow and lend at the risk-free rate.

We can derive a formula for the CML algebraically. Based on the assumption of homogeneous expectations regarding the inputs in the portfolio construction process, all investors can create an efficient portfolio consisting of w_f placed in the risk-free asset and w_M in the market portfolio, where w represents the corresponding percentage (weight) of the portfolio allocated to each asset. Thus, $w_f + w_M = 1$. As the expected return of the portfolio, $E(R_p)$, is equal to the weighted average of the expected returns of the two assets, we have

$$E(R_p) = w_f R_f + w_M E(R_M)$$

Since we know that $w_f = 1 - w_M$, we can rewrite $E(R_p)$ as

$$E(R_p) = (1 - w_M) R_f + w_M E(R_M)$$

which can be simplified to

$$E(R_p) = R_f + w_M [E(R_M) - R_f]$$

Since the return of the risk-free asset and the return of the market portfolio are uncorrelated and the variance of the risk-free asset is equal to zero, the variance of the portfolio consisting of the risk-free asset and the market portfolio is given by

$$\sigma_p^2 = \text{var}(R_p) = w_f^2 \text{var}(R_f) + w_M^2 \text{var}(R_M) + 2 w_f w_M (R_f, R_M)$$
$$= w_M^2 \text{var}(R_M)$$
$$= w_M^2 \sigma_M^2$$

In other words, the variance of the portfolio is represented by the weighted variance of the market portfolio.

Since the standard deviation is the square root of the variance, we can write

$$w_M = \frac{\sigma_p}{\sigma_M}$$

If we substitute the above result and rearrange terms, we get the explicit expression for the CML

$$E(R_p) = R_f + \left[\frac{E(R_M) - R_f}{\sigma_M}\right]\sigma_p$$

Equilibrium Market Price of Risk

The bracketed portion of the second term in the equation for the CML

$$\left[\frac{E(R_M) - R_f}{\sigma_M}\right]$$

is often referred to as the *risk premium.*

Let us examine the economic meaning of this risk premium. The numerator of the bracketed expression is the expected return from investing in the market beyond the risk-free return. It is a measure of the reward for holding the risky market portfolio rather than the risk-free asset. The denominator is the market risk of the market portfolio. Thus, the first factor, or the slope of the CML, measures the reward per unit of market risk. Since the CML represents the return offered to compensate for a perceived level of risk, each point on the CML is a balanced market condition, or equilibrium. The slope of the CML determines the additional return needed to compensate for a unit change in risk, which is why it is also referred to as the *equilibrium market price of risk.*

In other words, the CML says that the expected return on a portfolio is equal to the risk-free rate plus a risk premium, where the risk premium is equal to the market price of risk (as measured by the reward per unit of market risk) times the quantity of risk for the portfolio (as measured by the standard deviation of the portfolio). Summarizing, we can write

$$E(R_p) = R_f + \text{Market price of risk} \times \text{Quantity of risk}$$

SELECTION OF THE OPTIMAL PORTFOLIO WHEN THERE IS A RISK-FREE ASSET

Given the Markowitz efficient frontier or the CML (which replaces the efficient frontier when a risk-free asset is included), how does one select the optimal portfolio? That is, how does one determine the optimal point on the efficient frontier or the optimal combination of the market portfolio and the risk-free asset in which to invest? Investors have different preferences and tolerances for risk. In order to formalize these concepts, we first introduce the notion of utility functions and indifference curves. Thereafter, we show how the optimal portfolio is chosen within this framework.

Utility Functions and Indifference Curves

There are many situations where entities (i.e., individuals and firms) face two or more choices. The economic "theory of choice" uses the concept of a utility function to describe the way entities make decisions when faced with a set of choices. A *utility function*[30] assigns a (numeric) value to all possible choices faced by the entity. These values, often referred to as the *utility index*, have the property that *a* is preferred to *b*, if and only if, the utility of *a* is higher than that of *b*. The higher the value of a particular choice, the greater the utility derived from that choice. The choice that is selected is the one that results in the maximum utility given a set of constraints faced by the entity.

The assumption that an investor's decision-making process can be represented as optimization of a utility function goes back to Pareto in the 18th century. However, it was not until 1944 that utility theory was mathematically formalized by von Neumann and Morgenstern.[31] Utility functions can represent a broad set of preference orderings. The precise conditions under which a preference ordering can be expressed through a utility function have been widely explored in the literature.[32]

In portfolio theory, entities are faced with a set of choices. Different portfolios have different levels of expected return and risk—the higher the level of expected return, the larger the risk. Entities are faced with the decision of choosing a portfolio from the set of all possible risk/

---

[30] Strictly speaking, a utility function is a twice continuously differentiable function u from the set of all choices to the real line with the requirements that $u' > 0$ and $u'' \leq 0$.

[31] John von Neumann and Oskar Morgenstern, *Theory of Games and Economic Behavior* (Princeton: Princeton University Press, 1944).

[32] See, for example, Akira Takayama, *Mathematical Economics* (Cambridge: Cambridge University Press, 1985).

return combinations. Whereas they like return, they dislike risk. There-fore, entities obtain different levels of utility from different risk/return combinations. The utility obtained from any possible risk/return combi-nation is expressed by the utility function, expressing the preferences of entities over perceived risk and expected return combinations.

A utility function can be presented in graphical form by a set of indifference curves. Exhibit 2.10 shows indifference curves labeled u_1, u_2, and u_3. By convention, the horizontal axis measures risk and the vertical axis measures expected return. Each curve represents a set of portfolios with different combinations of risk and return. All the points on a given indifference curve indicate combinations of risk and expected return that will give the same level of utility to a given investor. For example, on utility curve u_1 there are two points u and u', with u having a higher expected return than u', but also having a higher risk.

EXHIBIT 2.10   Indifference Curves

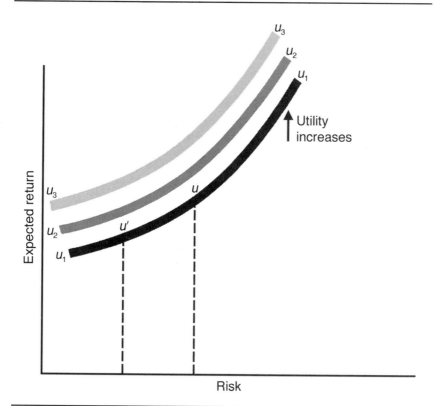

Because the two points lie on the same indifference curve, the investor has an equal preference for (or is indifferent between) the two points, or, for that matter, any point on the curve. The positive slope of an indifference curve reflects that, to obtain the same level of utility, the investor requires a higher expected return in order to accept higher risk. For the three indifference curves shown in Exhibit 2.10, the utility the investor receives is greater the further the indifference curve is from the horizontal axis, because that curve represents a higher level of return at every level of risk. Thus, among the three indifference curves shown in the exhibit, u_3 has the highest utility and u_1 the lowest.

The Optimal Portfolio

A reasonable assumption is that investors are risk averse. A risk averse investor is an investor who, when faced with choosing between two investments with the same expected return but two different risks, prefers the one with the lower risk.

In selecting portfolios, an investor seeks to maximize the expected portfolio return given his tolerance for risk. Given a choice from the set of efficient portfolios, the optimal portfolio is the one that is preferred by the investor. In terms of utility functions, the optimal portfolio is the efficient portfolio that has the maximum utility.

The particular efficient portfolio that the investor will select will depend on the investor's risk preference. This can be seen in Exhibit 2.11, which is the same as Exhibit 2.10 but has both the investor's indifference curves and the efficient frontier included. The investor will select the portfolio P^*_{CML} on the CML that is tangent to the highest indifference curve, u_3 in the exhibit.

Notice that without the risk-free asset, an investor could only get to u_2, which is the indifference curve that is tangent to the Markowitz efficient frontier. This portfolio is denoted by P^*_{MEF} in the exhibit. Thus, the opportunity to borrow or lend at the risk-free rate results in a capital market where risk-averse investors will prefer to hold portfolios consisting of combinations of the risk-free asset and the tangency portfolio M on the Markowitz efficient frontier.

MORE ON UTILITY FUNCTIONS: A GENERAL FRAMEWORK FOR PORTFOLIO CHOICE

In the classical Markowitz framework an investor chooses a certain desired trade-off between risk and return. As we saw above, this preference relation can also be expressed by utility functions. Utility functions

EXHIBIT 2.11 Optimal Portfolio and the Capital Market Line

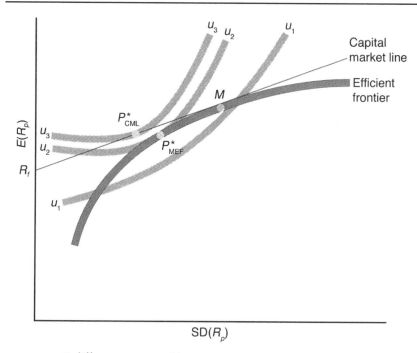

u_1, u_2, u_3 = Indifference curves with $u_1 < u_2 < u_3$
M = Market portfolio
R_f = Risk-free rate
P^*_{CML} = Optimal portfolio on capital market line
P^*_{MEF} = Optimal portfolio on efficient frontier

allow us to generalize the mean-variance framework into a much wider class of problems, *expected utility maximization problems.*

This general framework is based upon the idea that a rational investor with utility u and initial wealth W_0 chooses his portfolio $\mathbf{w}$ as to maximize his expected utility one period ahead,

$$\max_{\mathbf{w}} \ Eu(W_0(1 + \mathbf{w}'\mathbf{R}))$$

subject to

$$\mathbf{w}'\iota = 1, \iota' = [1, 1, ...,1]$$

where $\mathbf{R}$ is the vector of the individual asset returns.

To get comfortable with this framework, let us consider two special cases. First, let us assume that asset returns are jointly normally distributed (that is, fully described by the mean and the variance). Then for any utility function u, $Eu(\mathbf{w}'\mathbf{R})$ is just a function of the portfolio mean and standard deviation. Therefore, this special case resembles classical portfolio theory.

Second, we make an assumption about the investor's utility function, namely, we assume that an investor's utility function is given by the *quadratic utility*

$$u(x) = x - \frac{b}{2}x^2, \quad b > 0$$

so that

$$
\begin{aligned}
Eu(W_0(1 + \mathbf{w}'\mathbf{R})) &= E\left[W_0(1 + \mathbf{w}'\mathbf{R}) - \frac{b}{2}W_0^2(1 + \mathbf{w}'\mathbf{R})^2\right] \\
&= u(W_0) + W_0 E(\mathbf{w}'\mathbf{R}) - \frac{b}{2}W_0^2[2E(\mathbf{w}'\mathbf{R}) + E(\mathbf{w}'\mathbf{R})^2] \\
&= u(W_0) + W_0\mu_p(1 - bW_0) - \frac{b}{2}W_0^2(\sigma_p^2 - \mu_p^2)
\end{aligned}
$$

where μ_p and σ_p are the expected return and standard deviation of the portfolio, respectively. Consequently, we see that also in this case the objective function only depends on the mean and the variance of the portfolio. Thus, this special case is equivalent to mean-variance analysis.

For a general utility function, the optimization problem described above will no longer be equivalent to the classical mean-variance analysis, but often leads to more complex formulations. For a utility function it is common to require that $u' > 0$ and $u'' \le 0$. This means that an investor always prefers more to less utility, but that marginal utility decreases with increasing wealth. In this setting, an investor's aversion to risk is measured by his *absolute* and *relative risk aversion*, given by

$$r_A(x) = -\frac{u''(x)}{u'(x)}$$

and

$$r_R(x) = -\frac{xu''(x)}{u'(x)}$$

EXHIBIT 2.12   Different Utility Functions

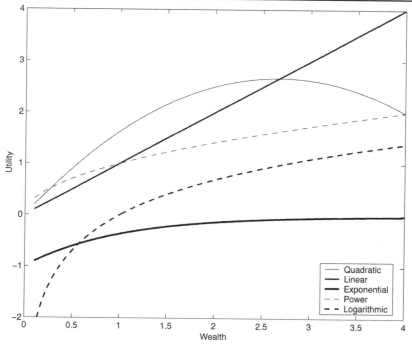

These measures express the intuitive fact that the "more curved" the utility function is, the more risk-averse the investor is. Some of the commonly used utility functions are listed below, and depicted in Exhibit 2.12:

■ *Linear utility function*

$$u(x) = a + bx, \quad r_A(x) = r_R(x) = 0$$

The risk aversions are zero and therefore the linear utility function is referred to as risk-neutral.

■ *Quadratic utility function*[33]

$$u(x) = x - \frac{b}{2}x^2, \quad b > 0$$

---

[33] This utility function satisfies $u' > 0$ only when $x < 1/b$, which implies that there are certain states where the investor would choose less wealth over more. This is a problem with the quadratic utility function.

$$r_A(x) = \frac{b}{1-bx}, \quad r_R(x) = \frac{bx}{1-bx}$$

■ *Exponential utility function*

$$u(x) = -\frac{1}{\lambda}e^{-\lambda x}, \quad \lambda = 0$$

$$r_A(x) = \lambda, \quad r_R(x) = \lambda x$$

This utility function is often referred to as *constant absolute risk aversion* (CARA) because the absolute risk aversion is constant.

■ *Power utility function*

$$u(x) = x^\alpha, \quad 0 < \alpha < 1$$

$$r_A(x) = \frac{1-\alpha}{x}, \quad r_R(x) = 1-\alpha$$

This utility function is often referred to as *constant relative risk aversion* (CRRA) because the relative risk aversion is constant.

■ *Logarithmic utility function*

$$u(x) = \ln(x)$$

$$r_A(x) = \frac{1}{x}, \quad r_R(x) = 1$$

This utility function is often referred to as *constant relative risk aversion* (CRRA) because the relative risk aversion is constant.[34]

In practice, the choice of utility function depends on the particular application at hand, together with computational considerations. With the computational resources available today it is possible, at least for smaller portfolios, to solve the expected utility maximization through simulation for any of the utility functions given above.[35] In many practi-

---

[34] As a matter of fact, the logarithmic utility function provides an extension of the power utility function for $\alpha = 0$ by the nature of the equality

$$\lim_{\alpha \to 0} \frac{x^\alpha - 1}{\alpha} = \ln(x)$$

[35] See for example, Paul Samuelson, "When and Why Mean-variance Analysis Generically Fails," forthcoming in the *American Economic Review*; Andrew Ang and Geert Bekaert, "International Asset Allocation With Regime Shifts," *Review of Financial Studies* 15, no. 4 (2002), pp. 1137–1187.

cal portfolio management applications there is a trade-off: computational convenience and speed versus modeling error and accuracy.

Levy and Markowitz showed how to approximate power utility functions using quadratic utility and compared their performance with the approximations on a sample of mutual fund returns.[36] They concluded that mean-variance approximations to power utility functions do well for returns from –30% to about 60%. Several other studies (e.g., Pulley,[37] Kroll et al.,[38] and Cremers et al.[39]) compare portfolio allocation using more general utility functions along with the empirical return distribution to mean-variance optimization, and conclude that the approximation error and the resulting performance differences from only using means and variances are very small.

Kallberg and Ziemba compared different utility functions and how they affect the optimal composition of portfolios.[40] Their study provides empirical support for portfolio allocations using utility functions that have different functional forms and parameter values but similar absolute risk aversion result in similar optimal portfolios. Their findings suggest that the portfolio optimization problem is relatively robust with respect to changes of utility function, provided that the level of absolute risk aversion remains the same.

These results show that in many practical applications, we can choose the utility function that allows for the most efficient numerical solution. Being the computationally most easily tractable utility function, it is not a surprise that quadratic utility is by far the most commonly used in practice today.

We note, however, that most of the studies above were performed using assets exhibiting return distributions not too far away from normality. For so-called elliptical distributions such as the normal, Student-*t*, and Levy distributions, it has been demonstrated that the mean-vari-

---

[36] Haim Levy and Harry Markowitz, "Approximating Expected Utility by a Function of Mean and Variance," *American Economic Review* 69, no. 3 (1979), pp. 308–318.

[37] Lawrence M. Pulley, "A General Mean-Variance Approximation to Expected Utility for Short Holding Periods," *Journal of Financial and Quantitative Analysis* 16 (1981), pp. 361–373.

[38] Yoram Kroll, Haim Levy, and Harry M. Markowitz, "Mean-Variance Versus Direct Utility Maximization," *Journal of Finance* 39, no. 1 (1984), pp. 47–61.

[39] Jan-Hein Cremers, Mark Kritzman, and Sebastien Page, "Portfolio Formation with Higher Moments and Plausible Utility," Revere Street Working Papers 272–12, undated.

[40] Jerry G. Kallberg and William T. Ziemba, "Comparison of Alternative Utility Functions in Portfolio Selection Problems," *Management Science* 29, no. 11 (November 1983), pp. 1257–1276.

ance approximation of the expected utility is exact for all utility functions.[41] This offers a possible explanation for the good performance of the classical mean-variance formulation in the studies. Furthermore, it was pointed out by Cremers *et al.* that higher moments do not seem to matter very much for investors with power utility.

When asset returns in a particular portfolio exhibit skew, fat tails, and high correlation—such as is the case with some stocks and many derivative securities—higher moments do matter. We discuss this in more detail in Chapter 5.

SUMMARY

- Markowitz quantified the concept of diversification through the statistical notion of covariance between individual securities, and the overall standard deviation of a portfolio.
- The basic assumption behind modern portfolio theory is that an investor's preferences can be represented by a function (utility function) of the expected return and the variance of a portfolio.
- The basic principle underlying modern portfolio theory is that for a given level of expected return a rational investor would choose the portfolio with minimum variance from amongst the set of all possible portfolios. We presented three equivalent formulations: (1) the minimum variance formulation, (2) the expected return maximization formulation, and (3) the risk aversion formulation.
- Minimum variance portfolios are called mean-variance efficient portfolios. The set of all mean-variance efficient portfolios is called the *efficient frontier*. The efficient frontier with only risky assets has a parabolic shape in the expected return/standard deviation coordinate system.
- The portfolio on the efficient frontier with the smallest variance is called the global minimum variance portfolio.
- The mean-variance problem results in an optimization problem referred to as a quadratic program.
- The efficient frontier widens as the number of (not perfectly correlated) securities increases. The efficient frontier shrinks as constraints are imposed upon the portfolio.

---

[41] Guy Chamberlain, "A Characterization of the Distributions That Imply Mean-Variance Utility Functions," *Journal of Economic Theory* 29, no. 1 (1983), pp. 185–201.

■ With the addition of a risk-free asset, the efficient frontier becomes a straight line in the expected return/standard deviation coordinate system. This line is called the *capital market line*.

■ The tangency point of the efficient frontier with only risky assets and the capital market line is called the *tangency portfolio*.

■ The *market portfolio* is the portfolio that consists of all assets available to investors in the same proportion as each security's market value divided by the total market value of all securities. Under certain assumptions it can be shown that the tangency portfolio is the same as the market portfolio.

■ The excess expected return of the market portfolio (the expected return of the market portfolio minus the risk-free rate) divided by the standard deviation of the market portfolio is referred to as the *equilibrium market price of risk*.

■ The capital market line expresses that the expected return on a portfolio is equal to the risk-free rate plus a portfolio specific risk premium. The portfolio specific risk premium is the market price of risk multiplied by the risk (standard deviation) of the portfolio.

■ A utility function is a numerical function that assigns a value to all possible choices faced by an entity. A *utility function* is a preference ordering that allows us to rank different choices from most to least preferred. The concept of utility functions allows us to consider a more general framework for portfolio choice, beyond that of just the mean and the variance.

■ The quadratic utility function provides a good approximation for many of the standard utility functions such as exponential, power, and logarithmic utility.

CHAPTER 3

Transaction and Trading Costs

In Chapter 1 we discussed the importance of formulating a rigorous investment program. We addressed four key aspects: (1) producing realistic and reasonable return expectations and forecasts; (2) controlling and managing risk exposure; (3) managing trading and transaction costs; and (4) monitoring and managing the total investment process. The first two areas will be covered in Chapters 8 and 9. In this chapter we focus on the third point.

Trading and executing are integral components of the investment process. A poorly executed trade can eat directly into portfolio returns. This is because financial markets are not frictionless and transactions have a cost associated to them. Costs are incurred when buying or selling securities in the form of, for example, brokerage commissions, bid-ask spreads, taxes, and market impact costs.

In recent years, portfolio managers have started to more carefully consider transaction costs. Partly, this is due to the flat performance of equities, often just in the single digits, after the period in the 1990s where the stock market returned about 20% per year. In a sideway market, portfolio managers become more careful about the costs that their trades and decisions bring about. If portfolio returns can be increased by 100 to 200 basis points (bps) by reducing trading costs, that can translate into a sizable amount, especially during tougher years. Consider for example a $1 billion equity fund that has an annual turnover of 100%.[1] Transaction costs in the order of 40 basis points per trade for this fund would result in an annual turnover cost of $8 million ($1 billion × 1 × 0.004 × 2).

The literature on market microstructure, analysis and measurement of transaction costs, and market impact costs on institutional trades is

---

[1] By turning over a security is meant both buying and later selling the security. This amounts to two transactions.

51

rapidly expanding.[2] One way of looking at transaction costs is to categorize them in terms of *explicit costs* such as brokerage and taxes, and *implicit costs,* which include market impact costs, price movement risk, and opportunity cost. *Market impact cost* is, broadly speaking, the price an investor has to pay for obtaining liquidity in the market, whereas *price movement risk* is the risk that the price of an asset increases or decreases from the time the investor decides to transact in the asset until the transaction actually takes place.

Opportunity cost is the cost suffered when a trade is not executed. Another way of seeing transaction costs is in terms of *fixed costs* versus *variable costs.* Whereas commissions and trading fees are fixed—bid-ask spreads, taxes and all implicit transaction costs are variable.

In this chapter, we will first present a simple taxonomy of trading costs. The specification is not new and has appeared in several forms in the literature before.[3] We then discuss the linkage between transaction costs and liquidity as well as the measurement of these quantities.

Portfolio managers and traders need to be able to effectively model the impact of trading costs on their portfolios and trades. In particular, if possible, they would like to minimize the total transaction costs. To address these issues we introduce several approaches for the modeling of transaction costs. We conclude the chapter by providing an introduction to optimal execution strategies.

A TAXONOMY OF TRANSACTION COSTS

Probably the easiest way to understand and distinguish transaction costs is to categorize them in terms of fixed versus variable transaction costs, and explicit versus implicit transaction costs as shown below as suggested by Kissell and Glantz:[4]

---

[2] See, for example, Ian Domowitz, Jack Glen, and Ananth Madhavan, "Liquidity, Volatility, and Equity Trading Costs Across Countries and Over Time," *International Finance* 4, no. 2 (2001), pp. 221–255 and Donald B. Keim and Ananth Madhavan, "The Costs of Institutional Equity Trades," *Financial Analysts Journal* 54, no. 4 (July/August 1998) pp. 50–69.
[3] See, Robert Kissell and Morton Glantz, *Optimal Trading Strategies* (New York: AMACOM, 2003); Bruce M. Collins and Frank J. Fabozzi, "A Methodology for Measuring Transaction Costs," *Financial Analysts Journal* 47 (1991), pp. 27–36; Ananth Madhavan, "Market Microstructure: A Survey," *Journal of Financial Markets* 3 (2000), pp. 205–258; *The Transaction Cost Challenge* (New York: ITG, 2000).
[4] Kissell and Glantz, *Optimal Trading Strategies.*

	Fixed	Variable
Explicit	Commissions	Bid-Ask Spreads
	Fees	Taxes
Implicit		Delay Cost
		Price Movement Risk
		Market Impact Costs
		Timing Risk
		Opportunity Cost

Fixed transaction costs are independent of factors such as trade size and market conditions.[5] In contrast, variable transaction costs depend on some or all of these factors. In other words, while the fixed transaction costs are "what they are," portfolio managers and traders can seek to reduce, optimize, and efficiently manage the variable transaction costs.

Explicit transaction costs are those costs that are observable and known upfront such as commissions and fees, and taxes. Implicit transaction costs, on the other hand, are nonobservable and not known in advance. Examples of transaction costs in this category are market impact costs and opportunity cost. The implicit costs make up the larger part of the total transaction costs in most cases.

Explicit Transaction Costs

Trading commissions and fees, taxes, and bid-ask spreads are explicit or observable transaction costs.

Commissions and Fees

Commissions are paid to brokers to execute trades.[6] Normally, commissions on securities trades are negotiable. Fees charged by an institution that holds the securities in safekeeping for an investor are referred to as *custodial fees*. When the ownership over a stock is transferred, the investor is charged a *transfer fee*.

---

[5] However, we emphasize that different exchanges and trading networks may have different fixed costs. Furthermore, the fixed costs may also vary depending upon whether a trade is an agency trade or a principal trade.

[6] For a more detailed discussion of commissions, see Alan D. Biller, "A Plan Sponsor's Guide to Commissions," Chapter 10 in Frank J. Fabozzi (ed.), *Pension Fund Investment Management: Second Edition* (Hoboken, NJ: John Wiley & Sons, 1997).

Taxes

The most common taxes are *capital gains tax* and *tax on dividends*. The tax law distinguishes between two types of capital gains taxes: *short-term* and *long-term*. The former is according to the investor's tax bracket, whereas the latter currently stands at 15%. In the United States, the tax law as of this writing requires that an asset must be held for at least one full year to qualify for the lower long-term capital gains rate. Although tax planning is an important component of any investment strategy this topic is outside the scope of this book.[7]

Bid-Ask Spreads

The distance between the quoted sell and buy order is called the *bid-ask spread*. The bid-ask spread is the immediate transaction cost that the market charges anyone for the privilege of trading. High immediate liquidity is synonymous with small spreads. We can think about the bid-ask spread as the price charged by dealers for supplying immediacy and short-term price stability in the presence of short-term order imbalances. Dealers act as a buffer between the investors that want to buy and sell, and thereby provide stability in the market by making sure a certain order is maintained. In *negotiated markets* such as the New York Stock Exchange (NYSE), market-makers and dealers maintain a certain minimum inventory on their books. If the dealer is unable to match a buyer with a seller (or vice versa), he has the capability to take on the exposure on his book.

However, the bid-ask spread does not necessarily represent the best prices available, and the "half spread" is, therefore, not always the minimal cost for immediate buy or sell executions. Certain price improvements are possible and occur, for example, because:

- NYSE specialists fill the incoming market orders at improved prices.[8]
- The market may have moved in favor during the time it took to route the order to the market center (a so-called "lucky saving").

---

[7] Although historically tax planning has only been part of the investment strategies of institutions and wealthy individuals, this is no longer the case. In recent years, there is a trend in the mutual fund industry to provide greater availability to tax efficient mutual funds as the demand for tax efficient vehicles for individual investors has increased. See for example, Brad M. Barber and Terrance Odean, "Are Individual Investors Tax Savvy? Evidence from Retail and Discount Brokerage Accounts," *Journal of Public Economics* 88, no. 1–2 (2004), pp. 419–442.

[8] See for example, Lawrence E. Harris and Venkatesh Panchapagesan, "The Information Content of the Limit Order Book: Evidence from NYSE Specialist Trading Decisions," *Journal of Financial Markets* 8 (2005), pp. 25–67.

■ The presence of hidden liquidity.[9]
■ Buy and sell orders can be "crossed."[10]

The bid-ask spread is misleading as a true liquidity measure because it only conveys the price for small trades. For large trades, due to price impact, as we will see the actual price will be quite different. We will elaborate more on the linkage between liquidity, trading costs, and market impact costs later in this chapter.

Implicit Transaction Costs

Investment delay, market impact cost, price movement risk, market timing, and opportunity cost are implicit or nonobservable transaction costs.

Investment Delay

Normally, there is a delay between the time when the portfolio manager makes a buy/sell decision of a security and when the actual trade is brought to the market by a trader. If the price of the security changes during this time, the price change (possibly adjusted for general market moves) represents the *investment delay cost*, or the cost of not being able to execute immediately. We note that this cost depends on the investment strategy. For example, modern quantitative trading systems that automatically submit an electronic order after generating a trading decision are exposed to smaller delay costs. More traditional approaches where investment decisions first have to be approved by, for example, an investment committee, exhibit higher delay costs. Some practitioners view the investment delay cost as part of the opportunity cost discussed below.

Market Impact Costs

The *market impact cost* of a transaction is the deviation of the transaction price from the market (mid) price[11] that would have prevailed had the trade not occurred. The price movement is the cost, *the market*

---

[9] For example, on *electronic communications networks* (ECNs) and on NASDAQ, although it is possible to view the limit order book, a significant portion of the book cannot be seen. This is referred to as *hidden* or *discretionary orders*.

[10] A *cross order* is an offsetting or noncompetitive matching of the buy order of one investor against the sell order of another investor. This practice is permissible only when executed in accordance with the Commodity Exchange Act, CFTC regulations and the rules of the particular market. See for example, Joel Hasbrouck, George Sofianos, and Deborah Sosebee, "New York Stock Exchange Systems and Trading Procedures," Working Paper 93-01, New York Stock Exchange, 1993, pp. 46–47.

[11] Since the buyer buys at the ask and the seller sells at the bid, this definition of market impact cost ignores the bid/ask spread which is an explicit cost.

impact cost, for demanding liquidity or immediacy. We note that the price impact of a trade can be negative if, for example, a trader buys at a price below the no-trade price (i.e., the price that would have prevailed had the trade not taken place). In general, liquidity providers experience negative costs while liquidity demanders will face positive costs.

We distinguish between two different kinds of market impact costs, temporary and permanent. Total market impact cost is computed as the sum of the two. Exhibit 3.1 illustrates the different components of the market impact costs of a buy order. The temporary price impact cost is of transitory nature and can be seen as the additional *liquidity concession* necessary for the liquidity provider (for example, the market maker) to take the order, *inventory effects* (price effects due to broker/dealer inventory imbalances), or *imperfect substitution* (for example, price incentives to induce market participants to absorb the additional shares).

The permanent price impact cost, however, reflects the persistent price change that results as the market receives the information provided by the trade. Intuitively, a buy transaction reveals to the market that the security may be undervalued, whereas a sell transaction signals that the security may be overpriced. Security prices change when market participants adjust their views and perceptions as they observe the information contained in the new trades throughout the trading day.

Although market impact costs are not constant throughout time, in general, by extending the trading horizon, they will decrease. For example, a trader executing a less urgent trade can buy/sell his position in smaller portions over a period and make sure that each portion only constitutes a small percentage of the average volume.

EXHIBIT 3.1   Market Impact Costs (Buy Order)

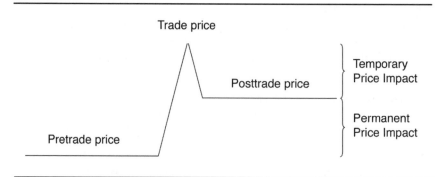

Source: Figure 1 on page 23 in "ITG ACE—Agency Cost Estimator: A Model Description," 2003, www.itginc.com.

Market impact costs are often *asymmetric*; that is they vary between buy and sell orders. For instance, Bikker and Spierdijk estimated the price impact costs from a data sample consisting of 3,728 worldwide equity trades executed during the first quarter of 2002 at the Dutch pension fund Algemeen Burgerlijk Pensioenfonds (ABP).[12] The trades, of which 1,963 were buys and 1,765 sales, had a total transaction value of €5.7 billion. They concluded that the temporary and persistent price effects of buy orders were 7.2 basis points and 12.4 basis points, respectively. For sell orders, on the other hand, these price effects were –14.5 basis points and –16.5 basis points.

This and many other empirical studies suggest that price impact costs are generally higher for buy orders. Nevertheless, while buy costs might be higher than sell costs, this empirical fact is most likely due to observations during rising/falling markets, rather than any *true* market microstructure effects. For example, a study by Hu shows that the difference in market impact costs between buys and sells is an artifact of the trade benchmark.[13] (We discuss trade benchmarks later in this chapter.) When a pretrade measure is used, buys (sells) have higher implicit trading costs during rising (falling) markets. Conversely, if a posttrade measure is used, sells (buys) have higher implicit trading costs during rising (falling) markets. In fact, both pretrade and posttrade measures are highly influenced by market movement, whereas during- or average-trade measures are neutral to market movement.

Despite the enormous global size of equity markets, the impact of trading is important even for relatively small funds. In fact, a sizable fraction of the stocks that compose an index might have to be excluded or their trading severely limited. For example, RAS Asset Management, which is the asset manager arm of the large Italian insurance company RAS, has determined that single trades exceeding 10% of the daily trading volume of a stock cause an excessive price impact and have to be excluded, while trades between 5% and 10% need execution strategies distributed over several days.

To appreciate the impact of these restrictions on portfolio management strategies, Exhibit 3.2 illustrates the distribution of trading volume in the MSCI Europe in the period September–December 2004 below €5 million, €7.5 million, and €10 million.

---

[12] Jacob A. Bikker, Laura Spierdijk, and Pieter Jelle van der Sluis, "Market Impact Costs of Institutional Equity Trades," Technical Report, Financial Engineering Laboratory and the Department of Applied Mathematics, University of Twente, 2004.
[13] Gang Hu, "Measures of Implicit Trading Costs and Buy-Sell Asymmetry," Working Paper, Babson College, 2005.

EXHIBIT 3.2   Distribution of Trading Volumes in the MSCI Europe in the Three-Month Period Ending 16-December 2004 (Data Courtesy of RAS Asset Management)

	Average daily trading volume < €5 million	Average daily trading volume < €7.5 million	Average daily trading volume < €10 million
Percentage of stocks in the MCSI Europe	17.76%	24.33%	33.75%

According to RAS Asset Management estimates, in practice funds managed actively with quantitative techniques and with market capitalization in excess of €100 million can operate only on the fraction of the market above the €5 million, splitting trades over several days for stocks with average daily trading volume in the range from €5 million to €10 million. They can freely operate only on two thirds of the stocks in the MSCI Europe.

Price Movement Risk

In general, the stock market exhibits a positive drift that gives rise to price movement risk. Similarly, individual stocks, at least temporarily, trend up or down. A trade that goes in the same direction as the general market or an individual security is exposed to price risk. For example, when a trader is buying in a rising market, he might pay more than he initially anticipated to fully satisfy the order. In practice, it can be difficult to separate price movement risk from the market impact cost. Typically, the price movement risk for a buy order is defined as the price increase during the time of the trade that is attributed to the general trend of a security, whereas the remaining part is market impact costs.

Market Timing Costs

The market timing costs are due to the movement in the price of a security at the time of the transaction that can be attributed to other market participants or general market volatility. Market timing cost is higher for larger trades, in particular when they are divided up into smaller blocks and traded over a period of time. Practitioners often define market timing costs to be proportional to the standard deviation of the security returns times the square root of the time anticipated in order to complete the transaction.

Opportunity Costs

The cost of not transacting represents an opportunity cost. For example, when a certain trade fails to execute, the portfolio manager misses an opportunity. Commonly, this cost is defined as the difference in performance between a portfolio manager's desired investment and his actual investment after transaction costs. Opportunity costs are in general driven by price risk or market volatility. As a result, the longer the trading horizon, the greater the exposure to opportunity costs. Later in this chapter we will discuss how a trader can try to find an optimal balance between market impact costs and opportunity costs.

Identifying Transaction Costs: An Example[14]

We now consider an example to highlight the key cost components of an equity trade. Following the completion of an institutional trade, suppose that the ticker tape for XYZ stock reveals that 6,000 shares of XYZ stock were purchased at $82.00.

Although 6,000 XYZ shares were bought, Exhibit 3.3 indicates what may have happened behind the scenes—beginning with the initial security selection decision by the manager (the investment idea), to the release of the buy order by the equity trader, to the subsequent trade execution by the broker (the essential elements of trading implementation).

We can assess the cost of trading XYZ stock as follows. The commission charge is the easiest to identify—namely, $0.045 per share, or $270 on the purchase of 6,000 shares of XYZ stock.

Since the trade desk did not release the order to buy XYZ stock until it was selling for $81, the assessed trader timing cost is $1 per share. Also, the price impact costs is $1 per XYZ share traded, as the stock was selling for $81 when the order was received by the broker—just prior to execution of the 6,000 XYZ shares at $82.

EXHIBIT 3.3   XYZ Trade Decomposition

Equity manager wants to buy 10,000 shares of XYZ at current price of $80. Trade desk releases 8,000 shares to broker when price is $81. Broker purchases 6,000 shares of XYZ stock at $82 plus $0.045 (per share) commission. XYZ stock jumps to $85, and remainder of order is canceled. 15 days later the price of XYZ stock is $88.

Source: Exhibit 1 in Chapter 11 of Frank J. Fabozzi and James L. Grant, *Equity Portfolio Management* (Hoboken, NJ: John Wiley & Sons, 1999), p. 309

---

[14] This illustration is similar to the example provided in Wayne H. Wagner and Mark Edwards, "Implementing Investment Strategies: The Art and Science of Investing," Chapter 11 in Frank J. Fabozzi (ed.), *Active Equity Portfolio Management* (Hoboken, NJ: John Wiley & Sons, 1998). The example used here is taken from Frank J. Fabozzi and James L. Grant, *Equity Portfolio Management* (Hoboken, NJ: John Wiley & Sons, 1999), pp. 309–310.

The opportunity cost—resulting from unexecuted shares—of the equity trade is somewhat more problematic. Assuming that the movement of XYZ stock price from $80 to $88 can be largely attributed to information used by the equity manager in his security selection decision, it appears that the value of the investment idea to purchase XYZ stock was 10% ($88/$80 − 1) over a 15-day trading interval. Since 40% of the initial buy order on XYZ stock was "left on the table," the opportunity cost of not purchasing 4,000 shares of XYZ stock is 4% (10% × 40%).

The basic trading cost illustration in Exhibit 3.3 suggests that without efficient management of the equity trading process, it is possible that the value of the manager's investment ideas (gross alpha) is impacted negatively by sizable trading costs in addition to commission charges, including trader timing, price or market impact cost, and opportunity cost. Moreover, trading cost management is especially important in a world where active equity managers are hard pressed to outperform a simple buy and hold approach such as that employed in a market index fund.

LIQUIDITY AND TRANSACTION COSTS

Liquidity is created by agents transacting in the financial markets when they buy and sell securities. Market makers and brokers/dealers do not create liquidity; they are intermediaries who facilitate trade execution and maintain an orderly market.

Liquidity and transaction costs are interrelated. A highly liquid market is one were large transactions can be immediately executed without incurring high transaction costs. In an indefinitely liquid market, traders would be able to perform very large transactions directly at the quoted bid-ask prices. In reality, particularly for larger orders, the market requires traders to pay more than the ask when buying, and pays them less than the bid when selling. As we discussed above, this percentage degradation of the bid-ask prices experienced when executing trades is the market impact cost.

The market impact cost varies with transaction size: the larger the trade size the larger the impact cost. Impact costs are not constant in time, but vary throughout the day as traders change the limit orders that they have in the limit order book. A *limit order* is a conditional order; it is executed only if the limit price or a better price can be obtained. For example, a buy limit order of a security XYZ at $60 indicates that the assets may be purchased only at $60 or lower. Therefore, a limit order is very different from a *market order*, which is an unconditional order to execute at the current best price available in the market (guarantees execution, not price). With a limit order a trader can improve the execution price relative to the market order price, but the execution is neither certain nor immediate (guarantees price, not execution).

Notably, there are many different limit order types available such as pegging orders, discretionary limit orders, IOC orders, and fleeting orders. For example, fleeting orders are those limit orders that are cancelled within two seconds of submission. Hasbrouck and Saar find that fleeting limit orders are much closer substitutes for market orders than for traditional limit orders.[15] This suggests that the role of limit orders has changed from the traditional view of being liquidity suppliers to being substitutes for market orders.

At any given instant, the list of orders waiting in the limit order book embodies the liquidity that exists in a particular market. By observing the entire limit order book, impact costs can be calculated for different transaction sizes. The limit order book reveals the prevailing supply and demand in the market.[16] Therefore, in a pure limit order market we can obtain a measure of liquidity by aggregating limit buy orders (representing the demand) and limit sell orders (representing the supply).[17]

We start by sorting the bid and ask prices, $p_1^{bid}, ..., p_k^{bid}$ and $p_1^{ask}, ..., p_l^{ask}$, (from the most to the least competitive) and the corresponding order quantities $q_1^{bid}, ..., q_k^{bid}$ and $q_1^{ask}, ..., q_l^{ask}$.[18] We then combine the sorted bid and ask prices into a supply and demand schedule according to Exhibit 3.4. For example, the block (p_2^{bid}, q_2^{bid}) represents the second best sell limit order with price p_2^{bid} and quantity q_2^{bid}.

We note that unless there is a gap between the bid (demand) and the ask (supply) sides, there will be a match between a seller and buyer, and

---

[15] Joel Hasbrouck and Gideon Saar, "Technology and Liquidity Provision: The Blurring of Traditional Definitions," Working Paper, New York University, 2004.

[16] Note that even if it is possible to view the entire limit order book it does not give a *complete* picture of the liquidity in the market. This is because hidden and discretionary orders are not included. For a discussion on this topic, see Laura A. Tuttle, "Hidden Orders, Trading Costs and Information," Working Paper, Ohio State University, 2002.

[17] Ian Domowitz and Xiaoxin Wang, "Liquidity, Liquidity Commonality and Its Impact on Portfolio Theory," Smeal College of Business Administration, Pennsylvania State University, 2002; Thierry Foucault, Ohad Kadan, and Eugene Kandel, "Limit Order Book As a Market for Liquidity," School of Business Administration, Hebrew University, 2001.

[18] In this chapter, we diverge slightly form the notation used elsewhere in this book. Instead, we use the notation that is common in the trading and transaction cost literature and denote price by p, order quantity by q, and trade size by Q (or V).

a trade would occur. The larger the gap, the lower the liquidity and the market participants' desire to trade. For a trade of size Q, we can define its *liquidity* as the reciprocal of the area between the supply and demand curves up to Q (i.e., the "dotted" area in Exhibit 3.4).

However, few order books are publicly available and not all markets are pure limit order markets. In 2004, the NYSE started selling information on its limit order book through its new system called the *NYSE OpenBook*®. The system provides an aggregated real-time view of the exchange's limit-order book for all NYSE-traded securities.[19]

In the absence of a fully transparent limit order book, expected market impact cost is the most practical and realistic measure of market liquidity. It is closer to the true cost of transacting faced by market participants as compared to other measures such as those based upon the bid-ask spread.

EXHIBIT 3.4   The Supply and Demand Schedule of a Security

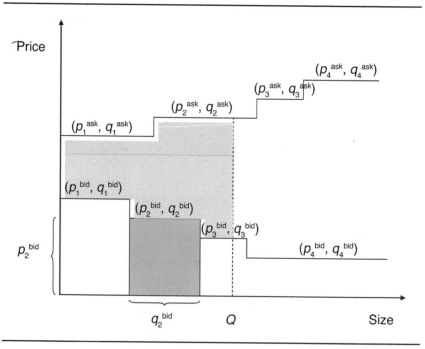

Source: Figure 1A on page 38 in Ian Domowitz and Xiaoxin Wang, "Liquidity, Liquidity Commonality and Its Impact on Portfolio Theory," Smeal College of Business Administration, Pennsylvania State University, 2002.

---

[19] NYSE and Securities Industry Automation Corporation, *NYSE OpenBook*®, Version 1.1, 2004.

MARKET IMPACT MEASUREMENTS AND EMPIRICAL FINDINGS

The problem with measuring implicit transaction costs is that the true measure, which is the difference between the price of the stock in the absence of a money manager's trade and the execution price, is not observable. Furthermore, the execution price is dependent on supply and demand conditions at the margin. Thus, the execution price may be influenced by competitive traders who demand immediate execution or by other investors with similar motives for trading. This means that the execution price realized by an investor is the consequence of the structure of the market mechanism, the demand for liquidity by the marginal investor, and the competitive forces of investors with similar motivations for trading.

There are many ways to measure transaction costs. However, in general this cost is the difference between the execution price and some appropriate benchmark, a so-called *fair market benchmark*. The fair market benchmark of a security is the price that would have prevailed had the trade not taken place, the *no-trade price*. Since the no-trade price is not observable, it has to be estimated. Practitioners have identified three different basic approaches to measure the market impact:[20]

- *Pretrade measures* use prices occurring before or at the decision to trade as the benchmark, such as the opening price on the same-day or the closing price on the previous day.
- *Posttrade measures* use prices occurring after the decision to trade as the benchmark, such as the closing price of the trading day or the opening price on the next day.
- *Same-day* or *average measures* use average prices of a large number of trades during the day of the decision to trade, such as the *volume-weighted average price* (VWAP) calculated over all transactions in the security on the trade day.[21]

The volume-weighted average price is calculated as follows. Suppose that it was a trader's objective to purchase 10,000 shares of stock XYZ. After completion of the trade, the trade sheet showed that 4,000 shares were purchased at $80, another 4,000 at $81, and finally 2,000

---

[20] Bruce M. Collins and Frank J. Fabozzi, "A Methodology for Measuring Transaction Costs," *Financial Analysts Journal* 47 (1991), pp. 27–36; Louis K. C. Chan and Joseph Lakonishok, "Institutional Trades and Intraday Stock Price Behavior," *Journal of Financial Economics* 33 (1993), pp. 173–199; and, Fabozzi and Grant, *Equity Portfolio Management*.

[21] Strictly speaking, VWAP is not the benchmark here but rather the transaction type.

at \$82. In this case, the resulting VWAP is $(4{,}000 \times 80 + 4{,}000 \times 81 + 2{,}000 \times 82)/10{,}000 = \$80.80$.

We denote by χ the indicator function that takes on the value 1 or -1 if an order is a buy or sell order, respectively. Formally, we now express the three types of measures of *market impact* (MI) as follows

$$\mathrm{MI}_{\mathrm{pre}} = \left(\frac{p^{\mathrm{ex}}}{p^{\mathrm{pre}}} - 1 \right) \chi$$

$$\mathrm{MI}_{\mathrm{post}} = \left(\frac{p^{\mathrm{ex}}}{p^{\mathrm{post}}} - 1 \right) \chi$$

$$\mathrm{MI}_{\mathrm{VWAP}} = \left(\frac{\displaystyle\sum_{i=1}^{k} V_i \cdot p_i^{\mathrm{ex}}}{\displaystyle\sum_{i=1}^{k} V_i} \Big/ p^{\mathrm{pre}} - 1 \right) \chi$$

where p^{ex}, p^{pre}, and p^{post} denote the execution price, pretrade price, and posttrade price of the stock, and k denotes the number of transactions in a particular security on the trade date. Using this definition, for a stock with market impact *MI* the resulting *market impact cost* for a trade of size V, *MIC*, is given by

$$\mathrm{MIC} = \mathrm{MI} \cdot V$$

It is also common to adjust market impact for general market movements. For example, the pretrade market impact with market adjustment would take the form

$$\mathrm{MI}_{\mathrm{pre}} = \left(\frac{p^{\mathrm{ex}}}{p^{\mathrm{pre}}} - \frac{p_M^{\mathrm{ex}}}{p_M^{\mathrm{pre}}} \right) \chi$$

where p_M^{ex} represent the value of the index at the time of the execution, and p_M^{pre} the price of the index at the time before the trade. Market adjusted market impact for the posttrade and same-day trade benchmarks are calculated in an analogous fashion.

The above three approaches to measure market impact are based upon measuring the fair market benchmark of stock at a point in time. Clearly, different definitions of market impact lead to different results. Which one should be used is a matter of preference and is dependent on the application at hand. For example, Elkins/McSherry, a financial consulting firm that provides customized trading costs and execution analysis, calculates a same-day benchmark price for each stock by taking the mean of the day's open, close, high and low prices. The market impact is then computed as the percentage difference between the transaction price and this benchmark. However, in most cases VWAP and the Elkins/McSherry approach lead to similar measurements.[22]

As we analyze a portfolio's return over time an important question to ask is whether we can attribute good/bad performance to investment profits/losses or to trading profits/losses. In other words, in order to better understand a portfolio's performance it can be useful to decompose investment decisions from trading execution. This is the basic idea behind the *implementation shortfall approach*.[23]

In the implementation shortfall approach we assume that there is a separation between investment and trading decisions. The portfolio manager makes decisions with respect to the investment strategy (i.e., what should be bought, sold, and held). Subsequently, these decisions are implemented by the traders.

By comparing the actual portfolio profit/loss (P/L) with the performance of a hypothetical "paper" portfolio in which all trades are made at hypothetical market prices, we can get an estimate of the implementation shortfall. For example, with a paper portfolio return of 6% and an actual portfolio return of 5%, the implementation shortfall is 1%.

There is considerable practical and academic interest in the measurement and analysis of international trading costs. Domowitz, Glen, and Madhavan[24] examine international equity trading costs across a broad sample of 42 countries using quarterly data from 1995 to 1998. They find that the mean total one-way trading cost is 69.81 basis points. However, there is an enormous variation in trading costs across countries. For example, in their study the highest was Korea with 196.85

---

[22] John Willoughby, "Executions Song," *Institutional Investor* 32, no. 11 (1998), pp. 51–56; and Richard McSherry, "Global Trading Cost Analysis," mimeo, Elkins/McSherry Co., Inc., 1998.

[23] Andre. F. Perold, "The Implementation Shortfall: Paper Versus Reality," *Journal of Portfolio Management* 14 (1998), pp. 4–9.

[24] Ian Domowitz, Jack Glen, and Ananth Madhavan, "International Equity Trading Costs: A Cross-Sectional and Time-Series Analysis," Technical Report, Pennsylvania State University, International Finance Corp., University of Southern California, 1999.

basis points whereas the lowest was France with 29.85 basis points. Explicit costs are roughly two-thirds of total costs. However, one exception to this is the United States where the implicit costs are about 60% of the total costs.

Transaction costs in emerging markets are significantly higher than those in more developed markets. Domowitz, Glen, and Madhavan argue that this fact limits the gains of international diversification in these countries explaining in part the documented "home bias" of domestic investors.

In general, they find that transaction costs declined from the middle of 1997 to the end of 1998, maybe with the exception of Eastern Europe. It is interesting to notice that this reduction in transaction costs happened despite the turmoil in the financial markets during this period. A few explanations that Domowitz *et al.* suggest are that (1) the increased institutional presence has resulted in a more competitive environment for brokers/dealers and other trading services; (2) technological innovation has led to a growth in the use of low-cost electronic crossing networks (ECNs) by institutional traders; and (3) soft dollar payments[25] are now more common.

Based on nearly 700,000 trades by over 50 different management firms during the second half of 1996, research by Wagner and Edwards[26] points to an "iceberg" of equity trading costs that consists of both explicit and implicit trading cost elements. Exhibit 3.5 presents the typical range of trading costs in basis points faced by institutional investors. In particular, we see that commission charges average about 15 basis points, whereas price impact varies quite dramatically from −103 basis points (for a liquidity demanding trade) to about +36 basis points (for a liquidity in supplying trade). We also observe from the exhibit that there is an asymmetry in trading costs between the cost of liquidity demanding and liquidity supplying trades.

Trade timing is another large component of the "iceberg" of equity trading costs. As shown in the exhibit, these costs range from −327 basis points for a liquidity demanding trade, to +316 basis points when the trading desk is handing a liquidity supplying trade. At −60 basis points for a liquidity neutral trade, the trader timing cost is about 2.6 times (60/23) the normal trading costs associated with the price impact.

The final cost of trading is opportunity cost—that portion of the "iceberg" of equity trading costs that is never seen, but possibly the most

---

[25] These are payments where broker/dealers return a part of the commissions to institutional investors in the form of research and other services.

[26] Wagner and Edwards, "Implementing Investment Strategies: The Art and Science of Investing."

EXHIBIT 3.5   The "Iceberg" of Trading Costs (in basis points)

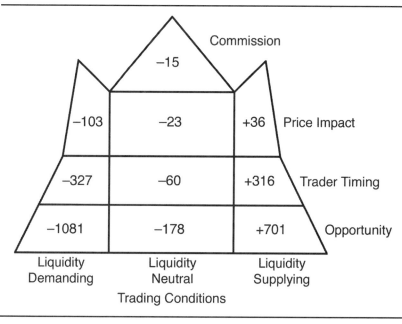

Source: Exhibit 2 in Wayne H. Wagner and Mark Edwards, "Implementing Investment Strategies: The Art and Science of Investing," Chapter 11 in Frank J. Fabozzi (ed.), *Active Equity Portfolio Management* (Hoboken, NJ: John Wiley & Sons, 1998), p. 186.

damaging to investment performance. As revealed in Exhibit 3.5, the opportunity cost of unexecuted trades ranges from a whopping –1,081 basis points (10.81% drain on investment performance when compared to costless trading) to +701 basis points for a liquidity supplying trade. With liquidity neutral trades, the opportunity cost from failed trades is –178 basis points. The resulting inefficiency due to opportunity cost might cause an active equity manager—with otherwise positive alpha— to have an *ex post*[27] performance that is either the same as—or possibly short of—the return to passive indexing.

---

[27] Latin for "after the fact." In models where there is uncertainty that is resolved during the course of events, the *ex post* values (realized returns for example) are the actual (realized) values. Compare this to *ex ante* which is Latin for "beforehand." In models where there is uncertainty that is resolved during the course of events, the ex ante values (expected returns for example) are forecasts of the actual (future) values.

FORECASTING AND MODELING MARKET IMPACT

In this section we describe a general methodology for constructing forecasting models for market impact. These types of models are very useful in predicting the resulting trading costs of specific trading strategies and in devising optimal trading approaches.

As we discussed above, the explicit transaction costs are relatively straightforward to estimate and forecast. Therefore, our focus in this section is to develop a methodology for the implicit transaction costs, and more specifically, market impact costs. The methodology is a linear factor based approach where market impact is the dependent variable. We distinguish between *trade-based* and *asset-based* independent variables or forecasting factors.

Trade-Based Factors

Some examples of trade-based factors include:

- Trade size
- Relative trade size
- Price of market liquidity
- Type of trade (information or noninformation trade)
- Efficiency and trading style of the investor
- Specific characteristics of the market or the exchange
- Time of trade submission and trade timing
- Order type

Probably the most important market impact forecasting variables are based on absolute or relative trade size. Absolute trade size is often measured in terms of the number of shares traded, or the dollar value of the trade. Relative trade size, on the other hand, can be calculated as number of shares traded divided by average daily volume, or number of shares traded divided by the total number of shares outstanding. Note that the former can be seen as an explanatory variable for the temporary price impact and the latter for the permanent price impact. In particular, we expect the temporary price impact to increase as the trade size to the average daily volume increases because a larger trade demands more liquidity.

Each type of investment style requires a different need for immediacy.[28] Technical trades often have to be traded at a faster pace in order to capitalize on some short-term signal and therefore exhibits higher market

---

[28] Donald B. Keim, and Ananth Madhavan, "Transaction Costs and Investment Style: An Inter-Exchange Analysis of Institutional Equity Trades," *Journal of Financial Economics* 46 (1997), pp. 265–292.

impact costs. In contrast, more traditional long-term value strategies can be traded more slowly. These type of strategies can in many cases even be liquidity providing, which might result in negative market impact costs.

Several studies show that there is a wide variation in equity transaction costs across different countries.[29] Markets and exchanges in each country are different, and so are the resulting market microstructures. Forecasting variables can be used to capture specific market characteristics such as liquidity, efficiency, and institutional features.

The particular timing of a trade can affect the market impact costs. For example, it appears that market impact costs are generally higher at the beginning of the month as compared to the end of it.[30] One of the reasons for this phenomenon is that many institutional investors tend to rebalance their portfolios at the beginning of the month. Because it is likely that many of these trades will be executed in the same stocks, this rebalancing pattern will induce an increase in market impact costs. The particular time of the day a trade takes place does also have an effect. Many informed institutional traders tend to trade at the market open as they want to capitalize on new information that appeared after the market close the day before.

As we discussed earlier in this chapter, market impact costs are asymmetric. In other words, buy and sell orders have significantly different market impact costs. Separate models for buy and sell orders can therefore be estimated. However, it is now more common to construct a model that includes dummy variables for different types of orders such as buy/sell orders, market orders, limit orders, and the like.

Asset-Based Factors

Some examples of asset-based factors are:

- Price momentum
- Price volatility
- Market capitalization
- Growth versus value
- Specific industry or sector characteristics

---

[29] See Domowitz, Glen, and Madhavan, "Liquidity, Volatility, and Equity Trading Costs Across Countries and Over Time," and Chiraphol N. Chiyachantana, Pankaj K. Jain, Christine Jian, and Robert A. Wood, "International Evidence on Institutional Trading Behavior and Price Impact," *Journal of Finance* 59 (2004), pp. 869–895.
[30] F. Douglas Foster and S. Viswanathan, "A Theory of the Interday Variations in Volume, Variance, and Trading Costs in Securities Markets," *Review of Financial Studies* 3 (1990), pp. 593–624.

For a stock that is exhibiting positive price momentum, a buy order is liquidity demanding and it is, therefore, likely that it will have higher price impact cost than a sell order.

Generally, trades in high volatility stocks result in higher permanent price effects. It has been suggested by Chan and Lakonishok[31] and Smith et al.[32] that this is because trades have a tendency to contain more information when volatility is high. Another possibility is that higher volatility increases the probability of hitting and being able to execute at the liquidity providers' price. Consequently, liquidity suppliers display fewer shares at the best prices to mitigate adverse selection costs.

Large-cap stocks are more actively traded and therefore more liquid in comparison to small-cap stocks. As a result, market impact cost is normally lower for large-caps.[33] However, if we measure market impact costs with respect to relative trade size (normalized by average daily volume, for instance) they are generally higher. Similarly, growth and value stocks have different market impact cost. One reason for that is related to the trading style. Growth stocks commonly exhibit momentum and high volatility. This attracts technical traders that are interested in capitalizing on short-term price swings. Value stocks are traded at a slower pace and holding periods tend to be slightly longer.

Different market sectors show different trading behaviors. For instance, Bikker and Spierdijk show that equity trades in the energy sector exhibit higher market impact costs than other comparable equities in non-energy sectors.[34]

A Factor-Based Market Impact Model

One of the most common approaches in practice and in the literature in modeling market impact is through a linear factor model of the form

$$MI_t = \alpha + \sum_{i=1}^{I} \beta_i x_i + \varepsilon_t$$

---

[31] Louis K. C. Chan and Joseph Lakonishok, "Institutional Equity Trading Costs: NYSE versus Nasdaq," *Journal of Finance* 52 (1997), pp. 713–735.

[32] Brian F. Smith, D. Alasdair S. Turnbull, and Robert W. White, "Upstairs Market for Principal and Agency Trades: Analysis of Adverse Information and Price Effects," *Journal of Finance* 56 (2001), pp. 1723–1746.

[33] Keim and Madhavan, "Transaction Costs and Investment Style," and Laura Spierdijk, Theo Nijman, and Arthur van Soest, "Temporary and Persistent Price Effects of Trades in Infrequently Traded Stocks," Working Paper, Tilburg University and Center, 2003.

[34] Bikker, Spierdijk, and van der Sluis, "Market Impact Costs of Institutional Equity Trades."

where α, β_i are the factor loadings and x_i are the factors. Frequently, the error term ε_t is assumed to be independently and identically distributed. Recall that the resulting market impact cost of a trade of (dollar) size V is then given by $MIC_t = MI_t \cdot V$. However, extensions of this model including conditional volatility specifications are also possible. By analyzing both the mean and the volatility of the market impact, we can better understand and manage the trade-off between the two. For example, Bikker and Spierdijk use a specification where the error terms are jointly and serially uncorrelated with mean zero, satisfying

$$\mathrm{Var}(\varepsilon_t) = \exp\left(\gamma + \sum_{j=1}^{J} \delta_j z_j\right)$$

where γ, δ_j, and z_j are the volatility, factor loadings, and factors, respectively.

Although the price impact function is linear, this does of course not mean that the dependent variables have to be. In particular, the factors in the specification above can be nonlinear transformations of the descriptive variables.

Consider, for example, factors related to trade size (e.g., trade size and trade size to daily volume). It is well known that market impact is nonlinear in these trade size measures. One of the earliest studies in this regard was performed by Loeb,[35] who showed that for a large set of stocks the market impact is proportional to the square root of the trade size, resulting in a market impact cost proportional to $V^{3/2}$. Typically, a price impact function linear in trade size will underestimate the price impact of small to medium-sized trades whereas larger trades will be overestimated.

Chen, Stanzl, and Watanabe suggest to model the nonlinear effects of trade size (dollar trade size V) in a price impact model by using the Box-Cox transformation;[36] that is,

$$\mathrm{MI}(V_t) = \alpha_b + \beta_b \frac{V_t^{\lambda_b} - 1}{\lambda_b} + \varepsilon_t$$

---

[35] Thomas F. Loeb, "Trading Costs: The Critical Link between Investment Information and Results," *Financial Analysts Journal* 39, no. 3 (1983), pp. 39–44.
[36] Zhiwu Chen, Werner Stanzl, and Masahiro Watanabe, "Price Impact Costs and the Limit of Arbitrage," Yale School of Management, International Center for Finance, 2002.

$$\mathrm{MI}(V_\tau) = \alpha_s + \beta_s \frac{V_\tau^{\lambda_s} - 1}{\lambda_s} + \varepsilon_\tau$$

where t and τ represent the time of transaction for the buys and the sells, respectively. In their specification, they assumed that ε_t and ε_τ are independent and identically distributed with mean zero and variance σ^2. The parameters α_b, β_b, λ_b, α_s, β_s, and λ_s were then estimated from market data by nonlinear least squares for each individual stock. We remark that λ_b, $\lambda_s \in [0,1]$ in order for the market impact for buys to be concave and for sells to be convex.

In their data sample (NYSE and Nasdaq trades between January 1993 and June 1993), Chen et al. report that for small companies the curvature parameters λ_b, λ_s are close to zero, whereas for larger companies they are not far away from 0.5. Observe that for $\lambda_b = \lambda_s = 1$ market impact is linear in the dollar trade size. Moreover, when $\lambda_b = \lambda_s = 0$ the impact function is logarithmic by the virtue of

$$\lim_{\lambda \to 0} \frac{V^\lambda - 1}{\lambda} = \ln(\lambda)$$

As just mentioned, market impact is also a function of the characteristics of the particular exchange, where the securities are traded as well as of the trading style of the investor. These characteristics can also be included in the general specification outlined above. For example, Keim and Madhavan proposed the following two different market impact specifications[37]

1. $\mathrm{MI} = \alpha + \beta_1 \chi_{\mathrm{OTC}} + \beta_2 \frac{1}{p} + \beta_3 |q| + \beta_4 |q|^2 + \beta_5 |q|^3 + \beta_6 \chi_{\mathrm{Up}} + \varepsilon$

    where
    χ_{OTC} is a dummy variable equal to one if the stock is an OTC traded stock or zero otherwise;
    p is the trade price;
    q is the number of shares traded over the number of shares outstanding; and

---

[37] Donald B. Keim and Ananth Madhavan, "Transactions Costs and Investment Style: An Inter-Exchange Analysis of Institutional Equity Trades," *Journal of Financial Economics* 46 (1997), pp. 265–292; and Donald B. Keim and Ananth Madhavan, "The Upstairs Market for Large-Block Transactions: Analysis and Measurement of Price Effects," *Review of Financial Studies* 9 (1996), pp. 1–36.

χ_{Up} is a dummy variable equal to one if the trade is done in the upstairs[38] market or zero otherwise.

2. $MI = \alpha + \beta_1 \chi_{Nasdaq} + \beta_2 q + \beta_3 \ln(MCap) + \beta_4 \dfrac{1}{p} + \beta_5 \chi_{Tech} + \beta_6 \chi_{Index} + \varepsilon$

where

χ_{NASDAQ} is a dummy variable equal to one if the stock is traded on NASDAQ or zero otherwise;

q is the number of shares traded over the number of shares outstanding, MCap is the market capitalization of the stock;

p is the trade price;

χ_{Tech} is a dummy variable equal to one if the trade is a short-term technical trade or zero otherwise; and

χ_{Index} is a dummy variable equal to one if the trade is done for a portfolio that attempts to closely mimic the behavior of the underlying index or zero otherwise.

These two models provide good examples for how nonlinear transformations of the underlying dependent variables can be used along with dummy variables that describe specific market or trade characteristics.

Several vendors and broker/dealers such as MSCI Barra[39] and ITG[40] have developed commercially available market impact models. These are sophisticated multi-market models that rely upon specialized estimation techniques using intraday data or tick-by-tick transaction based data. However, the general characteristics of these models are similar to the ones described in this section.

We emphasize that in the modeling of transaction costs it is important to factor in the objective of the trader or investor. For example, one market participant might trade just to take advantage of price movement and hence will only trade during favorable periods. His trading cost is different from an investor who has to rebalance a portfolio within a fixed time period and can therefore only partially use an opportunistic or liquidity searching strategy. In particular, this investor has to take into account the *risk of not completing* the transaction within a specified time period. Consequently, even if the market is not favorable,

---

[38] A securities transaction not executed on the exchange but completed directly by a broker in house is referred to an upstairs market transaction. Typically, the upstairs market consists of a network of trading desks of the major brokerages and institutional investors. The major purpose of the upstairs market is to facilitate large block and program trades.

[39] Nicolo G. Torre and Mark J. Ferrari, "The Market Impact Model," Barra Research Insights.

[40] "ITG ACE—Agency Cost Estimator: A Model Description," 2003, www.itginc.com.

he may decide to transact a portion of the trade. The market impact models described above assume that orders will be fully completed and ignore this point.

INCORPORATING TRANSACTION COSTS IN ASSET-ALLOCATION MODELS

Standard asset-allocation models generally ignore transaction costs and other costs related to portfolio and allocation revisions. As we have seen in this chapter, transaction costs are far from being insignificant. On the contrary, if transaction costs are not taken into consideration they can eat into a significant part of the returns. Whether transaction costs are being handled efficiently or not by the portfolio or fund manager can therefore make all the difference in attempting to outperform the peer group or a particular benchmark.

The typical asset-allocation model consists of one or several forecasting models for expected returns and risk. Small changes in these forecasts can result in reallocations which would not occur if transaction costs had been taken into account. Therefore, it is to be expected that the inclusion of transaction costs in asset-allocation models will result in a reduced amount of trading and rebalancing.

In this section we demonstrate how transaction costs models can be incorporated into standard asset-allocation models. For simplicity, we will use the mean-variance model to describe the basic approach. However, it is straightforward to extend this approach into other frameworks.

In 1970, Pogue gave one of the first descriptions in the literature of an extension of the mean-variance framework including transaction costs.[41] Several other authors including, for example, Schreiner,[42] Adcock and Meade,[43] Lobo, Fazel, and Boyd,[44] Mitchell and Braun,[45]

---

[41] Gerry A. Pogue, "An Extension of the Markowitz Portfolio Selection Model to Include Variable Transactions' Costs, Short Sales, Leverage Policies and Taxes," *Journal of Finance*, 25 (1970), pp. 1005–1027.

[42] John Schreiner, "Portfolio Revision: A Turnover-Constrained Approach," *Financial Management*, Spring 1980, pp. 67–75.

[43] Christopher J. Adcock and Nigel Meade, "A Simple Algorithm to Incorporate Transaction Costs in Quadratic Optimization," *European Journal of Operational Research*, 79 (1994), pp. 85–94.

[44] Miguel Sousa Lobo, Maryam Fazel, and Stephen Boyd, "Portfolio Optimization with Linear and Fix Transaction Costs and Bounds on Risk," Information Systems, Technical Report, Stanford University, 2000.

[45] John E. Mitchell and Stephen Braun, "Rebalancing an Investment Portfolio in the Presence of Transaction Costs," Technical Report, Department of Mathematical Sciences, Rensselaer Polytechnic Institute, 2002.

have provided further extensions and modifications to this basic approach. These formulations can be summarized by the mean-variance risk aversion formulation with transaction costs, given by

$$\max_{\mathbf{w}} \mathbf{w}'\boldsymbol{\mu} - \lambda \mathbf{w}'\boldsymbol{\Sigma}\mathbf{w} - \lambda_{\mathrm{TC}} \cdot TC$$

subject to $\boldsymbol{\iota}'\mathbf{w} = 1$, $\boldsymbol{\iota} = [1,1,\ldots,1]'$ where TC denotes a transaction cost penalty function and λ_{TC} a transaction cost aversion parameter. In other words, the objective is to maximize expected return less the cost of risk and transaction costs. The transaction costs term in the utility function introduces resistance or friction in the rebalancing process that makes it costly to reach the mean-variance portfolio, which would have been the result had transaction costs not been taken into account. We can imagine that as we increase the transaction costs, at some point it will be optimal to keep the current portfolio.

One of the most common simplifications to the transaction cost penalty function is to assume that it is a separable function dependent only on the portfolio weights $\mathbf{w}$, or more specifically on the portion to be traded $\mathbf{x} = \mathbf{w} - \mathbf{w}_0$, where $\mathbf{w}_0$ is the original portfolio and $\mathbf{w}$ is the new portfolio after rebalancing. Mathematically, we can express this as

$$TC(\mathbf{x}) = \sum_{i=1}^{N} TC_i(x_i)$$

where TC_i is the transaction cost function for security i and x_i is the portion of security i to be traded. The transaction cost function TC_i is often parameterized as a quadratic function of the form

$$TC_i(x_i) = \alpha_i \cdot \chi_{\{x_i \neq 0\}} + \beta_i |x_i| + \gamma_i |x_i|^2$$

where the coefficients α_i, β_i, and γ_i may be different for each asset, and $\chi_{\{x_i \neq 0\}}$ is the indicator function that is equal to one when $x_i \neq 0$ and zero otherwise.

When all $\alpha_i = 0$, the resulting optimization problem is a quadratic optimization problem of the form

$$\max_{\mathbf{w}} \mathbf{w}'\boldsymbol{\mu} - \lambda \mathbf{w}'\boldsymbol{\Sigma}\mathbf{w} - \lambda_{\mathrm{TC}}(\boldsymbol{\beta}'|\mathbf{x}| + \Gamma|\mathbf{x}|^2)$$

subject to the usual constraints, where $\boldsymbol{\beta}' = (\beta_1, \ldots, \beta_N)$ and

$$
\Gamma = \begin{bmatrix} \gamma_1 & 0 & \cdots & \cdots & 0 \\ 0 & \gamma_2 & \ddots & & \vdots \\ \vdots & \ddots & \ddots & \ddots & \vdots \\ \vdots & & \ddots & \ddots & 0 \\ 0 & \cdots & \cdots & 0 & \gamma_N \end{bmatrix}
$$

In particular, as this is a quadratic optimization problem, it can be solved with exactly the same software that is capable of solving the classical mean-variance optimization problem.

As we saw in previous sections in this chapter, transaction cost models can involve complicated nonlinear and nonconvex functions. Although optimization software is available for general nonlinear optimization problems, the computational time required for their solution is often too long for realistic investment management and portfolio management applications.

Very efficient optimization software is available for linear and quadratic optimization problems. It is therefore common in practice to approximate a complicated nonlinear optimization problem by simpler problems that can be solved quickly. In particular, as we described above, in the mean-variance framework portfolio managers often employ piecewise linear and quadratic approximations of the transaction cost penalty function.[46] We will discuss numerical optimization and issues related thereto further in Chapter 6.

A Simple Example

We now consider an example using 18 countries in the MSCI World Index over the period January 1980–May 2004.[47] For simplicity, we assume that the round-trip transaction costs are 50 basis points for all of the countries.

When we rebalance our portfolio, we solve the risk aversion formulation of the mean-variance problem described above with $\lambda = 1$, and with the transaction cost penalty function taking the form

---

[46] See for example, Andre F. Perold, "Large-Scale Portfolio Optimization," *Management Science* 30 (1984), pp. 1143–1160; and Hiroshi Konno and Annista Wijayanayake, "Portfolio Optimization Problem under Concave Transaction Costs and Minimal Transaction Unit Constraints," *Mathematical Programming* 89 (2001), pp. 233–250.

[47] An overview of this data set along with its basic statistical properties is provided in Appendix C.

$$TC(\mathbf{x}) = 0.005 \cdot \sum_{i=1}^{N} |x_i|$$

We let the transaction cost aversion parameter take the values $\lambda_{TC} = 0$, 0.1, 0.2, 1.

Each month, when we rebalance our portfolio, we use the historical sample means and covariances calculated from five years of daily data as our forecasts.[48] The first five years of the sample, January 1980 to December 1984, are used to construct the first estimates used in the simulation in January 1985. By the rebalancing at the end of each month, we calculate the realized portfolio return subject to transaction costs and the realized portfolio volatility. The results are depicted in Exhibits 3.6 through 3.8.

EXHIBIT 3.6   Growth of Equity for $\lambda_{TC} = 0$, 0.1, 0.2

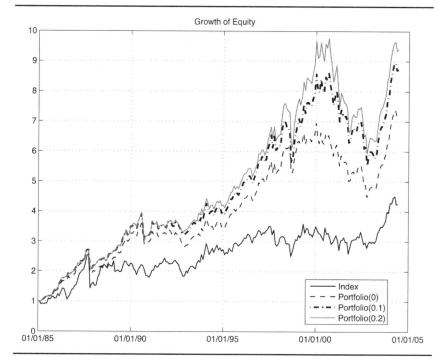

---

[48] We do not claim that these are "good" forecasts, but use them here merely for illustrative purposes. As we will see in Chapters 8 and 9, simple historical means and covariances are often suboptimal. In these chapters we also discuss forecasting techniques that provide more robust estimates that have, in general, proven to work better than historical estimates.

EXHIBIT 3.7 Annualized Sharpe Ratios for the Different Strategies with $\lambda_{TC} = 0$, 0.1, 0.2, 1 and the Index

	Start Date	End Date	λ_{TC} 0	0.1	0.2	1	Index
1st Quarter	Feb-85	Dec-89	1.41	1.60	1.65	1.67	0.70
2nd Quarter	Jan-90	Dec-94	0.30	0.21	0.29	0.32	0.29
3rd Quarter	Jan-95	Dec-99	0.88	0.99	0.78	0.92	0.38
4th Quarter	Jan-00	May-04	−0.07	−0.07	−0.20	−0.20	0.33
1st Half	Feb-85	Dec-94	0.84	0.87	0.93	0.95	0.53
2nd Half	Jan-95	May-04	0.40	0.47	0.32	0.35	0.36
Full	Feb-85	May-04	0.65	0.68	0.63	0.65	0.45

EXHIBIT 3.8 Monthly Volatility for $\lambda_{TC} = 0$, 0.1, 0.2

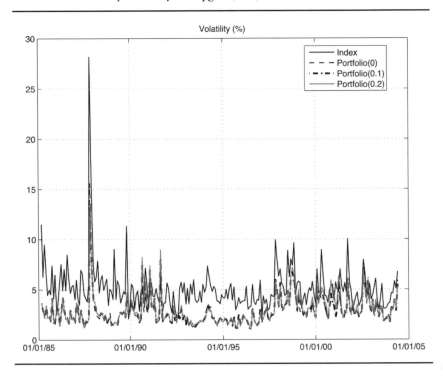

We observe that in this setting the mean-variance optimization performs better than the index, even on a risk-adjusted basis. The realized full sample annual Sharpe ratios are 0.65, 0.68, 0.63, and 0.65 (for λ_{TC} = 0, 0.1, 0.2, 1), and 0.45 for the index.

The transaction cost penalty function has a great impact on the portfolio turnover. In this simulation for λ_{TC} = 0, 0.1, 0.2, 1 the monthly portfolio turnover was 5.7%, 1.1%, 0.6%, and 0.01%, respectively. Exhibit 3.9 shows how the allocation to Belgium changes as a function of transaction costs. In particular, we observe that when no transaction costs are taken into account, the change from month-to-month can sometimes be substantial. As the effects of transaction costs increase, the allocation becomes more stable over time. At some point, when the simulated transaction costs are high enough, it is no longer optimal to allocate to Belgium. In other words, when we consider the trade-off between risk, return and transaction costs of Belgium on a relative basis, there are other countries that are more attractive.

EXHIBIT 3.9   Portfolio Weights for Belgium for λ_{TC} = 0, 0.1, 0.2, 1

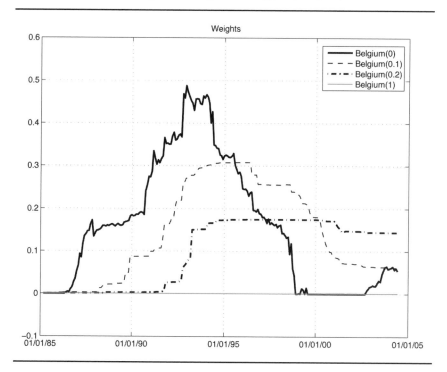

OPTIMAL TRADING

The decisions of the portfolio manager and the trader are based upon different objectives. The portfolio manager constructs the optimal portfolio to reflect the best trade-off between expected returns and risk, given his assessment of the prevailing trading costs. The trader decides on the timing of the execution of the trades based upon the trade-off between opportunity costs and market impact costs.

One way of reducing market impact cost is to delay the trade until the price is right. However, this process will also lead to missed investment opportunities. This trade-off between market impact and opportunity costs is illustrated in Exhibit 3.10. The vertical axis represents unit cost, where the units could be cents per share, basis points, or dollars. The horizontal axis represents the time periods, which could be ticks, minutes, hours, days and so on. First, we observe that market impact

EXHIBIT 3.10   Cost Trade-Offs: Market Impact Versus Opportunity Cost

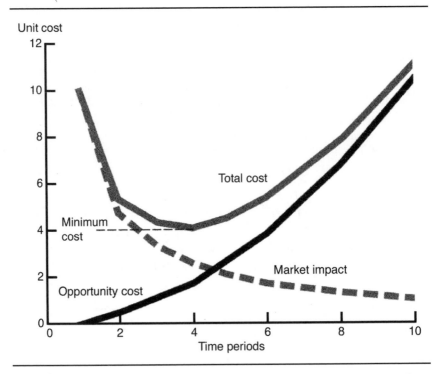

Source: Exhibit 2 in Chapter 11 of Frank J. Fabozzi and James L. Grant, *Equity Portfolio Management* (Hoboken, NJ: John Wiley & Sons, 1999), p. 313.

cost declines over time as it is positively related to the immediacy of execution. In other words, if a trader can "work an order" over time the resulting transaction costs are expected to be lower. Second, opportunity cost increases over time as it is positively related to the delay in execution. This means that if a trader waits too long, a part of the "alpha" of the investment opportunity might disappear. Taken together, these two basic mechanisms give a total cost that is shaped like a parabola. As the exhibit suggests, the total cost can be minimized by appropriately trading off market impact and opportunity costs.

Schematically, we can formulate this idea as an optimization problem where we attempt to minimize the expected total transaction costs. In general, this problem is a complicated *stochastic and dynamic optimization problem.* For example, Bertsimas, Hummel and Lo[49] and Almgren and Chriss[50] develop continuous time models for optimal execution that minimize average transaction costs over a specific time horizon. In particular, Almgren and Chriss assume that securities prices evolve according to a random-walk process. Given that most empirical studies have rejected the random-walk hypothesis, this assumption might be too stringent. Nevertheless, their article is an important contribution as it is one of the first of its kind that considers a dynamic model with market impact costs in which transactions occur over time.

As these techniques are rather involved mathematically, we describe only the basic ideas behind them. Realized transaction costs can deviate substantially from expected or average transaction costs. Therefore, it is convenient to use an objective function that takes this risk into account. Price volatility creates uncertainty in the realized trading costs in the same way it creates uncertainty in the realized return for an investment strategy. Therefore, we can think about opportunity costs as represented by the variance of the total transaction costs. More specifically, we define an *optimal execution strategy* to be a strategy that is a solution to the optimization problem[51]

$$\min \ (1 - \lambda)E(\text{TC}) - \lambda\text{var}(\text{TC})$$

---

[49] Dimitris Bertsimas, Paul Hummel, and Andrew W. Lo, "Optimal Control of Execution Costs for Portfolios," MIT Sloan School of Management, 1999.

[50] Robert Almgren and Neil Chriss, "Optimal Execution of Portfolio Transactions," Courant Institute of Mathematical Sciences, 2000; and Robert F. Almgren, "Optimal Execution with Nonlinear Impact Functions and Trading-Enhanced Risk," University of Toronto, 2001.

[51] This particular formulation was introduced by ITG in "ITG ACE—Agency Cost Estimator: A Model Description," 2003, www.itginc.com.

where $E(TC)$ and var(TC) denote the expectation and the variance of the total transaction costs, and λ is a risk aversion parameter. A solution to this problem is given by a trading schedule for the security, or a sequence of trades $(n_{ij})_{i\,=\,1,...,T, j\,=\,1,...,K}$ (trade sizes) where each trade n_{ij} is to be performed on day i over time window j.

In order to solve the optimization problem above, we have to make assumptions on the evolution of security prices. For example, in ITG's model, ITG ACE, security prices are assumed to evolve according to the process[52]

$$p_{i,j} = p_{i,j-1} + \gamma_j(n_{ij}) + \sigma_j \varepsilon_{i,j}, \, i = 1, \, ...,T, \, j = 1, \, ...,13$$

where T represents the trading horizon in days and each trading day is divided into 13 equal windows, and γ_j is the market impact cost due to trading. Furthermore, the innovations $\varepsilon_{i,j}$ are assumed to be independent and identically distributed. Both the volatility σ_j and the market impact cost γ_j are different for each window j.

For large λ, the penalty contribution from the opportunity cost is high. This will lead to execution strategies that tend to quickly fill the positions at the cost of slightly increasing the costs associated with market impact. In contrast, for small λ the resulting execution strategies attempt to minimize market impact cost by trading over a longer horizon and thereby increase the opportunity cost. Exhibit 3.11 illustrates these results by comparing different execution strategies for buying 300,000 shares of Boeing calculated with ITG ACE by solving the optimization problem above.

INTEGRATED PORTFOLIO MANAGEMENT: BEYOND EXPECTED RETURN AND PORTFOLIO RISK[53]

Equity trading should not be viewed separately from equity portfolio management. On the contrary, the management of equity trading costs is an integral part of any successful investment management strategy. In this context, MSCI Barra points out that superior investment performance is based on careful consideration of four key elements:[54]

---

[52] This is not the complete dynamics used in ITG ACE, but a great simplification thereof.

[53] This section draws from Fabozzi and Grant, *Equity Portfolio Management*, p. 320.

[54] The trading cost factor model described in this section is based on MSCI Barra's Market Impact Model™. A basic description of the model is covered in a three-part newsletter series. See Nicolo Torre, "The Market Impact Model™," Equity Trading: Research, Barra Newsletters 165–167 (Barra, 1998).

EXHIBIT 3.11   A Comparison of Different Execution Strategies for Buying 300,000 Shares of Boeing

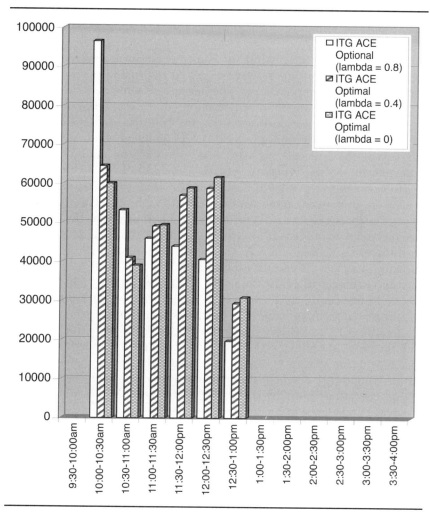

Note: The exhibit shows optimal execution strategies calculated by ITG ACE for buying 300,000 shares of Boeing. For comparison, three different risk aversion parameters were used: 0, 0.4 and 0.8. The trading period was constrained to be between 10 A.M. and 1 P.M.

Source: "ITG ACE—Agency Cost Estimator: A Model Description" (2003), p. 29, www.itginc.com.

- Forming realistic return expectations
- Controlling portfolio risk
- Efficient control of trading costs
- Monitoring total investment performance

Unfortunately, most discussions of equity portfolio management focus solely on the relationship between expected return and portfolio risk—with little if any emphasis on whether the selected securities in the "optimal" or target portfolio can be acquired in a cost efficient manner.

To illustrate the seriousness of the problem that can arise with suboptimal portfolio decisions, Exhibit 3.12 highlights what MSCI Barra refers to as the "typical" versus "ideal" approach to (equity) portfolio management. In the typical approach (top portion of Exhibit 3.12), portfolio managers engage in fundamental and/or quantitative research to identify investment opportunities—albeit with a measure of investment prudence (risk control) in mind. Upon completion, the portfolio manager reveals the list of securities that form the basis of the target portfolio to the senior trader. At this point, the senior trader informs the portfolio manager of certain nontradable positions—which causes the portfolio manager to adjust the list of securities either by hand or some other ad hoc procedure. This, in turn, causes the investor's portfolio to be suboptimal from an integrated portfolio management perspective.

Exhibit 3.12 also shows that as the trader begins to fill the portfolio with the now suboptimal set of securities, an additional portfolio imbalance may occur as market impact costs cause the prices of some securities to "run away" during trade implementation. It should be clear that any *ad hoc* adjustments by the trader at this point will in turn build a systematic imbalance in the investor's portfolio—such that the portfolio manager's actual portfolio will depart permanently from that which would be efficient from a return-risk and trading cost perspective.

According to MSCI Barra, the ideal approach to equity portfolio management (lower portion of Exhibit 3.12) requires a systematic integration of portfolio management and trading processes. In this context, the returns forecast, risk estimates, and trading cost program are jointly combined in determining the optimal investment portfolio. In this way, the portfolio manager knows up front if (complete) portfolio implementation is either not feasible or is too expensive when accounting for trading costs.

Accordingly, the portfolio manager can incorporate the appropriate trading cost information into the portfolio construction and risk control process—before the trading program begins. The portfolio manager can then build a portfolio of securities whereby actual security positions are consistent with those deemed to be optimal from an integrated portfolio context.

EXHIBIT 3.12   Typical Versus Ideal Portfolio Management

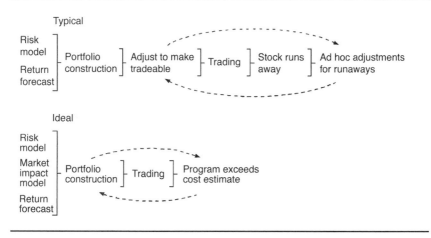

Source: Figure 4 in Nicolo Torre, "The Market Impact Model™—First in a Series: The Market Impact Problem," Equity Trading: Research, Barra Newsletters 165 (Barra, 1998), pp. 7–8.

SUMMARY

- Trading and execution are integral components of the investment process. A poorly executed trade can eat directly into portfolio returns because of transaction costs.
- Transaction costs are typically categorized in two dimensions: *fixed costs* versus *variable costs*, and *explicit costs* versus *implicit costs.*
- In the first dimension, fixed costs include commissions and fees. Bid-ask spreads, taxes, delay cost, price movement risk, market impact costs, timing risk, and opportunity cost are variable trading costs.
- In the second dimension, explicit costs include commissions, fees, bid-ask spreads, and taxes. Delay cost, price movement risk, market impact cost, timing risk, and opportunity cost are implicit transaction costs.
- Implicit costs make up the larger part of the total transaction costs. These costs are not observable and have to be estimated.
- Liquidity is created by agents transacting in the financial markets by buying and selling securities.
- Liquidity and transaction costs are interrelated: In a highly liquid market, large transactions can be executed immediately without incurring high transaction costs.

■ A limit order is an order to execute a trade only if the limit price or a better price can be obtained.

■ A market order is an order to execute a trade at the current best price available in the market.

■ In general, trading costs are measured as the difference between the execution price and some appropriate fair market benchmark. The fair market benchmark of a security is the price that would have prevailed had the trade not taken place.

■ Typical forecasting models for market impact costs are based on a statistical factor approach. Some common trade based factors are: trade size, relative trade size, price of market liquidity, type of trade, efficiency and trading style of the investor, specific characteristics of the market or the exchange, time of trade submission, trade timing, and order type. Some common asset based factors are: price momentum, price volatility, market capitalization, growth versus value, and specific industry/sector characteristics.

■ Transaction costs models can be incorporated into standard asset-allocation models such as the mean-variance framework.

■ Optimal trading and execution systems rely on mathematical models that determine the timing of the execution of the trades by balancing the trade-off between opportunity costs and market impact costs.

■ Efficient equity portfolio management requires a systematic integration of trading costs management, trading execution, and portfolio management.

CHAPTER 4

Applying the Portfolio Selection Framework in Practice

Markowitz's seminal paper on portfolio selection has undoubtedly had a major impact not only on academic research but also on the financial industry as a whole. It shifted the focus of investment analysis away from individual security selection and toward the concept of diversification and the impact of individual securities on a portfolio's risk-return characteristics. In the mean-variance optimization framework, efficient portfolios are formed by choosing an asset based upon its interaction with other assets in the portfolio as well as on its contribution to the overall portfolio, and not only on the basis of its standalone performance.

Nevertheless, for portfolio management in practice, the classical mean-variance framework only serves as a starting point. The original approach proposed by Markowitz is often extended in several different directions. First, being a single-period (myopic) model it has to be modified in order to account for changing market conditions over multiple periods. Second, portfolio management objectives and policies do often impose further restrictions beyond those of the original model. It is common practice to amend the mean-variance framework with various types of constraints that take specific investment guidelines and institutional features into account. We discuss these two important topics in more detail in this chapter. Specifically, we start by describing the rebalancing process using mean-variance optimization and provide a realistic example illustrating the approach. Thereafter, we outline a simple classification of the most common portfolio constraints used in practice. In particular, we discuss linear, quadratic and integer/combinatorial constraints along with two illustrations. The first one shows how an index tracking portfolio can be constructed by minimizing its tracking error relative to the index. The second one illustrates the usage of more complicated combinatorial restrictions such as so-called minimal holdings and cardinality constraints. In Chapters 5, 8, and 9, we cover other topics of importance in practice, such as—but not limited to—estimation of input parameters, factor models, the incorporation of higher moments, and robust techniques.

We mention in passing that the inclusion of transaction costs and tax effects in the portfolio selection problem may provide a challenge to the portfolio manager. We discuss transaction costs, transaction costs measurement and modeling separately in Chapter 3.

Capital gains taxes can make a strategy that is profitable on a pretax basis into a losing one on an after-tax basis. Therefore, it is important for the portfolio manager to factor tax consequences into the investment decision. What makes this problem more complicated is the fact that different investors are in different tax brackets, and therefore have different effective tax rates. The after-tax allocation problem is a large topic by itself and is beyond the scope of this book.[1]

REBALANCING IN THE MEAN-VARIANCE OPTIMIZATION FRAMEWORK

After the asset allocation decision (a strategic decision), portfolio rebalancing (a tactical decision) is probably the second most important decision for an investment portfolio. As the economic environment and the asset mix change, portfolio managers rebalance their portfolios to incorporate their new views on expected returns and risks.

A study by Arnott and Lovell suggests that disciplined rebalancing can improve returns as much as a fairly large shift in the investment policy mix can.[2] For example, in their study the choice between 60% or 50% in equities is less important than the decision as to how and when to rebalance. Elton et al. find that active managers with low turnover outperform managers with high turnover.[3] They provide evidence that the difference in performance is due to the increased transaction costs

---

[1] A good starting point for this topic is in the following papers by Don Mulvihill appearing in Bob Litterman and the Quantitative Resources Group of Goldman Sachs Asset Management, *Modern Investment Management: An Equilibrium Approach* (Hoboken, NJ: John Wiley & Sons, 2003): "Investing for Real After-Tax Results" (Chapter 29); "Asset Allocation and Location" (Chapter 31); and "Equity Portfolio Structure" (Chapter 32).

[2] Robert D. Arnott and Robert M. Lovell, "Rebalancing: Why? When? How Often?" *Journal of Investing* (Spring 1993), pp. 5–10.

[3] Edwin J. Elton, Martin J. Gruber, Sanjiv Das, and Matthew Hlavka, "Efficiency with Costly Information: A Reinterpretation of Evidence from Managed Portfolios," *Review of Financial Studies* 1 (1993), pp. 1–22.

for the managers with high turnover. They also show that the same results apply to individual investors. A study by Barber and Odean suggests that individual investors who trade the most (in their study defined by the investors that trade more than 48 times per year) have the lowest gross return as well as the lowest net return.[4]

Rebalancing using an optimizer opens up new opportunities. If dynamic forecasting models are used, the asset allocation will be adjusted over time depending on changes in the market and economy. The allocation decision relies on current forecasts as well as on the optimal blend of investments, such that risk and return targets are met.

As an example, consider an investor who maximizes the Sharpe ratio of his portfolio over one month.[5] We saw in Chapter 2 that the optimal portfolio for this investor is equal to the market portfolio. One month later, this investor revisits his portfolio decision. If the statistical properties of the asset returns for the new period are the same as those in the previous one, and returns in the new and the previous periods are uncorrelated, then the new portfolio weights will be the same as in the previous period. But because prices might have moved during the month, the market capitalization weights (the weights of the market portfolio) no longer have to be the same. Therefore, the investor's portfolio will no longer correspond to the market portfolio. This result is a contradiction: The one-period Markowitz approach in this example gives the same portfolio weights from period to period, however, the market capitalization weights change.

This problem arises because the Markowitz approach is myopic. One way of resolving this contradiction is to develop a full multi-period approach that allows for rebalancing.[6] In this section, we will discuss the issue of rebalancing within the Markowitz framework.

In the example above, we assumed that the statistical properties of the asset returns were constant over the two periods. This assumption,

[4] Brad Barber and Terrance Odean, "The Common Stock Investment Performance of Individual Investors," Working Paper, Graduate School of Management, University of California, Davis, 1998.
[5] In Chapter 7 we will see that the CAPM assumptions lead to the same conclusions.
[6] An excellent introduction to multistage stochastic optimization is found in John M. Mulvey, William R. Pauling, and Ronald E. Madey, "Advantages of Multiperiod Portfolio Models," *Journal of Portfolio Management* (Winter 2003), pp. 35–45. See also the following chapters in Erricos J. Kontoghiorghes, Berc Rustem, and Stavros Siokos, *Computational Methods in Decision-Making, Economics, and Finance, Optimization Models* (Boston, MA: Kluwer Academic Publishers, 2002): John M. Mulvey and Koray Simsek, "Rebalancing Strategies" (Chapter 2) and Nalan Gulpinar, Berc Rustem, and Reuben Settergren, "Multistage Stochastic Programming in Computational Finance" (Chapter 3).

as we saw in Appendix C—where we provide some of the basic statistical properties of the MSCI World Index and its constituents—rarely holds in practice, especially over longer horizons. In particular, asset return distributions change—though maybe not drastically—over time, due to changes in the economic environment. The statistical summaries also show that asset returns are not necessarily normally distributed but exhibit nontrivial skew and kurtosis and, as a consequence, some investors may include higher moments in their utility functions.

So then, why would anyone want to use the mean-variance framework? The short answer is because it works reasonably well as an approximation and it is straightforward to implement for large-scale portfolio management applications with thousands of assets. But, of course, simplicity does not validate the approach or guarantee that it always works in practice. As we discussed in Chapter 2, more general utility functions can be approximated by the quadratic utility with reasonable accuracy. The problem of changing asset return distributions can, in most situations, be satisfactorily circumvented by reestimating the underlying statistical properties on a periodic basis and subsequently rebalancing the portfolio.

A certain level of predictability of the asset return distributions (for example, of their first two moments) opens up the opportunity for dynamic trading strategies. Typical strategies rely on forecasting asset returns using lagged asset returns and other economic variables.[7] The forecasting variables are referred to as "dependent" or "conditioning" variables as the forecasts are produced as a result of some relationship (condition) or dependence to them. Consequently, when the dependent variables change, forecasts change, which in turn results in the need to rebalance the portfolio. Mean-variance analysis is often used in these cases for portfolio construction and rebalancing, and can be further extended to incorporate conditional information.[8]

We have seen that the portfolio may need to be rebalanced because with the passage of time, new information becomes available that changes our forecasts of risk and returns, or the investment choices simply change. Furthermore, the prices of the assets in the portfolio change and hence also the constitution of the portfolio. A portfolio having a tar-

---

[7] See, for example, Donald B. Keim and Robert F. Stambaugh, "Predicting Returns in the Stock and Bond Markets," *Journal of Financial Economics* 17 (1986), pp. 357–390 and Werner F. M. De Bondt, and Richard H. Thaler, "Does the Stock Market Overreact?" *Journal of Finance* 40 (1985), pp. 793–805.

[8] Lars P. Hansen and Scott F. Richard, "The Role of Conditioning Information in Deducing Testable Restrictions Implied by Dynamic Asset Pricing Models," *Econometrica* 55 (1987), pp. 587–613.

get of 50/50 in equities and bonds may be distributed 55/45 after a stock market rally. By rebalancing, the portfolio could be brought back to the original target. Mean-variance framework—being a single-period model—is extended to a multiperiod setting by "rolling over" or rebalancing the portfolio using a mean-variance optimization for each period.

So how often should a portfolio be rebalanced? The answer to this question is determined by factors such as the type of investment strategy, targeted tracking error, transaction costs, and simply the amount of work required by portfolio managers in the rebalancing process.[9] Developing the appropriate automated processes is crucial for larger portfolios. Finding a balance between tracking error on the one hand and transaction costs on the other is very important: Portfolios targeting lower tracking error require more frequent rebalancing, which in turn increases transaction costs. In general, we can distinguish the following three different approaches to portfolio rebalancing:

1. *Calendar rebalancing.* Rebalance the portfolio back to the optimal allocation at a certain frequency such as weekly, monthly, quarterly, and so on.
2. *Threshold rebalancing.* Rebalance the portfolio back to its optimal composition once it is outside a certain range. For example, the portfolio could be rebalanced when the portfolio weights differ more than, say, 10% from its optimal weight. Another type of threshold rebalancing is based upon the rebalancing of the portfolio when the expected tracking error exceeds a predetermined target.
3. *Range rebalancing.* Rebalance the portfolio back to a predetermined range once it has deviated from it. For example, suppose that an optimal mix of 60/40 equities and bonds is established as the target. A 10% tolerance would imply an allowed range of 54% through 66% for equities. In this case, if equity investment would drift away to, say, 68% then it should be rebalanced to bring it back within the allowed range.

The range rebalancing approach takes into account that portfolios within a certain range are statistically equivalent. We will elaborate more on this concept when we cover measurement errors, portfolio resampling, and robust portfolio optimization in Chapter 9.

As mentioned in the introduction to this chapter, trading and transaction costs may have a significant effect on the rebalancing decision. If we take transaction costs into account, recent research on dynamic trading strategies for asset allocation has shown that there is a so-called *no-*

---

[9] Transaction costs modeling is discussed in Chapter 3.

trade region around the optimal target portfolio weights.[10] If the portfolio weights lie inside this region, no trade is necessary. However, when the portfolio weights lie outside, Leland has demonstrated that it is optimal to trade but only to the extent of bringing the portfolio weights back to the nearest edge of the no-trade region rather than to the optimal allocation. Theoretically, it has been shown that the optimal strategy reduces transaction costs by about 50%. Nonetheless, to calculate the optimal allocation involves the solution of a high-dimensional partial differential equation, making this technique of limited use for practical applications.

Sun et al. have proposed a different framework that minimizes the cost of rebalancing in terms of risk-adjusted returns net of transaction costs based upon *dynamic programming*.[11] They apply the concept of *certainty equivalents* to translate the risk preferences embedded in a specific utility function into an equivalent certain return.[12] The basic idea is that given an expected utility, it is possible to find a "risk-free rate" (also referred to as the *certainty equivalent return*) that produces the same expected utility. If the investment portfolio, $\mathbf{w}$, is suboptimal then its utility $U(\mathbf{w})$ will be lower than the utility of the optimal portfolio $U(\mathbf{w}^*)$. In particular, for the certainty equivalent returns it holds that $r_{CE}(\mathbf{w}) \leq r_{CE}(\mathbf{w}^*)$. Consequently, we can interpret the difference $D(\mathbf{w}) = r_{CE}(\mathbf{w}^*) - r_{CE}(\mathbf{w})$ as an adjusted risk-free return that we give up for not holding the optimal portfolio. It is now a straightforward matter to translate this difference into the dollar numeraire and compare it to actual dollar transaction costs.

The authors apply dynamic programming to find the rebalancing strategy that minimizes the transaction costs and the costs associated with not holding the optimal portfolio. In simulation experiments they show that their method is over 25% more efficient compared to calendar, threshold and range rebalancing. Although computationally intensive, this approach appears to have great future potential.

---

[10] Hayne E. Leland. Optimal portfolio management with transaction costs and capital gains taxes. Haas School of Business Technical Report, University of California—Berkeley, December 1999.

[11] Walther Sun, Ayres Fan, Li-Wei Chen, Tom Schouwenaars, and Marius A. Albota, "Optimal Rebalancing Strategy Using Dynamic Programming for Institutional Portfolios," Working Paper, Laboratory for Information and Decision Systems, Massachusetts Institute of Technology, 2005.

[12] Daniel Bernoulli, "Exposition of a New Theory on the Measurement of Risk," *Econometrica* 22 (1954), pp. 23–36. See also, Jan-Hein Cremers, Mark Kritzman, and Sebastien Page, "Portfolio Formation with Higher Moments and Plausible Utility," Revere Street Working Paper, 2003, Working Paper Series, *Financial Economics* 272, no. 12 (2003).

Example: Rebalancing the MSCI World Index Portfolio

Let us take a look at a portfolio example using 18 countries from the MSCI World Index over the period January 1980 through May 2004.[13] We compare three simple approaches of monthly rebalancing of a portfolio containing the different country indices with the overall index:

1. Hold an equal proportion of each asset throughout the whole sample.
2. Rebalance the portfolio on a monthly basis by calculating the global minimum variance portfolio, not allowing for short-selling.
3. Rebalance the portfolio on a monthly basis using the risk aversion formulation of the mean-variance optimization problem with a risk aversion coefficient, λ, equal to 2, not allowing for short-selling.

For convenience, we will refer to these three approaches as "Equal," "GMV," and "RiskAver." We will simply refer to the MSCI World Index as the "Index." Each time we rebalance the portfolios, we need a forecast of the monthly covariance matrix for GMV, and a forecast of the monthly expected returns and of the covariance matrix for RiskAver. Here, we use the historical sample means and covariances calculated from five years of daily data. In other words, at the beginning of each month, we use the last five years of available daily data to compute our estimates.[14] For example, the first five years of the sample, from January 1980 to December 1984, are used to construct the first estimates used in the simulation in January 1985. Before rebalancing at the end of each month, we calculate the realized portfolio return and its volatility. The results are depicted in Exhibits 4.1 and 4.2, and portfolio summary statistics of the different approaches and of the index itself are presented in Exhibits 4.3 to 4.6.

We observe that the three approaches outperform the index. In particular, the full period alphas range from 4.1% to 4.7% and the Sharpe ratios are 0.82 (GMV), 0.78 (Equal), 0.59 (RiskAver), and 0.45 (Index). However, only the index has a significant positive return (6.1%) during the last quarter of the simulation. All portfolios and the index have negative skew, where the largest full period skew of –0.34 is achieved by RiskAver. The portfolios all have smaller full period kurtosis than the

---

[13] A description and basic statistical properties of this data set are provided in Appendix C.

[14] We do not claim these forecasts to be "good" forecasts, but use them here merely for illustrative purposes. As we will see in Chapters 8 and 9, simple historical means and covariances are often suboptimal. In these chapters we will also discuss forecasting techniques that provide more robust estimates that have, in general, proven to work better than historical estimates.

EXHIBIT 4.1   Growth of Equity Invested on January 1985 in each of the Different Portfolios and in the MSCI World Index

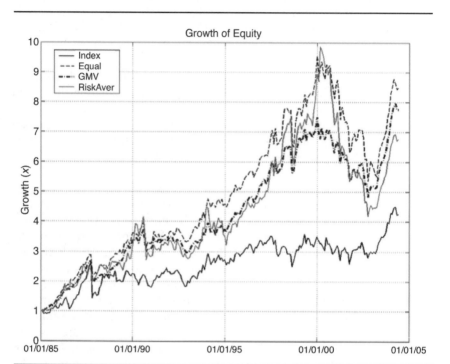

Note: "Equal" refers to an equally weighted portfolio; "GMV" refers to the global minimum variance portfolio; "RiskAver" refers to the risk aversion formulation of the mean-variance optimization problem with risk aversion coefficient $\lambda = 2$.

index, due to the fact that the most negative return of the index is almost a devastating –45%! It is, however, somewhat disappointing and discouraging that the portfolios relying upon mean-variance optimization do not perform much better than the portfolio using naïve equal weights. The risk aversion optimization actually performs worse.

Should not the portfolios relying on optimization be "optimal"? The reason for this problem is in the inputs to the optimization, the forecast of expected returns, and the covariance matrix. Intuitively speaking, when these forecasts have a large estimation error, the performance of the resulting portfolios will be anything less than desired. Optimizers are often cynically referred to as "error maximizers" as they overweight the estimation error in the inputs. In particular, assets with large expected returns and low standard deviations will be overweighted and, conversely, assets with low

EXHIBIT 4.2   Portfolio Volatility of the Different Portfolios and the MSCI World Index

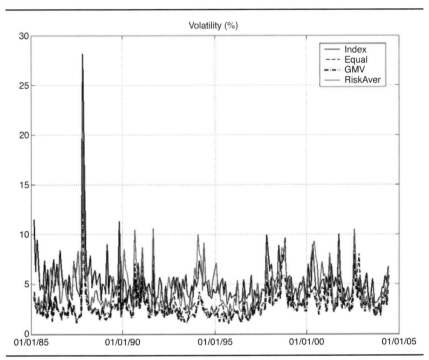

Note: "Equal" refers to an equally weighted portfolio; "GMV" refers to the global minimum variance portfolio; "RiskAver" refers to the risk aversion formulation of the mean-variance optimization problem with risk aversion coefficient $\lambda = 2$.

expected returns and high standard deviations will be underweighted. Therefore, estimation errors both in expected returns and variances/covariances will introduce errors in the optimal portfolio weights.

In practice, for forecasts with large estimation errors (which is unfortunately *not* uncommon), it is well known that equally weighted portfolios often outperform mean-variance optimized portfolios over time.[15] It turns out that the uncertainty in the expected return of forecasts tends to have more influence than the covariance matrix in the mean-variance optimization.[16] This is consistent with the finding in this

---

[15] John D. Jobson and Robert M. Korkie, "Putting Markowitz Theory to Work," *Journal of Portfolio Management* 7 (1981), pp. 70–74.
[16] Vijay K. Chopra and William T. Ziemba, "The Effect of Errors in Means, Variances, and Covariances on Optimal Portfolio Choice," *Journal of Portfolio Management* 19 (1993), pp. 6–11.

EXHIBIT 4.3 Portfolio Summary Statistics of the Equally Weighted Portfolio

	Start Date	End Date	Mean	Volatility	Sharpe Ratio	Skew	Kurtosis	Min	Max	Alpha	Beta
1st Qtr	Feb-85	Dec-89	27.8%	16.5%	1.69	-2.14	12.14	-21.7%	9.8%	15.3%	0.30
2nd Qtr	Jan-90	Dec-94	5.8%	14.6%	0.40	-0.25	3.64	-12.1%	9.6%	0.5%	0.45
3rd Qtr	Jan-95	Dec-99	15.8%	14.0%	1.12	-0.87	6.65	-14.9%	11.7%	9.6%	0.61
4th Qtr	Jan-00	May-04	-1.2%	17.1%	-0.07	-0.44	3.02	-12.2%	10.5%	-6.5%	0.72
1st Half	Feb-85	Dec-94	16.7%	15.8%	1.06	-1.21	7.60	-21.7%	9.8%	7.5%	0.34
2nd Half	Jan-95	May-04	7.8%	15.7%	0.50	-0.68	4.33	-14.9%	11.7%	2.1%	0.67
Full	Feb-85	May-04	12.4%	15.8%	0.78	-0.94	5.91	-21.7%	11.7%	4.7%	0.44

Notes: The columns Mean, Volatility, Sharpe Ratio, and Alpha are the annualized mean returns, volatilities, Sharpe ratios, and alphas of the portfolio over the different periods. Min and Max are the daily minimum and maximum portfolio returns, respectively. Skew and Kurtosis are calculated as the third and fourth normalized centered moments. Alphas and betas are calculated using one-month LIBOR.

EXHIBIT 4.4 Portfolio Summary Statistics of the Global Minimum Variance Portfolio Rebalanced Monthly

	Start Date	End Date	Mean	Volatility	Sharpe Ratio	Skew	Kurtosis	Min	Max	Alpha	Beta
1st Qtr	Feb-85	Dec-89	26.4%	16.2%	1.63	−3.03	18.82	−24.4%	9.6%	13.7%	0.31
2nd Qtr	Jan-90	Dec-94	2.9%	13.2%	0.22	−0.35	3.60	−10.4%	9.1%	−2.4%	0.46
3rd Qtr	Jan-95	Dec-99	14.8%	12.4%	1.19	−1.25	6.25	−13.1%	8.6%	8.7%	0.53
4th Qtr	Jan-00	May-04	1.7%	14.1%	0.12	−0.45	2.66	−9.4%	7.1%	−3.2%	0.62
1st Half	Feb-85	Dec-94	14.6%	15.1%	0.97	−1.83	11.98	−24.4%	9.6%	5.3%	0.36
2nd Half	Jan-95	May-04	8.7%	13.3%	0.65	−0.83	4.00	−13.1%	8.6%	3.1%	0.57
Full	Feb-85	May-04	11.7%	14.2%	0.82	−1.41	8.99	−24.4%	9.6%	4.1%	0.42

Notes: The columns Mean, Volatility, Sharpe Ratio, and Alpha are the annualized mean returns, volatilities, Sharpe ratios, and alphas of the portfolio over the different periods. Min and Max are the daily minimum and maximum portfolio returns, respectively. Skew and Kurtosis are calculated as the third and fourth normalized centered moments. Alphas and betas are calculated using one-month LIBOR.

EXHIBIT 4.5 Portfolio Summary Statistics of the Risk Aversion Formulation of the Mean-Variance Portfolio Rebalanced Monthly with Risk Aversion Coefficient $\lambda = 2$

	Start Date	End Date	Mean	Volatility	Sharpe Ratio	Skew	Kurtosis	Min	Max	Alpha	Beta
1st Qtr	Feb-85	Dec-89	25.4%	20.5%	1.24	-0.35	3.25	-16.1%	14.0%	13.9%	0.24
2nd Qtr	Jan-90	Dec-94	5.3%	24.4%	0.22	-0.18	4.35	-22.4%	19.4%	0.0%	0.57
3rd Qtr	Jan-95	Dec-99	20.3%	16.7%	1.21	-0.82	5.30	-16.7%	11.2%	14.2%	0.52
4th Qtr	Jan-00	May-04	-4.8%	17.6%	-0.27	-0.23	3.11	-11.1%	13.2%	-9.8%	0.63
1st Half	Feb-85	Dec-94	15.3%	22.7%	0.67	-0.30	4.06	-22.4%	19.4%	6.2%	0.32
2nd Half	Jan-95	May-04	8.5%	17.4%	0.49	-0.52	3.87	-16.7%	13.2%	3.0%	0.57
Full	Feb-85	May-04	12.0%	20.3%	0.59	-0.34	4.26	-22.4%	19.4%	4.5%	0.40

Notes: The columns Mean, Volatility, Sharpe Ratio, and Alpha are the annualized mean returns, volatilities, Sharpe ratios, and alphas of the portfolio over the different periods. Min and Max are the daily minimum and maximum portfolio returns, respectively. Skew and Kurtosis are calculated as the third and fourth normalized centered moments. Alphas and betas are calculated using one-month LIBOR.

EXHIBIT 4.6   Summary Statistics of the MSCI World Index

	Start Date	End Date	Mean	Volatility	Sharpe Ratio	Skew	Kurtosis	Min	Max
1st Qtr	Feb-85	Dec-89	23.1%	33.0%	0.70	−2.02	11.05	−44.7%	17.6%
2nd Qtr	Jan-90	Dec-94	5.4%	18.6%	0.29	0.20	2.12	−9.6%	11.1%
3rd Qtr	Jan-95	Dec-99	6.4%	16.9%	0.38	−0.67	3.81	−13.7%	10.1%
4th Qtr	Jan-00	May-04	6.1%	18.6%	0.33	0.01	3.22	−12.9%	14.1%
1st Half	Feb-85	Dec-94	14.1%	26.7%	0.53	−1.68	12.10	−44.7%	17.6%
2nd Half	Jan-95	May-04	6.3%	17.6%	0.36	−0.30	3.50	−13.7%	14.1%
Full	Feb-85	May-04	10.3%	22.7%	0.45	−1.40	12.12	−44.7%	17.6%

Notes: The columns Mean, Volatility, and Sharpe Ratio are the annualized mean returns, volatilities, and Sharpe ratios of the index over the different periods. Min and Max are the daily minimum and maximum Index returns, respectively. Skew and Kurtosis are calculated as the third and fourth normalized centered moments.

example that the GMV portfolio performs better than the risk aversion portfolio: The GMV only relies upon the covariance matrix. We will get back to these important issues, and to this example, again in Chapter 9.

PORTFOLIO CONSTRAINTS COMMONLY USED IN PRACTICE

Institutional features and investment policy decisions often lead to more complicated constraints and portfolio management objectives than those present in the original formulation of the mean-variance problem. For example, many mutual funds are managed relative to a particular benchmark or asset universe (e.g., S&P 500, Russell 1000) such that their tracking error relative to the benchmark is kept small. A portfolio manager might also be restricted on how concentrated the investment portfolio can be in a particular industry or sector. These restrictions, and many more, can be modeled by adding constraints to the original formulation.

In this section, we describe constraints that are often used in combination with the mean-variance problem in practical applications. Specifically, we distinguish between linear, quadratic, nonlinear, and combinatorial/integer constraints.

Throughout this section, we denote the current portfolio weights by $\mathbf{w}_0$ and the targeted portfolio weights by $\mathbf{w}$, so that the amount to be traded is $\mathbf{x} = \mathbf{w} - \mathbf{w}_0$.

Linear and Quadratic Constraints

Some of the more commonly used linear and quadratic constraints are described below.

Long-Only Constraints

When short-selling is not allowed we require that $\mathbf{w} \geq 0$. This is a frequently used constraint, as many funds and institutional investors are prohibited from selling stocks short.

Turnover Constraints

High portfolio turnover can result in large transaction costs that make portfolio rebalancing inefficient. One possibility is to limit the amount of turnover allowed when performing portfolio optimization. The most common turnover constraints limit turnover on each individual asset

$$|x_i| \leq U_i$$

or on the whole portfolio

$$\sum_{i \in I} |x_i| \leq U_{\text{portfolio}}$$

where I denotes the available investment universe. Turnover constraints are often imposed relative to the *average daily volume* (ADV) of a stock. For example, we might want to restrict turnover to be no more than 5% of average daily volume. Modifications of these constraints, such as limiting turnover in a specific industry or sector are also frequently applied.

Holding Constraints

A well-diversified portfolio should not exhibit large concentrations in any specific assets, industries, sectors, or countries. Maximal holdings in an individual asset can be controlled by the constraint

$$L_i \leq w_i \leq U_i$$

where L_i and U_i are vectors representing the lower and upper bounds of the holdings of asset i. To constrain the exposure to a specific set I_i (e.g., industry or country) of the available investment universe I, we can introduce constraints of the form

$$L_i \leq \sum_{j \in I_i} w_j \leq U_i$$

where L_i and U_i denote the minimum and maximum exposures to I_i.

Risk Factor Constraints

In practice, it is very common that portfolio managers use factor models to control for different risk exposures to risk factors such as market, size, and style.[17] Let us assume that security returns have a factor structure with K risk factors, that is

$$R_i = \alpha_i + \sum_{k=1}^{K} \beta_{ik} F_k + \varepsilon_i$$

---

[17] We discuss risk factors and factor models in more detail in Chapter 8.

where F_k, $k = 1, \ldots, K$ are the K factors common to all the securities, β_{ik} is the sensitivity of the i-th security to the k-th factor, and ε_i is the non-systematic return for the i-th security.

To limit a portfolio's exposure to the k-th risk factor, we can impose the constraint

$$\sum_{i=1}^{N} \beta_{ik} w_i \le U_k$$

where U_k denotes maximum exposure allowed. To construct a portfolio that is neutral to the k-th risk factor (for example, market neutral) we would use the constraint

$$\sum_{i=1}^{N} \beta_{ik} w_i = 0$$

Benchmark Exposure and Tracking Error Constraints

In practice, many portfolio managers are faced with the objective of managing their portfolio relative to a benchmark. This is the typical situation for index fund managers and passive managers who are trying to deliver a small outperformance relative to a particular benchmark, such as the Russell 1000 or the S&P 500.

Let us denote by w_b the market capitalization weights (sometimes also referred to as the *benchmark weights*) and $\mathbf{R}$ the vector of returns of the individual assets, so that $R_b = w_b' \cdot \mathbf{R}$ is the return on the benchmark. A portfolio manager might choose to limit the deviations of the portfolio weights from the benchmark weights by imposing

$$\|\mathbf{w} - \mathbf{w}_b\| \le M$$

or, similarly, for a specific industry I_i require that

$$\sum_{j \in I_i} w_j - w_{bj} \le M_i$$

However, the most commonly used metric to measure the deviation from the benchmark is the *tracking error*. The tracking error is defined by the variance of the difference between the return of the portfolio $R_p = \mathbf{w}' \cdot \mathbf{R}$ and the return of the benchmark $R_b = \mathbf{w}_b' \cdot \mathbf{R}$, that is, $\text{TEV}_p = \text{var}(R_p - R_b)$. Expanding this definition, we get

$$
\begin{aligned}
\mathrm{TEV}_p &= \mathrm{var}(R_p - R_b) \\
&= \mathrm{var}(\mathbf{w'R} - \mathbf{w}_b'\mathbf{R}) \\
&= (\mathbf{w} - \mathbf{w}_b)'\mathrm{var}(\mathbf{R})(\mathbf{w} - \mathbf{w}_b) \\
&= (\mathbf{w} - \mathbf{w}_b)'\mathbf{\Sigma}(\mathbf{w} - \mathbf{w}_b)
\end{aligned}
$$

where $\mathbf{\Sigma}$ is the covariance matrix of the asset returns. In order to limit the tracking error, a constraint of the form

$$
(\mathbf{w} - \mathbf{w}_b)'\mathbf{\Sigma}(\mathbf{w} - \mathbf{w}_b) \leq \sigma_{\mathrm{TE}}^2
$$

can be added to the portfolio optimization formulation. In the next section, we provide an example that shows how the tracking error constraint formulation can be used for index tracking.

Note that a pure tracking-error constrained portfolio ignores total portfolio risk or *absolute* risk. In practice, this can result in very inefficient portfolios (in a mean-variance sense) unless additional constraints on total volatility are imposed.[18]

General Linear and Quadratic Constraints

The constraints described in this section are all linear or quadratic, i.e. they can be cast either as

$$
\begin{aligned}
\mathbf{A}_w \mathbf{w} &\leq \mathbf{d}_w \\
\mathbf{A}_x \mathbf{x} &\leq \mathbf{d}_x \\
\mathbf{A}_b(\mathbf{w} - \mathbf{w}_b) &\leq \mathbf{d}_b
\end{aligned}
$$

or as

$$
\begin{aligned}
\mathbf{w}'\mathbf{Q}_w \mathbf{w} &\leq \mathbf{q}_w \\
\mathbf{x}'\mathbf{Q}_x \mathbf{x} &\leq \mathbf{q}_x \\
(\mathbf{w} - \mathbf{w}_b)'\mathbf{Q}_b(\mathbf{w} - \mathbf{w}_b) &\leq \mathbf{q}_b
\end{aligned}
$$

These types of constraints can be dealt with directly within the quadratic programming framework, and there are very efficient algorithms available that are capable of solving practical portfolio optimization problems with thousands of assets in a matter of seconds. In Chapter 6

---

[18] Philippe Jorion, "Portfolio Optimization with Tracking-Error Constraints," *Financial Analysts Journal* 59 (2003), pp. 70–82.

we provide a survey of some of the standard approaches to the solution of these optimization problems.

Example: Minimizing Index Tracking Error

The wide acceptance of portfolio theory has provided for the growth in the use of passive portfolio management techniques and the enormous popularity of index funds. A very simple classification of portfolio and fund management is into *active* and *passive* approaches. In active management, it is assumed that markets are not fully efficient and that a fund manager can outperform standard indices by using specific information, knowledge, and experience. Passive management, in contrast, relies on the assumption that financial markets are efficient and that return and risk are fully reflected in asset prices. In this case, an investor should invest in a portfolio that mimics the market.

John Bogle used this basic idea in 1975 when he proposed to the board of directors of the newly formed Vanguard Group to create the first index fund. The objective of the mutual fund that he suggested was not to try to beat the S&P 500 index, but instead to mirror the index as closely as possible by buying each of the index's 500 stocks in amounts equal to the weights in the index itself. Today, indexing is a very popular form of mutual fund investing.

The index tracking problem is the problem of reproducing or mimicking the performance of a stock market index, but without purchasing all of the stocks that make up the index. Here we construct a *tracking portfolio* of the MSCI World Index over the period January 1980–May 2004 by minimizing the tracking error of a portfolio of some of the individual country equity indices to the index portfolio.[19] In other words, we solve the optimization problem

$$\min_{\mathbf{w}} (\mathbf{w} - \mathbf{w}_b)' \mathbf{\Sigma} (\mathbf{w} - \mathbf{w}_b)$$

subject to the usual constraint that

$$\mathbf{w}' \iota = 1 , \iota' = [1, 1, ..., 1]$$

where $\mathbf{w}_b$ are the market capitalization weights.

Each month, when we rebalance our portfolio, we use the historical covariances calculated from five years of daily data. The first five years of the sample, from January 1980 to December 1984, are used to con-

---

[19] A description and basic statistical properties of this data set are provided in Appendix C.

struct the first estimates used in the simulation in January 1985. We consider three different portfolios each with 6, 13, and all countries in the MSCI World Index. The specific countries in the portfolios with 6 and 13 assets were drawn at random. The number of assets in the index varies over time (typically, between 23 to 26 countries) as the constitution of the MSCI World Index changes.

By the rebalancing at the end of each month, we calculate the realized tracking error. The results are depicted in Exhibits 4.7 and 4.8. In particular, we observe that as the number of assets in the tracking portfolio increases, the tracking error decreases, as expected. With only six assets we are able to track the index with an annualized tracking error of about 2.5%.

The reason why the tracking error is not equal to zero when we are using all the assets is that the weights in the tracking portfolio are constant throughout the month (they are only rebalanced monthly) whereas the market capitalization weights can change daily.

EXHIBIT 4.7 Monthly Tracking Error of the Index Replicating Portfolio with 6, 13, and All Assets Rebalanced Monthly

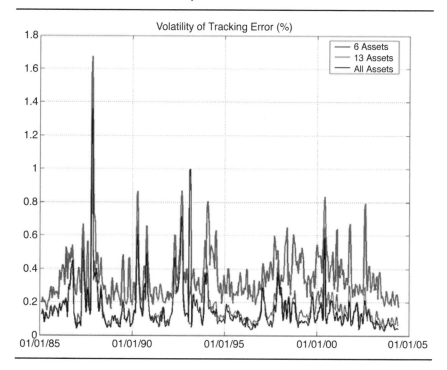

EXHIBIT 4.8   Average Yearly Tracking Error Over the Period January 1985 through May 2004 for a Tracking Portfolio of Different Numbers of Assets.

Number of Assets	Average TE
1	5.44%
2	4.48%
3	3.68%
6	2.50%
12	2.29%
18	1.70%
25	0.15%

Combinatorial and Integer Constraints

The following binary decision variable is useful in describing some combinatorial and integer constraints:

$$\delta_i = \begin{cases} 1, & \text{if } w_i \neq 0 \\ 0, & \text{if } w_i = 0 \end{cases}$$

where w_i denotes the portfolio weight of the i-th asset.

Minimum Holding and Transaction Size Constraints

The classical mean-variance optimization problem often results in a few large and many small positions. In practice, due to transaction costs and other ticket charges, small holdings are undesirable. In order to eliminate small holdings, threshold constraints of the following form are often used

$$|w_i| \geq L_{w_i} \delta_i \quad i = 1, ..., N$$

where L_{w_i} is the smallest holding size allowed for asset i.

Similarly, because of the fixed costs related to trading each individual security, it is desirable to avoid small trades. Therefore, a portfolio manager might also want to eliminate new trades, **x**, smaller than a prespecified amount

$$|x_i| \geq L_{x_i} \delta_i \quad i = 1, ..., N$$

where L_{x_i} is the smallest transaction size permitted for asset i.

In practice, few portfolio managers go to the extent of including constraints of this type in their optimization framework. Instead, a standard mean-variance optimization problem is solved and then, in a "postoptimization" step, generated portfolio weights or trades that are smaller than a certain threshold are eliminated. This simplification leads to small, but often negligible, differences compared to a full optimization using the threshold constraints. Given that the mean-variance optimization problem with threshold constraints is much more complicated to solve from a numerical and computational point of view, this small discrepancy is often ignored by practitioners. In Chapter 6, we discuss the numerical optimization techniques used in solving these types of constraints and address some of the computational difficulties.

Cardinality Constraints

In practice, a portfolio manager might want to restrict the number of assets allowed in a portfolio. This could be the case when, for example, attempting to construct a portfolio tracking a benchmark using a limited set of assets. The cardinality constraint takes the form

$$\sum_{i=1}^{N} \delta_i = K$$

where K is a positive integer significantly less than the number of assets in the investment universe, N.

Minimum holding and cardinality constraints are related. Both of them attempt to reduce the number of small trades and the number of portfolio positions. Therefore, it is not uncommon that both constraints are used simultaneously in the same portfolio optimization. There are situations in which imposing only cardinality constraints will lead to some small trades. Conversely, with only minimum holding constraints the resulting portfolio might still contain too many positions, or result in too many trades. Portfolio managers often have the desire not to keep the number of assets too large and at the same time make sure that all of their holdings are larger than a certain threshold.

Round Lot Constraints

For the most part, portfolio selection models proposed in the literature are based on the assumption of a perfect "fractionability" of the investments, in such a way that the portfolio weights for each security could be represented by real numbers. In reality, securities are transacted in multiples of a minimum transaction lots, or rounds (e.g., 100 or 500 shares). In order to model transaction round lots explicitly in the optimization problem, portfolio weights can be represented as

$$w_i = z_i \cdot f_i, \quad i = 1, \dots, N$$

where f_i is a fraction of portfolio wealth and z_i is an integer number of round lots. For example, if the total portfolio wealth is \$10 million and stock i trades at \$86 in round lots of 100, then

$$f_i = \frac{86 \cdot 100}{10^7} = 8.6 \times 10^{-4}$$

In applying round lot constraints, the budget constraint

$$\sum_{i=1}^{N} w_i = 1$$

may not be exactly satisfied. To accommodate this situation, the budget constraint is relaxed with "undershoot" and "overshoot" variables, ε^- and ε^+, so that

$$\sum_{i=1}^{N} f_i z_i + \varepsilon^- - \varepsilon^+ = 1$$

This formula can be written in a more compact way as

$$z'\Lambda\iota + \varepsilon^- - \varepsilon^+ = 1, \quad \iota' = [1, 1, \dots, 1]$$

where $\Lambda = \mathrm{diag}(f_1, f_2, \dots, f_N)$, that is, the diagonal matrix of the fractions of portfolio wealth.

The undershoot and overshoot variables are to be made as small as possible at the optimal point, and therefore, they are penalized in the objective function, yielding the following optimization problem:

$$\max_{z} \; z'\Lambda\mu - \lambda z'\Lambda\Sigma\Lambda z - \gamma(\varepsilon^- + \varepsilon^+)$$

subject to

$$z'\Lambda\iota + \varepsilon^- + \varepsilon^+ = 1, \quad \iota' = [1, 1, ..., 1]$$

where λ and γ are parameters chosen by the portfolio manager.

In general, the inclusion of round lot constraints to the mean-variance optimization problem normally only produces a small increase in risk for a prespecified expected return. Furthermore, the portfolios obtained in this manner cannot be obtained by simply rounding the portfolio weights from a standard mean-variance optimization to the nearest round lot.

In order to represent threshold and cardinality constraints we have to introduce binary (0/1) variables, and for round lots we need integer variables. In effect, the original *quadratic program* (QP) resulting from the mean-variance formulation becomes a *quadratic mixed integer program* (QMIP). Therefore, these combinatorial extensions require more sophisticated and specialized algorithms that often require significant computing time.

Example: A Combinatorial Problem in Asset Allocation

To illustrate the difficulty encountered in these combinatorial problems, we consider the four-asset example from Chang et al.[20] with the expected returns, standard deviations, and correlation matrix given in Exhibit 4.9.

First, we consider the problem of calculating the efficient frontier subject to no short-selling and proportional minimum holding constraints $L_{w_i} = 0.24$ for all *i*. The result is presented in Exhibit 4.10. We observe that the efficient frontier is discontinuous, unlike the classical

EXHIBIT 4.9 Expected Returns, Standard Deviations, and Correlations of Stock 1 through 4

Asset	Return (weekly)	Std. Dev. (weekly)	Correlation Matrix			
			1	2	3	4
1	0.48%	4.64%	1			
2	0.07%	3.06%	0.12	1		
3	0.32%	3.05%	0.14	0.16	1	
4	0.14%	0.04%	0.25	0.10	0.08	1

Source: T.-J. Chang, N. Meade, J. E. Beasley, and Y. M. Sharaiha, "Heuristics for Cardinality Constrained Portfolio Optimization," *Computers and Operations Research* 27 (2000), p. 1279. Reprinted with permission from the authors.

---

[20] T.-J. Chang, N. Meade, J. E. Beasley, and Y. M. Sharaiha, "Heuristics for Cardinality Constrained Portfolio Optimization," *Computers and Operations Research*, 27 (2000), pp. 1271–1302. We are grateful to the authors for allowing us to use their examples here.

EXHIBIT 4.10   Efficient Frontier with a Minimum Proportion of 0.24

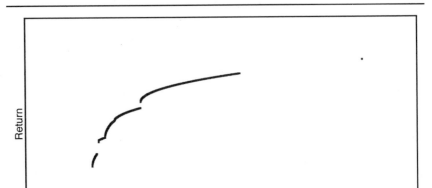

Source: Figure 6 in T.-J. Chang, N. Meade, J. E. Beasley, and Y. M. Sharaiha, "Heuristics for Cardinality Constrained Portfolio Optimization," *Computers and Operations Research* 27 (2000), p. 1282.

mean-variance efficient frontier. This implies that there are certain expected portfolio returns that no rational investor would consider because there are portfolios available with less risk and greater return.

Next, let us consider the cardinality constrained problem and using the four stocks in Exhibit 4.9 calculate the efficient frontier of portfolios containing only two stocks. With only four stocks, we can proceed in the following way. First, we calculate the efficient frontier of all feasible combinations of two assets,

$$\binom{4}{2} = \frac{4!}{(4-2)!} = 6$$

In Exhibit 4.11, six line segments representing each a two-asset efficient frontier are shown. The exhibit depicts the complete universe of feasible two-asset portfolios. We observe that certain portfolios are dominated. For example, the portfolio consisting of assets 1 and 2, and assets 1 and 4, are dominated by the portfolio consisting of assets 1 and 3. By eliminating all dominated portfolios, we obtain the efficient frontier consisting of the set of efficient portfolios of two assets, shown in Exhibit 4.12. As with the minimum holding constraints, the cardinality constrained efficient frontier is discontinuous.

EXHIBIT 4.11   Feasible Combinations of Two Assets

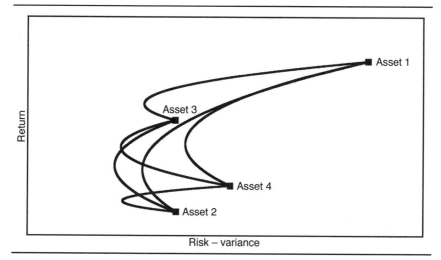

Source: Figure 2 in T.-J. Chang, N. Meade, J. E. Beasley, and Y. M. Sharaiha, "Heuristics for Cardinality Constrained Portfolio Optimization," *Computers and Operations Research* 27 (2000), p 1279.

EXHIBIT 4.12   Cardinality Constrained Efficient Frontier

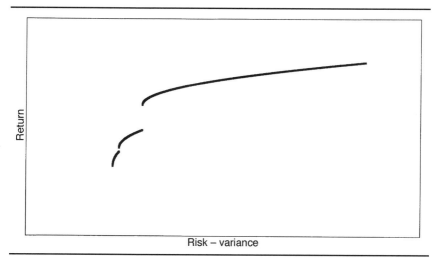

Source: Figure 3 in T.-J. Chang, N. Meade, J. E. Beasley, and Y. M. Sharaiha, "Heuristics for Cardinality Constrained Portfolio Optimization," *Computers and Operations Research* 27 (2000), p 1280.

In this four-asset case, the solution is obtained by enumeration. However, as the number of assets grows, simple enumeration techniques become computationally unfeasible as the number of combinations to be considered becomes too large. As a matter of fact, portfolio optimization problems with minimum holding constraints, cardinality constraints, or round lot constraints are so-called NP-complete (nondeterministic polynomial time)[21] problems.[22] For the practical solution of these problems, heuristics and other approximation techniques are often used.[23] Bartholomew-Biggs and Kane have proposed a penalty approach for solving the portfolio optimization problem with constraints for minimum holdings and round lots.[24] Their approach results in an objective function with multiple local optima. Therefore, a combination of local and global optimization techniques is used in order to find the global optima.[25] In general, this type of approach works for smaller problems where fewer assets are involved. However, when the number of assets increases, this technique becomes too burdensome computationally.

---

[21] A formal definition of NP-completeness is technical and outside the scope of this book. However, for our purposes, it suffices to loosely define it as algorithms of exponential complexity, that is, algorithms where the time required grows exponentially with the size of the problem. For a formal definition, refer to Michael Garey, *Computers and Intractability: A Guide to NP-completeness* (New York: W. H. Freeman, 1979).

[22] Renata Mansini and Maria Grazia Speranza, "Heuristic Algorithms for the Portfolio Selection Problem with Minimum Transaction Lots," *European Journal of Operational Research* 114 (1999), pp. 219–233.

[23] Norbert J. Jobst, Michael D. Horniman, Cormac A. Lucas, and Guatam Mitra, "Computational Aspects of Alternative Portfolio Selection Models in the Presence of Discrete Asset Choice Constraints," *Quantitative Finance* 1 (2001), pp. 1–13; and Hans Kellerer, Renata Mansini, and Maria Grazia Speranza, "Selecting Portfolios with Fixed Costs and Minimum Transaction Lots," *Annals of Operations Research* 99 (2000), pp. 287–304.

[24] Michael Bartholomew-Biggs and Stephen Kane, "A Global Optimization Problem in Portfolio Selection," School of Physics Astronomy and Mathematics, University of Hertfordshire, Technical Report, undated.

[25] Global optimization techniques as well as heuristics used in order to solve combinatorial and integer optimization problems do not guarantee that the global optima is found. Typically, these algorithms set out to find the "best" local optima. For practical purposes, however, this normally delivers a satisfactory solution at a reasonable computational cost.

SUMMARY

- Changes in return and risk forecasts, security prices, and in the investment universe available to the portfolio manager make it necessary to rebalance a portfolio.
- A disciplined rebalancing policy can improve performance significantly.
- In general, we can distinguish three different criteria to rebalancing: (1) calendar rebalancing, (2) threshold rebalancing, and (3) range rebalancing.
- The mean-variance framework is straightforward to use in the rebalancing of a portfolio. Since it is a single-period framework, it has its drawbacks, but its simplicity makes it attractive. More sophisticated multiperiod techniques have better properties, but are often more complicated to implement in practice.
- Trading and transaction costs significantly influence the rebalancing decision.
- Some of the most common constraints used in practice are no short-selling constraints, turnover constraints, maximum holding constraints, and tracking error constraints. These constraints can be handled in a straightforward way by the same type of optimization algorithms used for solving the mean-variance problem.
- Integer constraints or constraints of combinatorial nature are more difficult to handle and do often require more specialized optimization algorithms. Some examples of these type of constraints are minimum holding constraints, transaction size constraints, cardinality constraints (number securities permitted in the portfolio), and round lot constraints.

CHAPTER 5

Incorporating Higher Moments and Extreme Risk Measures

The portfolio manager may use his or her experience in stock picking or rely upon quantitative modeling techniques in the portfolio selection process. However, generally speaking, the main objective of portfolio selection is the construction of portfolios that maximize expected returns at a certain level of risk. For example, in the classical mean-variance framework, discussed in Chapter 2, estimates of the expected returns and the covariance matrix of the assets were used to calculate the optimal portfolio. Nonetheless, it is now well known that asset returns are not normal, and therefore the mean and the variance alone do not fully describe the characteristics of the joint assets return distribution. Indeed, many risks and undesirable scenarios faced by a portfolio manager cannot be captured solely by the variance of the portfolio. Consequently, especially in cases of significant nonnormality, the classical mean-variance approach will not be a satisfactory portfolio allocation model.

Since about the mid-1990s, considerable thought and innovation in the financial industry have been directed towards creating a better understanding of risk and its measurement, and to improve the management of risk in financial portfolios. From the statistical point of view, a key innovation is the attention paid to the ratio between the bulk of the risk and the risk of the tails. The latter has become a key statistical determinant of risk management policies. Changing situations and different portfolios may require alternative and new risk measures. The "race" for inventing the best risk measure for a given situation or portfolio is still ongoing. Maybe we will never find a completely satisfactory answer to the question of which risk measure to use, and this choice to some extent remains an art form.

We mention in passing, that one source that can lead to highly non-normal return distributions with fat tails and nonnegligible higher moments is regime changes. Commonly, these are modeled by regime and Markov switching techniques (see Chapter 16). These types of models are often data-hungry and computationally intensive as they have to be solved by simulation and dynamic programming techniques. Although they are typically out of reach for practical portfolio management situations, they provide an alternative to the models discussed in this chapter and show promise for the modeling of dynamic portfolio allocation and time-varying investment opportunities sets.[1]

In this chapter we examine some of the most common alternative portfolio risk measures used in practice for asset allocation. We begin by discussing dispersion and downside measures. Then, we turn to modifications to the generalized utility based framework. In particular, we study techniques based upon expansions of the utility function in higher moments such as its mean, variance, skew, and kurtosis.

The empirical estimation of higher moments and other alternative risk measures is often very sensitive to estimation errors. We discuss and illustrate some of the most common pitfalls.

One possibility that helps circumvent, to some extent, the error-prone measurement of higher moments and sensitive risk measures is to make stronger assumptions on the multivariate distribution of the asset returns. We conclude the chapter by describing a novel technique developed by Malevergne and Sornette that relies upon this idea.[2]

DISPERSION AND DOWNSIDE MEASURES

Simplistically speaking, we distinguish between two different types of risk measures: (1) dispersion and (2) downside measures. In this section we provide a brief overview of the most common dispersion and downside measures and their usage.[3]

---

[1] See, for example, Andrew Ang and Geert Bekaert, "International Asset Allocation with the Regime Shifts," Working Paper, Columbia University and NBER, 2001.

[2] Yannick Malevergne and Didier Sornette, "High-Order Moments and Cumulants of Multivariate Weibull Asset Returns Distributions: Analytical Theory and Empirical Tests: II," *Finance Letters* [Special Issue: Modeling of the Equity Market] 3 (2005), pp. 54–63 and "Higher-Moment Portfolio Theory: Capitalizing on Behavioral Anomalies of Stock Markets," *Journal of Portfolio Management* (Summer 2005), pp. 49–55.

[3] For a further discussion, see Sergio Ortobelli, Svetlozar T. Rachev, Stoyan Stoyanov, Frank J. Fabozzi, and Almira Biglova, "The Correct Use of Risk Measures in Portfolio Theory" forthcoming in *International Journal of Theoretical and Applied Finance*.

Dispersion Measures

Dispersion measures are measures of uncertainty. Nonetheless, uncertainty does not necessarily quantify risk. In contrast to downside measures, dispersion measures entail *both* positive and negative deviations from the mean and consider those deviations as equally risky. In other words, overperformance relative to the mean is penalized as much as underperformance. In this section we review the most popular and important portfolio dispersion measures such as mean standard deviation, mean absolute deviation, and mean absolute moment.

Mean Standard Deviation and the Mean-Variance Approach

For historical reasons, portfolio standard deviation (or portfolio variance) is probably the most well-known dispersion measure. The mean-variance framework, also referred to as classical portfolio theory, which we covered in Chapter 2, was pioneered by Markowitz in the 1950s.

Mean Absolute Deviation

Konno[4] introduced the *mean-absolute deviation* (MAD) approach in 1988. Rather than using squared deviations as is the case for the mean-variance approach, here the dispersion measure is based on the absolution deviations from the mean; that is,

$$MAD(R_p) = E\left(\left|\sum_{i=1}^{N} w_i R_i - \sum_{i=1}^{N} w_i \mu_i\right|\right)$$

where

$$R_p = \sum_{i=1}^{N} w_i R_i$$

R_i, and μ_i are the portfolio return, the return on asset i, and the expected return on asset i, respectively.

The computation of optimal portfolios in the case of the mean absolute deviation approach is significantly simplified as the resulting optimization problem is linear and can be solved by standard linear programming routines.

---

[4] Hiroshi Konno, "Portfolio Optimization Using L1 Risk Function," IHSS Report 88-9, Institute of Human and Social Sciences, Tokyo Institute of Technology, 1988. See, also, Hiroshi Konno, "Piecewise Linear Risk Functions and Portfolio Optimization," *Journal of the Operations Research Society of Japan* 33 (1990), pp. 139–156.

We note that it can be shown that under the assumption that the individual asset returns are multivariate normally distributed, then

$$MAD(R_p) = \sqrt{\frac{2}{\pi}} \sigma_p$$

where σ_p is the standard deviation of the portfolio.[5] That is, when asset returns are normally distributed, the mean absolute deviation and the mean-variance approaches are equivalent.

Mean-Absolute Moment

The mean-absolute moment (MAM_q) of order q is defined by

$$MAM_q(R_p) = \left(E(|R_p - E(R_p)|^q) \right)^{1/q}, q \geq 1$$

and is a straightforward generalization of the mean standard deviation ($q = 2$) and the mean absolute deviation ($q = 1$) approaches.

Downside Measures

The objective in these models is the maximization of the probability that the portfolio return is above a certain minimal acceptable level, often also referred to as the *benchmark level* or *disaster level*.

Despite the theoretical appeal of these measures, downside or safety-first risk measures are often computationally more complicated to use in a portfolio context. Downside risk measures of individual securities cannot be easily aggregated into portfolio downside risk measures as their computation requires knowledge of the entire joint distribution of security returns. Often, one has to resort to computationally intensive nonparametric estimation, simulation, and optimization techniques. Furthermore, the estimation risk of downside measures is usually higher than for standard mean-variance approaches. By the estimation of downside risk measures we only use a portion of the original data— maybe even just the tail of the empirical distribution—and hence the estimation error increases.[6] Nevertheless, these risk measures are very useful in assessing the risk for securities with asymmetric return distri-

---

[5] Hiroshi Konno and Hiroaki Yamazaki, "Mean-Absolute Deviation Portfolio Optimization Model and its Application to Tokyo Stock Market," *Management Science* 37 (1991), pp. 519–531.

[6] For further discussion of these issues, see Henk Grootveld and Winfried G. Hallerbach, "Variance Versus Downside Risk: Is There Really That Much Difference?" *European Journal of Operational Research* 11 (1999), pp. 304–319.

butions such as call and put options, as well as other derivative contracts.

We discuss some of the most common safety-first and downside risk measures below such as Roy's safety-first, semivariance, lower partial moment, Value-at-Risk, and conditional Value-at-Risk.

Roy's Safety-First

Two very important papers on portfolio selection were published in 1952: first, Markowitz's[7] paper on portfolio selection and classical portfolio theory; second, Roy's[8] paper on *safety first*, which laid the seed for the development of downside risk measures.[9]

Let us first understand the difference between these two approaches.[10] According to classical portfolio theory, an investor constructs a portfolio that represents a trade-off between risk and return. The trade-off between risk and return and the portfolio allocation depend upon the investor's utility function. It can be hard or even impossible to determine an investor's actual utility function.

Instead, Roy argued that an investor rather than thinking in terms of utility functions, first wants to make sure that a certain amount of the principal is preserved. Thereafter, he decides on some minimal acceptable return that achieves this principal preservation. Roy pointed out that an investor prefers the investment opportunity with the smallest probability of going below a certain target return or disaster level. In essence, this investor chooses this portfolio by solving the following optimization problem

$$\min_{\mathbf{w}} P(R_p \le R_0)$$

subject to

$$\mathbf{w}'\mathbf{\iota} = 1\,,\mathbf{\iota}' = [1, 1, ..., 1]$$

[7] Harry M. Markowitz, "Portfolio Selection," *Journal of Finance* 7 (1952), pp. 77–91.
[8] Andrew D. Roy, "Safety-First and the Holding of Assets," *Econometrica* 20 (1952), pp. 431–449.
[9] See, for example, Vijay S. Bawa, "Optimal Rules for Ordering Uncertain Prospects," *Journal of Financial Economics* 2 (1975), pp. 95–121; and Vijay S. Bawa, "Safety-First Stochastic Dominance and Portfolio Choice," *Journal of Financial and Quantitative Analysis* 13 (1978), pp. 255–271.
[10] For a more detailed description of these historical events, we refer the reader to David Nawrocki, "A Brief History of Downside Risk Measures," College of Commerce and Finance, Villanova University, Faculty Research, Fall 2003.

where P is the probability function and

$$R_p = \sum_{i=1}^{N} w_i R_i$$

is the portfolio return. Most likely the investor will not know the true probability function. However, by using Tchebycheff's inequality we obtain[11]

$$P(R_p \leq R_0) \leq \frac{\sigma_p^2}{(\mu_p - R_0)^2}$$

where μ_p and σ_p denote the expected return and the variance of the portfolio, respectively. Therefore, not knowing the probability function, the investor will end up solving the approximation

$$\min_w \frac{\sigma_p}{\mu_p - R_0}$$

subject to

$$\mathbf{w'\iota} = 1, \iota' = [1, 1, ..., 1]$$

We note that if R_0 is equal to the risk-free rate, then this optimization problem is equivalent to maximizing a portfolio's Sharpe ratio.

---

[11] For a random variable x with expected value μ and variance σ_x^2, Tchebycheff's inequality states that for any positive real number c, it holds that

$$P(|x - \mu| > c) \leq \frac{\sigma_x^2}{c^2}$$

Applying Tchebycheff's inequality, we get

$$P(R_p \leq R_0) = P(\mu_p - R_p \geq \mu_p - R_0)$$

$$\leq \frac{\sigma_p^2}{(\mu_p - R_0)^2}$$

Semivariance

In his original book, Markowitz proposed the usage of *semivariance* to correct for the fact that variance penalizes overperformance and underperformance equally.[12] When receiving his Nobel prize in Economic Science, Markowitz stated that ". . . it can further help evaluate the adequacy of mean and variance, or alternative practical measures, as criteria." Furthermore, he added "Perhaps some other measure of portfolio risk will serve in a two parameter analysis. . . . Semivariance seems more plausible than variance as a measure of risk, since it is concerned only with adverse deviations."[13]

The portfolio semivariance is defined as

$$\sigma^2_{p,\,min} = E\left(min\left(\sum_{i=1}^{N} w_i R_i - \sum_{i=1}^{N} w_i \mu_i, 0 \right) \right)^2$$

where

$$R_p = \sum_{i=1}^{N} w_i R_i,$$

R_i, and μ_i are the portfolio return, the return on asset i, and the expected return on asset i, respectively. Jin, Markowitz, and Zhou provide some of the theoretical properties of the mean-semivariance approach both in the single-period as well as in the continuous-time setting.[14] A generalization to the semivariance is provided by the lower partial moment risk measure that we discuss in the next subsection.

Lower Partial Moment

The *lower partial moment risk measure* provides a natural generalization of semivariance that we described above (see, for example, Bawa[15] and Fishburn[16]). The lower partial moment with *power index q* and the *target rate of return* R_0 is given by

---

[12] Harry Markowitz, *Portfolio Selection—Efficient Diversification of Investment* (New York: Wiley, 1959).

[13] Harry Markowitz, "Foundations of Portfolio Theory," *Journal of Finance* 46 (1991), pp. 469–477.

[14] Hanqing Jin, Harry Markowitz, and Xunyu Zhou, "A Note on Semivariance," Forthcoming in *Mathematical Finance*.

[15] Vijay S. Bawa, "Admissible Portfolio for All Individuals," *Journal of Finance* 31 (1976), pp.1169–1183.

[16] Peter C. Fishburn, "Mean-Risk Analysis with Risk Associated with Below-Target Returns," *American Economic Review* 67 (1977), pp. 116–126.

$$\sigma_{R_p, q, R_0} = \left(E(\min(R_p - R_0, 0)^q)\right)^{1/q}$$

where

$$R_p = \sum_{i=1}^{N} w_i R_i$$

is the portfolio return. The target rate of return R_0 is what Roy termed the *disaster level*.[17] We recognize that by setting $q = 2$ and R_0 equal to the expected return, the semivariance is obtained. Fishburn demonstrated that $q = 1$ represents a risk neutral investor, whereas $0 < q \leq 1$ and $q > 1$ correspond to a risk seeking and a risk-averse investor, respectively.

Value-at-Risk (VaR)

Probably the most well-known risk measure, besides the standard deviation, is *Value-at-Risk* (VaR) first developed by JP Morgan and made available through the RiskMetrics™ software in October 1994.[18] VaR is related to the percentiles of loss distributions and measures the predicted maximum loss at a specified probability level (for example, 95%) over a certain time horizon (for example, 10 days).

Formally, VaR is defined as

$$VaR_\alpha(R_p) = \min \{R \,|\, P(R_p \leq R) \geq \alpha\}$$

where P denotes the probability function. Typical values of α that commonly are considered are 90%, 95%, and 99%. Some of the practical and computational issues related to using VaR are discussed in Alexander and Baptista,[19] Gaivoronski, and Pflug,[20] and Mittnik, Rachev, and Schwartz et al.[21] Chow and Kritzman discuss the usage of VaR in

---

[17] Roy, "Safety-First and the Holding of Assets."
[18] JP Morgan/Reuters, *RiskMetrics™—Technical Document*, 4th ed. (New York: Morgan Guaranty Trust Company of New York, 1996). See also http://www.riskmetrics.com.
[19] Gordon J. Alexander and Alexandre M. Baptista, "Economic Implications of Using a Mean-VaR Model for Portfolio Selection: A Comparison with Mean-Variance Analysis," *Journal of Economic Dynamics & Control* 26 (2002), pp. 1159–1193.
[20] Alexei A. Gaivoronski, and Georg Pflug, "Value At-Risk in Portfolio Optimization: Properties and Computational Approach," *Journal of Risk* 7 (Winter 2004–2005), pp. 1–31.
[21] Stefan Mittnik, Svetlotzar Rachev, and Eduardo Schwartz, "Value At-Risk and Asset Allocation with Stable Return Distributions," *Allgemeines Statistisches Archiv* 86 (2003), pp. 53–67.

formulating risk budgets, and provide an intuitive method for converting efficient portfolio allocations into value at risk assignments.[22] In a subsequent article, they discuss some of the problems with the simplest approach for computing VaR of a portfolio.[23] In particular, the common assumption that the portfolio itself is lognormally distributed can be somewhat problematic, especially for portfolios that contain both long and short positions.

In April 1993, the Basel Committee proposed several amendments to the original so-called 1988 Basel Accord that regulates the minimal capital requirements for banks. While previously the Basel Accord had covered only credit risk (deposits and lending), the new proposal that was taken into effect in 1998 also covers market risk including organization-wide commodities exposures (measured by 10 day 95% VaR).[24] Today VaR is used by most financial institutions to both track and report the market risk exposure of their trading portfolios.

Despite its popularity, VaR has several undesirable properties.[25] First, it is not subadditive. In other words, for VaR it *does not* hold that $\rho(R_1 + R_2) \leq \rho(R_1) + \rho(R_2)$ for all returns R_1, R_2. This property is the mathematical description of the diversification effect. For risk measures that are not subadditive, it may happen that a more diversified portfolio has higher risk. Needless to say, nonsubadditive risk measures are highly undesirable. Second, when VaR is calculated from scenario generation or simulation, it turns out to be a nonsmooth and nonconvex function of the portfolio holdings. As a consequence, the VaR function calculated this way has multiple stationary points, making it computationally both difficult and time-consuming to find the global optimal point.[26] Third, VaR does not take the *magnitude* of the losses beyond the VaR value into account. For example, it is very unlikely that an investor will be indifferent between two portfolios with identical expected return and VaR when the return distribution of one portfolio has a short left tail and the other has a long

---

[22] George Chow and Mark Kritzman, "Risk Budgets—Converting Mean-Variance Optimization into VaR Assignments," *Journal of Portfolio Management* (Winter 2001), pp. 56-60.

[23] George Chow and Mark Kritzman, "Value at Risk for Portfolios with Short Positions," *Journal of Portfolio Management* (Spring 2002), pp. 73–81.

[24] Basel Committee on Banking Supervision, "Amendment to the Capital Accord to Incorporate Market Risks," 1996.

[25] Hans Rau-Bredow, "Value-at-Risk, Expected Shortfall and Marginal Risk Contribution," in Giorgio Szegö (ed.) *Risk Measures for the 21st Century* (Chichester: John Wiley & Sons, 2004), pp. 61–68.

[26] For some possible remedies and fixes to this problem see, Henk Grootveld and Winfried G. Hallerbach, "Upgrading Value-at-Risk from Diagnostic Metric to Decision Variable: A Wise Thing to Do?" in *Risk Measures for the 21st Century*, pp. 33–50.

left tail. These undesirable features motivated the development of conditional Value-at-Risk that we discuss next.

Conditional Value-at-Risk

The deficiencies of Value-at-Risk lead Artzner et al. to propose a set of natural properties that a reasonable measure of risk should satisfy.[27] This led to the introduction of so-called *coherent risk measures*.[28] *Conditional Value-at-Risk* (CVaR) is a coherent risk measure defined by the formula

$$CVaR_\alpha(R_p) = E(-R_p|-R_p \geq VaR_\alpha(R_p))$$

In the literature, this risk measure is also referred to as *expected short-fall*,[29] *expected tail loss* (ETL), and *tail VaR*. As with VaR, the most commonly considered values for α are 90%, 95%, and 99%.

Before we formulate the mean-CVaR optimization problem, we first proceed by discussing some mathematical properties of the CVaR measure. To this end, let us denote by **w** the N-dimensional portfolio vector such that each component w_i equals the number of shares held in asset i. Further, we denote by **y** a random vector describing the uncertain outcomes (also referred to as *market variables*) of the economy. We let the function $f(\mathbf{w},\mathbf{y})$ (also referred to as the *loss function*) represent the loss associated with the portfolio vector **w**. Note that for each **w** the loss function $f(\mathbf{w},\mathbf{y})$ is a one-dimensional random variable. We let $p(\mathbf{y})$ be the probability associated with scenario **y**.

---

[27] Philippe Artzner, Freddy Delbaen, Jean-Marc Eber, David Heath, "Coherent Measures of Risk," *Mathematical Finance*, 3 (1999), pp. 203–228.

[28] A risk measure ρ is called a *coherent measure of risk* if it satisfies the following properties:

  1. *Monotonicity.* If $X \geq 0$, then $\rho(X) \leq 0$
  2. *Subadditivity.* $\rho(X + Y) \leq \rho(X) + \rho(Y)$
  3. *Positive homogeneity.* For any *positive* real number c, it holds $\rho(cX) = c\rho(X)$
  4. *Translational invariance.* For any real number c, it holds $\rho(X + c) \leq \rho(X) - c$

where X and Y are random variables. In words, these properties can be interpreted as: (1) If there are only positive returns, then the risk should be non-positive; (2) the risk of a portfolio of two assets should be less than or equal to the risk of the individual assets; (3) if the portfolio is increased c times, the risk also becomes c times larger; and (4) cash or another risk-free asset does not contribute to portfolio risk.

[29] Strictly speaking, expected shortfall is defined in a different way, but is shown to be equivalent to CVaR (see, Carlo Acerbi and Dirk Tasche, "On the Coherence of Expected Shortfall," *Journal of Banking and Finance* 6 (2002), pp. 1487–1503).

Now, assuming that all random values are discrete, the probability that the loss function does not exceed a certain value γ is given by the cumulative probability

$$\Psi(\mathbf{w}, \gamma) = \sum_{\{\mathbf{y}|f(\mathbf{w}, \mathbf{y}) \leq \gamma\}} p(\mathbf{y})$$

Using this cumulative probability, we see that

$$\text{VaR}_\alpha(\mathbf{w}) = \min\{\gamma | \Psi(\mathbf{w}, \gamma) \geq \alpha\}$$

Since CVaR of the losses of portfolio $\mathbf{w}$ is the expected value of the losses conditioned on the losses being in excess of VaR, we have that

$$\text{CVaR}_\alpha(\mathbf{w}) = E(f(\mathbf{w}, \mathbf{y}) | f(\mathbf{w}, \mathbf{y}) > \text{VaR}_\alpha(\mathbf{w}))$$

$$= \frac{\displaystyle\sum_{\{\mathbf{y}|f(\mathbf{w}, \mathbf{y}) > \text{VaR}_\alpha(\mathbf{w})\}} p(\mathbf{y})f(\mathbf{w}, \mathbf{y})}{\displaystyle\sum_{\{\mathbf{y}|f(\mathbf{w}, \mathbf{y}) > \text{VaR}_\alpha(\mathbf{w})\}} p(\mathbf{y})}$$

The continuous equivalents of these formulas are

$$\Psi(\mathbf{w}, \mathbf{y}) = \int_{f(\mathbf{w}, \mathbf{y}) \leq \gamma} p(\mathbf{y})dy$$

$$\text{VaR}_\alpha(\mathbf{w}) = \min\{\gamma | \Psi(\mathbf{w}, \gamma) \geq \alpha\}$$

$$\text{CVaR}_\alpha(\mathbf{w}) = E(f(\mathbf{w}, \mathbf{y}) | f(\mathbf{w}, \mathbf{y}) \geq \text{VaR}_\alpha(\mathbf{w}))$$

$$= (1 - \alpha)^{-1} \int_{f(\mathbf{w}, \mathbf{y}) \geq \text{VaR}_\alpha(\mathbf{w})} f(\mathbf{w}, \mathbf{y})p(\mathbf{y})dy$$

We note that in the continuous case it holds that $\Psi(\mathbf{w}, \gamma) = \alpha$ and therefore the denominator

$$\sum_{\{\mathbf{y}|f(\mathbf{w}, \mathbf{y}) > \text{VaR}_\alpha(\mathbf{w})\}} p(\mathbf{y})$$

in the discrete version of CVaR becomes $1 - \alpha$ in the continuous case. Moreover, we see that

$$
\begin{aligned}
\mathrm{CVaR}_\alpha(\mathbf{w}) &= (1-\alpha)^{-1} \int\limits_{f(\mathbf{w},\mathbf{y}) \geq \mathrm{VaR}_\alpha(\mathbf{w})} f(\mathbf{w},\mathbf{y}) p(\mathbf{y}) dy \\
&\geq (1-\alpha)^{-1} \int\limits_{f(\mathbf{w},\mathbf{y}) \geq \mathrm{VaR}_\alpha(\mathbf{w})} \mathrm{VaR}_\alpha(\mathbf{w}) p(\mathbf{y}) dy \\
&= \mathrm{VaR}_\alpha(\mathbf{w})
\end{aligned}
$$

because

$$
(1-\alpha)^{-1} \int\limits_{f(\mathbf{w},\mathbf{y}) \geq \mathrm{VaR}_\alpha(\mathbf{w})} p(\mathbf{y}) dy = 1
$$

In other words, CVaR is always at least as large as VaR but as we mentioned above, CVaR is a coherent risk measure whereas VaR is not. It can also be shown that CVaR is a concave function and, therefore, has a unique minimum. However, working directly with the above formulas turns out to be somewhat tricky in practice as they involve the VaR function (except for those rare cases when one has an analytical expression for VaR). Fortunately, a simpler approach was discovered by Rockefellar and Uryasev.[30]

Their idea is that the function

$$
F_\alpha(\mathbf{w}, \xi) = \xi + (1-\alpha)^{-1} \int\limits_{f(\mathbf{w},\mathbf{y}) \geq \gamma} (f(\mathbf{w},\mathbf{y}) - \xi) p(\mathbf{y}) dy
$$

can be used instead of CVaR. Specifically, they proved the following three important properties:

Property 1. $F_\alpha(\mathbf{w}, \xi)$ is a convex and continuously differentiable function in ξ.
Property 2. $\mathrm{VaR}_\alpha(\mathbf{w})$ is a minimizer of $F_\alpha(\mathbf{w}, \xi)$.
Property 3. The minimum value of $F_\alpha(\mathbf{w}, \xi)$ is $\mathrm{CVaR}_\alpha(\mathbf{w})$.

In particular, we can find the optimal value of $\mathrm{CVaR}_\alpha(\mathbf{w})$ by solving the optimization problem

---

[30] See, Stanislav Uryasev, "Conditional Value-at-Risk: Optimization Algorithms and Applications," *Financial Engineering News*, No. 14 (February 2000), pp. 1–5; and R. Tyrrell Rockefellar and Stanislav Uryasev, "Optimization of Conditional Value-at-Risk," *Journal of Risk* 2 (2000), pp. 21–41.

$$\min_{\mathbf{w}, \xi} F_\alpha(\mathbf{w}, \xi)$$

Consequently, if we denote by $(\mathbf{w}^*, \xi^*)$ the solution to this optimization problem, then $F_\alpha(\mathbf{w}^*, \xi^*)$ is the optimal CVaR. In addition, the optimal portfolio is given by $\mathbf{w}^*$ and the corresponding VaR is given by ξ^*. In other words, in this fashion we can compute the optimal CVaR *without* first calculating VaR.

Often, in practice, the probability density function $p(\mathbf{y})$ is not available or is very difficult to estimate. Instead, we might have M different scenarios $Y = \{\mathbf{y}_1, ..., \mathbf{y}_M\}$ that are sampled from the density or that have been obtained from computer simulations. Evaluating the auxiliary function $F_\alpha(\mathbf{w}, \xi)$ using the scenarios Y, we obtain

$$F_\alpha^Y(\mathbf{w}, \xi) = \xi + (1 - \alpha)^{-1} M^{-1} \sum_{i=1}^{M} \max(f(\mathbf{w}, \mathbf{y}_i) - \xi, 0)$$

Therefore, in this case the optimization problem

$$\min_{\mathbf{w}} \mathrm{CVaR}_\alpha(\mathbf{w})$$

takes the form

$$\min_{\mathbf{w}, \xi} \xi + (1 - \alpha)^{-1} M^{-1} \sum_{i=1}^{M} \max(f(\mathbf{w}, \mathbf{y}_i) - \xi, 0)$$

Replacing $\max(f(\mathbf{w}, \mathbf{y}_i) - \xi, 0)$ by the auxiliary variables z_i along with appropriate constraints, we finally obtain the equivalent optimization problem

$$\min \xi + (1 - \alpha)^{-1} M^{-1} \sum_{i=1}^{M} z_i$$

subject to

$$z_i \geq 0, \, i = 1, ..., M$$

$$z_i \geq f(\mathbf{w}, \mathbf{y}_i) - \xi, \, i = 1, ..., M$$

along with any other constraints on $\mathbf{w}$, such as no short-selling constraints or any of the constraints discussed in Chapter 4. Under the assumption that $f(\mathbf{w},\mathbf{y})$ is linear in $\mathbf{w}$,[31] the above optimization problem is linear and can, therefore, be solved very efficiently by standard linear programming techniques.[32]

The formulation discussed above can be seen as an extension of calculating the *global minimum variance portfolio* (GMV) (see Chapter 2) and can be used as an alternative when the underlying asset return distribution is asymmetric and exhibits fat tails.

Moreover, the representation of CVaR given by the auxiliary function $F_\alpha(\mathbf{w},\xi)$ can be used in the construction of other portfolio optimization problems. For example, the mean-CVaR optimization problem

$$\max_{\mathbf{w}} \; \boldsymbol{\mu}'\mathbf{w}$$

subject to

$$\text{CVaR}_\alpha(\mathbf{w}) \le C_0$$

along with any other constraints on $\mathbf{w}$ (represented by $\mathbf{w} \in C_{\mathbf{w}}$) where $\boldsymbol{\mu}$ represents the vector of expected returns, would result in the following approximation

$$\max_{\mathbf{w}} \; \boldsymbol{\mu}'\mathbf{w}$$

subject to

$$\xi + (1-\alpha)^{-1} M^{-1} \sum_{i=1}^{M} z_i \le C_0$$

$$z_i \ge 0, \; 0 = 1, ..., M$$
$$z_i \ge f(\mathbf{w}, \mathbf{y}_i) - \xi, \; 0 = 1, ..., M$$
$$\mathbf{w} \in C_{\mathbf{w}}$$

To illustrate the mean-CVaR optimization approach we consider an example from Palmquist, Uryasev, and Krokhmal.[33] They considered two-

---

[31] This is typically the case as the loss function in the discrete case is chosen to be

$$f(\mathbf{w}, \mathbf{y}) = -\sum_{i=1}^{N} w_i(y_i - x_i)$$

where x_i is the current price of security i.

[32] See Chapter 6 for further discussion on numerical optimization.

[33] Pavlo Krokhmal, Jonas Palmquist, and Stanislav Uryasev, "Portfolio Optimization with Conditional Value-At-Risk Objective and Constraints," *Journal of Risk* 4, no. 2 (2002), pp. 11–27.

week returns for all the stocks in the S&P 100 Index over the period July 1, 1997 to July 8, 1999 for scenario generation. Optimal portfolios were constructed by solving the mean-CVaR optimization problem above for a two-week horizon for different levels of confidence. In Exhibit 5.1 we see three different mean-CVaR efficient frontiers corresponding to $\alpha = 90\%$, 95%, and 99%. The two-week rate of return is calculated as the ratio of the optimized portfolio value divided by the initial value, and the risk is calculated as the percentage of the initial portfolio value that is allowed to be put at risk. In other words, when the risk is 7% and α is 95%, this means that we allow for no more than a 7% loss of the initial value of the portfolio with a probability of 5%. We observe from the exhibit that as the CVaR constraint decreases (i.e., the probability increases) the rate of return increases.

It can be shown that for a normally distributed loss function, the mean-variance and the mean-CVaR frameworks generate the same efficient frontier. However, when distributions are nonnormal these two approaches are significantly different. On the one hand, in the mean-variance approach risk is defined by the variance of the loss distribution, and because the vari-

EXHIBIT 5.1   Efficient Frontiers of Different Mean-CVaR Portfolios

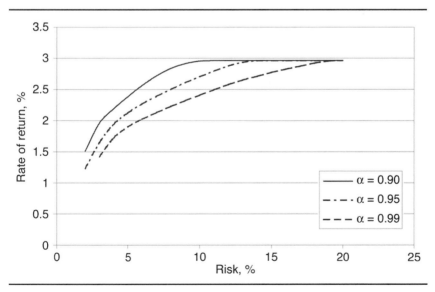

Source: Pavlo Krokhmal, Jonas Palmquist, and Stanislav Uryasev, "Portfolio Optimization with Conditional Value-At-Risk Objective and Constraints," *The Journal of Risk* 4, no. 2 (2002), p. 21. This copyrighted material is reprinted with permission from Incisive Media Plc, Haymarket House, 28-29 Haymarket, London, SW1Y 4RX, United Kingdom.

ance incorporates information from both the left as well as the right tail of the distribution, both the gains and losses are contributing equally to the risk. On the other hand, the mean-CVaR methodology only involves the part of the tail of the distribution that contributes to high losses.

In Exhibit 5.2 we can see a comparison between the two approaches for $\alpha = 95\%$. The same data set is used as in the illustration above. We note that in return/CVaR coordinates, as expected, the mean-CVaR efficient frontier lies above the mean-variance efficient frontier. Nevertheless, in this particular example the two efficient frontiers are close to each other and are similarly shaped. Yet with the inclusion of derivative assets such as options and credit derivatives, this will no longer be the case.[34]

EXHIBIT 5.2   Comparison Mean-CVaR95% and Mean-Variance Efficient Portfolios

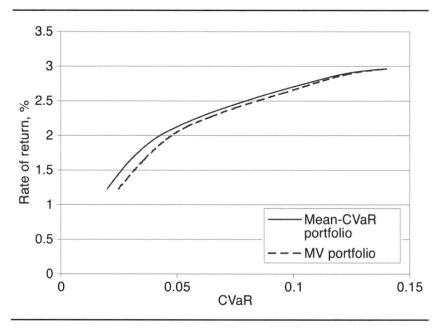

Source: Pavlo Krokhmal, Jonas Palmquist, and Stanislav Uryasev, "Portfolio Optimization with Conditional Value-At-Risk Objective and Constraints," *The Journal of Risk* 4, no. 2 (2002), p. 23. This copyrighted material is reprinted with permission from Incisive Media Plc, Haymarket House, 28-29 Haymarket, London, SW1Y 4RX, United Kingdom.

---

[34] Nicklas Larsen, Helmut Mausser, and Stanislav Uryasev, "Algorithms for Optimization of Value-at-Risk," on P. Pardalos and V. K. Tsitsiringos (eds.), *Financial Engineering, e-commerce and Supply Chain* (Boston: Kluwer Academic Publishers, 2002), pp. 129–157.

PORTFOLIO SELECTION WITH HIGHER MOMENTS THROUGH EXPANSIONS OF UTILITY

As we saw in Chapter 2, the mean-variance framework is a special case of general utility maximization that arises when investors have a quadratic utility or when asset returns are normally distributed. Many return distributions in the financial markets exhibit fat tails and asymmetry that cannot be described by their mean-variances alone. In many instances, the tails of the return distribution significantly affect portfolio performance.[35] Harvey and Siddique have shown that skew in stock returns is relevant to portfolio selection.[36] In particular, if asset returns exhibit nondiversifiable coskew, investors must be rewarded for it, resulting in increased expected returns. They also showed that in the presence of positive skew, investors may be willing to accept a negative expected return. Several other studies have shown that skew is an important factor in asset pricing (see for example, Arditti and Levy,[37] Jondeau and Rockinger,[38] Kraus and Litzenberger,[39] and Nummelin[40]).

To illustrate the effect of skew and kurtosis in the portfolio selection process, we consider three two-asset portfolios: Australia/Singapore, Australia/United Kingdom, and Australia/United States. For each portfolio, the mean, standard deviation, skew, and kurtosis is computed based on the empirical return distribution over the period January 1980 through May 2004 and depicted in Exhibit 5.3. First, we observe that while the return is a linear function of the weight, w, of the first asset[41] and the standard deviation is convex, the qualitative behavior of the skew and the kurtosis is very different for the three portfolios. Clearly, the skew and kurtosis are highly nonlinear functions that can exhibit multiple maxima and minima. Second, we see that in the case of Australia/Singapore, the

---

[35] Norbert J. Jobst and Stavros A. Zenios, "The Tail That Wags the Dog: Integrating Credit Risk in Asset Portfolios," *Journal of Risk Finance* (Fall 2001), pp. 31–44.

[36] Campbell R. Harvey and Akhtar Siddique, "Conditional Skewness in Asset Pricing Tests," *Journal of Finance* 55 (2000), pp. 1263–1295.

[37] Fred Arditti and Haim Levy, "Portfolio Efficiency Analysis in Three Moments: The Multi Period Case," *Journal of Finance* 30 (1975), pp. 797–809.

[38] Eric Jondeau and Michael Rockinger, "Conditional Volatility, Skewness, and Kurtosis: Existence, Persistence, and Comovements," *Journal of Economic Dynamics and Control* 27 (2003), pp. 1699–1737.

[39] Alan Kraus and Robert Litzenberger, "Skewness Preference and the Valuation of Risk Assets," *Journal of Finance* 33 (1976), pp. 303–310.

[40] Kim Nummelin, "Global Coskewness and the Pricing of Finnish Stocks: Empirical Tests," *Journal of International Financial Markets, Institutions and Money* 7 (1997), pp. 137–155.

[41] The weight of the second asset is $1 - w$ such that the portfolio weights add up to 1.

EXHIBIT 5.3   The Effect of Skew and Kurtosis on the Three Two-Asset Portfolios: Australia/Singapore, Australia/United Kingdom, and Australia/United States

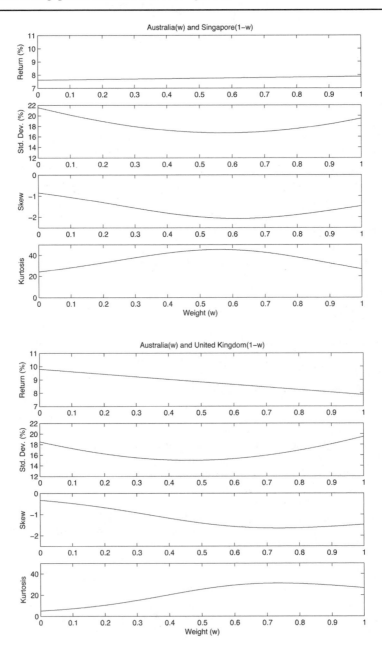

EXHIBIT 5.3 (Continued)

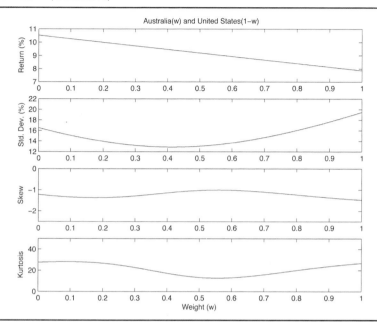

portfolio that minimizes the standard deviation also approximately minimizes the skew and maximizes the kurtosis. Given that an investor will prefer a higher to a lower skew and a lower to a higher kurtosis, the global minimum variance portfolio in this case is undesirable. In the case of Australia/United States, the minimum-variance portfolio comes closer to achieving a more desirable objective of minimizing variance and kurtosis, and maximizing skew. It is clear from this simple example that with the introduction of skew and kurtosis preferences, the classical mean-variance approach would deliver suboptimal portfolios.

Given the computational power available today, it is possible to construct portfolios (at least of moderate size) by maximizing expected utility and the empirical distribution of security returns. In practice, however, this approach is unheard of. Typically, practitioners rely upon mean-variance approximations of a chosen utility function.

Levy and Markowitz compared the performance of portfolio allocation by maximizing expected power utility with that of the standard mean-variance optimization. They found that mean-variance approximations perform very well.[42]

---

[42] Haim Levy and Harry M. Markowitz, "Approximating Expected Utility by a Function of Mean and Variance," *American Economic Review* 69 (1979), pp. 308–317.

Cremers, Kritzman, and Page[43] show empirically that the log and power utility functions are fairly insensitive to higher moments, and therefore, mean-variance optimization performs very well for investors with log or power utility. However, for discontinuous or S-shaped utility functions,[44] this result no longer holds and mean-variance optimization shows significant loss in utility compared to an optimization of the full utility function. Of course, in these cases the loss of utility depends on the exact form of the utility function. Nevertheless, it is to be expected that in the future it will become more common to use more realistic ("real-world") utility functions in making portfolio allocation decisions.

In this section, we derive a generalization of the mean-variance framework that incorporates higher moments such as skew and kurtosis, but that is significantly easier than solving the general expected utility maximization problem. The first attempt to extend the classical mean-variance optimization to higher moments was done by Jean in the early 1970s.[45] Later, more general and rigorous treatments have been presented by several authors (see for example, Athayde and Flôres[46] and Harvey et al.[47]). We provide a review of these approaches.

By expanding the expected utility of the end of period wealth

$$W = W_0(1 + \mathbf{w'R}) = W_0(1 + R_p)$$

in a Taylor series around the expected end of period wealth

---

[43] Jan-Hein Cremers, Mark Kritzman, and Sebastien Page, "Portfolio Formation with Higher Moments and Plausible Utility," 272-12 Revere Street Working Papers, November 22, 2003; and Jan-Hein Cremers, Mark Kritzman, and Sebastien Page, "Optimal Hedge Fund Allocations—Do Higher Moments Matter?" *Journal of Portfolio Management* (Spring 2005), pp. 70–81.

[44] Daniel Kahneman and Amos Tversky, "Prospect Theory: An Analysis of Decision under Risk," *Econometrica* 47 (1979), pp. 263–290.

[45] William H. Jean, "The Extension of Portfolio Analysis to Three or More Parameters," *Journal of Financial and Quantitative Analysis* 6 (1971), pp. 505–515 and "More on Multidimensional Portfolio Analysis," *Journal of Financial and Quantitative Analysis* 8 (1973), pp. 475–490.

[46] See Gustavo M. Athayde and Renato G. Flôres Jr., "Finding a Maximum Skewness Portfolio—A General Solution to Three-Moments Portfolio Choice," *Journal of Economic Dynamics and Control* 28 (2004), pp. 1335–1352; "The Portfolio Frontier with Higher Moments: The Undiscovered Country," *Computing in Economics and Finance 2002*, Society for Computational Economics, 2002, and "Certain Geometric Aspects of Portfolio Optimization with Higher Moments," EPGE/Fundaçao Getulio Vargas, 2002.

[47] Campbell R. Harvey, John C. Liechty, Merril W. Liechty, and Peter Mueller, "Portfolio Selection with Higher Moments, Duke University, Working Paper, 2003.

$$\overline{W} = W_0(1 + \mathbf{w}'\boldsymbol{\mu}) = W_0(1 + \mu_p)$$

where $\boldsymbol{\mu} = E(\mathbf{R})$, we get

$$
\begin{aligned}
Eu(W) &= u(\overline{W}) + u'(\overline{W})E(W - \overline{W}) + \frac{1}{2}u''(\overline{W})E(W - \overline{W})^2 \\
&\quad + \frac{1}{3!}u^{(3)}(\overline{W})E(W - \overline{W})^3 + \frac{1}{4!}u^{(4)}(\overline{W})E(W - \overline{W})^4 + O(W^5) \\
&= u(\overline{W}) + \frac{1}{2}u''(\overline{W})E(W - \overline{W})^2 + \frac{1}{3!}u^{(3)}(\overline{W})E(W - \overline{W})^3 \\
&\quad + \frac{1}{4!}u^{(4)}(\overline{W})E(W - \overline{W})^4 + O(W^5)
\end{aligned}
$$

where the second equality follows from $E(W - \overline{W}) = 0$. The functions $E(W - \overline{W})^k$, $k = 2, 3, \dots$ are called the central moments of the random variable W. In particular, we recognize that the second central moment is just the variance of W. Further, the third and fourth central moments are referred to as the *skew* and *kurtosis* of W.[48]

Using the following notation,

$$
\begin{aligned}
\mu_p &= E(R_p) \\
\sigma_p^2 &= E(R_p - \mu_p)^2 = E(W - \overline{W})^2 \\
s_p^3 &= E(R_p - \mu_p)^3 = E(W - \overline{W})^3 \\
\kappa_p^4 &= E(R_p - \mu_p)^4 = E(W - \overline{W})^4
\end{aligned}
$$

where $R_p = \mathbf{w}'\mathbf{R}$, we have

$$Eu(W) = u(\overline{W}) + \frac{1}{2}u''(\overline{W})\sigma_p^2 + \frac{1}{3!}u^{(3)}(\overline{W})\sigma_p^3 + \frac{1}{4!}u^{(4)}(\overline{W})\kappa_p^4 + O((W - \overline{W})^5)$$

For example, for logarithmic utility $u(x) = \ln(x)$ (a CRRA investor, see Chapter 2) we have

---

[48] This is slightly different from the standard definition of skew and kurtosis that are given by the *standardized third and fourth central moments*

$$E\left(\frac{W - \overline{W}}{\sigma_p}\right)^3 \text{ and } E\left(\frac{W - \overline{W}}{\sigma_p}\right)^4$$

$$E \ln(W) = \ln(\overline{W}) - \frac{1}{2\overline{W}^2}\sigma_p^2 + \frac{1}{3\overline{W}^3}s_p^3 - \frac{1}{4\overline{W}^4}\kappa_p^4 + O((W - \overline{W})^5)$$

$$\approx \ln(\overline{W}) - \frac{1}{2\overline{W}^2}\sigma_p^2 + \frac{1}{3\overline{W}^3}s_p^3 - \frac{1}{4\overline{W}^4}\kappa_p^4$$

The portfolio choice problem for this investor could be formulated as the optimization problem

$$\max_{\mathbf{w}} \left(\ln(\overline{W}) - \frac{1}{2\overline{W}^2}\sigma_p^2 + \frac{1}{3\overline{W}^3}s_p^3 - \frac{1}{4\overline{W}^4}\kappa_p^4 \right)$$

subject to

$$\mathbf{w}'\iota = 1, \; \iota' = [1, 1, ..., 1]$$

where $\overline{W} = W_0(1 + \mathbf{w}'\boldsymbol{\mu})$.

Similarly, we note that the "generic" optimization problem for investors with preferences described by the first four moments takes the form

$$\max_{\mathbf{w}} \mathbf{w}'\boldsymbol{\mu} - \lambda_1\sigma_p^2 + \lambda_2 s_p^3 - \lambda_3\kappa_p^4$$

subject to

$$\mathbf{w}'\iota = 1$$
$$\iota' = [1, 1, ..., 1]$$

The parameters λ_1, λ_2, and λ_3 are determined by the choice of utility function (as in the example with the logarithmic utility function above) or simply by the level of risk aversion or risk preference an investor has for each individual moment. For example, one can calibrate the parameters λ_1, λ_2, and λ_3 using historical data so that portfolio backtests with historical data meet the desired investment goals.

The formulation above involving higher moments of the underlying asset returns provides more freedom in describing investors' preferences than the classical mean-variance framework. A rational investor's preference is high odd moments, as this would decrease extreme values on the side of losses and increase them on the side of gains. Similarly, the investor prefers low even moments, as this implies decreased dispersion and therefore less uncertainty of returns.[49]

The Mathematics of Portfolio Selection with Higher Moments

Dealing with the third and higher portfolio moments quickly becomes cumbersome algebraically and can also be computationally inefficient unless caution is used. It is convenient to have similar formulas for the skew and kurtosis as for the portfolio mean and standard deviation

$$r_p = \mathbf{w}'\boldsymbol{\mu}$$
$$\sigma_p^2 = \mathbf{w}'\boldsymbol{\Sigma}\mathbf{w}$$

where $\boldsymbol{\mu}$ and $\boldsymbol{\Sigma}$ are the vector of expected returns and the covariance matrix of returns of the assets. In full generality, each moment of a random vector can be mathematically represented as a *tensor*. In the case of the second moment, the second moment tensor is the familiar $N \times N$ covariance matrix, whereas the third moment tensor, the so-called *skew tensor*, can intuitively be seen as a three-dimensional cube with height, width, and depth of N. The fourth moment tensor, the *kurtosis tensor*, can similarly be visualized as a four-dimensional cube.

When dealing with higher moments in the portfolio choice problem, it is convenient to "slice" the higher moment tensors and create one big matrix out of the slices. For example, the skew tensor (a three-dimensional cube) with N^3 elements and the kurtosis tensor (a fourth-dimensional cube) with N^4 elements, can each be represented by an $N \times N^2$ and an $N \times N^3$ matrix, respectively. Formally, we denote the $N \times N^2$ and $N \times N^3$ skew and kurtosis matrices by[50]

$$\mathbf{M}_3 = (s_{ijk}) = E[(\mathbf{R}-\boldsymbol{\mu})(\mathbf{R}-\boldsymbol{\mu})' \otimes (\mathbf{R}-\boldsymbol{\mu})']$$
$$\mathbf{M}_4 = (\kappa_{ijkl}) = E[(\mathbf{R}-\boldsymbol{\mu})(\mathbf{R}-\boldsymbol{\mu})' \otimes (\mathbf{R}-\boldsymbol{\mu})' \otimes (\mathbf{R}-\boldsymbol{\mu})']$$

where each element is defined by the formulas

$$s_{ijk} = E[(R_i-\mu_i)(R_j-\mu_j)(R_k-\mu_k)], \, i, j, k = 1, \ldots, N$$

$$\kappa_{ijk} = E[(R_i-\mu_i)(R_j-\mu_j)(R_k-\mu_k)(R_l-\mu_l)], \, i, j, k, l = 1, \ldots, N$$

---

[49] For a theoretical formalization and justification of this result, see Robert C. Scott and Philip A. Horvath, "On the Direction of Preference for Moments of Higher Order Than Variance," *Journal of Finance* 35 (1980), pp. 915–919.

[50] The symbol $\otimes$ is referred to as the *Kronecker symbol*.

For example, when $N = 3$ the skew matrix takes the form

$$
\mathbf{M}_3 = \left[\begin{array}{ccc|ccc|ccc}
s_{111} & s_{112} & s_{113} & s_{211} & s_{212} & s_{213} & s_{311} & s_{312} & s_{313} \\
s_{121} & s_{122} & s_{123} & s_{221} & s_{222} & s_{223} & s_{321} & s_{322} & s_{323} \\
s_{131} & s_{132} & s_{133} & s_{231} & s_{232} & s_{233} & s_{331} & s_{332} & s_{333}
\end{array} \right]
$$

Just like for the covariance matrix, the third and fourth moment tensors are symmetric. In fact, out of the N^3 and N^4 elements the number of different skew and kurtosis components in each tensor are given by[51]

$$
\binom{N+2}{3} \text{ and } \binom{N+3}{4}
$$

For example, if the number of assets considered is three, then the covariance matrix has six different elements, the skew matrix has 10 different elements, and the kurtosis matrix has 15 different elements. Taking the symmetries into account is important in practical applications involving many securities, as it significantly speeds up numerical computations and simulations.

Using the tensor notation we can restate the generic four-moment optimization problem in the form

$$
\max_{\mathbf{w}} \mathbf{w}'\boldsymbol{\mu} - \lambda_1 \mathbf{w}'\boldsymbol{\Sigma}\mathbf{w} + \lambda_2 \mathbf{w}'\mathbf{M}_3(\mathbf{w} \otimes \mathbf{w}) - \lambda_3 \mathbf{w}'\mathbf{M}_4(\mathbf{w} \otimes \mathbf{w} \otimes \mathbf{w})
$$

subject to

$$
\boldsymbol{\iota}'\mathbf{w} = 1, \; \boldsymbol{\iota}' = [1, 1, ..., 1]
$$

This formulation can be efficiently solved by nonlinear programming packages.[52] In general, as the objective function is a polynomial of fourth order in the portfolio weights, the problem is no longer convex and may therefore exhibit multiple local optima. A geometric characterization of the efficient set of the above portfolio choice problem involving the first three moments has been provided by Athayde and Flôres.[53]

---

[51] This fact follows from the symmetry relationships $s_{ijk} = s_{jik} = s_{kji} = s_{ikj}$ and $\kappa_{ijkl} = \kappa_{jikl} = \kappa_{kjil} = \kappa_{ljki} = \kappa_{ikjl} = \kappa_{ilkj} = \kappa_{ijlk}$.
[52] We discuss nonlinear optimization further in Chapter 6.
[53] Athayde and Flôres, "Finding a Maximum Skewness Portfolio—A General Solution to Three-Moments Portfolio Choice."

POLYNOMIAL GOAL PROGRAMMING FOR PORTFOLIO OPTIMIZATION WITH HIGHER MOMENTS

In this section we discuss an approach to the portfolio optimization problem with higher moments that is referred to as the *polynomial goal programming* (PGP) approach.[54] We suggested in the previous section that investors have a preference for positive odd moments, but strive to minimize their exposure to even moments. For example, an investor may attempt to, on the one hand, maximize expected portfolio return and skewness, while on the other, minimize portfolio variance and kurtosis. Mathematically, we can express this by the multiobjective optimization problem:

$$\max_{\mathbf{w}} O_1(\mathbf{w}) = \mathbf{w}'\boldsymbol{\mu}$$

$$\min_{\mathbf{w}} O_2(\mathbf{w}) = \mathbf{w}'\boldsymbol{\Sigma}\mathbf{w}$$

$$\max_{\mathbf{w}} O_3(\mathbf{w}) = \mathbf{w}'M_3(\mathbf{w} \otimes \mathbf{w})$$

$$\min_{\mathbf{w}} O_4(\mathbf{w}) = \mathbf{w}'M_4(\mathbf{w} \otimes \mathbf{w} \otimes \mathbf{w})$$

subject to desired constraints. The notation used in this formulation was introduced in the previous section. This type of problem, which addresses the trade-off between competing objectives, is referred to as a *goal programming* (GP) problem. The basic idea behind goal programming is to break the overall problem into smaller solvable elements and then iteratively attempt to find solutions that preserve, as closely as possible, the individual goals.

Because the choice of the relative percentage invested in each asset is the main concern in the portfolio allocation decision, the portfolio weights can be rescaled and restricted to the unit variance space $\{\mathbf{w} \mid \mathbf{w}'\boldsymbol{\Sigma}\mathbf{w} = 1\}$. This observation allows us to formulate the multiobjective optimization problem as follows:

---

[54] See, for example, Pornchai Chunhachinda, Krishnan Dandapani, Shahid Hamid, and Arun J. Prakash, "Portfolio Selection and Skewness: Evidence from International Stock Markets," *Journal of Banking and Finance* 21 (1997), pp. 143–167; Qian Sun and Yuxing Yan, "Skewness Persistence with Optimal Portfolio Selection," *Journal of Banking and Finance* 27 (2003), pp. 1111–1121; Arun J. Prakash, Chun-Hao Chang, and Therese E. Pactwa, "Selecting a Portfolio with Skewness: Recent Evidence from U.S., European, and Latin American Equity Markets," *Journal of Banking and Finance* 27 (2003), pp. 1375–1390; and Ryan J. Davies, Harry M. Kat, and Sa Lu, "Fund of Hedge Funds Portfolio Selection: A Multiple-Objective Approach," Working Paper, ISMA Centre, University of Reading, 2004.

$$\max_{\mathbf{w}} O_1(\mathbf{w}) = \mathbf{w}'\boldsymbol{\mu}$$

$$\max_{\mathbf{w}} O_3(\mathbf{w}) = \mathbf{w}'M_3(\mathbf{w} \otimes \mathbf{w})$$

$$\min_{\mathbf{w}} O_4(\mathbf{w}) = \mathbf{w}'M_4(\mathbf{w} \otimes \mathbf{w} \otimes \mathbf{w})$$

subject to

$$\boldsymbol{\iota}'\mathbf{w} = 1\,, \boldsymbol{\iota}' = [1, 1, ..., 1]$$

$$\mathbf{w}'\Sigma\mathbf{w} = 1$$

In general, there will not be a single solution of this problem that can maximize both $O_1(\mathbf{w})$ and $O_3(\mathbf{w})$, and minimize $O_4(\mathbf{w})$. Instead, the solution to the multiobjective optimization problem has to be obtained in a two-step procedure. First, optimal values of each individual objective are calculated separately, that is, we maximize $O_1(\mathbf{w})$ and $O_3(\mathbf{w})$, and minimize $O_4(\mathbf{w})$ subject to the constraints. Let us denote the optimal values so obtained by O_1^*, O_3^*, and O_4^*. In the second step, the optimization problem that has to be solved is one that attempts to simultaneously minimize the deviations of each individual objective from its optimal value

$$\min_{\mathbf{w}} O(\mathbf{w}) = (d_1(\mathbf{w}))^{p_1} + (d_3(\mathbf{w}))^{p_3} + (d_4(\mathbf{w}))^{p_4}$$

subject to the constraints

$$\boldsymbol{\iota}'\mathbf{w} = 1\,, \boldsymbol{\iota}' = [1, 1, ..., 1]$$

$$\mathbf{w}'\Sigma\mathbf{w} = 1$$

where $d_i(\mathbf{w}) = O_i^* - O_i(\mathbf{w})$ for $i = 1, 3, 4$ and p_1, p_3, p_4 are chosen parameters expressing the investor's preference for each moment.[55]

Trivially, this optimization problem collapses to a standard mean-variance optimization problem if we give no weight to the skew and kurtosis terms. The preference parameters p_1, p_3, p_4 have an explicit economic interpretation in that they are directly associated with the *marginal rate of substitution* (MRS),

---

[55] Alternatively, from a computational perspective it is sometimes more convenient to use the objective function $O_{(\mathbf{w})} = d_1(\mathbf{w}) + \lambda_3 d_3(\mathbf{w}) + \lambda_4 d_4(\mathbf{w})$.

$$MRS_{ij} = \frac{\partial O}{\partial d_i} \bigg/ \frac{\partial O}{\partial d_j} = \frac{p_i}{p_j} \frac{d_i(\mathbf{w})^{p_i-1}}{d_j(\mathbf{w})^{p_j-1}}$$

which measures the desirability of foregoing objective O_i in order to gain from objective O_j.

SOME REMARKS ON THE ESTIMATION OF HIGHER MOMENTS

From a practical point of view, when models involve estimated quantities, it is important to understand how accurate these estimates really are. It is well known that the sample mean and variance, computed via averaging, are very sensitive to outliers. The measures of skew and kurtosis of returns,

$$\hat{s}^3 = \frac{1}{N} \sum_{i=1}^{N} \left(R_i - \hat{R} \right)^3$$

$$\hat{k}^4 = \frac{1}{N} \sum_{i=1}^{N} \left(R_i - \hat{R} \right)^4$$

where

$$\hat{R} = \frac{1}{N} \sum_{i=1}^{N} R_i$$

are also based upon averages. These measures are therefore also very sensitive to outliers. Moreover, it is well known that the standard error of estimated moments of order n is proportional to the square root of the moment of order $2n$.[56] Consequently, the accuracy of moments beyond $n = 4$ is often too low for practical purposes.

As a matter of fact, the impact of outliers is magnified in the above measures of skew and kurtosis due to the fact that observations are raised to the third and fourth powers. Therefore, we have to use these

---

[56] Maurice G. Kendall, Alan Stuart, J. Keith Ord, Steven F. Arnold, and Anthony O'Hagan, *Kendall's Advanced Theory of Statistics: Volume 1: Distribution Theory* (London: Arnold Publishers, 1998).

measures with tremendous caution. For example, in the data set of MSCI World Index and United States returns from January 1980 through May 2004, the skews are –0.37 and –1.22, respectively. Similarly, the kurtosis for the same period is 9.91 for the MSCI World Index and 27.55 for the United States. However, recomputing these measures after removing the single observation corresponding to the October 19, 1987 stock market crash, the skews are –0.09 and –0.04, while the kurtosis are 6.78 and 5.07, for the MSCI World Index and the United States indices, respectively. That is a dramatic change, especially in the U.S. market, after removing a single observation. This simple example illustrates how sensitive higher moments are to outliers. The problem of estimating the higher moments (and even the variance) gets worse in the presence of heavy-tailedness, which is not uncommon in financial data. In practice, it is desirable to use more robust measures of these moments.

In the statistics literature, several robust substitutes for mean and variance are available. However, robust counterparts for skew and kurtosis have been given little attention. Many practitioners eliminate or filter out large outliers from the data. The problem with this approach is that it is done on an *ad hoc* basis, often by hand, without relying upon methods of statistical inference. Several robust measures of skew and kurtosis are surveyed and compared in a paper by Kim and White.[57] They carried out Monte Carlo simulations to compare the conventional measures with several robust measures. Their conclusion was that the conventional measures have to be viewed with skepticism. We recommend that in applications involving higher moments, robust measures should at least be computed for comparison along with traditional estimates.

THE APPROACH OF MALEVERGNE AND SORNETTE[58]

The mean-variance approach and the generalized formulation with higher moments described earlier in this chapter rely upon empirical

---

[57] Tae-Hwan Kim and Halbert White, "On More Robust Estimation of Skewness and Kurtosis," *Finance Research Letters* 1 (2004), pp. 56–73.

[58] For the remaining part of this section, we will use the notation of Malevergne and Sornette. Yannick Malevergne and Didier Sornette, "High-Order Moments and Cumulants of Multivariate Weibull Asset Returns Distributions: Analytical Theory and Empirical Tests: II," *Finance Letters, Special Issue: Modeling of the Equity Market* 3 (2005), pp. 54–63. In particular, we denote security returns by r in the one-dimensional case, and $\mathbf{r}$ in the N-dimensional case. Similarly, we write q in the one-dimensional case and $\mathbf{q}$ in the N-dimensional case, for the transformed variable and vector, respectively.

estimates of expected returns and risk, that is, centered moments or cumulants. In principle, these could all be estimated empirically. However, the estimation errors of higher moments quickly get very large. In particular, the standard error of the estimated moment of order n is proportional to the square root of the moment of order $2n$, so that for daily historical times series of returns, which with a decent length amount to about a few thousand observations, moments of order greater than six often become unreasonable to empirically estimate.[59] One way to proceed is to make stronger assumptions on the multivariate distribution of the asset returns. We describe a technique developed by Malevergne and Sornette for this particular problem.[60]

First, we recall from statistical theory that the dependence between random variables is completely described by their joint distribution. Therefore, for a complete description of the returns and risks associated with a portfolio of N assets we would need the knowledge of the multivariate distribution of the returns. For example, assume that the joint distribution of returns is Gaussian; that is,

$$p(\mathbf{r}) = \frac{1}{(2\pi)^{N/2}\sqrt{\det(\mathbf{\Sigma})}} \exp\left(-\frac{1}{2}(\mathbf{r}-\mathbf{\mu})'\mathbf{\Sigma}^{-1}(\mathbf{r}-\mathbf{\mu})\right)$$

with $\mathbf{\mu}$ and $\mathbf{\Sigma}$ being the mean and the covariance of the returns r. Then we would be back in the mean-variance world described in Chapter 2, because in the Gaussian case the joint distribution is completely described by the mean and the covariance matrix of returns.

In general, the joint distribution of asset returns is not normal. We attempt to represent their multivariate distribution by

$$p(\mathbf{r}) = F((\mathbf{r}-\mathbf{\mu})'\mathbf{\Sigma}(\mathbf{r}-\mathbf{\mu}))$$

where F is an arbitrary function. We see immediately that if we chose $F(x) = \exp(x)$ we would retrieve the Gaussian distribution. Malevergne and Sornette suggest constructing the function F in such a way that each return r_i is transformed into a Gaussian variable q_i.

[59] See, for example, Maurice G. Kendall, Alan Stuart, J. Keith Ord, Steven F. Arnold, and Anthony O'Hagan, *Kendall's Advanced Theory of Statistics: Volume 1: Distribution Theory* (London: Arnold Publishers, 1998).
[60] Malevergne and Sornette, "High-Order Moments and Cumulants of Multivariate Weibull Asset Returns Distributions: Analytical Theory and Empirical Tests: II."

The One-Dimensional Case

Let us assume that the probability density function of an asset's return r is given by $p(r)$. The transformation $q(r)$ that produces a normal variable q from r is determined by the conservation of probability:

$$p(r)dr = \frac{1}{\sqrt{2\pi}} e^{-\frac{q^2}{2}} dq$$

If we integrate this equation from minus infinity up to r, we get

$$F(r) = \frac{1}{2}\left[1 + \text{erf}\left(\frac{q}{\sqrt{2}} \right) \right]$$

where $F(r)$ is defined by

$$F(r) = \int_{-\infty}^{r} p(r')dr'$$

and erf is the so-called *error function* given by

$$\text{erf}(x) = \frac{2}{\sqrt{\pi}} \int_{0}^{x} e^{-t^2} dt$$

If we solve for q, we obtain

$$q(r) = \sqrt{2}\,\text{erf}^{-1}(2F(r) - 1)$$

In the case where the probability density function of r only has one maximum, it can be shown that there exists a function $f(x)$ such that the above change of variables takes the form[61]

---

[61] $f(x)$ is defined by the so-called Von Mises variables

$$p(r)dr = C\frac{f'(r)}{\sqrt{|f(r)|}} e^{-\frac{f(r)}{2}} dr$$

where C is a normalizing constant. This representation is valid if the pdf of r has a single maximum, that is, the pdf is so-called unimodal. (See Paul Embrechts, Claudia Kluppelberg, Thomas Mikosh, "Modelling Extremal Events for Insurance and Finance," *Applications of Mathematics*, vol. 33 (Berlin and Heidelberg: Springer, 1997).

$$q(r) = \text{sgn}(r)\sqrt{|f(r)|}$$

By construction, the new variable q is standard normal (i.e., $q(r) \sim N(0,1)$). Let us now see how we would use this transformation in the multidimensional case.

The Multidimensional Case

By virtue of the transformation described earlier, we can map each component r_i of the random vector $\mathbf{r}$ (representing asset returns) into a standard normal variable q_i. If these variables were all independent, we could simply calculate the joint distribution as the product of the marginal distributions. Of course, in practice the components will not be independent and it becomes important to describe their dependence. We can do this by calculating the covariance matrix $\mathbf{\Sigma_q}$ of $\mathbf{q}$ by standard techniques (see, Chapter 8).

Given the covariance matrix $\mathbf{\Sigma_q}$, using a classical result of information theory[62] the best joint distribution of $\mathbf{q}$ in the sense of entropy maximization is given by

$$p(\mathbf{q}) = \frac{1}{(2\pi)^{N/2}\sqrt{\det(\mathbf{\Sigma_q})}}\exp\left(-\frac{1}{2}\mathbf{q}'\mathbf{\Sigma_q^{-1}}\mathbf{q}\right)$$

By a transformation of variables, we obtain the joint distribution of $\mathbf{r}$,

$$p(\mathbf{r}) = p(\mathbf{q})\left|\frac{\partial\mathbf{q}}{\partial\mathbf{r}'}\right|$$

where

$$\left|\frac{\partial\mathbf{q}}{\partial\mathbf{r}'}\right|$$

denotes the determinant of the Jacobian. Observing that[63]

---

[62] C. Radhakrishna Rao, *Linear Statistical Inference and Its Applications* (New York: Wiley-Interscience, 2002).

[63] Here, δ_{ij} is the Dirac delta function defined by

$$\delta_{ij} = \begin{cases} 1, i = j \\ 0, i \neq j \end{cases}$$

$$\left|\frac{\partial q_i}{\partial r_j}\right| = \sqrt{2\pi}\,p_j(r_j)e^{\frac{1}{2}q_i^2}\gamma_{ij}$$

we immediately obtain

$$\left|\frac{\partial \mathbf{q}}{\partial \mathbf{r'}}\right| = (2\pi)^{\frac{N}{2}}\prod_{i=1}^{N}p_i(r_i)e^{\frac{1}{2}q_i^2}$$

Therefore, the joint distribution of $\mathbf{r}$ becomes

$$p(\mathbf{r}) = \frac{1}{\sqrt{\det(\boldsymbol{\Sigma}_\mathbf{q})}}\exp\left(-\frac{1}{2}\mathbf{q}(\mathbf{r})'(\boldsymbol{\Sigma}_\mathbf{q}^{-1}-\mathbf{I})\mathbf{q}(\mathbf{r})\right)\prod_{i=1}^{N}p_i(r_i)$$

where $p_i(r_i)$ is the marginal density function of r_i. We note that if all the components of $\mathbf{q}$ were independent then $\boldsymbol{\Sigma}_\mathbf{q} = \mathbf{I}$, and $p(\mathbf{r})$ would simply be the product of the marginal distributions of r_i.

It can also be shown that in this framework, where the arbitrary random variables $\mathbf{r}$ are transformed into the standard normal variables $\mathbf{q}$, that the new transformed variables conserve the structure of correlation of the original ones as measured by copula functions. In particular, we have that

$$p(r_1, ..., r_N) = c(F_1(r_1), ..., F_N(r_N))\prod_{i=1}^{N}p_i(r_i)$$

where

$$c(x_1, ..., x_N) = \frac{1}{\det(\boldsymbol{\Sigma}_\mathbf{q})}\exp\left(-\frac{1}{2}\mathbf{q}(\mathbf{x})'(\boldsymbol{\Sigma}_\mathbf{q}^{-1}-\mathbf{I})\mathbf{q}(\mathbf{x})\right)$$

and $F_i(r_i)$ are the marginal distribution functions of F. The function c: $R^N \to R$ is the density of the Gaussian copula[64] function C, that is,

$$c(x_1, ..., x_N) = \frac{\partial C(x_1, ..., x_N)}{\partial x_1, ..., \partial x_N}$$

---

[64] Copulas are described in Appendix B.

This property shows that this approach is based on the assumption of arbitrary marginal distributions with a Gaussian copula. We obtained the Gaussian copula from the transformation of the arbitrary marginal distributions to Gaussian marginal distributions under the assumption that the covariance matrix is constant. Finally, we remark that Malevergne and Sornette tested the Gaussian copula hypothesis for financial assets and found that it holds well for equities.[65]

SUMMARY

- The mean-variance framework only takes the first two moments, the mean and the variance, into account. When investors have preferences beyond the first two moments, it is desirable to extend the mean-variance framework to include higher moments.
- Two different types of risk measures can be distinguished: dispersion and downside measures.
- Dispersion measures are measures of uncertainty. In contrast to downside measures, dispersion measures entail both positive and negative deviations from the mean and consider those deviations as equally risky.
- Some common portfolio dispersion approaches are mean standard deviation, mean-variance, mean-absolute deviation, and mean-absolute moment.
- Some common portfolio downside measures are Roy's safety-first, semivariance, lower partial moment, Value-at-Risk, and Conditional Value-at-Risk.
- In principle, optimal portfolio allocations—at least for moderately sized portfolios—can be calculated by maximizing expected utility under the empirical distribution of security returns.
- Approximations to the expected utility framework can be derived by expanding the utility function in a Taylor series. In this fashion, portfolio optimization problems can be formulated that includes moments of desirable order. Typically, the mean, variance, skew, and kurtosis are considered.
- Higher order moments are very sensitive to estimation error.
- The approach by Malevergne and Sornette is based on the idea of transforming an arbitrary marginal distribution function to a Gaussian marginal distribution function (under the assumption of a Gaussian copula).

---

[65] Yannick Malevergne and Didier Sornette, "Testing the Gaussian Copula Hypothesis for Financial Assets Dependences," *Quantitative Finance* 3 (2003), pp. 231–250.

CHAPTER 6

Mathematical and Numerical Optimization

The concept of optimization is fundamental to finance theory. The seminal work of Harry Markowitz demonstrated that financial decision-making for a rational agent is essentially a question of achieving an optimal trade-off between risk and returns.

From an application perspective, mathematical programming allows the rationalization of many business or technological decisions. Nevertheless, in practice, the computational tractability of the resulting analytical models is a key issue. It does not make much sense to formulate models that we are not able to solve in a reasonable timeframe. The simplex algorithm, developed in 1947 by George Dantzig, was one of the first tractable mathematical programming algorithms to be developed for linear programming. Its subsequent successful implementation contributed to the acceptance of optimization as a scientific approach to decision-making, and initiated the field known today as operations research.

As we showed in Chapter 4, today's portfolio allocation models often involve more complicated functional forms and constraints than the classical mean-variance optimization problem. The inclusion of transaction costs such as those discussed in Chapter 3 has added yet another level of complexity. The asset universe available today is also much larger than what it was when Markowitz originally developed his theory.

All these factors make the resulting optimization problems more difficult to solve, maybe not from the theoretical but from the practical point of view. Until recently, complicated large-scale portfolio optimization problems could only be solved on supercomputers. However, due to the increased computational power and the tremendous algorithmic development by researchers in operations research during the last 10 to 15 years or so, today many of these problems are solved routinely on desktop computers.

The area of optimization is highly technical and we do not aspire to provide a full theoretical treatment in this chapter.[1] Instead, our purpose is to provide a general understanding of the field, develop intuition for how some of the most common algorithms work, and show how they can be used in practice.

This chapter is structured as follows. We start off with a general discussion of mathematical optimization and provide a standard classification of different subclasses of optimization problems. Since today's optimization software is highly specialized and relies on specific features of a particular problem, a thorough understanding of this standard taxonomy is important for the successful use of optimization software. Thereafter, we outline the necessary conditions for optimality: the standard gradient condition in the unconstrained case and the so-called Karush-Kuhn-Tucker conditions in the constrained case. We provide a discussion to the basic workings of different types of optimization algorithms, attempting to develop a more intuitive understanding rather than provide a full theoretical treatment. In particular, we discuss the simplex algorithm, line search methods, Newton-type methods, barrier and interior-point methods, sequential quadratic programming, and combinatorial and integer programming approaches. We cover the most commonly used publicly and commercially available optimization software, and then close the chapter by discussing several practical considerations that are important when using optimization software.

MATHEMATICAL PROGRAMMING

An optimization problem consists of three basic components:

- An objective function, denoted by f
- A set of unknown variables, denoted by the vector $\mathbf{x}$
- A set of constraints

The objective function is a mathematical expression of what we want to optimize (minimize or maximize) that depends upon the unknown

---

[1] For a more complete treatment of mathematical programming, see David G. Luenberger, *Linear and Nonlinear Programming* (Reading, MA: Addison-Wesley, 1984) and Jorge Nocedal and Stephen J. Wright, *Numerical Optimization* (New York: Springer Verlag, 1999).

variables. Constraints are sometimes provided for all or a subset of the unknown variables. For example, in the risk aversion formulation of the classical mean-variance optimization problem, the objective function is given by

$$f(\mathbf{w}) = \mathbf{w}'\boldsymbol{\mu} - \lambda \mathbf{w}'\boldsymbol{\Sigma}\mathbf{w}$$

where $\boldsymbol{\Sigma}$ is the covariance matrix, $\boldsymbol{\mu}$ is the expected return vector, λ is the risk aversion coefficient, and the unknown variables are the portfolio weights $\mathbf{w}$. If we do not allow for short-selling, we would express this constraint on the portfolio weights by the long-only constraint $\mathbf{w} \geq 0$. We discussed some of the most commonly used constraints in portfolio management in Chapter 4.

The area of mathematical and numerical optimization is devoted to the study of both theoretical properties and practical solution techniques for optimization problems of various forms. The starting point for the subject is the *nonlinear programming* (NLP) problem:

$$\min_{\mathbf{x}} f(\mathbf{x})$$
$$s.t. \ g_i(\mathbf{x}) \leq 0 \quad i = 1, ..., I$$
$$h_j(\mathbf{x}) = 0 \quad j = 1, ..., J$$

where f, g_i, and h_j are smooth functions of the N-dimensional variable $\mathbf{x}$ and referred to as the *objective function*, the *inequality constraints*, and the *equality constraints*, respectively. We note that a problem that involves finding the maximum of a function f can be recast in this form simply by minimizing $-f$.

In practice, situations are encountered where it might be desirable to optimize several objectives simultaneously. For example, in Chapter 5 where we discuss portfolio optimization with higher moments, we argue that a portfolio manager might want to maximize the mean and the skew, and at the same time minimize the variance and the kurtosis. Optimization problems with multiple objectives are typically reformulated as a single objective problem and then transformed into a standard optimization problem.

The nonlinear programming above, in comparison, is a large class of optimization problems. In subsequent sections, we will also take a closer look at some subclasses that are important in real-world modeling.

When there are no constraints, the problem is referred to as an *unconstrained optimization problem*. In this case, we would search for candidates to the solution over the whole N–dimensional space, where

N is the number of decision variables. However, in the presence of constraints, not all points in the N–dimensional space are possible candidates. We say that a point $\mathbf{x}$ is *feasible* (or a *feasible point*) if it satisfies all the constraints of the optimization problem.

In mathematical programming, we distinguish between two different types of solutions, global and local solutions. We say that a feasible point $\mathbf{x}^*$ is a *global solution* to the optimization problem above if $f(\mathbf{x}^*) \leq f(\mathbf{x})$ for all feasible points $\mathbf{x}$. Further, we say that a feasible point $\mathbf{x}^*$ is a *local solution* to the optimization problem above if $f(\mathbf{x}^*) \leq f(\mathbf{x})$ for all feasible points $\mathbf{x}$ in a small neighborhood of (points close to) $\mathbf{x}^*$.

One could, with good reason, argue that in most situations we are interested in the global solution. So why do we make this distinction? To intuitively see that this distinction is important we take a look at the objective function depicted in Exhibit 6.1. Obviously, the problem has the three local solutions indicated by A, B, and C. In this case, the global solution is located at A. If we constrain solutions to be within the interval [0, 5] the global solution is located at B. However, if we change

EXHIBIT 6.1   Local versus Global Solutions

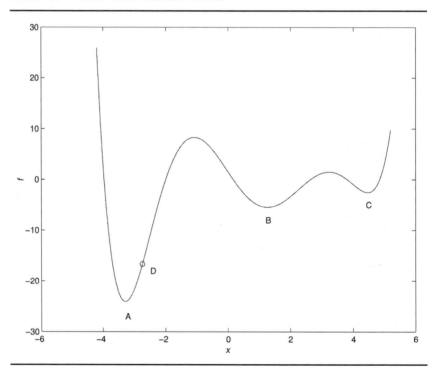

the feasible region of $\mathbf{x}$ to be the interval $[-2.75, 5]$ the global solution will be located at D, which is the left-end point of the interval. This simple illustration shows that even for a relatively simple function locating and distinguishing the local and global solutions requires some care.

Most efficient modern optimization algorithms available today attempt to find only a local solution. In general, finding the global optimal solution can be very difficult, in principle, and it requires an exhaustive search that first locates all local optimal solutions and then chooses the best one among those. There is no general efficient algorithm for the global optimization problem currently available, but rather specialized algorithms that rely upon unique properties of the objective function and constraints. Global optimization is an active research area, but it is outside the scope of this book.[2]

Although a vast set of problems can be formulated as nonlinear programs, in practice many problems possess further structure and have properties that if, taken into account, will deliver stronger mathematical results as well as more efficient algorithms. Therefore, it makes sense to categorize optimization problems based upon their properties. Typically, problems are classified according to the form of the objective function and the functions defining the constraints. A mathematical program can be formulated in many different but equivalent ways. Thus, it is reasonable to introduce standardized formulations, *standard forms*, in which a particular class of optimization problems can be expressed. The nonlinear program introduced above is one such standard form. We discuss some of the more common classes and their standard forms next.

Linear Programming

Linear programming (LP) refers to the problem of minimizing a linear function subject to linear equality and inequality constraints. The standard form of a linear program is given by

$$\min_{\mathbf{x}} \mathbf{c}'\mathbf{x}$$

$$s.t.\ A\mathbf{x} = b$$
$$\mathbf{x} \geq 0$$

---

[2] We refer the interested reader to Christodoulos A. Floudas and Panos M. Pardalos, *Recent Advances in Global Optimization* (Princeton: Princeton University Press, 1992) and Panos M. Pardalos and H. Edwin Romeijn, *Handbook of Global Optimization* (Dordrecht: Kluwer Academic Publishers, 2002).

where **c** is an N-dimensional vector, **A** is a $J \times N$ matrix, and **b** is a J-dimensional vector.

The linear programming problem is maybe the best known and the most frequently solved optimization problem in the real world. Some examples of when linear programming arises in financial applications are when determining whether there exist static arbitrage opportunities in current market prices,[3] calculating the smallest cost hedging portfolio, pricing American options,[4] and solving portfolio optimization problems with linear risk measures such as *mean-absolute deviation* (MAD), CVaR or portfolio shortfall.[5]

Quadratic Programming

Minimizing a quadratic objective function subject to linear equality and inequality constraints is referred to as *quadratic programming* (QP). This problem is represented in standard form as

$$\min_{\mathbf{x}} \; (\tfrac{1}{2}\mathbf{x}'\mathbf{Q}\mathbf{x} + \mathbf{c}'\mathbf{x})$$

$$s.t. \; \mathbf{A}\mathbf{x} = \mathbf{b}$$
$$\mathbf{x} \geq 0$$

where **Q** is an $N \times N$ matrix, **c** is an N-dimensional vector, **A** is a $J \times N$ matrix, and **b** is a J-dimensional vector.

We can assume that **Q** is symmetric. If this is not the case, we can replace **Q** by $\tfrac{1}{2}(\mathbf{Q} + \mathbf{Q}')$ without changing the value of the objective function since $\mathbf{x}'\mathbf{Q}\mathbf{x} = \mathbf{x}'\mathbf{Q}'\mathbf{x}$. If the matrix **Q** is positive semidefinite or positive definite, then this becomes a convex programming problem. In this case, *any local optimum is a global optimum*, and the problem can be solved by many of the standard algorithms for convex quadratic programming. When the matrix **Q** is indefinite (i.e., has both positive and negative eigenvalues), the problem can have several stationary points and local solutions and therefore becomes more difficult to solve.

---

[3] Stefano Herzel, "Arbitrage Opportunities on Derivatives: A Linear Programming Approach," Technical Report, Department of Economics, University of Perugia, 2000.

[4] Michael A. H. Dempster, James P. Hutton, and Darren G. Richards, "LP valuation of Exotic American Options Exploiting Structure," *Computational Finance* 2, no. 1 (1998), pp. 61–84.

[5] Dimitris Bertsimas, Geoffrey J. Lauprete, and Alexander Samarov, "Shortfall As Risk Measure: Properties, Optimization, and Applications," *Journal of Economic Dynamics and Control* 28, no. 7 (2004), pp. 1353–1381; and Chapter 5 in this book.

In finance, quadratic programs are a very important class of problems encountered in, for example, portfolio allocation problems (mean-variance optimization, Sharpe ratio maximization), model estimation through *ordinary least squares* (OLS) and *generalized least squares* (GLS), as well as subproblems when solving more general nonlinear programming problems through *sequential quadratic programming*, which is discussed later in this chapter.

Convex Programming

Convex programming is a large class of optimization problems that contains subclasses such as *semidefinite programs* (SPD), *second-order cones programs* (SOCP), *geometric programs* (GP), *least squares* (LS), *convex quadratic programming* (QS), and *linear programming* (LP). A convex program in standard form is given by

$$\min_{\mathbf{x}} f(\mathbf{x})$$

$$s.t. \ g_i(\mathbf{x}) \le 0, \quad i = 1, \dots, I$$
$$\mathbf{A}\mathbf{x} = \mathbf{b}$$

where f and g_i are convex[6] functions, $\mathbf{A}$ is a $J \times N$ matrix, and $\mathbf{b}$ is a J-dimensional vector. Furthermore, we require that the set of all feasible points is convex.

The most fundamental property of convex programs (unlike general nonlinear programs) is that *local optimal solutions are also global optimal solutions*. Unfortunately, checking that a given optimization problem is convex is in general far from straightforward and might even be more difficult than solving the problem itself.

However, many problems in financial applications are convex by design. Some examples of convex programs that occur in finance include robust linear and quadratic programming, mean-variance optimization with quadratic constraints or loss risk constraints,[7] and some portfolio allocation problems with trading cost models.

---

[6] A subset D of the N-dimensional space is said to be convex if for every $\mathbf{x}, \mathbf{y} \in D$, all convex combinations $\alpha\mathbf{x} + (1 - \alpha)\mathbf{y}$, where $0 < \alpha < 1$, are in D. A function $f: R^N \to R$ defined on a convex set D is said to be convex if for every $\mathbf{x}, \mathbf{y} \in D$ it holds that $f(\alpha\mathbf{x} + (1 - \alpha)\mathbf{y}) \le \alpha f(\mathbf{x}) + (1 - \alpha)f(\mathbf{y})$ where $0 \le \alpha \le 1$.

[7] Loss risk constraints are of the form $\Pr(r_p \le r_0) \le \varepsilon$ where r_p is the return on a portfolio (assumed to be normally distributed), r_0 is a given undesired return level (for example, for a loss of 10% we would set $r_0 = -0.1$), and ε is the maximum probability for the undesired return.

Many efficient algorithms for these types of problems are available. In particular, during the last decade or so the development of so-called *interior-point methods* for convex programming has been tremendous.[8] The name of this family of algorithms comes from the fact that they operate strictly in the interior of the feasible region. The first interior-point algorithm for solving linear programs was developed by Karmarkar.[9] Interior-point methods made the logical tie between linear and nonlinear programs clearer and now provide for a more systematic treatment of these classes of problems. We provide an introduction to some of these algorithms below.

Conic Optimization

By replacing the nonnegativity constraints in the standard form of a linear program with so-called *conic inclusion constraints*, we obtain the conic optimization problem

$$\min_{\mathbf{x}} \mathbf{c}'\mathbf{x}$$

$$s.t. \ \mathbf{A}\mathbf{x} = \mathbf{b}$$
$$\mathbf{x} \in C$$

where $\mathbf{c}$ is an N-dimensional vector, $\mathbf{A}$ is a $J \times N$ matrix, $\mathbf{b}$ is a J-dimensional vector, and C is a closed convex cone.[10]

Virtually any convex program can be represented as a conic optimization problem by appropriately specifying C. When $C = R_+^N$, the problem reduces to the linear programming problem in standard form that we are familiar with from above. One important class of cones is the so-called *second-order cones* ("ice cream cones")

$$C = \left\{ (x_1, \ldots, x_N) \in R^N : \left(x_1 \geq \sqrt{\sum_{i=2}^{N} x_i^2} \right) \right\}$$

---

[8] For a thorough treatment of interior-point algorithms, see for example, Yinyu Ye, *Interior Point Algorithms: Theory and Practice* (New York: John Wiley & Sons, 1997); Stephen J. Wright. *Primal Dual Interior Point Methods* (Philadelphia: Society of Industrial and Applied Mathematics Publications, 1999); and James Renegar, *A Mathematical View of Interior-Point Methods in Convex Optimization* (Philadelphia: Society of Industrial and Applied Mathematics Publications, 2001).

[9] Narendra Karmarkar, "A New Polynomial-Time Algorithm for Linear Programming," *Combinatorica* 4 (1984), pp. 373–395.

[10] A set C is a cone if for all $\mathbf{x} \in C$ it follows that $\alpha\mathbf{x} \in C$ for all $\alpha \geq 0$. A convex cone is a cone with the property that $\mathbf{x} + \mathbf{y} \in C$ for all $\mathbf{x}, \mathbf{y} \in C$.

and Cartesian products of second-order cones. The resulting *second-order cone program* (SOCP) occurs frequently in practice and takes the form

$$\min_{\mathbf{x}} \mathbf{c}'\mathbf{x}$$

$$s.t. \ \mathbf{Ax} = \mathbf{b}$$

$$\|\mathbf{C}_i\mathbf{x} + \mathbf{d}_i\| \le \mathbf{c}_i'\mathbf{x} + e_i \, , \ i = 1, ..., I$$

where $\mathbf{c}$ is an N-dimensional vector, $\mathbf{A}$ is a $J{\times}N$ matrix, $\mathbf{b}$ is a J-dimensional vector, $\mathbf{C}_i$ are $I_i{\times}N$ matrices, $\mathbf{d}_i$ are I_i-dimensional vectors, and e_i are scalars.

This problem is general enough to contain a large class of optimization problems such as linear programs, convex quadratic programs, and quadratically constrained convex quadratic programs, but at the same time share many of the same properties as linear programs, making optimization algorithms very efficient and highly scalable. Many robust portfolio allocation problems can be formulated as SOCPs.

Several primal-dual interior-point methods have been developed in the last few years for SOCPs.[11] For example, Lobo et al. show theoretically that the number of iterations required to solve a SOCP grows at most as the square root of the problem size, while their practical numerical experiments indicate that the typical number of iterations ranges between 5 and 50—more or less independent of the problem size.[12]

Integer and Combinatorial Programming

So far our discussion has focused on optimization problems where the variables are continuous. When they are only allowed to take on discrete values such as binary values (0, 1) or integer values (..., –2, –1, 0, –1, 2, ...), we refer to the resulting mathematical programming problem as a

---

[11] Details on the theory and applications of SOCP can be found in Farid Alizadeh and Donald Goldfarb, "Second Order Cone Programming," Technical Report 51-2001, RUTCOR, Rutgers University, 2001; Miguel Sousa Lobo, Lieven Vandenberghe, Stephen Boyd and Hervé Lebret, "Applications of Second-Order Cone Programming," *Linear Algebra and its Applications*, 284 (1998), pp. 193–22; and Yurii E. Nesterov and Arkadii Nemirovski, "Interior Point Polynomial Methods in Convex Programming," *Studies in Applied Mathematics*, vol. 13 (Philadelphia: SIAM, 1994).

[12] Miguel Sousa Lobo, Lieven Vandenberghe, Stephen Boyd, and Hervé Lebret, "Applications of Second-order Cone Programming," Technical Report, Information Systems Laboratory and the Electrical Engineering Department, Stanford University, 1998.

combinatorial, discrete, or *integer programming* (IP) *problem.* If some variables are continuous and others are discrete, the resulting optimization problem is called a *mixed-integer programming* (MIP) *problem.*

As shown in Chapter 4, some common extensions to the classical portfolio problems may include formulations where some variables are allowed to take on only discrete values. For example, round lot and cardinality constraints are combinatorial in nature and the resulting mean-variance problem is a mixed-integer quadratic program. Furthermore, portfolio optimization with transaction cost models with both fixed and proportional costs are often formulated as mixed-integer programs.

Integer and combinatorial programs are solved by branch and bound, branch and cut, disjunctive programming, special-purpose heuristics, and cutting planes algorithms. Due to the computational complexity of general combinatorial and integer programs, problem specific algorithms are often used. Later in this chapter, we briefly discuss the general ideas behind the branch and bound, and the branch and cut approaches.

NECESSARY CONDITIONS FOR OPTIMALITY FOR CONTINUOUS OPTIMIZATION PROBLEMS

In calculus we learn that optimal points of a smooth function have a simple derivative characterization: the derivative of the function must be zero at every optimal point. This result is easy to understand in the one-dimensional case. Let us assume that x^* is a local minimum and $f'(x) > 0$ for some point $x > x^*$. By moving a small amount to the left, $x - \varepsilon$, where $\varepsilon > 0$, we would be able to decrease the value of f until we reach $f(x^*)$.

In the general case of the unconstrained optimization problem

$$\min_{\mathbf{x}} \ f(\mathbf{x})$$

where f is an N-dimensional function, the necessary condition for a local optimal solution is given by the *gradient condition*

$$\nabla f(\mathbf{x}^*) = \left(\frac{\partial}{\partial x_1} f(\mathbf{x}^*), \dots, \frac{\partial}{\partial x_N} f(\mathbf{x}^*) \right) = 0$$

If equality constraints $h_i(\mathbf{x}) = 0$, $i = 1, \dots, I$ are present, then we can convert the resulting optimization problem into an unconstrained problem by using Lagrange multipliers λ_i, $i = 1, \dots, I$ with a resulting objective function of the form

$$\min_{\mathbf{x}} f(\mathbf{x}) + \sum_{i=1}^{I} \lambda_i h_i(\mathbf{x})$$

The gradient condition can then be applied to this unconstrained problem for each one of the vectors $\mathbf{x}$ and $\boldsymbol{\lambda}$.

In the presence of both equality and inequality constraints, $h_j(\mathbf{x}) = 0$, $j = 1, ..., J$ and $g_i(\mathbf{x}) \leq 0$, $i = 1, ..., I$, the extension of the gradient condition is given by the so-called Karush-Kuhn-Tucker (KKT) conditions:

Karush-Kuhn-Tucker Conditions: Suppose that $\mathbf{x}^*$ is a local minimum of the nonlinear programming problem and that the gradient vectors $\nabla h_j(\mathbf{x}^*)$ for all j and $\nabla g_i(\mathbf{x}^*)$ for all indices i for which $g_i(\mathbf{x}^*) = 0$ are linearly independent. Then there exist vectors $\boldsymbol{\lambda} \in \mathbb{R}^J$ and $\boldsymbol{\mu} \in \mathbb{R}^I$ such that

$$\nabla f(\mathbf{x}^*) + \sum_{j=1}^{J} \lambda_j \nabla h_j(\mathbf{x}^*) + \sum_{i=1}^{I} \mu_i \nabla g_i(\mathbf{x}^*) = 0$$

$$h_j(\mathbf{x}^*) = 0, j = 1, ..., J$$
$$g_i(\mathbf{x}^*) \leq 0, i = 1, ..., I$$
$$\mu_i \geq 0, i = 1, ..., I$$
$$\mu_i g_i(\mathbf{x}^*) = 0, i = 1, ..., I$$

The vectors $\boldsymbol{\lambda}$ and $\boldsymbol{\mu}$ are called *Lagrange multipliers.*

Any point that satisfies the KKT conditions is called a *KKT point*. It can be shown that if $\mathbf{x}^*$ is an optimal solution of the nonlinear programming problem, then it must be a KKT point. However, the converse is not true in general. In other words, the KKT conditions are necessary for all nonlinear programming problems, but not sufficient. But for the subclass of convex nonlinear programs, the KKT conditions are also sufficient.

We observe that the KKT conditions for general nonlinear programs takes the form of a system of nonlinear equations. Many optimization algorithms are based upon solving this set of nonlinear equations.

HOW DO OPTIMIZATION ALGORITHMS WORK?

Today, optimization packages are built upon rather sophisticated algorithms. It is hard for the nonexpert to learn and understand in detail how particular algorithms work. Although a basic understanding is useful, it is often unnecessary in order to make efficient use of optimization software.

In this section, we provide an intuitive overview of some of the basic principles underlying numerical optimization techniques. For further details, we refer the reader to some of the many references quoted in the text.

Optimization algorithms are of an iterative nature. That is, the algorithm or the "solver" generates a sequence of approximate solutions x_0, x_1, x_2, ... that gets closer and closer to the true solution x^*. We say that the sequence of approximate solutions converges to the true solution if

$$\|x_k - x^*\| \to 0 \text{ as } k \to \infty$$

However, since the true solution is not known and the solver cannot go on indefinitely, the iterative process is ended when a *termination criterion* or *convergence criterion* is satisfied. One of the more common convergence criteria is to stop when no longer any progress is being made; that is when

$$\|x_k - x_{k+1}\| < TOL$$

where TOL is a user-defined tolerance (typically a small number).

Linear Programming

Linear problems with tens or hundreds of thousands of continuous variables can today be solved efficiently. The tractable size of linear integer programs is significantly smaller but, as a general rule hundreds or thousands of variables and constraints can normally be handled without a problem.

There are two basic approaches to solving linear problems: *simplex methods* and *interior-point methods*. Both visit a progressively improving series of approximate solutions, until a solution that satisfies some convergence criteria is reached.

Simplex methods, introduced by Dantzig in the 1940s, visit so-called basic feasible solutions computed by fixing enough of the variables at their bounds to reduce the constraints $Ax = b$, where A is a $J \times N$ matrix, to a square system. This square system can then be uniquely solved for the remaining variables. Basic feasible solutions represent extreme boundary points of the feasible region, defined by $Ax = b$, $x \geq 0$, and the simplex method can be viewed as moving from one corner to another along the edges of this boundary. We give a more detailed description of the simplex method next.

The simplex method is highly efficient for most practical problems. Typically, the method requires about $2N$ to $3N$ (where N is the number of variables in the problem) iterations until the solution is found. However, theoretically speaking, the simplex method has exponential complexity (i.e., the computational time is proportional to an exponential function of the size of the problem). Therefore, it is possible to encounter problems that can be very difficult to solve computationally.[13]

It was not until the end of the 1970s when Khachiyan first discovered a method with polynomial complexity for the linear programming problem. Karmarkar described the first practical algorithm in 1984. In contrast to the simplex method, which moves along the edges of the boundary of the feasible region, Karmarkar's algorithm approaches the solution from within the interior of the feasible region and is therefore called an *interior-point method*. We give a more detailed description of interior-point methods when we discuss nonlinear problems in the next section.

The Simplex Method

The *feasible set* of a linear programming problem is the set C of points that satisfies the constraints; that is $C = \{\mathbf{x}: \mathbf{Ax} = \mathbf{b}, \mathbf{x} \geq 0\}$. We assume that the $J \times N$ matrix $\mathbf{A}$ defining the linear constraints has full rank. If this is not the case, we can use standard linear algebra techniques to reduce the matrix into a new matrix that satisfies this assumption.

The geometric shape of the feasible set is that of a *polytope*. The simplex method searches for optima on the vertices of the polytope.

Suppose that $\mathbf{x} = (x_1, \ldots, x_N) \in C$, with at most J nonzero components. We denote by $I(\mathbf{x})$ the set of nonzero components of $\mathbf{x}$. In other words, for $i \in I(\mathbf{x})$ it holds that $x_i > 0$, and for $j \notin I(\mathbf{x})$ it follows that $x_j = 0$. We say that $\mathbf{x}$ is a *basic feasible solution* if the $J \times J$ matrix made up of the columns of $\mathbf{A}$ corresponding to the nonzero components of $\mathbf{x}$, that is

$$\mathbf{B} = [\mathbf{A}_i]_{i \in I(\mathbf{x})}$$

is nonsingular.

So how are the basic feasible solutions related to the solution of the linear programming problem? In fact, it is possible to demonstrate the following important results, which are often referred to as the *fundamental theorem of linear programming*:

---

[13] A classical example is the one constructed by Victor Klee and George J. Minty, "How Good Is the Simplex Algorithm?" in Oved Shisha (ed.), *Inequalities* (New York: Academic Press, 1972), pp. 159–175, where the simplex method has to visit every single vertex of a polytope with 2^N vertices, N being the number of unknowns.

- If the linear program is feasible and bounded, then there is at least one optimal solution. Furthermore, at least one of the optimal solution corresponds to one of the vertices of the feasible set.
- If the linear program is feasible, then there is a basic feasible solution.
- If the linear program has solutions, then at least one of these solutions is a basic feasible solution.

The first result implies that in order to obtain an optimal solution of the linear program, we can limit our search to the set of points corresponding to the vertices of the feasible polytope. The last two results imply that each of these points is determined by selecting a set of basic variables, with cardinality equal to the number of the constraints of the linear program and the additional requirement that the (uniquely determined) values of these variables are nonnegative. This further implies that the set of extreme points for a linear program in standard form, with N variables and J constraints can have only a finite number of extreme points.

A naïve approach in solving the problem would be to enumerate the entire set of extreme points and select the one that minimizes the objective function over this set. However, since there are

$$\binom{N}{J} = \frac{N!}{J!(N-J)!}$$

vertices, this approach would be very inefficient even for relatively small problem sizes. Hence a more systematic method to organize the search is needed. The simplex algorithm provides such systematic approach.

At the *k-th* iteration of the simplex method, the basic feasible solution $\mathbf{x}_k$ is known. We can partition this vector into the two subvectors

$$\mathbf{x}_B = [x_{ki}]_{i \in I(\mathbf{x}_k)} \quad \text{and} \quad \mathbf{x}_N = [x_{ki}]_{i \in I^c(\mathbf{x}_k)}$$

where $I^c(\mathbf{x}_k) = \{1, 2, ..., N\} \setminus I(\mathbf{x}_k)$ and where, for simplicity, we have dropped the superscript. Similarly, we also partition the vector $\mathbf{c}$ in the objective function and the constraint matrix $\mathbf{A}$ such that

$$\mathbf{B} = [\mathbf{A}_i]_{i \in I(\mathbf{x}_k)}, \mathbf{N} = [\mathbf{A}_i]_{i \in I(\mathbf{x}_k)}, \mathbf{c}_B = [c_i]_{i \in I(\mathbf{x}_k)}, \text{and } \mathbf{c}_N = [c_i]_{i \in I^c(\mathbf{x}_k)}$$

To construct the next basic feasible solution $\mathbf{x}_{k+1}$ we exchange one component from $\mathbf{x}_B$ and $\mathbf{x}_N$ and vice versa. What happens geometrically during this swapping process is that we move from one vertex of the feasible set to an adjacent one. However, there are many components that we could pick, so which one should be chosen?

We observe that with the notation introduced above, $\mathbf{A}\mathbf{x} = \mathbf{b}$ implies that

$$\mathbf{B}\mathbf{x}_B + \mathbf{N}\mathbf{x}_N = \mathbf{b}$$

so that

$$\mathbf{x}_B = \mathbf{B}^{-1}(\mathbf{b} - \mathbf{N}\mathbf{x}_N)$$

By writing

$$\mathbf{c}'\mathbf{x} = \mathbf{c}'_B\mathbf{x}_B + \mathbf{c}'_N\mathbf{x}_N$$

and substituting the expression for x_B above into this expression, we have

$$\mathbf{c}'\mathbf{x} = \mathbf{c}'_B\mathbf{B}^{-1}\mathbf{b} + (\mathbf{c}'_N - \mathbf{c}'_B\mathbf{B}^{-1}\mathbf{N})\mathbf{x}_N = \mathbf{c}'_B\mathbf{B}^{-1}\mathbf{b} + \mathbf{d}'_B\mathbf{x}_N$$

where $\mathbf{d}_N = \mathbf{c}_N - \mathbf{N}'(\mathbf{B}^{-1})'\mathbf{c}_B$ is referred to as the *reduced cost vector*.

From this decomposition we see that if some component, say i, of $\mathbf{d}_N$ is negative, we decrease the value of the objective function, $\mathbf{c}'\mathbf{x}$, by allowing the i-th component of $\mathbf{x}_N$ to become positive and simultaneously adjusting $\mathbf{x}_B$ to make sure that $\mathbf{x}$ stays feasible. If there is more than one negative component of $\mathbf{d}_N$, we would typically choose the one that leads to the largest decrease in the objective function. This approach is referred to as *Dantzig's rule*. However, several other strategies have been devised. When there are no negative entries in the reduced cost vector, the current basic feasible solution is the optimal solution.

From the description above it is clear that the algorithm will terminate in a finite number of steps. Nevertheless, there are a few special pathological cases when convergence problems can occur, but well designed solvers are normally able to overcome these difficulties.

Nonlinear Programming

Earlier in this chapter we saw that the general Karush-Kuhn-Tucker optimality conditions for a nonlinear program take the form of a system of nonlinear equations. For that reason, in order to solve the optimization problem, the majority of algorithms apply either some variant of the Newton method to this system of equations or solve a sequence of approximations of this system.

In this section, we first take a look at *line-search* and *Newton-type* methods as they provide some of the foundation for unconstrained nonlinear programming. Thereafter, we discuss two very important classes of methods for constrained nonlinear programming: *interior-point methods* and *sequential quadratic programming*.

Line-Search and Newton Type Methods

We first describe the Newton method for the one-dimensional unconstrained optimization problem

$$\min_{x} f(x)$$

where we assume that the first and second order derivatives of f exist. Further, let us assume that we have an approximation x_k of the optimal solution x^* and we want to compute a "better" approximation x_{k+1}. The Taylor series expansion around x_k is given by

$$f(x_k + h) = f(x_k) + f'(x_k)h + \tfrac{1}{2}f''(x_k)h^2 + O(h^3)$$

where h is some small number.

If we assume h is small enough, we can ignore third and higher order terms in h. Since x_k is known, we can rewrite the original optimization problem as

$$\min_{h} f(x_k) + f'(x_k)h + \tfrac{1}{2}f''(x_k)h^2$$

This is a simple quadratic optimization problem in h, so by taking derivatives with respect to h, we have that

$$f'(x_k) + f''(x_k)h = 0$$

Solving for h we then obtain

$$h = -\frac{f'(x_k)}{f''(x_k)}$$

Therefore, we define the new approximation x_{k+1} by

$$x_{k+1} = x_k + h = x_k - \frac{f'(x_k)}{f''(x_k)}$$

This is the Newton method for the one-dimensional unconstrained optimization problem above. Given a starting value x_0, we can calculate x_1 and so forth by iteration.

The Newton method is easily extended to N-dimensional problems and then takes the form

$$\mathbf{x}_{k+1} = \mathbf{x}_k - [\nabla^2 f(\mathbf{x}_k)]^{-1} \nabla f(\mathbf{x}_k)$$

where $\mathbf{x}_{k+1}$, $\mathbf{x}_k$ are N-dimensional vectors, and $\nabla f(\mathbf{x}_k)$ and $\nabla^2 f(\mathbf{x}_k)$ are the gradient and the Hessian of f at x_k, respectively. We emphasize that $[\nabla^2 f(\mathbf{x}_k)]^{-1} \nabla f(\mathbf{x}_k)$ is shorthand for solving the linear system

$$\nabla^2 f(\mathbf{x}_k)\mathbf{h} = \nabla f(\mathbf{x}_k)$$

The Newton method is a so-called *line search strategy*: After the k-th step, $\mathbf{x}_k$ is given and the $(k + 1)$-th approximation is calculated according to the iterative scheme

$$\mathbf{x}_{k+1} = \mathbf{x}_k + \gamma \mathbf{p}_k$$

where $\mathbf{p}_k \in R^N$ is the *search direction* chosen by the algorithm. Of course, in the case of the Newton method, the search direction is chosen to be $\mathbf{p}_k = -[\nabla^2 f(\mathbf{x}_k)]^{-1} \nabla f(\mathbf{x}_k)$ and $\gamma = 1$. Other search directions lead to algorithms with different properties.

For example, in the *method of steepest descent* the search direction is chosen to be $\mathbf{p}_k = -\nabla f(\mathbf{x}_k)$. The name of this method comes from the fact that at point $\mathbf{x}_k$ the direction given by $-\nabla f(\mathbf{x}_k)$ is the direction in which the function f decreases most rapidly. The step size γ can be chosen in a variety of ways.

One advantage of steepest descent is that it only requires the first-order derivatives of the function f, and not second-order derivatives as the Newton method does. Therefore, a steepest descent iteration is computationally less burdensome to perform than a Newton iteration.

However, it turns out that steepest descent and the Newton method have different convergence properties. The rate of convergence to a solution is faster for the Newton method. In particular, the Newton method has *second-order convergence* (or *quadratic convergence*) in a local neighborhood of the solution $\mathbf{x}^*$, such that for all k sufficiently large it holds that

$$\left\| \mathbf{x}_{k+1} - \mathbf{x}^* \right\| \leq C \left\| \mathbf{x}_k - \mathbf{x}^* \right\|^2$$

for some constant $C > 0$. Steepest descent, in contrast, has *first-order convergence* (or *linear convergence*) in a local neighborhood of the solution $\mathbf{x}^*$, which means that for all k sufficiently large it holds that

$$\left\| \mathbf{x}_{k+1} - \mathbf{x}^* \right\| \leq c \left\| \mathbf{x}_k - \mathbf{x}^* \right\|$$

for some constant $0 < c < 1$.

The main advantage of the standard Newton method is its fast local convergence. *Local convergence* means that if we are sufficiently close to a solution, the method guarantees finding it. Although the method of steepest descent converges slower than the Newton method, it always guarantees to decrease the value of the objective function.[14] Therefore, steepest descent and Newton-type of methods are sometimes combined in the same optimization routine making it one of the most efficient tools for smooth unconstrained minimization.

The main drawback of the Newton-type methods is their relatively high computational cost. At each iteration, we have to compute the Hessian of the objective function and solve an $N \times N$ linear system. If the objective function is computationally costly to evaluate or the dimension of the problem, N, is large, then the Newton method might no longer be competitive. Although the method might have fast convergence, in this situation each iteration takes time to calculate. The method also requires that the Hessian is stored, which can be an issue for large problems. Modified Newton, quasi-Newton, and conjugate gradient methods are often computationally more efficient for large problems and converge faster than the method of steepest descent. Simplistically, modified and quasi-Newton methods use a search direction given by

$$\mathbf{p}_k = -\mathbf{B}_k^{-1} \nabla f_k$$

---

[14] The Newton method can be shown to always guarantee that the value of the objective function decreases with each iteration when the Hessian matrices $\nabla^2 f(x_k)$ are positive definite and have condition numbers that can be uniformly bounded. For the method of steepest descent, these requirements do not have to be valid for the same property to hold.

where $\mathbf{B}_k$ is a positive definite approximation of the true Hessian. In one of the most successful and widely used general-purpose quasi-Newton methods known as *BFGS* (Broyden, Fletcher, Goldfarb, and Shanno), the approximations are calculated according to

$$\mathbf{B}_{k+1} = \mathbf{B}_k + \frac{\mathbf{q}_k \mathbf{q}_k'}{\mathbf{q}_k' \mathbf{s}_k} - \frac{\mathbf{B}_k' \mathbf{s}_k' \mathbf{s}_k \mathbf{B}_k}{\mathbf{s}_k' \mathbf{B}_k \mathbf{s}_k}, \mathbf{B}_0 = \mathbf{I}$$

where $\mathbf{I}$ is the $N \times N$ identity matrix, and

$$\mathbf{s}_k = \mathbf{x}_{k+1} - \mathbf{x}_k$$
$$\mathbf{q}_k = \nabla f(\mathbf{x}_{k+1}) - \nabla f(\mathbf{x}_k)$$

Modern nonlinear optimization methods mimic the performance of the Newton method even though they calculate and store only a small fraction of the derivative information required by the original approach. Several other improvements have also been made for constrained problems, such as a better usage of the Lagrange multipliers (often referred to as the *dual variables*) in order to speed up and improve the performance of the algorithm.

Barrier and Interior-Point Methods

In this section we describe the idea behind interior-point methods for the solution of the convex optimization problem in standard form:

$$\min_{\mathbf{x}} f(\mathbf{x})$$

$$s.t.\ g_i(\mathbf{x}) \leq 0, \quad i = 1, ..., I$$
$$\mathbf{A}\mathbf{x} = \mathbf{b}$$

where f and g_i are convex functions, $\mathbf{A}$ is a $J \times N$ matrix, and $\mathbf{b}$ is a J-dimensional vector.

We assume that the problem is (strictly) feasible so that a unique solution $\mathbf{x}^*$ exists. Then the KKT conditions for this problem guarantee that there exist vectors $\boldsymbol{\lambda}$ (J-dimensional) and $\boldsymbol{\mu}$ (I-dimensional) such that

$$\nabla f(\mathbf{x}^*) + \sum_{i=1}^{I} \mu_i \nabla g_i(\mathbf{x}^*) + \mathbf{A}'\boldsymbol{\lambda} = 0$$

$$\mathbf{Ax}^* = \mathbf{b}$$
$$g_i(\mathbf{x}^*) \le 0, \, i = 1, \ldots, I$$
$$\mu_i \ge 0, \, i = 1, \ldots, I$$
$$\mu_i g_i(\mathbf{x}^*) = 0, \, i = 1, \ldots, I$$

In a nutshell, interior-point methods solve the optimization problem by either applying the Newton method to a sequence of equality-constrained approximations of the original problem or to a sequence of slightly modified versions of these KKT conditions. First, we will describe one type of interior-point method called the *barrier method*. Thereafter, we briefly outline the so-called primal-dual interior-point method.

A Barrier Method   In the barrier method, the idea is to convert the general problem with both equality and inequality constraints into a sequence of equality constrained approximations, which then can be solved by the Newton method.

By introducing the indicator function

$$\chi_{R_-}(x) = \begin{cases} 0, \, x \le 0 \\ \infty, \, x > 0 \end{cases}$$

we can rewrite the original problem as

$$\min_{\mathbf{x}} f(\mathbf{x}) + \sum_{i=1}^{I} \chi_{R_-}(g_i(\mathbf{x}))$$

$$s.t. \quad \mathbf{Ax} = \mathbf{b}$$

In particular, we see that the domain of the function

$$\Phi(\mathbf{x}) = \sum_{i=1}^{I} \chi_{R_-}(g_i(\mathbf{x}))$$

coincides with the interior of $G = \{\mathbf{x} \in R^N : g_i(\mathbf{x}) \le 0, \, i = 1, \ldots, I\}$. However, the problem with this formulation is that the new objective function is in general *not* differentiable. The reason for this is that the indicator function χ_{R_-} is neither smooth nor differentiable at zero. The "trick" is therefore to approximate the indicator function with a smooth and differentiable function.

A common choice is to use the approximation

$$\Phi^{\varepsilon}(\mathbf{x}) = -\varepsilon \sum_{i=1}^{I} \log(-g_i(\mathbf{x})) = \varepsilon \cdot \Psi_{\log}(\mathbf{x})$$

where

$$\Psi_{\log}(\mathbf{x}) = -\sum_{i=1}^{I} \log(-g_i(\mathbf{x}))$$

is referred to as the *logarithmic barrier function*. We note that the logarithmic barrier function possesses the following important properties:

- It is convex and differentiable.
- Its domain is the set of points that *strictly* satisfy the inequality constraints.
- $\Psi\log(\mathbf{x}) \to \infty$ when $g_i(\mathbf{x}) \to 0$ for any i.

The resulting nonlinear programming problem with equality constraints

$$\min_{\mathbf{x}} f(\mathbf{x}) + \varepsilon \cdot \Psi_{\log}(\mathbf{x})$$

$$s.t. \quad \mathbf{Ax} = \mathbf{b}$$

turns out to be a good approximation of the original problem and can be solved by the Newton method. In fact, one can show that the approximation improves incrementally as ε gets closer to zero. However, when ε is small, the resulting Hessian changes drastically when $\mathbf{x}$ takes on values such that $g_i(\mathbf{x})$ is close to zero. This behavior makes it difficult to minimize the objective function with the Newton method. The way to circumvent this problem is by solving a sequence of approximations and steadily decreasing the value of ε for each new step. At each step, the starting point for the Newton iteration is the solution of the approximation for the previous value of ε. We will see how that works below.

To apply the Newton method, we first form the Lagrangian

$$F(\mathbf{x}, \boldsymbol{\lambda}) = \frac{1}{\varepsilon}f(\mathbf{x}) + \Psi_{\log}(\mathbf{x}) + \boldsymbol{\lambda}'(\mathbf{A}\mathbf{x} - \mathbf{b})$$

where, for mathematical convenience, we first divide the objective function by ε. The gradient and the Hessian of F are easily calculated at the point $(\mathbf{x}_k, \boldsymbol{\lambda}_k)$

$$\nabla F(\mathbf{x}_k, \boldsymbol{\lambda}_k) = \begin{bmatrix} \frac{1}{\varepsilon}\nabla f(\mathbf{x}_k) + \nabla \Psi_{\log}(\mathbf{x}_k) + \boldsymbol{\lambda}'\mathbf{A} \\ \mathbf{A}\mathbf{x}_k - \mathbf{b} \end{bmatrix}$$

and

$$\nabla^2 F(\mathbf{x}_k, \boldsymbol{\lambda}_k) = \begin{bmatrix} \frac{1}{\varepsilon}\nabla^2 f(\mathbf{x}_k) + \nabla^2 \Psi_{\log}(\mathbf{x}_k) & \mathbf{A}' \\ \mathbf{A} & 0 \end{bmatrix}$$

If we already have $(\mathbf{x}_k, \boldsymbol{\lambda}_k)$ and we now want to calculate $(\mathbf{x}_{k+1}, \boldsymbol{\lambda}_{k+1})$, using the Newton method we would proceed as follows:

1. Solve the linear system

$$\nabla^2 F(\mathbf{x}_k, \boldsymbol{\lambda}_k)\begin{bmatrix} \Delta\mathbf{x} \\ \Delta\boldsymbol{\lambda} \end{bmatrix} = \nabla F(\mathbf{x}_k, \boldsymbol{\lambda}_k)$$

for the search direction $(\Delta\mathbf{x}, \Delta\boldsymbol{\lambda})'$
2. Update

$$\begin{bmatrix} \mathbf{x}_{k+1} \\ \boldsymbol{\lambda}_{k+1} \end{bmatrix} = \begin{bmatrix} \mathbf{x}_k \\ \boldsymbol{\lambda}_k \end{bmatrix} - \begin{bmatrix} \Delta\mathbf{x} \\ \Delta\boldsymbol{\lambda} \end{bmatrix}$$

3. If convergence criteria is not satisfied, decrease ε and go back to step 1.

The direction $(\Delta\mathbf{x}, \Delta\boldsymbol{\lambda})'$ is often referred to as the *barrier method search direction*.

A Primal-Dual Interior-Point Method   It is not difficult to show that the method derived above is equivalent to applying the Newton method directly to the modified KKT equations

$$\nabla f(\mathbf{x}) + \sum_{i=1}^{I} \mu_i \nabla g_i(\mathbf{x}) + \mathbf{A}'\boldsymbol{\lambda} = 0$$

$$\mathbf{A}\mathbf{x} = \mathbf{b}$$
$$-\mu_i g_i(\mathbf{x}) = \varepsilon, \, i = 1, ..., I$$

Nevertheless, the method used above is not the only approach to solve this system of nonlinear equations.

Another possibility is to apply the Newton method directly on the nonlinear system of equations with the unknown the vector $(\mathbf{x}, \boldsymbol{\mu}, \boldsymbol{\lambda})$ where $\mathbf{x} \in \mathbf{R}^N$, $\boldsymbol{\mu} \in \mathbf{R}^I$, and $\boldsymbol{\lambda} \in \mathbf{R}^J$. Written in a somewhat more compact form, the Newton method would be used on the nonlinear system

$$\mathbf{H}(\mathbf{x}, \boldsymbol{\lambda}, \boldsymbol{\mu}) = \begin{bmatrix} \nabla f(\mathbf{x}) + J_g(\mathbf{x})'\boldsymbol{\mu} + \mathbf{A}'\boldsymbol{\lambda} \\ -\boldsymbol{\Lambda}\mathbf{g}(\mathbf{x}) - \varepsilon \mathbf{I} \\ \mathbf{A}\mathbf{x} - \mathbf{b} \end{bmatrix} = 0$$

where $\mathbf{I}$ is the $J \times J$ identity matrix and

$$\boldsymbol{\Lambda} = \begin{bmatrix} \lambda_1 & & \\ & \ddots & \\ & & \lambda_J \end{bmatrix}$$

This is referred to as a primal-dual interior-point method. We see that both this and the barrier method are very closely related. The resulting search direction, $(\Delta \mathbf{x}, \Delta \boldsymbol{\mu}, \Delta \boldsymbol{\lambda})$ is called the *primal-dual search direction*. It is common in the primal-dual interior-point method to take a modified Newton step

$$\begin{bmatrix} \mathbf{x}_{k+1} \\ \boldsymbol{\mu}_{k+1} \\ \boldsymbol{\lambda}_{k+1} \end{bmatrix} = \begin{bmatrix} \mathbf{x}_k \\ \boldsymbol{\mu}_k \\ \boldsymbol{\lambda}_k \end{bmatrix} + \gamma \begin{bmatrix} \Delta \mathbf{x} \\ \Delta \boldsymbol{\mu} \\ \Delta \boldsymbol{\lambda} \end{bmatrix}$$

where γ is chosen via a line search.

General Nonlinear Programming Problems: The Sequential Quadratic Programming Approach

In this section we provide an intuitive introduction of the *sequential quadratic programming* (SQP) approach (also referred to as *recursive quadratic programming*) for solving general nonlinear programming problems. In this approach, a sequence of approximate solutions to the original problem are generated by solving a series of quadratic programming problems. SQP methods can handle small and large optimization problems with significant nonlinearities.

We start by considering the nonlinear programming problem

$$\min_{\mathbf{x}} f(\mathbf{x})$$

$$\text{s.t. } g_i(\mathbf{x}) \le 0 \quad i = 1, \ldots, I$$
$$h_j(\mathbf{x}) = 0 \quad j = 1, \ldots, J$$

where f, g_i, and h_j are smooth functions of the N-dimensional variable $\mathbf{x}$. Like we did for the Newton method above, let us assume that we have calculated an approximate solution $\mathbf{x}_k$ to the nonlinear programming problem. We now define a subproblem by approximating the objective function with a quadratic function and linearizing the inequality and equality constraints[15]

$$\min_{\mathbf{d}} \frac{1}{2}\mathbf{d}'\mathbf{B}_k\mathbf{d} + \nabla f(\mathbf{x}_k)\mathbf{d}$$

$$\text{s.t. } \nabla h_i(\mathbf{x}_k)\mathbf{d} + h_i(\mathbf{x}_k) = 0 \quad i = 1, \ldots, I$$
$$\nabla g_j(\mathbf{x}_k)\mathbf{d} + g_j(\mathbf{x}_k) \le 0 \quad j = 1, \ldots, J$$

where $\mathbf{B}_k = \nabla^2 f(\mathbf{x}_k)$ is the Hessian of the objective function at $\mathbf{x}_k$.

---

[15] We obtain the approximations through the second and first-order Taylor expansions

$$f(\mathbf{x}_k + \mathbf{d}) = f(\mathbf{x}_k) + \nabla f(\mathbf{x}_k)\mathbf{d} + \frac{1}{2}\mathbf{d}'\nabla^2 f(\mathbf{x}_k)\mathbf{d} + O(\|\mathbf{d}\|^3)$$

$$h_i(\mathbf{x}_k + \mathbf{d}) = h_i(\mathbf{x}_k) + \nabla h_i(\mathbf{x}_k)\mathbf{d} + O(\|\mathbf{d}\|^2), i = 1, \ldots, I$$

$$g_j(\mathbf{x}_k + \mathbf{d}) = g_j(\mathbf{x}_k) + \nabla g_j(\mathbf{x}_k)\mathbf{d} + O(\|\mathbf{d}\|^2), j = 1, \ldots, J$$

We note that by using a first-order Taylor expansion of the objective function we would get a linear approximation to the nonlinear programming problem. This is the basic idea behind *sequential linear programming* (SLP), in which a sequence of linear approximations are each solved by linear programming to produce a final solution of the nonlinear programming problem.

In principle, any quadratic programming algorithm can be used to solve this quadratic subproblem. However, the particular method chosen is important for large problems where otherwise the lack of computational efficiency and numerical robustness quickly becomes noticeable. Today, many SQP implementations are based on fast interior-point methods for the quadratic subproblem.

One complication that might arise is that $B_k = \nabla^2 f(x_k)$ may not be positive definite unless x_k is sufficiently close to the solution. In this case, the quadratic programming problem is no longer convex and a unique solution of the subproblem may no longer exist. One possibility is to modify the Hessian to make it positive definite at each iteration as is done in Han and Powell's version of the quasi-Newton method.[16]

Combinatorial and Integer Programming

Integer models come essentially in two different flavors: pure integer programs or mixed integer programs. In pure integer programs, the variables are restricted to either binary values, 0 or 1, or the integers ..., −2, −1, 0, 1, 2, ... Mixed-integer programs are problems that require only some of the variables to take integer values whereas others can be continuous.

Integer problem with many variables can be very difficult to solve. In contrast to continuous programs, for an integer program it can be very hard to prove that a particular solution is indeed the optimal one. Therefore, in many cases, the user might have to be satisfied with an approximate solution with a provable upper bound on its distance from optimality.

In this section we make the somewhat simplifying assumption that we are dealing with a pure integer program. Our purpose is to give general ideas and provide intuition for how integer programs are solved.

The nonlinear discrete or integer programming problem has the same form as the nonlinear programming problem with the additional requirement that all variables can only take on discrete or integer values

$$\min_z f(z)$$

$$s.t.\ g_i(z) \leq 0 \quad i = 1, ..., I$$
$$h_j(z) = 0 \quad j = 1, ..., J$$
$$z: \text{integer}$$

Many integer problems that occur in practice are either linear or convex quadratic problems. To simplify the discussion, we will drop the equality constraints and therefore consider the problem

---

[16] See, for example, Luenberger, *Linear and Nonlinear Programming*.

$$\min_{\mathbf{z}} f(\mathbf{z})$$

$$s.t.\ g_i(\mathbf{z}) \leq 0 \quad i = 1, \ldots, I$$

$$\mathbf{z}: \text{integer}$$

One approach for solving these problems is by exhaustive search. For example, if for simplicity we assume that we are dealing with a 0–1 program with N variables, then we could calculate the value of the objective function for all feasible combinations of the binary 0–1 vector. Possibly, we would then have to compare 2^N candidates and choose the one that has the smallest value. Clearly, this is only possible for very small problems.

Branch and Bound

Typically, general-purpose integer programming routines are based on a procedure called "branch-and-bound." An optimal integer solution is arrived at by solving a sequence of so-called *continuous relaxations* organized in an *enumeration tree* with two branches at each node.

Starting at the root, we would solve the optimization problem removing the requirement that variables take on integer values

$$\min_{\mathbf{z}} f(\mathbf{z})$$

$$s.t.\ g_i(\mathbf{z}) \leq 0 \quad i = 1, \ldots, I$$

This can be done with a suitable continuous optimization algorithm. In general, the solution to the root problem, $\mathbf{x}$, will not have all integer components.

In the next step we will perform a branching in which we partition the problem (the "parent") into two mutually exclusive problems. First, we choose some noninteger component x_j of $\mathbf{x}$ and round this to the closest integer, $I_j = \lfloor x_j \rfloor$. Then, we define the two subproblems, also referred to as the "children,"

1. $\min_{\mathbf{z}} f(\mathbf{z})$

    $s.t.\ g_i(\mathbf{z}) \leq 0 \quad i = 1, \ldots, I$

    $\qquad z_j \leq I_j$

2. $\min_{\mathbf{z}} f(\mathbf{z})$

    $s.t.\ g_i(\mathbf{z}) \leq 0 \quad i = 1, \ldots, I$

    $\qquad z_j \geq I_j + 1$

These two subproblems with the additional constraints are now solved and a new branching is performed. In this way, each of the subproblems leads to two new children. If we repeat this process, sooner or later, when enough bounds have been introduced, integer solutions to the different subproblems are obtained.

At this point, we need to keep track of the best integer solution, z^*, that so far has given the smallest value of the objective function. Doing so allows us to "prune" the binary enumeration tree. For example, if another subproblem at another branch has been solved and its final objective value is greater than $f(z^*)$, then all its children will also be greater than $f(z^*)$. This is because at each iteration we are making the feasible set smaller by adding more constraints, so the minimum we can find over the reduced set can be only worse than the minimum at the parent node. As we will not obtain any improvements along that particular branch, we can prune it (i.e., get rid of it).

The branching and the pruning are the two basic components in branch and bound. Implementations differ in how the branching components are selected.[17] In a worst-case situation we might, however, end up solving all of the subproblems. Therefore, branch and bound is normally combined with other techniques such as cutting planes.[18]

Cutting Planes

The branch and bound technique is often used in conjunction with cutting plane algorithms that introduce further linear constraints to the relaxed continuous problem. These linear constraints, also referred to as *cutting planes*, are constructed based upon the underlying structure of the problem in such a way that the set of continuous feasible points, but not the set of integer feasible points, is reduced.[19] In effect, these linear constraints "cut off" part of the continuous feasible set without affecting the integer feasible set.

---

[17] See, for example, Brian Borchers and John E. Mitchell, "An Improved Branch and Bound Algorithm for Mixed Integer Nonlinear Programs," *Computers and Operations Research* 21, no. 4 (1994), pp. 359–367.

[18] See, for example, Daniel Bienstock, "Computational Study of a Family of Mixed-Integer Quadratic Programming Problems," *Mathematical Programming* 74, no. 2 (1996), pp. 121–140.

[19] The interested reader might want to consult one of the following standard references: Laurence A. Wolsey, *Integer Programming* (New York: Wiley-Interscience, 1998); Laurence A. Wolsey and George L. Nemhauser, *Integer and Combinatorial Optimization* (New York: Wiley-Interscience, 1999); and, Christos H. Papadimitriou and Kenneth Steiglitz, *Combinatorial Optimization: Algorithms and Complexity* (Mineola, NY: Dover, 1998).

OPTIMIZATION SOFTWARE

Choosing and purchasing optimization software can be both very costly and time-consuming. It is important to evaluate different kinds of solvers for the applications in mind. Some solvers work better for a certain type of problem than others. Unfortunately, often the only way to find out how well a solver works for a particular problem is through extensive testing.

Today's optimization software is very sophisticated and can therefore be difficult to use for the nonexpert. However, most optimization packages can today be accessed by using a more user-friendly modeling language that provides a more convenient interface for specifying problems and that automates many of the underlying mathematical and algorithmic details. In particular, a modeling language allows the user to specify particular optimization problems in a generic fashion and independent of the specific algorithmic and input requirements of optimization routines. Some of the most widespread modeling languages are AMPL,[20] GAMS,[21] and LINGO.[22]

So where do we find software for a particular problem? Before settling on specific software, we recommend studying several of the optimization software guides that are available.[23] Hans Mittelmann has made his Decision Tree for Optimization Software[24] available online. Also very useful is Stephen Nash's nonlinear programming software survey[25] from 1998. Arnold Neumaier maintains a summary of public domain and commercially available software for both local and global optimization.[26]

One of the main projects at the Optimization Technology Center at Argonne National Laboratory and Northwestern University is NEOS—the Network Enabled Optimization System. NEOS consists of the NEOS Guide[27]

---

[20] See http://www.ampl.com and Robert Fourer, David M. Gay, NS Brian W. Kernighan, *AMPL: A Modeling Language for Mathematical Programming* (Belmont, CA: Duxbury Press, 2002).
[21] See http://www.gams.com and Enrique Castillo, Antonio J. Conejo, Pablo Pedregal, Ricardo García, and Natalia Alguacil, *Building and Solving Mathematical Programming Models in Engineering and Science* (New York: Wiley-Interscience, 2001).
[22] See http://www.lindo.com, Lindo Systems, Inc. LINGO version 9.0, 2004.
[23] Jorge J. Moré and Stephen J. Wright, *Optimization Software Guide, Frontiers in Applied Mathematics*, vol. 14 (Philadelphia: Society of Industrial and Applied Mathematics Publications, 1993).
[24] The guide can be accessed online at http://plato.asu.edu/guide.html.
[25] Stephen G. Nash, "Software Survey: NLP," *OR/MS Today* 25, no. 3 (1998).
[26] For global optimization, http://www.mat.univie.ac.at/~neum/glopt/software_g.html; for local optimization, http://www.mat.univie.ac.at/~neum/glopt/software_l.html.
[27] The NEOS Guide can be accessed online at http://www-fp.mcs.anl.gov/otc/Guide/index.html.

and the NEOS Server.[28] The NEOS Guide is a comprehensive guide to public and commercial optimization algorithms and software covering more than 100 software packages for linear programming, quadratic programming, nonlinear programming, and integer programming with or without constraints.

The NEOS Server provides free Internet access to over 50 optimization software packages that can solve a large class of unconstrained and nonlinearly constrained optimization problems. Optimization problems can be submitted online in a programming language such as Fortran and C, modeling languages such as AMPL and GAMS, or a wide variety of other low-level data formats.

In the rest of this section we briefly discuss some available optimization software. For further details we refer to the optimization guides provided earlier in this section.

While noncommercial optimization packages typically are slower than the best commercial optimization packages, they often show a much greater degree of flexibility and extendibility as the source code can often be obtained. This is especially important for users who want to develop customized solvers. For some noncommercial libraries, the documentation is sparse at best. However, many users will be fully satisfied with the noncommercial codes.

Spreadsheet programs such as Microsoft Excel and Corel Quattro Pro are equipped with general-purpose optimization algorithms for linear, integer, and nonlinear programming problems. These routines work well for small-scale problems, up to about a few hundred decision variables.

GNU Octave[29] and MATLAB[30] are two high-level technical computing and interactive environments for model development, data visualization, data analysis, and numerical simulation. The Optimization Toolbox available for MATLAB can solve a variety of constrained and unconstrained optimization problems for linear programming, quadratic programming, nonlinear optimization, nonlinear equations, multi-objective optimization, and binary integer programming.

---

[28] The NEOS Server can be accessed online at http://www-neos.mcs.anl.gov and is described in the following references: Joseph Czyzyk, Michael P. Mesnier, and Jorge J. Moré, "The NEOS Server," *IEEE Journal on Computational Science and Engineering 5* (1998), pp. 68-75; William Gropp and Jorge J. Moré, "Optimization Environments and the NEOS Server," in Martin D. Buhmann and Arieh Iserles (eds.), *Approximation Theory and Optimization* (Cambridge: Cambridge University Press, 1997), pp. 167–182; and Elizabeth D. Dolan, *The NEOS Server 4.0 Administrative Guide*, Technical Memorandum ANL/MCS-TM-250, Mathematics and Computer Science Division, Argonne National Laboratory, May 2001.

[29] See http://www.octave.org.

[30] Trademarked and copyrighted by The MathWorks, Inc.

CPLEX,[31] LINDO,[32] and XPRESS[33] are robust and efficient commercial optimizers for large linear and convex quadratic programming. Both simplex and primal-dual interior-point methods are available. The software packages handle integer problems through a variety of branching and node selection techniques such as cuts, branch-and-cut algorithms, or heuristics. CBC is a noncommercial mixed-integer linear programming package that provides support for different kinds of branching.[34]

MOSEK is commercial optimizer for linear, quadratic, and convex quadratically constrained optimization problems well-known for speed and numerical stability.[35] The subroutine library is based upon an interior-point implementation that is capable of exploiting sparsity and special structure, which yields accurate and efficient results in many applications, from small to large scale.

The optimizer LOQO for smooth constrained optimization problems is based on an infeasible, primal-dual interior-point method applied to a sequence of quadratic approximations to the given problem.[36]

SeDuMi[37] and SDPT3[38] are publicly available Matlab libraries for solving optimization problems over symmetric cones. In other words, these software packages can handle not only linear constraints, but also quasiconvex-quadratic constraints and positive semi-definite constraints. Both are built upon a primal-dual interior-point method referred to as the *centering-predictor-corrector method* and can exploit sparse matrix structure, making them very efficient.[39]

---

[31] See http://www.ilog.com/products/cplex.

[32] See http://www.lindo.com.

[33] See http://www.dashopt.com.

[34] See http://www.coin-or.org.

[35] See http://www.mosek.com.

[36] Robert J. Vanderbei, "LOQO: An Interior Point Code for Quadratic Programming," *Optimization Methods and Software* 12 (1999), pp. 451–484; and Robert J. Vanderbei and D.F. Shanno, "An Interior-Point Algorithm for Nonconvex Nonlinear Programming," *Computational Optimization and Applications* 13 (1999), pp. 231–252.

[37] Jos F. Sturm, "Using SeDuMi 1.02, A MATLAB Toolbox for Optimization over Symmetric Cones," *Optimization Methods and Software* 11–12 (1999), pp. 625–653. SeDuMi is available online at http://sedumi.mcmaster.ca.

[38] Reha H. Tütüncü, Kim C. Toh, and Michael J. Todd, "SDPT3—A Matlab Software Package for Semidefinite-Quadratic-Linear Programming," Version 3.0, 2001. SDPT3 is available online at http://www.math.nus.edu.sg/~mattohkc/sdpt3.html.

[39] Jos F. Sturm, "Primal-Dual Interior Point Approach to Semidefinite Programming," Vol. 156 of Tinbergen Institute Research Series, Thesis Publishers, The Netherlands, 1997.

TOMLAB is a general purpose development environment in MATLAB for the practical solution of optimization problems.[40] TOMLAB supplies MATLAB solver algorithms, as well as interfaces to well-known state-of-the-art optimization software packages for mixed-integer linear and quadratic programming, nonlinear programming, semidefinite programming, and global optimization, such as CGO, CPLEX, MINLP, MINOS, PENOPT, SNOPT, Xpress, and so on.

Portfolio Precision 3.1™ by Axioma is a highly specialized portfolio optimizer that allows for investment models which include market impact, transaction costs, tax implications, minimum/maximum holdings, sector and industry bets, and many other common business and investment restrictions.[41] The software combines proprietary linear and quadratic programming solvers for both continuous and integer problems. A preprocessor automatically routes the problem to the appropriate solver based on the characteristics of the portfolio and the investment strategy. A branch-and-bound method along with specialized heuristics has been incorporated to handle common integer and combinatorial restrictions such as limits on the number of securities traded, limits on the total number of holdings, and round lots. The latest version also includes support for robust optimization to take estimation error into account.

Barra provides the Barra Aegis System™ to support the quantitative investment process.[42] The system is a comprehensive portfolio management software package for risk decomposition, portfolio optimization, and performance attribution, that is integrated with Barra's multiple-factor risk models.

ITG/Opt by ITG is a portfolio optimization platform that enables users to construct portfolios with optimal risk by taking transaction costs, taxes, and a wide variety of business and investment constraints into account.[43] The optimization engine is based on the CPLEX mixed-integer programming optimizer.

The "Numerical Recipes" books are useful for anyone developing computer models and running simulations.[44] They provide simple to use algorithms in languages such as Basic, C, C++, Fortran, and Pascal for a large range of numerical analysis problems such as linear algebra, inter-

---

[40] See http://tomlab.biz.

[41] See http://www.axiomainc.com.

[42] See http://www.barra.com.

[43] See http://www.itginc.com.

[44] See for example, William H. Press, Saul A. Teukolsky, William T. Vetterling, and Brian P. Flannery, *Numerical Recipes in C++: The Art of Scientific Computing* (Cambridge: Cambridge University Press, 2002). Numerical recipes are also freely available online at http://www.nr.com.

polation, special functions, random numbers, nonlinear sets of equations, optimization, eigenvalue problems, Fourier methods and wavelets, statistical tests, ordinary and partial differential equations, integral equations, and inverse problems.

The Netlib repository contains freely available software, documents, and databases of interest to the numerical, scientific computing, and other communities.[45] The repository is maintained by AT&T Bell Laboratories, the University of Tennessee, Oak Ridge National Laboratory, and colleagues worldwide. The collection is replicated at several sites around the world, automatically synchronized to provide reliable and network efficient service to the global community.

PRACTICAL CONSIDERATIONS WHEN USING OPTIMIZATION SOFTWARE

Today, numerical software for vast areas of problems is widely available both publicly as well as commercially. This makes modeling and problem solving easier and more convenient. The wheel does not have to be reinvented every time a similar problem is encountered.

We can solve financial models by using modeling languages and software packages such as Matlab, Mathematica, SPlus, and SAS or by using numerical subroutine libraries from the development environment at hand.

However, we have to be careful when using numerical routines as "black boxes." Despite available documentation, it is often very hard to understand exactly what methods and techniques sophisticated numerical subroutines may use. The incorrect usage of numerical software may lead to reduced efficiency, lack of robustness, and loss in accuracy.

We provide some general guidelines and rules of thumb in solving a mathematical programming problem with optimization software below.

The Solution Process

The solution process for solving an optimization problem can be divided into three parts:

- Formulating the problem
- Choosing an optimizer
- Solving the problem with the optimizer.

---

[45] Netlib can be accessed online at http://www.netlib.org.

Formulating the Problem

The first step in solving an optimization problem with numerical software is to identify its type. Sometimes this is straightforward because the problem might already be given in some standard form. However, more often than not this is not the case and the original problem has to be transformed into one of the standard forms. As long as we can transform a particular optimization problem into one of the standard forms, we are all set.

Choosing an Optimizer

When it comes to the choice of optimization algorithms, unfortunately, there is no single technique that is better or outperforms all the others. It is also unrealistic to expect to find one software package that will solve all optimization problems. Different approaches and software packages are often complementary and some are better suited for some problems than others. In practice, it is often recommended to try different algorithms on the same problem to see which one performs best as far as speed, accuracy, and stability are concerned.

Most optimization subroutines are designed to handle prototypical mathematical programs in some standard form. In particular, they handle a class of problems that have certain properties or specific structure. We can think about optimization algorithms for the different standard forms as a toolbox that is applied to solve a particular part of a problem. Indeed, not every problem can be solved with a hammer alone (although a carpenter might think so) but may also require a drill and a screwdriver.

Although it is possible to solve a simple linear program with a nonlinear programming algorithm, this is not necessarily advisable. In general, we can expect more specialized algorithms to solve the problem not just faster but also more accurately.

Constraints Whether a problem is constrained or unconstrained affects the choice of algorithm or technique that is used for its solution. In general, unconstrained optimization is somewhat simpler than constrained optimization. However, the type of constraints also matter. Problems with equality constraints are in general easier to deal with than inequality constraints, as are linear compared to nonlinear constraints.

Derivatives Many optimization routines use derivative information. Thus, it is best if some or all of the first-order derivatives (and sometimes also second-order derivatives) of the objective function and constraints are available analytically. If they are not available, but all the functions involved are differentiable, then the algorithm will have to calculate these derivatives numerically. As a general rule of thumb, if analytic derivatives can be supplied by the user, this will greatly speed-up each iteration. In most instances, analytic derivatives will also increase the numerical stability and accuracy of the algorithm.

Dense versus Sparse and Medium- versus Large-Size Problems When many decision variables are involved (for nonlinear problems more than thousand or tens of thousand, and for linear problems more than hundred thousand), we refer to the problem as a *large-scale optimization problem*. For efficiency reasons, large-scale numerical algorithms try to take advantage of the specific structure in a particular problem. For example, so-called *sparse matrix techniques* are often used if possible, in order to improve the efficiency of the linear algebra type of computations inside the routines.

User Interface and Settings By using one of the standard mathematical programming modeling languages, an optimization problem can be specified on a much higher level (much closer to the original mathematical formulation) than by using a lower level (much further away from the original mathematical formulation) programming language such as C, C++, and Fortran, etc. Furthermore, by making the user interface and the mathematical programming formulation independent of a particular optimizer, we obtain greater flexibility and portability of our model. Portability will make it easier to test the model with different optimizers.

Good optimization software allows the user to specify different options and settings of the algorithms such as the maximum number of iterations or function evaluations allowed, the convergence criteria and tolerances, etc.

Many optimization platforms also provide a pre-optimization phase. During this phase, the problem at hand is analyzed in order to select the best and most suitable algorithm. Normally, there is also software support for checking the correctness of the analytically supplied derivatives by comparing them with numerical approximations.

Solving the Problem with the Optimizer

The final step is solving the problem with the optimizer.

The Starting Vector Some optimizers expect a starting vector. This should be a good guess of the optimal solution. For some problems it is easy to find a natural candidate for a good starting point (for example, sometimes the analytical solution of a simplified problem works well), although in general it can be difficult. For optimizers that provide support in generating a good starting point (often a feasible point is generated), it is in general advisable to let the algorithm choose, unless the user knows that his information is superior. Numerical testing should confirm this.

Monitor Progress Valuable information can be obtained if we monitor the progress of the optimization process. In particular, the number of iterations and function evaluations tell us how quickly the problem is converging. The sizes of constraint and first-order optimality condition violations to some extent convey how far away we are from reaching the optimal point. The sizes of the Lagrange multipliers provide information on which constraints are most binding as well as on the sensitivity of the value of the objective function to the different constraints.

Analyze Results Even if the optimizer converges and produces a solution, we should not blindly believe that the output is correct. The best way to understand how a particular software behaves is through experimentation. Indeed, understanding the behavior of software is necessary in order to make practical decisions regarding algorithm selection and to confirm that the results are valid. It is often a good idea to rerun the optimization with more stringent settings (e.g., smaller tolerances) and evaluate whether the problem still converges. By performing a few reruns, we also should be able to confirm if the optimization converges according to what we expect from theory. If we have several optimizers available, we can compare the results we get from each one. Any discrepancy needs to be fully understood. To make sure that the software is used and is working correctly, it is good practice to begin by solving a simplified problem that has a known analytical solution.

Sometimes we do not know whether our problem has a single or multiple local optimal points. A simple way of checking if there is more than one optimal point is to rerun the optimizer with a number of different starting values. If they all converge to the same solution, then it is likely that we have found the one unique solution.

By having a computer model of our problem, we can test to see how sensitive the outputs are to changes in the inputs. In the case of the mean-variance optimization, we can study how the solution (the optimal solution) changes as we slightly perturb expected return and covariance forecasts. A simple experiment of this kind will show how sensitive our model is to measurement errors in the forecasts.

On a computer, real numbers can only be represented up to a certain level of precision. Beyond a certain point, real numbers have to be rounded. Therefore, a certain amount of information (or precision) is lost when operations are performed with real numbers. In most practical circumstances, rounding errors are not an issue. When dealing with poorly scaled and ill-conditioned problems, however, we need to keep in mind that errors due to rounding may have an effect.

Some Important Numerical Issues

In this section we elaborate more on some common pitfalls in the usage of numerical software. In particular, we discuss (1) scaling and ill-conditioning, and (2) the importance of smoothness and differentiability of the objective and constraint functions for optimization routines that rely upon derivative information.

Scaling and Ill-Conditioning

In numerical computations, the performance and accuracy of an algorithm may be affected by how the particular problem formulation is *scaled*. An optimization problem is poorly scaled if changes to the decision variable produce large changes to the objective or constraint functions for some components and not for others. For example, in the case of the function

$$f(\mathbf{x}) = (x_1 \ x_2) \begin{pmatrix} 10^2 & 10^{-9} \\ 10^{-9} & 10^{-8} \end{pmatrix} \begin{pmatrix} x_1 \\ x_2 \end{pmatrix}$$

changes in x_1 have a much larger effect than changes in x_2. Some optimization techniques such as steepest descent are very sensitive to poor scaling, whereas Newton-based methods normally handle poor scaling better. Well-designed algorithms and software will automatically rescale the original problem if scaling has an effect upon the method used.

Another problem that can be encountered in numerical computations is that of *ill-conditioning*. An optimization problem is well-conditioned if small changes in the in-data (the data that define the problem) only lead to small or minor changes in the out-data (the solution). In contrast, if this is not the case the problem is said to be ill-conditioned.

A First Example of Ill-Conditioning   The problem

$$\min_{\mathbf{x}} \frac{1}{2}\mathbf{x}'\mathbf{A}\mathbf{x} - \mathbf{x}'\mathbf{b}$$

with

$$\mathbf{A} = \begin{pmatrix} 1 & 1 \\ 1 & 1.0001 \end{pmatrix} \quad \text{and} \quad \mathbf{b} = \begin{pmatrix} 0.5 \\ 0.5 \end{pmatrix}$$

has the solution $\mathbf{x} = (0.5\ 0)'$. However, if we instead take

$$\mathbf{b} = \begin{pmatrix} 0.5 \\ 0.5001 \end{pmatrix}$$

(i.e., changing be the second component of the original $\mathbf{b}$ by only 0.02%), then the solution is $\mathbf{x} = (-0.5\ 1)'$. The reason for this is that the matrix $\mathbf{A}$ is ill-conditioned (its condition number is about 40,000— the condition number of a symmetric matrix is defined as the ratio of the largest to the smallest eigenvalue) and close to being singular. Although this example is highly simplified, this type of situation is not uncommon in portfolio optimization with highly correlated assets. We discuss some of these issues and their mitigation in Chapters 8 and 9.

A Second Example of Ill-Conditioning   Optimization problems with equality constraints can be recast as unconstrained problems by augmenting the objective function with a penalty function that includes the constraints. For example, the optimization problem

$$\min_{\mathbf{x}} f(\mathbf{x})$$

$$s.t.\ h_i(\mathbf{x}) = 0, \quad i = 1, \dots, I$$

can be rewritten as a constrained problem using the *quadratic penalty approach*

$$\min_{\mathbf{x}} F_\lambda(\mathbf{x}) = f(\mathbf{x}) + \frac{1}{2\lambda}\sum_i h_i^2(\mathbf{x})$$

where $\lambda > 0$ is the *penalty parameter*. As λ is chosen smaller and smaller, the penalty from unsatisfied constraints becomes larger and larger. Some problems can be treated efficiently in this manner by solving a sequence of problems $F_{\lambda_k}(\mathbf{x})$, where each λ_k is chosen such that $\lambda_k \le \lambda_{k-1}$. However, unless special techniques are used, often this type of approach runs into ill-conditioning problems when λ_k becomes small. Specifically, the Hessian $\nabla^2 F_{\lambda_k}(\mathbf{x})$, becomes ill-conditioned near the optimal solution, which might result in poor convergence or no convergence at all. In these cases, it is normally better to treat the constraints explicitly and not through the penalty approach.

Smoothness and Differentiability

Many optimization routines use derivative information, such as for example, first and sometimes also second order derivatives of the objective and constraint functions. If some function in the problem is nondifferentiable at some point, we might no longer be able to use a derivative-based routine.

In theory, there is nothing that prevents a nonsmooth convex program from being solved as efficiently as a smooth one, say, for example with interior-point techniques.[46] However, the performance of many standard optimization packages decreases for nonsmooth and nondifferentiable problems. Some very common nondifferentiable functions are the absolute value and the many different kinds of norms. If possible, it is recommended that points of nondifferentiability be eliminated by using Boolean variables.

Transformations of this sort are problem specific and not always straightforward. For example, the function

$$f(x) = \begin{cases} cx + d, & \text{if } x > 0 \\ 0, & \text{if } x = 0 \end{cases}$$

where $c, d > 0$, sometimes occurs in transaction cost models incorporating both fixed and proportional costs. The minimization of this function can be replaced by a mixed-integer linear program (MILP) by the introduction of the integer variable z, $0 \leq z \leq 1$, where z is equal to 1 whenever $x > 0$. The MILP would take the form

$$\min_x cx + dz$$

$$s.t. \ x \leq Uz$$
$$0 \leq z \leq 1, \text{ integer}$$

where U is some upper bound on x.

---

[46] Iu E. Nesterov, Arkadii Nemirovsky, and Yurii Nesterov, *Interior-Point Polynomial Algorithms in Convex Programming: Theory and Algorithms*, vol. 13 of Studies in Applied Mathematics (Philadelphia: Society of Industrial and Applied Mathematics Publications, 1993).

SUMMARY

- An optimization problem consists of three basic components: (1) an objective function, (2) a set of unknown (decision) variables, and (3) a set of constraints.
- A point is feasible if it satisfies all the constraints of the optimization problem. Otherwise, it is unfeasible.
- We distinguish between local and global solutions. If there is more than one local solution, most optimization algorithms will find one local solution that is not necessarily the global solution.
- Optimization problems are categorized according to the form of the objective function and the functions defining the constraints. Some examples of common optimization problems are linear programming, quadratic programming, convex programming, and nonlinear programming.
- For convex programs, a local optimal solution is also the global optimal solution.
- When the decision variables are not continuous but allowed to take on discrete values, the resulting optimization problem is referred to as a combinatorial, discrete or integer programming problem.
- The gradient condition is a necessary condition for a local optimal solution for continuous unconstrained optimization problems. The Karush-Kuhn-Tucker conditions are necessary conditions for a local optimal solution for continuous constrained optimization problems.
- Most optimization algorithms are iterative in nature. The number of iterations taken by an algorithm is determined by the convergence or stopping criteria.
- Today, linear problems with tens or hundreds of thousands of continuous variables can be solved efficiently. The tractable size of linear integer programs is around hundreds or thousands of variables.
- There are two basic approaches to solving linear problems: simplex methods and interior-point methods.
- Newton-type methods are common for solving unconstrained nonlinear problems. For constrained nonlinear problems, modern interior-point methods and sequential quadratic programming can be used.
- Combinatorial and integer programs are solved by branch and bound, branch and cut, disjunctive programming, special-purpose heuristics, and cutting planes techniques.
- Choosing and purchasing optimization software is often a costly and time-consuming process. While some solvers work better for a certain type of problem than others, often the only way to find out how well a solver works for a particular problem is through testing.

■ The solution process for solving an optimization problem has three parts: (1) formulating the problem, (2) choosing an optimizer, and (3) solving the problem with the optimizer.

■ In numerical calculations it is important to be aware of issues with poor scaling and ill-conditioning.

Managing Uncertainty in Practice

Equity Price Models

This chapter introduces a number of models for asset returns, considering time series in discrete time. The objective of the chapter is to introduce basic concepts in time series analysis and to develop some intuition for basic time series models, in particular random walk models and trend stationary models, describing some of their key properties.

DEFINITIONS

We begin our discussion of equity price models by introducing some definitions and fixing some notations. A financial *time series in discrete time* is a sequence of financial variables such as asset prices or returns observed at discrete points in time, for example, the end of a trading day or the last trading day of a month. Most models that we will consider in this book assume that the spacing between points is fixed, for example, models of daily returns assume that returns are observed between consecutive trading days. In order to recover fixed spacing between time points due to weekends, holidays or periods when trading is suspended, a sequence of trading days different from the sequence of calendar days is typically introduced. When dealing with international markets, special care is required as holidays and periods of suspension of trading might be different in different markets.

Not all financial variables can be represented with the fixed periodicity described here. For instance, in most markets intraday trades are randomly spaced as trading occurs when the correct match between buy and sell orders is found. When considering high frequency data (i.e., data related to individual trades) the assumption of periodic, fixed discrete time points must be abandoned.

191

Consider a time series of prices P_t of a financial asset, where t is a discrete sequence of points. Assume that there are no dividend payouts. The *simple net return* of an asset between periods $t - 1$ and t is defined as the percentage change of its price:

$$R_t = \frac{P_t - P_{t-1}}{P_{t-1}} = \frac{P_t}{P_{t-1}} - 1$$

The *gross return* is defined as

gross
return

$$1 + R_t = \frac{P_t}{P_{t-1}}$$

For example, if the closing price of a stock at the end of a given trading day is $10.00 and goes to $11.00 at the end of the following trading day, the simple net return of that stock in that day is 0.1 or 10%. The gross return is the ratio of prices in subsequent periods, equal to 1.1 in the above example.

From this definition it is clear that the *compound return* $R_t(k)$ over k periods is

$$R_t(k) = \frac{P_t}{P_{t-k}} - 1 = \frac{P_t}{P_{t-1}} \frac{P_{t-1}}{P_{t-2}} \cdots \frac{P_{t-k+1}}{P_{t-k}} - 1 = \prod_{i=0}^{k-1} (R_{t-i} + 1) - 1$$

or

$$R_t(k) + 1 = \prod_{i=0}^{k-1} (R_{t-i} + 1)$$

If there are dividend payouts, they must be added to the price change. For example, suppose that there is a dividend payout D_t made just prior to the moment when the price P_t is observed. The simple net return then becomes

$$R_t = \frac{P_t + D_t}{P_{t-1}} - 1$$

Note that the moment in which prices are observed is critical: asset prices change after dividends are paid. All other returns can be computed accordingly.

Now consider the logarithms of prices and returns:

$$p_t = \log P_t$$

The *log return* is defined as the natural logarithm of the gross return:

$$r_t = \log(1 + R_t)$$

Following standard usage, we denote prices and returns with upper case letters and their logarithms with lower case letters. As the logarithm of a product is the sum of the logarithms, we can write

$$r_t = \log(1 + R_t) = \log\frac{P_t}{P_{t-1}} = p_t - p_{t-1}$$

$$r_t(k) = \log(1 + R_t(k)) = r_t + \ldots + r_{t-k+1}$$

Note that for real-world price time series, if the time interval is small, the numerical value of returns will also be small. Therefore, as a first approximation, we can write

$$r_t = \log(1 + R_t) \approx R_t$$

THEORETICAL AND ECONOMETRIC MODELS

A model of returns is a mathematical representation of returns. In finance theory, different types of models are considered. There are models that represent the time evolution of returns and models that represent relationships between the returns of different assets at any given moment. The former is exemplified by a random walk model, the latter by conditions of no-arbitrage. The distinction is important because models that represent the time evolution of assets can be used to make probabilistic forecasts starting from initial conditions.

Financial models are *approximate* models, not only in the sense that they are probabilistic models but also in the sense that the probability distributions assumed in the models are idealizations of reality and therefore never completely accurate. As a consequence, many different

If the market is efficient then there is no possibility for arbitrage, → information for contracting -

models might compete to describe the same phenomena. Consider also that financial time series have only one realization. This fact poses severe restrictions on selecting and testing financial models as we will see in Chapter 14, on model estimation.

There might be a trade-off between accuracy and the span of life of a model insofar as different models, or the same model but with different parameters, might apply to the same variables in different periods. When estimating time-varying models, a time window for estimation has to be determined with appropriate criteria as we will see in Chapter 13.

We can also make a distinction between (1) models that are based on theoretical economic considerations and (2) models that are econometric hypotheses. Theoretical models include the general equilibrium theories, the *Capital Asset Pricing Model* (CAPM), and arbitrage pricing theories; econometric models include the random walk and multifactor models.

While it can be said that econometric models lack a theoretical basis, some qualification is required. In principle, an econometric hypothesis has the status of an economic theory; however, with a sufficient number of parameters, an econometric hypothesis can fit any data set with arbitrary accuracy. This is the major potential weakness. Because econometric models contain an arbitrary number of parameters (and, therefore, can fit any finite set of data), complementary principles from the theory of learning are required to constrain these models. In the next section, we introduce a basic and fundamental model, the random walk.

RANDOM WALK MODELS

The *random walk model* is a basic model of stock prices based on the assumption of market efficiency. The basic idea is that returns can be represented as unforecastable fluctuations around some mean return. This assumption implies that the distribution of the returns at time t is independent from, or at least uncorrelated with, the distribution of returns in previous moments.

There are several different random walk models which we describe below.[1]

Simple Random Walk Model

To gain an understanding of the random walk, let us first consider one type of random walk. Suppose that a sequence of discrete, equally

---

[1] The random walk model applies to many phenomena in economics as well as the social and physical sciences. We restrict our discussion to random walk models of asset prices.

spaced instants of time is given. Suppose that at every instant a stock price can only go up or down by a fixed amount Δ with probability ½ independent of previous steps. The price movement is an idealized representation of a pure random path. This type of random walk model is called *a simple random walk*.

Arithmetic Random Walk Model

The up or down price movement at each step can be represented as a *Bernoulli variable*. A Bernoulli variable is a random variable that can assume only two values, which we represent conventionally as 0 and 1, with probabilities p and $q = 1 - p$. The two values can represent outcomes such as success or failure, up and down, and so on. Consider a sample of n trials of a Bernoulli variable. The distribution of 0s and 1s follows a binomial distribution:

$$P(k \text{ zeros in } n \text{ trials}) = \binom{n}{k} p^k q^{n-k} = \frac{n!}{k!(n-k)!} p^k q^{n-k}$$

Central Limit Thm

For large n, the binomial distribution can be approximated by a normal distribution.

Call P_t the price after t steps; P_0 is the initial price where the random walk starts. The difference $P_t - P_0$ is the sum of t independent Bernoulli variables. It can assume discrete values:

$$P_t - P_0 = -t\Delta + 2m\Delta; \quad m = 0, 1, ..., t$$

in the range $[-t\Delta, +t\Delta]$. For example, at time $t = 1$ the price can assume only one of two values $P_0 - \Delta$; $P_0 + \Delta$, at time $t = 2$ the price can assume only one of three values $P_0 - 2\Delta$, P_0, $P_0 + 2\Delta$, and so on. Note that the price P_t can be equal at the starting price P_0 only at even numbers of steps: 0, 2, 4, ... The distribution of the sum of independent Bernoulli variables is called a *binomial distribution*. The binomial distribution can be written explicitly as

$$P(P_t - P_0 = -t\Delta + 2m\Delta) = \binom{t}{m}; \quad m = 0, 1, ..., t$$

After a sufficiently large number of steps, the Bernoulli distribution is well approximated by a normal distribution. Therefore, we can now generalize the simple random walk assuming that at each time step an asset price P_t moves up or down by an amount that follows a normal probability distribution with mean μ. The movement of the price P_t is called an *arithmetic random walk with drift*. Under this model, prices move up or down at each time step according to a normal distribution, independent from previous prices:

$$P_t - P_{t-1} = \mu + \eta_t$$

where η_t is a normal white noise term.

Strict white noise or *strong white noise* is defined as a sequence of *independent and identically distributed* (IID) random variables with zero mean and finite variance. A weaker definition of white noise is often given. According to this weaker definition, a weak white noise is a sequence of zero-mean, finite-variance uncorrelated variables. A weak white noise is often called simply a white noise. Note, however, that if noise is normally distributed the above distinction is useless. In fact, two normal variables are uncorrelated if and only if they are independent.

Suppose that noise is distributed as an IID sequence of zero-mean normal variables with variance σ^2. It is convenient to write the random walk model as follows:

$$\Delta P_t = P_t - P_{t-1} = \mu + \sigma \varepsilon_t$$

where ε_t is a sequence of IID normal variables with zero mean and unitary variance. The term μ is called the *drift*, the term σ is called the *volatility*.

We can see, therefore, that there are different possible definitions of random walks. An arithmetic random walk with normal increments is a model where the value of the price variable at time t is equal to the value at time $t - 1$ plus a constant (the drift) plus a totally unforecastable (i.e., independent from the past) normally distributed noise term. However, we can also define a random walk with nonnormal, uncorrelated increments. This type of random walk is not completely unforecastable. In fact, white noise with nonnormal uncorrelated terms exhibits some residual forecastability.[2]

Consider an arithmetic random walk with normal increments. From the above formulas we can immediately write

$$P_t = P_0 + t\mu + \sum_{i=1}^{t} \eta_i$$

---

[2] See Clive Granger and Paul Newbold, *Forecasting Economic Time Series: Second Edition* (New York: Academic Press, 1986).

From the same formula, we see that a realization of an arithmetic random walk can be thought of as being formed by the sum of two terms: a deterministic straight line $P_t = P_0 + t\mu$ plus the sum of all past noises, that is,

$$\sum_{i=1}^{t} \eta_i$$

As we will see in Chapter 12, every realization of a linear model can be thought of as the sum of a deterministic model which is the solution of the deterministic linear model plus the weighted sum of past noise. In the case of arithmetic random walks, the noise weights are all equal to one. Exhibit 7.1 provides a graphical illustration of one realization of an arithmetic random walk p with daily drift $\sigma = 0.00027$ and daily volatility $\sigma = 0.022$. Assuming that the variable p is the logarithm of a stock price process P, the daily drift and volatility correspond to a 7% yearly return and a 35% yearly volatility for the stock price process P.

EXHIBIT 7.1 One Realization of an Arithmetic Random Walk with $\mu = 0.00027$ and $\sigma = 0.022$ over 10,000 Days

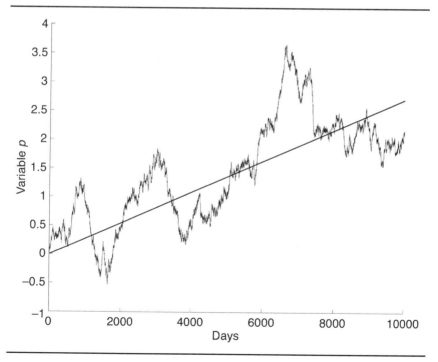

A number of observations are in order:

- In the arithmetic random walk random shocks (i.e., the noise terms) never decay, as in every moment the price level is affected by the sum of all past shocks, each with weight 1.
- Prices make "excursions" around the straight line $P_t = P_0 + t\mu$. This means that they depart from the straight line, meander, and then cross it again.
- These excursions are not periodic. They have neither a mean finite length nor a mean finite height. In other words, although a random walk crosses the straight line $P_t = P_0 + t\mu$ with probability one, the average time for crossing is infinite.
- Over a sufficiently long period of time, any parallel to the line $P_t = P_0 + t\mu$, however distant, will be crossed.
- In the arithmetic random walk model of prices, both the mean and the variance grow linearly with time. In fact, at time t, the mean of the prices is the deterministic term $P_t = P_0 + t\mu$ while the variance σ_t^2 is the sum of t terms:

$$\sum_{i=1}^{t} \varepsilon_i$$

whose variance is t times the variance of each term, $\sigma_t^2 = t\sigma^2$.

- As a consequence of the previous observation, the standard deviation of prices grows with the square root of time. In the presence of a positive drift, the ratio of the standard deviation and the mean of prices tend to zero. In the limit of infinite time, the risk associated with an arithmetic random walk process for prices becomes arbitrarily small.
- The assumption of normally distributed increments is not fundamentally limitative as long as noise is an IID sequence. In fact, the sum of finite-mean, finite-variance variables is asymptotically normal.

Geometric Random Walk Model

The arithmetic random walk model for prices has several drawbacks. First, it allows prices to become negative. In fact, as the normal variable extends from $-\infty$ to $+\infty$, the sum of random shocks can assume any real value. By appropriately choosing the drift and the volatility, the probability of negative prices can be made arbitrarily small. However, the probability of negative prices will never be zero. Negative prices could be prevented by setting "absorbing barriers" in the random walk models. An absorbing barrier in a time series model is a straight line placed at a given value such that the model stops if it crosses the barriers. In price models, these barriers can represent bankruptcies. However, in this way the random walk model looses its simplicity.

Second, the arithmetic random walk model conflicts with the empirical fact that the average size of price fluctuations grows with time. Over long periods of time, asset prices grow but so do fluctuations. Only price percentage changes seem to remain stationary. We could therefore assume that simple net returns are an IID sequence. Under this assumption, we can therefore write the following equation:

$$R_t = \frac{P_t - P_{t-1}}{P_{t-1}} = \mu + \eta_t$$

where η_t is a white noise term. If noise is distributed as a zero-mean normal variable with variance σ^2, we can write

$$R_t = \frac{P_t - P_{t-1}}{P_{t-1}} = \mu + \sigma \varepsilon_t$$

where ε_t is a sequence of independent normal variables with zero-mean and unitary variance.

The above random walk is called a *geometric random walk with drift*. It is a nonlinear model of prices as the noise term multiplies the price variable. In the geometric random walk, noise terms feed back into the process multiplicatively. Using the expression for the gross compound return we can represent prices as the product of gross returns:

$$P_t = \left(\frac{P_t}{P_{t-1}} \frac{P_{t-1}}{P_{t-2}} \cdots \frac{P_1}{P_0} \right) P_0 = \left(\prod_{i=0}^{t-1} (R_{t-i} + 1) \right) P_0$$

Exhibit 7.2 represents 10 realizations of a geometric random walk with $\mu = 0.00027$ and $\sigma = 0.022$ over 2,500 days that correspond approximately to 10 years.

Lognormal Model

The distribution of prices is a product of normal distributions; it is not a normal distribution itself. This is a major drawback of the geometric random walk model in discrete time. To avoid this problem, let us consider the logarithm of prices. Recall from the definitions given above

EXHIBIT 7.2   Ten Independent Realizations of a Geometric Random Walk with μ = 0.00027 and σ = 0.022 over 2,500 Days[a]

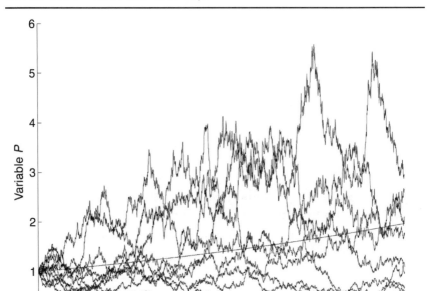

[a] The exponential line represents the process mean.

that the log returns are the differences of log prices. Now assume that log returns can be represented as an arithmetic random walk:

$$r_t = p_t - p_{t-1} = \mu + \varepsilon_t$$

If noise is distributed as a zero-mean normal variable with variance σ^2, we can also write

$$r_t = p_t - p_{t-1} = \sigma\varepsilon_t, \ \varepsilon_t \approx N_t(0, 1), \ E(\varepsilon_t\varepsilon_s) = 0 \text{ for } t \neq s$$

As $r_t = \log(1 + R_t)$, if log returns are normally distributed, simple gross returns are lognormally distributed. A random variable z is called lognormal if its logarithm $x = \log z$ is normally distributed. It can be demonstrated that if (μ, σ^2) are, respectively, the mean and the variance of x then the mean and the variance of z are, respectively,

$$\left(e^{\left(\mu + \frac{\sigma^2}{2}\right)}, e^{(2\mu + \sigma^2)}(e^{\sigma^2} - 1) \right)$$

If log returns are independent normal variables, log prices evolve as an arithmetic random walk. The prices themselves evolve as a geometric random walk but with lognormal increments. The mean of prices is an exponential:

$$P_t = P_0 e^{\left(\mu + \frac{\sigma^2}{2}\right)t}$$

Exhibits 7.3a and 7.3b represent 10 realizations of an arithmetic random walk for log prices and the corresponding ten realizations of prices.

EXHIBIT 7.3a Ten Realizations of an Arithmetic Random Walk for the Log Price Process[a]

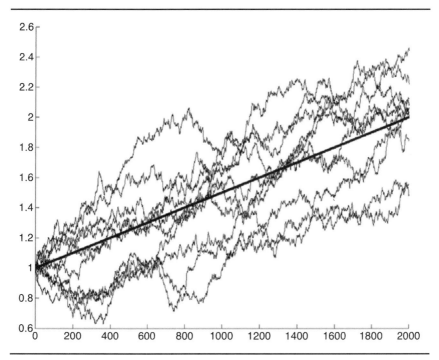

[a] As in Exhibit 7.2, if one time period corresponds to a day, the exhibit represents approximately eight years.

EXHIBIT 7.3b   Ten Realizations of the Price Process Corresponding to the Log Price Process of Exhibit 7.3a[a]

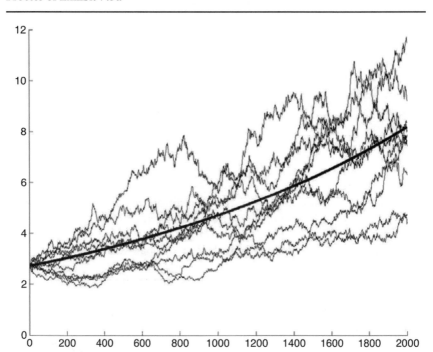

[a] Note the effect of compounding.

The effect of compounding of returns over very long periods is illustrated in Exhibits 7.4a and 7.4b; these represent respectively 10 realizations of an arithmetic random walk for log returns and the corresponding ten realizations of the price process over 10,000 time steps.

The assumption of normality of log returns is not required to justify the lognormal model. In fact, if the distribution of log returns is a nonnormal distribution with bounded variance, the sum of log returns will tend to a normally distributed variable. This is a key result of probability theory known as the *Central Limit Theorem* (CLT). The CLT can be stated in various ways. The Lindeberg-Levy form of the CLT, which suffices for our purpose, can be stated as follows. Suppose that X_t is a sequence of IID random variables with finite mean and variance (μ, σ^2), we can thus define the empirical mean:

$$\bar{X} = \frac{1}{T}\sum_t X_t$$

EXHIBIT 7.4a   Ten Realizations of an Arithmetic Random Walk for Log Return over 10,000 Steps

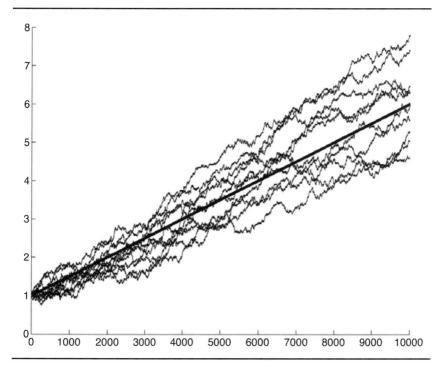

Then, the following relationship holds:

$$\frac{\overline{X} - \mu}{\sigma \sqrt{T}} \overset{D}{\Rightarrow} W \sim N(0, 1)$$

This result entails that if log returns are independent then the log return process is asymptotically normal. Stated differently, the log return process is approximately normal if we consider log returns on sufficiently long time intervals.

It should be clearly stated that the above does not imply that price processes are always asymptotically random walks. First, the CLT can be generalized to *independently distributed* (ID) processes (i.e., processes that have bounded but time-varying means and variances); however, additional conditions are required. Second, if the sequence X_t shows autocorrelation, the asymptotic validity of the CLT hinges on whether correlations decay sufficiently fast. If autocorrelations exhibit

EXHIBIT 7.4b   Ten Realizations of a Price Process Corresponding to the Log Price Processes in Exhibit H.4a

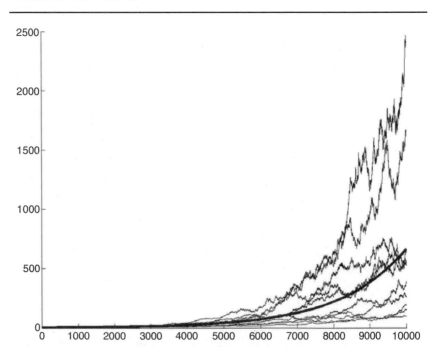

slow decay, the CLT does not hold. Ultimately, if the X_t variables have infinite variance, the CLT holds in a totally different form. In a nutshell, if log returns are either correlated or time-varying, two phenomena occur: (1) There can be short-term deviations from the lognormal behavior which might result in profit opportunities; and (2) the asymptotic behavior of the X_t sequence hinges on the asymptotic behavior of the autocorrelations and the time-dependence of means and variances.

In all these random walk models, the lack of forecastability means that the past does not influence the future. This statement should not be confused with the statement that the random walk model does not convey information. Actually, the information conveyed by a random walk model within a given time horizon can be arbitrarily high if the volatility is arbitrarily small.[3] However, the assumption of normally distributed noise terms entails fundamental simplifications when dealing with financial portfolios.

---

[3] This statement can be made precise within the theory of information. See Chapter 17.

Multivariate Random Walk

The models discussed so far are models of univariate price series, that is, they model any given individual price series independently from other price series. A model of this type is too simple to be empirically acceptable. If asset price series were independent random walks, then large portfolios would be fully diversified and therefore nearly deterministic. Empirically, this is not the case. Even large aggregates of stock prices, for example the S&P 500, exhibit random behavior.

This fact entails that there are mutual dependencies between returns or between log returns. If returns or log returns are jointly normally distributed, then dependencies can be fully accounted for by linear correlation coefficients.

This is not to say that the covariance matrix is able to capture *in full generality* the dependencies in a return process. First, correlations at lagged times (i.e., correlations of a dynamic nature) are not captured by the static covariance or correlation matrices. Second, there are forms of nonlinear dependency that are not captured by covariances and correlations. Alternative tools include *copula functions* (see Appendix B) and *transfer entropies* (see Chapter 17). Here we simply state that in the restricted case of a normal multivariate random walk, the covariance matrix captures all dependencies as all the process distributions—being normal multivariate distributions—can be fully expressed in terms of a vector of means and the covariance matrix.

Multivariate random walk models are fully described by a vector of means and by the variance-covariance matrix. Consider, for instance, a multivariate random walk model for log prices. Suppose there are n log price processes. In this case, log returns are a sequence of independent multivariate normal variables. In vector-matrix notation, the model is written as

$$\mathbf{r}_t = \mathbf{p}_t - \mathbf{p}_{t-1} = \mathbf{\mu} + \mathbf{\varepsilon}_t$$

where $\mathbf{r}_t$ is the n-vector of log returns, $\mathbf{p}_t$ is the n-vector of prices, $\mathbf{\mu} = (\mu, ..., \mu_n)$ is the n-vector of mean returns, and $\mathbf{\varepsilon}_t$ is a sequence of independent zero-mean, normal n-vectors with covariance matrix $[\sigma_{ij}]$.

If we consider a large number of assets—for example, all the assets in a universe such as the S&P 500 or the MSCI—the variance-covariance matrix has a huge number of entries. In order to reduce the dimensionality of multivariate random walk models, simplifications are called for, and factor models are an effective way to reduce the complexity. As we discuss in Chapter 14, model complexity has to be reduced to make estimates robust, not for computational reasons. A multifactor model of returns can be written in the following general form:

$$r_i(t) = \mu_i + \sum_{i=1}^{N} \beta_{i,j} f_j(t) + \varepsilon_i(t)$$

where the $f_j(t)$ are the factors and the $\beta_{i,j}$ are constants called *factor loadings* and the ε_i are zero-mean noise terms. Factors are multivariate random walks. If the noise terms satisfy the additional condition $E[\varepsilon_i(t)\varepsilon_j(t)] = 0$, the covariance structure of the model depends uniquely on the covariance structure of the factors.

Stationary and Trend-Stationary Models

Both the Geometric Random Walk and the Arithmetic Random Walk are models of *unpredictable* processes with time-varying variance. In this sense, they differ from stationary processes, which are characterized by constant variance and which can exhibit autocorrelation and dependence at different time lags.

Stationarity can be defined with varying degrees of strength. The strongest definition of stationarity requires that all finite dimensional distributions are invariant after time translation. According to this definition, a process $x(t)$ is called *strictly stationary* if

$$f(t_1, ..., t_n) = f(t_1 + \tau, ..., t_n + \tau), \forall \tau, \forall n, \forall (t_1, ..., t_n)$$

where f is any finite-dimensional distribution.

This definition is often too strong and is replaced by the weaker definition of *covariance stationarity.*[4] A process $x(t)$ is said to be covariance-stationary if

$$\text{mean}(x(t)) = \mu = \text{constant}, \forall t$$
$$\text{var}(x(t)) = \sigma^2 = \text{constant}, \forall t$$
$$\text{cov}(x(t), x(t + \tau)) = \lambda(\tau), \forall t$$

---

[4] In the econometric literature a strictly stationary process is sometimes called a *strongly stationary process* and a covariance stationary process is sometimes called a *weakly stationary process* or simply a *stationary process.* A covariance stationary process is sometimes also called a *second order stationary process* because second order moments are involved. It is possible to define a *l-th order stationary process* if all the joint *l*-th order moments are time invariant.

Consider a process $x(t)$ of the following form:

$$x(t) = \mu + \eta(t)$$

where $\eta(t)$ is a zero-mean stationary process. A process of this type is mean-reverting. Suppose that at time t the process assumes the value $x(t) \neq \mu$. The expectation at time $t + 1$ is μ. Simply stated, this means that a stationary process tends to revert to its mean. This is the case even if the process $\eta(t)$ is formed by a sequence of IID variables. This property is called the *regression effect*. Note that the regression effect of returns cannot in itself be exploited to earn a profit.[5] The ability to earn a profit would require true forecastability (i.e., conditional dependence) and not simply the regression effect. However, if *prices* were subject to a regression effect, returns would be forecastable; as a result excess gains could be realized.

A trend stationary process is a process of the following form:

$$x(t) = \mu(t) + \eta(t)$$

where $\mu(t)$ is a deterministic function and $\eta(t)$ is a zero-mean stationary process.

Returns are assumed to be stationary processes. While individual asset prices are not (in general) stationary, portfolios might have stationary values. We will see this in our discussion of cointegration in Chapter 12.

GENERAL EQUILIBRIUM THEORIES

General Equilibrium Theories[6] (GETs) are global mathematical models of an economy. They are based on two key principles:

---

[5] This statement needs qualification. The knowledge of the mean would indeed allow one to earn a profit if the mean is sufficiently high (or low if short selling is allowed). However, asset pricing theories constrain the mean to assume values that do not allow excess profit after adjusting for risk.

[6] The empirical adequacy of GETs has been questioned repeatedly. There are two key issues: (1) It was demonstrated by Harrison and Kreps that, in absence of arbitrage, any price process can be rationalized as a GET and (2) there is scant empirical evidence that GETs work in practice when specific utility functions are assumed. These questions are beyond the scope of this book. See Michael Harrison and David M. Kreps, "Martingale and Arbitrage in Multiperiod Securities Markets," *Journal of Economic Theory* 30 (1979), pp. 381–408.

■ Supply/demand equilibrium
■ Agent optimality

Let's consider the application of GETs to the problem of asset pricing. Consider an economy formed by agents that, at each time step, decide, within their budget constraints, the composition of their investment portfolio and the amount they consume. Suppose that agents are able to make a probabilistic forecast of dividends and prices, that is, suppose that each agent knows the joint probability distribution of prices for all future moments and all assets. Agents can order their preferences as regards consumption quantitatively through a utility function. We will consider a utility function as a numerical function of consumption. In Chapter 2 we defined the concept in more detail.

Each agent is characterized by a utility function. As prices are random variables, the utility function is a random variable. Agent decision making is characterized by the principle that each agent maximizes the expected value of his or her utility, choosing the portfolio that maximizes the expected utility derived by the stream of consumption. GETs apply to both finite and infinite time horizons. In the finite case, final wealth coincides with final consumption; in the infinite case, utility is defined over an infinite stream of consumption. The maximization of expected final wealth without intermediate consumption is a special case of maximizing a stream of consumption.

The quantity demanded and supplied depends on the price and dividend processes. In equilibrium, asset supply and demand originated by different agents must match. GETs seeks the price process that maximizes agent utility under equilibrium constraints.

The mathematical details of GETs are complex. The existence and uniqueness of the equilibrium solution is a delicate mathematical problem. A full treatment of GETs is well beyond the scope of this book. In the next section, however, we will discuss CAPM, the simplest example of GET.

CAPITAL ASSET PRICING MODEL (CAPM)

In Chapter 2 we introduced mean-variance portfolio selection. The Capital Asset Pricing Model is an equilibrium asset pricing model that hinges on mean-variance portfolio selection. The CAPM is an abstraction of the real-world capital markets based on the following assumptions:

■ Investors make investment decisions based on the expected return and variance of returns.
■ Investors are rational and risk-averse.

■ Investors subscribe to the Markowitz method of portfolio diversification.
■ Investors all invest for the same period of time.
■ Investors have the same expectations about the expected return and variance of all assets.
■ There is a risk-free asset and investors can borrow or lend any amount at the risk-free rate.
■ Capital markets are (perfectly) competitive and frictionless.

The first five assumptions deal with the way investors make decisions. The last two assumptions relate to characteristics of the capital market. All investors are assumed to make investment decisions over some single-period investment horizon. The CAPM is essentially a static relationship which, per se, does not imply a dynamics. Asset price dynamics must be added. The usual assumption is that returns are serially independent, that is, prices are random walks.

A risk-averse investor who makes decisions based on expected return and variance should construct an efficient portfolio using a combination of the market portfolio and the risk-free rate. The combinations are identified by the Capital Market Line. Based on this result, Sharpe derived an asset pricing model that shows how a risky asset should be priced. A powerful implication is that the appropriate risk that investors should be compensated for accepting is not the variance of an asset's return but some other quantity. Now we determine this risk measure.

First, we need to introduce the notion of *systematic* and *unsystematic risk*. Suppose asset returns are multivariate normal. We can leave undecided whether returns are simple net returns or log returns. Consider a portfolio P consisting of N assets; call w_i the weight of asset i in portfolio P. As w_i is the percentage of asset i in P,

$$\sum_{i=1}^{N} w_i = 1$$

The variance of portfolio P is

$$\text{var}(R_P) = \sum_{i=1}^{N} \sum_{j=1}^{N} w_i w_j \text{cov}(R_i, R_j)$$

If we substitute M (market portfolio) for P and denote by w_{iM} and w_{jM} the proportion invested in asset i and j in the market portfolio, then the above equation can be rewritten as

$$\text{var}(R_M) = \sum_{i=1}^{N}\sum_{j=1}^{N} w_{iM}w_{jM}\text{cov}(R_i, R_j)$$

Collecting terms, the above equation can be expressed as follows:

$$\text{var}(R_M) = w_{1M}\sum_{j=1}^{N} w_{jM}\text{cov}(R_1, R_j) + w_{2M}\sum_{j=1}^{N} w_{jM}\text{cov}(R_2, R_j)$$
$$+ \dots + w_{NM}\sum_{j=1}^{N} w_{NM}\text{cov}(R_N, R_j)$$

Given the linearity of the covariance, the covariance of asset i with the market portfolio is expressed as follows:

$$\text{cov}(R_i, R_M) = \sum_{j=1}^{N} w_{jM}\text{cov}(R_i, R_j)$$

Substituting the right-hand side of the left-hand side of the equation into the prior equation gives

$$\text{var}(R_M) = w_{1M}\text{cov}(R_1, R_M) + w_{2M}\text{cov}(R_2, R_M)$$
$$+ \dots + w_{NM}\sum_{j=1}^{N} w_{jM}\text{cov}(R_N, R_j)$$

Notice how the market portfolio variance can be represented as a function solely of the covariances of each asset with the market portfolio. Sharpe defines the degree to which an asset covaries with the market portfolio as the asset's *systematic risk*. More specifically, he defines systematic risk as the portion of an asset's variability that can be attributed to a common factor. Systematic risk is the minimum level of market risk that can be obtained for a portfolio by means of diversification across a large number of randomly chosen assets. As such, systematic risk is the risk that results from general market and economic conditions that cannot be diversified away. Sharpe defines the portion of an asset's variability that can be diversified away as *nonsystematic risk*. It is also sometimes called *unsystematic risk*, *diversifiable risk*, *unique risk*, *residual risk*, and *company-specific risk*. This is the risk that is unique to an asset.

Consequently, total risk (as measured by the variance) can be partitioned into systematic risk as measured by the covariance of asset i's return with the market portfolio's return and nonsystematic risk. The relevant risk is the systematic risk. The portfolio size needed to achieve diversification depends on market conditions. For example, during the TMT bubble this number significantly increased. The existence of systematic and unsystematic risk is a general property of large portfolios of assets subject to long-range correlations. In the absence of long-range correlations, there would not be any systematic risk and the Central Limit Theorem would hold.

Let us now suppose that the market is in equilibrium. As we have seen in Chapter 2, the *capital market line* (CML) represents an equilibrium condition in which the expected return on a portfolio of assets is a linear function of the expected return on the market portfolio. Individual assets do not fall on the CML. Instead, it can be demonstrated that the following relationship holds for individual assets:

$$E[R_i] = R_f + \frac{[E[R_M] - R_f]}{\text{var}(R_M)} \text{cov}(R_i, R_M)$$

This equation is called the *security market line* (SML). In equilibrium, the expected return of individual securities will lie on the SML and *not* on the CML. This is true because of the high degree of nonsystematic risk that remains in individual assets that can be diversified out of portfolios. In equilibrium, only efficient portfolios will lie on both the CML and the SML.

The ratio

$$\frac{\text{cov}(R_i, R_M)}{\text{var}(R_M)}$$

can be estimated empirically using return data for the market portfolio and the return on the asset. The empirical analogue for the above equation is the following linear regression, called the *characteristic line*:

$$R_{it} - R_{ft} = \beta_i [R_{Mt} - R_{ft}] + \varepsilon_{it}$$

where ε_{it} is the error term.

The beta term β_i in the above regression is the estimate of the ratio

$$\frac{\mathrm{cov}(R_i, R_M)}{\mathrm{var}(R_M)}$$

in the SML. Substituting β_i in the SML equation gives the beta-version of the SML:

$$E[R_i] = R_f + \beta_i[E[R_M] - R_f]$$

This is the CAPM. It states that, given the assumptions of the CAPM, the expected return on an individual asset is a positive linear function of its index of systematic risk as measured by beta. The higher the beta, the higher the expected return.[7]

ARBITRAGE PRICING THEORY (APT)

The arbitrage principle is perhaps the most fundamental principle in modern finance theory. Essentially it states that it is not possible to earn a risk-free return without investment. The *Arbitrage Pricing Theory* is a particular formulation of relative pricing theory based on the principle of absence of arbitrage. The APT places restrictions on the prices of a set of assets. Because APT is a multifactor model, we postpone discussion of it until Chapter 12 where we cover such models.

In the previous sections we introduced two families of models that we can consider benchmark models: the family of unpredictable random walks and the family of predictable trend-stationary models. We then discussed the conceptual rationalization of price processes in terms of GETs. In terms of predictability, realistic models are somewhere in between these extremes. We now briefly discuss the implications of GETs on price and return models.

Let's start with CAPM and APT models. These models are not dynamic models, but static models that place restrictions on the cross sections of returns. Both CAPM and APT are compatible with random walk models. They are also compatible with other models, but their typical implementation is based on the random walk model. Much of clas-

---

[7] The conditional CAPM is a version of CAPM where the CAPM regression equation at time t is conditional upon an information set known at time $t - 1$. The problem with Conditional CAPM, proposed by Jagannathan and Wang, is the difficulty of identifying the information set. (See Ravi Jagannathan and Zhenyu Wang, "The Conditional CAPM and the Cross-Section of Expected Returns," *Journal of Finance* 51 (1996) pp. 3–53.)

sical quantitative financial analysis is based on multivariate random walk models with restrictions dictated by either the CAPM or by linear factor models such as the APT model. Hence the fundamental importance of random walk models.

Dynamic models used in asset management are rarely the product of GETs; rather they are for the most part econometric models supported by theoretical insight. There is basically no evidence, empirical or theoretical, that the return process of individual securities can be represented as trend-stationary models. Different considerations apply to portfolios. Due to considerations of cointegration that will be developed in Chapter 15, cointegration implies that some portfolios are trend-stationary. In addition, there are predictors for equity return processes. This implies that it is possible to model trend stationarity by coupling return and price processes with exogenous variables.

Note that these considerations do not offer a free path to profitability. The profitability of dynamic strategies is, in fact, eroded by transaction costs. Only those strategies that generate profit well in excess of transaction costs can be considered truly profitable. The chapters in Part Two of this book are devoted to discussing how profitable information can be extracted from processes that are very close to multivariate random walks.

SUMMARY

- The arithmetic random walk is the basic model of unpredictable (i.e., random) processes. An *arithmetic* random-walk model is a linear model; this implies that it is formed by the addition of its stochastic and random parts.
- The stochastic part of an arithmetic random-walk model is such that random innovations never decay.
- An arithmetic random walk makes excursions that are not periodic and have infinite mean height and length. In other words, there is no reversion to the mean and it might take an unbounded time to recover losses.
- Though an arithmetic random-walk model is not a realistic model of equity prices, it can be a realistic model of the logarithms of prices (i.e., logprices).
- If logprices follow an arithmetic random walk, then prices follow (at least approximately) a lognormal model.
- A *geometric* random-walk model is a nonlinear model that approximates a lognormal model.

- A number of economic theories have been proposed to explain asset price processes, the most popular being the Capital Asset Pricing Model (CAPM) and Arbitrage Pricing Theory (APT).
- CAPM is the simplest general equilibrium theory; APT and factor models are econometric models.
- All three—CAPM, APT, and factor models—are compatible with multivariate random walks.
- While trend-stationary models are not a realistic representation of single stock price processes, they might well be a realistic representation of portfolios.

CHAPTER 8

Forecasting Expected Return and Risk

As explained in Chapter 1, to increase the likelihood of delivering stellar investment performance, a serious investment program must be formulated. The four key areas involve: (1) producing realistic and reasonable return expectations and forecasts; (2) controlling and managing risk exposure; (3) managing trading and transaction costs; and (4) monitoring and managing the total investment process.

Transaction cost measurement and modeling was covered in Chapter 3. In this chapter, and partly also in the following, we focus on the first two areas. More specifically, we discuss the estimation of the inputs required for portfolio asset allocation models. Our major focus will be on estimating expected asset returns and their covariances using classical and practically well probed techniques. In Chapters 14, 15, and 16 we turn to more recent developments. In particular, there we discuss more modern econometric approaches to constructing forecasts based upon regression models, dynamic models, and hidden variable models.

In the classical mean-variance framework, an investor's objective is to choose a portfolio of securities that has the largest expected return for a given level of risk, as measured by the portfolio volatility. By return (or expected return) of a security we mean the change (or expected change) in a security's price over the period, plus any dividends paid, divided by the starting price. Of course, since we do not know the true values of the securities' expected returns and covariance, these must be estimated or forecasted.

Historical data are often used for this purpose. For example, an analyst might proceed in the following way: observing weekly or monthly returns, he might use the past five years of historical data to estimate the

215

expected return and the covariance matrix by the sample mean and sample covariance matrix. He would then use these as inputs to the mean-variance optimization, along with any *ad hoc* adjustments to reflect his views about expected returns on future performance. Unfortunately this historical approach most often leads to counter-intuitive, unstable, or merely "wrong" portfolios. Better forecasts are necessary.

Statistical estimates can be very noisy and do typically depend on the quality of the data and the particular statistical techniques used. In general, it is desirable that an estimator of expected return and risk have the following properties:

- It provides a forward-looking forecast with some predictive power, not just a backward-looking historical summary of past performance.
- The estimate can be produced at a reasonable computational cost.
- The technique used does not amplify errors already present in the inputs used in the process of estimation.
- The forecast should be intuitive, that is, the portfolio manager or the analyst should be able to explain and justify them in a comprehensible manner.

The outline of this chapter is as follows. We begin by discussing techniques from traditional fundamental analysis that can be used for the estimation of expected returns. Specifically, our coverage includes dividend discount and residual income models.

Thereafter, we turn to the usage of the sample mean and covariance as a forecast of expected returns and future risk. The forecasting power of these estimators is typically poor, and for practical applications, modifications and extensions are necessary. We focus on some of the most common and widely used modifications.

Random matrix theory provides an explanation for the poor behavior of the sample covariance matrix: only a few "factors" carry real information about how different securities interact. This result suggests that security returns should be modeled with a small set of factors. Because of their practical importance, we devote considerable space to factor models, and provide several real-world examples.

Other approaches to volatility estimation and forecasting have been suggested. We provide an overview of forecasting techniques based upon implied volatilities, clustering techniques, and GARCH models.

We close the chapter by considering a few applications of the techniques and approaches to investment strategies and proprietary trading.

DIVIDEND DISCOUNT AND RESIDUAL INCOME VALUATION MODELS

By buying common stock, an investor receives an ownership interest in the corporation. Common stock is a perpetual security. The owner of the shares has the right to receive a certain portion of any cash flow from the company paid out in terms of dividends. The value of one share should equal the present value of all future cash flow (dividends) the owner of the stock expects to receive from that share. In turn, to value one share, the investor must project or forecast future dividends. This approach to the valuation of common stock is referred to as the *discounted cash flow approach*. In this section we will discuss the *dividend discount model* (DDM), and an extension, the *residual income valuation model* (RIM).

If for each time period we are given the expected dividends D_1, D_2, D_3, ..., for one share of stock, and the appropriate interest or discount rates R_1, R_2, R_3, ..., then the *dividend discount model price* of the stock (also referred to as *fair value* or *theoretical value*) is

$$P = \sum_{t=1}^{\infty} \frac{D_t}{(1 + R_t)^t}$$

Future dividends are not certain however, and whether or not a corporation will pay dividends is decided by its board of directors. Yet for a company that does not pay dividends (for example, a company that retains earnings), the same principle applies, as retained earnings should eventually turn into dividends. In this case, the fair value of a security is defined to be the present value of the discounted free cash flow stream FCF_1, FCF_2, FCF_3, ...

$$P = \sum_{t=1}^{\infty} \frac{FCF_t}{(1 + R_t)^t}$$

Historically, this was the form of the first dividend discount model as originated by John B. Williams in his book *The Theory of Investment Value* published in the 1930s.[1] After a decade of irrational exuberance and accounting scandals, his model was an attempt to bring more science to investing.

There are many variations on the above two basic DDMs such as two-stage, three-stage growth models, and stochastic DDMs that are beyond

---

[1] John B. Williams, *The Theory of Investment Value* (Cambridge, MA: Harvard University Press, 1938).

the scope of this book.[2] Instead, we are going to discuss how this basic framework can be used to construct estimates of the expected return (ER) on a security that can then be used as an input in mean-variance analysis.

First, if we assume the discount rate R is constant, and that the security would be sold after T periods for a price of P_T, the two formulas above would take the form

$$P = \sum_{t=1}^{T} \frac{D_t}{(1+R)^t} + \frac{P_T}{(1+R)^T}$$

and

$$P = \sum_{t=1}^{T} \frac{FCF_t}{(1+R)^t} + \frac{P_T}{(1+R)^T}$$

Now let us assume that the observed market price of a stock is P_A. Given the stock price after T periods and all dividends or free cash flows, we have

$$P_A = \sum_{t=1}^{T} \frac{D_t}{(1+ER)^t} + \frac{P_T}{(1+ER)^T}$$

and

$$P_A = \sum_{t=1}^{T} \frac{FCF_t}{(1+ER)^t} + \frac{P_T}{(1+ER)^T}$$

The price after T periods could come from an analyst's price expectations, or from any other pricing model. If all other inputs in the formulas above are known we can solve for the expected return, ER.

For example, consider the following inputs:

$D_1 = \$2.00$ $D_2 = \$2.20$ $D_3 = \$2.30$ $D_4 = \$2.55$ $D_5 = \$2.65$
$P_5 = \$26$ $T = 5$

[2] See for example, Pamela P. Peterson and Frank J. Fabozzi, "Traditional Fundamental Analysis III: Earnings Analysis, Cash Analysis, Dividends, and Dividend Discount Models," Chapter 11 in Frank J. Fabozzi and Harry M. Markowitz (eds.), *The Theory and Practice of Investment Management* (Hoboken, NJ: John Wiley & Sons, 2002).

and the market price to be $25.89. Then the expected return is found by solving the following equation for ER:

$$\$25.89 = \frac{\$2.00}{(1+ER)} + \frac{\$2.20}{(1+ER)^2} + \frac{\$2.30}{(1+ER)^3} + \frac{\$2.55}{(1+ER)^4}$$
$$+ \frac{\$2.65}{(1+ER)^5} + \frac{\$26.00}{(1+ER)^5}$$

By trial and error, it can be determined that the expected return is 9%.

The expected return is the discount rate that equates the present value of the expected future cash flows with the present value of the stock. This rate is also referred to as the *internal rate of return*. For a given set of future cash flows, the higher the expected return, the lower the current value. The relation between the market value of a stock and the expected return of a stock is shown in Exhibit 8.1.

EXHIBIT 8.1   The Relation Between the Market Value of a Stock and the Stock's Expected Return

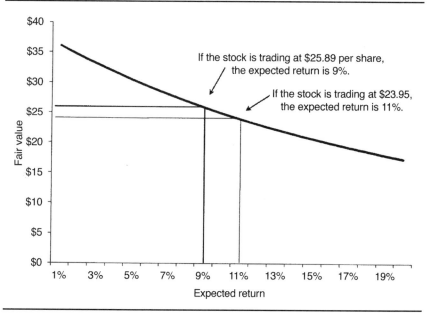

Source: Pamela P. Peterson and Frank J. Fabozzi, "Traditional Fundamental Analysis III: Earnings Analysis, Cash Analysis, Dividends, and Dividend Discount Models," Chapter 11 in Frank J. Fabozzi and Harry M. Markowitz (eds.), *The Theory and Practice of Investment Management* (Hoboken, NJ: John Wiley & Sons, 2002).

Although the dividend discount model is a useful framework for the estimation of expected returns, it can be very sensitive to the quality of the inputs. The determination of future dividends is often very hard, and analysts normally have to make various assumptions. For example, often it is assumed that future dividends grow at a constant growth rate g so that

$$D_t = D_{t-1}(1 + g) = D_1(1 + g)^{t-1}$$

Under this assumption, the basic DDM takes the form

Gordon Model

$$P = \frac{D_1}{ER - g}$$

which is referred to as the Gordon model.[3] Consequently, the expected return can be calculated as

$$ER = \frac{D_1}{P} + g$$

Several researchers have noted that the *residual income valuation model* (RIM) turns out to be much less sensitive to errors in the inputs than the basic DDM.[4] The residual income valuation model is also referred to as the *discounted abnormal earnings model* (DAEM) and the *Edwards-Bell-Ohlson model* (EBOM).[5] Due to their practical importance, we now give a brief overview of these models.[6]

---

[3] Myron Gordon, *The Investment, Financing, and Valuation of the Corporation* (Homewood, IL: Irwin Publishing, 1962).

[4] See, for example, Thomas K. Philips, "Estimating Expected Returns," *Journal of Investing* (Fall 2003), pp. 49–57; and James Claus and Jacob Thomas, "Equity Premia as Low as Three Percent? Evidence from Analysts' Earnings Forecasts for Domestic and International Stock Markets," *Journal of Finance* 56 (2001), pp. 1629–1666.

[5] So named for some of the researchers who worked on these types of models. See Edgar O. Edwards and Philip W. Bell, *Theory and Measurement of Business Income* (Berkeley, CA: University of California Press, 1961); Gerald A. Feltham and James A. Ohlson, "Valuation and Clean Surplus Accounting for Operating and Financial Activities," *Contemporary Accounting Research* 11 (1995), pp. 689–731; and James A. Ohlson, "Earnings, Book Values, and Dividends in Equity Valuation," *Contemporary Accounting Research* 11 (1995), pp. 681–687.

[6] For more details on the residual income valuation model, we refer the reader to John D. Stowe, Thomas R. Robinson, Jerald E. Pinto, and Dennis W. McLeavey, *Analysis of Equity Investments: Valuation* (Charlottesville, VA: Association for Investment Management and Research, 2002).

The basic idea that underlies the RIM is the so-called *clean surplus relation*

$$B_t = B_{t-1} + E_t - D_t$$

where B_t and E_t represent the book value per share, and the earnings per share of the company at time period t, respectively. This relationship reflects the fact that any item that enters onto a firm's balance sheet must first pass through its income statement. By recursively substituting this expression into the basic DDM above, we obtain the formula for the EBOM

$$P = B_0 + \sum_{t=1}^{\infty} \frac{E_t - ER \cdot B_{t-1}}{(1 + ER)^t}$$

In other words, the value of a stock is equal to its book value per share, plus the present value of expected future per-share residual income.

As before, given all inputs, we can solve for the expected return of the stock from the above equation. Nevertheless, due to the infinite sum, this formula can be hard to work with for practical purposes, and often various growth rate assumptions are used.

Under the assumption that the *return on equity* (ROE) and the spread between return on capital and the cost of capital are time invariant, Philips derives three equivalent formulas from the EBOM equation above,

$$ER = \frac{B_0(ROE_1 - g)}{P} + g$$
$$= \frac{FCF_1}{P} + g$$
$$= \frac{E_1 - gB_0}{P} + g$$

where ROE_1 is the return on equity for the first period.[7] We note that these expressions are of similar form as the Gordon model presented earlier. For purposes of calculating the expected return on a stock, the last expression is often the most convenient one to use, as future earnings, current book-to-price, and the growth rate (often chosen to be the growth of nominal GDP) are readily available. As compared to the DDM, Claus and Thomas show that the residual income estimate of

---

[7] Philips, "Estimating Expected Returns."

expected return is much less sensitive to errors under various growth rate assumptions.[8]

Of course, these "accounting valuation" techniques can also be used in cross-sectional rankings of stocks. For example, studies by Herzberg[9] and Frankel and Lee[10] show that these "accounting valuation" techniques have some merit in predicting cross-sectional stock returns. In the studies conducted by these researchers, they ranked their respective stock universes according to V/P, where V denotes the RIM fair value (using an appropriate discount rate) and P the current market value. They conclude that rankings based upon the V/P ratio perform better than the standard book-to-price ratio, and that these models perform best for holding periods of three to four years (although Herzberg reports that some superior performance is also found on horizons as short as three months).

THE SAMPLE MEAN AND COVARIANCE ESTIMATOR

The most commonly used approach for estimating security expected returns and covariances for portfolio allocation purposes is to calculate the sample analogues from historical data, the so-called sample mean and covariance estimators. It is important to remember that when we rely upon historical data for estimation purposes, we implicitly assume that the past provides a good estimate for the future.

However, it is well known that expected returns exhibit significant time variation (nonstationarity) and that realized returns are strongly influenced by changes in expected returns.[11] Consequently, extrapolated historical returns are in general poor forecasts of future returns, or as a typical disclaimer in any investment prospectus states: "Past performance is not an indication of future performance."

One problem of basing forecasts on historical performance is that markets and economic conditions change throughout time. For example, interest rates have varied substantially, all the way from the high

---

[8] Claus and Thomas, "Equity Premia as Low as Three Percent? Evidence from Analysts' Earnings Forecasts for Domestic and International Stock Markets."

[9] Martin M. Herzberg, "Implementing EBO/EVA® Analysis in Stock Selection," *Journal of Investing* 7 (1998), pp. 45–53.

[10] Richard Frankel and Charles M. C. Lee, "Accounting Valuation, Market Expectation, and Cross-Sectional Stock Returns," *Journal of Accounting and Economics* 25 (1998), pp. 283–319.

[11] See Eugene F. Fama and Kenneth R. French, "The Equity Risk Premium," *Journal of Finance* 57 (2002), pp. 637–659; and Thomas K. Philips, "Why Do Valuation Ratios Forecast Long-Run Equity Returns?" *Journal of Portfolio Management* (Spring 1999), pp. 39–44.

double digits to the low interest rate environment at the time of this writing. Other factors that change over time, and that can significantly influence the markets, include the political environment within and across countries, monetary and fiscal policy, consumer confidence, and the business cycle of different industry sectors and regions.

Of course, there are reasons why we can place more faith in statistical estimates obtained from historical data for some assets as compared to others. Different asset classes have varying lengths of histories available. For example, not only do the United States and the European markets have longer histories, but their data also tends to be more accurate. For emerging markets, the situation is quite different. Sometimes only a few years of historical data are available. As a consequence, based upon the quality of the inputs, we expect that for some asset classes we should be able to construct more precise estimates than others.

In practice, if portfolio managers believe that the inputs that rely on the historical performance of an asset class are not a good reflection of the future expected performance of that asset class, they may alter the inputs objectively or subjectively. Obviously, different portfolio managers may have different beliefs and therefore their "corrections" will be different.

Given the historical returns of two securities i and j, $R_{i,t}$ and $R_{j,t}$, where $t = 1, ..., T$, the sample mean and covariance are given by

$$\bar{R}_i = \frac{1}{T}\sum_{t=1}^{T} R_{i,t}$$

$$\bar{R}_j = \frac{1}{T}\sum_{t=1}^{T} R_{j,t}$$

$$\sigma_{ij} = \frac{1}{T-1}\sum_{t=1}^{T} (R_{i,t} - \bar{R}_i)(R_{j,t} - \bar{R}_j)$$

In the case of N securities, the covariance matrix can be expressed directly in matrix form:

$$\Sigma = \frac{1}{N-1}XX'$$

where

$$\mathbf{X} = \begin{bmatrix} R_{11} & \cdots & R_{1T} \\ \vdots & \ddots & \vdots \\ R_{N1} & \cdots & R_{NT} \end{bmatrix} - \begin{bmatrix} \bar{R}_1 & \cdots & \bar{R}_1 \\ \vdots & \ddots & \vdots \\ \bar{R}_N & \cdots & \bar{R}_N \end{bmatrix}$$

Under the assumption that security returns are *independent and identically distributed* (IID), it can be demonstrated that Σ is the maximum-likelihood estimator of the population covariance matrix and that this matrix follows a Wishart distribution with $N - 1$ degrees of freedom.[12]

As mentioned above, the risk-free rate R_f does change significantly over time. Therefore, when using a longer history, it is common that historical security returns are first converted into excess returns, $R_{i,t} - R_{f,t}$, and thereafter the expected return is estimated from

$$\bar{R}_i = R_{f,T} + \frac{1}{T} \sum_{t=1}^{T} (R_{i,t} - R_{f,t})$$

Alternatively, the expected excess returns may be used directly in a mean-variance optimization framework.

Unfortunately, for financial return series, the sample mean is a poor estimator for the expected return. The sample mean is the best linear unbiased estimator (BLUE) of the population mean for distributions that are not heavy-tailed. In this case, the sample mean exhibits the important property that an increase in the sample size always improves its performance. However, these results are no longer valid under extreme thick-tailedness and caution has to be exercised.[13] Furthermore, financial time series are typically *not* stationary, so the mean is not a good forecast of expected return. Moreover, the resulting estimator has a large

---

[12] Suppose $X_1, \ldots, X_N$ are independent and identically distributed random vectors, and that for each i it holds $\mathbf{X}_i \sim N_p(0, \mathbf{V})$ (that is, $E(\mathbf{X}_i) = 0$, where 0 is a p dimensional vector, and

$$\text{Var}(\mathbf{X}_i) = E(\mathbf{X}_i \mathbf{X}_i') = \mathbf{V}$$

where $\mathbf{V}$ is a $p \times p$ dimensional matrix). Then, the Wishart distribution with N degrees of freedom is the probability distribution of the $p \times p$ random matrix

$$\mathbf{S} = \sum_{i=1}^{N} \mathbf{X}_i \mathbf{X}_i'$$

and we write $\mathbf{S} \sim W_p(\mathbf{V}, N)$. In the case when $p = 1$ and $\mathbf{V} = 1$, then this distribution reduces to a chi-square distribution.

[13] Rustam Ibragimov, "On Efficiency of Linear Estimators Under Heavy-Tailedness," Discussion Paper Number 2085, Harvard Institute of Economic Research, Harvard University, 2005.

estimation error (as measured by the standard error), which significantly influences the mean-variance portfolio allocation process. For example:

- Equally-weighted portfolios often outperform mean-variance optimized portfolios.[14]
- Mean-variance optimized portfolios are not necessarily well diversified.[15]
- Uncertainty of returns tends to have more influence than risk in mean-variance optimization.[16]

These problems must be addressed from different perspectives. First, more robust or stable (lower estimation error) estimates of expected return should be used. One approach is to impose more structure on the estimator. Most commonly, practitioners use some form of factor model to produce the expected return forecasts (covered later in this chapter). Another possibility is to use Bayesian (such as the Black-Litterman model) or shrinkage estimators. Both are discussed further in Chapter 9.

Second, mean-variance optimization is very sensitive to its inputs. Small changes in expected return inputs often lead to large changes in portfolio weights. To some extent this is mitigated by using better estimators. However, by taking the estimation errors (whether large or small) into account in the optimization, further improvements can be made. In a nutshell, the problem is related to the fact that the mean-variance optimizer "does not know" that the inputs are statistical estimates and not known with certainty. When we are using classical mean-variance optimization, we are implicitly assuming that inputs are deterministic, and available with great accuracy. In other words, bad inputs lead to even worse outputs, or "garbage in, garbage out." We return to this issue when we discuss Monte Carlo simulation and robust optimization techniques for portfolio allocation in Chapter 9.

We will now turn to the sample covariance matrix estimator. Several authors (for example, Gemmill;[17] Litterman and Winkelmann;[18] and Pafka,

---

[14] J. D. Jobson and B. M. Korkie, "Putting Markowitz Theory to Work," *Journal of Portfolio Management* 7 (1981), pp. 70–74.

[15] Philippe Jorion, "International Portfolio Diversification with Estimation Risk," *Journal of Business* 58 (1985), pp. 259–278.

[16] Vijay K. Chopra and William T. Ziemba, "The Effect of Errors in Means, Variances, and Covariances on Optimal Portfolio Choice," *Journal of Portfolio Management* 9 (1993), pp. 6–11.

[17] Gordon Gemmill, *Options Pricing, An International Perspective* (London: McGraw-Hill, 1993).

[18] Robert Litterman and Kurt Winkelmann, "Estimating Covariance Matrices," *Risk Management Series*, Goldman Sachs, 1998.

Potters, and Kondor[19]) suggest improvements to this estimator using weighted data. The reason behind using weighted data is that the market changes and it makes sense to give more importance to recent, rather than to long past, information. If we give the most recent observation a weight of one and subsequent observations weights of d, d^2, d^3, ... where $d < 1$, then

$$
\sigma_{ij} = \frac{\displaystyle\sum_{t=1}^{T} d^{T-t}(R_{i,t} - \overline{R}_i)(R_{j,t} - \overline{R}_j)}{\displaystyle\sum_{t=1}^{T} d^{T-t}}
$$

$$
= \frac{1-d}{1-d^T} \sum_{t=1}^{T} d^{T-t}(R_{i,t} - \overline{R}_i)(R_{j,t} - \overline{R}_j)
$$

We observe that

$$
\frac{1-d}{1-d^T} \approx 1-d
$$

when T is large enough. The weighting (decay) parameter d can be estimated by maximum likelihood estimation, or by minimizing the out-of-sample forecasting error.[20]

Nevertheless, just like the estimator for expected returns, the covariance estimator suffers from estimation errors, especially when the number of historical return observations is small relative to the number of securities. These are poor estimators for anything but IID time series. In this particular case, the sample mean and covariance estimator are the maximum likelihood estimators of the true mean and covariance.[21]

The sample covariance estimator often performs poorly in practice. For instance, Ledoit and Wolf[22] argue against using the sample covari-

---

[19] Szilard Pafka, Marc Potters, and Imre Kondor, "Exponential Weighting and Random-Matrix-Theory-Based Filtering of Financial Covariance Matrices for Portfolio Optimization," Working Paper, Science & Finance, Capital Fund Management, 2004.
[20] See, Giorgio De Santis, Robert Litterman, Adrien Vesval, and Kurt Winkelmann, "Covariance Matrix Estimation," in Robert Litterman (ed.), *Modern Investment Management: An Equilibrium Approach* (Hoboken, NJ: John Wiley & Sons, 2003), pp. 224–248.
[21] See, for example, Fumio Hayashi, *Econometrics* (Princeton: Princeton University Press, 2000).
[22] Olivier Ledoit and Michael Wolf, "Honey, I Shrunk the Sample Covariance Matrix," *Journal of Portfolio Management* (Summer 2004), pp. 110–117.

ance matrix for portfolio optimization purposes. They stress that the sample covariance matrix contains estimation errors that will very likely perturb and produce poor results in a mean-variance optimization. As a substitute, they suggest applying shrinkage techniques to covariance estimation. We discuss this technique in more detail in Chapter 9.

The sample covariance matrix is a nonparametric (unstructured) estimator. An alternative is to make assumptions on what underlying economic variables or factors contribute to the movement of securities. This is, of course, the basic idea behind many asset pricing and factor models. We will turn to these approaches in a subsequent section.

Further Practical Considerations

The sample estimators discussed in this section can be further improved upon. In this subsection, we consider some techniques that are important for a more successful implementation of these, as well as other estimators encountered in practice.

Heteroskedasticity and Autocorrelation Consistent Covariance Matrix Estimation

Financial return series exhibit serial correlation and heteroskedasticity.[23] *Serial correlation*, also referred to as *autocorrelation*, is the correlation of the return of a security with itself over successive time intervals. The presence of heteroskedasticity means that variances/covariances are not constant but time-varying. These two effects introduce biases in the estimated covariance matrix. Fortunately, there are simple and straightforward techniques available that almost "automatically" correct for these biases.

Probably the most popular techniques include the approaches by Newey and West,[24] and its extension by Andrews,[25] often referred to as "Newey-West corrections" in the financial literature.[26]

---

[23] See John Y. Campbell, Andrew W. Lo, and A. Craig MacKinlay, *The Econometrics of Financial Markets* (Princeton: Princeton University Press, 1997).

[24] Whitney K. Newey and Kenneth D. West, "A Simple, Positive Semidefinite Heteroskedasticity and Autocorrelation Consistent Covariance Matrix," *Econometrica* 56 (1987), pp. 203–208.

[25] Donald W.K. Andrews, "Heteroskedasticity and Autocorrelation Consistent Covariance Matrix Estimation," *Econometrica* 59 (1991), pp. 817–858.

[26] However, these techniques can be traced back to work done by Jowett and Hannan in the 1950s. See G. H. Jowett, "The Comparison of Means of Sets of Observations from Sections of Independent Stochastic Series," *Journal of the Royal Statistical Society*, Series B, 17 (1955), pp. 208–227; and E.J. Hannan, "The Variance of the Mean of a Stationary Process," *Journal of the Royal Statistical Society*, Series B, 19 (1957), pp. 282–285.

Dealing with Missing and Truncated Data

In practice, we have to deal with the fact that no data series are perfect. There will be missing and errant observations, or just simply not enough data. If care is not taken, this can lead to poorly estimated models and inferior investment performance. Typically, it is tedious but very important work to clean data series for practical use. Some statistical techniques are available for dealing with missing observations; the so-called *expectation maximization* (EM) algorithm being among the most popular for financial applications.[27]

Longer daily return data series are often available from well-established companies in developed countries. However, if we turn to newer companies, or companies in emerging markets, this is often not the case. Say that we have a portfolio of 10 assets, of which five have a return history of 10 years, while the other five have only been around for three years. We could, for example, truncate the data series making all of them three years long and then calculate the sample covariance matrix. But by using the method proposed by Stambaugh,[28] we can do better than that. Simplistically speaking, starting from the truncated sample covariance matrix, this technique produces improvements to the covariance matrix that utilizes all the available data.

Data Frequency

Merton[29] shows that even if the expected returns are constant over time, a long history would still be required in order to estimate them accurately. The situation is very different for variances and covariances. Under reasonable assumptions, it can be shown that estimates of these quantities can be improved by *increasing the sampling frequency*.

However, not everyone has the luxury of having access to high-frequency or tick-by-tick data. An improved estimator of volatility can be achieved by using the daily high, low, opening, and closing prices, along with the transaction volume.[30] These types of estimators are typically referred to as *Garman-Klass estimators*.

---

[27] See Roderick J. A. Little and Donald B. Rubin, *Statistical Analysis with Missing Data* (New York: Wiley-Interscience, 2002); and Joe L. Schafer, *Analysis of Incomplete Multivariate Data* (Boca Raton, FL: Chapman & Hall/CRC, 1997).

[28] For a more detailed description of the technique, see Robert F. Stambaugh, "Analyzing Investments Whose Histories Differ in Length," *Journal of Financial Economics* 45 (1997), pp. 285–331.

[29] Robert C. Merton, "On Estimating the Expected Return on the Market: An Exploratory Investigation," *Journal of Financial Economics* 8 (1980), pp. 323–361.

[30] See, Mark B. Garman and Michael J. Klass, "On the Estimation of Security Price Volatilities from Historical Data," *Journal of Business* 53 (1980), pp. 67–78; and Michael Parkinson, "The Extreme Value Method for Estimating the Variance of the Rate of Return," *Journal of Business* 53 (1980), pp. 61–65.

Some guidance can also be gained from the option pricing literature. As suggested by Burghardt and Lane, when historical volatility is calculated for *option pricing purposes*, the time horizon for sampling should be equal to the time to maturity of the option.[31]

As Butler and Schachter point out, when historical data are used for volatility forecasting purposes, the bias found in the estimator tends to increase with the sample length.[32] However, it can be problematic in using information based on too short time periods. In this case, often the volatility estimator becomes highly sensitive to short-term regimes, such as over- and underreaction corrections.

An Argument Against Portfolio Variance

The most common critique levied against mean-variance optimization is the use of the portfolio variance as a measure of risk. Variance measures the dispersion of an asset's return from its expected return (or mean). As a result, by using the variance as a risk measure the returns, both above as well as below the expected return, are treated the same. However, an investor typically views returns that are higher than the expected return differently than the ones that are lower. On the one hand, an investor being long a particular asset obviously prefers returns above his expected return. On the other, an investor wants to avoid returns that are below his expected return.

Therefore, one can argue that risk measures should only consider unfavorable outcomes, or "downside" risk, and not outcomes where the return is above the expected return. For this purpose, Markowitz suggested the semivariance, calculated in a similar fashion as the variance but with the omission of returns above the expected return. Many other measures of downside risk are used by practitioners today, and we discussed some of the most common ones in Chapter 5.

Moreover, in classical portfolio theory, we do not consider higher moments such as skewness and kurtosis. In Chapter 5, we described some extensions to the mean-variance framework that incorporate higher moments. As we saw, however, the models increase in complexity, and it also becomes more difficult to obtain reliable estimates of higher moments. The beauty of Markowitz's portfolio theory is its simplicity. Despite the abundance of empirical evidence that asset returns are not normally distributed, some practitioners feel that in many practical applications, return distributions are not too far away from normal to be of concern.

---

[31] Galen Burghardt and Morton Lane, "How to Tell if Options Are Cheap," *Journal of Portfolio Management* (Winter 1990), pp. 72–78.

[32] John S. Butler, and Barry Schachter, "Unbiased Estimation of the Black-Scholes Formula," *Journal of Financial Economics* 15 (1986), pp. 341–357.

Chow et al. introduced a novel yet simple idea to incorporate outlier information into the covariance estimation.[33] They suggest the estimation of two separate covariance matrices. The first one computed from security returns during more quiet or less risky periods, and the second one calculated from outliers during more risky periods. They identify the two different regimes by examining the distance

$$d_t = (\mathbf{R}_t - \boldsymbol{\mu})\boldsymbol{\Sigma}^{-1}(\mathbf{R}_t - \boldsymbol{\mu})'$$

where $\mathbf{R}_t$, $\boldsymbol{\mu}$, and $\boldsymbol{\Sigma}^{-1}$ denote the vector of returns, the mean vector of the returns, and the standard sample covariance matrix of returns. Given a threshold parameter d_0, if $d_t < d_0$, the corresponding return vector is said to belong to the low-risk regime, and conversely, if $d_t \geq d_0$, it is said to belong to the high-risk regime. For each regime, a covariance matrix can be estimated, giving $\boldsymbol{\Sigma}_{\text{high}}$ and $\boldsymbol{\Sigma}_{\text{low}}$. The full sample covariance matrix is then defined to be

$$\boldsymbol{\Sigma} = p\boldsymbol{\Sigma}_{\text{low}} + (1 - p)\boldsymbol{\Sigma}_{\text{high}}$$

where p is the probability of falling within the low-risk regime and $1 - p$ is the probability of falling within the high-risk regime. The parameter p can be chosen by the portfolio manager, determined by estimation, or calibrated through historical backtests.

If the full sample covariance matrix is used, then in a period of higher or lower than normal volatility, the portfolio will be suboptimal. The blending of the two different covariance matrices mitigates this effect and gives the portfolio manager greater flexibility to control portfolio volatility.

In a subsequent paper, Kritzman et al.[34] use a two-state Markov chain regime switching model to determine and forecast the probability parameter p_t (p is now time-dependent). In this set-up, the resulting covariance matrix becomes

$$\boldsymbol{\Sigma}_t = p_t\boldsymbol{\Sigma}_{\text{low}} + (1 - p_t)\boldsymbol{\Sigma}_{\text{high}}$$

which can be used in the mean-variance framework to calculate regime-sensitive portfolios.

---

[33] George Chow, Eric Jacquier, Mark Kritzman, and Kenneth Lowry, "Optimal Portfolios in Good Times and Bad," *Financial Analysts Journal* (May/June 1999), pp. 65–73.
[34] Mark Kritzman, Kenneth Lowry, and Anne-Sophie Van Royen, "Risk, Regimes, and Overconfidence," *Journal of Derivative* (Spring 2001), pp. 32–42.

RANDOM MATRICES

In order to better understand the reason for the poor behavior of the sample covariance matrix, we introduce an area that developed in the 1950s by quantum physicists, called *Random Matrix Theory* (RMT).[35]

First, let us take a look at an example that demonstrates the instability of the sample covariance matrix for a larger number of assets. A simple test is the computation of the variance-covariance matrix over a moving window. If one performs this computation on a broad set of equities, such as the S&P 500, the result is a matrix that fluctuates in a nearly random way, although the average correlation level is high. Exhibit 8.2 illustrates the amount of fluctuations in a correlation matrix estimated over a moving window. The plot represents the average when the sampling window moves.

An evaluation of the random nature of the covariance matrix security returns was first proposed by Laloux, Cizeau, Bouchaud, and Pot-

EXHIBIT 8.2   Fluctuations of the Variance-Covariance Matrix

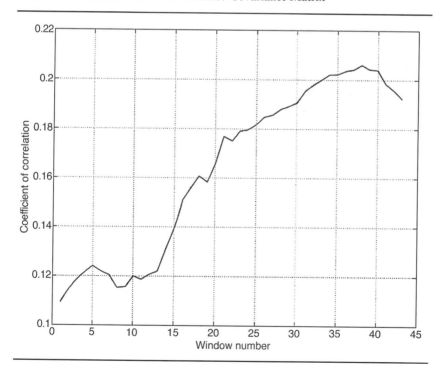

[35] Madan L. Mehta, *Random Matrix Theory* (New York: Academic Press, 1995).

ters, using random matrix theory.[36] A random matrix is the covariance matrix of a set of independent random walks. As such, its entries are a set of zero-mean, independent, and identically distributed variables. The mean of the random correlation coefficients is zero, as these coefficients have a symmetrical distribution in the range [−1,+1].

Interesting results can be shown in the case when both the number of sample points T and the number of time series N tend to infinity. Suppose that both T and N tend to infinity with a fixed ratio:

$$Q = T/N \geq 1$$

It can then be shown that the density of eigenvalues of the random matrix tends to

$$\rho(\lambda) = \frac{Q}{2\pi\sigma^2} \frac{\sqrt{(\lambda_{max} - \lambda)(\lambda_{min} - \lambda)}}{\lambda}$$

$$T, N \to \infty, Q = T/N \geq 1$$

$$\lambda_{max, min} = \sigma^2 \left[1 + \frac{1}{Q} \pm 2\sqrt{\frac{1}{Q}} \right]$$

where σ^2 is the average eigenvalue of the matrix. Exhibit 8.3 illustrates the theoretical function and a sample computed on 500 simulated independent random walks. The shape of the distribution of the eigenvalues is the signature of randomness.

If the covariance matrix entries do not have a zero mean, then the spectrum of the eigenvalues is considerably different. Malevergne and Sornette demonstrate that if the entries of the covariance matrix are all equal—with the obvious exception of the elements on the diagonal—then a very large eigenvalue appears, while all the others are equal to a single degenerate eigenvalue.[37] The eigenvector corresponding to the large eigenvalue has all components proportional to 1, that is, its components have equal weights.

---

[36] Laurent Laloux, Pierre Cizeau, Jean-Philippe Bouchaud, and Marc Potters, "Noise Dressing of Financial Correlation Matrices," *Physics Review Letter* 83 (1999), pp. 1467–1470.

[37] Yannick Malevergne and Didier Sornette, "Collective Origin of the Coexistence of Apparent RMT Noise and Factors in Large Sample Correlation Matrices," Cond-Mat 02/0115, 1, no. 4 (October 2002).

EXHIBIT 8.3 Theoretical Distribution of the Eigenvalues in a Random Matrix and Distribution of the Eigenvalues in a Sample of 500 Simulated Independent Random Walks

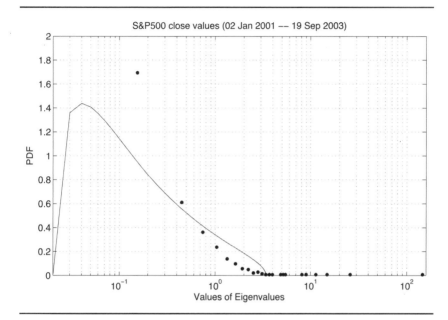

If the entries of the covariance matrix are random but with nonzero average, it can be shown that a large eigenvalue still appears. Nevertheless, a small number of large eigenvalues also appear, while the bulk of the distribution resembles that of a random matrix. The eigenvector corresponding to the largest eigenvalue includes all components with all equal weights proportional to 1.

If we compute the distribution of the eigenvalues of the covariance matrix of the S&P 500 over a window of two years, we obtain a distribution of eigenvalues which is fairly close to the distribution of a random matrix. In particular, the empirical distribution of eigenvalues fits well the theoretical distribution, with the exception of a small number of eigenvalues that have significantly higher values. Following the reasoning of Malevergne and Sornette, the existence of a large eigenvalue with a corresponding eigenvector of 1s in a large variance-covariance matrix arises naturally in cases where correlations have a random distribution with a nonzero mean.

This analysis shows that there is little information in the sample covariance matrix of a large portfolio. Only a few eigenvalues carry information, while the others are simply the result of statistical fluctuations in the sample correlation.

Therefore, developing alternative techniques for modeling the covariance matrix of security returns is critical. One possibility is to filter out the small eigenvalues and their corresponding eigenvectors.[38] This procedure also appears to be promising in reducing the effect of estimation error in the covariance matrix in the portfolio optimization context. Another interesting technique, proposed by Higham, relies upon computing the nearest correlation or covariance matrix in the Frobenius matrix norm, without having to calculate all its eigenvalues or principal components.[39] In this and the next chapter, we will discuss several other approaches, such as factor models, and Bayesian shrinkage estimation.

ARBITRAGE PRICING THEORY AND FACTOR MODELS

In well-functioning capital markets, an investor should be rewarded for accepting the various risks associated with investing in a security. Throughout this chapter we have been discussing these risks and how, if possible, to quantify them. In this, and in the following two sections, we consider the type of asset pricing models that practitioners refer to as *factor models*. These models are so-called because they attempt to model each exposure to risk as a separate factor. In these type of models, risks are also commonly referred to as "risk factors" or just "factors."

We begin with a general overview of the common characteristics of asset pricing models used in modern finance. Thereafter, we discuss the theoretical foundation for factor models laid by the *Arbitrage Pricing Theory* (APT). In the next two sections, we then cover the practical usage of factor models and provide several real-world illustrations.

Characteristics of Asset Pricing Models

We can express an asset pricing model in general terms as

---

[38] Laurent Laloux, Pierre Cizeau, Jean-Philippe Bouchaud, and Marc Potters, "Random Matrix Theory and Financial Correlations," *International Journal of Theoretical & Applied Finance* 3 (2000), pp. 391–397, 2000; and Vasiliki Plerou, Parameswaran Gopikrishnan, Bernd Rosenow, Luis A. Nunes Amaral, Thomas Guhr, and H. Eugene Stanley, "Random Matrix Approach to Cross Correlations in Financial Data," *Physical Review E* 65 (2002), pp. 1–18.
[39] Nicholas J. Higham, "Computing the Nearest Correlation Matrix—a Problem from Finance," *IMA Journal of Numerical Analysis* 22 (2002), pp. 329–343.

$$E(R_i) = f(F_1, F_2, F_3, \ldots, F_N)$$

where $E(R_i)$, F_k, and N denote the expected return on asset i, the k-th risk factor, and the number of risk factors, respectively.

By investing in an asset other than risk-free securities, investors will demand a premium over the risk-free rate. That is, the expected return that an investor will demand is

$$E(R_i) = R_f + \text{risk premium}$$

where R_f is the risk-free rate.

The "risk premium," or excess return expected over the risk-free rate, depends on the risk factors associated with investing in the asset. Thus, we can rewrite the general form of the asset pricing model given above as

$$E(R_i) = R_f + g(F_1, F_2, F_3, \ldots, F_N)$$

Risk factors can be divided into two general categories:

- *systematic*, or nondiversifiable risk factors
- *unsystematic*, or diversifiable risk factors

The first category refers to factors that cannot be diversified away via mean-variance techniques. The second category refers to risk factors that can be eliminated. These risk factors are not specific to any particular assets and can therefore be made to "cancel out" with other assets in the portfolio.

Example: The Capital Asset Pricing Model

The first asset pricing model derived from economic theory was developed by William Sharpe and is called the *capital asset pricing model* (CAPM)[40]

$$E(R_i) = R_f + \beta_i(E(R_M) - R_f)$$

---

[40] William F. Sharpe, "Capital Asset Prices," *Journal of Finance* (September 1964), pp. 425–442. See, also John Lintner, "The Valuation of Risk Assets and the Selection of Risky Investments in Stock Portfolio and Capital Budgets," *Review of Economics and Statistics* (February 1965), pp. 13–37; Jack L. Treynor, "Toward a Theory of Market Value of Risky Assets," Unpublished Paper, Arthur D. Little, Cambridge, MA, 1961; and, Jan Mossin, "Equilibrium in a Capital Asset Market," *Econometrica* (October 1966), pp. 768–783.

where $E(R_M)$ is the expected return on the market portfolio and

$$\beta_i = \frac{\text{cov}(R_i, R_M)}{\text{var}(R_M)}$$

denotes the measure of systematic risk of asset i relative to the market portfolio.[41]

The CAPM has only one systematic risk factor, the risk of the overall movement of the market. This risk factor is referred to as "market risk." So, in the CAPM, the terms "market risk" and "systematic risk" are used interchangeably. By "market risk" it is meant the risk associated with holding a portfolio consisting of all assets, called the "market portfolio" introduced in Chapter 2.

Given the risk-free return, the expected return on the market portfolio, and an asset's β, we can use the CAPM to derive an estimate of the expected return on the asset. Using return data for the market portfolio and the return on the asset, the β of each asset is typically estimated empirically by econometric techniques such as those described in Chapter 14. The empirical analogue of the CAPM is given by

$$r_{it} - r_{ft} = \beta_i [r_{Mt} - r_{ft}] + e_{it}, \, t = 1, ..., T$$

where e_{it} is the error term, and T is the length of the sample used in the estimation.

Arbitrage Pricing Theory

Stephen Ross derived, as an alternative to the capital asset pricing model just discussed, an asset pricing model based purely on arbitrage arguments called the *Arbitrage Pricing Theory* (APT).[42] This approach postulates that an asset's expected return is influenced by a variety of risk factors, as opposed to just market risk, as suggested by the CAPM. The APT states that the return on a security is linearly related to some K risk factors. However, the APT does *not* specify what these risk factors are, but it is assumed that the relationship between asset returns and the risk factors is linear. Moreover, unsystematic risk can be eliminated so that an investor is only compensated for accepting the systematic risk factors.

---

[41] We discussed the CAPM and its underlying assumptions in Chapter 7.
[42] Stephen A. Ross, "The Arbitrage Theory of Capital Asset Pricing," *Journal of Economic Theory* (December 1976), pp. 343–362.

Arbitrage Principle

Since the APT relies on arbitrage arguments, we will digress at this point to define what is meant by arbitrage. In its simple form, arbitrage is the simultaneous buying and selling of an asset at two different prices in two different markets. The arbitrageur profits, without taking any risk, by buying at a cheaper price in one market and simultaneously selling at a higher price in the other market. Investors do not hold their breath waiting for such situations to occur, because they are rare. In fact, a single arbitrageur with unlimited ability to sell short, could correct a mispricing condition by financing purchases in the underpriced market with the proceeds of short sales in the overpriced market. This means that in practice, riskless arbitrage opportunities are short lived.

Less obvious arbitrage opportunities exist in situations where a *portfolio of assets* can produce a payoff (expected return) identical to an asset that is priced differently. This arbitrage relies on a fundamental principle of finance called the *law of one price*, which states that a given asset must have the same price, regardless of the means by which one goes about creating that asset. The law of one price implies that if the payoff of an asset can be synthetically created by a portfolio of assets, the price of the portfolio, and the price of the asset whose payoff it replicates, must be equal.

When a situation is discovered whereby the price of the portfolio of assets differs from that of an asset with the same payoff, rational investors will trade these assets in such a way so as to restore price equilibrium. This market mechanism is assumed by the APT, and is founded on the fact that an arbitrage transaction does not expose the investor to any adverse movement in the market price of the assets in the transaction.

For example, let us consider how we can produce an arbitrage opportunity involving the three assets A, B, and C. These assets can be purchased today at the prices shown below, and can each produce only one of two payoffs (referred to as State 1 and State 2) a year from now:

Asset	Price	$ Payoff in State 1	$ Payoff in State 2
A	70	50	100
B	60	30	120
C	80	38	112

While it is not obvious from the data presented above, an investor can construct a portfolio of assets A and B that will have the identical return as asset C in both State 1 or State 2. Let w_A and w_B be the proportion of assets A and B, respectively, in the portfolio. Then the payoff (i.e., the terminal value of the portfolio) under the two states can be expressed mathematically as follows:

If State 1 occurs: $50 w_A + $30 w_B
If State 2 occurs: $100 w_A + $120 w_B

We can now create a portfolio consisting of A and B that will reproduce the payoff of C, regardless of the state that occurs one year from now. For either condition (State 1 and State 2), we set the expected payoff of the portfolio equal to the expected payoff for C, as follows:

State 1: $50 w_A + $30 w_B = $ 38
State 2: $100 w_A + $120 w_B = $112

We also know that $w_A + w_B = 1$.

If we solved for the weights for w_A and w_B that would simultaneously satisfy the above equations, we would find that the portfolio should have 40% in asset A (i.e., $w_A = 0.4$) and 60% in asset B (i.e., $w_B = 0.6$). The cost of that portfolio will be equal to

$$(0.4)(\$70) + (0.6)(\$60) = \$64$$

Our portfolio comprised of assets A and B has the same payoff in State 1 and State 2 as the payoff of asset C. The cost of asset C is $80 while the cost of the portfolio is only $64. This is an arbitrage opportunity that can be exploited by buying assets A and B, in the proportions given above, and short-selling asset C.

For example, suppose that $1 million is invested to create the portfolio with assets A and B. The $1 million is obtained by selling short asset C. The proceeds from the short sale of asset C provide the funds to purchase assets A and B. Thus, there would be no cash outlay by the investor. The payoffs for States 1 and 2 are shown as follows:

| Asset | Investment | $ Payoff in | |
		State 1	State 2
A	400,000	285,715	571,429
B	600,000	300,000	1,200,000
C	–1,000,000	–475,000	–1,400,000
Total	0	110,715	371,429

In either State 1 or 2, the investor profits without risk. The APT assumes that such an opportunity would be quickly eliminated by the market-place.

APT Formulation

Let us now suppose that there are N securities and that each have a return distribution according to the factor structure

$$R_i = \alpha_i + \sum_{k=1}^{K} \beta_{ik} F_k + \varepsilon_i$$

where we also assume that

$$E(\varepsilon_i) = E(F_k) = 0$$

$$E(\varepsilon_i \varepsilon_j) = E(\varepsilon_i F_j) = E(F_i F_j) = 0$$

and

$$E(\varepsilon_j^2) = \sigma^2$$

for all $i \neq j$.[43] Here F_k, $k = 1, 2, ..., K$ are the K factors common to all the securities, β_{ik} is the sensitivity of the i-th security to the k-th factor, and ε_i is the nonsystematic (idiosyncratic) return for the i-th security. In vector form, we can write the above relationship as

$$\mathbf{R} = \boldsymbol{\alpha} + \mathbf{BF} + \boldsymbol{\varepsilon}$$

where

$$\mathbf{R} = \begin{bmatrix} R_1 \\ \vdots \\ R_N \end{bmatrix}, \boldsymbol{\alpha} = \begin{bmatrix} \alpha_1 \\ \vdots \\ \alpha_N \end{bmatrix}, \boldsymbol{\varepsilon} = \begin{bmatrix} \varepsilon_1 \\ \vdots \\ \varepsilon_N \end{bmatrix},$$

---

[43] We choose to discuss a simplified version of the APT. Specifically, we assume that the nonsystematic errors are independent. In this case, returns are said to have a *strict factor structure*. Generalizations to an *approximate factor structure*, where the co-variance matrix satisfies cov($\boldsymbol{\varepsilon}$) = $\boldsymbol{\Omega}$ are possible, but technical. We also omit discussing approximate factor structures with infinitely many assets, which is the framework where the APT was originally established.

$$F = \begin{bmatrix} F_1 \\ \vdots \\ F_K \end{bmatrix}$$

and

$$B = \begin{pmatrix} \beta_{11} & \cdots & \beta_{1k} \\ \vdots & \ddots & \vdots \\ \beta_{k1} & \cdots & \beta_{kk} \end{pmatrix}$$

Ross showed that in the absence of arbitrage, the following relationship holds

$$E(R_i) = R_f + \sum_{k=1}^{K} \beta_{ik}(E(F_k) - R_f)$$

This is referred to as the APT.[44] The expression $E(F_k) - R_f$ is the excess return of the k-th systematic risk factor over the risk-free rate, and as such it can be thought of as the "price" (or risk premium) for the k-th systematic risk factor.

The APT asserts that investors want to be compensated for all the risk factors that *systematically* affect the return of a security. The compensation is the sum of the products of each risk factor's systematic risk β_{ik} and the risk premium assigned to it by the financial market, $E(F_k) - R_f$. As in the case of the CAPM, an investor is *not* compensated for accepting nonsystematic risk.

As a matter of fact, it turns out that the CAPM is actually a special case of the APT. If the only risk factor in the APT is market risk, the APT reduces to the CAPM.[45] Both say that investors are compensated

---

[44] Strictly speaking, this is not fully correct. In particular, the equality holds in the *mean-squared sense*, when the number of assets approaches infinity. That is, the APT states that in the absence of asymptotic arbitrage opportunities

$$\lim_{N \to \infty} \frac{1}{N} \sum_{k=1}^{K} \left(E(r_i) - R_f - \sum_{k=1}^{K} \beta_{ik}(E(F_k) - R_f) \right)^2 = 0$$

See, for example, Gur Huberman, "A Simple Approach to Arbitrage Pricing Theory," *Journal of Economic Theory* 28 (1982), pp. 183–191.

[45] Two necessary conditions for the two models to be asymptotically equivalent are: (1) The one factor must be uncorrelated with the residuals so that factor risk and specific risk can be separated; and (2) any specific risk must be diversified away in the market portfolio.

for accepting all systematic risk, but not nonsystematic risk. The CAPM states that systematic risk is market risk, while the APT does not specify what the systematic risk factors are.

How do the two different models differ? Supporters of the APT argue that it has several major advantages over the CAPM. First, it makes less restrictive assumptions about investor preferences toward risk and return. As explained in Chapter 7, the CAPM theory assumes investors trade-off between risk and return, solely on the basis of the expected returns, and standard deviations of prospective investments. The APT in contrast, simply requires some rather unobtrusive bounds be placed on potential investor utility functions. Second, the CAPM is a market equilibrium model, whereas APT relies upon the no-arbitrage condition. We note that while a market equilibrium implies no-arbitrage, no-arbitrage *does not* necessarily imply that the market is in equilibrium. Third, APT is a "relative" pricing model, in that it prices securities on the basis of the prices of other securities. Conversely, CAPM is an "absolute" pricing model that relates returns on the securities to the fundamental source of risk inherent in the portfolio of total wealth. Finally, in the APT, no assumptions are made about the distribution of asset returns besides the factor structure. Since the APT does not rely on the identification of the true market portfolio, the theory is potentially testable.[46]

FACTOR MODELS IN PRACTICE

The APT provides theoretical support for an asset pricing model where there is more than one risk factor. Consequently, models of this type are referred to as *multifactor risk models*. As we will see in the next section where these models are applied to equity portfolio management, they provide the tools for quantifying the risk profile of a portfolio relative to a benchmark, for constructing a portfolio relative to a benchmark, and controlling risk. Below, we provide a brief overview of the three different types

---

[46] In a paper by Richard Roll, he demonstrates that the CAPM is not testable unless (1) the exact composition of the "true" market portfolio is known; and (2) the only valid test of the CAPM is to observe whether the *ex ante* true market portfolio is mean-variance efficient. (Richard R. Roll, "A Critique of the Asset Pricing Theory's Tests, Part I: On Past and Potential Testability of the Theory," *Journal of Financial Economics* 4 (1977), pp. 129–176.) As a result of his findings, Roll states that he does not believe there ever will be an unambiguous test of the CAPM. He does not say that the CAPM is invalid, but rather that there is likely to be no unambiguous way to test the CAPM and its implications due to the nonobservability of the true market portfolio and its characteristics.

of multifactor risk models used in equity portfolio management: statistical factor models, macroeconomic factor models, and fundamental factor models.[47] The empirical estimation of factor models by linear regression and *maximum likelihood estimation* (MLE) is covered in Chapter 14.

Statistical Factor Models

In a *statistical factor model,* historical and cross-sectional data on stock returns are tossed into a statistical model. The goal of the statistical model is to best explain the observed stock returns with "factors" that are linear return combinations and uncorrelated with each other. This is typically accomplished by *principal component analysis* (PCA). In statistical factor models the number of factors is normally much smaller compared to macroeconomic and fundamental factor models.[48]

For example, suppose that monthly returns for 5,000 companies for ten years are computed. The goal of the statistical analysis is to produce factors that best explain the variance of the observed stock returns. For example, suppose that there are six factors that do this. These factors are statistical artifacts. The objective in a statistical factor model then becomes to determine the economic meaning of each of these statistically derived factors.

Because of the problem of interpretation, it is difficult to use the factors from a statistical factor model for valuation, portfolio construction, and risk control. Instead, practitioners prefer the two other models described next, which allow them to prespecify meaningful factors, and thus produce a more intuitive model.

Macroeconomic Factor Models

In a *macroeconomic factor model,* the inputs to the model are historical stock returns and observable macroeconomic variables. These variables are called *raw descriptors.* The goal is to determine which macroeconomic variables are persistent in explaining historical stock returns. Those variables that consistently explain the returns then become the factors and are included in the model. The responsiveness of a stock to these factors is estimated using historical time series data.

An example of a proprietary macroeconomic factor model is the *Burmeister, Ibbotson, Roll, and Ross* (BIRR) model.[49] In this model, there are

---

[47] Gregory Connor, "The Three Types of Factor Models: A Comparison of Their Explanatory Power," *Financial Analysts Journal* (May–June 1995), pp. 42–57.
[48] As a rule of thumb, practitioners often use 4 to 8 statistical factors. This is motivated by the results from random matrix theory.
[49] Edwin Burmeister, Roger Ibbotson, Richard Roll, and Stephen A. Ross, "Using Macroeconomic Factors to Control Portfolio Risk," Unpublished Paper.

five macroeconomic factors that reflect unanticipated changes in the following macroeconomic variables: investor confidence (confidence risk); interest rates (time horizon risk); inflation (inflation risk); real business activity (business cycle risk); and a market index (market risk). For each stock, the sensitivity of the stock to a factor risk is statistically estimated. In addition, for each factor risk, a market price for that risk is statistically estimated. Given these two estimates, the expected return can be projected.

Fundamental Factor Models

One of the most well-known fundamental factor models is the Fama-French three-factor model. Besides the market portfolio, the other two factors are the "size factor" and the "book-to-market factor."[50] The size factor is the return on a zero-cost portfolio that is long on small-cap stocks and short on large-cap stocks. The *book-to-market* (B/M) factor is the return on a zero-cost portfolio that is long on high B/M stocks and short on low B/M stocks. It turns out that the model explains the cross-sectional variation in stock returns fairly well.[51] However, the *forecasting power* of the model is less than satisfactory for most practical purposes. Therefore, it is common that practitioners extend the model with further factors.

Besides the three Fama-French factors, typical *fundamental factor models* use company and industry attributes and market data as raw descriptors. Examples are price/earnings ratios, estimated economic growth, trading activity, and liquidity. Other technical factors, such as volatility of total return and momentum, are also often included in modern factor models. The inputs into a fundamental factor model are stock returns and the raw descriptors about a company. Those fundamental variables about a company that are pervasive in explaining stock returns are then the raw descriptors retained in the model. Using cross-sectional analysis, the sensitivity of a stock's return to a raw descriptor is estimated.

There are several fundamental factor models available from vendors, and we will discuss the Barra model later in this chapter.

Practical Issues and Estimation

When developing factor models for practical applications, several considerations are important. In particular, it should be verified that all the factors used in the model are both statistically and economically signifi-

---

[50] Eugene F. Fama and Kenneth R. French, "Common Risk Factors in the Returns on Stocks and Bonds," *Journal of Financial Economics* 47 (1993), pp.427–465.
[51] Typical regressions have an R^2 of 0.6 or higher (see, for example, Eugene F. Fama and Kenneth R. French, "The Cross-Section of Expected Stock Returns," *Journal of Finance* 47 (1992), pp. 427–465).

cant. Some factors may only prove to have explanatory power for certain periods, and although a factor has worked for the last 20 years it is important to ask how well it has done for a more recent period, say the last three years. Persistent factors are often more desirable.

There is a trade-off between the number of factors being used. On the one hand, single factor models, such as the so-called *market model* first proposed by Sharpe, can be estimated with less estimation error but often tend to be severely biased and misspecified.[52] On the other hand, while multifactor models become more flexible, resulting in reduced bias, the estimation error and the complexity of the model typically increases. The choice of the number of factors to use is a trade-off between estimation error, bias, and ease of use.[53]

Simplistically speaking, there are two ways to estimate the factors' expected return, either via theory or by data. Both approaches have their own problems.

Theory is problematic to apply because we may not know what portfolio to use to represent a specific factor. In fact, as pointed out by Roll, we do not know what to use for the market portfolio in the CAPM, and we do not know what the factors are in the APT.[54] The market portfolio is unobservable and we have to use a proxy for it.

Nevertheless, in practice, the problem of not knowing or being able to observe the true market portfolio is not as severe as one might think. Typical candidates for the market portfolio are often very highly correlated. It can also be argued that even human capital, which is unobservable, should be highly correlated with portfolios of traded assets.[55]

Possibly, estimation from data is more problematic due to estimation error. Assuming that factors are stationary, we could mitigate this by using a long history to estimate the pricing of the factors. However, many typical factors used in practice are not stationary, but change significantly over time.[56]

---

[52] This approach is often referred to as the *single index model* or the *diagonal model.* See, William Sharpe, "A Simplified Model for Portfolio Analysis," *Management Science* 9 (1963), pp. 277–293.

[53] For statistical factor models, some theory is available in the determination of the number of factors. See, for example, Jushan Bai and Serena Ng, "Determining The Number of Factors in Approximate Factor Models," *Econometrica* 70 (2002), pp. 191–221; and George Kapetanios, "A New Method for Determining the Number of Factors in Factor Models with Large Datasets," Working Paper, Queen Mary, University of London, 2004.

[54] Roll, "A Critique Of the Asset Pricing Theory's Tests, Part I."

[55] See, Fischer Black, "Estimating Expected Return," *Financial Analysts Journal* 49 (1993), pp. 36–38.

[56] This has led to the introduction of dynamic factor models in finance. We discuss this development in Chapter 15.

FACTOR MODELS IN PRACTICE: AN EXAMPLE

In the previous two sections, we discussed the basic theory behind factor models, the different kinds of factor models, and how they are implemented. In this section we turn to the practical usage of factor models—and in particular, we provide several real-life illustrations.

There are many different factor models developed for the equity market, both commercially available as well as proprietary models developed by large investment houses. In this section, we will focus on one popular factor model, the MSCI Barra fundamental multifactor risk model. The specific version of the model we discuss is the "E3 model."[57] However, later versions have also been developed.

This multifactor risk model has 13 risk indices and 55 industry groups. The descriptors are the same variables that have been consistently found to be important in many well-known academic studies on risk factors. Exhibit 8.4 lists the 13 risk indices in the Barra model.[58] Also shown in the exhibit are the descriptors used to construct each risk index. The 55 industry classifications are further classified into sectors. For example, the following three industries comprise the energy sector: energy reserves and production, oil refining, and oil services. The consumer noncyclicals sector consists of the following five industries: food and beverages, alcohol, tobacco, home products, and grocery stores. The 13 sectors in the Barra model are: basic materials, energy, consumer noncylicals, consumer cyclicals, consumer services, industrials, utility, transport, health care, technology, telecommunications, commercial services, and financial services.

Given the risk factors, information about the exposure of every stock to each risk factor ($\beta_{i,k}$) is estimated using statistical analysis. For a given time period, the expected rate of return for each risk factor (R_j) can also be estimated using statistical analysis as:

$$E(R_i) = R_f + \sum_{k=1}^{K} \beta_{ik}(E(F_k) - R_f)$$

The forecast for the expected return can then be obtained for any stock. The nonfactor return (e_i) is found by subtracting the actual return for the period for a stock, from the return as predicted by the risk factors.

---

[57] Barra, *Risk Model Handbook United States Equity: Version 3* (Berkeley, CA: Barra, 1998). Barra is now MSCI Barra.

[58] For a more detailed description of each descriptor, see Appendix A in *Barra, Risk Model Handbook United States Equity: Version 3* (Berkeley, CA: Barra, 1998). A listing of the 55 industry groups is provided in Exhibit 8.12.

EXHIBIT 8.4 Barra E3 Model Risk Definitions

Descriptors in Risk Index	Risk Index
Beta times sigma	Volatility
Daily standard deviation	
High-low price	
Log of stock price	
Cumulative range	
Volume beta	
Serial dependence	
Option-implied standard deviation	
Relative strength	Momentum
Historical alpha	
Log of market capitalization	Size
Cube of log of market capitalization	Size Nonlinearity
Share turnover rate (annual)	Trading Activity
Share turnover rate (quarterly)	
Share turnover rate (monthly)	
Share turnover rate (five years)	
Indicator for forward split	
Volume to variance	
Payout ratio over five years	Growth
Variability in capital structure	
Growth rate in total assets	
Earnings growth rate over the last five years	
Analyst-predicted earnings growth	
Recent earnings change	
Analyst-predicted earnings-to-price	Earnings Yield
Trailing annual earnings-to-price	
Historical earnings-to-price	
Book-to-price ratio	Value
Variability in earnings	Earnings Variability
Variability in cash flows	
Extraordinary items in earnings	
Standard deviation of analyst-predicted earnings-to-price	
Market leverage	Leverage
Book leverage	
Debt to total assets	
Senior debt rating	
Exposure to foreign currencies	Currency Sensitivity
Predicted dividend yield	Dividend Yield
Indicator for firms outside US-E3 estimation universe	Nonestimation Universe Indicator

Adapted from Table 8-1 in Barra, *Risk Model Handbook United States Equity: Version 3* (Berkeley, CA: Barra, 1998), pp. 71–73. Adapted with permission from MSCI Barra.

Moving from individual stocks to portfolios, the predicted return for a portfolio can be computed. The exposure to a given risk factor of a portfolio is simply the weighted average of the exposure of each stock in the portfolio to that risk factor. For example, suppose a portfolio has 42 stocks. Suppose further that stocks 1 through 40 are equally weighted in the portfolio at 2.2%, stock 41 is 5% of the portfolio, and stock 42 is 7% of the portfolio. Then the exposure of the portfolio to risk factor k is

$$0.022 \ \beta_{1,k} + 0.022 \ \beta_{2,k} + \ldots + 0.022 \ \beta_{40,k} + 0.050 \ \beta_{41,k} + 0.007 \ \beta_{42,k}$$

The nonfactor error term is measured in the same way as in the case of an individual stock. However, in a well diversified portfolio, the nonfactor error term will be considerably less for the portfolio than for the individual stocks in the portfolio.

The same analysis can be applied to a stock market index because an index is nothing more than a portfolio of stocks.

Decomposition of Risk

The real usefulness of a linear multifactor model lies in the ease with which the risk of a portfolio with several assets can be estimated. Consider a portfolio with 100 assets. Risk is commonly defined as the variance of the portfolio's returns. So, in this case, we need to find the covariance matrix of the 100 assets. That would require us to estimate 100 variances (one for each of the 100 assets) and 4,950 covariances among the 100 assets. That is, in all we need to estimate 5,050 values, a very difficult undertaking. Suppose, instead, that we use a three-factor model to estimate risk. Then, we need to estimate (1) the three factor loadings for each of the 100 assets (i.e., 300 values); (2) the six values of the factor variance-covariance matrix; and (3) the 100 residual variances (one for each asset). That is, in all, we need to estimate only 406 values. This represents a nearly 90% reduction from having to estimate 5,050 values, a huge improvement. Thus, with well-chosen factors, we can substantially reduce the work involved in estimating a portfolio's risk.

Multifactor risk models allow a manager and a client to decompose risk in order to assess the *potential* performance of a portfolio to the risk factors and to assess the *potential* performance of a portfolio relative to a benchmark. This is the portfolio construction and risk control application of the model. Also, the *actual* performance of a portfolio relative to a benchmark can be monitored and assessed. This is the performance attribution analysis application of the model.

Barra suggests that there are various ways that a portfolio's total risk can be decomposed when employing a multifactor risk model.[59] Each decomposition approach can be useful to managers depending on the equity portfolio management that they pursue. The four approaches are (1) total risk decomposition; (2) systematic-residual risk decomposition; (3) active risk decomposition; and (4) active systematic-active residual risk decomposition. We describe each approach next and explain how managers, pursuing different strategies, find the decomposition helpful in portfolio construction and evaluation.

In all of these approaches to risk decomposition, the total return is first divided into the risk-free return and the total excess return. The *total excess return* is the difference between the *actual* return realized by the portfolio and the risk-free return. The risk associated with the total excess return, called *total excess risk*, is what is further partitioned in the four approaches.

Total Risk Decomposition

There are managers who seek to minimize total risk. For example, a manager pursuing a long-short or market neutral strategy, seeks to construct a portfolio that minimizes total risk. For such managers, it is useful to perform a total risk decomposition, breaking the total risk down into *common risk factors* (e.g., capitalization and industry exposures) and *specific risk factors*. This decomposition is shown in Exhibit 8.5. There is no provision for market risk, only risk attributed to the common factor risks and company-specific influences (i.e., risk unique to a particular company and therefore uncorrelated with the specific risk of other companies). Thus, the market portfolio is not a risk factor considered in this decomposition.

Systematic-Residual Risk Decomposition

There are managers who seek to time the market or who intentionally make bets to create a different exposure than that of a market portfolio. Such managers would find it useful to decompose total excess risk into systematic risk and residual risk as shown in Exhibit 8.6. Unlike in the total risk decomposition approach just described, this view brings market risk into the analysis.

Residual risk in the systematic-residual risk decomposition is defined in a different way than residual risk is in the total risk decomposition. In the systematic-residual risk decomposition, residual risk is risk

---

[59] See Chapter 4 in Barra, *Risk Model Handbook United States Equity: Version 3.* The subsequent discussion in this section follows that in this MSCI Barra publication.

EXHIBIT 8.5 Total Risk Decomposition

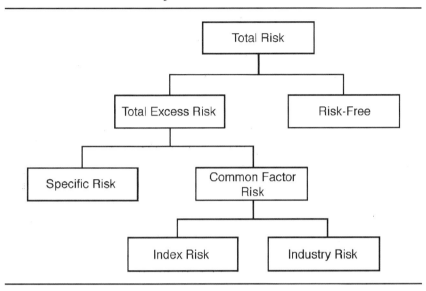

Source: Figure 4.2 in Barra, *Risk Model Handbook United States Equity: Version 3* (Berkeley, CA: Barra, 1998), p. 34. Reprinted with permission from MSCI Barra.

EXHIBIT 8.6 Systematic-Residual Risk Decomposition

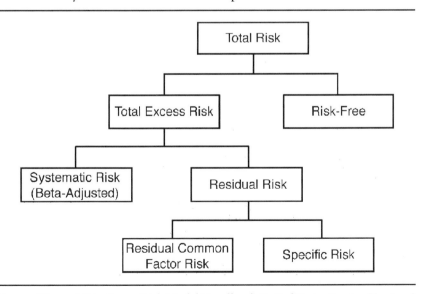

Source: Figure 4.3 in Barra, *Risk Model Handbook United States Equity: Version 3* (Berkeley, CA: Barra, 1998), p. 34. Reprinted with permission from MSCI Barra.

that is uncorrelated with the market portfolio. In turn, residual risk is partitioned into specific risk and common factor risk. Notice that the partitioning of risk described here is different from that in the Arbitrage Pricing Theory described earlier in this chapter. In that section, all risk factors that could not be diversified away were referred to as "systematic risks." In our discussion here, risk factors that cannot be diversified away are classified as market risk and common factor risk. Residual risk can be diversified to a negligible level.

Active Risk Decomposition

It is important to assess a portfolio's risk exposure and actual performance relative to a benchmark index. The active risk decomposition approach is useful for that purpose. In this type of decomposition, shown in Exhibit 8.7, the total excess return is divided into *benchmark risk* and *active risk*. Benchmark risk is defined as the risk associated with the benchmark portfolio.

Active risk is the risk that results from the manager's attempt to generate a return that will outperform the benchmark. Another name for active risk is *tracking error*, a concept covered in more detail in Chapter 4. The active risk is further partitioned into common factor risk and specific risk.

EXHIBIT 8.7 Active Risk Decomposition

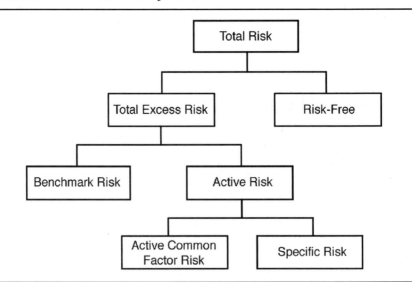

Source: Figure 4.4 in Barra, *Risk Model Handbook United States Equity: Version 3* (Berkeley, CA: Barra, 1998), p. 34. Reprinted with permission from MSCI Barra.

Active Systematic-Active Residual Risk Decomposition

There are managers who overlay a market-timing strategy on their stock selection. That is, they not only try to select stocks they believe will outperform but also try to time the purchase of the acquisition. For a manager who pursues such a strategy, it will be important in evaluating performance to separate market risk from common factor risks. In the active risk decomposition approach just discussed, there is no market risk identified as one of the risk factors.

Since market risk (i.e., systematic risk) is an element of active risk, its inclusion as a source of risk is preferred by managers. When market risk is included, we have the active systematic-active residual risk decomposition approach shown in Exhibit 8.8. Total excess risk is again divided into benchmark risk and active risk. However, active risk is further divided into active systematic risk (i.e., active market risk) and active residual risk. Then active residual risk is divided into common factor risks and specific risk.

Summary of Risk Decomposition

The four approaches to risk decomposition are just different ways of slicing up risk to help a manager in constructing and controlling the risk

EXHIBIT 8.8   Active Systematic-Active Residual Risk Decomposition

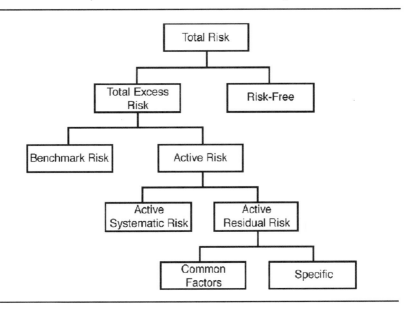

Source: Figure 4.5 in Barra, *Risk Model Handbook United States Equity: Version 3* (Berkeley, CA: Barra, 1998), p. 37. Reprinted with permission from MSCI Barra.

of a portfolio and for a client to understand how the manager performed. Exhibit 8.9 provides an overview of the four approaches to "carving up" risk into specific/common factor, systematic/residual, and benchmark/active risks.

Applications in Portfolio Construction and Risk Control

The power of a multifactor risk model is that given the risk factors and the risk factor sensitivities, a portfolio's risk exposure profile can be quantified and controlled. The three examples below show how this can be done so that the a manager can avoid making unintended bets. In particular, we discuss (1) how to assess the risk exposure of a portfolio; (2) the tracking of an index; and (3) the tilting a portfolio. In the examples, we use the Barra E3 factor model.[60] There are several other uses for factor models not discussed here. For some further examples and illustrations on performance attribution, see Fabozzi, Jones, and Vardharaj.[61]

EXHIBIT 8.9 Risk Decomposition Overview

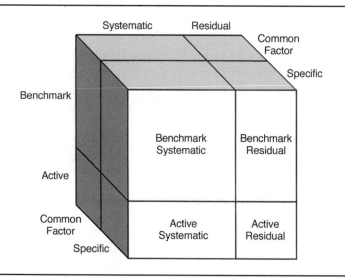

Source: Figure 4.6 in Barra, *Risk Model Handbook United States Equity: Version 3* (Berkeley, CA: Barra, 1998), p. 38. Reprinted with permission from MSCI Barra.

---

[60] The illustrations given are taken from Frank J. Fabozzi, Frank J. Jones, and Raman Vardharaj, "Multi-Factor Risk Models," Chapter 13 in Frank J. Fabozzi and Harry M. Markowitz (eds.), *The Theory and Practice of Investment Management* (Hoboken, NJ: John Wiley & Sons, 2002).

[61] Fabozzi, Jones, and Vardharaj, "Multi-Factor Equity Risk Models."

Assessing the Exposure of a Portfolio

A fundamental multifactor risk model can be used to assess whether the current portfolio is consistent with a manager's strengths. Exhibit 8.10 is a list of the top 15 holdings of Portfolio ABC as of September 30, 2000. Exhibit 8.11 is a risk-return report for the same portfolio. The portfolio had a total market value of over $3.7 billion, 202 holdings, and a predicted beta of 1.20. The risk report also shows that the portfolio had an active risk of 9.83%. This is its tracking error with respect to the benchmark, the S&P 500. Notice that over 80% of the active risk variance (which is 96.67) comes from the common factor risk variance (which is 81.34), and only a small proportion comes from the stock-specific risk variance (which is 15.33). Clearly, the manager of this portfolio has placed fairly large factor bets.

Exhibit 8.12a assesses the factor risk exposures of Portfolio ABC relative to those of the S&P 500, its benchmark. The first column shows the exposures of the portfolio, and the second column shows the exposures for the benchmark. The last column shows the active exposure, which is the difference between the portfolio exposure and the benchmark exposure. The exposures to the risk index factors are measured in units of standard deviation, while the exposures to the industry factors are measured in percentages. The portfolio has a high active exposure to the momentum risk index factor. That is, the stocks held in the portfolio have significant momentum. The portfolio's stocks were smaller than the benchmark average in terms of market cap. The industry factor exposures reveal that the portfolio had an exceptionally high active exposure to the semiconductor industry and electronic equipment industry. Exhibit 8.12b combines the industry exposures to obtain sector exposures. It shows that Portfolio ABC had a very high active exposure to the Technology sector. Such large bets can expose the portfolio to large swings in returns.

An important use of such risk reports is the identification of portfolio bets, both explicit and implicit. If, for example, the manager of Portfolio ABC did not want to place such a large Technology sector bet or momentum risk index bet, then he can rebalance the portfolio to minimize any such bets.

Index Tracking

In Chapter 4 we discussed index tracking. The objective is to match the performance of some specified stock market index with little tracking error. To do this, the risk profile of the indexed portfolio must match the risk profile of the designated stock market index. Put in other terms, the factor risk exposure of the indexed portfolio must match as closely as possible the exposure of the designated stock market index to the same factors. Any differences in the factor risk exposures result in tracking

EXHIBIT 8.10 Portfolio ABC's Holdings (Only the Top 15 Holdings Shown)

| Portfolio: | ABC Fund | Benchmark: | S&P500 | Model Date: | 2000-10-02 |
| Report Date: | 2000-10-15 | Price Date: | 2000-09-29 | Model: | U.S. Equity 3 |

Name	Shares	Price ($)	Weight (%)	Beta	Main Industry Name	Sector
General Elec. Co.	2,751,200	57.81	4.28	0.89	Financial Services	Financial
Citigroup, Inc.	2,554,666	54.06	3.72	0.98	Banks	Financial
Cisco Sys., Inc.	2,164,000	55.25	3.22	1.45	Computer Hardware	Technology
EMC Corp., Mass.	1,053,600	99.50	2.82	1.19	Computer Hardware	Technology
Intel Corp.	2,285,600	41.56	2.56	1.65	Semiconductors	Technology
Nortel Networks Corp. N	1,548,600	60.38	2.52	1.40	Electronic Equipment	Technology
Corning, Inc.	293,200	297.50	2.35	1.31	Electronic Equipment	Technology
International Business	739,000	112.50	2.24	1.05	Computer Software	Technology
Oracle Corp.	955,600	78.75	2.03	1.40	Computer Software	Technology
Sun Microsystems, Inc.	624,700	116.75	1.96	1.30	Computer Hardware	Technology
Lehman Bros. Hldgs. Inc.	394,700	148.63	1.58	1.51	Sec. & Asset Management	Financial
Morgan Stanley Dean Wi.	615,400	91.44	1.52	1.29	Sec. & Asset Management	Financial
Disney Walt Co.	1,276,700	38.25	1.32	0.85	Entertainment	Cnsmr. Services
Coca-Cola Co.	873,900	55.13	1.30	0.68	Food & Beverage	Cnsmr. (non-cyc.)
Microsoft Corp.	762,245	60.31	1.24	1.35	Computer Software	Technology

Source: Exhibit 13.7 in Frank J. Fabozzi, Frank J. Jones, and Raman Vardharaj, "Multi-Factor Risk Models," Chapter 13 in Frank J. Fabozzi and Harry M. Markowitz (eds.), *The Theory and Practice of Investment Management* (Hoboken, NJ: John Wiley & Sons, 2002), p. 353.

EXHIBIT 8.11 Portfolio ABC's Risk-Return Decomposition

RISK – RETURN

Number of Assets	202	Total Shares	62,648,570
		Average Share Price	$59.27
Portfolio Beta	1.20	Portfolio Value	$3,713,372,229.96

Risk Decomposition	Variance	Standard Deviation (%)
Active Specific Risk	15.33	3.92
Active Common Factor		
Risk Indices	44.25	6.65
Industries	17.82	4.22
Covariance	19.27	
Total Active Common Factor Risk[a]	81.34	9.02
Total Active[b]	96.67	9.83
Benchmark	247.65	15.74
Total Risk	441.63	21.02

[a] Equal to Risk Indices + Industries + Covariances
[b] Equal to Active Specific Risk + Total Active Common Factor Risk
Exhibit 13.8 in Frank J. Fabozzi, Frank J. Jones, and Raman Vardharaj, "Multi-Factor Risk Models," Chapter 13 in Frank J. Fabozzi and Harry M. Markowitz (eds.), *The Theory and Practice of Investment Management* (Hoboken, NJ: John Wiley & Sons, 2002), p. 353.

error. Identification of any differences allows the indexer to rebalance the portfolio to reduce tracking error.

To illustrate this, suppose that an index manager has constructed a portfolio of 50 stocks to match the S&P 500. Exhibit 8.13 shows output of the exposure to the Barra risk indices and industry groups of the 50-stock portfolio and the S&P 500. The last column in the exhibit shows the difference in the exposure. The differences are very small except for the exposures to the size factor and one industry (equity REIT). That is, the 50-stock portfolio has more exposure to the size risk index and equity REIT industry.

The illustration in Exhibit 8.13 uses price data as of December 31, 2001. It demonstrates how a multifactor risk model can be combined with an optimization model to construct an indexed portfolio when a given number of holdings is sought. Specifically, the portfolio analyzed in Exhibit 8.13 is the result of an application in which the manager wants a portfolio constructed that matches the S&P 500 with only 50

EXHIBIT 8.12 Analysis of Portfolio ABC's Exposures
a. Analysis of Risk Exposures to S&P 500

Factor Exposures

Risk Index Exposures (Std. Dev.)

	Mgd.	Bmk.	Act.		Mgd.	Bmk.	Act.
Volatility	0.220	−0.171	0.391	Value	−0.169	−0.034	−0.136
Momentum	0.665	−0.163	0.828	Earnings Variation	0.058	−0.146	0.204
Size	−0.086	0.399	−0.485	Leverage	0.178	−0.149	0.327
Size Nonlinearity	0.031	0.097	−0.067	Currency Sensitivity	0.028	−0.049	0.077
Trading Activity	0.552	−0.083	0.635	Yield	−0.279	0.059	−0.338
Growth	0.227	−0.167	0.395	Non-EST Universe	0.032	0.000	0.032
Earnings Yield	−0.051	0.081	−0.132				

Industry Weights (Percent)

	Mgd.	Bmk.	Act.		Mgd.	Bmk.	Act.
Mining and Metals	0.013	0.375	−0.362	Heavy Machinery	0.000	0.062	−0.062
Gold	0.000	0.119	−0.119	Industrial Parts	0.234	1.086	−0.852
Forestry and Paper	0.198	0.647	−0.449	Electric Utility	1.852	1.967	−0.115
Chemicals	0.439	2.386	−1.947	Gas Utilities	0.370	0.272	0.098
Energy Reserves	2.212	4.589	−2.377	Railroads	0.000	0.211	−0.211
Oil Refining	0.582	0.808	−0.226	Airlines	0.143	0.194	−0.051
Oil Services	2.996	0.592	2.404	Truck/Sea/Air Freight	0.000	0.130	−0.130
Food & Beverages	2.475	3.073	−0.597	Medical Services	1.294	0.354	0.940
Alcohol	0.000	0.467	−0.467	Medical Products	0.469	2.840	−2.370
Tobacco	0.000	0.403	−0.403	Drugs	6.547	8.039	−1.492
Home Products	0.000	1.821	−1.821	Electronic Equipment	11.052	5.192	5.860
Grocery Stores	0.000	0.407	−0.407	Semiconductors	17.622	6.058	11.564
Consumer Durables	0.165	0.125	0.039	Computer Hardware	12.057	9.417	2.640
Motor Vehicles & Parts	0.000	0.714	−0.714	Computer Software	9.374	6.766	2.608
Apparel & Textiles	0.000	0.191	−0.191	Defense & Aerospace	0.014	0.923	−0.909
Clothing Stores	0.177	0.308	−0.131	Telephone	0.907	4.635	−3.728
Specialty Retail	0.445	2.127	−1.681	Wireless Telecom.	0.000	1.277	−1.277
Department Stores	0.000	2.346	−2.346	Information Services	0.372	1.970	−1.598
Constructn. and Real Prop.	0.569	0.204	0.364	Industrial Services	0.000	0.511	−0.511
Publishing	0.014	0.508	−0.494	Life/Health Insurance	0.062	1.105	−1.044
Media	1.460	2.077	−0.617	Property/Casualty Ins.	1.069	2.187	−1.118
Hotels	0.090	0.112	−0.022	Banks	5.633	6.262	−0.630
Restaurants	0.146	0.465	−0.319	Thrifts	1.804	0.237	1.567
Entertainment	1.179	1.277	−0.098	Securities and Asst. Mgmt.	6.132	2.243	3.888
Leisure	0.000	0.247	−0.247	Financial Services	5.050	5.907	−0.857
Environmental Services	0.000	0.117	−0.117	Internet	3.348	1.729	1.618
Heavy Electrical Eqp.	1.438	1.922	−0.483	Equity REIT	0.000	0.000	0.000

Note: Mgd. = Managed; Bmk. = S&P 500 (the benchmark); Act. = Active = Managed − Benchmark

EXHIBIT 8.12 (Continued)
b. Analysis of Sector Exposures Relative to S&P 500

Sector Weights (Percent)

	Mgd.	Bmk.	Act.		Mgd.	Bmk.	Act.
Basic Materials	0.65	3.53	−2.88	Utility	2.22	2.24	−0.02
Mining	0.01	0.38	−0.36	Electric Utility	1.85	1.97	−0.12
Gold	0.00	0.12	−0.12	Gas Utility	0.37	0.27	0.10
Forest	0.20	0.65	−0.45	Transport	0.14	0.54	−0.39
Chemical	0.44	2.39	−1.95	Railroad	0.00	0.21	−0.21
Energy	5.79	5.99	−0.20	Airlines	0.14	0.19	−0.05
Energy Reserves	2.21	4.59	−2.38	Truck Freight	0.00	0.13	−0.13
Oil Refining	0.58	0.81	−0.23	Health Care	8.31	11.23	−2.92
Oil Services	3.00	0.59	2.40	Medical Provider	1.29	0.35	0.94
Cnsmr (non-cyc.)	2.48	6.17	−3.70	Medical Products	0.47	2.84	−2.37
Food/Beverage	2.48	3.07	−0.60	Drugs	6.55	8.04	−1.49
Alcohol	0.00	0.47	−0.47	Technology	53.47	30.09	23.38
Tobacco	0.00	0.40	−0.40	Electronic Equipment	11.05	5.19	5.86
Home Prod.	0.00	1.82	−1.82	Semiconductors	17.62	6.06	11.56
Grocery	0.00	0.41	−0.41	Computer Hardware	12.06	9.42	2.64
Cnsmr. (cyclical)	1.36	6.01	−4.66	Computer Software	9.37	6.77	2.61
Cons. Duarbles	0.17	0.13	0.04	Defense & Aerospace	0.01	0.92	−0.91
Motor Vehicles	0.00	0.71	−0.71	Internet	3.35	1.73	1.62
Apparel	0.00	0.19	−0.19	Telecommunications	0.91	5.91	−5.00
Clothing	0.18	0.31	−0.13	Telephone	0.91	4.63	−3.73
Specialty Retail	0.45	2.13	−1.68	Wireless	0.00	1.28	−1.28
Dept. Store	0.00	2.35	−2.35	Commercial Services	0.37	2.48	−2.11
Construction	0.57	0.20	0.36	Information Services	0.37	1.97	−1.60
Cnsmr Services	2.89	4.69	−1.80	Industrial Services	0.00	0.51	−0.51
Publishing	0.01	0.51	−0.49	Financial	19.75	17.94	1.81
Media	1.46	2.08	−0.62	Life Insurance	0.06	1.11	−1.04
Hotels	0.09	0.11	−0.02	Property Insurance	1.07	2.19	−1.12
Restaurants	0.15	0.47	−0.32	Banks	5.63	6.26	−0.63
Entertainment	1.18	1.28	−0.10	Thrifts	1.80	0.24	1.57
Leisure	0.00	0.25	−0.25	Securities/Asst. Mgmt.	6.13	2.24	3.89
Industrials	1.67	3.19	−1.51	Financial Services	5.05	5.91	−0.86
Env. Services	0.00	0.12	−0.12	Equity REIT	0.00	0.00	0.00
Heavy Electrical	1.44	1.92	−0.48				
Heavy Mach.	0.00	0.06	−0.06				
Industrial Parts	0.23	1.09	−0.85				

Note: Mgd = Managed; Bmk = Benchmark; Act = Active = Managed − Benchmark
Source: Exhibit 13.9 in Frank J. Fabozzi, Frank J. Jones, and Raman Vardharaj, "Multi-Factor Risk Models," Chapter 13 in Frank J. Fabozzi and Harry M. Markowitz (eds.), *The Theory and Practice of Investment Management* (Hoboken, NJ: John Wiley & Sons, 2002), pp. 355–356.

EXHIBIT 8.13　Factor Exposures of a 50-Stock Portfolio that
Optimally Matches the S&P 500

Risk Index Exposures (Std. Dev.)

	Mgd.	Bmk.	Act.		Mgd.	Bmk.	Act.
Volatility	−0.141	−0.084	−0.057	Value	−0.072	−0.070	−0.003
Momentum	−0.057	−0.064	0.007	Earnings Variation	−0.058	−0.088	0.029
Size	0.588	0.370	0.217	Leverage	−0.206	−0.106	−0.100
Size Nonlinearity	0.118	0.106	0.013	Currency Sensitivity	−0.001	−0.012	0.012
Trading Activity	−0.101	−0.005	−0.097	Yield	0.114	0.034	0.080
Growth	−0.008	−0.045	0.037	Non-EST Universe	0.000	0.000	0.000
Earnings Yield	0.103	0.034	0.069				

Industry Weights (Percent)

	Mgd.	Bmk.	Act.		Mgd.	Bmk.	Act.
Mining & Metals	0.000	0.606	−0.606	Heavy Machinery	0.000	0.141	−0.141
Gold	0.000	0.161	−0.161	Industrial Parts	1.124	1.469	−0.345
Forestry and Paper	1.818	0.871	0.947	Electric Utility	0.000	1.956	−1.956
Chemicals	2.360	2.046	0.314	Gas Utilities	0.000	0.456	−0.456
Energy Reserves	5.068	4.297	0.771	Railroads	0.000	0.373	−0.373
Oil Refining	1.985	1.417	0.568	Airlines	0.000	0.206	−0.206
Oil Services	1.164	0.620	0.544	Truck/Sea/Air Freight	0.061	0.162	−0.102
Food & Beverages	2.518	3.780	−1.261	Medical Services	1.280	0.789	0.491
Alcohol	0.193	0.515	−0.322	Medical Products	3.540	3.599	−0.059
Tobacco	1.372	0.732	0.641	Drugs	9.861	10.000	−0.140
Home Products	0.899	2.435	−1.536	Electronic Equipment	0.581	1.985	−1.404
Grocery Stores	0.000	0.511	−0.511	Semiconductors	4.981	4.509	0.472
Consumer Durables	0.000	0.166	−0.166	Computer Hardware	4.635	4.129	0.506
Motor Vehicles & Parts	0.000	0.621	−0.621	Computer Software	6.893	6.256	0.637
Apparel & Textiles	0.000	0.373	−0.373	Defense & Aerospace	1.634	1.336	0.297
Clothing Stores	0.149	0.341	−0.191	Telephone	3.859	3.680	0.180
Specialty Retail	1.965	2.721	−0.756	Wireless Telecom.	1.976	1.565	0.411
Department Stores	4.684	3.606	1.078	Information Services	0.802	2.698	−1.896
Constructn. & Real Prop.	0.542	0.288	0.254	Industrial Services	0.806	0.670	0.136
Publishing	2.492	0.778	1.713	Life/Health Insurance	0.403	0.938	−0.535
Media	1.822	1.498	0.323	Property/Casualty Ins.	2.134	2.541	−0.407
Hotels	1.244	0.209	1.035	Banks	8.369	7.580	0.788
Restaurants	0.371	0.542	−0.171	Thrifts	0.000	0.362	−0.362
Entertainment	2.540	1.630	0.910	Securities & Asst. Mgmt.	2.595	2.017	0.577
Leisure	0.000	0.409	−0.409	Financial Services	6.380	6.321	0.059
Environmental Services	0.000	0.220	−0.220	Internet	0.736	0.725	0.011
Heavy Electrical Eqp.	1.966	1.949	0.017	Equity REIT	2.199	0.193	2.006

Note: Mgd = Managed; Bmk = S&P 500 (the benchmark); Act = Active = Managed
− Benchmark
Source: Exhibit 13.10 in Frank J. Fabozzi, Frank J. Jones, and Raman Vardharaj,
"Multi-Factor Risk Models," Chapter 13 in Frank J. Fabozzi and Harry M.
Markowitz (eds.), *The Theory and Practice of Investment Management* (Hoboken,
NJ: John Wiley & Sons, 2002), p. 358.

stocks and that minimizes tracking error. Not only is the 50-stock portfolio constructed, but the optimization model combined with the factor
model indicates that the tracking error is only 2.19%. Because this is the
optimal 50-stock portfolio to replicate the S&P 500 that minimizes
tracking error risk, this tells the index manager that if he seeks a lower
tracking error, more stocks must be held. Note, however, that the optimal portfolio changes as time passes and prices move.

Tilting a Portfolio

Now let us look at how an active manager can construct a portfolio to
make intentional bets. Suppose that a portfolio manager seeks to construct a portfolio that generates superior returns relative to the S&P 500
by tilting it toward low P/E stocks. At the same time, the manager does
not want to increase tracking error significantly. An obvious approach
may seem to be to identify all the stocks in the universe that have a
lower-than-average P/E. The problem with this approach is that it introduces unintentional bets with respect to the other risk indices.

Instead, an optimization method combined with a multifactor risk
model can be used to construct the desired portfolio. The necessary
inputs to this process are the tilt exposure sought and the benchmark
stock market index. Additional constraints can be placed, for example,
on the number of stocks to be included in the portfolio. The Barra optimization model can also handle additional specifications such as forecasts of expected returns or alphas on the individual stocks.

In our illustration, the tilt exposure sought is towards low P/E
stocks, that is, high earnings yield stocks (since earnings yield is the
inverse of P/E). The benchmark is the S&P 500. We seek a portfolio that
has an average earnings yield that is at least 0.5 standard deviations
more than that of the earnings yield of the benchmark. We do not place
any limit on the number of stocks to be included in the portfolio. We
also do not want the active exposure to any other risk index factor
(other than earnings yield) to be more than 0.1 standard deviations in
magnitude. This way we avoid placing unintended bets. While we do
not report the holdings of the optimal portfolio here, Exhibit 8.14 provides an analysis of that portfolio by comparing the risk exposure of the
50-stock optimal portfolio to that of the S&P 500.

OTHER APPROACHES TO VOLATILITY ESTIMATION

There are several other estimation procedures for volatility that have
received considerable interest in finance in general, but not necessarily

EXHIBIT 8.14   Factor Exposures of a Portfolio Tilted Towards Earnings Yield

Risk Index Exposures (Std. Dev.)

	Mgd.	Bmk.	Act.		Mgd.	Bmk.	Act.
Volatility	-0.126	·-0.084	-0.042	Value	0.030	-0.070	0.100
Momentum	0.013	-0.064	0.077	Earnings Variation	-0.028	-0.088	0.060
Size	0.270	0.370	-0.100	Leverage	-0.006	-0.106	0.100
Size Nonlinearity	0.067	0.106	-0.038	Currency Sensitivity	-0.105	-0.012	-0.093
Trading Activity	0.095	-0.005	0.100	Yield	0.134	0.034	0.100
Growth	-0.023	-0.045	0.022	Non-EST Universe	0.000	0.000	0.000
Earnings Yield	0.534	0.034	0.500				

Industry Weights (Percent)

	Mgd.	Bmk.	Act.		Mgd.	Bmk.	Act.
Mining & Metals	0.022	0.606	-0.585	Heavy Machinery	0.000	0.141	-0.141
Gold	0.000	0.161	-0.161	Industrial Parts	1.366	1.469	-0.103
Forestry and Paper	0.000	0.871	-0.871	Electric Utility	4.221	1.956	2.265
Chemicals	1.717	2.046	-0.329	Gas Utilities	0.204	0.456	-0.252
Energy Reserves	4.490	4.297	0.193	Railroads	0.185	0.373	-0.189
Oil Refining	3.770	1.417	2.353	Airlines	0.000	0.206	-0.206
Oil Services	0.977	0.620	0.357	Truck/Sea/Air Freight	0.000	0.162	-0.162
Food & Beverages	0.823	3.780	-2.956	Medical Services	0.000	0.789	-0.789
Alcohol	0.365	0.515	-0.151	Medical Products	1.522	3.599	-2.077
Tobacco	3.197	0.732	2.465	Drugs	7.301	10.000	-2.699
Home Products	0.648	2.435	-1.787	Electronic Equipment	0.525	1.985	-1.460
Grocery Stores	0.636	0.511	0.125	Semiconductors	3.227	4.509	-1.282
Consumer Durables	0.000	0.166	-0.166	Computer Hardware	2.904	4.129	-1.224
Motor Vehicles & Parts	0.454	0.621	-0.167	Computer Software	7.304	6.256	1.048
Apparel & Textiles	0.141	0.373	-0.232	Defense & Aerospace	1.836	1.336	0.499
Clothing Stores	0.374	0.341	0.033	Telephone	6.290	3.680	2.610
Specialty Retail	0.025	2.721	-2.696	Wireless Telecom.	2.144	1.565	0.580
Department Stores	3.375	3.606	-0.231	Information Services	0.921	2.698	-1.777
Constructn. & Real Prop.	9.813	0.288	9.526	Industrial Services	0.230	0.670	-0.440
Publishing	0.326	0.778	-0.452	Life/health Insurance	1.987	0.938	1.048
Media	0.358	1.498	-1.140	Property/Casualty Ins.	4.844	2.541	2.304
Hotels	0.067	0.209	-0.141	Banks	8.724	7.580	1.144
Restaurants	0.000	0.542	-0.542	Thrifts	0.775	0.362	0.413
Entertainment	0.675	1.630	-0.955	Securities & Asst. Mgmt.	3.988	2.017	1.971
Leisure	0.000	0.409	-0.409	Financial Services	5.510	6.321	-0.811
Environmental Services	0.000	0.220	-0.220	Internet	0.434	0.725	-0.291
Heavy Electrical Eqp.	1.303	1.949	-0.647	Equity REIT	0.000	0.193	-0.193

Note: Mgd = Managed; Bmk = S&P 500 (the benchmark); Act = Active = Managed – Benchmark
Source: Exhibit 13.11 in Frank J. Fabozzi, Frank J. Jones, and Raman Vardharaj, "Multi-Factor Risk Models," Chapter 13 in Frank J. Fabozzi and Harry M. Markowitz (eds.), *The Theory and Practice of Investment Management* (Hoboken, NJ: John Wiley & Sons, 2002), p. 359.

to the area of portfolio management, in particular. We review implied volatility, clustering, GARCH, and stochastic volatility models below.

Implied Volatility

Another possibility to estimate the volatility of a stock is to solve for its implied volatility from the Black-Scholes formula. One can argue that volatility implied from option prices is more of a forward-looking measure than realized historical volatility. Since options on most stocks are available with different expirations, it makes sense to use the at-the-money option that has a maturity closest to the desired investment horizon. Alternatively, a weighted average of nearby in- and out-of-the-money options is a possibility.

Of course, there are not that many "correlation options" traded. Therefore, we can only expect to be able to gain insight about volatilities—not about correlations. Still, this information can be useful. For example, we may partition the covariance matrix according to

$$\Sigma = \Lambda C \Lambda'$$

where Λ is a diagonal matrix of the volatilities of returns and C is a correlation matrix. Hence, we see that the volatilities can be modified independently from the correlations.

A natural question is whether implied volatilities are better than historical volatilities in forecasting future volatility. Here, the results are mixed. Some studies conclude that implied volatilities provide an improved forecast, whereas others conclude the opposite.[62] Nevertheless, most of the available studies were done from the perspective of option pricing and these results can therefore not be directly extrapolated to portfolio management purposes.

Clustering

Focardi and Fabozzi discuss some of the uses of clustering in financial applications.[63] Clustering means forming groups that can be distinguished from each other by some rule, typically through a "distance

---

[62] See, for example, João Duque and Dean A. Paxson, "Empirical Evidence on Volatility Estimators," Working Paper, Universidade Técnica de Lisboa and University of Manchester, 1997; Linda Canina and Stephen Figlewski, "The Informational Content of Implied Volatility," Working Paper, New York University, Stern School of Business, 1991; and William K. H. Fung and David A. Hsieh, "Empirical Analysis of Implied Volatility Stocks, Bonds and Currencies," Proceedings of the 4th Annual Conference of the Financial Options Research Centre University of Warwick, Coventry, England, 19-20 July 1991.

function."[64] In particular, objects within each group are "similar," while two objects from two different groups are "dissimilar." One of the proposed applications use the detection of stable long-term relationships such as long-term correlations (cointegrating relationships) between time series that are much more persistent than classical correlations.

ARCH/GARCH Models

Volatility exhibits persistence in terms of serial correlation. For example, periods of high (low) volatility tends to stay around for a while before volatility goes down (up) again. Engle introduced the so-called *autoregressive conditionally heteroskedastic* processes (ARCH) to capture this phenomena.[65] Today, many different generalizations and extensions to these models exist. Probably the most well-known is the generalized ARCH (GARCH) model that first appeared in a paper by Bollerslev.[66] A univariate GARCH(p,q) (we discuss these models further in Chapter 12) is defined by:

$$\sigma_{T+1}^2 = \omega + \sum_{i=1}^{p} \alpha_i (R_{T-i} - \mu)^2 + \sum_{j=1}^{q} \beta_j R_{T-j}^2$$

where ω, μ, α_i ($i = 1, ..., p$), and β_j ($j = 1, ..., q$) are parameters that need to be estimated.

Noticeably, ARCH/GARCH models depend on the sampling frequency: They are not invariant under time aggregation. This means that the results of the model will change if, for example, we use daily data as opposed to weekly or monthly data.

Several multivariate extensions of GARCH have been proposed where the entire variance-covariance matrix is time-dependent. When considering large portfolios of stocks, the specification of models is critical. In fact, estimates are difficult to obtain given the exceedingly large number of parameters needed if one wants to estimate the entire vari-

---

[63] Sergio Focardi and Frank J. Fabozzi, "Clustering Economic and Financial Time Series: Exploring the Existence of Stable Correlation Conditions," *Finance Letters* 2 (2004), pp. 1–9.

[64] Clustering is a "data-mining" technique. We discuss data mining in Chapter 13. An excellent reference to this very broad topic is Richard O. Duda, Peter E. Heart, and David G. Stork, *Pattern Classification* (New York: John Wiley & Sons, 2001).

[65] Robert F. Engle, "Autoregressive Conditional Heteroskedasticity with Estimates of the Variance of U.K. Inflation," *Econometrica* 50 (1982), pp. 987–1008.

[66] Tim Bollerslev, "Generalized Autoregressive Conditional Heteroskedasticity," *Journal of Econometrics* 31 (1986), pp. 307–327.

ance-covariance matrix. A direct GARCH approach is therefore not practical, especially in a large portfolio context. One possible simplification that has been suggested is to assume that correlations are constant and model each individual variance with a univariate GARCH. The computational complexity of these models prevents all but the most sophisticated portfolio managers from using them. Different simplified approaches have been suggested, but there is yet no clear consensus about their effectiveness in portfolio management.

Stochastic Volatility Models

Recently, major developments have been achieved in so-called *structured stochastic volatility* (SV) models, by the introduction of dynamic factors and Bayesian analysis. Stochastic volatility models consider volatility as a variable term that should be forecasted. More generally, not only volatility but the entire covariance matrix can be regarded as a set of variable terms to forecast. But, as we know, estimates of the covariance matrix are not stable but vary with time. An early (and not entirely satisfactory) attempt to deal with this problem was covariance matrix discounting first introduced by Quintana and West.[67]

Covariance matrix discounting assumes that the covariance matrix changes with time. At any moment there is a "local" covariance matrix. The covariance matrix is estimated as a weighted average of past covariance matrices. Weighting factors typically decay exponentially with time. Since being introduced in the 1980s, covariance discounting has been used as a component of applied Bayesian forecasting models in financial applications.

However, covariance matrix discounting methods do not have any real predictive power: simplistically speaking, they provide exponentially smoothed estimates of the local covariance structure (i.e., the covariance matrix which is supposed to hold at a given moment) within the Bayesian modeling framework. They estimate change rather than forecast change. As a consequence, these models tend to work reasonably well in slow changing volatility environments, but do poorly in fast-moving markets or when structural change occurs.

Much greater flexibility is achieved by incorporating dynamic factor models or Bayesian dynamic factor models that can explicitly capture change through patterns of variation in process parameters throughout

---

[67] Jose M. Quintana and Michael West, "An Analysis of International Exchange Rates Using Multivariate DLMs," *The Statistician* 36 (1987), pp. 275–281; and Jose M. Quintana and Michael West, "Time Series Analysis of Compositional Data," in J. M. Bernardo, M. H. De Groot, D. V. Lindley, and A. F. M. Smith (eds.), *Bayesian Statistics, 3rd ed.* (Oxford: Oxford University Press, 1988), pp. 747–756.

time.[68] In other words, the covariance matrix is driven by a dynamic multifactor model. This approach has already shown significant improvement in short-term forecasting of multiple financial and economic time series, and appears to be a promising technique for intermediate and long-term horizons as well. Although Bayesian dynamic factor models are computationally demanding and often require time-consuming simulations, the availability of more powerful computers and recent advances in Markov Chain Monte Carlo methods will contribute to the growing use of these models for forecasting purposes.

APPLICATION TO INVESTMENT STRATEGIES AND PROPRIETARY TRADING

After the meltdown of Long-Term Capital Management (LTCM) in September 1998, when many well-known investment banks lost significant amounts of money, the view on the risk management of proprietary trading functions and hedge funds drastically changed. For example, in April 1999, the Clinton administration published a study on the LTCM crisis and its implications for systemic risk in financial markets entitled "Hedge Funds, Leverage, and the Lessons of Long-Term Capital Management."[69] This report describes the events around the LTCM crisis and provides an analysis of some of the implications.

As a consequence, not only are hedge funds more regulated today, but also hedge fund managers and proprietary traders themselves are more aware and cautious of their different risk exposures.

A deeper discussion of hedge funds and their management is beyond the scope of this book.[70] Nevertheless, the tools introduced in this book can be applied to analyze many of the relevant questions regarding proprietary trading and hedge fund strategies. We highlight a few issues below.

Risk constraints are typically imposed upon each strategy, such as capital requirements, expected standard deviation of the strategy, value at risk, liquidity constraints, and exposures to common risk factors (for example, standard equity and fixed income indices). On a second level, similar constraints are imposed upon the overall investment fund or

---

[68] Omar Aguilar and Mike West, "Bayesian Dynamic Factor Models and Variance Matrix Discounting for Portfolio Allocation," Working Paper, ISDS, Duke University, 1998.

[69] Report of The President's Working Group on Financial Markets, "Hedge Funds, Leverage, and the Lessons of Long-Term Capital Management," April 1999.

[70] We refer the interested reader to Stuart A. McCrary, *How to Create and Manage a Hedge Fund: A Professional's Guide* (Hoboken, NJ: John Wiley & Sons, 2002).

hedge fund. These risk constraints are also used for risk allocation purposes to determine what portion of the total fund should be invested in or exposed to a specific strategy.[71]

When it comes to quantitative trading strategies, the consideration of model risk is a very important issue. Proprietary traders commonly use loss targets to minimize that risk. For example, if more money than a specific target is lost in a specific strategy, then that strategy is closed down and reevaluated. We will come back to the topic of model risk in Chapter 13 when we discuss model selection and its pitfalls.

One should exercise caution when using complex forecasting or estimation techniques, especially if only limited data are available for estimation and backtesting. When there are too many parameters or factors that have to be estimated, it is easy to end up with an over-parameterized model that leads to poor out-of-sample performance. In many instances simple models with few parameters tend to perform much better out-of-sample, confirming the merit of simple and robust estimators.

There is an ongoing debate on whether one should develop either one or a few very good strategies, or combine many weaker strategies. Different portfolio managers, proprietary traders, and hedge fund managers diverge in opinion. The typical argument goes back to the correlation between the different strategies. From modern portfolio theory we know that it is possible to combine several uncorrelated trading models, each with a moderate Sharpe ratio (say 1, for example), to obtain an overall portfolio with a higher Sharpe ratio (say 2, for example). The proponents of using just a few strategies argue that models are often more correlated than we really think. In particular, in downward markets—especially during crashes—correlations of individual securities tend to increase, which makes many trading strategies interrelated.[72] Proponents of this argument therefore believe in developing only a few good strategies that are significantly different from each other.

SUMMARY

- ■ The value of one stock should equal the present value of all future dividends the owner of the stock expects to receive from that share. This is the essence behind *dividend discount models* (DDM).

---

[71] For a good discussion on this topic see Kurt Winkelmann, "Risk Budgeting: Managing Active Risk at the Total Fund Level," Investment Management Division, Goldman Sachs, 2000.

[72] Peter Muller, "Proprietary Trading: Truth and Fiction," *Quantitative Finance*, 1 (2001), pp. 6–8.

■ In order to apply the classical mean-variance framework an investor has to provide estimates of expected returns and covariances.

■ The sample means and covariances of financial return series are easy to calculate, but may exhibit significant estimation errors.

■ Serial correlation or autocorrelation is the correlation of the return of a security with itself over successive time intervals. Heteroskedasticity means that variances/covariances are not constant but changing over time.

■ In practical applications is important to correct the covariance estimator for serial correlation and heteroskedasticity.

■ The sample covariance estimator can be improved upon by increasing the sampling frequency. This is not the case for the sample expected return estimator whose accuracy can only be improved by extending the length of the sample.

■ There is little information in the covariance matrix of a large portfolio. Only a few eigenvalues or factors carry information while the others are simply the result of statistical fluctuations.

■ The *Arbitrage Pricing Theory* (APT) asserts that investors want to be compensated for the risk factors that systematically affect the return of a security.

■ The compensation in the APT is the sum of the products of each risk factor's systematic risk and the risk premium assigned to it by the financial market.

■ An investor is not compensated for accepting nonsystematic risk.

■ Factor models can be used for estimating expected returns and covariances of securities.

■ There are several other approaches to the estimation of the volatility of a security: implied volatility, clustering, GARCH, and stochastic volatility models.

CHAPTER 9

Robust Frameworks for Estimation and Portfolio Allocation

Markowitz first introduced portfolio selection using a quantitative optimization procedure that balances the trade-off between risk and return.[1] His work laid ground for the Capital Asset Pricing Model (CAPM), the most fundamental General Equilibrium Theory in modern finance, which we discussed in Chapters 7 and 8. However, more than 50 years after Markowitz's seminal work, it appears that full risk-return optimization at the portfolio level is done only at the more quantitative firms, where processes for automated forecast generation and risk control are already in place. Somewhat surprisingly, in many firms today portfolio management still remains a judgmental process based on qualitative, not quantitative, assessments.

Although optimization technology is considered to be mature, many asset managers have had problems applying it or have avoided it altogether. One reason is that, in practical applications, classical mean-variance optimization is very sensitive to the inputs (i.e., expected returns of each asset and their covariance matrix). For example, "optimal" portfolios often have extreme or nonintuitive weights for some of the individual assets. Generally, the practitioner's solution to this problem has been to add constraints to the original problem in order to limit extreme or nonintuitive portfolio weights. However, as a result, the constraints—instead of the forecasts—often determine the portfolio, making the risk-return optimization process pointless. Practitioners applying mean-variance portfolio allocation often face additional problems including:

---

[1] Harry M. Markowitz, "Portfolio Selection," *Journal of Finance* 7 (1952), pp. 77–91.

- Poor model *ex post* performance coupled in many instances with the risk of maximizing error rather than minimizing it
- Difficulty in estimating accurate expected returns and a stable covariance matrix of returns for a large number of assets
- Sensitivity of portfolio weights to small changes in expected return forecasts

In addressing these issues from a practical point of view, one important aspect is to make the portfolio allocation process more robust to different sources of risk—including estimation and model risk. The central theme of this chapter is to discuss the many improvements that have been proposed to make the mean-variance framework more robust for practical applications. In Chapter 17 we consider model and estimation risk from a more general perspective.

A common critique to the mean-variance optimization framework is its over-simplistic, unrealistic assumption that investors only care about the first two moments of the return distribution. It is well known that many return distributions in financial markets exhibit fat tails and other effects that can only be taken into account by incorporating higher moments, beyond the mean and variance. In Chapter 5 we covered several extensions to classical mean-variance optimization that incorporates the effect of higher moments.

Closely related to Bayesian modeling, *Random Coefficient Models* (RCM) have recently started to attract some attention.[2] We provide an introduction to these models in the context of mitigating model risk in Chapter 17.

The outline of the chapter is as follows. First, we provide a general overview of some of the common problems encountered in mean-variance optimization before we turn our attention to shrinkage estimators for expected returns and the covariance matrix. Within the context of Bayesian estimation, we then focus on the Black-Litterman model. We derive the model using so-called "mixed estimation" from classical econometrics. Introducing a simple cross-sectional momentum strategy, we then show how we can combine this strategy with market equilibrium using the Black-Litterman model in the mean-variance framework to rebalance the portfolio on a monthly basis. Finally, we discuss how estimation error in the inputs can be incorporated in the portfolio allocation process. In particular, we introduce the simulation technique referred to as portfolio resampling and cover a recent approach called robust portfolio optimization.

---

[2] Some standard references to this area include P. A. V. B. Swamy, *Statistical Inference in Random Coefficient Models* (New York: Springer-Verlag, 1971); and Cheng Hsaio, *Analysis of Panel Data* (New York: Cambridge University Press, 1986). The estimators developed by these authors are accordingly referred to as the Swamy estimator and Hsaio estimator.

PRACTICAL PROBLEMS ENCOUNTERED IN MEAN-VARIANCE OPTIMIZATION

The simplicity and the intuitive appeal of portfolio construction using modern portfolio theory have attracted significant attention both in academia and in practice. Yet, despite considerable effort it took many years until portfolio managers started using modern portfolio theory for managing real money. Unfortunately, in real world applications there are many problems with it, and portfolio optimization is still considered by many practitioners to be difficult to apply. In this section we consider some of the typical problems encountered in mean-variance optimization.

In Chapter 8, we mentioned that optimized portfolios do normally not perform as well in practice as one would expect from theory. For example, they are often outperformed by simple allocation strategies such the equally weighted portfolio[3] or the global minimum variance portfolio (GMV).[4] In fact, we saw in the illustration in Chapter 4 that the GMV and the equally weighted portfolios significantly outperformed the mean-variance portfolio. Simply put, the "optimized" portfolio is not optimal at all.

Portfolio weights are often not stable over time but change significantly each time the portfolio is reoptimized, leading to unnecessary turnover and increased transaction costs. Adding to this injury, these portfolios typically present extreme holdings ("corner solutions") in a few securities while other securities have close to zero weight. Consequently, these "optimized" portfolios are not necessarily well diversified and exposed to unnecessary *ex post* risk.[5]

The reason for these phenomena is not a sign that mean-variance optimization does not work, but rather that the modern portfolio theory framework is very sensitive to the accuracy in inputs. To some extent, this can be improved by using better forecasts or estimators. However, by taking the estimation errors, whether large or small, into account in the optimization, further improvements can be achieved. As we discussed in Chapter 8, this problem is related to the fact that the mean-variance optimizer "does not know" that the inputs are statistical estimates and therefore are uncertain. Implicitly, when we are using classical mean-variance optimization we are assuming that inputs are deterministic and known with certainty.

[3] J. D. Jobson and Bob M. Korkie, "Putting Markowitz Theory to Work," *Journal of Portfolio Management* 7 (1981), pp. 70–74.
[4] Philippe Jorion, "Bayesian and CAPM Estimators of the Means: Implications for Portfolio Selection," *Journal of Banking and Finance* 15 (1991), pp. 717–727.
[5] See Richard C. Green and Burton Hollifield, "When Will Mean-Variance Efficient Portfolios Be Well Diversified?" *Journal of Finance* 47 (1992), pp. 1785–1809 and Richard O. Michaud, "The Markowitz Optimization Enigma: Is 'Optimized' Optimal?" *Financial Analysts Journal* (January–February 1989), pp. 31–42.

In the remaining part of this section we elaborate on: (1) the sensitivity to estimation error; (2) the effects of uncertainty in the inputs in the optimization process; and (3) the large data requirement necessary for the mean-variance framework.

Sensitivity to Estimation Error

In a portfolio optimization context, securities with large expected returns and low standard deviations will be overweighted and conversely, securities with low expected returns and high standard deviations will be underweighted. Therefore, large estimation errors in expected returns and/or variances/covariances will introduce errors in the optimized portfolio weights. For this reason, people often cynically refer to optimizers as "error maximizers."

Uncertainty from estimation error in expected returns tends to have more influence than in the covariance matrix in a mean-variance optimization.[6] The relative importance depends on the investor's risk aversion, but as a general rule of thumb, errors in the expected returns are about 10 times more important than errors in the covariance matrix, and errors in the variances are about twice as important as errors in the covariances.[7] As the risk tolerance increases, the relative impact of estimation errors in the expected returns becomes even more important. Conversely, as the risk tolerance decreases, the relative impact between errors in expected returns and the covariance matrix becomes smaller. From this simple "rule," it follows that the major focus should be on providing good estimates for the expected returns, followed by the variances.

Broadly speaking, there are three different kinds of approaches that will decrease the impact of estimation errors in the mean-variance optimization, and as a side effect also lead to more diversified portfolio weights. One approach is to improve the accuracy of the inputs by using a more robust estimation framework. Part of this category is shrinkage and Bayesian estimators that we discuss in the next two sections. The

---

[6] See, Michael J. Best and Robert R. Grauer, "The Analytics of Sensitivity Analysis for Mean-Variance Portfolio Problems," *International Review of Financial Analysis* 1 (1992), pp. 17–37; and Michael J. Best and Robert R. Grauer, "On the Sensitivity of Mean-Variance-Efficient Portfolios to Changes in Assets Means: Some Analytical and Computational Results," *Review of Financial Studies* 4 (1991), pp. 315–342.

[7] Vijay K. Chopra and William T. Ziemba, "The Effect of Errors in Means, Variances, and Covariances on Optimal Portfolio Choice," *Journal of Portfolio Management* 19 (1993), pp. 6–11; and Jarl G. Kallberg and William T. Ziemba, "Misspecification in Portfolio Selection Problems" in G. Bamberg and K. Spremann (eds.), *Risk and Capital: Lecture Notes in Economics and Mathematical Systems* (New York: Springer-Verlag, 1984).

second approach is to constrain the portfolio weights in the optimization process. The third one is to incorporate estimation error directly into the optimization process. We discuss this last approach separately.

Constraining Portfolio Weights

Several studies have shown that the inclusion of constraints in the mean-variance optimization problem leads to better out-of-sample performance.[8] Practitioners often use no short-selling constraints or upper and lower bounds for each security to avoid overconcentration in a few assets. Gupta and Eichhorn suggest that constraining portfolio weights may also assist in containing volatility, increase realized efficiency, and decrease downside risk or shortfall probability.[9]

Jagannathan and Ma provide a theoretical justification for these observations.[10] Specifically, they show that the no short-selling constraints are equivalent to reducing the estimated asset covariances, whereas upper bounds are equivalent to increasing the corresponding covariances. For example, stocks that have high covariance with other stocks tend to receive negative portfolio weights. Therefore, when their covariance is decreased (which is equivalent to the effect of imposing no short-selling constraints), these negative weights disappear. Similarly, stocks that have low covariances with other stocks tend to get overweighted. Hence, by increasing the corresponding covariances the impact of these overweighted stocks decrease.

Furthermore, Monte Carlo experiments performed by Jagannathan and Ma indicate that when no-short-sell constraints are imposed, the sample covariance matrix has about the same performance (as measured by the global minimum variance portfolio) as a covariance matrix estimator constructed from a factor structure.

Care needs to be taken when imposing constraints for robustness and stability purposes. For example, if the constraints used are too "tight," they will completely determine the portfolio allocation—not the forecasts.

Instead of providing ad hoc upper and lower bounds on each security, as proposed by Bouchaud, Potters, and Aguilar one can use so-

---

[8] See, for example, Peter A. Frost and James E. Savarino, "For Better Performance: Constrain Portfolio Weights," *Journal of Portfolio Management* 15 (1988), pp. 29–34; Vijay K. Chopra, "Mean-Variance Revisited: Near-Optimal Portfolios and Sensitivity to Input Variations," Russell Research Commentary, December 1991; and Robert R. Grauer, and Frederick C. Shen, "Do Constraints Improve Portfolio Performance?" *Journal of Banking and Finance* 24 (2000), pp. 1253–1274.

[9] Francis Gupta and David Eichhorn, "Mean-Variance Optimization for Practitioners of Asset Allocation," Chapter 4 in Frank J. Fabozzi (ed.), *Handbook of Portfolio Management* (Hoboken, NJ: John Wiley & Sons, 1998).

[10] Ravi Jagannathan and Tongshu Ma, "Risk Reduction in Large Portfolios: Why Imposing the Wrong Constraints Helps," *Journal of Finance* 58 (2003), pp. 1651–1683.

called "diversification indicators" that measure the concentration of the portfolio.[11] These diversification indicators can be used as constraints in the portfolio construction phase to limit the concentration to individual securities. The authors demonstrate that these indicators are related to the information content of the portfolio in the sense of information theory.[12] For example, a very concentrated portfolio corresponds to a large information content (as we would only choose a very concentrated allocation if our information about future price fluctuations is "perfect"), whereas an equally weighted portfolio would indicate low information content (as we would not put "all the eggs in one basket" if our information about future price fluctuations is poor).

Importance of Sensitivity Analysis

In practice, in order to minimize dramatic changes due to estimation error, it is advisable to perform sensitivity analysis. For example, one can study the results of small changes or perturbations to the inputs from an efficient portfolio selected from a mean-variance optimization. If the portfolio calculated from the perturbed inputs drastically differ from the first one, this might indicate a problem. The perturbation can also be performed on a security by security basis in order to identify those securities that are the most sensitive. The objective of this sensitivity analysis is to identify a set of security weights that will be close to efficient under several different sets of plausible inputs.

Issues with Highly Correlated Assets

The inclusion of highly correlated securities (0.7 or higher) is another major cause for instability in the mean-variance optimization framework. For example, high correlation coefficients among common asset classes are one reason why real estate is popular in "optimized" portfolios. Real estate is one of the few asset classes that has a lower correlation with other common asset classes. But real estate does in general not have the liquidity necessary in order to implement these portfolios and may therefore fail to deliver the return promised by the real estate indices.

---

[11] Jean-Philippe Bouchaud, Marc Potters, and Jean-Pierre Aguilar, "Missing Information and Asset Allocation," working paper, Science & Finance, Capital Fund Management, 1997.
[12] The relationship to information theory is based upon the premise that the diversification indicators are generalized entropies. See, Evaldo M.F. Curado and Constantino Tsallis, "Generalized Statistical Mechanics: Connection with Thermodynamics," *Journal of Physics A: Mathematical and General* 2 (1991), pp. L69-L72, 1991 and Chapter 17.

The problem of high correlations typically becomes worse when the correlation matrix is estimated from historical data. Specifically, when the correlation matrix is estimated over a slightly different period, correlations may change, but the impact on the new portfolio weights may be drastic. In these situations, it may be a good idea to resort to a shrinkage estimator or a factor model to model covariances and correlations.

Incorporating Uncertainty in the Inputs into the Portfolio Allocation Process

In the classical mean-variance optimization problem, the expected returns and the covariance matrix of returns are uncertain and have to be estimated. After the estimation of these quantities, the portfolio optimization problem is solved as a deterministic problem—completely ignoring the uncertainty in the inputs. However, it makes sense for the uncertainty of expected returns and risk to enter into the optimization process, thus creating a more realistic model. Using point estimates of the expected returns and the covariance matrix of returns, and treating them as error-free in portfolio allocation, does not necessarily correspond to prudent investor behavior.

The investor would probably be more comfortable choosing a portfolio that would perform well under a number of different scenarios, thereby also attaining some protection from estimation risk and model risk. Obviously, to have some insurance in the event of less likely but more extreme cases (e.g., scenarios that are highly unlikely under the assumption that returns are normally distributed), the investor must be willing to give up some of the upside that would result under the more likely scenarios. Such an investor seeks a "robust" portfolio, that is, a portfolio that is assured against some worst-case model misspecification. The estimation process can be improved through robust statistical techniques such as shrinkage and Bayesian estimators discussed later in this chapter. However, jointly considering estimation risk and model risk in the financial decision-making process is becoming more important.

The estimation process does not deliver a point forecast (that is, one single number) but a full distribution of expected returns. Recent approaches attempt to integrate estimation risk into the mean-variance framework by using the expected return distribution in the optimization. A simple approach is to sample from the return distribution and average the resulting portfolios (Monte Carlo approach) as we will describe in more detail later on in this chapter. However, as a mean-variance problem has to be solved for each draw, this is computationally intensive for larger portfolios. In addition, the averaging does not guarantee that the resulting portfolio weights will satisfy all constraints.

Introduced in the late 1990s by Ben-Tal and Nemirovski[13] and El Ghaoui and Lebret,[14] the robust optimization framework is computationally more efficient than the Monte Carlo approach. This development in optimization technology allows for efficiently solving the robust version of the mean-variance optimization problem in about the same time as the classical mean-variance optimization problem. The technique explicitly uses the distribution from the estimation process to find a robust portfolio in one single optimization. It thereby incorporates uncertainties of inputs into a deterministic framework. The classical portfolio optimization formulations such as the mean-variance portfolio selection problem, the maximum Sharpe ratio portfolio problem, and the value-at-risk (VaR) portfolio problem all have robust counterparts that can be solved in roughly the same amount of time as the original problem.[15] We provide an introduction to Monte Carlo simulation techniques and the robust optimization framework in the last section of this chapter.

Large Data Requirements

In classical mean-variance optimization we need to provide estimates of the expected returns and covariances of all the securities in the investment universe considered. Typically, however, portfolio managers have reliable return forecasts for only a small subset of these assets. This is probably one of the major reasons why the mean-variance framework has not been adopted by practitioners in general. It is simply unreasonable for the portfolio manager to produce good estimates of all the inputs required in classical portfolio theory.

We will see later in this chapter that the Black-Litterman model provides a remedy in that it "blends" any views (this could be a forecast on just one or a few securities, or all them) the investor might have with the market equilibrium. When no views are present, the resulting Black-Litterman expected returns are just the expected returns consistent with the market equilibrium. Conversely, when the investor has views on some of the assets, the resulting expected returns deviate from market equilibrium.

---

[13] Aharon Ben-Tal and Arkadi S. Nemirovski, "Robust Convex Optimization," *Mathematics of Operations Research* 23 (1998), pp. 769–805; and Aharon Ben-Tal and Arkadi S. Nemirovski, "Robust Solutions to Uncertain Linear Programs," *Operations Research Letters* 25 (1999), pp. 1–13.

[14] Laurent El Ghaoui and Herve Lebret, "Robust Solutions to Least-Squares Problems with Uncertain Data," *SIAM Journal Matrix Analysis with Applications* 18 (1977), pp. 1035–1064.

[15] See, for example, Donald Goldfarb and Garud Iyengar, "Robust Portfolio Selection Problems," *Mathematics of Operations Research* 28 (2003), pp. 1–38.

SHRINKAGE ESTIMATION

It is well known since Stein's seminal work that biased estimators, often yield better parameter estimates than their generally preferred unbiased counterparts.[16] In particular, it can be shown that if we consider the problem of estimating the mean of an N-dimensional multivariate normal variable $(N > 2)$, $\mathbf{X} \in N(\mathbf{\mu},\mathbf{\Sigma})$ with known covariance matrix $\mathbf{\Sigma}$, the sample mean $\hat{\mathbf{\mu}}$ is not the best estimator of the population mean $\mathbf{\mu}$ in terms of the quadratic loss function

$$L(\mathbf{\mu}, \hat{\mathbf{\mu}}) = (\mathbf{\mu} - \hat{\mathbf{\mu}})'\mathbf{\Sigma}^{-1}(\mathbf{\mu} - \hat{\mathbf{\mu}})$$

For example, the so-called *James-Stein shrinkage estimator*

$$\hat{\mathbf{\mu}}_{JS} = (1 - w)\hat{\mathbf{\mu}} + w\mu_0\mathbf{\iota}$$

has a lower quadratic loss than the sample mean, where

$$w = \min\left(1, \frac{N - 2}{T(\hat{\mathbf{\mu}} - \mu_0\mathbf{\iota})'\mathbf{\Sigma}^{-1}(\hat{\mathbf{\mu}} - \mu_0\mathbf{\iota})} \right)$$

and $\mathbf{\iota} = [1,1,...,1]'$. Moreover, T is the number of observations, and μ_0 is an *arbitrary* number. The vector $\mu_0\mathbf{\iota}$ and the weight w are referred to as the shrinkage target and the shrinkage intensity (or shrinkage factor), respectively. Although there are some choices of μ_0 that are better than others, what is surprising with this result is that it could be *any* number! This fact is referred to as the *Stein paradox*.

In effect, shrinkage is a form of averaging different estimators where the shrinkage estimator typically consists of three components: (1) an estimator with little or no structure (like the sample mean above); (2) an estimator with a lot of structure (the shrinkage target); and (3) the shrinkage intensity. The shrinkage target is chosen with the following two requirements in mind. First, it should have only a small number of free parameters (robust and with a lot of structure). Second, it should have some of the basic properties in common with the unknown quantity being estimated. The shrinkage intensity can be chosen based on theoretical properties or simply by numerical simulation.

---

[16] Charles Stein, "Inadmissibility of the Usual Estimator for the Mean of Multivariate Normal Distribution," *Proceedings of the Third Berkeley Symposium on Mathematical Statistics and Probability* 1 (1956), pp. 197–206.

Probably the most well-known shrinkage estimator[17] used to estimate expected returns in the financial literature is the one proposed by Jorion,[18] where the shrinkage target is given by $\mu_g \iota$ with

$$\mu_g = \frac{\iota' \Sigma^{-1} \hat{\mu}}{\iota' \Sigma^{-1} \iota}$$

and

$$w = \frac{N+2}{N+2+T(\hat{\mu}-\mu_g\iota)'\Sigma^{-1}(\hat{\mu}-\mu_g\iota)}$$

We note that μ_g is the return on the minimum variance portfolio discussed in Chapter 2. Several studies document that for the mean-variance framework: (1) the variability in the portfolio weights from one period to the next decrease; and (2) the out-of-sample risk-adjusted performance improves significantly when using a shrinkage estimator as compared to the sample mean.[19]

We can also apply the shrinkage technique for covariance matrix estimation. This involves shrinking an unstructured covariance estimator toward a more structured covariance estimator. Typically the structured covariance estimator only has a few degrees of freedom (only a few nonzero eigenvalues) as motivated by Random Matrix Theory (see Chapter 8).

For example, as shrinkage targets, Ledoit and Wolf[20] suggest using the covariance matrix that follows from the single-factor model developed by Sharpe[21] or the constant correlation covariance matrix. In practice the single-factor model and the constant correlation model yield

[17] Many similar approaches have been proposed. For example, see Jobson and Korkie, "Putting Markowitz Theory to Work" and Frost and Savarino, "An Empirical Bayes Approach to Efficient Portfolio Selection."

[18] Philippe Jorion, "Bayes-Stein Estimation for Portfolio Analysis," *Journal of Financial and Quantitative Analysis* 21 (1986), pp. 279–292.

[19] See, for example, Michaud, "The Markowitz Optimization Enigma: Is 'Optimized' Optimal?" Jorion, "Bayesian and CAPM Estimators of the Means: Implications for Portfolio Selection," and Glen Larsen, Jr. and Bruce Resnick, "Parameter Estimation Techniques, Optimization Frequency, and Portfolio Return Enhancement," *Journal of Portfolio Management* 27 (2001), pp. 27–34.

[20] Olivier Ledoit and Michael Wolf, "Improved Estimation of the Covariance Matrix of Stock Returns with an Application to Portfolio Selection," *Journal of Empirical Finance* 10 (2003), pp. 603–621, 2003; and Olivier Ledoit and Michael Wolf, "Honey, I Shrunk the Sample Covariance Matrix," *Journal of Portfolio Management* 30 (2004), pp. 110–119.

similar results, but the constant correlation model is much easier to implement. In the case of the constant correlation model, the shrinkage estimator for the covariance matrix takes the form

$$\hat{\Sigma}_{LW} = w\hat{\Sigma}_{CC} + (1-w)\hat{\Sigma}$$

where $\hat{\Sigma}$ is the sample covariance matrix, and $\hat{\Sigma}_{CC}$ is the sample covariance matrix with constant correlation. The sample covariance matrix with constant correlation is computed as follows.

First, we decompose the sample covariance matrix according to

$$\hat{\Sigma} = \Lambda C \Lambda'$$

where Λ is a diagonal matrix of the volatilities of returns and C is the sample correlation matrix, that is,

$$C = \begin{bmatrix} 1 & \hat{\rho}_{12} & \cdots & & \hat{\rho}_{1N} \\ \hat{\rho}_{21} & \ddots & & \ddots & \vdots \\ \vdots & \ddots & & \ddots & \hat{\rho}_{N-1N} \\ \hat{\rho}_{N1} & \cdots & \hat{\rho}_{NN-1} & & 1 \end{bmatrix}$$

Second, we replace the sample correlation matrix with the constant correlation matrix

$$C_{CC} = \begin{bmatrix} 1 & \hat{\rho} & \cdots & \hat{\rho} \\ \hat{\rho} & \ddots & \ddots & \vdots \\ \vdots & \ddots & \ddots & \hat{\rho} \\ \hat{\rho} & \cdots & \hat{\rho} & 1 \end{bmatrix}$$

where $\hat{\rho}$ is the average of all the sample correlations, in other words

---

[21] William F. Sharpe, "A Simplified Model for Portfolio Analysis," *Management Science* 9 (1973), pp. 277-293, 1963. Elton, Gruber, and Urich proposed the single factor model for purposes of covariance estimation in 1978. They show that this approach leads to: (1) better forecasts of the covariance matrix; (2) more stable portfolio allocations over time; and (3) more diversified portfolios. They also find that the average correlation coefficient is a good forecast of the future correlation matrix. See, Edwin J. Elton, Martin J. Gruber, and Thomas J. Urich, "Are Betas Best?" *Journal of Finance* 33 (1978), pp. 1375–1384.

$$\hat{\rho} = \frac{2}{(N-1)N}\sum_{i=1}^{N}\sum_{j=i+1}^{N}\hat{\rho}_{ij}$$

The optimal shrinkage intensity can be shown to be proportional to a constant divided by the length of the history, T.[22]

---

[22] Although straightforward to implement, the optimal shrinkage intensity, w, is a bit tedious to write down mathematically. Let us denote by $r_{i,t}$ the return on security i during period t, $1 \le i \le N$, $1 \le t \le T$,

$$\bar{r}_i = \frac{1}{T}\sum_{t=1}^{T} r_{i,t} \text{ and } \hat{\sigma}_{ij} = \frac{1}{T-1}\sum_{t=1}^{T} (r_{i,t} - \bar{r}_i)(r_{j,t} - \bar{r}_j)$$

Then the optimal shrinkage intensity is given by the formula

$$w = \max\left\{0, \min\left\{\frac{\hat{\kappa}}{T}, 1\right\}\right\}$$

where

$$\hat{\kappa} = \frac{\hat{\pi} - \hat{c}}{\hat{\gamma}}$$

and the parameters $\hat{\pi}$, $\hat{c}$, $\hat{\gamma}$ are computed as follows. First, $\hat{\pi}$ is given by

$$\hat{\pi} = \sum_{i,j=1}^{N} \hat{\pi}_{ij}$$

where

$$\hat{\pi}_{ij} = \frac{1}{T}\sum_{t=1}^{T}\left((r_{i,t} - \bar{r}_i)(r_{j,t} - \bar{r}_j) - \hat{\sigma}_{ij}\right)^2$$

Second, $\hat{c}$ is given by

$$\hat{c} = \sum_{i=1}^{N}\hat{\pi}_{ii} + \sum_{\substack{i=1\\i\neq j}}^{N}\frac{\hat{\rho}}{2}\left(\sqrt{\hat{\rho}_{jj}/\hat{\rho}_{ii}}\,\hat{\vartheta}_{ii,ij} + \sqrt{\hat{\rho}_{ii}/\hat{\rho}_{jj}}\,\hat{\vartheta}_{jj,ij}\right)$$

where

$$\hat{\vartheta}_{ii,ij} = \frac{1}{T}\sum_{t=1}^{T}[((r_{i,t} - \bar{r}_i)^2 - \hat{\sigma}_{ii})((r_{i,t} - \bar{r}_i)(r_{j,t} - \bar{r}_j) - \hat{\sigma}_{ij})]$$

Finally, $\hat{\gamma}$ is given by

$$\hat{\gamma} = \|\mathbf{C} - \mathbf{C}_{CC}\|_F^2$$

where $\|\cdot\|_F$ denotes the Frobenius norm defined by

$$\|\mathbf{A}\|_F = \sqrt{\sum_{i,j=1}^{N} a_{ij}^2}$$

In their two articles, Ledoit and Wolf compare the empirical out-of-sample performance of their shrinkage covariance matrix estimators with other covariance matrix estimators, such as the sample covariance matrix, a statistical factor model based on the first five principal components, and a factor model based on the 48 industry factors[23] as defined by Fama and French.[24] The results indicate that when it comes to computing a global minimum variance portfolio, their shrinkage estimators are superior compared to the others tested, with the constant correlation shrinkage estimator coming out slightly ahead. Interestingly enough, it turns out that the shrinkage intensity for the single-factor model (the shrinkage intensity for the constant coefficient model is not reported) is fairly constant throughout time with a value around 0.8. This suggests that there is about four times as much estimation error present in the sample covariance matrix as there is bias in the single-factor covariance matrix.

Example: Using the James-Stein Shrinkage Estimator

To illustrate the use of the James-Stein shrinkage estimator, we extend the illustration provided in Chapter 4 where we considered the rebalancing of a portfolio of country indices in the MSCI World Index. Here, we use two new estimators beyond those introduced in Chapter 4 to estimate the expected returns of the different countries: (1) the James-Stein shrinkage estimator with the global minimum variance portfolio as the shrinkage target; and (2) the Black-Litterman model (introduced in the next section) using historical means as the views. For comparison, as in the earlier illustration, we use the global minimum variance portfolio (GMV).

For convenience we will refer to these three approaches as "Shrinkage GMV," "BL," and "GMV." For the Shrinkage GMV and BL simulations, the optimal portfolios were calculated using the risk aversion formulation of the mean-variance optimization problem with risk aversion coefficient $\lambda = 2$.[25] All other details remain the same as in the illustration in Chapter 4. The results are presented in Exhibits 9.1 through 9.4.

We observe that the full sample Sharpe ratios of the Shrinkage GMV and BL portfolios are very similar, at 0.71 and 0.72, respectively. Recall

---

[23] Besides some other proprietary and nonindustry-based factors, MSCI Barra's factor model discussed in the previous chapter uses these factors.

[24] Eugene F. Fama and Kenneth R. French, "Industry Costs of Equity," *Journal of Financial Economics* 43 (1997), pp. 153-193.

[25] We chose not to calibrate the risk aversion parameter but left it the same for both approaches. One could for example, calibrate this parameter such that both the Shrinkage GMV and BL portfolios have about the same realized volatility. Because we perform the comparison on a Sharpe ratio basis, this has no influence on the results.

EXHIBIT 9.1   Growth of Equity Invested on January 1985 in the GMV, Shrinkage GMV, and BL Portfolios

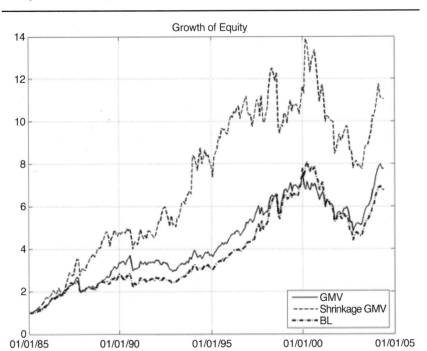

Note: GMV refers to the global minimum variance portfolio; Shrinkage GMV refers to the portfolio where the expected returns are estimated with the James-Stein shrinkage estimator with the global minimum variance portfolio as the shrinkage target; and BL refers to the portfolio where the expected returns are estimated with the Black-Litterman model using historical means as the views. In the last two cases, we use the risk aversion formulation of the mean-variance optimization problem with risk aversion coefficient $\lambda = 2$.

that the full sample Sharpe ratios of the other approaches presented in Chapter 4 were 0.82 (GMV), 0.78 (Equal), 0.59 (RiskAver), and 0.45 (Index). In other words, the new estimators clearly perform better than the risk aversion formulation using historical means, yet perform worse than both the global minimum variance portfolio and the equally weighted portfolio. These results are consistent with the findings by Jorion,[26] who used monthly returns on the stocks listed on the NYSE over the period January 1926 through December 1987.

---

[26] Jorion, "Bayesian and CAPM Estimators of the Means: Implications for Portfolio Selection."

EXHIBIT 9.2   Portfolio Volatility of the GMV, Shrinkage GMV, and BL Portfolios

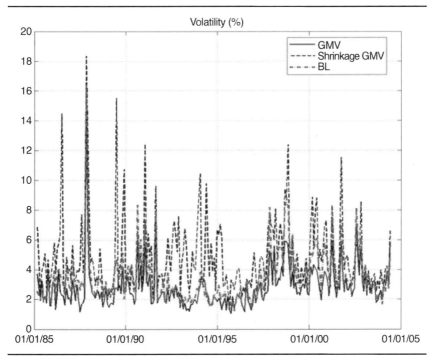

Note: GMV refers to the global minimum variance portfolio; Shrinkage GMV refers to the portfolio where the expected returns are estimated with the James-Stein shrinkage estimator and the global minimum variance portfolio as the shrinkage target; and BL refers to the portfolio where the expected returns are estimated with the Black-Litterman model using historical means as the views. In the last two cases, we use the risk aversion formulation of the mean-variance optimization problem with risk aversion coefficient $\lambda = 2$.

BAYESIAN APPROACHES

The classical approach to estimating future expected returns assumes that the "true" expected returns and covariances of returns are unknown and *fixed*. A point estimate (i.e., an estimate of the most likely return represented by a single number) is obtained using forecasting models of observed market data and proprietary data. However, it is difficult to make accurate estimates and the mean-variance portfolio allocation decision is influenced by the estimation error of the forecasts.

EXHIBIT 9.3 Portfolio Summary Statistics of the Portfolio Where the Expected Returns Are Estimated with the James-Stein Shrinkage Estimator with the Global Minimum Variance Portfolio as the Shrinkage Target

	Start Date	End Date	Mean	Volatility	Sharpe Ratio	Skew	Kurtosis	Min	Max	Alpha	Beta
1st Qtr	Feb-85	Dec-89	34.9%	21.9%	1.59	-0.94	5.16	-21.3%	15.3%	21.0%	0.39
2nd Qtr	Jan-90	Dec-94	12.0%	21.1%	0.57	1.21	7.02	-10.8%	27.3%	6.7%	0.45
3rd Qtr	Jan-95	Dec-99	9.4%	17.9%	0.53	-1.10	6.66	-20.6%	12.5%	3.2%	0.68
4th Qtr	Jan-00	May-04	0.7%	19.6%	0.03	0.63	6.96	-15.2%	22.8%	-4.4%	0.63
1st Half	Feb-85	Dec-94	23.3%	21.7%	1.08	0.10	5.27	-21.3%	27.3%	13.6%	0.41
2nd Half	Jan-95	May-04	5.3%	18.7%	0.28	-0.19	6.62	-20.6%	22.8%	-0.3%	0.65
Full	Feb-85	May-04	14.6%	20.4%	0.71	0.05	5.83	-21.3%	27.3%	6.7%	0.49

Notes: The columns Mean, Volatility, Sharpe Ratio, and Alpha are the annualized mean returns, volatilities, Sharpe ratios, and alphas of the portfolio over the different periods. Min and Max are the daily minimum and maximum portfolio returns, respectively. Skew and Kurtosis are calculated as the third and fourth normalized centered moments. Alphas and betas are calculated using 1-month LIBOR.

EXHIBIT 9.4 Portfolio Summary Statistics of the Portfolio Where the Expected Returns Are Estimated with the Black-Litterman Model Using Historical Means As the Views.

	Start Date	End Date	Mean	Volatility	Sharpe Ratio	Skew	Kurtosis	Min	Max	Alpha	Beta
1st Qtr	Feb-85	Dec-89	22.6%	16.6%	1.36	-0.85	5.10	-16.5%	10.4%	11.7%	0.19
2nd Qtr	Jan-90	Dec-94	3.2%	15.0%	0.21	-0.33	4.20	-13.8%	9.8%	-2.1%	0.43
3rd Qtr	Jan-95	Dec-99	19.4%	14.4%	1.35	-1.07	6.79	-15.5%	10.3%	13.4%	0.53
4th Qtr	Jan-00	May-04	-2.0%	15.0%	-0.14	-0.39	2.39	-9.1%	6.9%	-7.0%	0.61
1st Half	Feb-85	Dec-94	12.8%	16.0%	0.80	-0.55	4.44	-16.5%	10.4%	4.3%	0.26
2nd Half	Jan-95	May-04	9.4%	14.9%	0.63	-0.71	4.20	-15.5%	10.3%	3.8%	0.57
Full	Feb-85	May-04	11.1%	15.5%	0.72	-0.61	4.36	-16.5%	10.4%	3.9%	0.35

Notes: The columns Mean, Volatility, Sharpe Ratio, and Alpha are the annualized mean returns, volatilities, Sharpe ratios, and alphas of the portfolio over the different periods. Min and Max are the daily minimum and maximum portfolio returns, respectively. Skew and Kurtosis are calculated as the third and fourth normalized centered moments. Alphas and betas are calculated using 1-month LIBOR.

The Bayesian approach, in contrast, assumes that the "true" expected returns are unknown and *random*. Named after the English mathematician Thomas Bayes, the Bayesian approach is based on the *subjective* interpretation of probability. A probability distribution is used to represent an investor's belief on the probability that a specific event will actually occur. This probability distribution, called the "prior distribution," reflects an investor's knowledge about the probability before any data are observed. After more information is provided (e.g., data observed), the investor's opinions about the probability might change. Bayes' rule (see Chapter 17) is the formula for computing the new probability distribution, called the "posterior distribution". The posterior distribution is based on knowledge of the prior probability distribution plus the new data.

A posterior distribution of expected return is derived by combining the forecast from the empirical data with a prior distribution. For example, in the Black-Litterman model, which we will introduce later in this section, an estimate of future expected returns is based on combining market equilibrium (e.g., the CAPM equilibrium) with an investor's views. Such views are expressed as absolute or relative deviations from equilibrium together with confidence levels of the views (as measured by the standard deviation of the views).

The Black-Litterman expected return is calculated as a weighted average of the market equilibrium and the investor's views. The weights depend on (1) the volatility of each asset and its correlations with the other assets and (2) the degree of confidence in each forecast. The resulting expected return, which is the mean of the posterior distribution, is then used as input in the portfolio optimization process. Portfolio weights computed in this fashion tend to be more intuitive and less sensitive to small changes in the original inputs (i.e., forecasts of market equilibrium, investor's views, and the covariance matrix).

The ability to incorporate exogenous insight, such as a portfolio manager's judgment, into formal models is important: such insight might be the most valuable input used by the model. The Bayesian framework allows forecasting systems to use such external information sources and subjective interventions (i.e., modification of the model due to judgment) in addition to traditional information sources such as market data and proprietary data.

Because portfolio managers might not be willing to give up control to a "black box," incorporating exogenous insights into formal models through Bayesian techniques is one way of giving the portfolio manager better control in a quantitative framework. Forecasts are represented through probability distributions that can be modified or adjusted to incorporate other sources of information deemed relevant. The only restriction is that such additional information (i.e., the investor's "views") be combined with the existing model through the laws of probability. In effect, incorporating Bayesian views into a model allows one to "rationalize" subjectivity within a formal, quantitative framework. "[T]he rational investor is a Bayesian," as Markowitz noted.[27]

Interventions can be either feed-forward (anticipatory actions) or feed-back (corrective actions).[28] The Bayesian framework also allows for mixing, selecting, and switching among dynamic models in a common framework. In the first half of the last decade, progress in Bayesian modeling has put these general and powerful computational techniques within reach of practitioners in the financial markets.[29]

We discuss Bayesian techniques further in the context of modeling model risk in Chapter 17. In particular, we give examples of Bayesian autoregressive models in both univariate and multivariate settings.

The Black-Litterman Model

The basic feature of the Black-Litterman model that we will discuss in this and the following sections is that it combines an investor's views with the market equilibrium. Let us understand what this statement implies. In the classical mean-variance optimization framework an investor is required to provide estimates of the expected returns and covariances of all the securities in the investment universe considered. This is of course a humongous task, given the number of securities available today. Portfolio and investment managers are very unlikely to have a detailed understanding of all the securities, companies, industries, and sectors that they have at their disposal. Typically, most of them have a specific area of expertise that they focus on in order to achieve superior returns.

This is probably one of the major reasons why the mean-variance framework has not been adopted among practitioners in general. It is simply unrealistic for the portfolio manager to produce reasonable estimates (besides the additional problems of estimation error) of the inputs required in classical portfolio theory.

---

[27] See page 57 in Harry M. Markowitz, *Mean-Variance Analysis in Portfolio Choice and Capital Markets*, (Cambridge, MA, Basil Blackwell, 1987).

[28] See, for example, Michael West and P. Jeff Harrison, *Bayesian Forecasting and Dynamic Models*, (New York: Springer, 1989).

[29] See, for example, Bradley P. Carlin, Nicholas G. Polson, and David S. Stoffer, "A Monte Carlo Approach to Nonnormal and Nonlinear State-Space Modeling," *Journal of the American Statistical Association* 87 (1992), pp. 493–500; C. K. Carter and R. Kohn, "On Gibbs Sampling for State Space Models," *Biometrica* 81 (1994), pp. 541–553; and Sylvia Fruhwirth-Schnatter, "Data Augmentation and Dynamic Linear Models," *Journal of Time Series Analysis* 15 (1994), pp. 183–202.

Furthermore, many trading strategies used today cannot easily be turned into forecasts of expected returns and covariances. In particular, not all trading strategies produce views on *absolute* return, but rather just provide *relative* rankings of securities that are predicted to outperform/underperform other securities. For example, considering two stocks, A and B, instead of the *absolute view*, "the one-month expected return on A and B are 1.2% and 1.7% with a standard deviation of 5% and 5.5%, respectively," while a *relative view* may be of the form "B will outperform A with half a percent over the next month" or simply "B will outperform A over the next month." Clearly, it is not an easy task to translate any of these relative views into the inputs required for the modern portfolio theoretical framework. We will walk through and illustrate the usage of the Black-Litterman model in three simple steps.

Step 1: Basic Assumptions and Starting Point

One of the basic assumptions underlying the Black-Litterman model is that the expected return of a security should be consistent with market equilibrium *unless* the investor has a specific view on the security.[30] In other words, an investor who does not have any views on the market should hold the market.[31]

Our starting point is the CAPM model:[32]

$$E(R_i) - R_f = \beta_i(E(R_M) - R_f)$$

where $E(R_i)$, $E(R_M)$, and R_f are the expected return on security i, the expected return on the market portfolio, and the risk-free rate, respectively. Furthermore,

$$\beta_i = \frac{\text{cov}(R_i, R_M)}{\sigma_M^2}$$

---

[30] Fischer Black and Robert Litterman, *Asset Allocation: Combining Investor Views with Market Equilibrium*, Goldman, Sachs & Co., Fixed Income Research, September 1990.
[31] A "predecessor" to the Black-Litterman model is the so-called Treynor-Black model. In this model, an investor's portfolio is shown to consist of two parts (1) a passive portfolio/positions held purely for the purpose of mimicking the market portfolio, and (2) an active portfolio/positions based on the investor's return/risk expectations. This somewhat simpler model relies on the assumption that returns of all securities are related only through the variation of the market portfolio (Sharpe's Diagonal Model). See, Jack L. Treynor and Fischer Black, "How to Use Security Analysis to Improve Portfolio Selection," *Journal of Business* 46 (1973) pp. 66–86.
[32] See Chapters 7 and 8 for a review of this model.

where σ_M^2 is the variance of the market portfolio. Let us denote by $\mathbf{w}_b = (w_{b1}, \ldots, w_{bN})'$ the market capitalization or benchmark weights, so that with an asset universe of N securities[33] the return on the market can be written as

$$R_M = \sum_{j=1}^{N} w_{bj} R_j$$

Then by the CAPM, the expected excess return on asset i, $\Pi_i = E(R_i) - R_f$, becomes

$$\Pi_i = \beta_i (E(R_i) - R_f)$$

$$= \frac{\text{cov}(R_i, R_M)}{\sigma_M^2} (E(R_i) - R_f)$$

$$= \frac{E(R_M) - R_f}{\sigma_M^2} \sum_{j=1}^{N} \text{cov}(R_i, R_j) w_{bj}$$

We can also express this in matrix-vector form as

$$\mathbf{\Pi} = \delta \Sigma \mathbf{w}$$

where we define the market price of risk as

$$\delta = \frac{E(R_M) - R_f}{\sigma_M^2},$$

the expected excess return vector

$$\mathbf{\Pi} = \begin{bmatrix} \Pi_1 \\ \vdots \\ \Pi_N \end{bmatrix},$$

and the covariance matrix of returns

---

[33] For simplicity, we consider only equity securities. Extending this model to other assets classes such as bonds and currencies is fairly straightforward.

$$\Sigma = \begin{bmatrix} \text{cov}(R_1, R_1) & \cdots & \text{cov}(R_1, R_N) \\ \vdots & & \vdots \\ \text{cov}(R_N, R_1) & \cdots & \text{cov}(R_N, R_N) \end{bmatrix}$$

The true expected returns μ of the securities are unknown. However, we assume that our equilibrium model above serves as a reasonable estimate of the true expected returns in the sense that

$$\Pi = \mu + \varepsilon_\Pi, \ \varepsilon_\Pi \sim N(0, \tau\Sigma)$$

for some small parameter $\tau \ll 1$. We can think about $\tau\Sigma$ as our confidence in how well we can estimate the equilibrium expected returns. In other words, a small τ implies a high confidence in our equilibrium estimates and vice versa.

Because the market portfolio is on the efficient frontier, as we saw in Chapter 2, as a consequence of the CAPM an investor will be holding a portfolio consisting of the market portfolio and a risk-free instrument earning the risk-free rate. But let us now see what happens if an investor has a particular view on some of the securities.

Step 2: Expressing an Investor's Views

Formally, K views in the Black-Litterman model are expressed as a K-dimensional vector $\mathbf{q}$ with

$$\mathbf{q} = P\mu + \varepsilon_q, \ \varepsilon_q \sim N(0, \Omega)$$

where P is a $K \times N$ matrix (explained in the following example) and Ω is a $K \times K$ matrix expressing the confidence in the views. In order to understand this mathematical specification better, let us take a look at an example.

Let us assume that the asset universe that we consider has five stocks ($N = 5$) and that an investor has the following two views:

1. Stock 1 will have a return of 1.5%.
2. Stock 3 will outperform Stock 2 by 4%.

We recognize that the first view is an absolute view where as the second one is a relative view. Mathematically, we express the two views together as

$$\begin{bmatrix} 1.5\% \\ 4\% \end{bmatrix} = \begin{bmatrix} 1 & 0 & 0 & 0 & 0 \\ 0 & -1 & 1 & 0 & 0 \end{bmatrix} \begin{bmatrix} \mu_1 \\ \mu_2 \\ \mu_3 \\ \mu_4 \\ \mu_5 \end{bmatrix} + \begin{bmatrix} \varepsilon_1 \\ \varepsilon_2 \end{bmatrix}$$

The first row of the **P** matrix represents the first view, and similarly, the second row describes the second view. In this example, we chose the weights of the second view such that they add up to zero, but other weighting schemes are also possible. For instance, the weights could also be chosen as some scaling factor times one over the market capitalizations of the stock, some scaling factor times one over the stock price, or other variations thereof. We come back to these issues later in this section when we discuss how to incorporate time-series based strategies and cross-sectional ranking strategies.

We also remark at this point that the error terms ε_1, ε_2 do not explicitly enter into the Black-Litterman model—but their variances do. Quite simply, these are just the variances of the different views. Although in some instances they are directly available as a byproduct of the view or the strategy, in other cases they need to be estimated separately. For example,

$$\Omega = \begin{bmatrix} 1\%^2 & 0 \\ 0 & 1\%^2 \end{bmatrix}$$

corresponds to a higher confidence in the views, and conversely,

$$\Omega = \begin{bmatrix} 5\%^2 & 0 \\ 0 & 7\%^2 \end{bmatrix}$$

represents a much lower confidence in the views. We discuss a few different approaches in choosing the confidence levels below. The off diagonal elements of Ω are typically set to zero. The reason for this is that the error terms of the individual views are most often assumed to be independent of one another.

Step 3: Combining an Investor's Views with Market Equilibrium

Having specified the market equilibrium and an investor's views separately, we are now ready to combine the two together. There are two different, but equivalent, approaches that can be used to arrive to the Black-Litterman model. We will describe a derivation that relies upon standard econometrical techniques, in particular, the so-called *mixed estimation technique* described by Theil.[34] The approach based on Bayesian statistics has been explained in some detail by Satchel and Scowcroft.[35]

Let us first recall the specification of market equilibrium

$$\Pi = \mu + \varepsilon_\Pi, \ \varepsilon_\Pi \sim N(0, \tau\Sigma)$$

and the one for the investor's views

$$q = P\mu + \varepsilon_q, \ \varepsilon_q \sim N(0, \Omega)$$

We can "stack" these two equations together in the form

$$y = X\mu + \varepsilon, \ \varepsilon \sim N(0, V)$$

where

$$y = \begin{bmatrix} \Pi \\ q \end{bmatrix}, \ X = \begin{bmatrix} I \\ P \end{bmatrix}, \ V = \begin{bmatrix} \tau\Sigma & \\ & \Omega \end{bmatrix}$$

with I denoting the $N \times N$ identity matrix. We observe that this is just a standard linear model for the expected returns μ. Calculating the Generalized Least Squares (GLS) estimator (see Chapter 14) for μ, we obtain

$$\hat{\mu}_{BL} = (X'V^{-1}X)^{-1}X'V^{-1}y$$

$$= \left(\begin{bmatrix} I & P' \end{bmatrix} \begin{bmatrix} (\tau\Sigma)^{-1} & \\ & \Omega^{-1} \end{bmatrix} \begin{bmatrix} I \\ P \end{bmatrix} \right)^{-1} \begin{bmatrix} I & P' \end{bmatrix} \begin{bmatrix} (\tau\Sigma)^{-1} & \\ & \Omega^{-1} \end{bmatrix} \begin{bmatrix} \Pi \\ q \end{bmatrix}$$

$$= \left(\begin{bmatrix} I & P' \end{bmatrix} \begin{bmatrix} (\tau\Sigma)^{-1} \\ \Omega^{-1}P \end{bmatrix} \right)^{-1} \begin{bmatrix} I & P' \end{bmatrix} \begin{bmatrix} (\tau\Sigma)^{-1}\Pi \\ \Omega^{-1}q \end{bmatrix}$$

$$= [(\tau\Sigma)^{-1} + P'\Omega^{-1}P]^{-1}[(\tau\Sigma)^{-1}\Pi + P'\Omega^{-1}q]$$

The last line in the above formula is the Black-Litterman expected returns that "blend" the market equilibrium with the investor's views.

---

[34] Henri Theil, *Principles of Econometrics* (New York: Wiley and Sons, 1971).
[35] Stephen Satchel and Alan Scowcroft, "A Demystification of the Black-Litterman Model: Managing Quantitative and Traditional Portfolio Construction," *Journal of Asset Management* 1 (2000), pp. 138–150.

Some Remarks and Observations

Following are some comments are in order to provide a better intuitive understanding of the formula. We see that if the investor has no views (that is, $q = \Omega = 0$) or the confidence in the views is zero, then the Black-Litterman expected return becomes $\hat{\mu}_{BL} = \Pi$. Consequently, the investor will end up holding the market portfolio as predicted by the CAPM. In other words, the optimal portfolio in the absence of views is the defined market.

If we were to plug return targets of zero or use the available cash rates, for example, into an optimizer to represent the absence of views, the result would be an optimal portfolio that looks very much different from the market. The equilibrium returns are those forecasts that in the absence of any other views will produce an optimal portfolio equal to the market portfolio. Intuitively speaking, the equilibrium returns in the Black-Litterman model are used to "center" the optimal portfolio around the market portfolio.

By using $q = P\mu + \varepsilon_q$, we have that the investor's views alone imply the estimate of expected returns $\hat{\mu} = (P'P)^{-1}P'q$. Since $P(P'P)^{-1}P' = I$ where I is the identity matrix, we can rewrite the Black-Litterman expected returns in the form

$$\hat{\mu}_{BL} = [(\tau\Sigma)^{-1} + P'\Omega^{-1}P]^{-1}[(\tau\Sigma)^{-1}\Pi + P'\Omega^{-1}P\hat{\mu}]$$

Now we see that the Black-Litterman expected return is a "confidence weighted" linear combination of market equilibrium Π and the expected return $\hat{\mu}$ implied by the investor's views. The two weighting matrices are given by

$$w_\Pi = [(\tau\Sigma)^{-1} + P'\Omega^{-1}P]^{-1}(\tau\Sigma)^{-1}$$
$$w_q = [(\tau\Sigma)^{-1} + P'\Omega^{-1}P]^{-1}P'\Omega^{-1}P$$

where

$$w_\Pi + w_q = I$$

In particular, $(\tau\Sigma)^{-1}$ and $P'\Omega^{-1}P$ represent the confidence we have in our estimates of the market equilibrium and the views, respectively. Therefore, if we have low confidence in the views, the resulting expected returns will be close to the ones implied by market equilibrium. Conversely, with higher confidence in the views, the resulting expected returns will deviate from the market equilibrium implied expected returns. We say that we "tilt" away from market equilibrium.

It is straightforward to show that the Black-Litterman expected returns can also be written in the form

$$\hat{\mu}_{BL} = \Pi + \tau \Sigma P'(\Omega + \tau P \Sigma P')^{-1}(q - P\Pi)$$

where we now immediately see that we tilt away from the equilibrium with a vector proportional to $\Sigma P'(\Omega + \tau P \Sigma P')^{-1}(q - P\Pi)$.

We also mention that the Black-Litterman model can be derived as a solution to the following optimization problem:

$$\hat{\mu}_{BL} = \arg\min_{\mu} \{(\Pi - \mu)' \Sigma^{-1}(\Pi - \mu) + \tau(q - P\mu)' \Omega^{-1}(q - P\mu)\}$$

From this formulation we see that $\hat{\mu}_{BL}$ is chosen such that it is *simultaneously* as close to Π, and $P\mu$ is as close to q as possible. The distances are determined by Σ^{-1} and Ω^{-1}. Furthermore, the relative importance of the equilibrium versus the views is determined by τ. For example, for τ large the weight of the views is increased, whereas for τ small the weight of the equilibrium is higher. Moreover, we also see that τ is a "redundant" parameter as it can be absorbed into Ω.

It is straightforward to calculate the variance of the Black-Litterman combined estimator of the expected returns by the standard "sandwich formula," that is,

$$\begin{aligned} \text{var}(\hat{\mu}_{BL}) &= (X'V^{-1}X)^{-1} \\ &= [(\tau\Sigma)^{-1} + P'\Omega^{-1}P]^{-1} \end{aligned}$$

The most important feature of the Black-Litterman model is that it uses the mixed estimation procedure to adjust the *entire* market equilibrium implied expected return vector with an investor's views. Because security returns are correlated, views on just a few assets will, due to these correlations, imply changes to the expected returns on *all* assets. Mathematically speaking, this follows from the fact that although the vector q can have dimension $K << N$, $P'\Omega^{-1}$ is an $N \times K$ matrix that "propagates" the K views into N components, $P'\Omega^{-1}q$. This effect is stronger the more correlated the different securities are. In the absence of this adjustment of the expected return vector, the differences between the equilibrium expected return and an investor's forecasts will be interpreted as an arbitrage opportunity by a mean-variance optimizer and result in portfolios concentrated in just a few assets ("corner solutions"). Intuitively, any estimation errors are spread out over all assets, making the Black-Litterman expected return vector less sensitive to errors in individual views. This effect contributes to the mitigation of estimation risk and error maximization in the optimization process.

Practical Considerations and Extensions

In this subsection we discuss a few practical issues in using the Black-Litterman model. Specifically, we discuss how to incorporate factor models and cross-sectional rankings in this framework. Furthermore, we also provide some ideas on how the confidences in the views can be estimated in cases where these are not directly available.

It is straightforward to incorporate factor models in the Black-Litterman framework. Let us assume we have a factor representation of the returns of some of the assets. We use the same notation introduced in Chapter 8, and assume we have a factor model of the form:

$$R_i = \alpha_i + F\beta_i + \varepsilon_i, \ i \in I$$

where $I \subset \{1, 2, ..., N\}$. Typically, from a factor model it is easy to obtain an estimate of the residual variance, $\text{var}(\varepsilon_i)$. In this case, we set

$$q_i = \begin{cases} \alpha + F\beta_i, i \in I \\ 0, \text{ otherwise} \end{cases}$$

and the corresponding confidence

$$\omega_{ii}^2 = \begin{cases} \text{var}(\varepsilon_i), i \in I \\ 0, \text{ otherwise} \end{cases}$$

The **P** matrix is defined by

$$p_{ii} = \begin{cases} 1, i \in I \\ 0, \text{ otherwise} \end{cases}$$

$$p_{ij} = 0, i \neq j$$

Of course in a practical implementation we would omit rows with zeros.

Many quantitative investment strategies do not *a priori* produce expected returns, but rather just a simple ranking of the securities. Let us consider a ranking of securities from "best to worst" (from an outperforming to an underperforming perspective, etc.). For example, a value manager might consider ranking securities in terms of increasing book-to-price ratio (B/P), where a low B/P would indicate an undervalued stock (potential to increase in value) and high B/P an overvalued stock (potential to decrease in value). From this ranking we form a long-short portfolio where we purchase the top half of the stocks (the group that is expected to outperform) and we sell short the second half of stocks (the group that is expected to underperform). The view q in this case becomes a scalar, equal to the expected return on the long-short portfolio. The confidence of the view can be decided from backtests, as we describe below. Further, here the P matrix is a $1 \times N$ matrix of ones and minus ones. The corresponding column component is set to one if the security belongs to the outperforming group, or minus one if it belongs to the underperforming group.

In many cases we may not have a direct estimate of the expected return and confidence (variance) of the view. There are several different ways to determine the confidence level.

One of the advantages of a quantitative strategy is that it can be backtested. In the case of the long-short portfolio strategy discussed above, we could estimate its historical variance through simulation with historical data. Of course, we cannot completely judge the performance of a strategy going forward from our backtests. Nevertheless, the backtest methodology allows us to obtain an estimate of the Black-Litterman view and confidence for a particular view/strategy.

Another approach of deriving estimates of the confidence of the view is through simple statistical assumptions. To illustrate, let us consider the second view in the example above: "Stock 3 will outperform Stock 2 by 4%." If we don't know its confidence, we can come up with an estimate for it from the answers to a few simple questions. We start asking ourselves with what certainty we believe the strategy will deliver a return between 3% and 5% (4% ± α where α is some constant, in this case α = 1%). Let us say that we believe there is a chance of two out of three that this will happen, ⅔ ≈ 67%. If we assume normality, we can interpret this as a 67% confidence interval for the future return to be in the interval [3%, 5%]. From this confidence interval we calculate that the implied standard deviation is equal to about 0.66%. Therefore, we would set the Black-Litterman confidence equal to $(0.66\%)^2 = 0.43\%$.

Some extensions to the Black-Litterman model have been derived. For example, Satchel and Scowcroft propose a model where an investor's view on global volatility is incorporated in the prior views by assuming that τ is unknown and stochastic.[36] Idzorek introduces a new

---

[36] Satchel and Scowcroft, "A Demystification of the Black-Litterman Model: Managing Quantitative and Traditional Portfolio Construction."

idea for determining the confidence level of a view.[37] He proposes that the investor derives his confidence level indirectly by first specifying his confidence in the tilt away from equilibrium (the difference between the market capitalization weights and the weights implied by the view alone). Qian and Gorman describe a technique based on conditional distribution theory that allows an investor to incorporate his views on *any* or *all* variances.[38]

Of course other asset classes beyond equities and bonds can be incorporated into the Black-Litterman framework.[39] Some practical experiences and implementation details have been described by Bevan and Winkelman[40] and He and Litterman.[41] A Bayesian approach, with some similarity to the Black-Litterman model, to portfolio selection using higher moments has been proposed by Harvey et al.[42]

The Black-Litterman Model: An Example

In this section we provide an illustration of the Black-Litterman model by combining a cross-sectional momentum strategy with market equilibrium. The resulting Black-Litterman expected returns are subsequently fed into a mean-variance optimizer. We start by describing the momentum strategy before we turn to the optimized strategy.

A Cross-Sectional Momentum Strategy

Practitioners and researchers alike have identified several ways to successfully predict security returns based on the past history returns. Among these findings, perhaps the most popular ones are those of momentum and reversal strategies.

---

[37] Thomas M. Idzorek, "A Step-By-Step Guide to the Black-Litterman Model: Incorporating User-Specified Confidence Levels," Research Paper, Ibbotson Associates, Chicago, 2005.

[38] Edward Qian and Stephen Gorman, "Conditional Distribution in Portfolio Theory," *Financial Analysts Journal* 57 (2001), pp. 44–51.

[39] See, for example, Fischer Black and Robert Litterman, "Global Asset Allocation with Equities, Bonds, and Currencies," Fixed Income Research, Goldman Sachs 1991 and Robert Litterman, *Modern Investment Management: An Equilibrium Approach* (Hoboken, NJ: John Wiley & Sons, 2003).

[40] Andrew Bevan and Kurt Winkelmann, "Using the Black-Litterman Global Asset Allocation Model: Three Years of Practical Experience," *Fixed Income Research*, Goldman Sachs, 1998.

[41] Guangliang He and Robert Litterman, "The Intuition Behind Black-Litterman Model Portfolios," *Investment Management Division*, Goldman Sachs, 1999.

[42] Campbell R. Harvey, John C. Liechty, Merril W. Liechty, and Peter Mueller, "Portfolio Selection with Higher Moments," Duke University, Working Paper, 2003.

The basic idea of a momentum strategy is to buy stocks that have performed well and to sell the stocks that have performed poorly with the hope that the same trend will continue in the near future. This effect was first documented in academic literature by Jegadeesh and Titman[43] in 1993 for the U.S. stock market and has thereafter been shown to be present in many other international equity markets.[44] The empirical findings show that stocks that outperformed (underperformed) over a horizon of 6 to 12 months will continue to perform well (poorly) on a horizon of 3 to 12 months to follow. Typical backtests of these strategies have historically earned about 1% per month over the following 12 months.

Many practitioners rely on momentum strategies—both on shorter as well as longer horizons. Short-term strategies tend to capitalize on intraday buy and sell pressures, whereas more intermediate and long-term strategies can be attributed to over- and underreaction of prices relative to their fundamental value as new information becomes available.[45]

Momentum portfolios tend to have high turnover so transaction and trading costs become an issue. Most studies show that the resulting profits of momentum strategies decrease if transaction costs are taken into account. For example, Korajczyk and Sadka, taking into account the different costs of buying and short-selling stocks, report that depending on the method of measurement and the particular strategy, profits between 17 to 35 basis points per month (after transaction costs) are achievable.[46]

While researchers seem to be in somewhat of an agreement on the robustness and pervasiveness of the momentum phenomenon, the debate is still ongoing on whether the empirical evidence indicates market inefficiency or if it can be explained by rational asset pricing theories. This discussion is beyond the scope of this book. Instead, we provide an illustration of a simple cross-sectional momentum strategy using the country indices from the MSCI World Index.[47]

The cross-sectional momentum portfolio is constructed at a point in time t ("today") and held for one month. We sort the countries based on

---

[43] Narasimhan Jegadeesh and Sheridan Titman, "Returns to Buying Winners and Selling Losers: Implications for Stock Market Efficiency," *Journal of Finance* 48 (1993), pp. 65–91.

[44] K. Geert Rouwenhorst, "International Momentum Strategies," *Journal of Finance* 53 (1998), pp. 267–283.

[45] Kent D. Daniel, David Hirshleifer, and Avanidhar Subrahmanyam, "Investor Psychology and Security Market Under- and Overreactions," *Journal of Finance* 53 (1998), pp. 1839–1885.

[46] Robert A. Korajczyk and Ronnie Sadka, "Are Momentum Profits Robust to Trading Costs?" *Journal of Finance* 59 (2004), pp. 1039–1082.

[47] A more detailed description of the data is provided in Appendix C.

their "one-day lagged" past nine-month return normalized by their individual volatilities. In other words, the ranking is based on the quantity

$$z_{t,i} = \frac{P_{t-1\,\text{day},\,i} - P_{t-1\,\text{day}-9\,\text{months},\,i}}{P_{t-1\,\text{day}-9\,\text{months},\,i} \cdot \sigma_i}$$

where $P_{t-1\,\text{day},\,i}$, $P_{t-1\,\text{day}-9\,\text{months},\,i}$ and σ_i denote the prices of security i at one day before t, one day and nine months before t, and the volatility of security i, respectively. After the ranking, the securities in the top half are assigned a weight of

$$w_i = \frac{1}{\sigma_i \cdot \kappa}$$

where κ is a scaling factor chosen such that the resulting annual portfolio volatility is at a desirable level. In this example, we set it equal to 20%.[48] Similarly, the securities in the bottom half are assigned a weight of

$$w_i = -\frac{1}{\sigma_i \cdot \kappa}$$

We make the portfolio weights a function of the individual volatilities in order not to overweight the most volatile assets. This is not a zero cost long-short portfolio as the portfolio weights do not sum up to zero. It is straightforward to modify the weighting scheme to achieve a zero cost portfolio, but for our purposes this does not matter and will not significantly change the results. The results from this simple momentum strategy are given in Exhibits 9.5 through 9.8.[49]

The momentum strategy outperforms the index on both an "alpha" and a Sharpe ratio basis. The Sharpe ratio of the strategy over the full period is 0.88 versus 0.62 for the index. The full period-annualized alpha is 11.7%, consistent with the standard results in the momentum literature. We also see that the beta of the strategy is very low, only 0.05 for the full sample. The realized correlation between the momentum strategy and the index is 3.5%. In other words, this momentum strategy is more or less market neutral.

---

[48] κ can be estimated from past portfolio returns at each time of rebalancing. Typically, it's value does not change significantly from period to period.
[49] The first portfolio is constructed in January 1981, as we need the previous 9-month return in order to perform the ranking.

EXHIBIT 9.5   Growth of Equity for the Momentum Strategy and the MSCI World Index

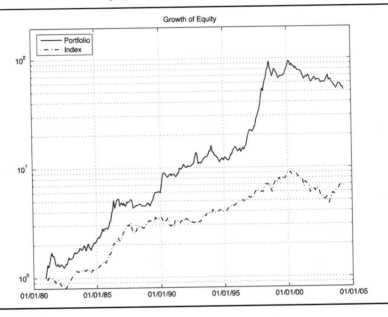

EXHIBIT 9.6   A Comparison of the Annualized Volatility of the Momentum Strategy and the Index

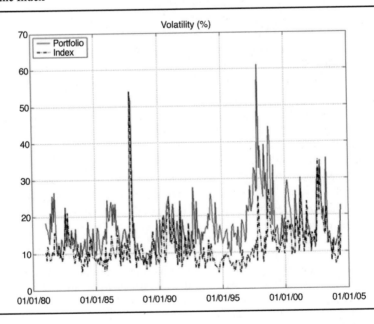

EXHIBIT 9.7 Summary Statistics of the Momentum Strategy

	Start Date	End Date	Mean	Volatility	Sharpe Ratio	Skew	Kurtosis	Min	Max	Alpha	Beta
1st Qtr	Jan-81	Dec-85	23.0%	19.4%	1.18	0.12	2.82	−10.4%	17.1%	11.7%	0.25
2nd Qtr	Jan-86	Dec-91	22.1%	21.7%	1.02	0.50	4.90	−14.9%	21.8%	14.3%	0.06
3rd Qtr	Jan-92	Dec-97	26.9%	20.9%	1.29	−0.09	4.87	−18.8%	20.2%	22.3%	−0.02
4th Qtr	Jan-98	May-04	3.7%	20.8%	0.18	0.54	3.33	−13.1%	16.9%	−0.1%	−0.05
1st Half	Jan-81	Dec-91	22.5%	20.6%	1.09	0.36	4.23	−14.9%	21.8%	12.9%	0.12
2nd Half	Jan-92	May-04	14.8%	21.1%	0.70	0.23	3.82	−18.8%	20.2%	10.7%	−0.03
Full	Jan-81	May-04	18.4%	20.9%	0.88	0.29	4.01	−18.8%	21.8%	11.7%	0.05

Notes: The columns Mean, Volatility, Sharpe Ratio, and Alpha are the annualized mean returns, volatilities, Sharpe ratios, and alphas of the portfolio over the different periods. Min and Max are the daily minimum and maximum portfolio returns, respectively. Skew and Kurtosis are calculated as the third and fourth normalized centered moments. Alphas and betas are calculated using 1-month LIBOR.

EXHIBIT 9.8 Summary Statistics of the MSCI World Index

	Start Date	End Date	Mean	Volatility	Sharpe Ratio	Skew	Kurtosis	Min	Max
1st Qtr	Jan-81	Dec-85	10.2%	11.5%	0.88	-0.29	2.70	-7.6%	7.7%
2nd Qtr	Jan-86	Dec-91	13.2%	16.4%	0.81	-0.21	4.05	-14.6%	12.8%
3rd Qtr	Jan-92	Dec-97	9.6%	9.8%	0.98	0.62	3.28	-3.9%	9.5%
4th Qtr	Jan-98	May-04	2.9%	17.2%	0.17	0.17	3.49	-12.3%	16.0%
1st Half	Jan-81	Dec-91	11.8%	14.3%	0.83	-0.21	4.22	-14.6%	12.8%
2nd Half	Jan-92	May-04	6.1%	14.1%	0.43	0.15	4.32	-12.3%	16.0%
Full	Jan-81	May-04	8.8%	14.2%	0.62	-0.02	4.22	-14.6%	16.0%

Notes: The columns Mean, Volatility, and Sharpe Ratio are the annualized mean returns, volatilities, and Sharpe ratios of the index over the different periods. Min and Max are the daily minimum and maximum Index returns, respectively. Skew and Kurtosis are calculated as the third and fourth normalized centered moments.

It turns out that this particular implementation has an average monthly portfolio turnover of 23.7% with a cross-sectional standard deviation of 9.3%. The United Kingdom has the highest average turnover (40.6%) and New Zealand has the lowest (10.8%). For a "real-world" implementation it would therefore be important to consider the impact of transaction costs.

An Optimized Cross-Sectional Momentum Strategy

In the previous section we introduced a simple cross-sectional momentum strategy. In this section we demonstrate how it can be combined with market equilibrium in a portfolio optimization framework by using the Black-Litterman model.

In this case, we only have one view—the momentum strategy. We use the approach described earlier where we discussed the "practical considerations and extensions" to specify the parameters for the Black-Litterman view.

The covariance matrices needed for the portfolio optimization are calculated from daily historical data with weighting (monthly decay parameter of $d = 0.95$) and with the correction for autocorrelation of Newey and West (2 lags).[50] We choose $\tau = 0.1$ for the Black-Litterman model.

After computing the implied Black-Litterman expected returns, we use the risk aversion formulation introduced in Chapter 2 of the mean-variance optimization problem with a risk aversion coefficient of $\lambda = 2$ (calibrated to achieve about the same volatility as the index) to calculate the optimal portfolio weights and rebalance the portfolio monthly. Before rebalancing at the end of each month, we calculate the realized portfolio return and its volatility. Results and summary statistics are presented in Exhibits 9.9 through 9.11. A comparison with the MSCI World Index is given in Exhibit 9.8.

The optimized strategy has a full sample Sharpe ratio of 0.92 versus 0.62 for the index and an "alpha" of 8.3%. We observe that in the last quarter the Sharpe ratio and the "alpha" of the strategy were negative, largely due to the general downturn in the market during that period. In contrast to the standalone momentum strategy that we discussed in the previous section, since the optimized strategy is a blend of momentum and market equilibrium, its resulting correlation with the index is significantly different from zero. For example, the full sample correlation with the index in this case is 0.36.[51]

---

[50] This particular covariance matrix estimator is described in Chapter 8.

[51] One possibility to decrease the correlation of the strategy with the index is to impose zero β constraints.

EXHIBIT 9.9   Growth of Equity of the Optimized Strategy and the MSCI World Index

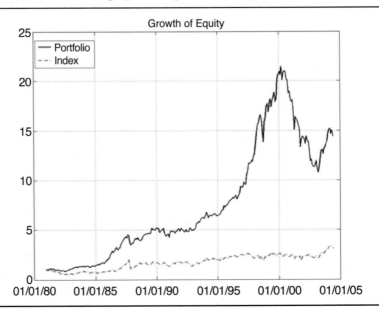

EXHIBIT 9.10   Monthly Portfolio Volatility of the Optimized Strategy Compared to Monthly Volatility of the MSCI World Index

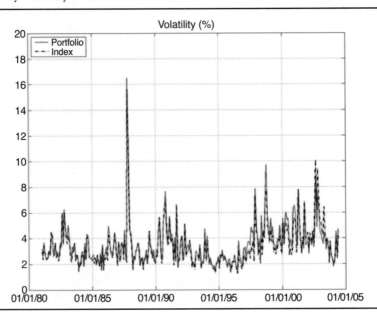

EXHIBIT 9.11 Portfolio Summary Statistics of the Optimized Strategy Rebalanced Monthly

	Start Date	End Date	Mean	Volatility	Sharpe Ratio	Skew	Kurtosis	Min	Max	Alpha	Beta
1st Qtr	Jan-81	Dec-89	18.9%	15.0%	1.26	-0.33	4.39	-15.1%	13.2%	9.2%	0.28
2nd Qtr	Jan-90	Dec-94	13.8%	13.7%	1.01	0.35	3.92	-9.4%	12.8%	11.23%	0.40
3rd Qtr	Jan-95	Dec-99	23.8%	14.0%	1.70	0.19	4.12	-9.1%	14.4%	18.1%	0.39
4th Qtr	Jan-00	May-04	-2.9%	15.3%	-0.19	-0.28	2.82	-11.9%	8.5%	-5.0%	0.65
1st Half	Jan-81	Dec-94	16.5%	14.6%	1.13	-0.09	4.08	-15.1%	13.2%	11.4%	0.31
2nd Half	Jan-95	May-04	11.4%	15.2%	0.75	-0.13	3.60	-11.9%	14.4%	6.3%	0.37
Full	Jan-81	May-04	13.6%	14.9%	0.92	-0.11	3.88	-15.1%	14.4%	8.3%	0.36

Notes: The columns Mean, Volatility, Sharpe Ratio, and Alpha are the annualized mean returns, volatilities, Sharpe ratios, and alphas of the portfolio over the different periods. Min and Max are the daily minimum and maximum portfolio returns, respectively. Skew and Kurtosis are calculated as the third and fourth normalized centered moments. Alphas and betas are calculated using 1-month LIBOR.

Albeit rudimentary, this illustration shows that it is possible to use portfolio theory and mean-variance optimization in the design of profitable investment strategies. We recall that in the illustrations presented earlier in this chapter as well as in Chapter 3, the standard textbook version of the mean-variance optimization always underperformed an equally weighted portfolio and the global minimum variance portfolio. There we argued that the problem of the classical mean-variance approach is in the estimation of the expected returns of the securities. The mixed estimation procedure used in the computation of the Black-Litterman implied expected returns by blending an investor's views with market equilibrium is, in practice, an effective way to mitigate estimation errors. Simply speaking, the Black-Litterman model manages to spread out any estimation errors in individual views over all assets and thereby makes the resulting expected returns more robust to estimation risk.

INCORPORATING ESTIMATION ERROR AND UNCERTAINTY IN THE PORTFOLIO ALLOCATION PROCESS

In the development of modern portfolio theory it is assumed that expected returns and covariances of the securities are known with certainty. Of course in practice this is not the case and the inputs have to be estimated. As we have discussed in this chapter, the estimation error in the forecasts may greatly influence the quality of the resulting optimized portfolio allocations. One way of tackling this problem that we have discussed in this chapter is to use "better and more robust" estimation techniques that increase the accuracy of the inputs. Nevertheless, even if they possibly are smaller, estimation errors will always be present.

In this section we discuss another possible route to handle this problem, namely by directly incorporating the estimation errors into the portfolio optimization process. In particular, we change the portfolio optimization problem in such a way that uncertainty in the inputs is taken into consideration.

In the first approach, estimation errors in the inputs are quantified through a Monte Carlo-type simulation, and in the second they are incorporated directly into the optimization process.

Portfolio Resampling Techniques

In this section we describe the basic idea behind the portfolio simulation techniques proposed in the literature (see, for example, Michaud,[52]

---

[52] Richard O. Michaud, *Efficient Asset Management: A Practical Guide to Stock Portfolio Optimization and Asset Allocation* (Oxford: Oxford University Press, 1998).

Jorion,[53] and Scherer[54]). It is based on resampling from the estimated inputs and is therefore also often referred to as *portfolio resampling*.

We start from our original estimates for the expected returns, $\hat{\mu}$, and the covariance matrix, $\hat{\Sigma}$ and first solve for the global minimum variance portfolio (GMV) and the maximum return portfolio (MR). Let us assume that the standard deviation of these portfolios are σ_{GMV} and σ_{MR} where per construction $\sigma_{GMV} < \sigma_{MR}$. Further, we define an equally spaced partition of the interval $[\sigma_{GMV}, \sigma_{MR}]$ in M points ($m = 1,...,M$), so that $\sigma_{GMV} = \sigma_1 < \sigma_2 < ... < \sigma_M = \sigma_{MR}$. For each one of these standard deviations, we solve for the corresponding minimum variance portfolio, and thereby obtain a representation of the efficient frontier with M portfolios. Let us denote the corresponding vectors of portfolio weights by $w_1, ..., w_M$. So far we have just been following the standard recipe for constructing the efficient frontier. Now, we will perform the portfolio resampling in the following steps:

Step 1: We draw T random samples from the multivariate distribution $N(\hat{\mu}, \hat{\Sigma})$ and use these to estimate a new expected return vector, $\hat{\mu}_i$, and covariance matrix, $\hat{\Sigma}_i$.

Step 2: Using $\hat{\mu}_i$ and $\hat{\Sigma}_i$ we solve for the corresponding global minimum variance and maximum return portfolios, $\sigma_{GMV,i}$ and $\sigma_{MR,i}$. Then, as before, we partition the interval $[\sigma_{GMV,i}, \sigma_{MR,i}]$ into M equally spaced points ($m = 1, ..., M$). For each standard deviation in the partition, we calculate the corresponding minimum variance portfolios, $w_{1,i}, ..., w_{M,i}$.

Step 3: We repeat steps 1 and 2 a total of I times.

Typically the parameter I is large, say around 100 or 500. After the portfolio resampling has been completed for each point in the partition, we calculate the *resampled portfolio weights* as the average

$$\bar{w}_M = \frac{1}{I}\sum_{i=1}^{I} w_{M,i}$$

[53] Philippe Jorion, "Portfolio Optimization in Practice," *Financial Analysts Journal* 48 (1992), pp. 68–74.
[54] Bernd Scherer, "Portfolio Resampling: Review and Critique," *Financial Analysts Journal* 58 (2002), pp. 98–109.

If we would recompute the efficient frontier using our original inputs, $\hat{\mu}$ and $\hat{\Sigma}$, and the new resampled portfolio weights, the new resampled efficient frontier would appear below the original one. This is because the weights $w_{1,i}, ..., w_{M,i}$ are efficient relative to $\hat{\mu}_i$ and $\hat{\Sigma}_i$ but inefficient relative to the original estimates $\hat{\mu}$ and $\hat{\Sigma}$. Therefore, the resampled portfolio weights is also inefficient relative to $\hat{\mu}$ and $\hat{\Sigma}$. By the sampling and reestimation that occurs at each step in the portfolio resampling process, the effect of estimation error is incorporated into the determination of the resampled portfolio weights.

Moreover, for each security in the asset universe, a distribution of the portfolio weight can be calculated from the simulated data. For example, a large standard deviation of a portfolio weight is an indication that the original portfolio weight is not very precise due to estimation error. This type of diagnostic can be generalized in the following way.

By introducing a test statistic, we can determine whether two portfolios are statistically different or not. For example, two natural test statistics are given by

$$d_1(w^*, w) = (w^* - w)' V_W^{-1} (w^* - w)$$

and

$$d_2(w^*, w) = (w^* - w)' \Sigma^{-1} (w^* - w)$$

where V_w and Σ are the covariance matrix of the resampled portfolio weights and the covariance matrix of returns, respectively. The first test statistic follows a chi-square (χ^2)-distribution with degrees of freedom equal to the number of securities considered. We notice that the second test statistic is the squared tracking error between two portfolios, w^* and w. Using one of these test statistics, we can determine which portfolio vectors calculated in the resampling process are statistically equivalent to the original portfolio vector. An important application of this idea is in the rebalancing of portfolios.

Let us assume that we are considering rebalancing our current holdings. Given our forecasts of expected returns and risk, we could calculate a set of new portfolios through the resampling procedure given above. The approach just discussed could now be used to determine whether these new portfolios are statistically different from our current holdings and, therefore, whether it would be worthwhile to rebalance or not. If we find the need to rebalance, we could do so using any of the statistically equivalent portfolios! Which one should we choose? One natural choice is to select the portfolio that would lead to the lowest transaction costs. We note that although we have described this idea in the context of portfolio resampling, it has a much wider application.

Some drawbacks have been identified with the resampled portfolio approach. We discuss some of them here.

Since the resampled portfolio is calculated through a simulation procedure in which, at each step, a portfolio optimization problem has to be solved, this approach can be computationally cumbersome—especially for large portfolios. It is important to find a good trade-off between the number of resampling steps to perform in a reasonable time; and at the same time achieve the necessary accuracy in order to measure the effects of estimation error on the optimized portfolios.

Due to the averaging in the calculation of the resampled portfolio, all assets will most likely obtain a nonzero weight. One possibility is to include constraints that would limit both the turnover as well as the number of assets with nonzero weights. Again however, due to the averaging process used in calculating the resampled portfolio, the resulting portfolio weights may no longer satisfy the imposed constraints. In general, only *linear* constraints imposed on each optimization will still be satisfied in the resampled portfolio. This is a serious limitation of the resampled portfolio approach for practical applications.

The resampled portfolio approach is suboptimal in terms of expected utility maximization, and therefore inconsistent with Von Neumann and Morgenstern[55] expected utility axioms and the behavior of a "rational investor."[56]

Markowitz and Usmen present a comparison between the resampled efficient frontier and classical mean-variance with forecasts derived from diffuse Bayesian priors.[57] In their simulation study based on returns drawn from a multivariate normal distribution, both methods overestimate the portfolio expected return. For example, for a risk aversion parameter $\lambda = 0.5$, the mean-variance approach forecasted an average annual growth rate of 18.05%, whereas the actual portfolios it chose had an average realized growth rate of 10.89%. The resampled efficient frontier forecasted an average annual growth rate of 15.09%, and the average realized growth rate was 11.46%. Nevertheless, in this study the resampled efficient frontier shows an improvement over the mean-variance approach.

[55] John Von Neumann and Oscar Morgenstern, *Theory of Games and Economic Behavior, 3rd ed.* (Princeton: Princeton University Press, 1953).
[56] Harvey, Liechty, Liechty, and Mueller. "Portfolio Selection with Higher Moments."
[57] Harry M. Markowitz and Nilufer Usmen, "Resampled Frontiers versus Diffuse Bayes: An Experiment," *Journal of Investment Management* 1 (2003), pp. 9–25.

Robust Portfolio Allocation

The inputs to the portfolio allocation process are unknown and have to be estimated. Therefore, it would appear to be natural if the portfolio optimization problem would be able to deal with the inputs given as ranges, or even as statistical distributions, rather than as the traditional point estimates that we are familiar with.

When solving for the efficient portfolios, ideally the differences in precision of the estimates should be explicitly incorporated into the analysis. But modern portfolio theory assumes that all estimates are as precise or imprecise and therefore *treats all securities equally.* Most commonly, practitioners of mean-variance optimization incorporate their beliefs on the precision of the estimates by imposing constraints on the maximum exposure of the securities in the portfolio. The securities on whom these constraints are imposed are generally those whose expected performances are either harder to estimate, or those whose performances are estimated less precisely.

We can only speculate as to why robust portfolio modeling, which we introduce below, is not more widely used by practitioners in the financial community. Probably, the major reason is that this technique is relatively new, considered too technical, and to a large extent only known and appreciated in the areas of optimization and operations research. In this section we hope to provide the intuition, and demystify the ideas, behind the robust optimization approach.

The Basic Ideas Behind Robust Optimization

Robust optimization is not a difficult concept. The basic idea is to consider the distribution of estimation errors directly in the optimization process. First, let us denote our estimate of the expected return by $\hat{\mu}$. For simplicity, we will assume that we can observe the true covariance matrix of returns, Σ. If we knew the true expected return, μ_{exact}, we could solve, for example, the risk aversion formulation of the portfolio allocation problem for the portfolio weights, that is,

$$\max_{\mathbf{w}} \mathbf{w}'\mu_{\text{exact}} - \lambda \mathbf{w}'\Sigma\mathbf{w}$$
$$s.t.\ \mathbf{w}'\iota = 1$$

where $\iota = [1,1,...,1]'$. But since we cannot observe and estimate the true expected return perfectly, we instead end up solving

$$\max_{\mathbf{w}} \mathbf{w}'\hat{\mu} - \lambda \mathbf{w}'\Sigma\mathbf{w}$$
$$s.t.\ \mathbf{w}'\iota = 1$$

where the estimated expected return $\hat{\mu}$ is subject to estimation error.

Let us assume that the estimated expected return is not too far away from the true expected return. In this case, suppose that for each component i of the estimated expected return vector there is some small number $\varepsilon_i > 0$ such that

$$\hat{\mu}_i - \varepsilon_i \leq \mu_{i,\,\text{exact}} \leq \hat{\mu}_i + \varepsilon_i$$

The ε_i's could be specified by assuming some confidence interval around the estimated expected return. For instance, assuming normality, we obtain a 95% confidence interval by setting $\varepsilon_i = 1.96\sigma_i/\sqrt{T}$ where σ_i is the standard deviation of $\hat{\mu}_i$ and T is the sample size used in the estimation.

Armed with this parametrization of the estimation error, we ask ourselves: What is the "worst" estimate of the expected return and how would we allocate our portfolio in this case? One possibility of mathematically expressing this is through the following optimization problem:

$$\max_{w} \min_{\mu} \ w'\mu - \lambda w'\Sigma w$$
$$s.t. \ w'\iota = 1$$
$$(\mu_i - \hat{\mu}_i)^2 \leq \varepsilon_i^2, i = 1, ..., N$$

The solution to this so-called "max-min problem" maximizes the expected utility (the minimum with respect to μ) for a given risk aversion parameter, $\lambda > 0$, in the worst-case realization of the uncertain expected return.

Since we are minimizing over the expected return, we observe that when the confidence is low for a particular security (i.e., the confidence interval is large), then the reliability in the estimated expected return is also low. But more importantly, in this case as we will see, the resulting portfolio weight for the security will be decreased. Conversely, when the confidence is high, the reliability in the estimated expected return is higher and, therefore, the resulting portfolio weight will be much closer to the weight that would be obtained from the classical mean-variance problem.

The set

$$U_\varepsilon(\hat{\mu}) = \left\{ \mu \mid (\mu_i - \hat{\mu}_i)^2 \leq \varepsilon_i^2, i = 1, ..., N \right\}$$

is referred to as an *uncertainty set*, and we may rewrite the optimization problem in the equivalent form

$$\max_{\mathbf{w}} \min_{\mu \in U_\varepsilon(\hat{\mu})} \mathbf{w}'\mu - \lambda \mathbf{w}'\Sigma\mathbf{w}$$

$$s.t. \ \mathbf{w}'\iota = 1$$

To get a better understanding of the properties of this problem, we will transform it into a more familiar form. For a fixed vector **w**, we first solve the "inner problem":

$$\min_{\mu} \ \mathbf{w}'\mu - \lambda \mathbf{w}'\Sigma\mathbf{w}$$

$$s.t. \ (\mu_i - \hat{\mu}_i)^2 \le \varepsilon_i^2, \ i = 1, \ldots, N$$

Denoting by μ^* the optimal solution of the inner problem, then by the Karush-Kuhn-Tucker (KKT) conditions (see, Chapter 6), a necessary condition for optimality is that there is a N-dimensional vector γ such that

$$\nabla_\mu L(\mu^*, \gamma) = 0$$

$$(\mu_i^* - \hat{\mu}_i)^2 - \varepsilon_i^2 \le 0, \ i = 1, \ldots, N$$

$$\gamma_i \ge 0, \ i = 1, \ldots, N$$

$$\gamma_i((\mu_i^* - \hat{\mu}_i)^2 - \varepsilon_i^2) = 0, \ i = 1, \ldots, N$$

where the Lagrangian takes the form

$$L(\mu, \gamma) = \mathbf{w}'\mu - \lambda \mathbf{w}'\Sigma\mathbf{w} - \frac{1}{2}\sum_{i=1}^{N} \gamma_i((\mu_i - \hat{\mu}_i)^2 - \varepsilon_i^2)$$

Differentiating the Lagrangian with respect to μ_i we obtain the first-order condition

$$w_i - \gamma_i(\mu_i - \hat{\mu}_i) = 0$$

and

$$\mu_i^* = \frac{w_i}{\gamma_i} + \hat{\mu}_i$$

We need to determine the Lagrange multiplier γ_i. Substituting the constraint $(\mu_i^* - \hat{\mu}_i)^2 \le \varepsilon_i^2$ into the formula for μ_i^*, we obtain

$$\gamma_i \geq \pm \frac{w_i}{\varepsilon_i}$$

Therefore, we conclude that

$$\mu_i^* = \hat{\mu}_i - \text{sign}(w_i)\varepsilon_i, \, i = 1, \ldots, N$$

is the solution to the "inner problem." Here, sign($\cdot$) is the sign function (that is, sign(x) = 1 when $x \geq 0$ and sign(x) = –1 when $x < 0$). For each security, we have obtained a representation of the worst-case expected returns μ_i as a function of the portfolio weights and the estimation error. By substituting this representation into the max-min problem, we get

$$\max_{\mathbf{w}} \, \mathbf{w}'(\hat{\mu} - \mu_{\varepsilon, \mathbf{w}}) - \lambda \mathbf{w}' \Sigma \mathbf{w}$$
$$s.t. \, \mathbf{w}' \iota = 1$$

where

$$\mu_{\varepsilon, \mathbf{w}} = \begin{bmatrix} \text{sign}(w_1)\varepsilon_1 \\ \vdots \\ \text{sign}(w_N)\varepsilon_N \end{bmatrix}$$

This optimization problem can be interpreted as a modification of the classical mean-variance problem where the expected return vector has been adjusted downwards to account for the uncertainty of its true value. The adjustment results in a shrinkage of the portfolio weights. Specifically, if a portfolio weight is positive then due to the adjustment the expected return is adjusted downwards, resulting in a smaller portfolio weight. Conversely, if a portfolio weight is negative then the expected return is adjusted upwards, resulting in a less negative portfolio weight.

By using the equality

$$w_i \text{sign}(w_i)\varepsilon_i = w_i \frac{w_i}{|w_i|}\varepsilon_i = \frac{w_i}{\sqrt{|w_i|}}\varepsilon_i \frac{w_i}{\sqrt{|w_i|}}$$

we can also write the max-min problem in the form

$$\max_{\mathbf{w}} \mathbf{w}'\hat{\boldsymbol{\mu}} - \lambda \mathbf{w}'\boldsymbol{\Sigma}\mathbf{w} - \tilde{\mathbf{w}}'\mathbf{E}\tilde{\mathbf{w}}$$
$$s.t. \ \mathbf{w}'\iota = 1$$

where

$$\tilde{\mathbf{w}} = \begin{bmatrix} \dfrac{w_1}{\sqrt{|w_1|}} \\ \vdots \\ \dfrac{w_N}{\sqrt{|w_N|}} \end{bmatrix}$$

and

$$\mathbf{E} = \begin{bmatrix} \varepsilon_1 & & \\ & \ddots & \\ & & \varepsilon_N \end{bmatrix}$$

We observe that this optimization problem is also a modification of the classical mean-variance problem. In particular, we see that a "risk-like" term $\tilde{\mathbf{w}}'\mathbf{E}\tilde{\mathbf{w}}$ has been added to the classical formulation. This term can be interpreted as a risk adjustment performed by an investor who is averse to estimation error. In other words, it models the effect of the uncertainty that stems from the estimation errors in the estimated expected returns. The exact form of the investor's *estimation risk aversion* is specified by the magnitude of the epsilons.

We chose a relatively simple representation of the uncertainty set above. More general uncertainty sets lead to more complicated optimization problems, although the basic interpretation and principles remain the same. For instance, if we consider the uncertainty set[58]

$$U_\varepsilon(\hat{\boldsymbol{\mu}}) = \{\boldsymbol{\mu} | (\boldsymbol{\mu} - \hat{\boldsymbol{\mu}})'\boldsymbol{\Sigma}^{-1}(\boldsymbol{\mu} - \hat{\boldsymbol{\mu}}) \le \varepsilon^2\}$$

---

[58] We remark that the covariance matrix $\boldsymbol{\Sigma}$ used in the definition of the uncertainty set for $\hat{\boldsymbol{\mu}}$ is in general not the same as the covariance matrix of returns. For example, if $\hat{\boldsymbol{\mu}}$ is calculated by the Black-Litterman model, then instead we may use $[(\tau\boldsymbol{\Sigma})^{-1} + \mathbf{P}'\boldsymbol{\Omega}^{-1}\mathbf{P}]^{-1}$. Here, to make the exposition simple and intuitive, we do not make this distinction.

then a similar analysis[59] shows that the max-min problem can be reformulated as

$$\max_{\mathbf{w}} \mathbf{w}'\hat{\boldsymbol{\mu}} - \lambda \mathbf{w}'\boldsymbol{\Sigma}\mathbf{w} - \varepsilon\sqrt{\mathbf{w}'\boldsymbol{\Sigma}\mathbf{w}}$$
$$s.t. \ \mathbf{w}'\boldsymbol{\iota} = 1$$

Just as in the previous problems above, we interpret the term $\varepsilon\sqrt{\mathbf{w}'\boldsymbol{\Sigma}\mathbf{w}}$ as the investor's aversion to estimation risk. In this case, ε represents the estimation risk aversion. We remark that this uncertainty set can be interpreted as an N-dimensional confidence region for the parameter vector $\hat{\boldsymbol{\mu}}$.

Notably, unlike the classical mean-variance problem, the forms of the two robust optimization problems introduced in this section are not

---

[59] The derivation goes as follows. First, we need to solve the "inner problem":

$$\min_{\boldsymbol{\mu}} \mathbf{w}'\boldsymbol{\mu} - \lambda \mathbf{w}'\boldsymbol{\Sigma}\mathbf{w}$$
$$s.t. \ (\boldsymbol{\mu} - \hat{\boldsymbol{\mu}})'\boldsymbol{\Sigma}^{-1}(\boldsymbol{\mu} - \hat{\boldsymbol{\mu}}) \leq \varepsilon^2$$

As before, by differentiating the Lagrangian

$$L(\boldsymbol{\mu}, \gamma) = \mathbf{w}'\boldsymbol{\mu} - \lambda \mathbf{w}'\boldsymbol{\Sigma}\mathbf{w} - \gamma(\varepsilon^2 - (\hat{\boldsymbol{\mu}} - \boldsymbol{\mu})'\boldsymbol{\Sigma}^{-1}(\hat{\boldsymbol{\mu}} - \boldsymbol{\mu}))$$

and solving the first-order condition, we obtain

$$\boldsymbol{\mu}^* = \hat{\boldsymbol{\mu}} - \frac{1}{2\gamma}\boldsymbol{\Sigma}\mathbf{w}$$

Substituting this back into the Lagrangian gives

$$L(\boldsymbol{\mu}^*, \gamma) = \mathbf{w}'\hat{\boldsymbol{\mu}} - \lambda \mathbf{w}'\boldsymbol{\Sigma}\mathbf{w} - \frac{1}{4\gamma}\mathbf{w}'\boldsymbol{\Sigma}\mathbf{w} - \gamma\varepsilon^2$$

Let us now consider the optimization problem with respect to $\mathbf{w}$ and γ,

$$\max_{\mathbf{w}, \gamma} L(\boldsymbol{\mu}^*, \gamma)$$
$$s.t. \ \mathbf{w}'\boldsymbol{\iota} = 1$$

Maximizing this with respect to γ, we obtain

$$\gamma^* = \frac{1}{2\varepsilon}\sqrt{\mathbf{w}'\boldsymbol{\Sigma}\mathbf{w}}$$

Substituting this back, results in an optimization problem only over $\mathbf{w}$

$$\max_{\mathbf{w}} \mathbf{w}'\hat{\boldsymbol{\mu}} - \lambda \mathbf{w}'\boldsymbol{\Sigma}\mathbf{w} - \varepsilon\sqrt{\mathbf{w}'\boldsymbol{\Sigma}\mathbf{w}}$$
$$s.t. \ \mathbf{w}'\boldsymbol{\iota} = 1$$

quadratic programming problems. Instead, in a simple and straightforward fashion they can be converted (see, for example, Alizadeh and Goldfarb,[60] Ben-Tal and Nemirovski,[61] and Lobo et al.[62]) into so-called *second-order cone programs* (SOCPs). This type of optimization problems can be solved in about the same time as the classical mean-variance problem by modern interior-point algorithms.[63]

Generalizations and Extensions

In the setup considered in the previous section, we only allowed for uncertainty in the expected returns. Several extensions to the robust framework have been developed. Simplistically speaking, they can be divided into four main areas:[64]

■ Modeling uncertainty in other inputs beyond the expected return
■ Incorporating different utility functions and risk measures in the robust framework
■ Using and specifying different uncertainty sets
■ Taking model risk into account beyond the uncertainty in the inputs

---

[60] Farid Alizadeh and Donald Goldfarb, "Second-Order Cone Programming." *Mathematical Programming* 95 (2003), pp. 3–51.
[61] Aharon Ben-Tal and Arkadi S. Nemirovski, *Lectures on Modern Convex Optimization: Analysis, Algorithms, and Engineering Applications*, MPS/SIAM Series on Optimization (Philadelphia: SIAM 2001).
[62] Miguel S. Lobo, Lieyen Vandenberghe, Stephen Boyd, and Herv Lebret, "Applications of Second-Order Cone Programming," *Linear Algebra and Its Applications* 284 (1998), pp. 193–228.
[63] See Chapter 6 for a further discussion of SOCPs and interior-point algorithms.
[64] See, for example, the following papers and the references therein: Laurent El Ghaoui, Maksim Oks, and Francois Oustry, "Worst-Case Value-At-Risk and Robust Portfolio Optimization: A Conic Programming Approach," *Operations Research* 51 (2003), pp. 543–556; Donald Goldfarb and Garud Iyengar, "Robust Portfolio Selection Problems," *Mathematics of Operations Research* 28 (2003), pp. 1–38; Bjarni V. Halldórsson and Reha H. Tütüncü, "An Interior-Point Method for a Class of Saddle Point Problems," Technical report, Carnegie Mellon University, Pittsburgh, PA, 2000; Miguel Sousa Lobo, "Robust and Convex Optimization Applications and Finance," Dissertation, Stanford University, 2000; Karthik Natarajan, Dessislava Pachamanova, and Melvyn Sim, "Constructing Risk Measures from Uncertainty Sets," Working Paper, National University of Singapore and Babson College, July 2005; Dessislava Pachamanova, "Handing Parameter Uncertainty in Portfolio Risk Minimization: The Robust Optimization Approach," Working Paper, Babson College, Babson Park, MA, 2004; and Reha H. Tütüncü and M. Koenig, "Robust Asset Allocation," Technical Report, Carnegie Mellon University and National City Investment Management Company, 2003.

The robust optimization framework offers a lot of flexibility and some new interesting applications. Much in the same fashion as in the section on portfolio resampling in this chapter, robust portfolio optimization can exploit the fact that there are statistically equivalent portfolios that are cheaper to trade into.[65] This becomes extremely important in large-scale portfolio management with many complex constraints such as transaction costs, turnover, and market impact. For instance, with robust optimization we can calculate the new portfolio that (1) minimizes trading costs with respect to the current holdings; and (2) has an expected portfolio return and variance that is statistically equivalent to the classical mean-variance portfolio. But maybe most importantly, robust mean-variance portfolios are more stable to changes in inputs and tend to offer performance superior to classical mean-variance portfolios.

We emphasize that in many portfolio allocation applications it may be too pessimistic to use the worst-case portfolio calculated through the robust framework. Indeed, since in the robust portfolio allocation framework described above, the net adjustment to the estimated portfolio expected return will always be downwards, this approach is in many cases too conservative. Furthermore, it is important to consider the impact of any other portfolio constraints used in the optimization on the resulting robust portfolio weights. We point out that the framework presented here is just a starting point, and many other alternative forms of robust portfolio optimization are possible.

An Example

To illustrate the practicality and usefulness of the robust portfolio optimization, we consider an illustration from Goldfarb and Iyengar that compares the performance between the robust and the classical approach using 43 stocks from the Dow Jones.[66] They chose the 43 stocks by picking the top companies from each one of the 10 industry categories in the Dow Jones in August 2000, and obtained daily return data from January 2, 1997 through December 29, 2000.[67] They point out that although the data suffers from *survivorship bias*, this bias should affect the two different strategies in a similar fashion and not have much impact on their relative comparison.

---

[65] Unlike portfolio resampling, robust mean-variance requires the solution of one optimization problem that takes about the same time to solve as the classical mean-variance formulation. Portfolio resampling is computationally intensive as it requires the solution of a large number of classical mean-variance problems.

[66] Goldfarb and Iyengar, "Robust Portfolio Selection Problems."

[67] The 10 industry categories are: aerospace, telecommunication, semiconductor, computer software, computer hardware, internet and online, biotech and pharmaceuticals, utilities, chemicals, and industrial goods. The top 4 to 5 companies from each category, as of August 2000, were chosen.

To forecast expected returns and the covariance matrix of returns they used a factor model with 10 factors: five major market indices (Dow Jones Composite, NASDAQ 100, S&P 500, Russell 2000, the 30-year bond) and the first five principal components from the covariance matrix of returns. The daily returns were divided into periods of 90 days, and the forecast of expected returns and covariance matrix for one period was based on the previous periods. In other words, the portfolios are rebalanced every 90 day period with a total of 10 investment periods. The two portfolio optimization problems that were considered were the classical and robust maximum Sharpe ratio problems:

Classical Maximum Sharpe Ratio Problem

$$\max_{w} \frac{w'\hat{\mu} - R_f}{\sqrt{w'\hat{\Sigma}w}}$$

$$s.t.\ w'\iota = 1$$
$$w \geq 0$$

where $\iota = [1,1,...,1]'$, and R_f, $\hat{\mu}$ and $\hat{\Sigma}$ denote the risk-free rate, the expected return vector and covariance matrix estimated by the factor model, respectively.

Robust Maximum Sharpe Ratio Problem

$$\max_{w}\ \min_{\substack{\mu \in U(\hat{\Omega}) \\ \Sigma \in V(\hat{\Sigma})}} \frac{w'\mu - R_f}{\sqrt{w'\Sigma w}}$$

$$s.t.\ w'\iota = 1$$
$$w \geq 0$$

where we use the same notation as in the problem above. Further, $U(\hat{\Omega})$ and $V(\hat{\Sigma})$ denote the uncertainty sets, that depend on the confidence level ω (similar to the ε we use previously in this chapter), of the estimated expected return and covariance matrix.[68]

---

[68] In order to keep this description from being too technical, we refrain from describing the full details of the specification of the uncertainty sets used. However, we emphasize that one of the major contributions of Goldfarb and Iyengar's study (that is of both practical and theoretical interest) is the modeling of the estimation errors in the factor model by translating confidence intervals implied by standard linear regression assumptions into so-called ellipsoidal uncertainty sets.

The change in wealth of the portfolios is calculated in each period and their relative performance is compared for different levels of confidence, ω, in the robust formulation.

Their results show that for low levels of confidence, as expected the classical and the robust portfolios have very similar performance. It is not until the confidence is more than 80% that the robust strategy outperforms the classical one—at least over this time period. In particular, for the 95% and 99% confidence levels, the final wealth of the robust portfolios is 40% and 50% higher than that of the classical portfolio, respectively.

These results are similar to the ones reported by Ceria.[69] His simulation experiments show an improvement in realized Sharpe ratios of portfolios rebalanced with robust mean-variance versus classical mean-variance of between 20% and 45% dependent on the aversion to estimation error (confidence level).

Let us now take a look at the difference in average turnover between the two portfolios over the investment horizon defined by

$$\frac{\frac{1}{10}\sum_{t=1}^{10}\left\|\mathbf{w}_{R,t}-\mathbf{w}_{R,t-1}\right\|_1}{\frac{1}{10}\sum_{t=1}^{10}\left\|\mathbf{w}_{c,t}-\mathbf{w}_{c,t-1}\right\|_1}$$

where

$$\|\mathbf{w}\|_1 = \sum_{i=1}^{N}|w_i|$$

The ratio of the average turnover of the robust and the classical portfolios is more or less constant (between about 1.005 to 1.015) up to the 90% confidence level. This means that the turnover of the robust portfolios is around 0.5% to 1.5% higher than the classical portfolio. However, for confidence levels greater than 90%, the turnover decreases monotonically. For example, at the 95% and 99% confidence levels, the turnover of the robust portfolios is 4% and 7% lower than the classical portfolio, respectively.

---

[69] Sebastian Ceria, "Overcoming Estimation Error in Portfolio Construction," Presentation at the Chicago Quantitative Alliance Las Vegas Conference, 2003.

Note that if the confidence level is chosen too high, the robust portfolio becomes very conservative. Typically, in this case, the portfolio weights will be close to those of the global minimum variance portfolio and not change drastically from period to period, thereby reducing turnover.

This example shows that the robust portfolio framework is very flexible and incorporates different trading styles. One possibility is to adjust the confidence level dynamically over time, for example by making it a function of volatility. In periods of high volatility—high risk— an investor might prefer a higher level of confidence and vice versa.

SUMMARY

- Classical mean-variance optimization is sensitive to estimation error and small changes in the inputs.
- In this chapter, the different approaches discussed to make the classical mean-variance framework more robust are: (1) improve the accuracy of the inputs; (2) use constraints for the portfolio weights; (3) use portfolio resampling to calculate the portfolio weights; and (4) apply the robust optimization framework to the portfolio allocation process.
- Typically, errors in the expected returns are about 10 times more important than errors in the covariance matrix, and errors in the variances are about twice as important as errors in the covariances.
- Estimates of expected return and covariances can be improved by using shrinkage estimation. Shrinkage is a form of averaging different estimators where the shrinkage estimator typically consists of three components: (1) an estimator with little or no structure; (2) an estimator with a lot of structure (the shrinkage target); and (3) the shrinkage intensity.
- Jorion's shrinkage estimator for the expected return shrinks towards the return of the global minimum variance portfolio.
- The sample covariance matrix should not be used as an input to the mean-variance problem. By shrinking it towards the covariance matrix with constant correlations, its quality will be improved.
- The Black-Litterman model combines an investor's views with the market equilibrium.
- The Black-Litterman expected return is a "confidence" weighted linear combination of market equilibrium and the investor's views. The confidence in the views and in market equilibrium determines the relative weighting.
- Factor models as well as simple ranking models can be simultaneously incorporated into the Black-Litterman model.

- Portfolio resampling is based on the idea of Monte Carlo simulation. By repeatedly drawing from the estimated distribution and for each draw solving a mean-variance problem, the effects of estimation error in the portfolio allocation process can be simulated.
- Robust portfolio optimization incorporates the distribution of estimation errors directly into the optimization process.
- A robust mean-variance problem can be seen as an "adjusted" classical mean-variance problem and can be solved by an optimization algorithm in about the same time as the classical mean-variance problem.

PART Three

Dynamic Models for Equity Prices

CHAPTER 10

Feedback and Predictors in Stock Markets

Now that we have presented static linear factor models, let us review some of the phenomena that they fail to explain. In particular, we discuss the concepts of time diversification, momentum, and feedback, all three phenomena that require *dynamic* extensions of static models. We also discuss how these phenomena can be explained with economic models based on multiple interacting agents.

RANDOM WALK MODELS AND THEIR SHORTCOMINGS

As discussed in Chapter 7, linear factor models are embodied in static linear relationships between returns that hold at any given moment. They do not entail time dynamics. The time dynamics must be added. If returns or logarithms of returns (log returns) are assumed to be a sequence of identical and independently distributed (IID) random variables, the actual dynamics of prices processes or logarithms of price processes are assumed to be, respectively, a multivariate geometric random walk or an arithmetic random walk. As we know from Chapter 7, the concept of random walk can be generalized. We can distinguish three main concepts of random walk:[1]

- Random walk with independent and identically distributed increments
- Random walk with independent but possibly nonidentically distributed increments

---

[1] John Y. Campbell, Andrew W. Lo, and A.Craig MacKinlay, *The Econometrics of Financial Markets* (Princeton, NJ: Princeton University Press, 1997).

■ Random walk with uncorrelated but possibly nonindependent increments.

The three concepts are progressively weaker in the sense that the first implies the second and the third and the second implies the third but not vice versa.

The random walk with uncorrelated increments can be further analyzed. The assumption of uncorrelated increments means that increments form a white-noise process. As discussed in Chapter 7, a white noise process is not completely unforecastable unless it is Gaussian. In a white-noise process the mean cannot be forecasted with linear forecasts but might be forecasted with nonlinear forecasts. In fact, at each step the conditional expectation of the process is not necessarily zero. If we assume that increments form a martingale difference sequence then expectations cannot be forecasted neither with linear nor with nonlinear forecasts.[2] In fact, in a martingale difference sequence, at each step the conditional expectation of the process is zero. In both white noise and martingale difference sequences, however, higher moments might be forecasted.

The assumption that increments form a martingale difference sequence is called a *weak form of market efficiency*. According to the weak form of market efficiency only permanent drifts can be determined but the expectation of price changes at time $t + 1$ cannot be forecasted with the information available at time t. The weak form of market efficiency, however, leaves open the possibility that higher moments are forecastable.

In this chapter we discuss three basic questions on stock price behavior:

■ Do individual equity price processes behave as random walks?
■ Do aggregates of equity price processes behave as multivariate random walks?
■ Are there long-range dependencies in equity price processes?

Later in this chapter, we will see that price processes can be individually random walks and yet still exhibit a joint dynamics due to cross auto-correlations and cointegration. Cointegration implies that there are feedbacks from prices to returns where prices are integrated processes and returns are stationary processes. The concepts of integration and cointegration can be generalized introducing the notion of long-range dependence through fractionally integrated and fractionally cointegrated processes. We begin by examining tests of the random walk hypothesis.

---

[2] See Chapter 11 for a definition and properties of martingale difference sequences.

Tests of the Random Walk Hypothesis for Univariate Price Processes

The random walk hypothesis of *individual* price processes is the simplest and most intuitive representation of market efficiency. As it is so central to finance theory, the random walk hypothesis has been extensively tested. As any other statistical hypothesis, the random walk hypothesis is tested by computing some statistics of the sample, that is, some function of the sample data. If the distribution of that statistic is known (or if at least its limit distribution for large samples it is known), critical values for the acceptance or rejection of the hypothesis can be computed. One can then compare the sample statistics with the critical values and accept or reject the hypothesis within a given confidence level.

Let us first consider the strongest assumption that increments of log prices, that is log returns, are a sequence of IID random variables. A number of classical tests of the random walk hypothesis with IID increments are based on testing the sequence of the signs of increments. Suppose increments are IID variables. The hypothesis of IID increments entails that, if the drift is zero, the signs of increments are Bernoulli variables; that is, positive and negative signs have the same probability, 1/2. In long sequences of increments, the ratio of sequences and reversals of sign should be equal to one. The absence of drift is critical as a drift induces a bias in the distribution of the sign of increments.

Another early test is based on the distribution of runs, that is sequences of increments with the same sign. Mood proved that the asymptotic distribution of runs is normal after appropriate normalization.[3] Extensive applications of the run test performed, for example by Fama,[4] on U.S. stock price data, have not found any appreciable correlation structure. An elegant generalization of the theory of runs, which also applies to non-IID sequences, was proposed by Aldous and Diaconis using permutation group theory.[5]

Now assume that returns are uncorrelated but not necessarily independent variables. Different tests of the hypothesis of absence of correlation have been proposed. Let's write a model of log returns as follows:

$$r(t) = p(t) - p(t-1) = \varepsilon(t)$$

---

[3] A. M. Mood, "The Distribution Theory of Runs," *Annals of Mathematical Statistics* 11 (1940), pp. 367–392.
[4] Eugene F. Fama, "The Behavior of Stock Market Prices," *Journal of Business* 38 (1965), pp. 34–105.
[5] D. Aldous and P. Diaconis, "Shuffling Cards and Stopping Times," *American Mathematical Monthly* 8 (1986), pp. 333–348.

where $\varepsilon(t)$ is a white-noise sequence, that is, a sequence of uncorrelated variables. Under the random walk assumption, the autocovariances $\gamma(t)$ and the autocorrelation coefficients $\rho(k)$ at lag k of the sequence $\varepsilon(t)$ are zero for every k. It is well known that we can estimate the autocovariances and the autocorrelation coefficients with the sample autocovariances and autocorrelation coefficients:

$$\hat{\gamma}(k) = \frac{1}{T} \sum_{t=1}^{T-k} ((r_t - \overline{r_T})(r_{t+k} + \overline{r_T}))$$

$$\overline{r_T} = \frac{1}{T} \sum_{t=1}^{T} r_t$$

$$\hat{\rho}(k) = \frac{\hat{\gamma}(k)}{\hat{\gamma}(0)}$$

The asymptotic distribution of the sample autocovariances and autocorrelation coefficients under the assumption of uncorrelated increments were determined by Fuller.[6] Fuller showed that sample autocovariances and autocorrelation coefficients are biased and proposed corrections to the sample estimates.

In 1970, Box and Pierce proposed the Q-test as a general way to test autocorrelation at every lag.[7] The Q-test is based on the following statistics:

$$Q_m = T \sum_{k=1}^{m} \frac{\rho^2(k)}{T-k}$$

They demonstrated that the asymptotic distribution of the Q-statistics is a χ_m^2 distribution. In 1978, Ljung and Box proposed the following small-sample correction:[8]

[6] Wayne A. Fuller, *Introduction to Statistical Time Series* (New York: John Wiley & Sons, 1976).

[7] G. Box and D. Pierce, "Distribution of Residual Autocorrelations in Autoregressive-Integrated Moving Average Time Series Models," *Journal of the American Statistical Association* 65 (1970), pp. 1509–1526.

[8] G. Ljung and G. Box, "On a Measure of Lack of Fit in Time Series Models," *Biometrika* 66 (1978), pp. 67–72.

$$Q_m = T(T+2) \sum_{k=1}^{m} \frac{\rho^2(k)}{T-k}$$

These tests are implemented in every time series software package and are widely used in applied statistical work.

Lo and MacKinlay proposed a different approach based on testing the linear growth of the process variance.[9] In fact, in the above model of log returns, the variance of log returns grows linearly with time. For example, consider the two-period return:

$$r_{t,2} = p_t - p_{t-2} = r_t + r_{t-1}$$

We can write

$$\mathrm{Var}(r_{t,2}) = \mathrm{Var}(r_t) + \mathrm{Var}(r_{t-1}) + 2\,\mathrm{Cov}(r_t, r_{t-1})$$

As the return process is assumed to be stationary, we can write the variance ratio

$$\frac{\mathrm{Var}(r_{t,2})}{2\,\mathrm{Var}(r_t)} = 1 + 2\rho(1)$$

If the process is a random walk, the correlation coefficient $\rho(1) = 0$ and the two-period return variance is twice the one-period variance. This formula can be generalized to any number of periods. The variance ratio for k periods can be written as follows:

$$\frac{\mathrm{Var}(r_{t,k})}{k\,\mathrm{Var}(r_t)} = 1 + 2\sum_{i=1}^{k-1}\left(1 - \frac{i}{k}\right)\rho(i)$$

It is now possible to conclude that the log return variance grows linearly if log prices follow an arithmetic random walk. Lo and MacKinlay derived the distribution of the variance ratio at different time horizons. Therefore, a random walk test is obtained comparing variances at different time horizons.

---

[9] Andrew W. Lo and A. Craig MacKinlay, "Stock Market Prices Do Not Follow Random Walks: Evidence from a Simple Specification Test," *Review of Financial Studies* 1 (1988), pp. 41–66.

Other tests of the random walk hypothesis are based on the fact that it is possible to engineer profitable trading strategies. In fact, under the random walk hypothesis, it is not possible to earn an extra profit using trading strategies based on the past history of prices. However these tests, which are based on filtering rules, are delicate to interpreted as the profit derived from trading strategies is itself stochastic.

Tests of the random walk hypothesis have not been conclusive. The empirical findings can be summarized as follows:

■ Tests of the random walk hypothesis do not systematically fail on randomly chosen price processes.
■ In large samples of price processes, most random walk tests fail with a frequency higher than that expected at corresponding confidence levels.
■ Average estimates yield parameters slightly different from those of random walks.

For example, Campbell, Lo, and MacKinlay report that the average autocorrelation coefficient in large sets of equity log return processes is slightly below one. It is fair to say that the universal validity of the random walk hypothesis can be rejected although evidence against the random walk hypothesis is not statistically very strong.

Tests of the Random Walk Hypothesis for Multivariate Price Processes

Thus far, we have considered tests of the random walk hypothesis for single processes. Consider next the hypothesis that *aggregates* of asset price processes behave as multivariate random walks. The evidence against the random walk hypothesis is much stronger in the case of portfolios than in the case of single asset prices. For example, there is empirical evidence, as documented in Lo et al. that the returns of large portfolios are strongly autocorrelated.[10]

Aggregates of price processes exhibit a type of behavior that can be much more complex than that of single price processes. In particular, as we will see in Chapter 12, it is possible that individual price processes are random walks but that the aggregate has a rich dynamical structure insofar as portfolios can be strongly autocorrelated. This behavior is known as *cointegration*.

We will postpone the discussion of tests of the random walk hypothesis for multivariate price processes until we have introduced the concepts of integration and cointegration and of long-range depen-

---

[10] Campbell, Lo, and MacKinlay, *The Econometrics of Financial Markets*.

dence. In the following two sections we discuss the theoretical motivations in favor and against the random walk hypothesis.

The Theory Behind the Random Walk Hypothesis

Let us now discuss the theoretical motivation which supports the random walk hypothesis. The random walk hypothesis is based on the intuitive principle that, in a competitive, efficient market, any forecastability that leads to a profit must be, at most, short lived. This occurs because profit opportunities based on price forecasts lead to market movements that tend to eliminate those same profit opportunities. Market forecastability thus tends to disappear. For example, if the price of an asset is forecast to rise, agents will tend to buy that asset. In doing so, they produce an excess demand that makes that asset price rise immediately rather than in the future. The forecast is thus invalidated. As a consequence, price movements are unforecastable. This idea was first expressed by Bachelier in his 1900 thesis[11] and restated in the more general context of market efficiency in the 1960s by Samuelson[12] and Fama.[13]

However, the above statements are simplistic to the point of being meaningless as forecasts are generally risky. The notion of forecastability and the notion of risk have to be made precise. To do so requires a dynamic model of asset returns. Call p_{t+1} the log prices at the next moment $t + 1$. Let's consider a theoretical model where, at every step, the probability distribution of p_{t+1} conditional on the information set I at step t is

$$f_t(p_{t+1}|I_t)$$

This model is very general—indeed every econometric model is a special instance of this model. Essentially, it assumes only that we know the conditional probability distribution of prices.

Under the above model, the statement that profit opportunities tend to disappear must be articulated with the consideration of risk and returns. We have seen in our discussion on mean-variance analysis in Chapter 2 how investors choose their portfolios in order to optimize their risk-return trade off. We have also seen in Chapter 7 where we discuss General Equilibrium Theories how the collective behavior of agents results in return

---

[11] Louis Bachelier, "Théorie de la Speculation" translated in Paul Cootner, *The Random Character of Stock Market Prices* (Cambridge, MA: MIT Press, 1964).
[12] Paul A. Samuelson, "Proof that Properly Anticipated Prices Fluctuate Randomly," *Industrial Management Review* 6 (1965), pp. 41–49.
[13] Eugene F. Fama, "Efficient Capital Markets: A Review of Theory and Empirical Work," *Journal of Finance* 25 (1970), pp. 383–417.

distributions that make all assets equivalent when risk and return are considered, though different risk and returns are possible.

We can now come back to the concept of market efficiency in terms of the principle of absence of arbitrage. *Absence of arbitrage* means that it is not possible to make a sure profit without an investment outlay. Absence of arbitrage is a fundamental principle of finance theory which does not require any specification of investors' preferences in terms of risk and returns. Amongst other things, it tells us that only one risk-free rate is possible.

The principle of absence of arbitrage is a strong principle on which much of relative asset pricing theory rests. For example, most derivatives pricing methods are based on it. However, the principle of absence of arbitrage is compatible with a vast class of price stochastic processes and does not require that returns are independent or uncorrelated sequences. In fact, it can be demonstrated that absence of arbitrage implies that all price processes become martingales after appropriate discounting. A *martingale* is a stochastic process such that, at every moment, the conditional expectation of the process is equal to the value of the process at that moment.

Based therefore on the consideration of market efficiency, we can state that price processes behave as martingales after discounting. If we want to characterize price processes more precisely, we need to know more about the risk-return preferences of agents. These preferences define what combinations of risk and returns are considered equivalent by the market.[14]

As they can exhibit correlation structures, martingales are not random walks. Therefore, theoretical considerations ultimately impose only absence of arbitrage; they do not require that price processes behave as random walks. In a stochastic dynamic environment, we no longer need assume that markets are completely unforecastable. Some residual forecastability in a probabilistic sense is compatible with absence of arbitrage. Dynamic models, which will be introduced in Chapter 12, do not violate the principle of no arbitrage although they do admit some level of forecastability. As we will see in the following section, complete absence of forecastability is not a tenable assumption given the fundamental principle of risk remuneration.

However, and this is the reason why random walk tests are inconclusive, there cannot be that much forecastability in the market. Though martingales admit an autocorrelation structure, the eventual existence of clear autocorrelation, given reasonable risk-return preferences for agents, would be immediately exploited. Though any martingale can

---

[14] For a lucid exposition of these concepts, see Michael Magill and Martine Qunzii, *Theory of Incomplete Markets* (Cambridge, MA: MIT Press, 1996).

represent price processes, in practice the set of admissible price processes is more severely constrained.

Consequences of Risk Premiums and Absence of Forecastability

The models discussed in the previous section entail that, at every step, we can determine the conditional probability distribution of returns. Random walk models require (1) that log price processes have a deterministic linear trend and (2) that log price increments are stationary and uncorrelated. These assumptions are too strong if we admit risk premiums. Consider, in fact, that we must assume that linear trends will be different for different assets. This occurs because agents are not indifferent to risk and, therefore, different return distributions entail different average returns, that is, there is a risk premium. If we consider risk premiums, multivariate random walk models of prices cannot be long-term models of asset prices.

To appreciate this point, consider the case where log returns are multivariate normal distributions:

$$\mathbf{r} = \boldsymbol{\mu} + \boldsymbol{\varepsilon}$$

where as usual, $\boldsymbol{\mu}$ is the vector of drifts and $\boldsymbol{\varepsilon}$ is a sequence of independent, identical, zero-mean normal variables. As remarked in Chapter 7, the assumption of normality for log returns is substantially not restrictive as long as we assume that return variance is finite. In general, each log price process $p_{i,t}$ will be characterized by a specific drift μ_i and variance σ_i^2. These drifts and variances are the constant one-step means and variances of the log returns which are a sequence of independent variables. This implies that each price process $P_{i,t}$ will be a lognormal process whose unconditional mean at time t is

$$P_{i,t} = P_{i,0} e^{\left(\mu_i + \frac{\sigma_i^2}{2}\right)t}$$

and whose unconditional variance at time t is:

$$\sigma_{i,t}^2 = e^{(2\mu_i + \sigma_i^2)t}\left(e^{\sigma_i^2 t} - 1\right)P_{i,0}^2$$

The above relationships imply that, if drifts are not all equal, the ratio between the means of price processes with different drifts and volatilities will diverge exponentially as

$$\frac{P_{i,t}}{P_{j,t}} = \frac{P_{i,0}}{P_{j,0}} e^{\left(\mu_i - \mu_j + \frac{\sigma_i^2 - \sigma_j^2}{2}\right)t}$$

Neither of these relationships is sustainable in the long run given the spread of drifts and volatilities estimated over shorter periods of time. For example, in the period January 2001–April 2004, the vector of estimated daily drifts of the S&P 500 covered the range –0.0032 to 0.0022, corresponding to yearly compounded returns of –55% and +73%, respectively. The average returns of the ten highest and lowest returns are –0.0026 and +0.0014, corresponding to yearly compounded returns of –48% and +45%, respectively. Over a period of 12 years, these drifts would translate into a relative compound return of approximately 800,000% for the highest-lowest pair and approximately 3,200% for the average of the ten highest and lowest. Compound relative returns of this type are not found empirically. Any long-term model must include feedback from prices to returns and thus deviations from joint random-walk behavior.[15]

Therefore, the hypothesis that price processes behave jointly as random walks is eventually tenable only as an approximation valid over short time horizons. In the practice of financial econometrics, factor models (which are ultimately multivariate random walk models) are estimated over relatively short moving windows—in the range of one to three years. The rationale behind this is that feedback (and ultimately mean reversion) is a slow process.

Integrated Processes and Long-Range Memory

It is now appropriate to introduce the concept of integrated processes, which plays a key role in dynamic models. Consider a simple log price process written as

$$p(t) = \rho p(t-1) + \eta(t), \quad t = 0, 1, 2, \ldots$$

where ρ is a constant coefficient and $\eta(t)$ is a stationary, possibly autocorrelated process. An *integrated process* is a process with $\rho = 1$; it is characterized by the fact that shocks never decay. In fact, we can write

---

[15] Consider that the problem of analyzing the long-run behavior of large aggregates of stock prices is made complex by the fact that companies are continuously being formed, merged, or closed. Any long-run model of stock prices must take this phenomenon into account. Estimating models on those processes that have "survived" for a long period of time introduces the "survivorship bias."

$$p(t) = p(t-1) + \eta(t) = p(t-2) + \eta(t-1) + \eta(t) = p(0) + \sum_{i=1}^{t} \eta(i)$$

If $|\rho| \le 1$, shocks would decay as we could write

$$p(t) = \rho p(t-1) + \eta(t) = \rho[\rho p(t-2) + \eta(t-1)] + \eta(t)$$
$$= \rho^t p(0) + \sum_{i=1}^{t} \rho^{t-i} \eta(i)$$

An integrated process is a process that becomes stationary after differencing. A process is said to be integrated on order d if it becomes stationary after differencing d times. Stationary processes are said to be processes integrated of order zero. Clearly, a random walk is an integrated process but the opposite is not true because the shocks of an integrated process can be autocorrelated. Tests for integrated processes are therefore not tests of the random walk hypothesis.

It is possible to define processes that are intermediate between integrated and stationary processes. Granger and Joyeux,[16] and Hosking[17] introduced *fractionally integrated processes*. Fractionally integrated processes are processes with a fractional integration order. Fractionally integrated processes exhibit long memory. This means that their autocorrelation function decays very slowly. The importance of fractionally integrated processes will become clearer after discussing cointegration in Chapter 12.

TIME DIVERSIFICATION

We have discussed the reasons for rejecting the assumption that, in the long run, price processes jointly behave as random walks. However, it is still possible to make the assumption that indexes behave as random walks, that is, that market averages are basically unpredictable at least at some forecasting horizon. (See below the section on time aggregation.) As we will see after discussing dynamic models, this assumption entails that in the very long run, risk premiums are all equal (at least on the average) with a first-order approximation. This raises the question

[16] C. Granger and R. Joyeaux, "An Introduction to Long Memory Time Series Models and Fractional Differencing," *Journal of Time Series Analysis* 1 (1980), pp. 15–29.
[17] J. Hosking, "Fractional Differencing," *Biometrika* 68 (1981), pp. 165–176.

of time diversification, a key concept which sets the stage for discussing feedback in price processes.

The concept of asset diversification was discussed in Chapter 2. Diversification is based on the fact that a linear combination of random variables can have a variance smaller than that of individual variables. A portfolio can thus be less risky than its component assets. The portfolio selection problem optimizes the weights in order to attain the optimum trade-off between portfolio return and variance according to some criteria. Time diversification consists in applying the same principle through time. Proponents of time diversification argue that if returns are IID random variables in long time series, the return should be very close to the theoretical average return.

We start by defining time diversification and models that exhibit time diversification.

Definition of Time Diversification

Time diversification is typically embodied in the statement that equity prices are less risky over long time horizons than over short time horizons. Proponents of time diversification argue that investing in stocks over long time horizons is less risky than investing in the same stocks over short time horizons. A corollary of this principle is that optimal asset allocation changes with aging: Young people are better off investing in stocks while old people should allocate their resources to bonds. The above cannot be considered a formal statement of the principle of time diversification insofar as it depends on the definition of risk that we adopt. Confusion about this point is a source of ambiguity as regards the reality of time diversification.

The concept of time diversification has been the subject of heated debate. A clear and nontechnical presentation of the principle of time diversification and its applicability can be found in Kritzman.[18] We will take a slightly more formal approach. Suppose we choose a model to represent asset price processes. The existence of time diversification in these asset price processes hinges on the following three questions:

■ How do we define time diversification?
■ Does the chosen model exhibit time diversification?
■ How empirically faithful is the chosen model?

Let us start with the question of how we define time diversification. In the Markowitz framework, portfolio risk is equated to portfolio vari-

---

[18] Mark Kritzman, "What Practitioners Need to Know About Time Diversification," *Financial Analysts Journal* 50 (1994), pp. 14–18.

ance of returns. If we assume that risk is measured by the portfolio variance, there is time diversification if the ratio between variance and mean decreases over time. In other words, there is time diversification if the level of risk relative to the level of returns decreases with time. Note that there are other considerations related to risk measures and utility functions. A clear discussion of time diversification from the point of view of risk measures and utility functions is presented by Kritzman. Our objective here is to keep the discussion on a basic level that does not require any specific assumption as regards the risk profile of agents.

Models Exhibiting Time Diversification

Let us discuss just what models exhibit time diversification. First suppose that prices follow arithmetic random walks. Starting from any given moment, returns

$$R_{\Delta t} = \frac{P(t + \Delta t) - P(t)}{P(t)}$$

are proportional to price increments at different time horizons.

Recall from Chapter 7 that the mean and the variance of an arithmetic random walk grow linearly with time while its standard deviation grows as the square root of time. A random walk without drift presents a standard deviation that grows as the square root of time and a variance that grows linearly with time. The distribution of an arithmetic random walk without drift becomes more widespread as time elapses. This can be seen in Exhibit 10.1 which shows the empirical probability density function $y = f(x)$ of 10,000 generated arithmetic random walk paths at 250 and 2,500 steps respectively.

Now add a drift. The mean and the variance of the random walk grows linearly while the standard deviation grows with the square root of time. The ratio of standard deviation to the mean tends to zero as time tends to infinity while the ratio of variance to the mean is constant. Though the standard deviation grows over time, the mean grows faster so that their ratio tends to zero. However, the variance grows linearly over time so that the ratio of the variance to the mean is a constant. The two statements are equivalent to the *Law of Large Num*bers and to the *Central Limit Theorem* (CLT) respectively.

There is no feedback and reversion to the mean. If, at a given moment, the arithmetic random walk reaches a level below the mean, the expected value at any time horizon is the mean minus that negative value. Note, however, that there is a probability one of crossing any negative or positive level provided that an unlimited amount of time is allowed.

EXHIBIT 10.1   Probability Density Function at 250 and 2,500 Steps

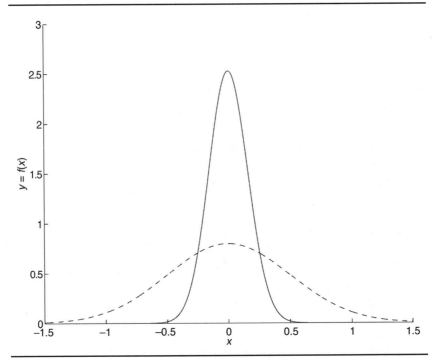

Note: The solid line represents the empirical pdf at 250 steps, the dotted line the empirical pdf at 2,500 steps.

We can therefore conclude that the arithmetic random walk with drift is a process that exhibits time diversification if we measure risk by the standard deviation of portfolio returns. If equity price processes do indeed follow arithmetic random walks, then the risk of investing, as measured by the standard deviation of portfolio returns, would decrease over time as the mean, which grows over time, prevails over deviations from the mean. However, if we measure the risk of investing in terms of the variance of portfolio returns, then there is no time diversification as the ratio of the variance to the mean remains constant. Clearly there is room for ambiguities in these definitions.

Suppose now that returns are an IID sequence of lognormal variables. Under this assumption, the logarithm of each price follows an arithmetic random walk with normal increments. The relative price process is therefore a lognormal process. While the mean and the variance of each log price grows linearly over time, the mean of each price process $P_{i,t}$ is an exponential,

$$P_{i,t} = P_{i,0}e^{\left(\mu + \frac{\sigma^2}{2}\right)t}$$

and its standard deviation $\sigma_{i,t}$ is another exponential,

$$\sigma_{i,t} = P_{i,0}e^{\left(\mu_i + \frac{\sigma^2}{2}\right)t}(e^{\sigma^2 t} - 1)^{\frac{1}{2}}$$

The ratio between the standard deviation and the mean diverges exponentially as

$$\frac{\sigma_{i,t}}{P_{i,t}} = \frac{P_{i,0}e^{\left(\mu_i + \frac{\sigma^2}{2}\right)t}(e^{\sigma^2 t} - 1)^{\frac{1}{2}}}{P_{i,0}e^{\left(\mu_i + \frac{\sigma^2}{2}\right)t}} = \left(e^{\sigma_i^2 t} - 1\right)^{\frac{1}{2}} \to e^{\frac{1}{2}\sigma_i^2 t}$$

The model with independent lognormal returns does not exhibit time diversification. Suppose an investor starts with a capital C_0. Under the assumption of lognormal independent returns, the expected value of this initial capital will grow exponentially, but the variance of the capital will grow at an even faster exponential rate. The same result obtains for a geometric random walk.

The above result is somewhat counterintuitive. In fact, for a large number of time steps, the proportion of returns above or below the average will be approximately the same. This consideration often leads to the erroneous conclusion that the lognormal model exhibits time diversification. The point is that returns do not add but multiply. Therefore, in the independent lognormal return model, returns over long horizons exhibit a large standard deviation, larger than the process mean at that horizon. In addition, the probability of negative returns is not negligible, as shown by Kritzman.

Let's now consider a model with mean reversion. The simplest example of a mean reverting model is *a trend stationary model*. A trend-stationary model that exhibits stationary fluctuations around a deterministic trend:

$$P_t = f(t) + \eta(t)$$

where f is a deterministic function and η is a zero mean stationary process. Suppose, for simplicity, that the deterministic trend is linear,

$$f(t) = \alpha + \beta t$$

and that the random disturbance is normally distributed.

Consider first the case where prices follow a trend-stationary process with a growing linear trend. As the stochastic disturbance η is a stationary process, its variance and standard deviation are constants. Therefore, as the linear trend grows, the ratio of the standard deviation to the mean tends to zero. The process shows a strong form of mean reversion and time reversion. This model is quite unrealistic as a long-term stock price model.

Now suppose that the logarithm of prices is trend-stationary. The mean of the logprices will be

$$E[p(t)] = \alpha + \beta t$$

and the standard deviation will be a constant σ as in the previous case. Consider next the price process. It will be a nonstationary lognormal process whose mean and standard deviations are respectively

$$P_t = P_0 e^{\beta t}$$

$$\sigma_t = P_0 e^{\beta t}(e^{\sigma^2} - 1)^{1/2}$$

In this case, the ratio between the standard deviation and the mean is constant. A mean-reverting logprice process translates into a price process with a constant risk figure as measured by the ratio (standard deviation)/mean. There is no time diversification—a result which is again quite counterintuitive as it is generally assumed that a mean-reverting process leads to time diversification.

The risk-return accounting provides a first rough indication that trend-stationary models for logprices can be an approximate model in the long run as they provide a reasonable account of risk and returns over long time horizons: The risk-to-return ratio remains constant. A geometric random walk, on the contrary, is unrealistic in the long run as it entails an exponential explosion of risk.

The above considerations apply to econometric models. Whether asset price processes actually do exhibit time diversification or not depends on just what model realistically describes price processes. Insofar it depends on the ability to make forecasts, time diversification is a question of modeling. Time diversification is the statement that we can model long-term behavior better than short-term behavior. However, the latter statement is ambiguous. The ability to make better forecasts on long as opposed to short time horizons might be a question of the Law of Large Numbers. Or we might have a better view of long time horizons because there are dynamic laws that pull prices close to some deterministic trend.

Consider, however, that one key modeling ingredient is missing: regime shifts or structural changes. It is quite unrealistic that a simple trend-stationary model can represent the variety of behavior in different periods. Take, for example, the U.S. stock market, where in the 20th century, the stock market experienced 20 periods of bull market and 20 periods of bear market. More likely, the structure of price processes is better approximated by a combination of trend-stationary models with regime shifts. The latter are embodied in models such as the Markov-switching models.

A MULTIAGENT ECONOMY: EFFECTS OF AGENT HETEROGENEITY AND INTERACTIONS

General Equilibrium Theories are based on the paradigm of perfectly rational optimizing agents. Agents are coordinated solely by a central price signal. This model can be seen under two different perspectives. First, as a pure mathematical model, its empirical adequacy is fundamentally unassailable. It has been demonstrated by Harrison and Kreps that any price process that does not exhibit arbitrage opportunities can be rationalized as a general equilibrium.[19]

However, if we want to interpret a General Equilibrium Theory as a theory descriptive of actual agent behavior, we encounter difficulties that cannot be resolved. Real agents make imperfect forecasts based on past data, have different information sets, and are subject to pairwise direct interactions. In addition, agents have finite resources that limit their ability to trade. At the aggregate level, the supply and demand for new investments is determined by macro considerations, in particular the availability of cash resources.

Many stylized facts that have been empirically discovered in financial markets are difficult to explain in a natural way within the General Equilibrium Theory framework. For example, it is difficult to explain how the fat tails of returns that have been empirically found in stock prices can be endogenously generated within the General Equilibrium Theory framework. Market crashes and bubbles are also difficult to

---

[19] Michael Harrison and David M. Kreps, "Martingale and Arbitrage in Multiperiod Securities Markets," *Journal of Economic Theory* 30 (1979), pp. 381–408.

explain within this framework. As observed above, any price process in the absence of arbitrage can be rationalized as a general equilibrium but the assumptions that one needs to make to justify fat tails, bubbles, and market crashes are unnatural *ad hoc* assumptions. Perhaps a more fundamental difficulty is presented by the widely discussed aggregation properties of General Equilibrium Theories. Under General Equilibrium Theories, aggregation destroys many individual properties. For example, individual processes can be negatively autocorrelated while the relative indexes can be positively autocorrelated.[20]

The paradigm of *multiple interacting agents* with bounded rationality was proposed to overcome some of the difficulties mentioned above. The paradigm of multiple interacting agents hypothesizes that the economy is a complex system made up of a multitude of agents that form a partial and imperfect representation of the world based on global signals as well as pairwise exchanges of information.

Mathematical models of the stock market developed through the joint efforts of economists and physicists have provided support for price and return distributions with heavy tails. This was done by modeling the interaction of market agents. Probably the most well-known model is the Santa Fe Stock Market Model.[21] There are others. Bak, Paczuski, and Shubik[22] and Lux [23]analyze the interaction between two categories of market agents: "rational investors" and "noise traders." Rational agents act on fundamental information in order to analyze risk-return opportunities and then optimize their utility function. "Noise" traders are market agents whose behavior is governed only by their analysis of market dynamics.[24] Their choice at which price to

---

[20] For a comprehensive treatment of the subject, see M. Forni and M. Lippi, *Aggregation and the Microfoundations of Dynamic Macroeconomics* (Oxford: Clarendon Press, 1997).

[21] W. B. Arthur, J. H. Hollan, B. LeBaron, R. Palmer, and P. Tayler, "Asset Pricing under Endogeneous Expectations in an Artificial Stock Market," in W.B. Arthur, S. Durlauf, and D. Lane (eds.), *The Economy as an Evolving Complex System, II*, vol. xxvii of SFI Studies in the Sciences of Complexit (Redwood, CA: Addison-Wesley. 1997).

[22] P. Bak, M. Paczuski, and M. Shubik, "Price Variations in a Stock Market with Many Agents," No 1132, Cowles Foundation Discussion Papers from, Cowles Foundation, Yale University, 1996.

[23] T. Lux, "The Socio-Economic Dynamics of Speculative Markets," *Journal of Economic Behavior and Organization* 33 (1998), pp. 143–165.

[24] Fischer Black introduced the concept of a noise trader. He described noise trading as "trading on noise as if it were information" even though "from an objective point they would be better off not trading." See Fischer Black, "Noise," *Journal of Finance* 41 (1986), pp. 351–368.

transact (buy or sell) may imitate the choice of other market agents. Cont and Bouchaud develop a model based on herding or crowd behavior that has been observed in financial markets.[25] Specifically, they suggest a relation between heavy tails, market order flows, and the tendency of market participants to mimic each other. While these mathematical models are by nature a gross simplification of real-world financial markets, they provide sufficient structure to analyze return distributions. Computer simulations of these models have been found to generate fat tails and other statistical characteristics that have been observed in real-world financial markets.

The theory of interacting agents presently offers theoretical justification for econometric models that would be difficult to justify within the classical framework. However, few applications based on the actual representation of the empirical structure of interactions have been proposed to date.

Dynamic Modeling: Feedback and Momentum

The concept of feedback was introduced in the 1950s and 1960s in the context of a discipline that was then called *cybernetics*. A *feedback* is a control signal that is activated when a system deviates from some target behavior. It is the basis of the modern theory of *servocontrols*.[26] Econometric models explored in previous chapters do not include feedbacks. Absence of feedback is responsible for the possibly exponentially diverging behavior exhibited by these models.

It is unlikely that a finite economy does not impose feedback on its price processes. As noted at the beginning of this chapter, there is some tension between two highly intuitive concepts. On the one hand, it seems reasonable to hold that markets reflect available information, making market fluctuations unpredictable events; there is no reason why market forecastability would be left unexploited. On the other hand, a sequence of unpredictable shocks applied to returns in a fundamentally growing economy that rewards risk would produce exponentially diverging behavior. This behavior runs against another highly intuitive concept: A finite market must implement feedback as it cannot grow indefinitely. Reconciling the two phenomena, thereby allowing for

---

[25] R. Cont and J. P. Bouchaud, "Herd Behavior and Aggregate Fluctuations in Financial Markets," *Macroeconomic Dynamics* 4 (2000), pp. 170–196.

[26] An engaging discussion of cybernetics in the scientific perspective of the 1960s can be found in *Cybernetics* by Norbert Wiener. A mathematician, Norbert Wiener is credited with, amongst many other fundamental contributions, the development of cybernetics. Though the term cybernetics is no longer used, cybernetic concepts such as feedback are ubiquitous in modern science and engineering.

controlled growth and some fundamental unpredictability, is an important challenge for financial econometrics.

For our purposes, it is convenient to divide feedbacks into two categories. The first category includes feedbacks that govern the market as an economic aggregate. This type of feedback is eventually responsible for the predictability of indexes and other market aggregates. Mean reversion of indexes is a feedback of this type. The second category includes relative feedbacks that govern the gains and losses of one asset with respect to others. The two types of feedbacks are interrelated. For example, relative feedbacks generally translate into index predictability. However, the modeling of the two types of feedback differs significantly. As a general rule, it is easier to model relative as opposed to absolute feedbacks.

Feedbacks are not the only dynamic effects present in financial markets. Momentum is another dynamic effect that has been discovered.[27] *Return momentum* means that both positive and negative return paths exhibit some level of permanence. For example, if the price of a stock begins to rise, it will continue to go up for a while. Different interpretations of momentum have been advanced. For example it has been proposed that momentum is a consequence of higher moments of return distributions.[28]

The discovery of momentum in returns was preceded by the discovery of momentum in volatility. This is the well-known volatility clustering (or ARCH/GARCH) effect. (Note that volatility clustering is model-dependent, insofar as one needs to identify a volatility parameter.) In plain English, the ARCH effect means that uncertainty in market behavior exhibits permanence: One finds extended periods of high uncertainty followed by extended periods of low uncertainty. Thus market predictability is not constant; there are regime changes.

Different modeling strategies have been proposed to model feedback and momentum. The most fundamental models are dynamic linear models based on rationalizing variances and covariances. Linear models are embodied in *Autoregressive Moving Average* (ARMA) models for univariate time series and *Vector Autoregressive Moving Average* (VARMA), and Vector Autoregressive (VAR) models for multivariate time series. ARMA and VARMA models posit that the value of the process at the next step is a linear function of previous values plus a random disturbance. This idea can be generalized to include nonlinear functions.

A different modeling strategy consists of adopting a simple basic model whose parameters are driven by another model. Examples of this

---

[27] Narasimhan Jegadeesh and Sheridan Titman, "Momentum," Working Paper, University of Illinois, October 23, 2001.

[28] Campbell R. Harvey and Akhtar Siddique, "Conditional Skewness in Asset Pricing Tests," *Journal of Finance* 55 (2000), pp. 1263–1296.

modeling strategy include the ARCH/GARCH family as well as Markov-switching models and stochastic volatility models. Models of this type are generally nonlinear models. In the following two chapters we will discuss autoregressive and vector autoregressive models and their properties.

MARKET PREDICTORS

In the previous sections, we saw that there are feedbacks in the market. The presence of feedbacks means that there are cross autocorrelations of price processes, that is to say, there are correlations between the price of different stocks at different time lags. Feedback naturally induces autocorrelations—and thus predictability—at the level of portfolios or indexes. We will better formalize this after introducing the concepts of cointegration and common trends in Chapter 12.

Let us now discuss the question of exogenous predictors of prices and returns other than lagged prices and returns. The quest for variables that allow one to predict future returns began in earnest in the 1930s with the work of Graham and Dodd on corporate valuation.[29] Graham and Dodd argued that high valuation ratios, that is high corporate valuation with respect to the actual stock price, are a predictor of future positive returns. In the 1980s, economists such as Fama and French[30] and Campbell and Shiller[31] identified valuation ratios as predictors of returns. Economic quantities such as dividend/price ratios, price/earnings ratios, or financial quantities related to corporate cash flows have been widely used by practitioners to identify underpriced stocks. Macroeconomic quantities such as unemployment rates and interest rates have also been considered. The advent of low-cost, high-performance computers ushered in a more systematic search for predictors. Using advanced analytical software, analysts can now explore the predictive power of hundreds of variables.

Recent academic studies have explored the predictive power of various valuation ratios.[32] (That is, ratios between the price of a stock and

---

[29] Benjamin Graham and David L. Dodd, *Security Analysis*, 1st ed. (New York: McGraw Hill, 1934).

[30] Eugene F. Fama and Kenneth R. French, "Dividend Yields and Expected Stock Returns," *Journal of Financial Economics* 22 (1988), pp. 3–25.

[31] John Y. Campbell, and Robert J. Shiller, "Stock Prices, Earnings, and Expected Dividends," *Journal of Finance* 43 (1988), pp. 661–676; and John Y. Campbell, and Robert J. Shiller, "Valuation Ratios and the Long-Run Stock Market Outlook," *Journal of Portfolio Management* (Winter 1998), pp. 11–26.

[32] John Y. Campbell and Samuel B. Thomson, "Predicting the Equity Premium Out of Sample: Can Anything Beat the Historical Average?" unpublished, 2005.

quantities related to its value computed from balance sheet data. Most studies have found that valuation ratios (and other financial indicators) do indeed have some predictive power. Other categories of predictors including momentum factors, market sentiment, and corporate quality have also been investigated.

The simplest predictor-based model is the linear regression. Using linear regression, the return of asset i is linearly regressed over a number of predictor variables that might include the asset return itself. A general form of the model is the following:

$$E(r_i(t)) = \mu_i + \beta_i x(t-1)$$

where β_i is a vector of coefficients specific to asset i and x is a vector of predictors. One component of x can be $r_i(t-1)$.

This linear regression model is very general. As any vector autoregressive (VAR) model is equivalent to a VAR(1) model (see Chapter 12), the above multiple regression includes all VAR models of returns as well as models that include exogenous regressors. Nonlinear generalizations of the above linear regression model include Markov-switching models (see Chapter 12), where the coefficients depend on a state variable that follows a Markov chain.

The validity of making linear regressions of returns over predictors has been questioned. Stambaugh[33] observes that many regressors used in practice have a high level of permanence, that is, they are not I(0) variables. This fact would invalidate linear regressions and thus the power of predictive models. Stambaugh also observes that the residuals are often correlated with returns; this induces additional biases. Recently, Goyal and Welch[34] argue that linear regressions on predictors systematically fail out of sample.

These criticisms have in turn been questioned. Campbell and Thomson challenged the view that linear regressions on predictors perform poorly out of sample. They found that there is a level of predictability over historical averages that is economically meaningful. Campbell and Yogo[35] propose a new test aimed at better filtering noise in regressions. Nonlinear conditional models[36] and Markov-switching models have

---

[33] Robert F. Stambaugh, "Predictive Regressions," *Journal of Financial Economics* 54 (1999), pp. 375–421.

[34] Amit Goyal and Ivo Welch, "A Comprehensive Look at the Empirical Performance of Equity Premium Prediction," NBER Working Paper 10483, 2004.

[35] John Y. Campbell and Motohiro Yogo, "Efficient Tests of Stock Return Predictability," NBER Working Paper No. 10026, October 2003.

[36] Eric H. Sorensen, Ronald Hua, and Edward Qian, "Contextual Fundamentals, Models, and Active Management," *Journal of Portfolio Management* (Fall 2005).

also been used to show that there is predictability in stock returns. Nonlinear models not only capture nonlinear relationships between expected returns and predictors, but also one allow to model nonnormal distributions (some of these nonlinear models are discussed in Chapter 12).

It is probably fair to say that the existence of market predictors has been empirically ascertained: Subject to risk, it might be possible to make probabilistic forecasts of future asset returns and earn a profit. However, linear regression might not be the optimal modeling tool; nonlinear models might yield better performance in terms of both predicting expected returns and managing risk.

TIME AGGREGATION

The time scale at which returns are forecasted is a fundamental parameter of forecasting models. Returns might be unforecastable at one time scale but have some forecastability at a different time scale. Similar considerations apply to higher moments. For example, volatility has different behavior at different time scales.

There are several explanations for the behavior of time aggregation. Consider the decay of the autocorrelation function of returns. This decay signals that beyond a given time horizon, returns can be considered independent. A process can be autocorrelated—and thus predictable—at short time horizons but behave as a random walk at longer time horizons. Arshanapalli et al. find that stock prices retain some forecastability when the time horizon is in the order of days, but become unforecastable at longer time horizons.[37] Over long time scales, regime shifts are more likely to affect time aggregation. It is not realistic to model price processes as if they were random walks over long time intervals; one should consider different models at different time horizons.

SUMMARY

- Though the hypothesis that price processes behave as a random walk has been extensively tested, tests are inconclusive to date.
- The hypothesis that multivariate price processes behave as multivariate random walks can be rejected. This is confirmed by the fact that some large portfolios are strongly autocorrelated.

---

[37] Bala Arshanapalli, Larry Belcher, K.C. Ma, and James Mallett, "Memory in World Stock Prices," *International Journal of Business* 9 (2004), pp. 1–13.

- The joint consideration of the random walk hypothesis and of risk remuneration leads to exponentially diverging price processes. However, exponentially diverging price processes are incompatible with the finite nature of financial markets.
- Time diversification is the hypothesis that stocks are less risky in the long run than in the short run.
- The reality of time diversification depends on the measure of risk one adopts. If risk is measured by the standard deviation normalized by price, random walks do not exhibit time diversification. If log prices behave as trend-stationary processes, normalized risk measured by the standard deviation normalized by price does not change with the time horizon.
- Price processes exhibit both momentum effects and feedbacks from prices to returns at different time lags.
- There are predictor variables for returns. However, the validity of predictors is weakened by the fact that some predictor variables exhibit permanence; that is, they have an autocorrelation coefficient close to 1.

CHAPTER 11

Individual Price Processes: Univariate Models

A s we saw in the previous chapter, the evidence for feedback and momentum calls for *dynamic models*. Dynamic models are models that describe a dynamics such as a price dynamics. Dynamics are described introducing relationships between the values of variables at different time lags. For example, a price dynamics can be established by linking future prices with the prices at previous dates up to the present. We start by discussing linear univariate dynamic models, analyzing their statistical properties and presenting their solutions. In particular, in this chapter we present the *Autoregressive Moving Average* (ARMA) family of univariate models, review their statistical properties, and show explicit solutions using the theory of difference equations. Looking at explicit solutions helps to understand the key properties of linear models and their applicability. Univariate models do not consider correlations and auto-cross correlations between variables. Though this is a serious limitation, the understanding of univariate models is an essential prerequisite for the understanding of multivariate models, which will be treated in Chapter 12, *Vector Autoregressive Moving Average Models* (VARMA).

Correlations and cross autocorrelations are fundamental properties of price and return processes. In the absence of correlation, large portfolios would be nearly deterministic due to diversification while cross autocorrelations are one of the major sources of profitable price dynamics. For these reasons, univariate dynamic models have found very limited application in equity portfolio management. However, univariate and multivariate linear systems based on difference equations share some common properties. First, solutions are the sum of a deterministic

347

and a stochastic part. Solutions themselves have the same general form as sums of exponentials and sinusoidal functions, eventually with polynomial weights. In this chapter, we discuss linear ARMA processes and present some of the key properties of linear systems in the univariate setting.

Difference equations are an important mathematical tool to understand dynamic econometric models: ARMA and VARMA models are expressed as linear difference equations with random disturbances added. Understanding the behavior of solutions of linear difference equations enhances one's intuition of the behavior of linear stochastic models. The theory of difference equations and the computation of the solution of different types of equations are provided in Appendix A.

TIME SERIES CONCEPTS

First we recall the concept and some properties of time series. A *time series* x_t is a sequence of random variables indexed by time. For example, the sequence of daily returns r_t of a given stock is a time series. The stochastic behavior of a time series x_t is completely determined by its *finite dimensional distributions,* which are the joint distributions of the series at different moments. That is, the finite dimensional distributions are all the joint distributions $p(x_{t_1}, ..., x_{t_m})$ for every collection of time indexes.

Recall from Chapter 7 that a time series x_t is called *strictly stationary* if all finite dimensional distributions are time invariant, that is, if the following property holds for every τ and for every set $(x_{t_1}, ..., x_{t_m})$:

$$p(x_{t_1}, ..., x_{t_m}) = p(x_{t_1 + r}, ..., x_{t_m + \tau})$$

A time series is called *covariance stationary* if only the mean and the covariances are time independent, that is, if the following property holds for every τ and every t:

$$E(x_t) = E(x_{t+\tau}) = \mu$$
$$E((x_t - \mu)(x_{t+\tau} - \mu)) = \gamma(\tau)$$

The function

$$\rho(\tau) = \frac{\gamma(\tau)}{\gamma(0)}$$

is called the autorrelation function of the time series. Note that a strictly stationary time series is not necessarily covariance stationary because the first two moments might not exist. A covariance-stationary time series is not necessarily strictly stationary as higher moments are unrestricted.

In general terms, a series x_t is said to be predictable if the distribution $p(x_t)$ depends on the information I_{t-1} known at time $t - 1$, in particular if it depends on the previous history of the same series. Conversely, a series is said to be unpredictable if the distribution $p(x_t)$ does not depend on the information I_{t-1} known at time $t - 1$, in particular if it does not depend on the previous history of the same series.

Specialized concepts of predictability can be defined. In particular, it is possible to define processes such that only the mean is unpredictable while the variance and eventually higher moments can be predicted. A series x_t is unpredictable in mean if the conditional expectation $E(x_t|I_{t-1})$ does not depend on I_{t-1} that is, if $E(x_t|I_{t-1}) = E(x_t)$. An example is the return process of a stock, whose mean is constant but whose variance is subject to clustering effects and thus predictable.

It is also possible to define processes where the conditional expectation is linearly unpredictable though it might be predictable in a broader sense. White noise is an example of a linearly unpredictable process.

The fundamental *Wold representation theorem* states that any stationary time series x_t can be decomposed in a unique way as the sum of two uncorrelated processes $x_t = s_t + w_t$, where s_t is a linearly deterministic process and w_t is an infinite moving average of error terms:

$$w_t = \sum_{i=0}^{\infty} h_i \varepsilon_{t-i}$$

where the errors are linearly unpredictable white noise. Note that the Wold theorem does not say that any series has a unique moving average representation. Actually a time series has many moving average representations but only one corresponds to the Wold decomposition.

The Wold theorem also does not specify any particular deterministic component. If we assume that the deterministic component is a constant, then any univariate stationary causal time series admits the following infinite moving average representation:

$$x_t = \sum_{i=0}^{\infty} h_i \varepsilon_{t-i} + m$$

where ε_{t-i} is a one-dimensional zero-mean white-noise process. A process of this type is called a *linear process*.[1]

A sufficient condition for stationarity is that the coefficients h_i are absolutely summable:

$$\sum_{i=0}^{\infty} |h_i|^2 < \infty$$

This is a *causal* time series because the present value of the series depends on the present and past values of the noise process.[2]

DIGRESSION ON WHITE NOISE AND MARTINGALE DIFFERENCE SEQUENCES

In this section we expand the discussion on the different concepts of white noise that we began in Chapter 7 and introduce the concept of *martingale difference sequences*.

In Chapter 7, we introduced two types of white noise: *strict white noise*, which is a sequence of independent and identically distributed (IID) zero-mean variables with finite variance, and the weaker concept of *white noise*, which is a sequence of zero-mean uncorrelated variables not necessarily independently distributed. We also observed that if white noise is normally distributed (i.e., all finite distributions are jointly normal), the two definitions coincide. In that chapter we also stated that the principle of absence of arbitrage implies that price processes are martingales after appropriate discounting. Our task now is to place these different concepts in an econometric perspective.

The concept of martingale implies that an *information structure*, or a *filtration* in continuous time, is defined. We will not formally define the concept information structure and conditional expectation here.[3] Suffice to recall that a *martingale* is a process such that its conditional expectation at the next step is equal to the present value of the process. We can write this condition as follows:

---

[1] See Chapter 9, Sergio M. Focardi and Frank J. Fabozzi, *The Mathematics of Financial Modeling and Investment Management* (Hoboken, NJ: John Wiley, 2004).

[2] A more general infinite moving-average representation would involve a summation that extends from $-\infty$ to $+\infty$. However, series of this type imply anticipation of information and are therefore not suitable for economic analysis.

[3] See Focardi and Fabozzi, *The Mathematics of Financial Modeling and Investment Management* for a discussion of the concepts of information structure and filtration.

$$E(x_{t+1}|I_t) = x_t$$

where I_t is the information set known at time t.

As mentioned, the information set is embodied in an information structure or a filtration. If only the past values of the process need to be considered and if the process starts at $t = 1$, then the martingale condition can be written as

$$E(x_{t+1}|x_t, ..., x_1) = x_t$$

an expression which has a rather intuitive meaning.[4]

Suppose that a time series x_t is a martingale. Consider the *martingale difference sequence* y_t defined as follows:

$$y_1 = x_1, y_2 = x_2 - x_1, ..., y_n = x_n - x_{n-1}, ...$$

Given the martingale property, it is possible to demonstrate that a martingale difference sequence is a zero-mean, uncorrelated process with the additional property that

$$E(y_{t+1}|y_t, y_{t-1}, ..., y_1) = 0$$

These properties can be used to *define* a martingale difference sequence, that is, a martingale difference sequence is a zero mean, uncorrelated process such that its conditional mean at every step is zero.

From this definition, we see that the definition of martingale difference sequence is more restrictive than the definition of white noise insofar as not only is zero its unconditional expectation, as in the white noise case, but its conditional expectation is zero at every step. In fact, we can establish the following implication chain.[5]

- ■ Any strict white noise process is a martingale difference sequence.
- ■ Any martingale difference sequence is a white noise.

The converse, however, is not true. In fact, there exist both the following:

---

[4] Though intuitive, these definitions can lead to logical errors. In fact, as the variables x typically assume a continuum of values, the probability of each individual value is zero and, therefore, the usual definitions of conditional probability cannot be used.
[5] Phoebus J. Dhrymes, *Topics in Advanced Econometrics* (New York: Springer Verlag, 1989).

- White noise processes that are not martingale difference sequences.
- Martingale difference sequences that are not IID sequences.

Both of the above are quite important. The first implies that there are white noise processes that have, for some time step, a conditional mean different from zero though the unconditional mean is always zero. The second implies that martingale difference sequences, though uncorrelated, are not independent and can therefore exhibit correlation in higher moments.

For normal processes, as already established, the three concepts coincide: white noise, strict white noise, and martingale difference sequences imply each other.

The above considerations are important if we are to distinguish between noise and innovation processes. In general, a stochastic model is formed by a predictable process and an unpredictable innovation process. In terms of means, given a univariate process x_t we can write

$$x_t = E(x_t|I_{t-1}) + v_t$$

where I_{t-1} is the history of the process up to time $t - 1$[6] and v_t is called a *mean innovation process*. If the distribution of v_t is independent of I_{t-1} then v_t is called an *innovation process*. The objective in modeling is to extract maximum information from noise (i.e., to separate the predictable process from the unpredictable innovation).

However, if we write our models with error terms that are only white noise, we do not necessarily separate the forecastable process from the unforecastable innovation. In fact, white noise terms, though they are not linearly forecastable, have residual forecastability as their conditional mean is not necessarily zero.[7]

From the above considerations one can infer that each strong random walk is a martingale. It is not true that any weak random walk is also a martingale. The converse is however true: Every martingale is a weak random walk. Therefore, perhaps surprisingly, we can conclude that the martingale condition is more restrictive than the weak random-walk condition.

Later in this chapter, we introduce the concept of integrated processes, which is more general than the weak random walk.

---

[6] These considerations can be extended immediately to multivariate processes.

[7] For a detailed treatment, see D. F. Hendry, *Dynamic Econometrics* (Oxford: Oxford University Press, 1996).

THE LAG OPERATOR *L*

Now we define the lag operator. The lag operator L is a linear operator that acts on doubly infinite time series by shifting positions by one place:

$$Lx_t = x_{t-1}$$

The difference operator $\Delta x_t = x_t - x_{t-1}$ can be written in terms of the lag operator as

$$\Delta x_t = (1 - L)x_t$$

Products and thus powers of the lag operator are defined as follows:

$$(L \times L)x_t = L^2 x_t = L(Lx_t) = x_{t-2}$$

From the previous definition, we can see that the *i*-th power of the lag operator shifts the series by *i* places:

$$L^i x_t = x_{t-i}$$

The lag operator is linear, that is, given scalars a and b we have

$$(aL^i + bL^j)x_t = ax_{t-i} + bx_{t-j}$$

Hence we can define the polynomial operator:

$$A(L) = (1 - a_1 L - \cdots - a_p L^p) \equiv \left(1 - \sum_{i=1}^{p} a_i L^i \right)$$

UNIVARIATE AUTOREGRESSIVE MOVING AVERAGE (ARMA) MODELS

The infinite moving average representation of a time series is useful from a theoretical point of view. However, in practice it is more convenient to work with a parsimonious time series model that is able to represent both stationary and nonstationary series with a finite number of parameters.

The ARMA family of models provides one such representation. An ARMA(p,q) model has the following general representation:

$$x_t - a_1 x_{t-1} - \cdots - a_p x_{t-p} = \varepsilon_t - b_1 \varepsilon_{t-1} - \cdots - b_q \varepsilon_{t-q}$$

where the a and b are constant coefficients.

Let us discuss the properties of ARMA models, starting with an autoregressive model of order p. An autoregressive process of order p – AR(p), is a process that follows a stochastic linear difference equation of the following form:

$$x_t - a_1 x_{t-1} - \cdots - a_p x_{t-p} = \varepsilon_t$$

Using the lag operator L notation, the ARMA(p,q) process can also be written as

$$A(L)x_t = (1 - a_1 L - \cdots - a_p L^p)x_t = B(L)\varepsilon_t = \varepsilon_t - b_1 \varepsilon_{t-1} - \cdots - b_q \varepsilon_{t-q}$$

and an AR(p) process as

$$A(L)x_t = (1 - a_1 L - \cdots - a_p L^p)x_t = \varepsilon_t$$

A literal interpretation of the above formula shows that the AR(p) process is defined by the property that, taking a linear combination of $p + 1$ terms of the series shifted in time, we can reconstruct a white noise process. However we can read the above formula in a more intuitive form as follows:

$$x_t = a_1 x_{t-1} + \cdots + a_p x_{t-p} + \varepsilon_t$$

This representation makes clear the autoregressive nature of the AR(p) process. It shows that the current value of the process is a linear combination of the past p terms of the series plus a white noise term, that is, the current value is obtained as a linear regression over past terms.

STATIONARITY CONDITIONS

An AR(p) process can be stationary or nonstationary. Let us investigate the conditions of stationarity. Consider the polynomial

$$A(z) = 1 - a_1 z - \cdots - a_p z^p$$

where z is a complex variable. The algebraic equation

$$A(z) = 1 - a_1 z - \cdots - a_p z^p = 0$$

is called the inverse characteristic equation. Suppose that φ_i, $i = 1, 2, \ldots,$ p are the p roots of the inverse characteristic equation. These roots are in general complex numbers not necessarily distinct. Given the polynomial $A(L) = 1 - a_1 L - \cdots - a_p L^p$ in the lag operator, the equation

$$B(z) = z^p - a_1 z^{p-1} - \ldots - a_{p-1} z - a_p = 0$$

is called the *characteristic equation.*

It can be verified by substitution that the roots λ_i, $i = 1, 2, \ldots, p$ of the characteristic equation are the reciprocal of the roots φ_i of the inverse characteristic equation. Recall that if a root λ_i of an algebraic equation is a complex number $\lambda_j = \alpha_j + i\beta_j$, where i is the imaginary unit, its complex conjugate

$$\overline{\lambda}_j = \alpha_j - i\beta_j$$

is also a root of the same equation. Note that we can expand the polynomial $A(z)$ as a product:

$$A(z) = 1 - a_1 z - \cdots - a_p z^p = (1 - \lambda_1 z) \times \ldots \times (1 - \lambda_p z) \equiv \prod_{i=1}^{p} (1 - \lambda_i z)$$

where the λ_i, $i = 1, 2, \ldots, p$ are the roots of the characteristic equation, that is, the reciprocals of the p roots φ_i, $i = 1, 2, \ldots, p$ of the inverse characteristic equation:

$$\lambda_i = \frac{1}{\varphi_i}, \quad i = 1, 2, \ldots, p$$

Using the linearity properties of the lag operator, we can write:

$$A(L) = (1 - a_1 L - \cdots - a_p L^p) = (1 - \lambda_1 L) \times \cdots \times (1 - \lambda_p L) = \prod_{i=1}^{p} (1 - \lambda_i L)$$

For example, if $A(L) = 1 - aL$, then the inverse characteristic equation is $A(z) = 1 - az = 0$ whose root is

$$\varphi = \frac{1}{a}$$

It can be demonstrated that if the roots φ_i, $i = 1, 2, ..., p$ of the inverse characteristic equation of the AR(p) process all have modulus greater than 1, then the process is stationary. Therefore, we can write the stationarity condition for an AR(p) process as

$$|\varphi_i| > 1 , i = 1, 2, ..., p$$

The AR(p) process is then called *invertible* because it can be formally inverted to yield an infinite moving average representation:

$$A(L)x_t = \varepsilon_t$$

$$x_t = \frac{1}{A(L)} \varepsilon_t = \left(\sum_{i=0}^{\infty} h_i L^i \right) \varepsilon_t = \sum_{i=0}^{\infty} h_i \varepsilon_{t-i}$$

The simplest example is the inversion of $A(L) = 1 - aL$ which, if

$$|\varphi| = \left| \frac{1}{a} \right| > 1$$

yields

$$\frac{1}{1 - aL} = \sum_{i=0}^{\infty} (aL)^i$$

Note that in the literature the above properties are often stated in terms of the characteristic equation. The stationarity condition prescribes that the roots λ_i, $i = 1, 2, ..., p$ of the characteristic equation of the AR(p) process all have modulus smaller than 1:

$$|\lambda_i| < 1, \quad i = 1, 2, ..., p$$

AUTO CORRELATIONS AT DIFFERENT LAGS

Suppose that the $AR(p)$ process

$$A(L)x_t = (1 - a_1 L - \cdots - a_p L^p)x_t = \varepsilon_t$$

satisfies the stationarity conditions. As the process is stationary, it is meaningful to compute the correlation coefficients between the variables x at different lags.

Consider the *Autocorrelation Function* (ACF) $\rho(\tau)$ that represents the correlation coefficient between variables x_t, $x_{t+\tau}$ which is independent from t. It can be demonstrated that the ACF $\rho(\tau)$ satisfies the following *Yule-Walker equations*:

$$\rho(\tau) = \sum_{i=1}^{p} a_i \rho(\tau - i)$$

These equations allow computation of $\rho(\tau)$ *recursively*. For example, consider an $AR(1)$ process:

$$x_t = a_1 x_{t-1} + \varepsilon_t$$

Its autocorrelation function satisfies the equation:

$$\rho(\tau) = a_1 \rho(\tau - 1)$$

$$\rho(0) = 1, \, \rho(1) = a_1, \cdots, \rho(\tau) = a_1^{\tau}$$

Note that the Yule-Walker equations show that the autocorrelations satisfy the same difference equation of the process itself. Therefore, for stationary autoregressive processes $AR(p)$, the autocorrelation function behaves as a mixture of damped exponentials and/or sine waves. Note also that the first p Yule-Walker equations can be solved in terms of the autocorrelations to yield the coefficients of the $AR(p)$ process.

In the analysis of the AR processes, it is also important to define the *Partial Autocorrelation Function* (PACF). When performing a regression of one dependent variable on n independent variables, we can evaluate the *partial correlations* between the dependent variable and each of the dependent variables. An autoregressive model is a regression of the variable x_t on its own lagged values. The PACF is defined as the partial correlation between x_t, x_{t-k}, $k \leq p$ after removing the effects of intermediate terms. The PACF is zero for $k > p$ and is obtained by solving the following system of linear equations for $k \leq p$:

$$\rho_\tau = \sum_{j=1}^{s} a_{sj}\rho_{\tau-j}, \tau = 1, 2, ..., s$$

The PACF is the a_{ss}.

SOLUTIONS OF AN AR(p) PROCESS

We can now write down the solutions of an AR(p) process, the simplest of the univariate linear autoregressive processes. In financial econometrics AR(p) processes can be thought of as a first approximation of many processes including, for example, high-frequency return data.[8]

As discussed above, an AR(p) process is stationary if the roots of its characteristic equation have modulus less than one. Under this hypothesis, the process is formally invertible as follows:

$$A(L)x_t = \varepsilon_t$$

$$x_t = \frac{1}{A(L)}\varepsilon_t = \left(\sum_{i=0}^{\infty} h_i L^i\right)\varepsilon_t = \sum_{i=0}^{\infty} h_i \varepsilon_{t-i}$$

Consider now that the solution of an AR(p) process is a time series, that is, a discrete time stochastic process such that each realization satisfies the difference equation: $A(L)x_t = \varepsilon_t$.[9] As we know from the theory of difference equations, the solution of this equation, when taken together with initial conditions, is the sum of the solution of the associated homogeneous equation $A(L)x_t$ and a particular solution. The behavior of solutions depends on how the system reacts to innovations ε_t.

[8] Dietmar Bauer, "Subspace Algorithms," in *Proceedings of the 13th IFAC SYSID Symposium* (Rotterdam: August 2003).
[9] Note that this property does not hold in the continuous-time limit as the definition of white noise cannot be extended to the continuous-time limit. For example, a path of a Brownian motion is not a solution of the corresponding differential equation. The pathwise definition of stochastic differential equation requires a fairly complex mathematical construction. See Focardi and Fabozzi, *The Mathematics of Financial Modeling and Investment Management* and references therein.

Stationary AR(p) Processes

If the AR(p) process is *stationary*, then its solution can be thought of as the pathwise solution of the difference equation $A(L)x_t = \varepsilon_t$ without initial conditions. Its solutions are

$$x_t = \sum_{i=0}^{\infty} ((\lambda_1 L)^i + i(\lambda_1 L)^i + \cdots + i^{n_1 - 1}(\lambda_1 L)^i + \cdots$$

$$+ (\lambda_m L)^i + i(\lambda_m L)^i + \cdots + i^{n_m - 1}(\lambda_m L)^i)\varepsilon_t$$

if the solutions of the characteristic equation are real, and

$$x_t = \sum_{i=1}^{\infty} (r^i(\cos(\omega i) + \sin(\omega i))\varepsilon_{t-i})$$

for each complex root. The above expressions are meaningful only if the roots or their modulus, if complex, is less than one.

AR(p) Processes that Start at Initial Conditions

The above discussion of difference equations provides the basic mathematical formalism of AR(p) processes and helps intuition in finding a solution. If the AR(p) process starts at given initial conditions, it is not stationary, though it can be asymptotically stationary. Its solution is the sum of the deterministic solution of the associated homogeneous difference equation plus a stochastic part, as in the previous case. The stochastic part is not influenced by initial conditions. The process is asymptotically stationary if the solutions of the characteristic equation are less than one in modulus.[10] Solutions can be written down explicitly as

$$x_t = C_1^1(\lambda)^t + C_2^1 t(\lambda)^t + \cdots + C_{n_1}^1 t^{n_1 - 1}(\lambda)^t + \cdots$$

$$+ C_1^m(\lambda)^t + C_2^m t(\lambda)^t + \cdots + C_{n_m}^m t^{n_m - 1}(\lambda)^t$$

$$+ \sum ((\lambda_1 L)^i + i(\lambda_1 L)^i + \cdots + i^{n_1 - 1}(\lambda_1 L)^i + \cdots$$

$$+ (\lambda_m L)^i + i(\lambda_m L)^i + \cdots + i^{n_m - 1}(\lambda_m L)^i)\varepsilon_t$$

in the case of real roots.

---

[10] See Focardi and Fabozzi, *The Mathematics of Financial Modeling and Investment Management* and references therein.

AR(p) processes admit solutions that are the sum of a deterministic part plus a weighted average of past noise terms.[11] The deterministic part is a sum of exponentials or a sum of sinusoidal functions with eventual exponential weights.

Exhibit 11.1 illustrates a realization of an AR(2) model based on the same difference equation as in Exhibit A.3 in Appendix A with the same initial conditions $x_1 = 1$, $x_2 = 1.5$ but with an exogenous Gaussian white noise:

$$(1 - 1.7L + 0.72L^2)x_t = u_t$$

The solution of the equation is the sum of the deterministic solution,

$$x_{d,t} = -7.5(0.8)^t + 7.7778(0.9)^t$$

EXHIBIT 11.1 A Realization of the AR(2) Model $(1 - 1.7L + 0.72L^2)x_t = u_t$ with Initial Conditions

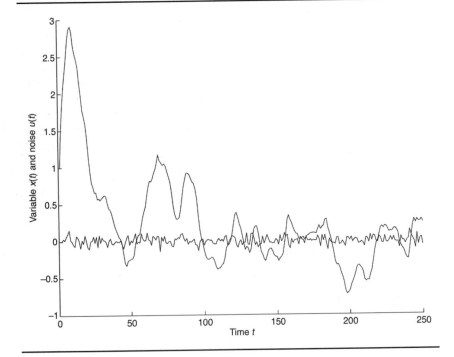

---

[11] This property is shared in general by all linear difference or differential stochastic equation systems.

plus a stochastic term,

$$x_{s,t} = \sum_{i=0}^{t-1} [((0.8)^i + (0.9)^i)u(t-i)]$$

Note that the noise term, shown in the Exhibit S.1, is greatly amplified by the model. The simulation runs for 250 steps.

Exhibit 11.2 illustrates a sample path of an AR(2) model based on the same difference equation as in Exhibit A.5 in Appendix A with the same initial conditions $x_1 = 1$, $x_2 = 1.5$ and with an exogenous Gaussian white noise:

$$(1 - 1.0L + 0.89L^2)x_t = u_t$$

The characteristic equation has two complex conjugate roots $0.5+i0.8$ and $0.5-i0.8$ and with modulus 0.9434. Each realization is the sum of the deterministic term,

EXHIBIT 11.2   Solutions of the Equation $(1 - 1.0L + 0.89L^2)x_t = u_t$ with Initial Conditions $x_1 = 1$, $x_2 = 1.5$

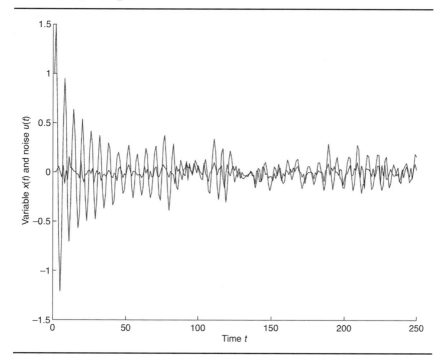

$$x_{d,t} = 0.9434^t(-0.5618\cos(1.0122t) + 1.6011\sin(1.0122t))$$

plus the stochastic term,

$$x_{s,t} = \sum_{i=0}^{t-1} [0.9434^i(\cos(1.0122i) + \sin(1.0122i))u(t-i)]$$

MA(*q*) MOVING AVERAGE MODELS

A *Moving Average model* of order q, MA(q), is a model written as follows:

$$x_t = C(L)\varepsilon_t = (1 + c_1 L + \cdots + c_q L^q)\varepsilon_t$$

$$x_t = \varepsilon_t + c_q \varepsilon_{t-1} + \cdots + c_q \varepsilon_{t-q}$$

In a MA(q) model, the present value x_t of the process is a moving average of the present and past q white-noise term. The MA(q) model can be considered an approximation truncated to the first q terms of the linear model:

$$x_t = \sum_{i=0}^{\infty} h_i \varepsilon_{t-i}$$

As ARMA are linear models, additive constants can be removed without changing their basic properties. Without loss of generality, we can assume that additive constants are zero.

MA processes that extend from $-\infty$ to $+\infty$ can be *inverted* in a way similar to AR processes. Consider a MA(q) model and suppose that the roots of the equation,

$$C(z) = 1 + c_1 z + \cdots + c_q z^q = 0$$

all lay outside the unit circle. The process can then be inverted to yield the following infinite autoregressive model:

$$C^{-1}(L)x_t = \left(\sum_{i=0}^{\infty} \phi_i L^i\right) = \varepsilon_t$$

ARMA(p,q) MODELS

We can combine AR and MA models to yield the *ARMA(p,q) models* written as follows:

$$\Phi(L)x_t = \Psi(L)\varepsilon_t$$

$$\Phi(L) = \sum_{i=0}^{p} \varphi_i L^i$$

$$\Psi(L) = \sum_{j=0}^{q} \psi_j L^j$$

Let us assume that the polynomials in the lag operator have constant coefficients. (We will discuss how this assumption can be relaxed in Chapters 12 and 16.) We can state the conditions of stationarity and invertibility for ARMA(p,q) models. Consider the equations

$$\Phi(z) = 0$$

$$\Psi(z) = 0$$

The following two properties can be stated:

- If the roots of the equation $\Phi(z) = 0$ lay outside the unit circle, then the process is stationary and invertible and can be written as an infinite moving average process:

$$x_t = \Phi^{-1}(L)\Psi(L)\varepsilon_t$$

- If the roots of the equation $\Psi(z) = 0$ lay outside the unit circle then the process is stationary and invertible and can be written as an infinite autoregressive process:

$$\Psi^{-1}(L)\Phi(L)x_t = \varepsilon_t$$

Explicit solutions of this process can be computed along the lines outlined in the AR and MA sections. However, explicit solutions are represented by complex expressions which do not add much to the intuition of these processes.

INTEGRATED PROCESSES

We can now introduce the key concept of integrated processes. Let us start with an intuitive definition. An integrated process is a process such that any shock to the system is permanent and never decays. In other words, the level of an integrated process is the sum of all past shocks. The most typical integrated process is the random walk. However not all integrated processes are random walks, as the process innovations need not be uncorrelated.

To give a more precise, formal definition of an integrated process, we first introduce the concept of *differencing*. The *difference operator* Δ $= (1 - L)$ is an operator that acts on an infinite series x_t, $-\infty < t < \infty$ to produce another series formed by the first differences:

$$\Delta x_t = x_t - x_{t-1}, -\infty < t < \infty$$

The difference operator can be applied to a series that starts at t_0 with the obvious convention that the differenced series starts at $t_0 + 1$.

The difference operator can be repeatedly applied, that is, it is possible to define powers of the difference operator. We can give the following recursive definition:

$$\Delta x_t = x_t - x_{t-1}$$
$$\Delta^2 x_t = \Delta(\Delta x_t) = (x_t - x_{t-1}) - (x_{t-1} - x_{t-2}) = x_t - 2x_{t-1} + x_{t-2}$$
$$\Delta^3 x_t = \Delta(\Delta^2 x_t) = (x_t - 2x_{t-1} + x_{t-2}) - (x_{t-1} - 2x_{t-2} + x_{t-3})$$
$$= x_t - 3x_{t-1} + 3x_{t-2} - x_{t-3}$$

$$\Delta^n x_t = \Delta(\Delta^{n-1} x_t)$$

We are now ready to define integrated processes. An integrated process is a ARMA process $\Phi(L)x_t = \Psi(L)\varepsilon_t$, which can be factorized as follows:

$$\Phi'(L)\Delta^d x_t = \Psi(L)\varepsilon_t$$

$$\Phi(L) = \Phi'(L)\Delta^d$$

where the roots of the polynomials $\Phi'(z)$, $\Psi(z)$ are all outside the unit circle. In other words, an integrated process of order d is a process that becomes stationary after differencing d times.

Now that we have acquired some fundamental intuition for univariate processes, in the next chapter we move on to the theory of *multivariate* ARMA processes, the latter being critical to equity portfolio management. In fact, price processes can be individually integrated processes while portfolios formed with the same processes exhibit stationary behavior.

SUMMARY

- Stationary processes can be represented as infinite moving averages of white-noise sequences.
- ARMA models are a finite, parsimonious representation of time series that include an autoregressive process and a moving-average process.
- A white noise is a sequence of zero-mean, uncorrelated variables, while a strict white noise is a sequence of zero-mean, identical, and independently distributed variables. If the white noise is Gaussian, the two definitions coincide.
- A martingale difference sequence is a zero-mean, uncorrelated sequence whose conditional mean is zero at every time step.
- An innovation process is the unpredictable residual of a process.
- A white-noise process is not necessarily an innovation process as the conditional mean of white noise is not necessarily zero and white noise retains residual forecastability.
- An autoregressive model is stable if the roots of the inverse characteristic equation have modulus larger than one.
- The solution of an autoregressive model is the solution of the corresponding difference equation.
- Solutions are sums of exponentials and sinusoidal functions weighted with exponentials.

CHAPTER 12

Multivariate Models

Having discussed univariate linear models in the previous chapter, we now discuss *multivariate* linear models and introduce the concepts of cointegration and dynamic factor analysis. Recall that in Chapter 10, we discussed the intuition for these models in financial econometrics, namely that these models capture the many feedbacks present in financial markets. By capturing feedbacks, dynamic multivariate models capture the (limited) forecastability in a fundamentally noisy and unpredictable environment (i.e., the markets). In the language of asset managers, while classical factor models focus on the betas (i.e., the stable relationships between risk and returns), dynamic models aim at capturing the elusive alphas on which profitable strategies can be built.

We will start our discussion by presenting a number of multivariate models that are widely used in macroeconomics and financial econometrics, namely *Vector Autoregressive* (VAR) models, *Vector Autoregressive Moving Average* (VARMA) models, *Error Correction Models* (ECM), and *State-Space* models.[1] We review their statistical properties and exhibit explicit solutions. In order to facilitate the intuition of these models, we will compute solutions of VAR models and simulate their realizations. The application of these processes to asset management and asset-liability management as well as their estimation will be discussed in Chapters 15 and 16.

---

[1] The dynamic multivariate models described in this chapter are implemented in major software packages such as E-Views, Mathematica, MatLab, PC-Give, and SPSS. The analyst need not program the models, only apply them. This, coupled with the computing power now available, has ushered in a new phase in financial econometrics: it is now possible to search for global properties of large portfolios of assets. Actually, this is also a problem: with today's computing power, it is easy to find patterns in virtually any large set of data. The key task is to find *stable* patterns that reveal *real* properties of asset prices, but these patterns are typically hidden in a large amount of noise. Thus the importance of searching for simple patterns and properties that are statistically significant over large aggregates.

DYNAMIC MODELS: A HISTORICAL PERSPECTIVE

Equity portfolio management depends, ultimately, on the ability to make forecasts, albeit probabilistic forecasts. While on the surface the Efficient Market Hypothesis seems to negate the possibility of making forecasts, what it effectively does is *restrict* the ability to forecast expected returns and volatility. It does this by imposing risk-return trade-off constraints on the amount of information that can be acquired through forecasting. Dynamic models that link future returns to present and past returns and to exogenous variables are key components of the financial modeler's toolbox. Let us first place dynamic models in their historical perspective.

Computer software to estimate dynamic models has been available for nearly three decades. In the 1970s, Box and Jenkins formalized a methodology for analyzing time series with linear autoregressive models. The Box and Jenkins methodology became very popular and was soon incorporated in many software packages, making it available to even relatively unsophisticated users.[2] However, the Box and Jenkins methodology estimates univariate (not multivariate) dynamic models. Because individual equity price processes are so close to random walks, they cannot be forecasted with univariate linear autoregressive models. The diffusion of dynamic models in equity modeling had to wait for the availability of models and software able to tackle multivariate time series.

On another front, the 1980s saw the development of the theory of nonlinear dynamics. The theory of nonlinear dynamics entailed two opposite conclusions. On the one hand, it demonstrated that nonlinear processes can be so sensitive to initial conditions as to be practically unpredictable; only statistical analysis can be performed.[3] On the other hand, the theory also demonstrated that, under specific conditions, the dynamics of a nonlinear process can be completely reconstructed from a finite number of samples. This is the essence of *Takens' theorem*.

Consequent to Takens' theorem, attempts were made to capture the deterministic dynamics of financial markets. A wide range of methodologies were developed. Takens' theorem itself is a constructive methodology which has been implemented in a number of forecasting applications.

---

[2] Box and Jenkins did not invent the methodology that bears their name. Their contribution was to assemble in a coherent methodological framework a number of results that were already known. They also had the intuition to propose the methodology where it might be applied in practice, namely sociology.

[3] Models of the weather are a typical example of nonlinear models very sensitive to initial conditions. The MIT meteorologist Lorenz is credited with being the first to discover this property. Lorenz observed that numerical solutions of a particular differential equation produced diverging results for changes in initial parameters due to rounding-off errors.

However, the nonlinear models that enjoyed the broadest diffusion were neural networks. Among the startups created to tackle the problem of forecasting financial quantities with nonlinear methods were The Prediction Company (Santa Fe, New Mexico) founded by the physicists Norman Packard and Doyne Farmer and Olsen & Associates (Zurich) founded by Richard Olsen.[4]

The 1990s saw the beginning of the wide diffusion of computerized linear multivariate models in equity management. Large multivariate linear econometric models had been used in macroeconomic studies since the 1960s, but these models were used primarily by government agencies and central banks. It was only in the second half of the 1990s that low-cost high-performance computing made dynamic models a realistic choice for asset management firms. Commercial products such as those developed by Barra and APT made multifactor models available to most users. Methods based on cointegration, such as pair trading, were used at some of the major Wall Street firms.[5] During the sharp market correction in the year 2000, many models performed quite poorly, as markets experienced a major structural break. In the quest for returns, asset management firms began to explore new classes of dynamic models and the use of a whole battery of models as opposed to one single model.[6]

A popular modeling choice is to use factors or signals to predict expected returns. Models of this type are dynamic insofar as the present and past values of factors are used as signals to predict returns one or more periods ahead. Note that factor models of this type are different from multifactor models such as the APT models. The latter establish relationships between factors and returns simultaneously and do not imply any specific dynamic.

Vector Autoregressive (VAR) models, which are the central subject of this chapter, are a broad family of linear dynamic models used to make joint forecasts of indexes and specially selected portfolios and to forecast

---

[4] The Prediction Company was later bought by Swiss Bank Corporation which was subsequently bought by UBS. Both Farmer and Packard have left the company, Farmer to become a professor at the Santa Fe Institute, Packard to start a new company to study artificial life.

[5] Pair trading is a trading strategy that looks for pairs of processes that are mean-reverting (i.e., cointegrated) around a common trend. Long-short positions are taken when prices are far apart and liquidated when they close up.

[6] A 2001 Intertek Research Note and the successive 2003 update outline the evolution of models in equity management after the downturn in the market in 2000. Market participants credit models with bringing a better discipline to the investment management process and enabling active risk control. Among the trends are the use of a set of factors, such as market sentiment, for integrating qualitative and quantitative views.

factor signals. Autoregressive models are also used to represent phenomena such as momentum and reversals. The nonlinear Markov-switching models, which belong to the VAR family of models, are used to model processes subject to structural breaks and regime changes. The following sections will describe the different autoregressive models and their applicability.

VECTOR AUTOREGRESSIVE MODELS

Vector autoregressive (VAR) models are, as suggested by their name, models where each variable is linearly regressed over its own lagged values as well as over the lagged values of the other variables. This means that the future values of the process will be a weighted sum of past and present values plus some noise plus eventual exogenous terms. For example, it is known that there are equity price "leaders" and equity price "laggards" in the sense that the returns of some portfolios of large-cap stocks anticipate the returns of large portfolios of small-cap stocks.[7] An analyst who wants to exploit this relationship for a specific pair of leader-laggard portfolios can create a simple linear regression model, that is, a proportionality constant, between the returns of the leader and laggard portfolios.

Suppose, for example, that portfolio A is a leader portfolio and portfolio B a laggard portfolio. The analyst can write the following model for returns:

$$R_A(t+1) = R_A(t) + \varepsilon_A(t+1)$$
$$R_B(t+1) = aR_A(t) + \varepsilon_B(t+1)$$

where $R_A(t)$, $R_B(t)$ are the returns of the two portfolios respectively. The first equation states that the price leader portfolio follows a random walk; the second equation states that the laggard portfolio follows a random walk but tends to follow the leader with a delay.

The above is a simple example of a multivariate extension of the VAR model. A Vector Autoregressive model of order p [VAR(p)] has the following general form:

$$\mathbf{x}_t = \mathbf{A}_1\mathbf{x}_{t-1} + \mathbf{A}_2\mathbf{x}_{t-2} + \cdots + \mathbf{A}_p\mathbf{x}_{t-p} + \mathbf{s}_t + \varepsilon_t$$

---

[7] See John Y. Campbell, Andrew W. Lo, and A. Craig MacKinlay, *The Econometrics of Financial Markets* (Princeton: Princeton University Press, 1997) and Angelos Kanas and George P. Kouretas, "A Cointegration Approach to the Lead-Lag Effect Among Sized-Sorted Equity Portfolios," Working Paper, Department of Economics, University of Crete, 2001.

where $\mathbf{x}_t = (x_{1,t}, ..., x_{n,t})'$ is a multivariate stochastic time series in vector notation, $\mathbf{A}_i$; $i = 1, 2, ..., p$ are deterministic $n \times n$ matrices; $\boldsymbol{\varepsilon}_t = (\varepsilon_{1,t}, ..., \varepsilon_{n,t})'$ is a multivariate white noise with variance-covariance matrix $\boldsymbol{\Omega} = (\omega_1, ..., \omega_n)$; and $\mathbf{s}_t = (s_{1,t}, ..., s_{n,t})'$ is a vector of deterministic terms.

Using the lag-operator L notation, a VAR(p) model can be written in the following form:

$$\mathbf{x}_t = (\mathbf{A}_1 L + \mathbf{A}_2 L^2 + ... + \mathbf{A}_p L^p)\mathbf{x}_t + \mathbf{s}_t + \boldsymbol{\varepsilon}_t$$

In most applications, the deterministic term will be a constant intercept term $\mathbf{s}_t = \mathbf{v}$ or a linear function. A deterministic term formed by a constant can produce a linear trend while a deterministic term formed by a linear trend can produce a quadratic or a linear trend. Polynomial trends can also appear in the case of multiple eigenvalues.

Let us first examine the stability and stationarity conditions of VAR models.

Stability, Stationarity, and Invertibility

Recall that a stochastic process is called *weakly stationary* or covariance-stationary if all expectations and variances-covariances are time-invariant. A process is called *strictly stationary* if all finite-dimensional distributions are time-invariant. However, in practical financial econometric applications, processes start at a given time. A process that starts at a specified moment cannot be stationary. This occurs not only because the process has a discontinuity at the origin but also because, in general, the process will exhibit initial conditions with a distribution different from that of the corresponding stationary process.

A process that starts at a time origin can, however, be asymptotically stationary. A process is called *asymptotically stationary* if its first and second moments (i.e., expectations and variances-covariances) converge to the expectations and variances-covariances of the corresponding stationary process.

Stationarity imposes a lot of structure on a stochastic process. The Swedish mathematician Herman Ole Andreas Wold was able to prove in 1938[8] a fundamental theorem known as the *Wold decomposition theorem*. The Wold decomposition theorem for multivariate time series is the following proposition:

---

[8] Herman Ole Andreas Wold, *A Study in the Analysis of Stationary Time Series* (Stockholm: Almqvist and Wiksell, 1938).

Any zero-mean, covariance stationary process $\mathbf{y}_t = (y_{1,t}, ..., y_{n,t})'$ can be represented in a unique way as the sum of a stochastic process and a linearly predictable deterministic process, that is,

$$\mathbf{y}_t = \boldsymbol{\mu}_t + \boldsymbol{\Psi}(L)\boldsymbol{\varepsilon}_t$$

where the stochastic part is represented as an infinite moving average,

$$\boldsymbol{\Psi}(L) = \sum_{i=0}^{\infty} \boldsymbol{\Psi}_i \boldsymbol{\varepsilon}_{t-i} \quad \boldsymbol{\Psi}_0 = \mathbf{I}_n$$

subject to the condition

$$\sum_{i=0}^{\infty} \boldsymbol{\Psi}_i \boldsymbol{\Psi}_i' < \infty$$

to ensure that the series is summable. The $\boldsymbol{\varepsilon}_t$ are the one step ahead linear forecast errors and the deterministic part is a linear deterministic process.

Note that the $\boldsymbol{\varepsilon}_t$'s are linear forecast errors for $\mathbf{y}_t$ but this does not necessarily imply $E(\boldsymbol{\varepsilon}_t | \mathbf{y}_{t-1}, ...) = 0$. In fact the conditional expectation is the best guess of $\mathbf{y}_t$ using linear and nonlinear combinations of lagged $\mathbf{y}_t$. Note also that the Wold representation is the unique representation of a covariance stationary time series in terms of linear predictors; however, other representations based on non-forecast errors are perfectly possible.

Consider a VAR(p) model:

$$\mathbf{x}_t = (\mathbf{A}_1 L + \mathbf{A}_2 L^2 + ... + \mathbf{A}_p L^p)\mathbf{x}_t + \mathbf{v} + \boldsymbol{\varepsilon}_t, t = \pm 0, \pm 1, \pm 2, ...$$

where the deterministic term is a constant and time extends from $-\infty$ to $+\infty$. Consider the matrix polynomial

$$\mathbf{A}(z) = \mathbf{I} - \mathbf{A}_1 z - \mathbf{A}_2 z^2 - \cdots - \mathbf{A}_p z^p, z \in \mathbb{C}$$

Consider now the equation

$$\det(\mathbf{A}(z)) = 0$$

This algebraic equation is called the *inverse characteristic equation* of the VAR model. It is the multivariate equivalent of the univariate inverse characteristic equation. Consider the matrix polynomial

$$\mathbf{B}(z) = \mathbf{I}z^p - \mathbf{A}_1 z^{p-1} - \mathbf{A}_2 z^{p-2} - \cdots - \mathbf{A}_p, z \in \mathbb{C}$$

The equation

$$\det(\mathbf{B}(z)) = 0$$

is called the *characteristic equation* of the VAR model. As in the univariate case, its solutions are the reciprocal of the solutions of the inverse characteristic equation.

Consider the characteristic equation of an n-variate VAR(p) model with s distinct solutions λ_i each with multiplicity m_i. The characteristic equation can then be written as follows:

$$(z - \lambda_1)^{m_1} \cdots (z - \lambda_s)^{m_s} = 0$$

Note that, though widely used, the above terminology is somewhat imprecise. In fact, we can state more precisely that the characteristic and inverse characteristic equations are associated with the *Vector Difference Equation* (VDE) that defines the VAR process.

If the roots of the inverse characteristic equation are strictly outside of the unit circle, then the VDE is said to be *stable*. We can now write the *stability conditions* as follows:

$$\det(\mathbf{A}(z)) \neq 0 \text{ for } |z| \leq 1$$

It can be demonstrated that, if a VDE satisfies the stability conditions, the relative VAR process is stationary if it extends on the entire time axis and it is asymptotically stationary if it starts from initial conditions. However, the converse is not true as there are stationary processes that are not stable. Though strictly speaking the stability condition applies to the VDE that defines a process, we generally make reference to a stable VAR process when there is no possibility of confusion between the process and its defining VDE.

To understand the meaning of the stability conditions, consider that, as detailed in the Appendix A and as we will see in the following section, the solutions of a VAR model are linear combinations of terms of the type λ^t, $\rho^t \cos(wt + \varphi)$ where λ, ρ are respectively the reciprocal of the solution or the modulus of the reciprocal of the solution of the inverse characteristic equation $\det(A(z)) = 0$. If the roots of the inverse characteristic equation are outside the unit circle, all past shocks will decay exponentially over time.

If a VAR process satisfies the stability conditions and is stationary, then the process is *invertible* in the sense that the process

$$(I - A_1 L - A_2 L^2 - ... - A_p L^p) x_t = v + \varepsilon_t$$

can be written in an *Infinite Moving Average* representation as follows:

$$x_t = (I - A_1 L - A_2 L^2 - ... - A_p L^p)^{-1} (v + \varepsilon_t)$$

$$= \left(\sum_{i=0}^{\infty} \Phi_i L^i \right) (v + \varepsilon_t)$$

$$\Phi_0 = I$$

where the Φ_i are $n \times n$ constant matrices.

It can be demonstrated that, if the process is stable, the matrix sequence Φ_i is *absolutely summable*. Therefore, the process

$$\left(\sum_{i=0}^{\infty} \Phi_i L^i \right) \varepsilon_t$$

is a well-defined process. We can rewrite the above process as

$$x_t = u + \left(\sum_{i=0}^{\infty} \Phi_i L^i \right) \varepsilon_t$$

where

$$u = \left(\sum_{i=0}^{\infty} \Phi_i \right) v$$

is the constant mean of the process

$$u = E[x_t]$$

If the process is not stable, then the mean is a function of time as we will see later in the section on the solutions of VAR processes. The above considerations show that, in the case of a VAR(p) process, the Wold decomposition coincides with the infinite moving average representation obtained by inverting the process and the shocks ε_t are the linear forecast errors.

Solutions of VAR(p) Models

Similar to what we did with univariate AR(p) models, we now write down the explicit solutions of multivariate VAR(p) models. Explicit solutions of VAR models provide the necessary intuition for the concepts of cointegration, error correction, and dynamic factors that are introduced later in this chapter.

As for any other linear model, solutions to a VAR model are the sum of a deterministic part plus a stochastic part. The deterministic part depends on the initial conditions and deterministic terms; the stochastic part depends on random shocks. The stochastic part of the solution is a weighted sum of past shocks. If the process is stable, then shocks in the distant past have only a negligible influence and the stochastic part is a weighted sum of the most recent shocks. If the process is integrated, then shocks never decay; the stochastic part is thus the cumulation of all past shocks. If the process is explosive, then shocks get amplified as time passes. We now develop solutions.

Equivalence of VAR(p) and VAR(1)

In order to compute explicit solutions of VAR(p) models, we make use of the key fact that any VAR(p) model is equivalent to some VAR(1) model after introducing appropriate additional variables. This is an important simplification as VAR(1) models can be characterized with simple intuitive formulas.

To illustrate this point, first write down a bivariate model of order one in matrix notation, that is,

$$\mathbf{x}_t = \mathbf{A}_1 \mathbf{x}_{t-1} + \mathbf{s}_t + \varepsilon_t$$

$$\begin{bmatrix} x_{1,t} \\ x_{2,t} \end{bmatrix} = \begin{bmatrix} a_{11} & a_{12} \\ a_{21} & a_{22} \end{bmatrix} \begin{bmatrix} x_{1,t-1} \\ x_{2,t-1} \end{bmatrix} + \begin{bmatrix} s_{1,t} \\ s_{2,t} \end{bmatrix} + \begin{bmatrix} \varepsilon_{1,t} \\ \varepsilon_{2,t} \end{bmatrix}$$

and explicitly

$$x_{1,t} = a_{11}x_{1,t-1} + a_{12}x_{2,t-1} + s_{1,t} + \varepsilon_{1,t}$$
$$x_{2,t} = a_{21}x_{1,t-1} + a_{22}x_{2,t-1} + s_{1,t} + \varepsilon_{2,t}$$

We observe that any VAR(1) model becomes an arithmetic multivariate random walk if $\mathbf{A}_1$ is an identity matrix and $s_t = (s_{1,t}, \ldots, s_{n,t})$ is a constant vector. In particular, in the bivariate case, a VAR(1) is a random walk if

$$\begin{bmatrix} a_{11} & a_{12} \\ a_{21} & a_{22} \end{bmatrix} = \begin{bmatrix} 1 & 0 \\ 0 & 1 \end{bmatrix}$$

and $\mathbf{s}_t = (s_1, s_2)$.

Consider now a bivariate VAR(2) model of order two:

$$\begin{bmatrix} x_{1,t} \\ x_{2,t} \end{bmatrix} = \begin{bmatrix} a_{11} & a_{12} \\ a_{21} & a_{22} \end{bmatrix} \begin{bmatrix} x_{1,t-1} \\ x_{2,t-1} \end{bmatrix} + \begin{bmatrix} b_{11} & b_{12} \\ b_{21} & b_{22} \end{bmatrix} \begin{bmatrix} x_{1,t-2} \\ x_{2,t-2} \end{bmatrix} + \begin{bmatrix} s_{1,t} \\ s_{2,t} \end{bmatrix} + \begin{bmatrix} \varepsilon_{1,t} \\ \varepsilon_{2,t} \end{bmatrix}$$

Let us introduce a new vector variable $\mathbf{z}_t = \mathbf{x}_{t-1}$. The VAR(2) model can then be rewritten as follows:

$$x_{1,t} = a_{11}x_{1,t-1} + a_{12}x_{2,t-1} + b_{11}z_{1,t-1} + b_{12}z_{2,t-1} + s_{1,t} + \varepsilon_{1,t}$$
$$x_{2,t} = a_{21}x_{1,t-1} + a_{22}x_{2,t-1} + b_{21}z_{1,t-1} + b_{22}z_{2,t-1} + s_{1,t} + \varepsilon_{2,t}$$
$$z_{1,t} = x_{1,t-1}$$
$$z_{2,t} = x_{2,t-1}$$

or in matrix form

$$\begin{bmatrix} x_{1,t} \\ x_{2,t} \\ z_{1,t} \\ z_{2,t} \end{bmatrix} = \begin{bmatrix} a_{11} & a_{12} & b_{11} & b_{12} \\ a_{21} & a_{22} & b_{21} & b_{22} \\ 1 & 0 & 0 & 0 \\ 0 & 1 & 0 & 0 \end{bmatrix} \begin{bmatrix} x_{1,t-1} \\ x_{2,t-1} \\ z_{1,t-1} \\ z_{2,t-1} \end{bmatrix} + \begin{bmatrix} 1 & 0 & 0 & 0 \\ 0 & 1 & 0 & 0 \\ 0 & 0 & 0 & 0 \\ 0 & 0 & 0 & 0 \end{bmatrix} \begin{bmatrix} s_{1,t} \\ s_{2,t} \\ 0 \\ 0 \end{bmatrix} + \begin{bmatrix} \varepsilon_{1,t} \\ \varepsilon_{2,t} \\ 0 \\ 0 \end{bmatrix}$$

The above considerations can be generalized. Any AR(p) or VAR(p) model can be transformed into a first-order VAR(1) model adding appropriate variables.[9] In particular an n-dimensional VAR(p) model of the form

---

[9] The theory of VAR models parallels the theory of systems of linear differential equations and of systems of linear stochastic differential equations.

$$\mathbf{x}_t = (\mathbf{A}_1 L + \mathbf{A}_2 L^2 + \dots + \mathbf{A}_p L^p)\mathbf{x}_t + \mathbf{s}_t + \varepsilon_t$$

is transformed into the following np-dimensional VAR(1) model

$$\mathbf{X}_t = \mathbf{A}\mathbf{X}_t + \mathbf{S}_t + \mathbf{W}_t$$

where

$$\mathbf{X}_t = \begin{bmatrix} \mathbf{x}_t \\ \mathbf{x}_{t-1} \\ \vdots \\ \mathbf{x}_{t-p+1} \end{bmatrix}, \ \mathbf{A} = \begin{bmatrix} \mathbf{A}_1 & \mathbf{A}_2 & \dots & \mathbf{A}_{p-1} & \mathbf{A}_p \\ \mathbf{I}_n & 0 & \dots & 0 & 0 \\ 0 & \mathbf{I}_n & \dots & 0 & 0 \\ 0 & 0 & \ddots & \vdots & \vdots \\ 0 & 0 & \dots & \mathbf{I}_n & 0 \end{bmatrix}, \ \mathbf{S}_t = \begin{bmatrix} \mathbf{s}_t \\ 0 \\ \vdots \\ 0 \end{bmatrix}, \ \mathbf{W}_t = \begin{bmatrix} \varepsilon_t \\ 0 \\ \vdots \\ 0 \end{bmatrix}$$

We can see from the above definitions that $\mathbf{X}_t$ is a $np \times 1$ vector, $\mathbf{A}$ is a $np \times np$ square matrix, and $\mathbf{S}_t$, $\mathbf{W}_t$ are $np \times 1$ vectors. In order to compute explicit solutions, we have therefore only to consider VAR(1) models.

It can be demonstrated that the inverse characteristic equation of this VAR(1) system and that of the original VAR(p) system have the same roots.

Solving Stable VAR(1) Processes

We can now proceed to show how solutions to stable VAR models can be computed. Given the equivalence between VAR(1) and VAR(p) models, we will only consider VAR(1) models. We consider, separately, stable processes that start in the infinite past and possibly unstable processes that start at a given time from initial conditions. We begin with stable processes.

Consider an n-dimensional VAR(1) model,

$$\mathbf{x}_t = \mathbf{A}\mathbf{x}_{t-1} + \mathbf{v} + \varepsilon_t, \ t = 0, \pm 1, \pm 2, \dots$$

where the deterministic term is a constant vector $\mathbf{v}$. Suppose that the roots of its characteristic equation lay inside the unit circle. Recall that in the case of a VAR(1) model, the characteristic equation is

$$\det(\mathbf{I}z - \mathbf{A}) = 0$$

The solutions of this equation are the eigenvalues of the matrix $\mathbf{A}$. Therefore, in the case of a stable process, all the eigenvalues of the matrix $\mathbf{A}$ have modulus less than one. Note that we express here the stability condition in terms of the characteristic equation while in a previous section we used the inverse characteristic equation.

As the VAR operator is stable, the process is stationary and invertible. Given that it is a VAR(1) process, the infinite moving average representation can be written as follows:

$$\frac{1}{I - AL} = \sum_{i=0}^{\infty} A^i L^i \qquad A^0 = I$$

The above relationship can be verified premultiplying both sides by $I - AL$.[10]

As we saw above when we discussed stability, stationarity, and invertibility, an invertible process can be represented as follows:

$$\mathbf{x}_t = \mathbf{u} + \left(\sum_{i=0}^{\infty} A^i L^i \right) \varepsilon_t$$

where

$$\mathbf{u} = \left(\sum_{i=0}^{\infty} A^i \right) \mathbf{v}$$

is the constant mean of the process

$$\mathbf{u} = E[\mathbf{x}_t]$$

We now compute the autocovariances of the process. It can be demonstrated that the time-invariant autocovariances of the process are

$$\Gamma_h = E[(\mathbf{x}_t - \mathbf{u})(\mathbf{x}_{t-h} - \mathbf{u})'] = \sum_{i=0}^{\infty} A^{i+h} \Omega (A^i)'$$

---

[10] In this book we frequently use fractions to express the inverse operator. For example, in the above formulas we used

$$\frac{1}{I - AL}$$

to express the inverse operator $(I - AL)^{-1}$. Strictly speaking, the fractional notation is meaningless. However, it is widely used in the literature because many operations on polynomial of the operator L are formally analogous to algebraic operations.

where $\boldsymbol{\Omega}$ is the variance-covariance matrix of the noise term. This expression involves an infinite sum of matrices. While it is not convenient for practical computations, it can be demonstrated that the following recursive matrix equations hold:

$$\boldsymbol{\Gamma}_h = \mathbf{A}\boldsymbol{\Gamma}_{h-1}$$

These equations are called *Yule-Walker equations*. They are the *multivariate* equivalent of the Yule-Walker equations that we defined for univariate ARMA processes.

Yule-Walker equations can be used to compute the process autocovariances recursively—provided that we know $\boldsymbol{\Gamma}_0$. Note that $\boldsymbol{\Gamma}_0$ is the variance-covariance matrix of the *process*, which is different from the variance-covariance matrix $\boldsymbol{\Omega}$ of the noise term. It can demonstrated that $\boldsymbol{\Gamma}_0$ satisfies the following equation:

$$\boldsymbol{\Gamma}_0 = \mathbf{A}\boldsymbol{\Gamma}_0(\mathbf{A})' + \boldsymbol{\Omega}$$

which allows to compute $\boldsymbol{\Gamma}_0$. It can be demonstrated that $\boldsymbol{\Gamma}_0$ admits the following closed-form expression:

$$\mathrm{vec}(\boldsymbol{\Gamma}_0) = (\mathbf{I} - \mathbf{A} \otimes \mathbf{A})^{-1}\mathrm{vec}(\boldsymbol{\Omega})$$

The vectoring operation and the tensor product $\otimes$ are defined in Chapter 15.

To explicitly compute solutions, consider separately the case of distinct roots and the case of at least two coincident roots. Suppose first that the matrix $\mathbf{A}$ has distinct real or complex eigenvalues $(\lambda_1, ..., \lambda_n)$ and distinct eigenvectors $(\xi_1, ..., \xi_n)$. The matrix $\mathbf{A}$ is thus nonsingular and can be represented as: $\mathbf{A} = \boldsymbol{\Xi}\boldsymbol{\Lambda}\boldsymbol{\Xi}^{-1}$ where $\boldsymbol{\Xi} = [\xi_1, ..., \xi_n]$ is a nonsingular matrix whose columns are the eigenvectors and

$$\boldsymbol{\Lambda} = \begin{pmatrix} \lambda_1 & & 0 \\ & \ddots & \\ 0 & & \lambda_n \end{pmatrix}$$

is a diagonal matrix whose diagonal elements are the eigenvalues.

Consider the process solution

$$\mathbf{x}_t = \mathbf{u} + \left(\sum_{i=0}^{\infty} \mathbf{A}^i L^i \right)\varepsilon_t$$

The infinite matrix series on the right-hand side converges as the eigenvalues of the matrix $\mathbf{A}$ have modulus less than one. In fact we can write

$$\mathbf{A} = \Xi \Lambda \Xi^{-1}$$

$$\mathbf{A}^i = \overbrace{\Xi \Lambda \Xi^{-1} \ldots \Xi \Lambda \Xi^{-1}}^{i \text{ times}} = \Xi \Lambda^i \Xi^{-1}$$

$$\Lambda^i = \begin{pmatrix} \lambda_1^i & & 0 \\ & \ddots & \\ 0 & & \lambda_n^i \end{pmatrix}$$

and

$$\frac{1}{\mathbf{I} - \mathbf{A}L} = \left(\sum_{i=0}^{\infty} \mathbf{A}^i L^i \right) = \sum_{i=0}^{\infty} \Xi \Lambda^i \Xi^{-1} L^i$$

The process solution can therefore be written as

$$\mathbf{x}_t = \mathbf{u} + \left(\sum_{i=0}^{\infty} \Xi \Lambda^i \Xi^{-1} L^i \right) \varepsilon_t$$

The process can be represented as a constant plus an infinite moving average of past noise terms weighted with exponential terms.

Suppose now that two or more roots are *coincident*. We know from Appendix A that in this case matrix $\mathbf{A}$ can be diagonalized only if it is normal, that is, if $\mathbf{A}^T \mathbf{A} = \mathbf{A} \mathbf{A}^T$. In all other cases, it can be put in Jordan canonical form:

$$\mathbf{A} = \mathbf{PJP}^{-1}$$

where the matrix $\mathbf{J}$ has the form $\mathbf{J} = \text{diag}[\mathbf{J}_1, \ldots, \mathbf{J}_k]$, that is, it is formed by *Jordan diagonal blocks*:

$$\mathbf{J} = \begin{bmatrix} \mathbf{J}_1 & \cdots & 0 \\ \vdots & \ddots & \vdots \\ 0 & \cdots & \mathbf{J}_k \end{bmatrix}$$

The process solution will be given by the following expression:

$$\mathbf{x}_t = \mathbf{u} + \left(\sum_{i=0}^{\infty} \mathbf{P} \mathbf{J}^i \mathbf{P}^{-1} L^i \right) \varepsilon_t$$

Details on how to compute $\mathbf{J}^i$ are given in Appendix A.

In summary, the solution of a stable VAR(1) model is a stationary process with a constant mean and constant autocovariances. The mean depends on the matrix $\mathbf{A}$ as well as on the constant intercept term $\mathbf{v}$. The mean is zero if the intercept is zero but the converse is not necessarily true. The autocovariances depend on the matrix $\mathbf{A}$ as well as on the variance-covariance matrix of the noise term.

Solving Stable and Unstable Processes with Initial Conditions

In the previous section we considered stable, stationary systems defined on the entire time axis. In practice, however, most models start at a given time. If the system starts at a given moment with given initial conditions, it need not be stable and stationary. Consider an n-dimensional VAR(1) model,

$$\mathbf{x}_t = \mathbf{A}\mathbf{x}_{t-1} + \mathbf{s}_t + \varepsilon_t, \quad t = 1, 2, \dots$$

together with initial conditions.

Consider $\mathbf{x}_0$. As in the previous case, we have to consider separately the case in which the roots of the characteristic equation are all distinct and the case where at least two roots coincide. See Appendix A for computational details. Recall that the roots of the characteristic equation are the eigenvalues of the matrix $\mathbf{A}$.

Suppose first that the matrix $\mathbf{A}$ has distinct real or complex eigenvalues ($\lambda_1, \dots, \lambda_n$) and distinct eigenvectors. The matrix $\mathbf{A}$ is thus nonsingular and can be represented as: $\mathbf{A} = \mathbf{\Xi}\mathbf{\Lambda}\mathbf{\Xi}^{-1}$ where $\mathbf{\Xi} = [\xi_1, \dots, \xi_n]$ is a nonsingular matrix whose columns are the eigenvectors and

$$\mathbf{\Lambda} = \begin{pmatrix} \lambda_1 & & 0 \\ & \ddots & \\ 0 & & \lambda_n \end{pmatrix}$$

is a diagonal matrix whose diagonal elements are the eigenvalues.

Suppose the VAR(1) model starts at $t = 0$ and suppose that the initial conditions $\mathbf{x}_0$ are given. The solution of the model, as detailed in Appendix A, is the sum of the general solution of the associated homogeneous system with the given initial conditions plus a particular solution. The *general* solution can be written as follows:

$$\mathbf{x}_G(t) = \Xi\Lambda^t\mathbf{c} = c_1\lambda_1^t\xi_1 + \dots + c_n\lambda_n^t\xi_n$$

with constants c determined in function of initial conditions. A *particular* solution can be written as

$$\mathbf{x}_t = \sum_{i=0}^{t-1}\Xi\Lambda^i\Xi^{-1}(\mathbf{s}_{t-i}+\boldsymbol{\varepsilon}_{t-i})$$

All solutions are a sum of a particular solution and the general solution. We can also see that the solution is a sum of the deterministic and stochastic parts:

$$\mathbf{x}_t = \overbrace{\Xi\Lambda^t\mathbf{c}+\sum_{i=0}^{t-1}\Xi\Lambda^i\Xi^{-1}\mathbf{s}_{t-i}}^{\text{Deterministic part}} + \overbrace{\sum_{i=0}^{t-1}\Xi\Lambda^i\Xi^{-1}\boldsymbol{\varepsilon}_{t-i}}^{\text{Stochastic part}}$$

From the above formulas, we can see that the modulus of eigenvalues dictates if past shocks decay, persist, or are amplified.

We now discuss the shape of the deterministic trend under the above assumptions. Recall that the deterministic trend is given by the mean of the process. Let us assume that the deterministic terms are either constant intercepts $\mathbf{s}_t = \mu$ or linear functions $\mathbf{s}_t = \gamma t + \mu$. Taking expectations on both sides of the above equation we can write

$$E[\mathbf{x}_t] = \Xi\Lambda^t\mathbf{c}+\sum_{i=0}^{t-1}\Xi\Lambda^i\Xi^{-1}\mu$$

in the case of constant intercepts, and

$$E[\mathbf{x}_t] = \Xi\Lambda^t\mathbf{c}+\sum_{i=0}^{t-1}\Xi\Lambda^i\Xi^{-1}(\gamma t + \mu)$$

in the case of a linear functions.

As the matrix Λ is diagonal, it is clear that the process deterministic trend can have different shapes in function of the eigenvalues. In both cases, the trend can be either a constant, a linear trend, or a polynomial of higher order. If the process has only one unitary root, then a constant intercept produces a linear trend, while a linear function might produce a constant, a linear, or a quadratic trend.

Now suppose that two or more roots are coincident. We know from Appendix A that in this case the matrix $\mathbf{A}$ can be diagonalized only if it is normal, that is if $\mathbf{A}^T\mathbf{A} = \mathbf{A}\mathbf{A}^T$. In this case all the eigenvectors are linearly independent. In all other cases, it can be put in Jordan canonical form:

$$\mathbf{A} = \mathbf{PJP}^{-1}$$

where the matrix $\mathbf{J}$ has the form $\mathbf{J} = \mathrm{diag}[\mathbf{J}_1, ..., \mathbf{J}_k]$, that is, it is formed by *Jordan diagonal blocks*:

$$\mathbf{J} = \begin{bmatrix} \mathbf{J}_1 & \cdots & 0 \\ \vdots & \ddots & \vdots \\ 0 & \cdots & \mathbf{J}_k \end{bmatrix}$$

The general solution of the system will be given by the following expression:

$$\mathbf{x}(t) = \mathbf{A}^t\mathbf{c} = \mathbf{PJ}^t\mathbf{P}^{-1}\mathbf{c}$$

while a fundamental matrix will be

$$\mathbf{\Phi}(t) = \mathbf{PJ}^t$$

A particular solution will be given by the following expression:

$$\mathbf{x}_t = \sum_{i=0}^{t-1} \mathbf{PJ}^i\mathbf{P}^{-1}(\mathbf{s}_{t-i} + \mathbf{\varepsilon}_{t-i})$$

Details on how to compute $\mathbf{J}^i$ are given in Appendix A.

As in the previous case, all solutions will be the sum of a deterministic part plus a stochastic part:[11]

---

[11] This property is shared by all systems of linear stochastic differential equations (see Sergio M. Focardi and Frank J. Fabozzi, *The Mathematics of Financial Modeling and Investment Management* (Hoboken, NJ: John Wiley & Sons, 2004)). Nonlinear systems such as GARCH do not have this property.

$$\overbrace{\text{Deterministic part}}^{} \qquad \overbrace{\text{Stochastic part}}^{}$$

$$\mathbf{x}_t = \overbrace{\mathbf{PJ}^t \widehat{\mathbf{c}} + \sum_{i=0}^{t-1} \mathbf{PJ}^i \mathbf{P}^{-1} \mathbf{s}_{t-i}}^{} + \overbrace{\sum_{i=0}^{t-1} \mathbf{PJ}^i \mathbf{P}^{-1} \boldsymbol{\varepsilon}_{t-i}}^{}$$

To illustrate the above, consider the following VAR(2) model:

$$x(t) = 0.6x(t-1) - 0.1y(t-1) - 0.7x(t-2) + 0.15y(t-2) + \varepsilon_x(t)$$
$$y(t) = -0.12x(t-1) + 0.7y(t-1) + 0.22x(t-2) - 0.8y(t-2) + \varepsilon_y(t)$$

with the following initial conditions at time $t = 1,2$:

$$x(1) = 1 \quad x(2) = 1.2 \quad y(1) = 1.5 \quad y(2) = -2$$

It can be transformed into a VAR(1) model as follows:

$$x(t) = 0.6x(t-1) - 0.1y(t-1) - 0.7z(t-1) + 0.15w(t-1) + \varepsilon_x(t)$$
$$y(t) = -0.12x(t-1) + 0.7y(t-1) + 0.22z(t-1) - 0.8w(t-1) + \varepsilon_y(t)$$
$$z(t) = x(t-1)$$
$$w(t) = y(t-1)$$

with the following initial conditions:

$$x(2) = 1.2 \quad y(2) = -2 \quad z(2) = 1 \quad w(2) = 1.5$$

Note that now we have defined four initial conditions at $t = 2$.
The coefficient matrix

$$\mathbf{A} = \begin{pmatrix} 0.6 & -0.1 & -0.7 & 0.15 \\ -0.12 & 0.7 & 0.22 & -0.8 \\ 1 & 0 & 0 & 0 \\ 0 & 1 & 0 & 0 \end{pmatrix}$$

has four distinct complex eigenvalues:

$$\Lambda = \begin{bmatrix} 0.2654+0.7011i & 0 & 0 & 0 \\ 0 & 0.2654-0.7011i & 0 & 0 \\ 0 & 0 & 0.3846+0.8887i & 0 \\ 0 & 0 & 0 & 0.3846-0.8887i \end{bmatrix}$$

The corresponding eigenvector matrix (columns are the eigenvectors) is

$$\Xi = \begin{bmatrix} 0.1571 + 0.4150i & 0.1571 - 0.4150i & -0.1311 - 0.3436i & -0.1311 + 0.3436i \\ 0.0924 + 0.3928i & 0.0924 - 0.3928i & 0.2346 + 0.5419i & 0.2346 - 0.5419i \\ 0.5920 & 0.5920 & -0.3794 + 0.0167i & -0.3794 + 0.0167i \\ 0.5337 + 0.0702i & 0.5337 - 0.0702i & 0.6098 & 0.6098 \end{bmatrix}$$

The general solution can be written as

$$\mathbf{x}_G = c_1 0.7497^t \cos(1.2090t + \rho_1) + c_2 0.9684^t \cos(1.1623t + \rho_2)$$

VECTOR AUTOREGRESSIVE MOVING AVERAGE MODELS (VARMA)

VARMA models combine an autoregressive part and a moving average part. In some cases, they can offer a more parsimonious modeling option than a pure VAR model. A VARMA(p,q) model is a model of the following general form:

$$\mathbf{A}(L)\mathbf{x}_t = \mathbf{B}(L)\boldsymbol{\varepsilon}_t$$
$$\mathbf{A}(L) = \mathbf{I} - \mathbf{A}_1 L - \mathbf{A}_2 L^2 - \cdots - \mathbf{A}_p L^p$$
$$\mathbf{B}(L) = \mathbf{I} + \mathbf{B}_1 L + \mathbf{B}_2 L^2 + \cdots + \mathbf{B}_q L^q$$

A VARMA model has two characteristic equations:

$$\det(\mathbf{A}(z)) = 0$$
$$\det(\mathbf{B}(z)) = 0$$

If the roots of the equation $\det(\mathbf{A}(z)) = 0$ are all strictly outside the unit circle, then the process is invertible and can be represented as an infinite moving average. If the roots of the equation $\det(\mathbf{B}(z)) = 0$ are all strictly outside the unit circle, then the process is invertible and can be represented as an infinite autoregressive process. Both representations require the process to be defined for $-\infty < t < \infty$.

If the process starts at $t = 0$, the theory developed above in our discussion of VAR models can be applied. The process can be reduced to VAR($1,q$) model and then solved with the same methods.

DISTRIBUTIONAL PROPERTIES

The distributional properties of VAR models of every order strictly depend on the distributional properties of the noise process. If the noise process is normally distributed, then it can be demonstrated that a VAR or VARMA process is a normal process in the sense that all process variables are normally distributed. If the noise process has finite variance but it is not normally distributed, the process will not be normal in general. There is no way to make general inferences on the process distributional properties. Each distributional assumption yields a different model.

Note that, as we will see in Chapter 15, VAR models can be estimated without making specific assumptions on the distributional properties of the variables or the noise term. In order to apply standard estimation methods, the only requirement is that the noise terms be uncorrelated with zero mean and finite variance. Under these assumptions, it is possible to estimate the coefficients of a VAR model. The estimated VAR yields the dynamics of the expected values of the process and allows one to estimate the variances.

If it is important to produce an estimate of higher moments or to recover the dynamics of the moments higher than the expected value, then additional modeling assumptions and different estimation techniques are called for. Estimation of higher moments might be important for portfolio management. In Chapter 5 we discussed the optimization process when variables are not normal.

COINTEGRATION

We first give an intuitive explanation of cointegration and its properties. Two or more processes are said to be *cointegrated* if they stay close to each other even if they "drift about" as individual processes. A colorful illustration is that of the drunken man and his dog: both stumble about aimlessly but never drift too far apart. Cointegration is an important concept both for economics and financial econometrics. It implements the notion that there are feedbacks, that is, servo-controls that keep variables mutually aligned. To introduce the notion of cointegration, recall the concepts of stationary processes and integrated processes.

Integrated Processes

A process is said to be *stationary* in the strict sense if all joint, finite-dimensional distributions are time-invariant. A process is said to be (weakly) second-order stationary or covariance-stationary if its first and second moments are time-invariant. Stationarity does not imply weak stationarity as distributions might have infinite second moments. A process described by a *vector difference equation* (VDE) is stationary if the VDE is stable, that is, if the solutions of the characteristic equations lie strictly outside the unit circle.

Note that stationarity is a transformation-invariant property. That is, a time series X_t is stationary if and only if the time series $f(X_t)$ is stationary. In addition, it can also be demonstrated that a time series X_t is stationary if and only if the finite-dimensional copulas of X_t are time-invariant. Copulas allow a better characterization of the dependence structure of time series than linear correlation coefficients. A general characterization of dependence structures using copulas has been obtained by de la Peña, Ibragimov, and Sharakhmetov.[12] Capturing the dependence structure of a time series is very important from the point of view of model risk as will be discussed in Chapter 17.

A process is said to be *integrated* of order one if its first differences form a stationary process. Recursively, we can define a process integrated of order n if its first differences are integrated of order $n - 1$. An arithmetic random walk is a process integrated of order one as its differences are stationary. However, not all integrated processes are random walks as the definition of stationarity does not assume that processes are generated as IID sequences. In other words, a stationary process can exhibit autocorrelation.

Consider a multivariate process $\mathbf{x}_t$. The process $\mathbf{x}_t$ is said to be integrated of order d if we can write

$$(I - L)^d \mathbf{x}_t = \mathbf{y}_t$$

where $\mathbf{y}_t$ is a stationary process. Suppose that $\mathbf{x}_t$ can be represented by a VAR process,

$$(\mathbf{I} - \mathbf{A}_1 L - \mathbf{A}_2 L^2 - \cdots - \mathbf{A}_p L^p)\mathbf{x}_t = \Phi(L)\mathbf{x}_t = \boldsymbol{\varepsilon}_t$$

The process $\mathbf{x}_t$ is said to be integrated of order d if we can factorize Φ as follows:

---

[12] Victor H. de la Peña, Rustam Ibragimov, and Shaturgun Sharakhmetov, "Characterizations of Joint Distributions, Copulas, Information, Dependence and Decoupling, with Applications to Time Series," in J. Rojo (ed.), *Proceedings of the Second Erich L. Lehmann Symposium—Optimality, IMS Lecture Notes—Monograph Series*, NSF-CBMS Regional Conference Series in Probability and Statistics, 2005.

$$\Phi(L)\mathbf{x}_t = (1-L)^d\Psi(L)\mathbf{x}_t = \boldsymbol{\varepsilon}_t$$

where $\Psi(L)$ is a stable VAR process that can be inverted to yield

$$(1-L)^d\mathbf{x}_t = \Psi(L)^{-1}\boldsymbol{\varepsilon}_t = \sum_{i=0}^{\infty} C_i\boldsymbol{\varepsilon}_{t-i}$$

In particular, an integrated process with order of integration $d = 1$ admits the following representation:

$$\Delta\mathbf{x}_t = (1-L)\mathbf{x}_t = \Psi(L)^{-1}\boldsymbol{\varepsilon}_t = \left(\sum_{i=0}^{\infty} \Psi_i L^i\right)\boldsymbol{\varepsilon}_t$$

The above definition can be generalized to allow for different orders of integration for each variable.

It is clear from the above definition that the characteristic equation of a process integrated of order d has a root equal to 1, that is a unit root, with multiplicity d.

Stochastic and Deterministic Trends

An integrated process is characterized by the fact that past shocks never decay. In more precise terms, we can demonstrate that an integrated process can be decomposed as the sum of three components: a deterministic trend, a stochastic trend, and a cyclic stationary process. To see this fact, consider first a process integrated of order 1, without a constant intercept, which we can write in the following form:

$$\Delta\mathbf{x}_t = \Psi(L) = \left(\sum_{i=0}^{\infty} \Psi_i L^i\right)\boldsymbol{\varepsilon}_t$$

Let's rewrite $\Psi(L)$ as follows:

$$\Psi(L) = \Psi + (1-L)\left(\sum_{i=0}^{\infty} \Psi_i^* L^i\right)$$

Note that in general $\Psi \neq \Psi_0$ and that $\Psi(1) = \Psi$. We can now write the process $\mathbf{x}_t$ as follows:

$$\Delta \mathbf{x}_t = (1-L)\mathbf{x}_t = \left[\mathbf{\Psi} + (1-L)\left(\sum_{i=0}^{\infty} \mathbf{\Psi}_i^* L^i \right) \right] \boldsymbol{\varepsilon}_t$$

and therefore, dividing by $(1-L)$:

$$\mathbf{x}_t = \frac{\mathbf{\Psi}}{(1-L)} \boldsymbol{\varepsilon}_t + \left(\sum_{i=0}^{\infty} \mathbf{\Psi}_i^* L^i \right) \boldsymbol{\varepsilon}_t$$

$$\mathbf{x}_t = \mathbf{\Psi} \sum_{i=1}^{t} \boldsymbol{\varepsilon}_i + \left(\sum_{i=0}^{\infty} \mathbf{\Psi}_i^* L^i \right) \boldsymbol{\varepsilon}_t$$

The process $\mathbf{x}_t$ is thereby decomposed into a stochastic trend,

$$\mathbf{\Psi} \sum_{i=1}^{t} \boldsymbol{\varepsilon}_i$$

and a stationary component

$$\left(\sum_{i=0}^{\infty} \mathbf{\Psi}_i^* L^i \right) \boldsymbol{\varepsilon}_t$$

The difference between the two terms should be clearly stated: The stochastic term is a sum of shocks that never decay, while in the stationary term past shocks decay due to the weighting matrices $\mathbf{\Psi}_i^*$. We explore the structure of the common trends in the cointegration section.

Any eventual deterministic trend is added to the stochastic trend and to the stationary component. A constant intercept produces a linear trend or a constant. In fact, if we add a constant intercept v we can write

$$\Delta \mathbf{x}_t = (1-L)\mathbf{x}_t = v + \left[\mathbf{\Psi} + (1-L)\left(\sum_{i=0}^{\infty} \mathbf{\Psi}_i^* L^i \right) \right] \boldsymbol{\varepsilon}_t$$

which implies

$$\mathbf{x}_t = \frac{\boldsymbol{\Psi}}{(1-L)}\boldsymbol{\varepsilon}_t + \left(\sum_{i=0}^{\infty} \boldsymbol{\Psi}_i^* L^i\right)\boldsymbol{\varepsilon}_t + \frac{\boldsymbol{\Psi}}{(1-L)}\mathbf{v}$$

$$\mathbf{x}_t = \boldsymbol{\Psi}\sum_{i=1}^{t} \boldsymbol{\varepsilon}_i + \left(\sum_{i=0}^{\infty} \boldsymbol{\Psi}_i^* L^i\right)\boldsymbol{\varepsilon}_t + t\mathbf{u}$$

where $\mathbf{u} = \boldsymbol{\Psi}\mathbf{v}$. The term $\mathbf{u}$ can be zero even if the intercept $\mathbf{v}$ is different from zero.

A process $\mathbf{x}_t$ is called *trend stationary* if it is the sum of a deterministic trend plus a stationary component, that is if

$$\mathbf{x}_t = \mathbf{s}_t + \boldsymbol{\Psi}_t$$

A process is called *difference stationary* if it becomes stationary after differencing. A difference-stationary process is the sum of a stochastic trend plus a stationary process.

Key Defining Properties Related to Cointegration

Let's now give an intuitive characterization to the concept of cointegration in the case of two stochastic processes. Cointegration can be understood in terms of its three key defining properties:

- Reduction of order of integration
- Regression
- Common trends

Let's take a look at each of these properties.

First, consider *reduction of order of integration*. Two or more stochastic processes that are integrated of order one or higher are said to be cointegrated if there are linear combinations of the processes with a *lower* order of integration. In financial econometrics, cointegration is usually a property of processes integrated of order one that admit linear combinations integrated of order zero (stationary). As we will see, it is also possible to define fractional cointegration between fractionally integrated processes.

Second, the concept of cointegration can be also stated in terms of *linear regression*. Two or more processes integrated of order one are said to be cointegrated if it is possible to make a meaningful linear regression of one process over the other(s). In general, it is not possible to make a meaningful linear regression of one integrated process over another. However, regression is possible if the two processes are cointegrated. Cointegration is that property that allows to regress one integrated process over other integrated processes.

Finally, a property of cointegrated processes is the presence of integrated *common trends*. Given n processes with r cointegrating relationships, it is possible to determine n-r common trends. Common trends are integrated processes such that any of the n original processes can be expressed as a linear regression on the common trends. Cointegration entails a dimensionality reduction insofar as common trends are the common drivers of a set of processes. By removing the trend, the concept of cointegration can be defined even if deterministic trends are present.

Long-Run Equilibrium

Given n processes integrated of order one, the processes are said to be cointegrated if there is a linear combination of the processes that is stationary. If the processes are stock prices, cointegration means that even if the stock prices are individually integrated of order one—for example arithmetic random walks—there are portfolios that are stationary. The linear relationships that produce stationary processes are called *cointegrating* relationships.

Cointegrated processes are characterized by a short-term dynamics and a long-run equilibrium. Note that this latter property does not mean that cointegrated processes *tend* to a long-term equilibrium. On the contrary, the relative behavior is stationary. Long-run equilibrium is the static regression function, that is, the relationship between the processes after eliminating the short-term dynamics.

In general, there can be many linearly independent cointegrating relationships. Given n processes integrated of order one, there can be a maximum of $n - 1$ cointegrating relationships. Cointegrating relationships are not uniquely defined: In fact, any linear combination of cointegrating relationships is another cointegrating relationship.

More Rigorous Definition of Cointegration

Let's now define cointegration in more rigorous terms. The concept of cointegration was introduced by Granger.[13] It can be expressed in the following way. Suppose that n time series $x_{i,t}$, integrated of the same order d are given. If there is a linear combination of the series

---

[13] Clive W.J. Granger, "Some Properties of Time Series Data and Their Use in Econometric Model Specification," *Journal of Econometrics* 16 (1981), pp. 121–130.

$$\delta_t = \sum_{i=1}^{n} \beta_i x_{i,t}$$

which is integrated of order $e < d$, then the series are said to be cointegrated. Any linear combination as the one above is called a cointegrating relationship. The most usual concept of cointegration in financial econometrics is between processes integrated of order $d = 1$ that exhibit stationary ($e = 0$) linear combinations.

The concept of cointegration can be extended to processes integrated of order d where d is a rational fraction. Such processes are called *fractionally integrated processes*. The reduction of the order of integration can be fractional too. For example, processes with order of integration $d = \frac{1}{2}$ are cointegrated if they exhibit linear combinations that are stationary.

Given n time series, there can be from none to at most $n - 1$ cointegrating relationships. The cointegration vectors $[\beta_i]$ are not unique. In fact, given two cointegrating vectors $[\alpha_i]$ and $[\beta_i]$ such that

$$\sum_{i=1}^{N} \alpha_i X_i, \quad \sum_{i=1}^{N} \beta_i X_i$$

are integrated of order e, any linear combination of the cointegrating vectors is another cointegrating vector as the linear combination

$$A \sum_{i=1}^{N} \alpha_i X_i + B \sum_{i=1}^{N} \beta_i X_i$$

is integrated of order e.

STOCHASTIC AND DETERMINISTIC COINTEGRATION

An important distinction has to be made between stochastic and deterministic cointegration. Following the definition of cointegration given above, a multivariate integrated process is cointegrated if there are linear combinations of its components that are stationary. Let us now look at how we define cointegration if the integrated process has a deterministic trend.

Suppose that the multivariate stochastic process x_t has a deterministic trend. The process x_t is said to be *stochastically cointegrated* if there are linear combinations of the process components, each including its own deterministic trend, that are trend stationary, that is stationary plus an eventual deterministic trend. In other words, stochastic cointegration removes stochastic trends but not necessarily deterministic trends.

The process x_t is said to be *deterministically cointegrated* if there are linear combinations of the process components, each including its own deterministic trend, that are stationary without any deterministic trend. In other words, deterministic cointegration removes both stochastic trends and deterministic trends.

COMMON TRENDS

Suppose there are n time series $x_{i,t}$, $i = 1, ..., n$ and $k < n$ cointegrating relationships. It can be demonstrated that there are $n - k$ integrated time series $u_{j,t}$, $j = 1, ..., n - k$, called *common trends*, such that every time series can expressed as a linear combination of the common trends plus a stationary disturbance:

$$x_{i,t} = \sum_{j=1}^{n-k} \gamma_j u_{j,t} + \eta_{i,t}$$

In other words, each process can be regressed over the common trends. Common trends are integrated processes; their existence was first observed by Stock and Watson.[14]

Let's now analyze how, in a cointegrated set of integrated processes, each process can be expressed in terms of a reduced number of common stochastic trends. The exposition follows the original work of Stock and Watson.[15] Suppose that the n-variate process x_t has no deterministic trend, is integrated of order 1, and admits $n - k$ linearly independent cointegrating relationships. This means that there are r vectors of coefficients $\beta_{i,j}$, $i = 1, 2, ..., n$ and $j = 1, 2, ..., r$ such that the processes

$$\sum_{i=1}^{n} \beta_{i,j} x_{i,t}$$

---

[14] James H. Stock and Mark W. Watson, "Diffusion Indexes," NBER Working Paper W6702, 1998; James H. Stock and Mark W. Watson, "New Indexes of Coincident and Leading Economic Indications," in O.J. Blanchard and S. Fischer (eds.), *NBER Macroeconomics Annual 1989* (Cambridge, MA: M.I.T. Press, 1989).
[15] James H. Stock and Mark W. Watson, "Testing for Common Trends," *Journal of the American Statistical Association* 83 (December 1988), pp. 1097–1107.

are stationary. As we initially suppose that the process has no deterministic trend, we do not have to make any distinction between stochastic and deterministic cointegration. If $\mathbf{x}_t$ represent stock prices, cointegration means that there are r portfolios that are stationary even if each individual price process is a random walk.

We arrange the cointegrating relationships in a $n \times r$ matrix:

$$\beta = \begin{pmatrix} \beta_{1,1} & \cdots & \beta_{1,n-k} \\ \vdots & \ddots & \vdots \\ \beta_{n,1} & \cdots & \beta_{n,n-k} \end{pmatrix}$$

This matrix has rank r given that its columns are linearly independent. Therefore the r-variate process $\beta' \mathbf{x}_t$ is stationary. Recall that the process can be represented as

$$\mathbf{x}_t = \Psi \sum_{i=1}^{t} \varepsilon_i + \left(\sum_{i=0}^{\infty} \Psi_i^* L^i \right) \varepsilon_t + \mathbf{x}_{-1}$$

It can be demonstrated that the assumption of r independent cointegrating relationships implies

$$\beta' \Psi = 0$$

Therefore, we can write

$$\beta' \mathbf{x}_t = \mathbf{z}_t = \beta' \left(\sum_{i=0}^{\infty} \Psi_i^* L^i \right) \varepsilon_t + \beta' \mathbf{x}_{-1}$$

where $\mathbf{z}_t$ is a r-variate stationary process. The stochastic trends have been removed.

Let's now explicitly express the process $\mathbf{x}_t$ in terms of common stochastic trends. Observe that the assumption of r cointegrating relationships entails that both $\beta' \Psi = 0$ and Ψ has rank $k = n - r$. In fact, if the rank of Ψ were smaller than $k = n - r$, then there would be one or more additional cointegrating relationships. Because Ψ has rank $k < n$ there is a $n \times r$ matrix H_1 such that $\Psi H_1 = 0$. Furthermore, if H_2 is a $n \times k$ matrix with rank k and columns orthogonal to the columns of H_1 then $A = \Psi H_2$ is a $n \times k$ matrix with rank k. The matrix $n \times n$ $H = [H_1 H_2]$ is non singular and $\Psi H = [0A]$. We can therefore write the representation in terms of common stochastic trends as follows:

$$\mathbf{x}_t = (\mathbf{\Psi H}) \left(\mathbf{H}^{-1} \sum_{i=1}^{t} \boldsymbol{\varepsilon}_i \right) + \left(\sum_{i=0}^{\infty} \mathbf{\Psi}_i^* L^i \right) \boldsymbol{\varepsilon}_t + \mathbf{x}_{-1} = \mathbf{A}\boldsymbol{\tau}_t + \left(\sum_{i=0}^{\infty} \mathbf{\Psi}_i^* L^i \right) \boldsymbol{\varepsilon}_t + \mathbf{x}_{-1}$$

$$\boldsymbol{\tau}_t = \mathbf{H}^{-1} \sum_{i=1}^{t} \boldsymbol{\varepsilon}_i$$

We expand on how to handle deterministic terms in Chapter 15 where we cover estimation.

ERROR CORRECTION MODELS

Having discussed cointegration and cointegrated processes, we now discuss their representation. Granger was able to demonstrate that a multivariate integrated process is cointegrated if and only if it can be represented in the *Error Correction Model* (ECM) form with appropriate restrictions.

First we rewrite a generic VAR model in error correction form. All VAR models can be written in the following error-correction form:

$$\Delta \mathbf{x}_t = (\mathbf{\Phi}_1 L + \mathbf{\Phi}_2 L^2 + \ldots + \mathbf{\Phi}_{n-1} L^{n-1}) \Delta \mathbf{x}_t + \mathbf{\Pi} L^n \mathbf{x}_t + D \mathbf{s}_t + \boldsymbol{\varepsilon}_t$$

where the first $n - 1$ terms are in first differences and the last term is in levels. The term in levels can be placed at any lag.

To see how this representation can be obtained, consider, for example, the following transformations of a VAR(2) model:

$$\mathbf{x}_t = \mathbf{A}_1 \mathbf{x}_{t-1} + \mathbf{A}_2 \mathbf{x}_{t-2} + D \mathbf{s}_t + \boldsymbol{\varepsilon}_t$$
$$= \mathbf{x}_t - \mathbf{x}_{t-1} = (\mathbf{A}_1 - \mathbf{I})\mathbf{x}_{t-1} - (\mathbf{A}_1 - \mathbf{I})\mathbf{x}_{t-2} + (\mathbf{A}_1 - \mathbf{I})\mathbf{x}_{t-2} + \mathbf{A}_2 \mathbf{x}_{t-2} + \mathbf{s}_t + \boldsymbol{\varepsilon}_t$$
$$= \Delta \mathbf{x}_t = (\mathbf{A}_1 - \mathbf{I})\Delta \mathbf{x}_{t-1} + (\mathbf{A}_1 + \mathbf{A}_2 - \mathbf{I})\mathbf{x}_{t-2} + \mathbf{s}_t + \boldsymbol{\varepsilon}_t$$
$$\mathbf{\Phi}_1 = (\mathbf{A}_1 - \mathbf{I}), \mathbf{\Pi} = (\mathbf{A}_1 + \mathbf{A}_2 - \mathbf{I})$$

with the term in level at lag 2, or

$$\mathbf{x}_t = \mathbf{A}_1 \mathbf{x}_{t-1} + \mathbf{A}_2 \mathbf{x}_{t-2} + D \mathbf{s}_t + \boldsymbol{\varepsilon}_t$$
$$= \mathbf{x}_t - \mathbf{x}_{t-1} = (\mathbf{A}_1 + \mathbf{A}_2 - \mathbf{I})\mathbf{x}_{t-1} - \mathbf{A}_2 \mathbf{x}_{t-1} + \mathbf{A}_2 \mathbf{x}_{t-2} + \mathbf{s}_t + \boldsymbol{\varepsilon}_t$$
$$= \Delta \mathbf{x}_t = (-\mathbf{A}_2)\Delta \mathbf{x}_{t-1} + (\mathbf{A}_1 + \mathbf{A}_2 - \mathbf{I})\mathbf{x}_{t-1} + \mathbf{s}_t + \boldsymbol{\varepsilon}_t$$
$$\mathbf{\Phi}_1 = -\mathbf{A}_2, \mathbf{\Pi} = (\mathbf{A}_1 + \mathbf{A}_2 - \mathbf{I})$$

with the term in level at lag 1. Clearly these transformations can be immediately generalized to any number of lags. Note that, though they mix differences and levels, these transformations do not assume any special property of the VAR model; they are simple rearrangements of terms which are always possible. Cointegration is expressed as restrictions on the matrix Π.

In fact, cointegration is expressed as the ECM representation of a multivariate process in first differences with corrections in levels as follows:

$$\Delta x_{t+1} = \left(\sum_{i=1}^{n-1} AL^i \right) \Delta \mathbf{x}_t + \alpha \beta' \mathbf{x}_t + \varepsilon_t$$

where α is a $p \times r$ matrix, β is a $p \times r$ matrix with $\alpha\beta' = \Pi$ and ε_t is a vector white noise.

In the above ECM representation, the $\beta'\mathbf{x}_t$ are the common trends while the α are the loading factors of the common trends. If $r = 0$, there is no common trend and no cointegration exists between the processes; if $r = p$, the processes are stationary; in the other cases $p > r > 0$, processes are integrated and there are cointegrating relationships.

FORECASTING WITH VAR MODELS

One of the key objectives of financial modeling is forecasting. Forecasting entails a criterion for forecasting as we have to concentrate a probability distribution in a point forecast. A widely used criterion is the minimization of the *mean square error* (MSE). Suppose that a process $\mathbf{y}_t$ is generated by a VAR(p) process. It can be demonstrated that the optimal h-step ahead forecast according to the MSE criterion is the conditional expectation:

$$E_t(\mathbf{y}_{t+h}) \equiv E(\mathbf{y}_{t+h} | \mathbf{y}_s, s \leq t)$$

If the error terms are strict white noise, then the optimal forecast of a VAR model can be computed as follows:

$$E_t(\mathbf{y}_{t+h}) = \mathbf{v} + \mathbf{A}_1 E_t(\mathbf{y}_{t+h-1}) + \cdots + \mathbf{A}_p E_t(\mathbf{y}_{t+h-p})$$

This formula remains valid if the noise term is a martingale difference sequence. However, if the error term is simply white noise, then the above forecasting formula will be valid only in the sense of the best linear predictor.

STATE-SPACE MODELS

All ARMA and VAR models can be formulated in the language of *State-Space Models*. State space and ARMA/VAR are equivalent formulations. However, the state-space language is more convenient in a number of cases, especially when a large number of processes are involved.

The general form of a state-space model is the following:

$$
\begin{aligned}
\mathbf{x}_t &= A\mathbf{z}_t + B\mathbf{u}_t + \boldsymbol{\varepsilon}_t \\
\mathbf{z}_{t+1} &= C\mathbf{z}_t + D\mathbf{u}_t + \boldsymbol{\eta}_t \\
t &= 1, 2, \dots
\end{aligned}
$$

where

- $\mathbf{x}_t$ is the n-dimensional vector of observable output series
- $\mathbf{z}_t$ is the s-dimensional vector of latent (nonobservable) state variables
- $\mathbf{u}_t$ is a m-dimensional vector of deterministic inputs
- $\boldsymbol{\varepsilon}_t$ is the n-dimensional observation white noise
- $\boldsymbol{\eta}_t$ is the m-dimensional transition equation white noise
- A is the $n \times s$ observation matrix
- B is the $n \times m$ input matrix of the observation equation
- C is the $s \times s$ transition matrix
- D is the $s \times m$ input matrix of the transition equation.

The first equation, called the *observation equation*, is a linear regression of the output variables over the state variables and the input variables, while the second equation, called the (*state*) *transition equation* is a VAR(1) model that describes the dynamics of the state variables. In general it is assumed that the system starts from a state $\mathbf{z}_0$ and an initial input $\mathbf{u}_0$.

The joint noise process

$$
\begin{bmatrix} \boldsymbol{\varepsilon}_t \\ \boldsymbol{\eta}_t \end{bmatrix}
$$

is a zero-mean, IID sequence with variance-covariance matrix

$$\begin{bmatrix} \Omega_\varepsilon & \Omega_{\varepsilon\eta} \\ \Omega_{\eta\varepsilon} & \Omega_\eta \end{bmatrix}$$

A number of observations are in order. First, observe that it is possible to write different variants of state-space models. For example, we could define state-space processes with only one noise process so that η_t = $\mathbf{H}\varepsilon_t$. Second, observe that output variables and state variables must be either stationary or cointegrated so that the regressions in the observation equations are meaningful. Third, observe that it is not restrictive to assume that the transition equation is a VAR(1) model. In fact, all VAR(p) models are equivalent to a larger VAR(1) model obtained adding variables for each additional lag.

Let's now establish the equivalence with ARMA/VAR models. To see the equivalence of state-space and ARMA models, consider the following ARMA(p,q) model:

$$x_t = \sum_{i=1}^{p} \varphi_i x_{t-i} + \sum_{j=0}^{q} \psi_j \varepsilon_{t-j}, \quad \psi_0 = 1$$

This model is equivalent to the following state-space model:

$$x_t = \mathbf{A} z_t$$
$$z_t = \mathbf{C} z_{t-1} + \varepsilon_t$$

where

$$\mathbf{A} = \begin{bmatrix} \varphi_1 \ldots \varphi_p & 1 & \psi_1 \ldots \psi_q \end{bmatrix}$$

$$z_t = \begin{bmatrix} x_{t-1} \\ \vdots \\ x_{t-p} \\ \varepsilon_t \\ \varepsilon_{t-1} \\ \vdots \\ \varepsilon_{t-q} \end{bmatrix}$$

and

$$C = \begin{bmatrix} \varphi_1 & \cdots & \varphi_p & 1 & \psi_1 & \cdots & \psi_{q-1} & \psi_q \\ 1 & \cdots & 0 & 0 & 0 & \cdots & 0 & 0 \\ \vdots & \vdots & \vdots & \vdots & \vdots & \vdots & \vdots & \vdots \\ 0 & \cdots & 1 & 0 & 0 & \cdots & 0 & 0 \\ 0 & \cdots & 0 & 0 & 0 & \cdots & 0 & 0 \\ \vdots & \vdots & \vdots & \vdots & \vdots & \vdots & \vdots & \vdots \\ 0 & \cdots & 0 & 0 & 0 & \cdots & 1 & 0 \end{bmatrix}$$

The converse also holds. It can be demonstrated that a state-space model admits a VARMA representation.

Neither ARMA nor state-space representations are unique. However, it can be demonstrated that a minimal ARMA and state-space representation exists for any model that admits an ARMA and state-space representation. A minimal representation is a state-space model of minimal dimensionality, that is, such that any other equivalent model cannot have smaller dimensionality.

The solutions of a state-space model are clearly determined by the transition equation. Therefore solutions of a state-space model are determined by the solutions of a VAR(1) model. We know from our above discussion of VAR models that these solutions are sums of exponentials and/or sinusoidal functions. Exhibit 12.1 shows the solutions of bivariate VAR(2) model. The two variables x and y exhibit oscillating behavior. This VAR(2) model is equivalent to a state-space model with four variables. Two of the variables are x and y while the other two are their lagged values.

AUTOREGRESSIVE DISTRIBUTED LAG MODELS

The *Autoregressive Distributed Lag* (ARDL) models are models formed by an autoregressive part plus a regression with distributed lags over a set of other variables. In other words, an ARDL model regresses a variable over its own past plus the present and past values of a number of exogenous variables. ARDL models are well-known models in a stationary framework.[16] Pesaran and Shin demonstrated that the ARDL framework can be extended to cointegrated processes.[17]

---

[16] See David F. Hendry, "Econometrics: Alchemy or Science?" *Economica* 47 (1980), pp. 387–406, reprinted in David F. Hendry, *Econometrics: Alchemy or Science?* (Oxford: Blackwell Publishers, 1993/Oxford University Press, 2000); David F. Hendry, *Dynamic Econometrics* (Oxford: Oxford University Press, 1995).

[17] M. Hashem Pesaran and Y. Shin, "An Autoregressive Distributed Lag Modeling Approach to Cointegration Analysis," Chapter 11 in S. Strom (ed.), *Econometrics and Economic Theory in the 20th Century: The Ragnar Fresh Centennial Symposium* (Cambridge: Cambridge University Press, 1999).

EXHIBIT 12.1   Solutions of a Bivariate VAR(2) Model

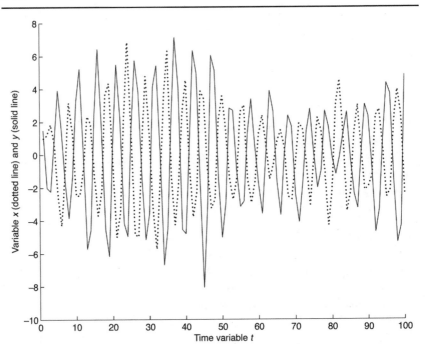

An ARDL model is a model of the following form:

$$x_t = \alpha_0 + \alpha_1 t + (\Phi_1 L + \Phi_2 L^2 + \ldots + \Phi_p L^p)x_t$$
$$+ \beta z_t + (\beta_1 L + \beta_2 L^2 + \ldots + \beta_q L^q)\Delta z + u_t$$
$$\Delta z_t = (P_1 L + P_2 L^2 + \ldots + P_s L^s)\Delta z + \varepsilon_t$$

where z_t is a vector of integrated variables such that the process in the first differences is stable and x is a variable cointegrated with z_t. The P_i are coefficient matrices of the z_t process and the Φ_j are the coefficients of the lagged x terms. In the above formulation we assume a linear trend. The cointegrating relationship ensures that the ARDL regression is meaningful.

Clearly the ARDL model can be cast in a state-space form. To see this point, first define

$$\mathbf{w}_t = \begin{bmatrix} w_{1,t} \\ w_{2,t} \\ \cdot \\ w_{s,t} \end{bmatrix} = \begin{bmatrix} z_t \\ z_{t-1} \\ \cdot \\ z_{t-s+1} \end{bmatrix}$$

which transforms the VAR$(s + 1)$ system

$$\Delta z_t = (P_1 L + P_2 L^2 + \ldots + P_s L^s)\Delta z + \varepsilon_t$$

into a VAR(1) system

$$\mathbf{w}_t = \mathbf{H}\mathbf{w}_{t-1} + \mathbf{K}\varepsilon_t$$

so that the ARDL model becomes

$$x_t = \alpha_0 + \alpha_1 t + (\Phi_1 L + \Phi_2 L^2 + \ldots + \Phi_p L^p)x_t + \Psi \mathbf{w}_t + u_t$$

$$\mathbf{w}_t = \mathbf{H}\mathbf{w}_{t-1} + \mathbf{K}\varepsilon_t$$

$$\Psi = \begin{bmatrix} \beta + \beta_1 \\ -(\beta_1 - \beta_2) \\ \cdot \\ -\beta_q \\ \cdot \\ 0 \end{bmatrix}$$

We can now perform a second step with the transformation:

$$\mathbf{y}_t = \begin{bmatrix} x_t \\ \cdot \\ x_t - p + 1 \\ \mathbf{w}_t \end{bmatrix}$$

and proceed as in the previous step.

DYNAMIC FACTOR MODELS

Dynamic factor models have a representation similar to that of ARDL models. In fact, a dynamic factor model has the following general representation:

$$\mathbf{p}_t = \mathbf{s}_t + \sum_{i=1}^{p} \mathbf{A}_i \mathbf{p}_{t-i} + \sum_{j=1}^{q} \mathbf{B}_j \mathbf{f}_{t-j} + \mathbf{u}_t$$

$$\mathbf{f}_{t+1} = \sum_{k=1}^{s} \mathbf{C}_k \mathbf{f}_{t-k} + \boldsymbol{\varepsilon}_t$$

where the processes $\mathbf{p}_t$ have an autoregressive distributed-lag dynamics, the factors $\mathbf{f}_t$ follow a VAR model, and the noise terms $\mathbf{u}_t$, $\boldsymbol{\varepsilon}_t$ are mutually uncorrelated zero-mean IID sequences. Dynamic factor models can be cast in a state-space form in the same way as ARDL models.

THE ARCH/GARCH FAMILY OF MODELS

The *Autoregressive Conditional Heteroscedastic* (ARCH) models were proposed by Engle as a model for inflation.[18] The empirical fact behind ARCH models is the clustering of volatility observed in many economic and financial series. If instantaneous volatility is defined as a hidden variable in a price model and estimated as the variance of returns over relatively long periods, one finds periods of high volatility followed by periods of low volatility and vice versa.

Note that a new strain of econometric literature deals with instantaneous volatility as an observed variable. The observability of volatility is made possible by the availability of high frequency data. In this case, there is a variety of models for the volatility process, in particular *long-memory fractional models*.[19] We maintain the classical definition of volatility as a hidden variable.

Engle proposed a model in the spirit of state-space modeling where volatility is modeled by an autoregressive process and then injected mul-

---

[18] Robert F. Engle, "Autoregressive Conditional Heteroscedasticity with Estimates of the Variance of United Kingdom Inflation," *Econometrica* 50 (July 1982), pp. 987–1007.

[19] Torben G. Andersen, Tim Bollerslev, Francis X. Diebold, and Paul Labys, "Modeling and Forecasting Realized Volatility," *Econometrica* 71 (2003), pp. 529–626.

tiplicatively in the price process. More precisely, the simplest ARCH model is defined as follows:

$$x_t = [\sqrt{\beta + \lambda x_{t-1}^2}]z_t$$

In the above equation, x is the process variable and the terms z form an IID sequence with zero mean and unitary variance. The parameters α and β must be nonnegative.

The ARCH model was extended by Bollerslev, who proposed the GARCH family of models.[20] In the *Generalized Autoregressive Conditional Heteroscedastic* (GARCH) models, volatility is modeled as a more general ARMA process and then treated as before:

$$x_t = \sigma_t z_t$$

$$\sigma_t^2 = \beta + \sum_{i=1}^{p} \lambda_i x_{t-i}^2 + \sum_{j=1}^{q} \delta_i \sigma_{t-j}^2$$

The key ingredients of ARCH modeling are an ARMA process for volatility and a regressive process where volatility multiplies a white-noise process. Consider a GARCH(1,1) process. If $\lambda_1 + \delta_1 = 1$ then the process is called IGARCH or integrated GARCH. The IGARCH process has a unit root in the sense that today's volatility affects the forecast of volatility in the indefinite future.

The GARCH(m,q) model can be further generalized to multivariate processes by modeling not only the process's volatility but the entire variance-covariance matrix. In this form the model is known as *multivariate GARCH*. Because multivariate GARCH becomes rapidly unmanageable with the number of assets, simplified forms have been proposed.

GARCH models are not necessarily stationary insofar as their stationarity depends on the coefficients of the ARMA process. For example, the IGARCH process is nonstationary.

While ARCH and GARCH models model volatility, asset pricing models require that returns depend on volatility as higher volatility commands a higher return. To capture the dependence of returns on volatility, Engle, Lilien, and Robins suggested adding an expected return term to the GARCH equations.[21] Equations then become

---

[20] Tim Bollerslev, "Generalized Autoregressive Conditional Heteroscedasticity," *Journal of Econometrics* 31 (1986), pp. 307–327.
[21] Robert Engle, David M. Lilien, and Russell P. Robins, "Estimating Time-Varying Risk Premia in the Term Structure: the ARCH-M Model," *Econometrica* 55 (1987), pp. 391–407.

$$r_t = \mu_t + \sigma_t \varepsilon_t$$

$$\mu_t = \gamma_0 + \gamma_1 \sigma_t^2$$

$$\sigma_t^2 = \sum_{i=1}^{m} \alpha_i \sigma_{t-i}^2 + \sum_{j=1}^{q} \beta_j r_{t-j}$$

This model is called *M-ARCH* or *ARCH in mean*.

NONLINEAR MARKOV-SWITCHING MODELS

A number of features of price and return processes might be difficult to explain within the domain of linear autoregressive models. Among the effects are asymmetries in distributions with asymmetric fat tails, asymmetries in correlations such as the fact that stocks are more correlated in bear markets than in bull markets as described in Longin and Solnik[22] and Ang and Chen.[23] The existence of different regimes has also been discussed, by Ang and Bekaert.[24]

Markov-switching models are a family of models which are, in principle, able to tackle many of these problems. Though Markov-switching models require large amounts of data for estimation, they are becoming increasingly popular in the financial econometrics literature as well as in many applications.

A Markov-switching model is a VAR model whose coefficients are driven by a Markov chain. Consider a VAR(p) model,

$$\mathbf{x}_t = \left(\sum_{i=1}^{p} \mathbf{A}_i^s L^i \right) \mathbf{x}_t + \varepsilon_t$$

where the matrices $\mathbf{A}_i^s$ are the coefficient of the process at lag i in state s and the noise terms ε_t are independent normal variables $\varepsilon_t \sim N(0, \varepsilon_t^s)$. The process is driven by a k-states Markov chain. A Markov chain is a discrete variable that can assume at each instant one of k possible values with transition probabilities:

---

[22] François Longin and Bruno Solnik, "Extreme Correlation of International Equity Markets," *Journal of Finance* 56, no. 2 (2001), pp. 649–676.

[23] Andrew Ang and Joseph Chen, "Asymmetric Correlations of Equity Portfolios," *Journal of Financial Economics* 63, no. 3 (2002), pp. 443–494.

[24] Andrew Ang and Geert Bekaert, "International Asset Allocation with Regime Shifts," *Review of Financial Studies* 15 (2002), pp. 1137–1187.

$$P(s_t = u \mid s_{t-1} = v) = p_{uv}$$

The realized state determines the coefficients and the vector of intercepts of the process at each moment. The state variable is a hidden (i.e., not observed) factor. As a result, the noise term is distributed as a mixture of Gaussian distributions. It is well known that mixtures of normal distributions allow to approximate practically every distribution.

SUMMARY

- With the availability of low-cost, high-performance computers and large databases of financial data, multivariate dynamic models have become a feasible modeling option.
- Vector autoregressive (VAR) models enjoy broad diffusion; they linearly regress a multivariate variable on its own lagged values.
- By adding variables, all VAR models can be made equivalent to VAR models with only one lag.
- The solutions of a VAR model are sums of exponentials, exponentially weighted sinusoidal functions, or polynomial functions.
- If the absolute values of the exponents are less than 1, then VAR models are stable and thus stationary.
- The solutions are determined by the characteristic equation of the VAR model.
- If the VAR models is not stable, then its solutions are integrated processes. An integrated process is a process such that it becomes stationary after differencing.
- VAR models that are not stable typically start from initial conditions.
- Cointegration is a property of integrated processes such that individual variables are integrated but linear combinations of those variables (e.g., portfolios) are stationary.
- Cointegration allows to make meaningful regressions of one integrated process on other integrated processes.
- Cointegration also implies the existence of a long-run dynamics superimposed on a short-run dynamics.
- Cointegrated processes can be represented as Vector Error Correction Models.
- VAR models can also be represented as state-space models. State-space models are formed by a VAR model that drives the dynamics of the nonobservable states and by linear regressions of the observables on the states.

- Nonlinear models of stock prices have been proposed, among which are the ARCH/GARCH and Markov-switching models.
- ARCH/GARCH models use an ARMA model to drive the volatility parameter.
- Markov-switching models use a Markov chain to drive the parameters of an autoregressive model.

CHAPTER 13

Model Selection and its Pitfalls

A financial modeler has to solve the critical problem of selecting or perhaps building the optimal model to represent the phenomena he or she wants to study. The task calls for a combination of personal creativity, theory, and machine learning. This chapter discusses methods for model selection and analyzes the many pitfalls of the model selection process.

MODEL SELECTION AND ESTIMATION

In his book *Complexity*, Mitchell Waldrop[1] describes the Global Economy Workshop held at The Santa Fe Institute[2] in Santa Fe, New Mexico in 1987. Organized by the economist Bryan Arthur and attended by distinguished economists and physicists, the seminar introduced the idea that economic laws might be better understood applying the principles of physics and, in particular, the newly developed theory of complex systems. The seminar proceedings were to become the influential book *The Economy as an Evolving Complex System*.[3]

An anecdote from the book is revealing of the issues specific to economics as a scientific endeavor. According to Waldrop, physicists

---

[1] Mitchell Waldrop, *Complexity* (New York: Simon & Schuster, 1992).
[2] The Santa Fe Institute is a research center dedicated to the study of complex phenomena and related issues. Though small in itself, the Institute is in the middle of one of the largest concentrations of research resources in the world. It is, in fact, close to the Los Alamos National Laboratories and the Sandia National Laboratories.
[3] Philip W. Anderson, Kenneth J. Arrow, and David Pines (eds.), *The Economy as an Evolving Complex System* (New York: Westview Press, 1988).

attending the seminar were surprised to learn that economists used highly sophisticated mathematics.

A physicist attending the seminar reportedly asked Kenneth Arrow, the 1972 Nobel prize winner in economics, why, given the lack of data to support theories, economists use such sophisticated mathematics. Arrow replied, "It is just because we do not have enough data that we use sophisticated mathematics. We have to ensure the logical consistency of our arguments." For physicists, on the other hand, *explaining* empirical data is the best guarantee of the logical consistency of theories. If theories work empirically, then mathematical details are not so important and will be amended later; if theories do not work empirically, no logical subtlety will improve them.

This anecdote is revealing of one of the key problems that any modeler of economic phenomena has to confront. On the one side, economics is an empirical science based on empirical facts. However, as data are scarce, many theories and models fit the same data. One is tempted to rely on "clear reasoning" to compensate for the scarcity of data.[4] In economics, there is always a tension between the use of pure reasoning to develop *ex ante* economic theories and the need to conform to generally accepted principles of empirical science. The development of high-performance computing has aggravated the problem, making it possible to discover subtle patterns in data and to build models that fit data samples with arbitrary precision. But patterns and models selected in this way are meaningless and reveal no true economic feature.

Given the importance of model selection, let us discuss this issue before actually discussing estimation issues. It is perhaps useful to compare again the methods of economics and of physics. In physics, the process of model choice is largely based on human creativity. Facts and partial theories are accumulated until scientists make a major leap forward, discovering a new unifying theory. Theories are generally expressed through differential equations and often contain constants (i.e., numerical parameters) to be empirically ascertained. Note that the discovery of laws and the determination of constants are separate moments. Theories are often fully developed before the constants are determined; physical constants often survive major theoretical overhauls in the sense that new theories must include the same constants plus, eventually, additional ones.

Physicists are not concerned with problems of "data snooping," that is, of fitting the data to the same sample that one wants to predict.

---

[4] The French philosopher René Descartes argued that the truth is revealed by clear reasoning. Physics, however, sides with David Hume, the father of modern empiricism.

In general, data are overabundant and models are not determined through a process of fitting and adaptation. Once a physical law that accurately fits all available data is discovered, scientists are confident that it will fit similar data in the future. The key point is that physical laws are known with a high level of precision. Centuries of theoretical thinking and empirical research have resulted in mathematical models that exhibit an amazing level of correspondence with reality. Any minor discrepancy from predictions to experiments entails a major scientific re-evaluation. Often new laws have completely different forms but produce quite similar results. Experiments are devised to choose the winning theory.

Now consider economics, where the conceptual framework is totally different. First, though apparently many data are available, these data come in vastly different patterns. For example, the details of economic development are very different from year to year and from country to country. Asset prices seem to wander about in random ways. Introducing a concept that plays a fundamental role later in the chapter, we can state that:

From the point of view of statistical estimation, economic data are always scarce given the complexity of their patterns.

Attempts to discover simple deterministic laws that accurately fit empirical economic data have proved futile. Furthermore, as economic data are the product of human artifacts, it is reasonable to believe that they will not follow the same laws for very long periods of time. Simply put, the structure of any economy changes too much over time to believe that economic laws are time-invariant laws of nature. One is, therefore, inclined to believe that only approximate laws can be discovered.

However the above considerations create an additional problem: The precise meaning of approximation must be defined. The usual response is to have recourse to probability theory. Here is the reasoning. Economic data are considered one realization of stochastic (i.e., random) data. In particular, economic time series are considered one realization of a stochastic process. The attention of the modeler has therefore to switch from discovering deterministic paths to determining the time evolution of probability distributions. In physics, this switch was made at the end of the 19th century, with the introduction of statistical physics. It later became an article of scientific faith that we can arrive at no better than a probabilistic description of nature.

The adoption of probability as a descriptive framework is not without a cost: Discovering probabilistic laws with confidence requires working with very large populations (or samples). In physics, this is not a problem as we have very large populations of particles.[5] In economics, however, populations are too small to allow for a safe estimate of probability laws; small changes in the sample induce changes in the laws. We can, therefore, make the following statement: *Economic data are too scarce to allow us to make sure probability estimates.*

For example, in 1998 Gopikrishnan, Meyer, Nunes Amaral, and Stanley conducted a study to determine the distribution of stock returns at short time horizons, from a few minutes to a few days.[6] They found that returns had a power tail distribution with exponent $\alpha \approx 3$. One would expect that the same measurement repeated several times over would give the same result. But this is not the case. Since the publication of the aforementioned paper, the return distribution has been estimated several times, obtaining vastly different results. Each successive measurement was made in *bona fide*, but a slightly different empirical setting produced different results.

As a result of the scarcity of economic data, many statistical models, even simple ones, can be compatible with the same data with roughly the same level of statistical confidence. For example, if we consider stock price processes, many statistical models—including the random walk—compete to describe each process with the same level of significance. Before discussing the many issues surrounding model selection and estimation, we will briefly discuss the subject of machine learning and the machine-learning approach to modeling.

THE (MACHINE) LEARNING APPROACH TO MODEL SELECTION

There is a fundamental distinction between (1) estimating parameters in a well-defined model and (2) estimating models through a process of learning. Models, as mentioned, are determined by human modelers using their creativity. For example, a modeler might decide that stock returns in a given market are influenced by a set of economic variables and then write a linear model as follows:

---

[5] This statement needs some qualification. Physics has now reached the stage where it is possible to experiment with small numbers of elementary particles. This poses problems of a nature different from those of classical statistical physics. The interested reader can consult one of the many books on quantum measurement, for example, Vladimir Borisovich Braginsky and Farid Y. Khalili, *Quantum Measurement* (Cambridge: Cambridge University Press, 1992).

[6] Parameswaran Gopikrishnan, Martin Meyer, Luís A. Nunes Amaral, and H. Eugene Stanley, "Inverse Cubic Law for the Distribution of Stock Price Variations," *The European Physical Journal B* 3 (1998), pp. 139–140.

$$r_{i,t} = \sum_{k=1}^{K} \beta_k f_{k,t}$$

where the f are stochastic processes that represent a set of given economic variables. The modeler must then estimate the β_k and test the validity of his model.

In the machine-learning approach to modeling—ultimately a by-product of the diffusion of computers—the process is the following:

- There is a set of empirical data to explain.
- Data are explained by a family of models that include an unbounded number of parameters.
- Models fit with arbitrary precision any set of data.

That models can fit any given set of data with arbitrary precision is illustrated by *neural networks*, one of the many machine learning tools used to model data that includes *genetic algorithms*. As first demonstrated by Cybenko, neural networks are universal function approximators.[7] If we allow a sufficient number of layers and nodes, a neural network can approximate any given function with arbitrary precision. The idea of universal function approximators is well known in calculus. The Taylor and Fourier series are universal approximators for broad classes of functions.

Suppose a modeler wants to model the unknown *data generation process* (DGP) of a time series $X(t)$ using a neural network. A DGP is a possibly nonlinear function of the following type:

$$X(t) = F(X(t-1), ..., X(t-k))$$

that links the present value of the series to its past. A neural network will try to learn the function F using empirical data from the series. If the number of layers and nodes is not constrained, the network can learn F with unlimited precision.

However, the key concept of the theory of machine learning is that a model that can fit any data set with arbitrary precision has *no* explanatory power, that is, it does not capture any true feature of the data, neither in a deterministic setting nor in a statistical setting. In an economic context, machine learning perfectly explains sample data but has no

---

[7] G. Cybenko, "Approximations by Superpositions of a Sigmoidal Function," *Mathematics of Control Signals & Systems* 2 (1989), pp. 303–314.

forecasting power. It is only a mathematical device; it does not correspond to any economic property.

We can illustrate this point in a simplified setting. Let us generate an autoregressive trend stationary process according to the following model:

$$X(i) = X(i-1) + \lambda(Di - X(i-1)) + \sigma\varepsilon(i)$$
$$\lambda = 0.1, D = 0.1, \sigma = 0.5$$

where $\varepsilon(i)$ are normally distributed zero-mean unit-variance random numbers generated with a random number generator. The initial condition is $X = 1$. This process is asymptotically trend stationary. Using the ordinary least squares (OLS) method, let us fit to the process X two polynomials of degree 2 and 20 respectively on a training window of 200 steps. We continue the polynomials five steps after the training window. Exhibit 13.1 represents the process plot and the two polynomials. Observe from the exhibit the different behavior of the two polynomials. The polynomial of degree 2 essentially repeats the linear trend, while the polynomial of

EXHIBIT 13.1   Polynomial Fitting of a Trend Stationary Process Using Two Polynomials of Degree 2 and 20 Respectively on a Training Window of 200 Steps

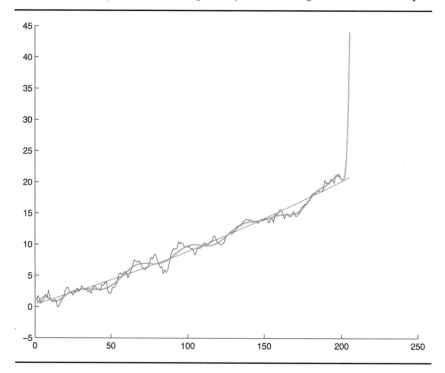

degree 20 follows the random fluctuations of the process quite accurately. Immediately after, however, the training window it diverges.

To address the problem, the theory of machine learning suggests criteria to constrain models so that they fit sample data only partially but, as a trade-off, retain some forecasting power. The intuitive meaning is the following: *The structure of the data and the sample size dictate the complexity of the laws that can be learned by computer algorithms.*

This is a fundamental point. If we have only a small sample data set we can learn only simple patterns, provided that these patterns indeed exist. The theory of machine learning constrains the dimensionality of models to make them adapt to the sample size and structure.[8]

In most practical applications, the theory of machine learning works by introducing a *penalty function* that constrains the models. The penalty function is a function of the size of the sample and of the complexity of the model. One compares models by adding the penalty function to the likelihood function (a definition of the likelihood function is provided later). In this way one can obtain an ideal trade-off between model complexity and forecasting ability.

Several proposals have been made as regards the shape of the penalty function. Three criteria are in general use:

- The Akaike Information Criterion (AIC)
- The Bayesian Information Criterion (BIC) of Schwartz
- The Maximum Description Length principle of Rissanen

These criteria will be described in Chapter 15.

More recently, Vapnik and Chervonenkis have developed a full-fledged quantitative theory of machine learning. While this theory goes well beyond the scope of this book, the practical implication of the theory of learning is important to note: Model complexity must be constrained in function of the sample.

Consider that some "learning" appears in most financial econometric endeavors. For example, determining the number of lags in an autoregressive model is a problem typically solved with methods of learning theory, that is, by selecting the number of lags that minimize

---

[8] The theory of machine learning is a fascinating chapter in modern mathematics and statistics with deep philosophical implications. The key question is: How do we distinguish data that are purely random from data that have a structure? One important answer is provided by the theory of algorithmic complexity developed by Chaitin and Kolmogorov and, in a slightly different context, by Rissanen: Random data cannot be compressed, that is, they cannot be generated by a short algorithm. However, data with a structure are "algorithmically compressible," that is, they can be generated by a short model.

the sum of the loss function of the model plus a penalty function. Ultimately, in modern computer-based financial econometrics, there is no clear-cut distinction between a learning approach versus a theory-based *a priori* approach.

Note, however, that the theory of machine learning offers no guarantee of success. To see this point, let's generate a random walk and fit two polynomials of degree 3 and 20, respectively. Exhibit 13.2 illustrates the random path and the two polynomials. The two polynomials appear to fit the random path quite well. Following the above discussion, the polynomial of order 3 seems to capture some real behavior of the data. But as the data are random, the fit is spurious. This is by no means a special case. In general, it is often possible to fit models to sample data even if the data are basically unpredictable.

Exhibits 13.1 and 13.2 are examples of the simplest cases of model fitting. One might be tempted to object that fitting a curve with a polynomial is not a good modeling strategy for prices or returns. This is true, as one should model a dynamic DGP. However, fitting a DGP

EXHIBIT 13.2   Polynomial Fitting of a Random Walk Using Two Polynomials of Degree 3 and 20 Respectively on a 100-Step Sample

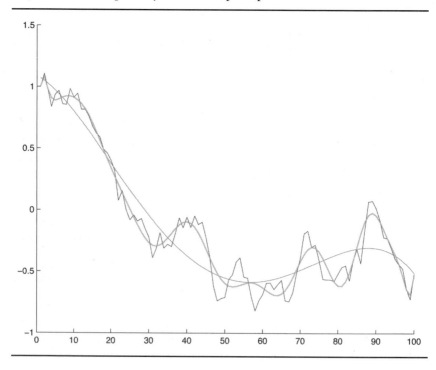

implies a multivariate curve fitting. For illustration purposes, we chose the polynomial fitting of a univariate curve: It is easy to visualize and contains all the essential elements of model fitting.

SAMPLE SIZE AND MODEL COMPLEXITY

Let us summarize the key conclusions reached thus far:

- Economic data are generally scarce for statistical estimation given the complexity of their patterns.
- Economic data are too scarce for sure statistical estimates.
- The scarcity of data means that the data might be compatible with many different models.
- There is a trade-off between model complexity and the size of data sample.

The last two considerations are critical. To illustrate the quantitative trade-off between the size of a data sample and model complexity, consider an apparently straightforward case: estimating a correlation matrix.

It is well known from the theory of random matrices that the eigenvalues of the correlation matrix of independent random walks are distributed according to the following law:

$$\rho(\lambda) = \frac{Q}{2\pi\sigma^2} \frac{\sqrt{(\lambda_{max} - \lambda)(\lambda_{min} - \lambda)}}{\lambda}$$

where Q is the ratio between the number N of sample points and the number M of time series. Exhibit 13.3 illustrates the theoretical distribution of eigenvalues for three values of Q: $Q = 1.8$, $Q = 4$, and $Q = 16$.

As can be easily predicted by examining the above formula, the distribution of eigenvalues is broader when Q is smaller. The corresponding λ_{max} is larger for the broader distribution. The λ_{max} are respectively:

$$\lambda_{max} = 3.0463 \text{ for } Q = 1.8$$

$$\lambda_{max} = 2.2500 \text{ for } Q = 4$$

$$\lambda_{max} = 1.5625 \text{ for } Q = 16$$

EXHIBIT 13.3   The Theoretical Distribution of Eigenvalues for Three Values of Q: $Q = 1.8$, $Q = 4$, and $Q = 16$

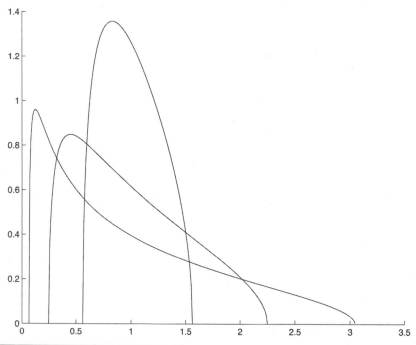

The eigenvalues of a random matrix do not carry any true correlation information. If we now compute the eigenvalues of an empirical correlation matrix of asset returns with a given Q (i.e., the ratio between number of samples and the number of series), we find that only a few eigenvalues carry information as they are outside the area of pure randomness corresponding to the Q. In fact, with good approximation, λ_{max} is the cut-off point that separates meaningful correlation information from noise.[9] Therefore, as the ratio of sample points to the number of asset prices grows (i.e., we have more points for each price process) the "noise area" gets smaller.

To show the effects of the ratio Q on the estimation of empirical correlation matrices, let's compute the correlation matrix for three sets of

---

[9] The application of random matrices to the estimation of correlation and covariance matrices is developed in Vasiliki Plerou, Parameswaran Gopikrishnan, Bernd Rosenow, Luis A. Nunes Amaral, Thomas Guhr, and H. Eugene Stanley, "Random Matrix Approach to Cross Correlations in Financial Data," *Physical Review E 65*, 066126.

900, 400, and 100 stock prices that appeared in the MSCI Europe in a six-year period from December 1998 to February 2005. The return series contain in total 1,611 sample points, each corresponding to a trading day.

First we compute the correlation matrices. The average correlation (excluding the diagonal) is approximately 10% for the three sets of 100, 400, and 900 stocks. Then we compute the eigenvalues. The plot of sorted eigenvalues for the three samples is shown in Exhibit 13.4, 13.5, and 13.6. One can see from these exhibits that when the ratio Q is equal to 16 (i.e., we have more sample points per stock price process), the plot of eigenvalues decays more slowly.

Now compare the distribution of empirical eigenvalues with the theoretical cut-off point λ_{max} that we computed above. The parameter Q was chosen to approximately represent the ratios between 1,611 sample points and 100, 400, and 900 stocks. Results are tabulated in Exhibit 13.7. This exhibit shows that the percentage of meaningful eigenvalues grows as the ratio between the number of sample points and the number of processes increases. If we hold the number of sample points constant (i.e., 1,611) and increase the number of time series from 100 to 900, a larger percent-

EXHIBIT 13.4 Plot of Eigenvalues for 900 Prices, Q = 1.8

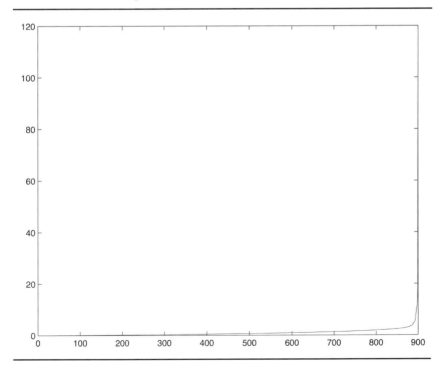

EXHIBIT 13.5   Plot of Eigenvalues for 400 Prices, $Q = 4$

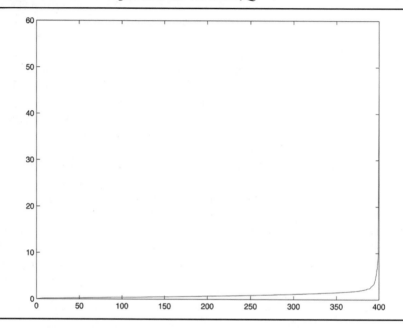

EXHIBIT 13.6   Plot of Eigenvalues for 100 Prices, $Q = 16$

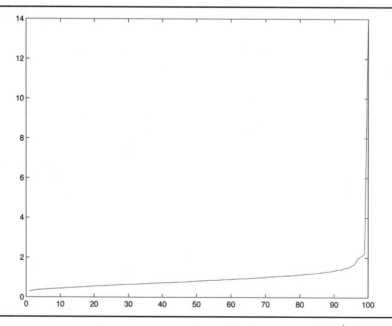

EXHIBIT 13.7 Comparison of the Distribution of Empirical Eigenvalues with the Theoretical Cut-Off Point for Different Values of Q

Number of processes	Average correlation	Max eigenvalue	Number of meaningful eigenvalues	Percentage of meaningful eigenvalues
900; $Q = 1.8$	10%	118	26	0.029
400; $Q = 4$	9.5%	50	15	0.038
100; $Q = 16$	9.8%	14	6	0.06

age of eigenvalues becomes essentially noise (i.e., they do not carry information). Obviously the number of meaningful eigenvalues increases with the number of series, but, due to loss of information, it does so more slowly than does the number of series due to loss of information.

Two main conclusions can be drawn from Exhibit 13.7:

■ Meaningful eigenvalues represent a small percentage of the total, even when $Q = 16$.
■ The ratio of meaningful eigenvalues to the total grows with Q, but the gain is not linear.

The above considerations apply to estimating a correlation matrix. As we will see, however, they carry over, at least qualitatively, to the estimation of any linear dynamic model. In fact, the estimation of linear dynamic models is based on estimating correlation and covariance matrices.

DANGEROUS PATTERNS OF BEHAVIOR

One of the most serious mistakes that a financial modeler can make is to look for rare or unique patterns that look profitable in-sample but produce losses out-of-sample. This mistake is made easy by the availability of powerful computers that can explore large amounts of data: Any large data set contains a huge number of patterns, many of which look very profitable. Otherwise expressed, any large set of data, even if randomly generated, can be represented by models that appear to produce large profits. To see the point, perform the following simple experiment. Using a good random number generator,[10] generate a large number of independent random walks with zero drift. In sample, these random

---

[10] Random number generators are deterministic algorithms that generate patterns so complex to be practically random.

walks exhibit large profit opportunities. There are numerous reasons for this. In fact, if we perform a sufficiently large number of simulations, we will generate a number of paths that are arbitrarily close to any path we want. Many paths will look autocorrelated and will be indistinguishable from trend-stationary processes. In addition, many stochastic trends will be indistinguishable from deterministic drifts.

There is nothing surprising in the above phenomena. A stochastic process or a discrete time series is formed by all possible paths. For example, a trend stationary process and a random walk are formed by the same paths. What makes the difference between a trend-stationary process and a random walk are not the paths—which are exactly the same—but the probability assignments. Suppose processes are discrete, for example because time is discrete and prices move by only discrete amounts. Any computer simulation is ultimately a discrete process, though the granularity of the process is very small. In this discrete case, we can assign a discrete probability to each path. The difference between processes is the probability assigned to each path. In a large sample, even low probability paths will occur, albeit in small numbers.

In a very large data set, almost any path will be approximated by some path in the sample. If the computer generates a sufficiently large number of random paths, we will come arbitrarily close to any given path, including, for example, to any path that passes the test for trend stationarity. In any large set of price processes, one will therefore always find numerous interesting paths, such as cointegrated pairs and trend-stationary processes.

To avoid looking for ephemeral patterns, we must stick rigorously to the paradigm of machine learning and statistical tests. This sounds conceptually simple, but it is very difficult to do in practice. It means that we have to decide the level of confidence that we find acceptable and then compute probability distributions *for the entire sample*. This has somewhat counterintuitive consequences. We illustrate this point using as an example the search for cointegrated pairs; the same reasoning applies to any statistical property.

Suppose that we have to decide whether a given pair of time series is cointegrated or not. We can use one of the many cointegration tests. If the time series are short, no test will be convincing; the longer the time series, the more convincing the test. The problem with economic data is that no test is really convincing as the confidence level is generally in the range of 95% or 99%. Whatever confidence level we choose, given one or a small number of pairs, we decide the cointegration properties of each pair individually. For example, in macroeconomic studies where only a few time series are given, we decide if a given pair of time series is cointegrated or not by looking at the cointegration test for that pair.

Does having a large number of data series, for example 500 price time series, require any change in the testing methodology? The answer, in fact, is that *additional* care is required: in a large data set, for the reasons we outlined above, any pattern can be approximated. One has to look at the probability that a pattern will appear in that data set. In the example of cointegration, if one finds, say, ten cointegrated pairs in 500 time series, the question to ask is: What is the probability that in 500 time series 10 time series are cointegrated? Answering this question is not easy because the properties of pairs are not independent. In fact, given three series a, b, and c we can form three distinct pairs whose cointegration properties are not, however, mutually independent. This makes calculations difficult.

To illustrate the above, let us generate a simulated random walk using the following formula:

$$X(i) = X(i-1) + \varepsilon(i)$$
$$X(1) = 1$$

where $X(i)$ is a random vector with 500 elements, and the noise term is generated with a random number generator as 500 independent normally distributed zero-mean unitary-variance numbers. Now run simulations for 500 steps. Next, eliminate linear trends from each realization.[11] A sample of three typical realizations of the random walks is illustrated in Exhibit 13.8 and the corresponding residuals after detrending in Exhibit 13.9.

Now run the cointegration test at a 99% confidence level on each possible pair. In a sample of 10 simulation runs, we obtain the following number of pairs that pass the cointegration test: 74, 75, 89, 73, 65, 91, 91, 93, 84, 62. There are in total

$$\binom{500}{2} = \frac{500 \times 499}{2} = 124{,}750 \text{ distinct pairs}$$

If cointegration properties of pairs were independent, given 500 random walks, on the average we should find 124 pairs that pass the cointegration test at the 99% confidence level. However, cointegration properties of pairs are not independent for the reasons mentioned above. This explains why we obtained a smaller number of pairs than expected. This example illustrates the usefulness of running Monte Carlo experiments to determine the number of cointegrated pairs found in random walks.

---

[11] Cointegration tests can handle linear trends. We detrended for clarity of illustrations.

EXHIBIT 13.8   A Sample of Three Typical Realizations of a 500-Step Random Walk with Their Trends

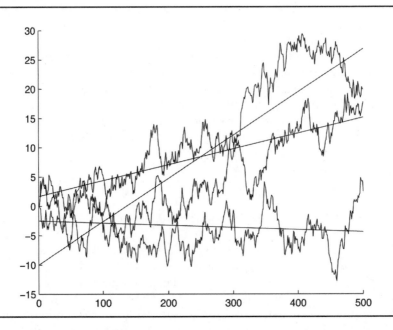

EXHIBIT 13.9   The Residuals of the Same Random Walks after Detrending

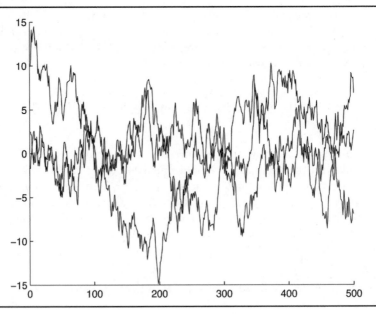

If, however, the patterns we are looking for are all independent, calculations are relatively straightforward. Suppose we are looking for stationary series applying an appropriate test at a 99% confidence interval. This means that a sample random walk has a 1% probability of passing the test (i.e., to be wrongly accepted as stationary) and a 99% probability of being correctly rejected. In this case, the probability distribution of the number of paths that pass the stationarity test given a sample of 500 generated random walks is a binomial distribution with probabilities $p = 0.01$ and $q = 1 - p = 0.99$ and mean 5.

We apply criteria of this type very often in our professional and private lives. For example, suppose that an inspector has to decide whether to accept or reject a supply of spare parts. The inspector knows that on average one part in 100 is defective. He randomly chooses a part in a lot of 100 parts. If the part is defective, he is likely to ask for additional tests before accepting the lot. Suppose now that he tests 100 parts from 100 different lots of 100 parts and finds only one defective part. He is likely to accept the 100 lots because the incidence of faulty parts is what he expected it to be, that is, one in 100. The point is that we are looking for statistical properties, not real identifiable objects.

A profitable price time series is not a recognizable object. We find what seems to be a profitable time series but we cannot draw any conclusion because the level of the "authenticity test" of each series is low. When looking at very large data sets, we have to make data work for us and not against us, examining the entire sample. For example, a modeler who would define a "pair trading strategy"[12] based on the cointegrated pair in the previous example would be disappointed.[13]

We can conclude that it is always good practice is to test any model or pattern recognition method against a surrogated random sample generated with the same statistical characteristics as the empirical ones. For example, it is always good practice to test any model and any strategy intended to find excess returns on a set of computer-generated random walks. If the proposed strategy finds profit in computer-generated random walks, it is highly advisable to rethink the strategy.

---

[12] In a pair trading strategy, an investor selects pairs from a stock universe and maintains a market neutral (i.e., zero beta) long-short portfolio of several pairs of stocks with a mean-reverting spread. When there are imbalances in the market causing the spread to diverge, the investor seeks to determine the reason for the divergence. If the investor believes that the spread will revert, he or she takes a position in the two stocks to capitalize on the reversion.

[13] We ran extensive Monte Carlo simulations to compare the number of cointegrated pairs among the stocks in the S&P 500 index for the period 2001–2004 and in computer-generated random walks. We found that the number of cointegrated pairs is slightly larger in the real series than in the simulated random walks.

DATA SNOOPING

Given the scarcity of data and the basically uncertain nature of any econometric model, it is generally required to calibrate models on some data set, the so-called *training set*, and test them on another data set, the *test set*. In other words, it is necessary to perform an out-of-sample validation on a separate test set. The rationale for this procedure is that any machine-learning process—or even the calibration mechanism itself —is a heuristic methodology, not a true discovery process. Models determined through a machine-learning process must be checked against the reality of out-of-sample validation. Failure to do so is referred to as *data snooping*, that is, performing training and tests on the same data set.

Out-of-sample validation is typical of machine-learning methods. Learning entails models with unbounded capabilities of approximation constrained by somewhat artificial mechanisms such as a penalty function. This learning mechanism is often effective but there is no guarantee that it will produce a good model. Therefore, the learning process is considered *discovery heuristics*. The true validation test, say the experiments, has to be performed on the test set. Needless to say, the test set must be large and cover all possible patterns, at least in some approximate sense. For example, in order to test a trading strategy one would need to test data in many different market conditions: with high volatility and low volatility, in expansionary and recessionary economic periods, under different correlation situations, and so on.

Data snooping is not always easy to understand or detect. Suppose that a modeler wants to build the DGP of a time series. A DGP is often embodied in a set of difference equations with parameters to be estimated. Suppose that four years of data of a set of time series are available. A modeler might be tempted to use the entire four years to perform a "robust" model calibration and to "test" the model on the last year. This is an example of data snooping that might be difficult to recognize and to avoid. In fact, one might (erroneously) reason as follows. If there is a true DGP, it is more likely that it is "discovered" on a four-year sample than on shorter samples. If there is a true DGP, data snooping is basically innocuous and it is therefore correct to use the entire data set. On the other hand, if there is no stable DGP, then it does not make sense to calibrate models as their coefficients would be basically noise.

This reasoning is wrong. In general, there is no guarantee that, even if a true DGP exists, a learning algorithm will learn it. Among the reasons for learning failure are (1) the slow convergence of algorithms which might require more data than that available and (2) the possibility of getting stuck in local optima. However, the real danger is the possibility that no true DGP exists. Should this be the case, the learning algorithm might converge to a false solution or not converge at all. We illustrated this fact earlier in this chapter where we showed how it is possible to successfully fit a low dimensionality polynomial to a randomly generated path.

There are other forms of data snooping. Suppose that a modeling team works on a sample of stock price data to find a profitable trading strategy. Suppose that they respect all of the above criteria of separation of the training set and the data set. Different strategies are tried and those that do not perform are rejected. Though sound criteria are used, there is still the possibility that by trial and error the team hits a strategy that performs well in sample but poorly when applied in the real world. Another form of hidden data snooping is when a methodology is finely calibrated to sample data. Again, there is the possibility that by trial and error one finds a calibration parameterization that works well in sample and poorly in the real world.

There is no sound theoretical way to avoid this problem *ex ante*. In practice, the answer is to separate the sets of training data and test data, and to decide on the existence of a DGP in function of performance on the test data. However, this type of procedure requires a lot of data. "Resampling" techniques have been proposed to alleviate the problem. Intuitively, the idea behind resampling methods is that a stable DGP calibrated on any portion of the data should work on the remaining data. Widely used resampling techniques include "leave-one-out" and "bootstrapping." The bootstrap technique creates surrogated data from the initial sample data.[14]

Data snooping is a defect of training processes which must be controlled but which is very difficult to avoid given the size of data samples currently available. Suppose samples in the range of ten years are available.[15] One can partition these data and perform a single test free from data snooping biases. However, if the test fails, one has to start all over again and design a new strategy. The process of redesigning the modeling strategy might have to be repeated several times over before an acceptable solution is found. Inevitably, repeating the process on the same data includes the risk of data snooping. The real danger in data snooping is the

---

[14] The bootstrap is an important technique but its description goes beyond the scope of this book. For a useful review of bootstrapping, see A. C. Davison and D. V. Hinkley, *Bootstrap Methods and their Application* (Cambridge: Cambridge University Press, 1997). The name "bootstrap" is given to this methodology because of the initial skepticism on its soundness: The name comes from the fictional character, the Baron of Munchausen, who pulled himself out of a well climbing on his own bootstrap.

[15] Technically much longer data sets on financial markets, up to 50 years of price data, are available. While useful for some applications, these data are useless for most asset management applications given the changes in the structure of the economy.

possibility that by trial and error or by optimization, one hits upon a model that casually performs well on the sample data but that will perform poorly in real-world forecasts. Fabozzi, Focardi, and Ma explore at length different ways in which data snooping and other biases might enter the model discovery process and propose a methodology to minimize the risk of biases as will be explained in the last section of this chapter.[16]

SURVIVORSHIP BIASES AND OTHER SAMPLE DEFECTS

We now examine possible defects of the sample data themselves. In addition to errors and missing data, one of the most common (and dangerous) defects of sample data are the so-called *survivorship biases*. The survivorship bias is a consequence of selecting time series, in particular asset price time series, based on criteria that apply at the end of the period. For example, suppose a sample contains 10 years of price data for all stocks that are in the S&P 500 today and that existed for the last 10 years. This sample, apparently well-formed, is however biased: The selection, in fact, is made on the stocks of companies that are in the S&P 500 today, that is, those companies that have "survived" in sufficiently good shape to still be in the S&P 500 aggregate. The bias comes from the fact that many of the surviving companies successfully passed through some difficult period. Surviving the difficulty is a form of reversion to the mean that produces trading profits. However, at the moment of the crisis it was impossible to predict which companies in difficulty would indeed have survived.

To gauge the importance of the surviroship bias, consider a strategy that goes short on a fraction of the assets with the highest price and long on the corresponding fraction with the lowest price. This strategy might appear highly profitable in sample. Looking at the behavior of this strategy, however, it becomes clear that profits are very large in the central region of the sample and disappear approaching the present day. This behavior should raise flags. Although any valid trading strategy will have good and bad periods, profit reduction when approaching the present day should command heightened attention.

Avoiding the survivorship bias seems simple in principle: It might seem sufficient to base any sample selection at the moment where the forecast begins, so that no invalid information enters the strategy prior to trading. However, the fact that companies are founded, merged, and closed plays havoc with simple models. In fact, calibrating a simple

---

[16] Frank J. Fabozzi, Sergio M. Focardi, and Christopher K. Ma, "Implementable Quantitative Research and Investment Strategies," *Journal of Alternative Investment* 8 (Fall 2005), pp. 71–79.

model requires data of assets that exist over the entire training period. This in itself introduces a potentially substantial training bias.

A simple model cannot handle processes that start or end in the middle of the training period. On the other hand, models that take into account the foundation or closing of firms cannot be simple. Consider for example, a simple linear autoregressive model. Any addition or deletion of companies introduces a nonlinearity in the model and precludes using standard tools such as the OLS method (see Chapters 15 and 16).

There is no ideal solution. Care is required in estimating possible performance biases consequent to sample biases. Suppose that we make a forecast of return processes based on models trained on the past three or four years of returns data on the same processes that we want to forecast. Clearly there is no data snooping, as we use only information available prior to forecasting. However, it should be understood that we are estimating our models on data that contain biases. If the selection of companies to forecast is subject to strong criteria, for example companies that belong to a major index, it is likely that the model will suffer a loss of performance. This is due to the fact that models will be trained on spurious past performance. If the modeler is constrained to work on a specific stock selection, for example because he has to create an active strategy against a selected benchmark, he might want to consider Bayesian techniques to reduce the biases.[17]

The survivorship bias is not the only possible bias of sample data. More in general, any selection of data contains some bias. Some of these biases are intentional. For example selecting large caps or small caps introduces special behavioral biases that are intentional. However, other selection biases are more difficult to appreciate. In general, any selection based on belonging to indexes introduces index-specific biases in addition to the survivorship bias. Consider that presently thousands of indexes are in use—the FTSE alone has created some 60,000. Institutional investors and their consultants use these indexes to create asset allocation strategies and then give the indexes to asset managers for active management.

Anyone creating active management strategies based on these indexes should be aware of the biases inherent in the indexes when building their strategies. Data snooping applied to carefully crafted stock selection can result in poor performance because the asset selection process inherent in the index formation process can produce very good results in sample; these results vanish out-of-sample as "snow under the sun."

---

[17] Bayesian techniques, named after the 18th century English statistician Thomas Bayes, consider probability distributions uncertain and allow the consideration of prior information that one might have about a given set of phenomena.

MOVING TRAINING WINDOWS

Thus far we assumed that the DGP exists as a time-invariant model. Can we also assume that the DGP varies and that it can be estimated on a moving window? If yes, how can it be tested? These are complex questions that do not admit an easy answer. It is often assumed that the economy undergoes "structural breaks" or "regime shifts" (i.e., that the economy undergoes discrete changes at fixed or random time points).

If the economy is indeed subject to breaks or shifts and the time between breaks is long, models would perform well for a while and then, at the point of the break, performance would degrade until a new model is learned. If regime changes are frequent and the interval between the changes short, one could use a model that includes the changes. The result is typically a nonlinear model such as the Markov-switching models (see Chapters 12 and 16). Estimating models of this type is very onerous given the nonlinearities inherent in the model and the long training period required.

There is however another possibility which is common in modeling. Consider a model which has a defined structure, for example a linear VAR model, but whose coefficients are allowed to change in time with the moving of the training window. In practice, most models used work in this way as they are periodically recalibrated. The rationale of this strategy is that models are assumed to be approximate and sufficiently stable for only short periods of time. Clearly there is a trade-off between the advantage of using long training sets and the disadvantage that a long training set includes too much change.

Intuitively, if model coefficients change rapidly, this means that the model coefficients are noisy and do not carry genuine information. We have seen an example above in the simple case of estimating a correlation matrix. Therefore, it is not sufficient to simply reestimate the model: One must determine how to separate the noise from the information in the coefficients. For example, a large VAR model used to represent prices or returns will generally be unstable. It would not make sense to reestimate the model frequently; one should first reduce model dimensionality with, for example, factor analysis. Once model dimensionality has been reduced, coefficients should change slowly. If they continue to change rapidly, the model structure cannot be considered appropriate. One might, for example, have ignored fat tails or essential nonlinearities.

How can we quantitatively estimate an acceptable rate of change for model coefficients? Are we introducing a special form of data snooping in calibrating the training window? Clearly the answer depends on the nature of the true DGP—assuming that one exists. It is easy to construct artificially DGPs that change slowly in time so that the learning process can progressively adapt to them. It is also easy to construct true DGPs that will play havoc with any method based on a moving training window. For example, if one constructs a linear model where coefficients change systematically at a frequency comparable with a minimum training window, it will not be possible to estimate the process as a linear model estimated on a moving window.

Calibrating a training window is clearly an empirical question. However, it is easy to see that calibration can introduce a subtle form of data snooping. Suppose a rather long set of time series is given, say six to eight years, and that one selects a family of models to capture the DGP of the series and to build an investment strategy. Testing the strategy calls for calibrating a moving window. Different moving windows are tested. Even if training and test data are kept separate so that forecasts are never performed on the training data, clearly the methodology is tested on the same data on which the models are learned.

Other problems with data snooping stem from the psychology of modeling. A key precept that helps to avoid biases is the following: modeling hunches should be based on theoretical reasoning and not on looking at the data. This statement might seem inimical to an empirical enterprise, an example of the danger of "clear reasoning" mentioned above. Still it is true that by looking at data too long one might develop hunches that are sample-specific. There is some tension between looking at empirical data to discover how they behave and avoiding to capture the idiosyncratic behavior of the available data.

In his best-seller *Chaos: Making a New Science*, James Gleick reports that one of the initiators of chaos theory used to spend long hours flying planes (at his own expense) just to contemplate clouds to develop a feeling for their chaotic movement. Obviously there is no danger of data snooping in this case as there are plenty of clouds on which any modeling idea can be tested. In other cases, important discoveries have been made working on relatively small data samples. The 20th century English hydrologist Harold Hurst developed his ideas of rescaled range analysis from the yearly behavior of the Nile River, approximately 500 years of sample data, not a huge data sample.

Clearly simplicity (i.e., having only a small number of parameters to calibrate) is a virtue in modeling. A simple model that works well should be favored over a complex model that might produce unpredictable results. Nonlinear models in particular are always subject to the danger of unpredictable chaotic behavior. It was a surprising discovery that even simple maps originate highly complex behavior. The conclusion is that every step of the discovery process has to be checked for empirical, theoretical, and logical consistency.

MODEL RISK

As we have seen above, any model choice and estimation process might result in biases and poor performance. In other words, any model selection process is subject to *model risk*. One might well ask if it is possible to mitigate model risk. In statistics, there is a long tradition, initiated by the 18th century English mathematician Thomas Bayes, of considering uncertain not only individual outcomes but the probability distribution itself. It is therefore natural to see if ideas from Bayesian statistics and related concepts could be applied to mitigate model risk.

A simple idea which is widely used in practice is to take the average of different models. This idea can take different forms. Suppose that we have to estimate a variance-covariance matrix. It makes sense to take radically different estimates such as noisy empirical estimates and Capital Asset Pricing Model (CAPM) estimates that only consider covariances with the market portfolio and average. Averaging is done with the principle of *shrinkage*, that is, one does not form a pure average but weights the two matrices with weights a and $1 - a$ choosing a according to some optimality principle. This idea can be extended to dynamic models, weighting all coefficients in a model with a probability distribution. We will describe these concepts in more details in Chapter 17. Here, however, we want to make some additional qualitative considerations that lead to strategies in model selection.

There are two principal reasons for applying model risk mitigation. First, we might be uncertain as to which model is best, and so mitigate risk by diversification. Second, perhaps more cogent, we might believe that different models will perform differently under different circumstances. By averaging, we hope to reduce the volatility of our forecasts. It should be clear that averaging model results or working to produce an average model (i.e., averaging coefficients) are two different techniques. The level of difficulty involved is also different.

Averaging results is a simple matter. One estimates different models with different techniques, makes forecasts and then averages the forecasts. This simple idea can be extended to different contexts. For example, in rating stocks one might want to do an exponential averaging over past ratings, so that the *proposed* rating today is an exponential average of the *model* rating today and *model* ratings in the past. Obviously parameters must be set correctly, which again forces a careful analysis of possible data snooping biases. Whatever the averaging process one uses, the methodology should be carefully checked for statistical consistency. For example, one obtains quite different results applying methodologies based on averaging to stationary or nonstationary processes. The key principle is that averaging is used to eliminate noise, not genuine information.

Averaging models is more difficult than averaging results. In this case, the final result is a single model which is, in a sense the average of other models. Shrinkage of the covariance matrix is a simple example of averaging models. We will describe shrinkage and other techniques in Chapter 17.

MODEL SELECTION IN A NUTSHELL

It is now time to turn all the caveats into some positive approach to model selection. As remarked in Fabozzi, Focardi, and Ma,[18] any process of model selection must start with strong economic intuition. Data mining and machine learning alone are unlikely to produce significant positive results. The possibility that scientific discovery, and any creative process in general, can be "outsourced" to computers is still far from today's technological reality. A number of experimental Artificial Intelligence (AI) programs have indeed shown the ability to "discover" scientific laws. For example, the program KAM developed by Yip[19] is able to analyze nonlinear dynamic patterns and the program TETRAD[20] developed at Carnegie Mellon is able to discover causal relationships in data. However, practical applications of machine intelligence use AI as a tool to help perform specific tasks.

Economic intuition clearly entails an element of human creativity. As in any other scientific and technological endeavor, it is inherently dependent on individual abilities. Is there a body of true, shared science that any modeler can use? Or do modelers have to content themselves with only partial and uncertain findings reported in the literature? As of the writing of this book, the answer is probably a bit of both.

One would have a hard time identifying economic laws that have the status of true scientific laws. Principles such as the absence of arbitrage are probably what comes closest to a true scientific law but it is not, *per se*, very useful in finding, say, profitable trading strategies. Most economic findings are of an uncertain nature and are conditional on the structure of the economy or the markets.

---

[18] Fabozzi, Focardi, and Ma, "Implementable Quantitative Research and Investment Strategies."

[19] Kenneth Man-kam Yip, *KAM: Automatic Planning and Interpretation of Numerical Experiments Using Geometrical Methods*, PhD. Thesis, MIT, 1989.

[20] Clark Glymour, Richard Scheines, Peter Spirtes, and Kevin Kelly, *Discovering Causal Structure* (Orlando, FL: Academic Press, 1987).

It is fair to say that economic intuition is based on a number of broad economic principles plus a set of findings of an uncertain and local nature. Economic findings are statistically validated on a limited sample and probably hold only for a finite time span. Consider, for example, findings such as volatility clustering. One might claim that volatility clustering is ubiquitous and that it holds for every market. In a broad sense this is true. However, no volatility clustering model can claim the status of a law of nature as all volatility clustering models fail to explain some essential fact.

It is often argued that profitable investment strategies can be based only on secret proprietary discoveries. This is probably true but its importance should not be exaggerated. Secrecy is typically inimical to knowledge building. Secrets are also difficult to keep. Historically, the largest secret knowledge-building endeavors were related to military efforts. Some of these efforts were truly gigantic, such as the Manhattan project to develop the first atomic bomb. Industrial projects of a non-military nature are rarely based on a truly scientific breakthrough. They typically exploit existing knowledge.

Financial econometrics is probably no exception. Proprietary techniques are, in most cases, the application of more or less shared knowledge. There is no record of major economic breakthroughs made in secrecy by investment teams. Some firms have advantages in terms of data. Custodian banks, for example, can exploit data on economic flows which are not available to (or in any case are very expensive for) other entities. Until the recent past, availability of computing power was also a major advantage, reserved to only the biggest Wall Street firms; however computing power is now a commodity.

As a consequence, it is fair to say that economic intuition can be based on a vast amount of shared knowledge plus some proprietary discovery or interpretation. In the last 20 years, a number of computer methodologies were experimented with in the hope of discovering potentially important sources of profits. Among the most fascinating of these were nonlinear dynamics and chaos theory, as well as neural networks and genetic algorithms. None has lived up to initial expectations. With the maturing of techniques, one discovers that many new proposals are only a different language for existing ideas. In other cases, there is a substantial equivalence between theories.

After using intuition to develop an *ex ante* hypothesis, the process of model selection and calibration begins in earnest. This implies selecting a sample free from biases and determining a quality-control methodology. In the production phase, an independent risk control mechanism will be essential. A key point is that the discovery process should be linear. If at any point the development process does not meet the quality standards one should resist the temptation of adjusting parameters and go back to develop new economic intuition.

This process implies that there is plenty of economic intuition to work on. The modeler must have many ideas to develop. Ideas might range from the intuition that certain market segments have some specific behavior to the discovery that there are specific patterns of behavior with unexploited opportunities. In some cases it will be the application of ideas that are well known but have never been applied on a large scale.

A special feature of the model selection process is the level of uncertainty and noise. Models capture small amounts of information in a vast "sea of noise." Models are always uncertain, and so is their potential longevity. The psychology of discovery plays an important role. These considerations suggest the adoption of a rigorous objective research methodology. Exhibit 13.10 illustrates the work flow for a sound process of discovery of profitable strategies.[21]

An analyst working in financial econometrics is always confronted with the risk of finding an artifact that does not, in reality, exist. And, as we have seen, paradoxically one cannot look too hard at the data; this risks introducing biases formed by available but insufficient data sets. Even trying too many possible solutions, one risks falling into the trap of data snooping.

SUMMARY

- Model selection in financial econometrics requires a blend of theory, creativity, and machine learning.
- The machine-learning approach starts with a set of empirical data that we want to explain. Data are explained by a family of models that include an unbounded number of parameters and are able to fit data with arbitrary precision.
- There is a trade-off between model complexity and the size of the data sample. To implement this trade-off, ensuring that models have forecasting power, the fitting of sample data is constrained to avoid fitting noise. Constraints are embodied in criteria such as the *Akaike Information Criterion* (AIC) or the *Bayesian Information Criterion* (BIC).
- Economic data are generally scarce given the complexity of their patterns. This scarcity introduces uncertainty as regards our statistical estimates. It means that the data might be compatible with many different models with the same level of statistical confidence.

---

[21] For a further discussion, see Fabozzi, Focardi, and Ma, "Implementable Quantitative Research and Investment Strategies."

EXHIBIT 13.10   Process of Quantitative Research and Investment Strategy

Quantitative Research

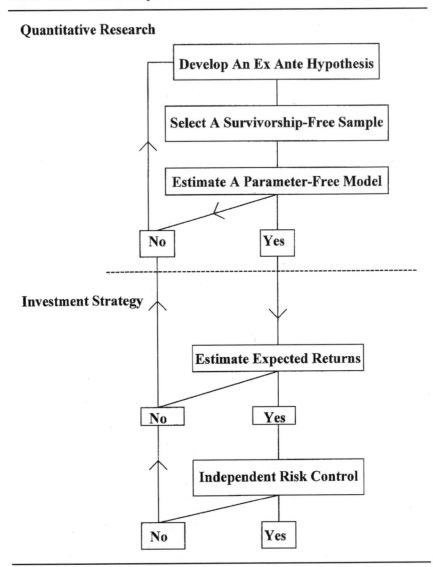

Source: Exhibit 1 in Frank J. Fabozzi, Sergio M. Focardi, and Christopher K. Ma, "Implementable Quantitative Research and Investment Strategies," *Journal of Alternative Investments* 8 (Fall 2005), p. 73.

- A serious mistake in model selection is to look for models that fit rare or unique patterns; such patterns are purely random and lack predictive power.

- Another mistake in model selection is data snooping, that is, fitting models to the same data that we want to explain. A sound model selection approach calls for a separation of sample data and test data: models are fitted to sample data and tested on test data.

- Because data are scarce, techniques have been devised to make optimal use of data; perhaps the most widely used of such techniques is bootstrapping.

- Financial data are also subject to "survivorship bias", that is, data are selected using criteria known only a posteriori, for example companies that are presently in the S&P 500. Survivorship bias induces biases in models and results in forecasting errors.

- Model risk is the risk that models are subject to forecasting errors in real data. Techniques to mitigate model risk include Bayesian techniques, averaging/shrinkage, and random coefficient models.

- A sound model selection methodology includes strong theoretical considerations, the rigorous separation of sample and testing data, and discipline to avoid data snooping.

Model Estimation and Model Risk Mitigation

Estimation of Regression Models

In previous chapters we described a number of probabilistic models that are used in finance. These models have to be estimated from empirical data, and this is where the concepts and methods of statistics come in. In this chapter, we learn how to make a link between empirical data, for example time series of prices or returns, and the probabilistic models that we believe represent them.

PROBABILITY THEORY AND STATISTICS

There is an important conceptual and practical distinction between probability theory and statistics. The former is the mathematical theory that formalizes the notion of uncertainty; the latter is the applied science used to estimate probabilities from data and make decisions under uncertainty. The idea of a quantitative measurement of uncertainty (i.e., probability) started in full earnest in the Renaissance. Much of the initial effort in the study of probability was motivated by the desire to realize gains in gambling.[1] The 16th century Italian mathematician, physician, philosopher, and gambler Girolamo Cardano was the first to write extensively on probability. Among his numerous writings, Car-

---

[1] Before modern times, the study of probability was considered a moral fault: It was associated with gambling and thought to encourage the concept of uncertainty and relativism as opposed to the quest for unassailable truth. In his preface to *Percolation and Disordered Systems*, Geoffrey Grimmett quotes the *Encyclopedie* of Diderot and D'Alembert published in Geneva in 1778 where probability is described as "the abominable doctrine of opinions made probable by the decision of a probabilist" (in *Lectures in Probability Theory and Statistics, Ecole d'Eté de Probabilités de Saint-Flour XXVI-1996*, Springer Lecture Notes in Maths no. 1665, P. Bernard (ed.), 1997).

dano left us a treatise on gambling called *Liber de Ludo Aleae (Book on Games of Chance)*.[2]

The concept of probability has provoked much philosophical debate, the essence of which is: Does probability represent our ignorance or is it a true feature of the world? Einstein's widely quoted phrase, "God does not play dice," epitomizes the classical side of the debate: Things happen according to a predetermined order and probability is a measure of our ignorance. The so-called *Copenhagen School*, formed around Niels Bohr and which represents mainstream quantum mechanics, takes the other side: Uncertainty is an ineliminable feature of the world.[3] Finance theory considers uncertainty ineliminable: Adding variables and observations might reduce uncertainty, but never eliminates it.

Statistics—a methodology to make inferences from a sample to the entire "population," for example to forecast future returns from past returns—is a more recent discipline; it dates from the 18th century. Its center of interest is real-life problems. Early probabilists were not much concerned with statistics. Their interest was to make inferences from basically equiprobable outcomes such as those found in the throwing of dice. Nor was statistics of interest to physicists who, at the time of Newton, were concerned with exact laws such as the movement of the planets.

Newton's friend, the French mathematician Abraham De Moivre (1667–1754) was the first to describe what was later called the Gaussian (or normal) distribution, now ubiquitous in financial modeling.[4] It is interesting to note that De Moivre made a meager living teaching mathematics to currency traders on an open-air bench in London. Next came the introduction of crucial concepts such as *prior information* and the theorem on *conditional probabilities* that we owe to the 18th century English mathematician Thomas Bayes. Today Bayesian statistics is a

---

[2] Peter Bernstein's *Against the Gods: The Remarkable Story of Risk* (New York: John Wiley & Sons, 1996) offers a lively account of Cardano's life and the development of the ideas of probability and risk.

[3] Things have become more complicated as physicists now question the reality of the physical world. According to the Copenhagen School, the laws of physics are only "recipes" to predict experiments without any interpretation in terms of a physical reality. What is deeply puzzling today is that even the spatial localization of physical laws is under question. The interested reader can consult, for example, Bernard d'Espagnat, *A la Recherche du Réel* (Paris: Gauthier-Villars, 1985); Alistair Rae, *Quantum Physics: Illusion or Reality?* (Cambridge: Cambridge University Press, 1986); or, at a higher mathematical level, Michael Redhead, *Incompleteness, Nonlocality, and Realism* (Oxford: Clarendon Press, 1987).

[4] De Moivre predicted the date of his own death. He observed that he slept 15 more minutes per day each day. Using progression, he calculated when he would have slept exactly 24 hours. He was right!

fundamental tool in financial modeling, used in mainstream applications such as the Black-Litterman model.

The end of the 18th century witnessed a number of other important discoveries for statistics. The German physicist and mathematician Carl Frederick Gauss and his French colleague Adrien Marie Legendre introduced the concept of *regression* and the *Ordinary Least Squares* (OLS) method. Gauss was later to prove that OLS estimates are the best unbiased linear estimators. The importance of OLS estimates in financial modeling can hardly be overestimated: many linear models are estimated with this method, now implemented in every popular statistical software package.

It was only in the 19th century that statistics was formalized as a scientific methodology. Scientists began collecting large amounts of data on phenomena that escape description in terms of exact laws, such a human genetics and biometrics. The British explorer, anthropologist, and cousin of James Darwin, Francis Galton (1822–1911) collected and statistically described a vast amount of data on hereditary phenomena making use of regressions.[5] The methodology of collecting data and testing hypotheses was to be described by Ronald Fisher (1890–1962). William Gosset (1876–1937), a Guinness brewery chemist writing under the pen name Student, introduced the Student-t sample distribution and invented the t-test. Both are widely used today in financial estimation. Following on the work of Galton, Karl Pearson (1857–1936) made two important contributions to regression analysis: he introduced the correlation coefficient and invented the chi-squared test.[6]

Fisher and Pearson were to clash bitterly on questions of statistical theory. Pearson was mainly interested in deriving correlations from a large sample; following Gosset, Fisher was interested in finding causal laws from small samples. The distinction between causation as opposed to mere correlation is of great importance in both applied and theoretical work in financial modeling and in economics. A crucial clarification of the concept of causation was provided by Nobel prize winner Clive Granger, who introduced a concept of causation now called *Granger causality* (or causality in the sense of Granger).[7] Granger causality is essentially dynamic in the sense that a variable X does not cause Y in the

---

[5] Today Galton's reputation is tarnished by his interest in eugenics. Hoping to improve the quality of human beings, Galton became an advocate of eugenics, including the imposition of breeding restrictions.

[6] We owe the invention of fingerprinting to Pearson.

[7] Clive Granger shared the 2003 Nobel Memorial Prize in Economic Sciences with Robert Engle.

sense of Granger if the value of Y at time t is independent of the values of X prior to time t.[8]

Other important contributions were to come from Jerzy Neyman (1894–1981), who introduced the concept of confidence intervals, so widely used today in measurements such as Value-at-Risk (VaR). The study of autoregressive time series was introduced by the Scot George Udny Yule (1871–1951), and factor analysis by Harold Hotelling (1895–1973). The Hungarian mathematician Abraham Wald (1902–1950) made seminal contributions to time series analysis, introducing a basic representation of time series, and to decision theory where he formalized the notion of sequential analysis. The Norwegian mathematician Herman Ole Andreas Wold (1908–1992) proved a basic representation theorem for stationary time series.

Though most modern statistical conceptual tools were well known before we had computers, it was the advent of high-performance computing and cheap storage devices in the later part of the 20th century that enabled a much wider use of statistics in science and business. Without today's storage capability and fast computers, going beyond simple regression analysis was simply not possible. In finance, the availability of tapes with daily closing stock prices was considered a major achievement in the 1960s. Today, we have high-frequency (or intraday) data on individual transactions. These data sets are several thousand times bigger than daily closing data sets. Information technology has changed the science of statistics, allowing the use of dynamic models such as the Autoregression Conditional Heteroschedastic (ARCH)/ Generalized ARCH (GARCH) models, stochastic volatility models, Vector Autoregressive (VAR) models, and the cointegration models discussed in previous chapters.

POPULATIONS OF PRICES AND RETURNS

We now discuss the role of statistics in financial modeling. As remarked above, statistics makes inferences from a sample to a population. By "population" we mean a set of possible observations, real or idealized. The term population derives from the early use of statistics, when phenomena being studied were human populations. It is perhaps a bit curious in finance where populations are ensembles of observations of prices, returns, rates, and other economic data, but we will use the term which is, by now, conventional. In most practical statistical applica-

---

[8] Granger causality is in the spirit of classical physics where causation means that dynamic differential equations perfectly determine the evolution of a system from initial and boundary conditions.

tions, the population is identified with a physical reality that is too big to be directly analyzed. For example, in medicine "population" refers to the entire human population of the area under study, say a nation or a continent. Because it is practically impossible to reach the entire population, a statistical study is performed on a much smaller sample.

In financial modeling, however, the population is an idealization as we have only one realization of each time series which is, in itself, supposed to be extracted from a population of time series. For example, portfolio managers and quantitative analysts are generally interested in forecasting future prices. They might use long series of past data to make predictions on a short time horizon. Suppose an analyst uses three years of past price data, say from January 1, 2002 to December 31, 2004, to make predictions about the next three months of data, say from January 1, 2005 to March 30, 2005. What is the sample and what is the population? It would be a mistake to believe that the entire population is the period from January 1, 2002 to March 30, 2005. The population is an idealization, from which all data used are supposedly extracted. In practice, as observed in Chapter 13, this implies that financial predictions can never be properly tested.

One might object that the true population is always an idealization and that the link between any real population and the abstract probability distribution is regulated by special principles. This is true. From a mathematical point of view, probability is based on a triple (Ω, F, P) where Ω is the set of possible outcomes, F is the set of possible events, and P is a set function that represents probabilities. The link between these abstract concepts and any empirical quantity is not prescribed either by mathematics or by empirical observations. *Ad hoc* assumptions are required.

In practice, the usual assumption is that, in very large samples, probabilities and relative frequencies are very close. Although any empirical population is compatible with any theoretical distribution, in applied work we consider very unlikely events to be impossible. This might sound confusing because in applied work we do consider unlikely events, for example extreme tail events in financial risk analysis. Consider, however, that in estimating the probability of tail events we assume that very unlikely tail events do not (or are not supposed to) occur. Note that this is not the same as the Law of Large Numbers (LLN), which is a purely logical statement. Consider, however, that in finance empirical populations are usually too small to offer frequencies very close to any theoretical distribution.

ESTIMATION AT WORK

In making financial predictions, the interest is not in the raw distribution of financial quantities such as prices or returns but in the idealized, underlying mechanism that is supposed to generate the data, that is, the data generating process or DGP. This means that a typical population in financial modeling is formed taking n-tuples of consecutive data, say n-tuples of consecutive prices or returns. The distribution of interest is the joint distribution of these data, or, better, the conditional distribution of present data given past data. Distributions of this type are assumed to be sufficiently time-invariant to be learnable from past data.

Whether or not there is indeed a true DGP impinges on whether the future repeats the past. This question is ever-present in the context of our ability to forecast financial values: Is past performance a guarantee of future performance? It should be remarked that, to make any knowledge possible, the future must somehow repeat the past. If the future does not repeat the past, at least at the level of DGP, no knowledge is possible. However, we cannot take a naive view that would have the future repeat the past in a simple sense. For example, we cannot assume that a stock price will keep going up because it has been going up for some time. What eventually remains stable is the generating mechanism, that is, the DGP. The problem with financial modeling is that we do not know what repeats what, that is, we do not know what the correct DGP is. In addition, any DGP is subject to possibly abrupt and unpredictable changes.

The starting point of financial modeling is generally a tentative DGP. To illustrate the point, suppose, that the DGP is a linear model, say a bivariate Vector Autoregressive model, denoted by VAR(2)

$$X_i = a_{11}X_{i-1} + a_{12}Y_{i-1} + \varepsilon_{1,i}$$
$$Y_i = a_{21}X_{i-1} + a_{22}Y_{i-1} + \varepsilon_{2,i}$$
$$i = 1, 2, ..., T$$

The objective of the estimation process is (1) to estimate the model parameters (the a_{ij}) and (2) to estimate the parameters of the distributions of X, Y and of the noise term. One might or might not assume a specific form for the distributions.

This calls for the discussion of the following key statistical concepts:

- Estimators
- Sample distribution
- Critical values and confidence intervals.

Let us start with estimators.

ESTIMATORS

To estimate a statistical model is to estimate its parameters from sample data. For example, given a sample of historical stock returns R_i, $i = 1, 2, \ldots, T$, a portfolio manager might want to estimate the standard deviation of their distribution. Or, as mentioned above, an analyst might want to estimate the coefficients in a VAR model. The latter are a vector of parameters that describe the conditional distribution embodied in the VAR model. The process of estimation can be described as follows. Suppose that a population with a distribution f is given and that μ is a constant parameter or a vector of constant parameters of the distribution f. Now consider a sample of N elements X_i, $i = 1, 2, \ldots, N$ extracted from the population. An estimator $\hat{\mu}$ of the parameter μ is a function $\hat{\mu} = g(X_1, \ldots, X_N)$ of the sample which produces numbers close to the parameter μ.

In the case of VAR systems, it is convenient to estimate the model parameters from the joint distribution of the noise random vector. For example, rewrite the VAR(2) model of the example above as follows:

$$X_i - a_{11}X_{i-1} - a_{12}Y_{i-1} = \varepsilon_{1,i}$$
$$Y_i - a_{21}X_{i-1} - a_{22}Y_{i-1} = \varepsilon_{2,i}$$

The distribution of the noise vector is a multivariate distribution whose parameters are the model parameters:

$$\varepsilon = (\varepsilon_{1,i}\,\varepsilon_{2,i})' \sim D(x, y, v, w \,|\, a_{11}, a_{12}, a_{21}, a_{22})$$

Any estimator is characterized by several important properties, among which the following two are fundamental:

- ■ An estimator $\hat{\mu}$ is called *unbiased* if the mean of the estimator equals the true parameter μ: $E(\hat{\mu}) = \mu$ for any sample size.
- ■ An estimator $\hat{\mu}$ is called *consistent* if the limit in probability of the estimator equals the true parameter μ: plim $(\hat{\mu}) = \mu$.

Note that the above are *theoretical properties* of the distribution f and of the estimators. They are not facts that can be ascertained empirically; that is, there is no logical leap from probability to real data. For example, an estimator is unbiased if the probabilistic *mean* of the estimator equals the true parameter. Note also that an estimator can be consistent but biased as the bias might progressively disappear as the sample size grows.

SAMPLING DISTRIBUTIONS

Any estimation process yields results that depend on the specific sample data. As sample data are random variables, estimated parameters that are functions of the sample data are also random variables. Consider, for example, the estimation of a VAR(2) model:

$$X_i = a_{11}X_{i-1} + a_{12}Y_{i-1} + \varepsilon_{1,i}$$
$$Y_i = a_{21}X_{i-1} + a_{22}Y_{i-1} + \varepsilon_{2,i}$$
$$i = 1, 2, ..., T$$

from empirical time series data. The empirical data that form the empirical time series must be considered a sample extracted from a population. As a consequence, the model parameters estimated on the sample (i.e., the a_{ij}) are random variables characterized by a probability distribution.

Sampling distributions is critical for testing and choosing hypotheses because, in general, we do not know if the model we are estimating is the correct model: Any model is only a scientific hypothesis. Often two competing models explain the same data. We have to choose which of the models is more faithful. We therefore formulate a hypothesis and decide on the basis of observations. For example, we formulate the hypothesis that a given time series is integrated. If a series is integrated, its autocorrelation coefficient is unity. But because samples vary, no observation will yield exactly unity, even if the series is indeed integrated. However, if we know the sampling distribution, we can formulate a decision rule which allows us to determine if a series is integrated even if the estimated autocorrelation parameter has a value other than one.

The probability distributions of a model's parameters depend on the estimation method. In some cases, they can be expressed as explicit functions of the sample data. For example, as we will see in the section on regression, the regression parameters are algebraic functions of sample data. In other cases, however, it might be impossible to express estimators as explicit functions of sample data. For example, some estimators used in the popular *Augmented Dickey-Fuller* (ADF) test for determining if a series is integrated or not are functionals of Wiener processes.

The probability distribution of estimators clearly depends on the probability distribution of sample data. Determining the distribution of parameters is a rather difficult task. In cases such as simple regressions, one might assume that variables have given distributions, for example normal distributions. However, in complex models, one cannot assume an arbitrary distribution for sample data. For example, data generated by a VAR(2) model are constrained by the model itself. One has to assume a distribution of initial values and a distribution for the noise terms.

We illustrate the problem of sampling distributions with the simple case of determining the parameters of a normal distribution. Consider a sample of N elements X_i, $i = 1, 2, \ldots, N$ extracted independently from a normally distributed population with distribution $N(\mu, \sigma^2)$. In this case, it is known that the empirical mean

$$\bar{\mu} = \frac{1}{N} \sum_{i=1}^{N} X_i$$

and the empirical variance

$$\bar{\sigma}^2 = \frac{1}{N} \sum_{i=1}^{N} (X_i - \mu)^2$$

are unbiased estimators of μ and σ^2 respectively.[9]

If we assume that the sample data are independent random draws from the sample population, then the empirical mean is the rescaled sum of normally distributed data and is therefore normally distributed. The empirical variance is the sum of the square of independent, normally distributed variables. The distribution of the sum of the square of k independent normal variables is known as a Chi-square distribution with k degrees of freedom (or χ^2-distribution with k degrees of freedom). For large values of k, the χ^2 distribution is approximated by a normal distribution. Therefore, for large samples, both the empirical mean and the empirical variance are normally distributed.

To illustrate the above, we generated 2 million random numbers extracted from a normal distribution with mean 0 and unitary variance. We then computed the mean and variance on 100,000 samples of 20 points, each selected from the given population. Mean and variance change from sample to sample as shown in Exhibit 14.1. The distribution of sample variance is not normal but is approximated by a χ^2 distribution. If we repeat the same calculations on samples of 100 points each, we see that both empirical mean and variance are normally distributed as shown in Exhibit 14.2.

Though sampling distributions can be very complex, they typically simplify in the limit of very large samples. The asymptotic theory of estimators studies the distribution of estimators in large samples. We

---

[9] The empirical mean and the empirical variance are unbiased estimators of the true mean and variance not only for the normal distribution but also for any distribution with finite second moments.

EXHIBIT 14.1 Sampling Distribution of the Mean and Variance for a Sample of 20 Elements Each

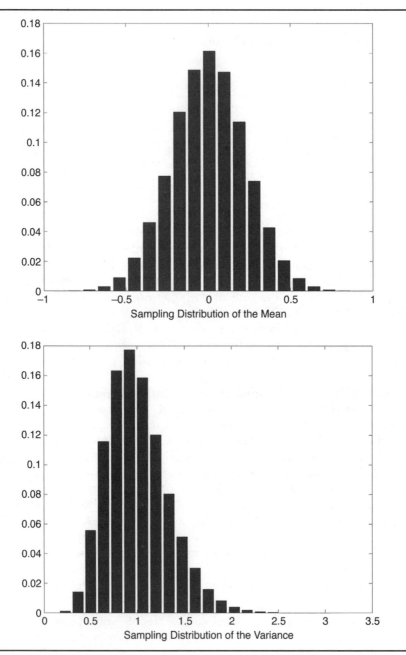

EXHIBIT 14.2   Sampling Distribution of the Mean and Variance for a Sample of 100 Elements Each

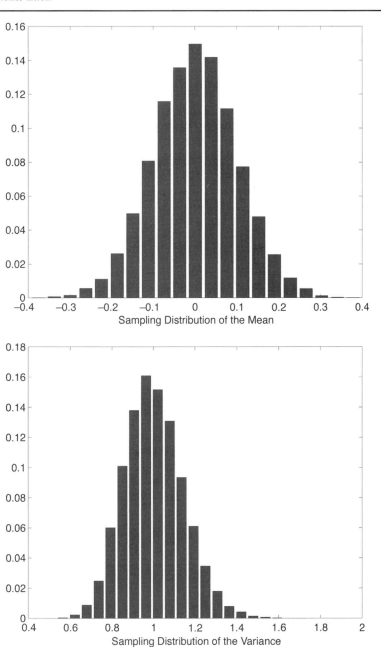

consider sample distributions for different models in our discussion of the models themselves.

CRITICAL VALUES AND CONFIDENCE INTERVALS

An estimator is a random variable characterized by a distribution that depends on the population distribution. If the estimator distribution is known, it is possible to determine *critical values*, that is, the numbers that allow one to reject or accept any hypothesis that bears on that estimator. The reasoning is the following. Suppose a statistical hypothesis on a given population depends on a parameter. In general, the parameter will vary with the sample. For example, an AR(1) process is integrated if the autoregressive coefficient is 1.

Even if a process is truly integrated, its autoregressive parameter estimated from any given sample will be slightly different from 1. However, if we know the distribution of the autoregressive parameter, we can establish the interval within which any estimate of the autoregressive parameter falls with a given probability. For example, we can estimate in what interval around 1 the autoregressive parameter will fall with a 99% probability. If the autoregressive parameter falls outside of the critical value at 99%, we can conclude that the process is not integrated at a 99% confidence interval. If the estimated autoregressive parameter is less than the critical value, we cannot say that the process is integrated with 99% confidence. The process might in fact, follow a different dynamics that could produce the same result by chance.

Each estimated parameter is associated with a confidence interval. The confidence interval can be established *a priori* as in the case of testing if a series is integrated where, in fact, we were interested in the special value 1 for the autoregressive parameter. If, however, after estimating a parameter, we know the sample distribution of that parameter, we can determine a confidence interval such that, if the model is correctly specified, the true parameter falls within that interval with a given probability. For example, suppose the estimated autoregressive parameter is 0.9. Given the sample distribution, we can determine the probability that the true autoregressive parameter falls between, say, 0.85 and 0.95. The assumption that the model is correctly specified is critical.

MAXIMUM LIKELIHOOD, OLS, AND REGRESSIONS

We now discuss a fundamental principle, the *Maximum Likelihood* (ML) principle of estimation, and see its links with *Ordinary Least*

Squares (OLS) estimation. We will illustrate the links in the case of linear regressions. The ML principle is very intuitive. Suppose you flip a coin 1,000 times and you get 700 heads. Would you draw the conclusion that the coin is biased or that the coin is fair and that you have experienced a particularly unlikely stream of outcomes? It is reasonable to expect that you conclude that the coin is biased with a 70% probability of heads. In other words you rule out the possibility that very unlikely things occur in practice.

The ML principle generalizes the above idea. Suppose that a sample is randomly and independently extracted from a distribution which contains a number of parameters, for example a binomial distribution with an unknown probability parameter. The ML principle prescribes that the estimate of the distribution parameters should maximize the (*a priori*) probability of the sample given the distribution. In the previous example of the coin, it is easy to see that 0.7 is the binomial probability value that maximizes the probability of a sample with 700 heads and 300 tails.

It should be clear that the ML principle is a *decision rule*; it is not possible to demonstrate the ML principle. There is no theoretical reason why the sample we are considering should not be a low-probability sample. There is no way to go from a decision rule to a factual demonstration or, as stated in the preface of the book by Chow and Teicher: Once one is in the world of probability, there is no way to get out of it.[10] One might be tempted to think that the systematic adoption of the ML principle reduces the number of mistakes in estimation over repeated estimation processes. However, it is easy to see that this reasoning is circular, as it simply assumes that sequences of unlikely events do not occur. Ultimately there is no way to demonstrate that we are not experiencing a very unlikely event.[11]

---

[10] Y.S. Chow and H. Teicher, *Probability Theory* (New York: Springer-Verlag, 1997).

[11] The ML principle touches upon questions of scientific methodology. The notion of uncertainty and estimation is different in economics and in the physical sciences. In general, the physical sciences tend to have a "deterministic" view of uncertainty in the sense that individual events are uncertain, but aggregates are certain and probability distributions are empirically ascertained with great precision given the astronomical size of the samples involved. In economics, uncertainty is more fundamental as the entire theory of economics is uncertain. However, there are theoretical subtleties in the physical sciences that we cannot discuss here. The interested reader can consult, for example, David Ruelle, *Hasard et Chaos* (Paris: Odile Jacob, 1991), Lawrence Sklar, *Physics and Chance: Philosophical Issues in the Foundations of Statistical Mechanics* (Cambridge: Cambridge University Press, 1993), or more technical treatises such as R. F. Streater, *Statistical Dynamics* (London: Imperial College Press, 1995).

We now formally state the ML principle. Suppose that a sample of N observations $\mathbf{X}_i = (X_{1,i}, \ldots, X_{p,i})'$, $i = 1, 2, \ldots, N$ is given. Suppose that the sample is characterized by a global multivariate probability distribution density $f(\mathbf{X}_1, \ldots, \mathbf{X}_N; \alpha_1, \ldots, \alpha_q)$ which contains q parameters $\alpha_1, \ldots, \alpha_q$. The distribution parameters have to be estimated.

The *likelihood function* L is any function proportional to f:

$$L(\alpha_1, \ldots, \alpha_q | \mathbf{X}_1, \ldots, \mathbf{X}_N) \propto f(\mathbf{X}_1, \ldots, \mathbf{X}_N | \alpha_1, \ldots, \alpha_q)$$

In the sequel, we will choose the constant of proportionality equal to 1. If the sample is formed by random independent extractions from a population with a density f, then the likelihood function L is the product of f computed on the different elements of the sample:

$$L(\alpha_1, \ldots, \alpha_q | \mathbf{X}_1, \ldots, \mathbf{X}_N) = \prod_{i=1}^{N} f(\mathbf{X}_i; \alpha_1, \ldots, \alpha_q)$$

The ML principle states that the optimal estimate of parameters $\alpha_1, \ldots, \alpha_q$ maximizes L:

$$(\hat{\alpha}_1, \ldots, \hat{\alpha}_q) = \mathrm{argmax}(L(\alpha_1, \ldots, \alpha_q))$$

As the log function is strictly monotone, we can replace the likelihood function with the log-likelihood defined as the logarithm of L. The ML principle states equivalently that the optimal estimate of parameters $\alpha_1, \ldots, \alpha_q$ maximizes the log-likelihood $\log L$:

$$(\hat{\alpha}_1, \ldots, \hat{\alpha}_q) = \mathrm{argmax}(\log L(\alpha_1, \ldots, \alpha_q))$$

In the case of independent samples, the transformation to the logarithms has the advantage of replacing a product with a sum, which is easier to compute.

$$\log(L(\alpha_1, \ldots, \alpha_q)) = \log \prod_{i=1}^{N} f(X_{1,i}, \ldots, X_{p,i}; \alpha_1, \ldots, \alpha_q)$$

$$= \sum_{i=1}^{N} \log f(X_{1,i}, \ldots, X_{p,i}; \alpha_1, \ldots, \alpha_q)$$

Observe that if the distribution is continuous, the probability of an individual sample is zero. Maximizing the probability of an individual sample is thus meaningless. However, we can approximate the probability of a small interval around any observed value with the product of the density times the size of the interval. We can now maximize the probability of small fixed intervals, which entails the likelihood maximization as stated above.

THE FISHER INFORMATION MATRIX AND THE CRAMER-RAO BOUND

ML estimators are usually biased. This is a consequence of the equivariance property of ML estimators: a function of an estimator is the estimator of the function. An interesting aspect of unbiased ML estimators is the possibility to estimate, in advance, bounds to the precision of estimates. Consider the q-vector $\boldsymbol{\alpha} = (\alpha_1, ..., \alpha_q)'$ of parameters that determine the population distribution $f(\mathbf{X}_1, ..., \mathbf{X}_N; \alpha_1, ..., \alpha_q)$. Suppose that $\hat{\boldsymbol{\alpha}}$ is an unbiased ML estimator of $\boldsymbol{\alpha}$. Then it can be demonstrated that the variance of the sampling distribution of $\hat{\boldsymbol{\alpha}}$ has a lower limit given by the Cramer-Rao bound,

$$\text{var}(\hat{\boldsymbol{\alpha}}) \geq \{\mathbf{J}^{-1}(\boldsymbol{\alpha})\}_{ii}$$

where $\{\mathbf{J}^{-1}(\boldsymbol{\alpha})\}_{ii}$ are the diagonal elements of the inverse $\mathbf{J}^{-1}(\boldsymbol{\alpha})$ of the *Fisher Information Matrix* $\mathbf{J}(\boldsymbol{\alpha})$.

To define the Fisher Information Matrix, let's first define the *score*. The score $\mathbf{q}$ is defined as the vector formed by the first derivatives of the log-likelihood with respect to the parameters $\boldsymbol{\alpha}$, that is,

$$\mathbf{q}(\hat{\boldsymbol{\alpha}}) = \frac{\partial(l(\boldsymbol{\alpha}|\mathbf{X}))}{\partial\boldsymbol{\alpha}}$$

The score is a random vector. It can be demonstrated that the expectation of the score is zero:

$$E(\mathbf{q}(\hat{\boldsymbol{\alpha}})) = 0$$

The covariance matrix of the score is the Fisher Information Matrix (also called the *Fisher Information*):

$$J(\hat{\alpha}) = E[\mathbf{q}\mathbf{q}']$$

It can be demonstrated that the Fisher Information Matrix is also the expected value of the Hessian of the log-likelihood:

$$J(\hat{\alpha}) = -E\left[\left.\frac{\partial^2 l}{\partial\alpha_i\partial\alpha_j}\right|_{\alpha=\hat{\alpha}}\right]_{1\le i\le q,\,1\le j\le q}$$

Intuitively, Fisher Information is the amount of information that an observable random variable carries about a nonobservable parameter. There is a profound connection between Fisher Information and Shannon Information which will be defined in Chapter 17.

REGRESSIONS

We now see how the ML principle applies to a regression problem. We will discuss regressions, in particular linear regressions, in detail because linear regressions are themselves a fundamental tool of financial modeling and because any linear dynamic model is ultimately a regression model. For example, the Capital Asset Pricing Model (CAPM) and static factor models are regression models while VAR models can be interpreted in terms of regressions. Understanding the issues surrounding the estimation of regressions, including the fundamental link between ML and OLS estimates, is essential for understanding the estimation of linear dynamic models.

Essentially, regressions express a functional dependency between two or more variables when data are affected by random disturbances. Expressing the link between two or more variables is a fundamental task of science.[12] In the simplest case, the link between two or more variables can be assumed to be a deterministic function. For example, the height of the sun on the horizon in different moments of the day at a given date can be assumed to be a deterministic function of time. However, in economic modeling the empirical data will be random in the sense that the observed pairs will not be linked by any simple functional

---

[12] However, science was able to make a fundamental leap forward only when it learned to link variables and their rate of variations, that is, to use differential equations. The corresponding leap in finance is from static regressions to dynamic models.

form. For example, empirical data on two variables might be scattered in the plane as in the Exhibit 14.3. The scatter plot in Exhibit 14.3 shows the spatial distribution of 1,000 points randomly drawn from a bivariate normal distribution with zero means and covariance matrix: $\Omega = I$, where I is the identity matrix.

There is no obvious functional dependency between the data as in the exhibit. The idea of regression is to assume that the data are random draws from a bivariate probability distribution with joint density $f(x,y)$. Let's factorize the density $f(x,y)$ as: $f_{y|x}(y|X = x)f_x(x)$. Alternatively, we can ignore the distribution of x and consider only the conditional distribution. The regression function is then defined as the conditional expectation $r(x) = E_x[f_{y|x}(y|X = x)]$. The intuition behind regression is that there is a functional dependence between variables plus some noise:

$$y = r(x) + \varepsilon$$

EXHIBIT 14.3 Scatter Plot of 1,000 Points Randomly Drawn From a Bivariate Normal Distribution

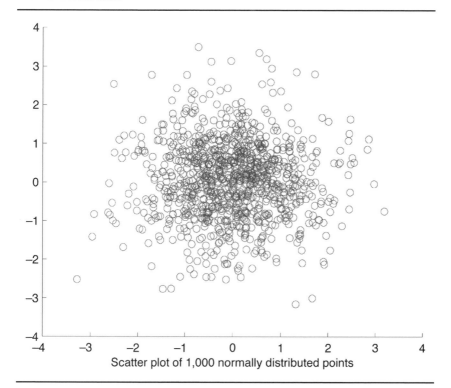

Scatter plot of 1,000 normally distributed points

The regression problem greatly simplifies if we can assume that the functional relationship is linear with normally distributed noise. We first discuss linear regressions with normally distributed white noise and then extend the discussion to nonnormal distributions and possibly correlated noise.

LINEAR REGRESSIONS

In this and the following sections we discuss two major estimation questions:

- The estimation of the linear regression parameters
- The sampling distributions of linear regression parameters.

We start with the case of a linear regression in one variable. Suppose we want to estimate the regression parameters β_1, β_2 of a linear regression:

$$ Y = \beta_1 X + \beta_2 + \varepsilon $$

where the noise term ε is Gaussian white noise. We assume that we are given a sample of T pairs Y_i, X_i generated according to the model $Y_i = \beta_1 X_i + \beta_2 + \varepsilon$ and we want to estimate the unknown coefficients β_1, β_2. In other words, we know that the data are linked by a noisy linear relationship and we want to estimate the parameters of this linear relationship. Note that this problem is different from the problem of understanding if and how a generic set of data can be approximated with a linear relationship. Here we assume that data are generated by a linear regression whose parameters are unknown. We want to estimate the parameters.

The pairs Y_i, X_i can be generated in two different settings: They can be generated by a normal bivariate distribution or they can be conditionally normal. Suppose, first, as detailed in Appendix B, that the variables X, Y are jointly normally distributed with a bivariate normal distribution $N(\mu, \Omega)$ with correlation coefficient ρ.

The conditional distribution of Y given X is a univariate normal distribution with the following parameters:

$$ f_{y|x}(Y|X = x) \sim N\left[\mu_y - \frac{\sigma_{xy}}{\sigma_{xx}^2}(\mu_x - x), \sigma_{yy}^2 - \frac{(\sigma_{xy})^2}{\sigma_{xx}^2} \right] $$

The regression function, defined as the conditional mean of one variable in function of the other, is

$$y \equiv E(Y|X = x) = \mu_y - \frac{\sigma_{xy}}{\sigma_{xx}^2}(\mu_x - x)$$

Given a sample of N pairs Y_i, X_i, we can estimate either the bivariate distribution $f(x,y)$ or the conditional distribution $f_{y|x}(Y|X = x)$. The two estimations are conceptually different and, on small samples, might lead to different regression functions. Choosing one or the other depends on the empirical setting. The distribution of sample data can be conditionally normal but not jointly normal. For example, the variable X can be arbitrarily determined in some experimental setting.

Suppose first that we want to estimate the joint distribution $f(x,y)$. In order to form the likelihood function, we need the joint density of the sample. Assuming that the pairs Y_i, X_i are independent random draws, the log-likelihood function has the following expression:

$$\log L = \log \left[\frac{1}{2\pi\sigma_{xx}\sigma_{yy}\sqrt{1 - \rho^2}} \right]$$

$$+ \sum_{i=1}^{T} \left(-\frac{1}{2(1 - \rho^2)} \right) \left[\frac{(X_i - \mu_x)^2}{\sigma_{xx}^2} - 2\rho\frac{(X_i - \mu_x)(Y_i - \mu_y)}{\sigma_{xx}\sigma_{yy}} + \frac{(Y_i - \mu_y)^2}{\sigma_{yy}^2} \right]$$

We can determine the distribution parameters finding the maximum of the log-likelihood function. In this case, that is in the case of normal variables, it can be demonstrated that the maximum is reached where the first derivatives of the log-likelihood function with respect to the parameters are zero and the Hessian determinant is positive. We have, therefore, to solve the equations

$$\frac{\partial \log L}{\partial \mu_x} = 0, \frac{\partial \log L}{\partial \sigma_{xx}} = 0, \frac{\partial \log L}{\partial \rho} = 0$$

$$\frac{\partial \log L}{\partial \mu_y} = 0, \frac{\partial \log L}{\partial \sigma_{yy}} = 0$$

and check the positiveness of the Hessian in each system's solutions. Having determined the joint distribution $f(x,y)$, one can derive the regression function.

Note that the assumption of independence of samples is critical. If samples are not independent, the above estimation is no longer valid and the regression equation is not applicable. We come back to this important issue after first discussing regression.

Estimating the joint distribution $f(x,y)$ is not necessary if the objective is only to estimate the regression model:

$$Y = \beta_1 X + \beta_2 + \varepsilon$$

In this case, it does not make sense to consider the joint distribution $f(x,y)$; we have to consider the univariate conditional distribution $f_{y|x}(Y|x)$, where x is not the value assumed by a random variable but a parameter.

To this end, we can estimate the univariate parametric normal distribution

$$f_{y|x}(Y|X = x) \sim N[y - \beta_1 x - \beta_2, \sigma_\varepsilon^2]$$

If samples are independent we can form the log-likelihood function $\log L(\beta_1, \beta_2, \sigma_\varepsilon)$ as follows:

$$\log L = -\frac{T}{2}\log(2\pi) - \frac{T}{2}\log(\sigma_\varepsilon^2) - \sum_{i=1}^{T}\left[\frac{(Y_i - \beta_1 X_i - \beta_2)^2}{2\sigma_\varepsilon^2}\right]$$

Maximizing the log-likelihood function entails solving the equations

$$\frac{\partial \log L}{\partial \beta_1} = 0, \frac{\partial \log L}{\partial \beta_2} = 0, \frac{\partial \log L}{\partial \sigma_\varepsilon^2} = 0$$

The first two equations can be explicitly written as follows:

$$\sum_{i=1}^{T}(Y_i - \beta_1 X_i - \beta_2) = 0$$

$$\sum_{i=1}^{T} X_i(Y_i - \beta_1 X_i - \beta_2) = 0$$

We define the following notation:

$$\overline{X} = \frac{1}{T}\sum_{t=1}^{T} X_t, \ \overline{Y} = \frac{1}{T}\sum_{i=1}^{T} Y_i, \ \overline{XY} = \frac{1}{T}\sum_{t=1}^{T} X_t Y_t,$$

$$\sigma_x^2 = \frac{1}{T}\sum_{i=1}^{T} (X_i - \overline{X})^2, \ \sigma_y^2 = \frac{1}{T}\sum_{i=1}^{T} (Y_i - \overline{Y})^2,$$

$$\sigma_{xy} = \sigma_{yx} = \frac{1}{T}\sum_{i=1}^{T} (X_i - \overline{X})(Y_i - \overline{Y}), \ r = \frac{\sigma_{xy}}{\sigma_x \sigma_y}$$

A little algebra shows that solving this system yields

$$\hat{\beta}_1 = \frac{\overline{XY} - \overline{X}\,\overline{Y}}{\sigma_x^2} = r\frac{\sigma_y}{\sigma_x}$$

$$\hat{\beta}_2 = (\overline{Y} - \beta_1 \overline{X})$$

In fact,

$$\sum_{i=1}^{T} X_i(Y_i - \beta_1 X_i - \beta_2) = \sum_{i=1}^{T} X_i Y - \beta_1 \sum_{i=1}^{T} X_i^2 - \beta_2 \sum_{i=1}^{T} X_i$$

$$= \sum_{i=1}^{T} X_i Y_i - \beta_1 \sum_{i=1}^{T} X_i^2 - (\overline{Y} - \beta_1 \overline{X}) \sum_{i=1}^{T} X_i = 0$$

$$\overline{XY} - \beta_1 \sum_{i=1}^{T} X_i^2 - \overline{X}\,\overline{Y} + \beta_1 \overline{X}^2 = 0$$

Solving

$$\frac{\partial \log L}{\partial \sigma_\varepsilon^2} = 0$$

and inserting $\hat{\beta}_1, \hat{\beta}_2$ yields the estimate of the variance of the residuals: $\hat{\sigma}_\varepsilon^2 = \sigma_{xy}(1 - r^2)$. This estimate is biased.

We now discuss a widely used reformulation of the regression problem in matrix form. Place the given data in a vector $\mathbf{Y}$ and a matrix $\mathbf{X}$,

$$\mathbf{Y} = \begin{pmatrix} Y_1 \\ \vdots \\ Y_T \end{pmatrix}, \mathbf{X} = \begin{pmatrix} X_1 & 1 \\ \vdots & \vdots \\ X_T & 1 \end{pmatrix}$$

the regression coefficients in a vector,

$$\boldsymbol{\beta} = \begin{pmatrix} \beta_1 \\ \beta_2 \end{pmatrix}$$

and the noise terms in a vector $\boldsymbol{\varepsilon} = (\varepsilon_1, \ldots, \varepsilon_T)'$,

$$\boldsymbol{\varepsilon} \sim N(0, \sigma_\varepsilon \mathbf{I})$$

The regression equation can be written as

$$Y_1 = \beta_1 X_1 + \beta_2 + \varepsilon_1$$
$$\dots\dots\dots\dots\dots\dots\dots\dots$$
$$Y_T = \beta_1 X_T + \beta_2 + \varepsilon_T$$

or in matrix form as

$$\mathbf{Y} = \mathbf{X}\boldsymbol{\beta} + \boldsymbol{\varepsilon}$$

The regression equation can also be written $E(\mathbf{Y}|\mathbf{X}) = \mathbf{X}\boldsymbol{\beta}$, which entails $E(\mathbf{X}\varepsilon) = 0$.

These latter conditions are very strong. For example, if $\mathbf{Y}, \mathbf{X}$ are observations of two time series, so that Y_t, X_t are the observations of the two time series at time t, the above conditions imply that there is no autocorrelation in the series. These conditions can be weakened in large samples, as we see next.

Next we establish the relationship between the MLE principle and OLS. The latter is a general method to approximate a relationship between two or more variables. Suppose a set of T pairs Y_i, X_i is given. We want to approximate the relationship between the two variables with a linear function $Y = \beta_1 X + \beta_2$. OLS finds the parameters β_1, β_2 by minimizing the sum of the squares of the residuals, that is by minimizing the expression:

$$\sum_{i=1}^{T} (Y_i - \beta_1 X_i - \beta_2)^2$$

Now consider the expression for the log-likelihood established above in the case of independent and normally distributed residuals:

$$\log L = -\frac{T}{2}\log(2\pi) - \frac{T}{2}\log(\sigma_\varepsilon^2) - \sum_{i=1}^{T}\left[\frac{(Y_i - \beta_1 X_i - \beta_2)^2}{2\sigma_\varepsilon^2}\right]$$

It is clear from this formula that maximizing the log-likelihood function is equivalent to minimizing the sum of the residuals. We can then establish the fundamental result that, for linear regressions with independent and normally distributed residuals, the MLE principle and the OLS method coincide.

We can summarize the above discussion as follows. Suppose a set of bivariate data is given. If they are generated by a linear regression of the type

$$Y = \beta_1 X + \beta_2 + \varepsilon$$

we can estimate the regression parameters with the following estimators:

$$\hat{\beta}_1 = \frac{\overline{XY} - \overline{X}\,\overline{Y}}{\overline{\sigma}_x^2}$$

$$\hat{\beta}_2 = (\overline{Y} - \beta_1 \overline{X})$$

We can now generalize the discussion to multiple regressions. As in the bivariate case above, we can consider multiple linear regressions in two different settings. The first is the case of a sample extracted from a multivariate normal distribution. Consider a normally distributed random vector:

$$\mathbf{X} = (X_1, ..., X_{N+1})'$$

Under the assumption of joint normality, we can write the joint density as

$$f(\mathbf{x}) = \left[(2\pi)^{N+1}|\mathbf{\Omega}|\right]^{-\frac{1}{2}} \exp\left[-\frac{1}{2}(\mathbf{x}-\mathbf{\mu})'\mathbf{\Omega}^{-1}(\mathbf{x}-\mathbf{\mu})\right]$$

where, as usual, $\mathbf{\mu} = (\mu_{x_1}, \ldots, \mu_{x_{N+1}})'$ is the vector of expected values and $|\mathbf{\Omega}|$ is the determinant of the covariance matrix (see Appendix B).

If we partition $\mathbf{x}$, $\mathbf{\mu}$, and $\mathbf{\Omega}$ conformably in the following way:

$$\mathbf{X} = \begin{pmatrix} Y \\ Z \end{pmatrix}, \mathbf{x} = \begin{pmatrix} y \\ z \end{pmatrix}, \mathbf{\mu} = \begin{pmatrix} \mu_z \\ \mu_z \end{pmatrix}, \mathbf{\Omega} = \begin{pmatrix} \sigma_{yy} & \sigma_{zy} \\ \sigma_{yz} & \mathbf{\Omega}_{zz} \end{pmatrix}$$

The conditional density $(Y|Z = z)$ has the following expression:

$$(Y|Z = z) \sim N(\alpha + \mathbf{\beta}'z, \sigma)$$

where

$$\mathbf{\beta} = \mathbf{\Omega}_{zz}^{-1}\sigma_{zy}$$
$$\alpha = \mu_y - \mathbf{\beta}'\mu_z$$
$$\sigma = \sigma_{yy} - \sigma_{yz}\mathbf{\Omega}_{zz}^{-1}\sigma_{zy}$$

and the regression function can be written as follows:

$$y = \alpha + \mathbf{\beta}'z$$

In the second setting, data are only conditionally normal, that is, data are a sample extracted from the following family of conditionally normal distributions:

$$(Y|Z = z) \sim N(\alpha + \mathbf{\beta}'z, \sigma)$$

without any assumption on the distribution of the variables Z. The variables Z can also be deterministic, as is the case in an experimental setting.

Suppose therefore that a data sample extracted in one of the previous settings is given. We can organize data in matrix form,

$$Y = \begin{pmatrix} Y_1 \\ \vdots \\ Y_T \end{pmatrix}, \ W = \begin{bmatrix} z_{11} & \cdots & z_{N1} \\ \vdots & \ddots & \vdots \\ z_{1T} & \cdots & z_{NT} \end{bmatrix}$$

and the regression coefficients and error terms in the vectors,

$$\beta = \begin{pmatrix} \beta_1 \\ \vdots \\ \beta_N \end{pmatrix}, \ \varepsilon = \begin{pmatrix} \varepsilon_1 \\ \vdots \\ \varepsilon_N \end{pmatrix}$$

The matrix W which contains all the regressors is called the *design matrix*. One of the columns can be formed by 1s to allow for a constant term (intercept). We want to explain data as a linear regression:

$$Y = \beta' z + \varepsilon$$

Note that on the right side of the equation, we use lower case letters to emphasize that we do not make any assumption on the distribution of the Z. We assume that $\varepsilon \sim N[0, \sigma^2 I]$ and that noise is uncorrelated with the Z.

Using the above notation, the regression equation can be compactly written in matrix form as follows:

$$Y = W\beta + \varepsilon$$

We can now estimate the regression coefficients using the MLE or OLS methods. It can be demonstrated that under the above assumptions both methods yield the same estimators, that is, the OLS estimators are also ML estimators. The Gauss-Markov theorem demonstrates that the OLS estimators are the Best Linear Unbiased Estimators (BLUE). The OLS estimators of the regression coefficients are obtained minimizing the following expression:

$$(Y - W\beta)'(Y - W\beta)$$

It can be demonstrated that the minimum is attained for

$$\hat{\beta} = (W'W)^{-1}W'Y$$

It is straightforward to show that, in the univariate case, this expression reduces to

$$\hat{\beta}_1 = \frac{\overline{XY} - \overline{X}\,\overline{Y}}{\overline{\sigma}_x^2}$$

$$\hat{\beta}_2 = (\overline{Y} - \beta_1 \overline{X})$$

SAMPLING DISTRIBUTIONS OF REGRESSIONS

Estimated regression parameters depend on the sample. They are random variables whose distribution we want to determine. We discuss separately the case where the regressors are considered given nonrandom variables and the case where the regressors are random variables.

Suppose the regressors are given non-random variables. The $\hat{\beta}$ are unbiased estimators and therefore $E[\hat{\beta}] = \beta$ holds. It can also be demonstrated that the following expression for the variance of $\hat{\beta}$ holds

$$E[(\beta - \hat{\beta})(\beta - \hat{\beta})'] = \sigma^2 (\mathbf{W}'\mathbf{W})^{-1}$$

and that an unbiased estimate s^2 of σ^2 is given by

$$s^2 = \frac{(\mathbf{Y} - \mathbf{W}\beta)'(\mathbf{Y} - \mathbf{W}\beta)}{(T - N)}$$

In other words, the variance of the error term is the empirical variance but with a correction to take into account the number of parameters. Without this correction the estimator still holds but it is biased, as we saw in the univariate case. Under the assumption of normality of the noise term, it can be demonstrated that the regression coefficients are jointly normally distributed as follows:

$$\hat{\beta} \sim N_N[\beta, \sigma^2 (\mathbf{W}'\mathbf{W})^{-1}]$$

Now suppose that the regressors are random variables. Under the assumption $E(\mathbf{Z}\varepsilon) = 0$, it can be demonstrated that the variance of the estimators $\hat{\beta}$ can be written as follows:

$$V_S(\beta) = E[(\mathbf{W}'\mathbf{W})^{-1}] V(\mathbf{W}'\varepsilon) E[(\mathbf{W}'\mathbf{W})^{-1}]$$

where the terms $E[(\mathbf{W}'\mathbf{W})^{-1}]$ and $V(\mathbf{W}'\boldsymbol{\varepsilon})$ have to be intended as the empirical expectation of $(\mathbf{W}'\mathbf{W})^{-1}$ and the empirical variance of $\mathbf{W}'\boldsymbol{\varepsilon}$, respectively. This estimator is called the *sandwich estimator* (or the *robust estimator* or *White estimator*) of the variance.[13] Consider that if the regressors are a large sample, the sandwich and the classical estimators are close to each other.

To illustrate the above, we computer-generated 5,000 populations, each formed by 1,000 pairs X,Y. In each sample, the X are generated as random draws from the normal distribution $N(0,1)$ while the Y are generated as $5X + e$ where the e are again random draws from a zero mean normal distribution with unitary variance. We then computed the linear regression parameter for each of the 5,000 samples and we constructed the distribution of the regression coefficients. Exhibit 14.4 shows the distribution of the regression coefficients.

EXHIBIT 14.4   Sampling Distribution of the Regression Coefficients

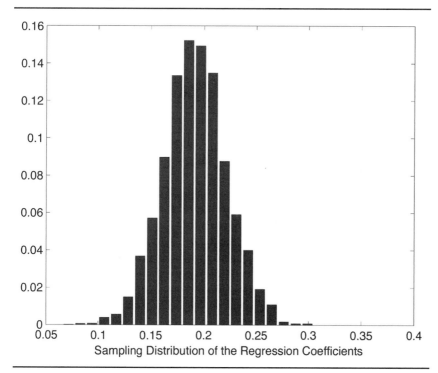

---

[13] The term "sandwich" estimator is due to the fact that the term $V(\mathbf{W}'\boldsymbol{\varepsilon})$ is sandwiched between the terms $E[(\mathbf{W}'\mathbf{W})^{-1}]$.

Finally, it can be demonstrated that, under the assumption of normally distributed noise terms, the estimator s^2 of the noise variance σ^2 is independent from the estimator of the regression parameters and that the quantity

$$(T - N)\frac{s^2}{\sigma^2}$$

is distributed as a χ^2 distribution with $T - N$ degrees of freedom.

Determining the Explanatory Power of a Regression

The previous computations to estimate regression parameters were carried out under the assumption that data were indeed generated by a linear regression function with uncorrelated and normally distributed noise. In general, we do not know if this is indeed the case. Though we can always estimate a linear regression model on any data sample by applying the estimators discussed above, we must now ask the question: When is a linear regression applicable and how can one establish the goodness of fit (i.e., the explanatory power) of a linear regression?

Quite obviously, a linear regression model is applicable if the relationship between the variables is approximately linear. How can we check if this is indeed the case? What happens if we fit a linear model to variables that have nonlinear relationships, or if distributions are not normal? A number of tests have been devised to help answer these questions.

Intuitively, a measure of the quality of approximation offered by a linear regression is given by the variance of the residuals. The variance of the residuals is the sum of the squared residuals given that the sum of residuals is zero. If residuals are large, the regression model has little explanatory power. However, the size of the average residual in itself is meaningless as it has to be compared with the range of the variables. For example, if we regress stock prices over an index, other things being equal, the residuals will be numerically different if the price is in the range of dollars or in the range of hundreds of dollars.

A widely used measure of the quality and usefulness of a regression model is given by the *coefficient of determination*, denoted by R^2. The idea behind R^2 is the following. The dependent variable Y has a total variation given by the following expression:

$$S_Y^2 = \frac{1}{T}\sum_{i=1}^{T}(Y_i - \bar{Y})^2, \; S_\varepsilon^2 = \frac{1}{T}\sum_{i=1}^{T}\varepsilon_t^2$$

$$S_R^2 = S_Y^2 - S_\varepsilon^2, \ \overline{Y} = \frac{1}{T} \sum_{i=1}^{T} Y_i$$

This total variation is the sum of the variation of the variable Y due to the variation of the regressors plus the variation of noise. We can therefore define

$$R^2 = \frac{S_R^2}{S_Y^2}, \ 1 - R^2 = \frac{S_\varepsilon^2}{S_Y^2}$$

as the percentage of the total fluctuation of the dependent variable explained by the regression relation. R^2 is a number between 0 and 1: $R^2 = 0$ means that the regression has no explanatory power, $R^2 = 1$ means that the regression has perfect explanatory power. The quantity R^2 is computed by software packages that perform linear regressions.

The quantity R^2 as a measure of the usefulness of a regression model suffers from the problem that a regression might fit data very well in-sample but have no explanatory power. This occurs if the number of regressors is too high. Therefore, an adjusted R^2 is sometimes used. The latter is defined as R^2 corrected by a penalty function that takes into account the number p of regressors in the model:

$$\text{Adjusted } R^2 = \frac{T-1}{T-N-1} \frac{\sigma_R^2}{\sigma_Y^2}$$

The square root of R^2 is called the *correlation coefficient*. The correlation coefficient is a number between −1 and +1. If a linear relationship is assumed, the correlation coefficient has the usual product-moment expression,

$$r = \frac{\overline{XY} - \overline{X}\,\overline{Y}}{\overline{\sigma}_y \overline{\sigma}_x}$$

where $\overline{\sigma}_x, \overline{\sigma}_y$ are the empirical standard deviations of the sample variables X, Y, respectively. It can be demonstrated that the coefficient of determination R^2 is distributed as a Student F distribution.

RELAXING THE NORMALITY AND UNCORRELATED NOISE ASSUMPTIONS

In the above discussion we assumed that the noise term is Gaussian white noise and that there is no correlation between the noise term and the regressors. Let us now relax these assumptions.

If the noise term is not normally distributed, then the equivalence of ML and OLS estimators breaks down. In fact, recall from previous sections that the special form of the normal distribution was instrumental in showing the equivalence. However, if the variance of the distribution is finite, we can still estimate regression parameters with OLS methods and the estimators will still be the best linear unbiased estimators, that is,

$$\hat{\beta} = (W'W)^{-1}W'Y$$

still holds and it is BLUE, though the sampling distributions will be different. Many quantities—including returns—cannot be considered normally distributed. If we estimate regressions involving returns, we can use OLS methods quite confidently.

The correlation of the noise terms is more critical from the point of view of estimation. Correlation of residuals is quite common in financial estimation where we regress quantities that are time series. Recall from the previous section that we organized regressor data in a matrix called the *design matrix*. Suppose that both regressors and the variable Y are time series data, that is, every row of the design matrix corresponds to a moment in time. If residuals are correlated, with $E(u) = 0$, $E(u, u') = \sigma^2\Omega$, Ω symmetric, positive definite matrix, the regression parameters can still be estimated without biases using the formula:

$$\hat{\beta} = (W'W)^{-1}W'Y$$

This estimate will, however, not be optimal: The optimal linear unbiased estimator is now Aitken's *Generalized Least Squares* (GLS) estimator:

$$\hat{\beta} = (W'\Omega^{-1}W)^{-1}W'\Omega^{-1}Y$$

It can also be demonstrated that the variance of the GLS estimator is given by the following "sandwich" formula:

$$V(\bar{\beta}) = E((\beta - \bar{\beta})(\beta - \bar{\beta})') = \sigma^2(W'\Omega^{-1}W)^{-1}$$

Unfortunately, the latter cannot be estimated without first knowing the regression coefficients. The correlation matrix of residuals can be explicitly computed in a number of cases including serial autocorrelation of residuals in time series analysis. Consider the regression model

$$Y_t = \beta X_t + u_t$$
$$u_t = \rho u_{t-1} + \varepsilon_t$$
$$E(\varepsilon) = 0, E(\varepsilon, \varepsilon') = \sigma^2 I$$

which is a regression model of the time series Y_t, X_t with autocorrelated residuals. In this case the following relationships hold:

$$E(\mathbf{u}) = 0$$

$$E(\mathbf{u}, \mathbf{u}') = \sigma^2 \Omega = \frac{\sigma^2}{1-\rho^2}
\begin{bmatrix}
1 & \rho & \cdots & \rho^{T-1} \\
\rho & 1 & \cdots & \rho^{T-2} \\
\vdots & \vdots & \ddots & \vdots \\
\rho^{T-1} & \rho^{T-2} & \cdots & 1
\end{bmatrix}$$

and, therefore, the generalized regression can be estimated.

How do we detect the autocorrelation of residuals? Suppose, for example, that we believe that there is a reasonable linear relationship between two variables, for instance a stock's returns and some fundamental variable. We then perform a linear regression between the two variables and estimate regression parameters with the usual OLS methods. After estimating the regression parameters, we can compute the sequence of residuals. At this point, we can apply tests such as the Durbin-Watson test or the Dickey-Fuller test to gauge the autocorrelation of residuals. If residuals are autocorrelated, we should modify the model.

PITFALLS OF REGRESSIONS

Linear autoregressive models are regression models. It is important to understand when regressions are correctly applicable and when they are not. In addition to the autocorrelation of residuals, there are other situations where regressions cannot be applied. In particular, we analyze the following cases which represent possible pitfalls of regressions:

■ Spurious regressions with integrated variables

■ Collinearity

■ Increasing the number of regressors.

Spurious Regressions

The phenomenon of spurious regressions, observed by Yule in 1927, led to the study of cointegration. We encounter spurious regressions when we perform an apparently meaningful regression between variables that are independent. A typical case is regression between two independent random walks. Regressing two independent random walks, one might find very high values of R^2 even if the two processes are independent. More in general, one might find high values of R^2 in the regression of two or more integrated variables, even if residuals are highly correlated.

As we will see in Chapter 15, testing for regressions implies testing for cointegration. Anticipating what will be discussed there, it is always meaningful to perform regressions between stationary variables. When variables are integrated, regressions are possible only if variables are cointegrated. This means that residuals are a stationary (though possibly autocorrelated) process.

Collinearity

Collinearity occurs when two or more regressors have a linear deterministic relationship. For example, there is collinearity if the design matrix

$$\mathbf{W} = \begin{bmatrix} z_{11} & \cdots & z_{N1} \\ \vdots & \ddots & \vdots \\ z_{1T} & \cdots & z_{NT} \end{bmatrix}$$

exhibits two or more columns that are perfectly proportional. Collinearity is essentially a numerical problem. Intuitively, it is clear that it creates indeterminacy as we are regressing twice on the same variable.

In principle, collinearity can be easily resolved eliminating one or more regressors. The problem with collinearity is that some variables might be very close to collinearity, thus leading to numerical problems and indeterminacy of results. In practice, this might happen for many different numerical artefacts.

Increasing the Number of Regressors

We begin our discussion on the number of regressors by reviewing the econometric theorem called *Pyrrho's lemma*.[14] Pyrrho's lemma states

---

[14] T.K. Dijkstra, "Pyrrho's Lemma, or Have it Your Way," *Metrica* 42 (1995), pp. 119–225.

that, by adding one special regressor to a linear regression, it is possible to arbitrarily change the size and sign of regression coefficients as well as to obtain an arbitrary goodness of fit. This rather technical result seems artificial because the regressor is an artificially constructed variable. It is, however, a perfectly rigorous result. It tells us that, if we add regressors without a proper design and testing methodology, we risk obtaining totally spurious results.

Pyrrho's lemma is the proof that modeling results can be arbitrarily manipulated in-sample even in the simple context of linear regressions. In fact, by adding regressors one might obtain an excellent fit in-sample though these regressors might have no predictive power out-of-sample. In addition, the size and even the sign of the regression relationships can be artificially altered in-sample.

The above observations are especially important for those financial models that seek to forecast prices, returns, or rates based on regressions over economic or fundamental variables. With modern computers, by trial and error, one might find a complex structure of regressions that give very good results in-sample but have no real forecasting power.

THE METHOD OF MOMENTS AND ITS GENERALIZATIONS

The *method of moments* and its generalizations, the *linear instrumental variables method*, and the *generalized method of moments* are powerful estimation methods that are often used in financial econometrics when the LS and the ML methods are not applicable. Though the applications involve a number of technical points, the general ideas are simple.

Method of Moments

To explain the method of moments, Suppose that

- n observations $(Y_1, \ldots, Y_n)$ of a random variable Y are given
- these observations are extracted from a population with a distribution $f(y; \lambda_1, \ldots, \lambda_k)$ that depends on a vector Λ of k parameters $\Lambda = (\lambda_1, \ldots, \lambda_k)'$
- the k parameters $(\lambda_1, \ldots, \lambda_k)$ are functions of the first k moments of the distribution: $\Lambda = F(m_1, \ldots, m_k)$ where the moments are defined as usual:

$$m_1 = E(Y), \cdots, m_k = E(Y^k)$$

The moments $m_1, \cdots, m_k$ can be estimated with the corresponding empirical moments:

$$\overline{m}_1 = \frac{1}{n} \sum_{i=1}^{n} Y_i, \cdots, \overline{m}_k = \frac{1}{n} \sum_{i=1}^{n} Y_i^k$$

The idea of the method of moments is to estimate the parameters $(\lambda_1, \ldots, \lambda_k)$ using the function $\mathbf{F}$ of the corresponding estimates of moments: $\overline{\mathbf{\Lambda}} = \mathbf{F}(\overline{m}_1, \ldots, \overline{m}_k)$. For example, consider n independent random sample from an exponential distribution $Exp(\lambda) = \lambda e^{-\lambda y}$, $y > 0$. The mean of an exponentially distributed variable is the reciprocal of the distribution parameter:

$$E(Y) = \frac{1}{\lambda}$$

The method of moments computes the parameters λ as follows:

$$\lambda = \frac{1}{E(Y)} = \frac{1}{\overline{Y}} = \frac{n}{\displaystyle\sum_{i=1}^{n} Y_i}$$

Linear Instrumental Variables Method

The linear instrumental variables method is a generalization of the method of moments. Suppose that there is a linear relationship between a dependent variable Y and k independent variables X_i, $i = 1, \ldots, k$:

$$Y = \sum_{i=1}^{k} \lambda_i X_i + u$$

n observations are given:

$$Y_j = \sum_{i=1}^{k} \lambda_i X_{j,i} + u_j, j = 1, \ldots, n$$

and the vector $\mathbf{\Lambda} = (\lambda_1, \ldots, \lambda_k)'$ represents the true value of the parameters.

In a number of cases, the usual OLS estimators could not be used. This arises, for example, if the condition $E(\mathbf{Z}\varepsilon) = 0$ does not hold. However, suppose that n observations of other variables are available. In particular, suppose that we have available h variables Z_i, $i = 1, ..., h$ that might eventually include some of the variables X_j. To simplify, suppose that all the variables,

$$(u_j, X_{j,\,1}, ..., X_{j,\,k}, Z_{i,\,1}, ..., Z_{j,\,h})\,, j = 1, ..., n$$

are independent, follow the same distribution, and have finite first and second order moments.

A variable Z_i is called an *instrumental variable* or an *instrument* if $E(Z_i u) = 0$, that is, if it is uncorrelated with the noise terms. The system of variables Z_i, $i = 1, ..., h$ is called a *system of instrumental variables* if each variable is an instrument. In other words, a system of instrumental variables is a system of variables orthogonal to the noise terms.

We can now express the orthogonality condition in terms of the observables. In fact, we can write the noise terms as follows:

$$u = Y - \sum_{i=1}^{k} \lambda_i X_i$$

and rewrite the orthogonality condition as

$$E(Z_j Y) = \sum_{i=1}^{k} \lambda_i E(Z_j X_i)\,, j = 1, ..., h$$

We now distinguish three cases.

Case 1: If $h < k$, that is, if the number of instruments Z if less than the number of explicatory variables X, then estimation process is not feasible.

Case 2: If the number of instruments is equal to the number of explicatory variables, then the above system will in general admit a unique solution. If we stack the observations and the instruments in matrix form as we did in the case of regressions, it can be demonstrated that the linear instrumental variables estimator can be written as follows:

$$\bar{\Lambda} = (\mathbf{Z}'\mathbf{X})^{-1}\mathbf{Z}'\mathbf{Y}$$

Observe that if we choose $Z = X$, we find the same estimation formula that we have determined in the case of regressions. In this case, the instrumental variables coincide with the regressors.

Case 3: If $h > k$, the problem is in general impossible to solve because there are more equations than unknown variables. This fact will result in incompatible equations if we replace theoretical moments with estimated moments. The number of equations has to be reduced by choosing a subset of instruments.

Alternatively, one could try to find an approximate solution by minimizing the following quadratic form:

$$\left[\frac{1}{n}u'Z\right]W_n\left[\frac{1}{n}u'Z\right]'$$

where W_n is a weighting matrix that needs to be estimated. The solution for $\bar{\Lambda}$ becomes

$$\bar{\Lambda} = (X'HW_nH'Z'X)^{-1}X'HW_nH'Z'Y$$

In order to study the asymptotic distribution of the instrumental variables estimators, additional conditions are required. Suppose $h = k$. If the conditional mean of the error terms given the instruments is zero and if the error term is homoskedastic, that is, if $E(u|Z) = 0$, $Var(u|Z) = \sigma_0^2$, then the asymptotic distribution of the estimators is a normal distribution:

$$N(0, \sigma_0^2 E[Z'X]^{-1}E(Z'Z)E[X'Z]^{-1})$$

Generalized Method of Moments

The methods of linear instrumental variables was further generalized by Hansen who introduced the generalized method of moments.[15] This method generalizes the method of moments insofar as it allows:

- Nonlinear relationships between the variables and not only between linear regressions
- Multivariate vectors as well as scalars in the error terms
- Heteroskedasticity in the error terms

---

[15] Lars P. Hansen, "Large Sample Properties of Generalized Method of Moments Estimators," *Econometrica* 50 (1982), pp. 1029–1054.

We only outline the method which includes many technical details.[16] We replace the relationship

$$u = Y - \sum_{i=1}^{k} \lambda_i X_i$$

with a general equation,

$$\mathbf{u} = \mathbf{u}(\mathbf{X}, \boldsymbol{\Lambda})$$

where $\mathbf{u}$ is now a vector of noise terms possibly correlated and possibly heteroskedastic, $\mathbf{X}$ includes all the variables, and the function is possibly non-linear. The instruments $\mathbf{Z}$ are defined as in the case of linear instrumental variables. Next we form the tensor product $\mathbf{F} = \mathbf{Z} \otimes \mathbf{u}$. In analogy with the case of linear instrumental variables, we write the orthogonality conditions $E(\mathbf{F}) = 0$.

We form now the sample mean of the elements of $\mathbf{F}$ as follows:

$$\mathbf{G} = \frac{1}{n}\sum \mathbf{F}$$

The generalized method of moments is based on minimizing the quadratic form:

$$Q_n = \mathbf{G}'\mathbf{W}_n\mathbf{G}$$

where $\mathbf{W}_n$ is a weighting matrix that needs to be estimated. Hansen has derived the optimality conditions and the asymptotic distribution of the estimators.

SUMMARY

- The objective of statistics is the make inference from a sample to the entire population.
- Statistics developed in the 19th century in the context of the social sciences but made real progress only with the development of computer technology.

---

[16] The interested reader should consult the original work of Hansen.

■ In applied statistics, a population often indicates a physical population; in financial econometrics, populations are generally idealized populations while samples are unique realizations of time series extracted from an ideal population.

■ To estimate a model is to estimate its parameters; an estimator is a function of sample data that approximates a given parameter.

■ An unbiased estimator is an estimator such that the mean of the estimator coincides with the true value of the parameter.

■ A consistent estimator is an estimator that tends to the true parameter value for an infinite sample.

■ Estimators are functions of random sample data and are, therefore, random variables themselves.

■ The sampling distribution is the distribution of the estimator when sample data vary.

■ Knowing the sampling distribution it is possible to determine statistical hypotheses and establish confidence intervals.

■ Two important estimation methods are the Maximum Likelihood Estimation (MLE) method and the Ordinary Least Squares (OLS) method. The MLE method maximizes the likelihood (i.e., the distribution computed on data samples); the OLS method minimizes the square of the residuals.

■ The Cramer-Rao bound prescribes a bound to the accuracy of estimators.

■ The variance of an estimator cannot be less than the Fisher Information Matrix, defined as the expected value of the Hessian determinant (i.e., determinant of second derivatives) of the distribution.

■ The regression function represents the functional dependence of the conditional mean of the dependent variable in function of the independent variables.

■ Estimators of the regression parameters are algebraic functions of the sample data; estimators of the regression coefficients are normally distributed.

■ The explanatory power of a regression can be established by evaluating its coefficient of determination which gives the percentage of total variation explained by the regression.

■ There are many pitfalls in applying regressions. Pitfalls include the use of too many regression parameters; this makes the regression meaningless.

■ The method of moments estimates model parameters as functions of empirical moments.

■ The linear instrumental variables method estimates model parameters using a set of additional variables orthogonal to the noise terms of the model.

CHAPTER 15

Estimation of Linear Dynamic Models

In this and the following chapter we discuss estimation methods for dynamic models, focusing on two broad classes of models which appear frequently in the financial econometric literature and are used at asset management firms: linear Vector Autoregressive (VAR) models and nonlinear Markov-switching models. Methods and issues related to estimating VAR models are discussed in this chapter. The next chapter discusses methods and issues related to estimating nonlinear Markov-switching models. We will also identify a number of application areas for both classes of dynamic models.

AN APPROACH TO ESTIMATION

In our discussion on model selection in Chapter 13, we remarked that economic intuition is the starting point in building a portfolio management application. One major intuition is that returns can somehow be predicted, through what we call "predictor variables." The idea that returns can be predicted, albeit within a large margin of error, is supported by a vast body of econometric literature. These predictor variables might include, for example, economic variables, financial valuation ratios or market sentiments, or they might be determined through a process of endogenous factorization. As the search space of possible predictors is so large, a data-mining approach to selecting predictors is not feasible; economic intuition is used to suggest just what factors should be explored. A widely adopted approach uses models where asset returns are linearly regressed on a set of variables.

Forecasting requires models that link variables at different time lags, that is to say, forecasting requires dynamic models. This entails that dynamic models link variables with their rates of change.[1] In particular, future returns are regressed over the present and past values of regressors. There is a wide choice of dynamic models: regressors might be the lagged values of those variables that we are trying to predict, exogenous variables, or a combination of the two. In Chapter 13, we outlined a number of criteria that might guide us in selecting models. After using economic intuition and finance theory to select a set of possible factors and a family of models, econometric analysis validates intuition and finalizes parameter estimation. The key estimation issues are:

1. Estimating the model coefficients
2. Estimating the number of lags
3. Checking the "whiteness" of residuals
4. Checking normality versus nonnormality of the model
5. Checking the quality of forecasts
6. Checking the robustness of the selected model to model misspecification

Estimation techniques for VAR models are implemented in most statistical software packages. While the analyst need not know the details of the estimation processes, he must know how to interpret the results and read the diagnostics. In addition, different packages implement different techniques: familiarity with the econometric principles underlying models is therefore needed to select the correct approach. For these reasons, it is useful to discuss in some detail the estimation process. After introducing unit root tests, we discuss stable and unstable VAR processes.

UNIT ROOT TESTING

One of the key issues in financial econometrics is to decide whether time series are integrated and, if so, what order of integration they have. An integrated time series admits the following representation:

$$y_t = s_t + \rho y_{t-1} + u_t, \rho = 1$$

---

[1] The idea of linking a variable to its rate of change in a single equation is the basis of differential equations which mark the birth of modern science. The process of discretizing a differential equation to compute its solutions yields discrete dynamic models such as those discussed in these two chapters.

where s_t is a deterministic term and u_t is a possibly autocorrelated process. Integrated processes are said to exhibit a unit root $\rho = 1$. If $|\rho| < 1$, the process is stationary. Random walks have a unit root, but unit root processes are not necessarily random walks as the errors can be autocorrelated. Testing for unit roots is not the same thing as testing for random walk behavior.

There are two types of unit root tests: tests where the null is the hypothesis that the series is integrated, that is the null is $\rho = 1$, and tests where the null is the hypothesis that the series is not integrated. To test for unit roots, one might want to test the null $\rho = 1$ or to difference the series and test the null of absence of unit roots.

There are many unit root tests and there is a vast literature on unit root tests.[2] Here we can only give an idea of the type of issues in unit root testing by describing the Dickey-Fuller test and the Augmented Dickey-Fuller test.

The *Dickey-Fuller test* (DF test) computes the autoregressive coefficient ρ with maximum likelihood methods and compares it with a table of critical values. Critical values cannot be easily obtained because the asymptotic distribution of the autoregressive coefficient is a complicated distribution. In fact, the asymptotic autoregressive coefficient is distributed as a functional of the Brownian motion. Critical values have been tabulated; the DF test is implemented in most time series software packages.

The *Augmented Dickey-Fuller test* (ADF test) replaces the simple autoregressive equation with an AR(p) process. The AR process is estimated with standard methods and the autoregressive coefficient is tested against critical values. The distribution of the unit root coefficient is again a functional of the Brownian motion. Critical values are tabulated. The ADF test is available on most time series software packages.

Issues in unit root testing include the handling of drifts, linear trends, or other deterministic trends. These trends need to be removed before tests are applied. Overdifferencing is also an issue. In fact, if we difference a series to remove unit roots, we might difference too many times, in the sense that we might difference a series which is already stationary. Overdifferencing can invalidate tests.

ESTIMATION OF LINEAR REGRESSION MODELS

Linear regression models of returns represent returns as a linear regression over a set of N regressors f_s called factors or predictors:

---

[2] See G.S. Maddala and In-Moo Kim, *Unit Roots, Cointegration, and Structural Change* (Cambridge: Cambridge University Press, 1998).

$$r_{t+1} = \alpha + \sum_{s=1}^{N} \beta_s f_{s,t} + \varepsilon_{t+1}$$

We allow a constant intercept which represents some basic return level, for example the risk-free return. In this formulation, r_{t+1} is the return of a stock or an index at time $t + 1$:

$$r_{t+1} = \frac{p(t+1) - p(t)}{p(t)}$$

while factors are observed at time t.

Factors can represent a broad class of variables, including company-specific indicators such as the P/E ratio as well as indexes and macroeconomic variables. Factors can also be quantities of a more abstract nature such as momentum or market sentiment.

In this generic unconstrained formulation, the model can be estimated as a linear regression where the training set is formed by a set of past observations of factors and returns. If residuals are uncorrelated, the model can be estimated with Ordinary Least Squares (OLS) methods as detailed in Chapter 14. Suppose that T empirical samples of the returns and of the N factors are available. As we saw in Chapter 14, we can compactly write the estimators as closed-form algebraic formulas. Using the same notation introduced in that chapter,[3] we stack all the sample returns in a $T \times 1$ vector, all the sample factors in the $T \times N$ design matrix of the model, all the sample innovations in a $T \times 1$ vector, and all the regression coefficients in $(N + 1) \times 1$ vector:

$$\mathbf{r} = \begin{pmatrix} r_2 \\ \vdots \\ r_{T+1} \end{pmatrix}, \quad \mathbf{w} = \begin{pmatrix} 1 & f_{1,1} & \cdots & f_{N,1} \\ \vdots & \vdots & \ddots & \vdots \\ 1 & f_{1,T} & \cdots & f_{N,T} \end{pmatrix},$$

$$\mathbf{u} = \begin{pmatrix} \varepsilon_1 \\ \vdots \\ \varepsilon_T \end{pmatrix}, \quad \boldsymbol{\beta} = \begin{pmatrix} \alpha \\ \beta_1 \\ \vdots \\ \beta_N \end{pmatrix}$$

---

[3] This type of notation is standard in the analysis of regressive and autoregressive models. We will use it consistently through this chapter.

With this notation we can compactly write the regression model as $r = w\beta + u$. The estimator of the regression coefficients is that already established in Chapter 14:

$$\hat{\beta} = (w'w)^{-1}w'r, \hat{\beta}' = r'w(w'w)^{-1}$$

The regression models can be easily generalized to include multiple lags of the factors. In this case, the model will have the form:

$$r_{t+1} = \alpha + \sum_{s=1}^{N} \beta_{s,1} f_{s,t} + \cdots + \sum_{s=1}^{N} \beta_{s,p} f_{s,t-p+1} + \varepsilon_t$$

Adding more lags allows the model to represent the return sensitivity to both the values of the factors and their rates of change. If residuals are uncorrelated, the model is a multivariate regression model that can be estimated with OLS methods as the previous regression model. We write down the estimator explicitly as it will help familiarize us with the rather intricate notation. Therefore, we stack all the sample returns in a $T \times 1$ vector, all the sample factors in the $T \times (Np)$ design matrix of the model, all the sample innovations in a $T \times 1$ vector, and all the regression coefficients in $(Np + 1) \times 1$ vector:

$$r = \begin{pmatrix} r_2 \\ \vdots \\ r_{T+1} \end{pmatrix}, w = \begin{pmatrix} 1 & f_{1,1} & \cdots & f_{N,1} & \cdots & f_{1,1-p+1} & \cdots & f_{N,1-p+1} \\ \vdots & \vdots & \ddots & \vdots & \ddots & \vdots & \ddots & \vdots \\ 1 & f_{1,T} & \cdots & f_{N,T} & \cdots & f_{1,T-p+1} & \cdots & f_{N,T-p+1} \end{pmatrix},$$

$$u = \begin{pmatrix} \varepsilon_1 \\ \vdots \\ \varepsilon_T \end{pmatrix}, \beta = \begin{pmatrix} \alpha \\ \beta_{1,1} \\ \vdots \\ \beta_{N,1} \\ \vdots \\ \beta_{1,1-p+1} \\ \vdots \\ \beta_{N,1-p+1} \end{pmatrix}$$

Note that we now need $T + p - 1$ samples of the factors. Using this notation, the regression equation and the formulas that yield the estimators of the regression coefficients are the same as above:

$$\mathbf{r} = \mathbf{w}\boldsymbol{\beta} + \mathbf{u}$$

$$\hat{\boldsymbol{\beta}} = (\mathbf{w}'\mathbf{w})^{-1}\mathbf{w}'\mathbf{r}, \; \hat{\boldsymbol{\beta}}' = \mathbf{r}'\mathbf{w}(\mathbf{w}'\mathbf{w})^{-1}$$

Pure regressive models have limited forecasting abilities. However, as we will see later in this chapter, recent studies show that forecasting ability can be enhanced by adding an autoregressive component to models. Returns can, therefore, be represented through one of the vector autoregressive models that we introduced in Chapter 12. The following sections discuss the estimation of vector autoregressive models.

ESTIMATION OF STABLE VECTOR AUTOREGRESSIVE (VAR) MODELS

When discussing the estimation of regression models in Chapter 14, we introduced two main methods for estimating linear regressions: the least squares method and the maximum likelihood method. These methods apply immediately to unrestricted stable VAR models. Note that models are said to be "unrestricted" if the estimation process is allowed to determine any possible outcome, and "restricted" if the estimation process is allowed to determine parameters that satisfy given conditions, that is, restrictions on their possible range of values.

Suppose that an empirical time series is given and that the Data Generation Process (DGP) of the series is a finite dimensional VAR(p) model. Recall that a VAR(p) model has the following form:

$$\mathbf{x}_t = \mathbf{A}_1\mathbf{x}_{t-1} + \mathbf{A}_1\mathbf{x}_{t-1} + \cdots + \mathbf{A}_1\mathbf{x}_{t-1} + \mathbf{v} + \boldsymbol{\varepsilon}_t$$

where $\mathbf{x}_t = (x_{1,t}, \ldots, x_{N,t})'$ is a N–dimensional stochastic time series in vector notation, $\mathbf{A}_i = (a_{s,t}^i)$, $i = 1, 2, \ldots, p$, $s, t = 1, 2, \ldots, N$ are deterministic $N \times N$ matrices, $\boldsymbol{\varepsilon}_t = (\varepsilon_{1,t}, \ldots, \varepsilon_{N,t})'$ is a multivariate white noise with variance-covariance matrix $\Sigma = (\sigma_1, \ldots, \sigma_N)'$, and $\mathbf{v} = (v_1, \ldots, v_N)'$ is a vector of deterministic terms.

Though deterministic terms might be time-dependent deterministic vectors, in this section we will limit our discussion to the case of a constant intercept as this is the case commonly encountered in financial econometrics. As we have seen in Chapter 12, a constant intercept in a stable VAR model yields a nonzero mean of the process. Only in the section on the estimation of cointegrated models we will have to consider linear deterministic terms as well as a constant intercept.

The above model can be written in lag notation as

$$\mathbf{x}_t = (\mathbf{A}_1 L + \mathbf{A}_2 L^2 + \cdots + \mathbf{A}_p L^p)\mathbf{x}_t + \mathbf{v} + \varepsilon_t$$

Consider the matrix polynomial

$$\mathbf{A}(z) = \mathbf{I} - \mathbf{A}_1 z - \mathbf{A}_2 z^2 - \cdots - \mathbf{A}_p z^p, z \in \mathbb{C}$$

and consider the inverse characteristic equation

$$\det(\mathbf{A}(z)) = 0$$

In this section we assume that stability conditions hold

$$\det(\mathbf{A}(z)) \neq 0 \text{ for } |z| \leq 1$$

that is, the roots of the inverse characteristic equation are strictly outside of the unit circle. The result is that the VAR(p) model is stable and the corresponding process stationary. As discussed in Chapter 7, the property of stationarity applies only to processes that extend on the entire real axis, as a process that starts at a given point cannot be strictly time-invariant. In general, we will consider processes that start at $t = 1$, assuming that p initial conditions are given: $\mathbf{x}_{-p+1}, \ldots, \mathbf{x}_0$.[4] In this case, stable VAR models yield asymptotically stationary processes. When there is no risk of confusion, we will not stress this distinction.

Recall also that the above N-dimensional VAR(p) model is equivalent to the following Np-dimensional VAR(1) model:

$$\mathbf{X}_t = \mathbf{A}\mathbf{X}_{t-1} + \mathbf{V} + \mathbf{U}_t$$

where

$$\mathbf{X}_t = \begin{bmatrix} \mathbf{x}_t \\ \mathbf{x}_{t-1} \\ \vdots \\ \mathbf{x}_{t-p+1} \end{bmatrix}, \mathbf{A} = \begin{bmatrix} \mathbf{A}_1 & \mathbf{A}_2 & \cdots & \mathbf{A}_{p-1} & \mathbf{A}_p \\ \mathbf{I}_N & 0 & \cdots & 0 & 0 \\ 0 & \mathbf{I}_N & \cdots & 0 & 0 \\ 0 & 0 & \ddots & \vdots & \vdots \\ 0 & 0 & \cdots & \mathbf{I}_N & 0 \end{bmatrix}, \mathbf{V} = \begin{bmatrix} \mathbf{v} \\ 0 \\ \vdots \\ 0 \end{bmatrix}, \mathbf{U}_t = \begin{bmatrix} \varepsilon_t \\ 0 \\ \vdots \\ 0 \end{bmatrix}$$

---

[4] As in this chapter we assume that the entire time series is empirically given, the distinction between initial conditions and the remaining data is made only to simplify notation.

The matrix $\mathbf{A}$ is called the *companion matrix* of the VAR(p) system.

Note that in this section we do not place any *a priori* computational restrictions on the model parameters, though we do assume that the model is stable. The assumption of model stability ensures that the process is stationary. This, in turn, ensures that the covariances are time-invariant. As the above VAR(p) model is unrestricted, it can be estimated as a linear regression; it can therefore be estimated with the estimation theory of linear regression. As we consider only consistent estimators, the estimated parameters (in the limit of an infinite sample) satisfy the stability condition. However on a finite sample, the estimated parameters might not satisfy the stability condition.

We will first show how the estimation of a VAR(p) model and its VAR(1) equivalent can be performed with least squares methods or with maximum likelihood methods. To do so we apply the estimation theory developed in Chapter 14, estimating the model coefficients either by the multivariate Least Squares method or by the Maximum Likelihood method. To see how both methods work, we need to establish some notation.

Vectoring Operators and Tensor Products

We first define the *vectoring operator*. Given an $m \times n$ matrix,

$$A = \begin{pmatrix} a_{11} & \cdots & a_{1n} \\ \vdots & \ddots & \vdots \\ a_{m1} & \cdots & a_{mn} \end{pmatrix}$$

the vectoring operator, written as vec($\mathbf{A}$),[5] stacks the matrix columns in a vector as follows:

$$\text{vec}(\mathbf{A}) = \begin{pmatrix} a_{11} \\ \vdots \\ a_{m1} \\ \vdots \\ a_{1n} \\ \vdots \\ a_{mn} \end{pmatrix}$$

Next it is useful to define the Kronecker product. Given the $m \times n$ matrix

---

[5] The vec operator should not be confused with the vech operator which is similar but not identical. The vech operator stacks the terms below and on the diagonal.

$$A = \begin{pmatrix} a_{11} & \cdots & a_{1n} \\ \vdots & \ddots & \vdots \\ a_{m1} & \cdots & a_{mn} \end{pmatrix}$$

and the $p \times q$ matrix

$$B = \begin{pmatrix} b_{11} & \cdots & b_{1q} \\ \vdots & \ddots & \vdots \\ b_{p1} & \cdots & b_{pq} \end{pmatrix}$$

we define the Kronecker product $C = A \otimes B$ as follows:

$$C = A \otimes B = \begin{pmatrix} a_{11}B & \cdots & a_{1n}B \\ \vdots & \ddots & \vdots \\ a_{m1}B & \cdots & a_{mn}B \end{pmatrix}$$

The Kronecker product, also called the *direct product* or *the tensor product*, is an $(mp) \times (nq)$ matrix. It can be demonstrated that the tensor product satisfies the associative and distributive property and that, given any four matrices A, B, C, D of appropriate dimensions, the following properties hold:

$$\text{vec}(A \otimes B) = (B' \otimes I)\text{vec}(A)$$

$$(A \otimes B)(C \otimes D) = (AC) \otimes (BD)$$

$$(A \otimes B)' = (A') \otimes (B')$$

$$\text{Trace}(A'BCD') = (\text{vec}(A))'(D \otimes B)\text{vec}(C)$$

Next we discuss estimation of the model parameters using the multivariate least squares estimation method.

Multivariate Least Squares Estimation

Conceptually, the multivariate *least squares* (LS) estimation method is equivalent to that of a linear regression (see Chapter 14); the notation, however, is more complex. This is because we are dealing with multiple time series and because there are correlations between noise terms. Similar to what we did in estimating regressions (Chapter 14), we now represent the autoregressive process applied to the sample and presample data as a single-matrix equation. Note that the VAR(p) process is an autoregressive process where the variables $\mathbf{x}_t$ are regressed over their own lagged values: The regressors are the lagged values of the dependent variable. We will introduce two different but equivalent notations.

Suppose that a sample of T observations of the N-variate variable $\mathbf{x}_t$, $t = 1, \ldots, T$ and a pre-sample of p initial conditions $\mathbf{x}_{-p+1}, \ldots, \mathbf{x}_0$ are given. We first stack all observations $\mathbf{x}_t$, $t = 1, \ldots, T$ in a vector as was done in the case of regressions:

$$
\mathbf{x} = \begin{pmatrix} x_{1,1} \\ \vdots \\ x_{N,1} \\ \vdots \\ \vdots \\ x_{1,T} \\ \vdots \\ x_{N,T} \end{pmatrix}
$$

Introducing a notation that will be useful later, we can also write

$$
\mathbf{x} = \mathrm{vec}(\mathbf{X})
$$

$$
\mathbf{X} = (\mathbf{x}_1, \ldots, \mathbf{x}_T) = \begin{pmatrix} x_{1,1} & \cdots & x_{1,T} \\ \vdots & \ddots & \vdots \\ x_{N,1} & \cdots & x_{N,T} \end{pmatrix}
$$

In other words, $\mathbf{x}$ is a $(NT \times 1)$ vector where all observations are stacked, while $\mathbf{X}$ is a $(N \times T)$ matrix where each column represents an N-variate observation.

Proceeding analogously with the innovation terms, we stack the innovation terms in a $(NT \times 1)$ vector as follows:

$$
\mathbf{u} = \begin{pmatrix} \varepsilon_{1,1} \\ \vdots \\ \varepsilon_{N,1} \\ \vdots \\ \varepsilon_{1,T} \\ \vdots \\ \varepsilon_{N,T} \end{pmatrix}
$$

which we can represent alternatively as follows:

$$\mathbf{u} = \text{vec}(\mathbf{U})$$

$$\mathbf{U} = \begin{pmatrix} \varepsilon_{1,1} & \cdots & \varepsilon_{1,T} \\ \vdots & \ddots & \vdots \\ \varepsilon_{N,1} & \cdots & \varepsilon_{N,T} \end{pmatrix}$$

where $\mathbf{U}$ is a $(N \times T)$ matrix such that each column represents an N-variate innovation term.

The innovation terms have a nonsingular covariance matrix,

$$\Sigma = [\sigma_{i,j}] = E[\varepsilon_{i,t}\varepsilon_{j,t}]$$

while $E[\varepsilon_{i,t}\varepsilon_{j,s}] = 0$, $\forall i, j, t \neq s$. The covariance matrix of $\mathbf{u}$, $\Sigma_{\mathbf{u}}$ can now be written as

$$\Sigma_{\mathbf{u}} = \mathbf{I}_T \otimes \Sigma = \begin{pmatrix} \Sigma & \cdots & 0 \\ \vdots & \ddots & \vdots \\ 0 & \cdots & \Sigma \end{pmatrix}$$

In other words, the covariance matrix of $\mathbf{u}$ is a block-diagonal matrix where all diagonal blocks are equal to Σ. This covariance structure reflects the assumed white-noise nature of innovations that precludes autocorrelations and cross autocorrelations in the innovation terms.

In discussing the case of multivariate single-equation regressions (Chapter 14), we stacked the observations of the regressors in a matrix where each column represented all the observations of one regressor. Here we want to use the same technique but there are two differences: (1) In this case, there is no distinction between the observations of the regressors and those of the dependent variables; and (2) the multiplicity of equations requires special care in constructing the matrix of regressors. One possible solution is to construct the $(NT \times (N^2p + N))$ matrix of observations of the regressors shown in Exhibit 15.1.

EXHIBIT 15.1 The Matrix of Observations of the Regressors

$$
\mathbf{w} = \begin{bmatrix}
1 & \cdots & 0 & x_{1,0} & \cdots & 0 & \cdots & \cdots & \cdots & x_{N,0} & \cdots & 0 & \cdots & \cdots & \cdots & x_{1,1-p} & \cdots & 0 & \cdots & \cdots & \cdots & x_{N,1-p} & \cdots & 0 \\
\vdots & \ddots & \vdots & \vdots & \ddots & \vdots & \vdots & \ddots & \vdots & \vdots & \ddots & \vdots & \vdots & \ddots & \vdots & \vdots & \ddots & \vdots & \vdots & \ddots & \vdots & \vdots & \ddots & \vdots \\
0 & \cdots & 1 & 0 & \cdots & x_{1,0} & \cdots & \cdots & \cdots & 0 & \cdots & x_{N,0} & \cdots & \cdots & \cdots & 0 & \cdots & x_{1,1-p} & \cdots & \cdots & \cdots & 0 & \cdots & x_{N,1-p} \\
1 & \cdots & 0 & x_{1,1} & \cdots & 0 & \cdots & \cdots & \cdots & x_{N,1} & \cdots & 0 & \cdots & \cdots & \cdots & x_{1,2-p} & \cdots & 0 & \cdots & \cdots & \cdots & x_{N,2-p} & \cdots & 0 \\
\vdots & \ddots & \vdots & \vdots & \ddots & \vdots & \vdots & \ddots & \vdots & \vdots & \ddots & \vdots & \vdots & \ddots & \vdots & \vdots & \ddots & \vdots & \vdots & \ddots & \vdots & \vdots & \ddots & \vdots \\
0 & \cdots & 1 & 0 & \cdots & x_{1,1} & \cdots & \cdots & \cdots & 0 & \cdots & x_{N,1} & \cdots & \cdots & \cdots & 0 & \cdots & x_{1,2-p} & \cdots & \cdots & \cdots & 0 & \cdots & x_{N,2-p} \\
\vdots & \cdots & \vdots & \vdots & \cdots & \vdots & & & & \vdots & \cdots & \vdots & & & & \vdots & \cdots & \vdots & & & & \vdots & \cdots & \vdots \\
\vdots & \ddots & \vdots & \vdots & \ddots & \vdots & & \ddots & & \vdots & \ddots & \vdots & & \ddots & & \vdots & \ddots & \vdots & & \ddots & & \vdots & \ddots & \vdots \\
\vdots & \cdots & \vdots & \vdots & \cdots & \vdots & & & & \vdots & \cdots & \vdots & & & & \vdots & \cdots & \vdots & & & & \vdots & \cdots & \vdots \\
1 & \cdots & 0 & x_{1,T-2} & \cdots & 0 & \cdots & \cdots & \cdots & x_{N,T-2} & \cdots & 0 & \cdots & \cdots & \cdots & x_{1,T-p-1} & \cdots & 0 & \cdots & \cdots & \cdots & x_{N,T-p-1} & \cdots & 0 \\
\vdots & \ddots & \vdots & \vdots & \ddots & \vdots & \vdots & \ddots & \vdots & \vdots & \ddots & \vdots & \vdots & \ddots & \vdots & \vdots & \ddots & \vdots & \vdots & \ddots & \vdots & \vdots & \ddots & \vdots \\
0 & \cdots & 1 & 0 & \cdots & x_{1,T-2} & \cdots & \cdots & \cdots & 0 & \cdots & x_{N,T-2} & \cdots & \cdots & \cdots & 0 & \cdots & x_{1,T-p-1} & \cdots & \cdots & \cdots & 0 & \cdots & x_{N,T-p-1} \\
1 & \cdots & 0 & x_{1,T-1} & \cdots & 0 & \cdots & \cdots & \cdots & x_{N,T-1} & \cdots & 0 & \cdots & \cdots & \cdots & x_{1,T-p} & \cdots & 0 & \cdots & \cdots & \cdots & x_{N,T-p} & \cdots & 0 \\
\vdots & \ddots & \vdots & \vdots & \ddots & \vdots & \vdots & \ddots & \vdots & \vdots & \ddots & \vdots & \vdots & \ddots & \vdots & \vdots & \ddots & \vdots & \vdots & \ddots & \vdots & \vdots & \ddots & \vdots \\
0 & \cdots & 1 & 0 & \cdots & x_{1,T-1} & \cdots & \cdots & \cdots & 0 & \cdots & x_{N,T-1} & \cdots & \cdots & \cdots & 0 & \cdots & x_{1,T-p} & \cdots & \cdots & \cdots & 0 & \cdots & x_{N,T-p}
\end{bmatrix}
$$

This matrix can be written compactly as follows: $\mathbf{w} = (\mathbf{W}' \otimes \mathbf{I}_N)$, where

$$
\mathbf{W} = \begin{bmatrix}
1 & 1 & \cdots & 1 & 1 \\
\mathbf{x}_0 & \mathbf{x}_1 & \cdots & \mathbf{x}_{T-2} & \mathbf{x}_{T-1} \\
\mathbf{x}_{-1} & \mathbf{x}_0 & \cdots & \mathbf{x}_{T-3} & \mathbf{x}_{T-2} \\
\vdots & \vdots & \ddots & \vdots & \vdots \\
\mathbf{x}_{p-1} & \mathbf{x}_{p-2} & \cdots & \mathbf{x}_{T-p-1} & \mathbf{x}_{T-p}
\end{bmatrix}
$$

$$
= \begin{bmatrix}
1 & 1 & \cdots & 1 & 1 \\
x_{1,0} & x_{1,1} & \cdots & x_{1,T-2} & x_{1,T-1} \\
\vdots & \vdots & \ddots & \vdots & \vdots \\
x_{N,0} & x_{N,1} & \cdots & x_{N,T-2} & x_{N,T-1} \\
x_{1,-1} & x_{1,0} & \cdots & x_{1,T-3} & x_{1,T-2} \\
\vdots & \vdots & \ddots & \vdots & \vdots \\
x_{N,-1} & x_{N,0} & \cdots & x_{N,T-3} & x_{N,T-2} \\
\vdots & \vdots & \ddots & \vdots & \vdots \\
\vdots & \vdots & \ddots & \vdots & \vdots \\
x_{1,1-p} & x_{1,2-p} & \cdots & x_{1,T-p-1} & x_{1,T-p} \\
\vdots & \vdots & \ddots & \vdots & \vdots \\
x_{N,1-p} & x_{N,2-p} & \cdots & x_{N,T-p-1} & x_{N,T-p}
\end{bmatrix}
$$

is a $((Np + 1) \times T)$ matrix and $\mathbf{I}_N$ is the N-dimensional identity matrix.

Let us arrange all the model coefficients in a single $(N \times (Np + 1))$ matrix as

$$
\mathbf{A} = (\mathbf{v}, \mathbf{A}_1, ..., \mathbf{A}_p)
$$

$$
= \begin{pmatrix}
v_1 & a_{11}^1 & \cdots & a_{1N}^1 & \cdots & \cdots & \cdots & a_{11}^p & \cdots & a_{1N}^p \\
\vdots & \vdots & \ddots & \vdots & \vdots & \ddots & \vdots & \vdots & \ddots & \vdots \\
v_N & a_{N1}^1 & \cdots & a_{NN}^1 & \cdots & \cdots & \cdots & a_{N1}^p & \cdots & a_{NN}^p
\end{pmatrix}
$$

and construct the $(N(Np + 1) \times 1)$ vector as

$$\beta = \text{vec}(\mathbf{A}) = \begin{pmatrix} v_1 \\ \vdots \\ v_N \\ a_{11}^1 \\ \vdots \\ a_{N1}^1 \\ \vdots \\ a_{1N}^p \\ \vdots \\ a_{NN}^p \end{pmatrix}$$

Using the notation established above, we can now compactly write the VAR(p) model in two equivalent ways as follows:

$$\mathbf{X} = \mathbf{AW} + \mathbf{U}$$

$$\mathbf{x} = \mathbf{w}\beta + \mathbf{u}$$

The first is a matrix equation where the left and right sides are $N \times T$ matrices such that each column represents the VAR(p) equation for each observation. The second equation, which equates the two NT vectors on the left and right sides, can be derived from the first as follows, using the properties of the vec operator and the Kronecker product established above:

$$\text{vec}(\mathbf{X}) = \text{vec}(\mathbf{AW}) + \text{vec}(\mathbf{U})$$

$$\text{vec}(\mathbf{X}) = (\mathbf{W}' \otimes \mathbf{I}_N)\text{vec}(\mathbf{A}) + \text{vec}(\mathbf{U})$$

$$\mathbf{x} = \mathbf{w}\beta + \mathbf{u}$$

This latter equation is the equivalent of the regression equation established in Chapter 14.

To estimate the model, we have to write the sum of the squares of residuals as we did for the sum of the residuals in a regression (see Chapter 14). However, as already mentioned, we must also consider the multivariate nature of the noise terms and the presence of correlations.

Our starting point will be the regression equation $\mathbf{x} = \mathbf{w}\beta + \mathbf{u}$ which we can rewrite as $\mathbf{u} = \mathbf{x} - \mathbf{w}\beta$. As the innovation terms exhibit a correlation structure, we have to proceed as in the case of Generalized Least Squares. We write the squared residuals as follows:

$$S = u'\Sigma_u^{-1}u = \sum_{t=1}^{T} \varepsilon_t'\Sigma^{-1}\varepsilon_t$$

For a given set of observations, the quantity S is a function of the model parameters $S = S(\beta)$. The function S admits the following alternative representation:

$$S(\beta) = \text{trace}[(X - AW)'\Sigma_u^{-1}(X - AW)] = \text{trace}[U'\Sigma_u^{-1}U]$$

In fact, we can write the following derivation:

$$S = u'\Sigma_u^{-1}u = (\text{vec}(U))'(I_T \otimes \Sigma)^{-1}\text{vec}(U)$$

$$= (\text{vec}(X - AW))'(I_T \otimes \Sigma^{-1})\text{vec}(X - AW)$$

$$= \text{trace}[(X - AW)'\Sigma_u^{-1}(X - AW)] = \text{trace}[U'\Sigma_u^{-1}U]$$

These expressions are recurrent in the theory of estimation of VAR processes and multiple regressions.

We are now ready to estimate the model parameters, imposing the least squares condition: the estimated parameters $\hat{\beta}$ are those that minimize $S = S(\beta)$. The minimum of S is attained for those values of β that equate to zero the partial derivatives of S:

$$\frac{\partial S(\beta)}{\partial \beta} = 0$$

Equating these derivatives to zero yields the so-called *normal equations* of the LS method that we can derive as follows:

$$S = u'\Sigma_u^{-1}u = (x - w\beta)'\Sigma_u^{-1}(x - w\beta)$$

$$= x'\Sigma_u^{-1}x + \beta'w'\Sigma_u^{-1}w\beta - 2\beta'w'\Sigma_u^{-1}x.$$

Hence the normal equations

$$\frac{\partial S(\beta)}{\partial \beta} = 2w'\Sigma_u^{-1}w\beta - 2w'\Sigma_u^{-1}x = 0$$

In addition, the Hessian is positive as

$$\frac{\partial^2 S(\beta)}{\partial\beta\partial\beta'} = 2\mathbf{w}'\Sigma_{\mathbf{u}}^{-1}\mathbf{w}$$

Consequently, the LS estimator is

$$\hat{\beta} = (\mathbf{w}'\Sigma_{\mathbf{u}}^{-1}\mathbf{w})^{-1}\mathbf{w}'\Sigma_{\mathbf{u}}^{-1}\mathbf{x}$$

This expression—which has the same form as the Aitkin GLS estimator—is a fundamental expression in LS methods. However in this case, due to the structure of the regressors, further simplifications are possible. In fact, the LS estimator can be also written as follows:

$$\hat{\beta} = ((\mathbf{WW}')^{-1}\mathbf{W} \otimes \mathbf{I}_N)\mathbf{x}$$

To demonstrate this point, consider the following derivation:

$$
\begin{aligned}
\hat{\beta} &= (\mathbf{w}'\Sigma_{\mathbf{u}}^{-1}\mathbf{w})^{-1}\mathbf{w}'\Sigma_{\mathbf{u}}^{-1}\mathbf{x} \\
&= ((\mathbf{W}' \otimes \mathbf{I}_N)'(\mathbf{I}_T \otimes \Sigma)^{-1}(\mathbf{W}' \otimes \mathbf{I}_N))^{-1}(\mathbf{W} \otimes \mathbf{I}_N)(\mathbf{I}_T \otimes \Sigma)^{-1}\mathbf{x} \\
&= ((\mathbf{W} \otimes \mathbf{I}_N)(\mathbf{I}_T \otimes \Sigma^{-1})(\mathbf{W}' \otimes \mathbf{I}_N))^{-1}(\mathbf{W} \otimes \mathbf{I}_N)(\mathbf{I}_T \otimes \Sigma)^{-1}\mathbf{x} \\
&= ((\mathbf{WI}_T) \otimes (\mathbf{I}_N\Sigma^{-1})(\mathbf{W}' \otimes \mathbf{I}_N))^{-1}(\mathbf{WI}_T) \otimes (\mathbf{I}_N\Sigma^{-1})\mathbf{x} \\
&= ((\mathbf{W} \otimes \Sigma^{-1})(\mathbf{W}' \otimes \mathbf{I}_N))^{-1}(\mathbf{W} \otimes \Sigma^{-1})\mathbf{x} \\
&= ((\mathbf{WW}')^{-1} \otimes (\Sigma^{-1}))(\mathbf{W} \otimes \Sigma)\mathbf{x} \\
&= ((\mathbf{WW}')^{-1}\mathbf{W}) \otimes (\Sigma^{-1}\Sigma)\mathbf{x} \\
&= ((\mathbf{WW}')^{-1}\mathbf{W} \otimes \mathbf{I}_N)\mathbf{x}
\end{aligned}
$$

The above shows that, in the case of a stable unrestricted VAR process, the multivariate LS estimator is the same as the OLS estimator obtained by minimizing the quantity $S = \mathbf{u}'\mathbf{u}$. We can therefore state that in the case of VAR processes, the LS estimators are the same as the OLS estimators computed equation by equation. Computationally, this entails a significant simplification.

We can also write another expression for the estimators. In fact, we can write the following estimator for the matrix **A**:

$$\hat{A} = XW'(WW')^{-1}$$

The above relationship is obtained from:

$$\hat{\beta} = ((WW')^{-1}W \otimes I_N)x$$

$$\text{vec}\left(\hat{A}\right) = ((WW')^{-1}W \otimes I_N)\text{vec}(X)$$

$$= \text{vec}(XW'(WW')^{-1})$$

To summarize, we have obtained the following results:

1. Given a VAR(p) process, the multivariate LS estimator is the same as the OLS estimator computed equation by equation.
2. The following three expressions for the estimator are equivalent:

$$\hat{\beta} = (w'\Sigma_u^{-1}w)^{-1}w'\Sigma_u^{-1}x$$

$$\hat{\beta} = ((WW')^{-1}W \otimes I_N)x$$

$$\hat{A} = XW'(WW')^{-1}$$

We next discuss the large-sample (asymptotic) distribution of these estimators.

The Asymptotic Distribution of LS Estimators

In Chapter 14 we observed that estimators depend on the sample and have therefore to be considered random variables. To assess the quality of the estimators, the distribution of the estimators must be determined. The properties of these distributions are not the same in small and large samples.

It is difficult to calculate the small sample distributions of the LS estimators of the stationary VAR process determined earlier. Consider that the only restriction placed on the distribution of the white noise process is that it has a non-singular covariance matrix. Small sample properties of a stationary VAR process can be approximately ascertained using Monte Carlo methods.

Significant simplifications hold approximately in large samples and hold asymptotically when the sample size becomes infinite. The essential result is that the distribution of the model estimators becomes normal. The asymptotic properties of the LS estimators can be established under additional assumptions on the white noise. Suppose that the white-noise process has finite and bounded fourth moments and that noise variables at different times are independent and not merely uncorrelated as we have assumed thus far. (Note that these conditions are automatically satisfied by any Gaussian white noise.). Under these assumptions, it can be demonstrated that the following properties hold:

■ The $((Np + 1) \times (Np + 1))$ matrix

$$\Gamma : = \text{plim}\frac{\mathbf{W}\mathbf{W}'}{T}$$

exists and is nonsingular.

■ The $(N(Np + 1) \times 1)$ vector $\hat{\boldsymbol{\beta}}$ of estimated model parameters is jointly normally distributed:

$$\sqrt{T}\left(\hat{\boldsymbol{\beta}} - \boldsymbol{\beta}\right) \xrightarrow{d} N(0, \Gamma^{-1} \otimes \Sigma)$$

The $(N(Np + 1) \times N(Np + 1))$ matrix $\Gamma^{-1} \otimes \Sigma$ is the covariance matrix of the parameter distribution.

From the above, in any large but finite sample, we can identify the following estimators for the matrices Γ, Σ:

$$\hat{\Gamma} = \frac{\mathbf{W}\mathbf{W}'}{T}$$

$$\hat{\Sigma} = \frac{1}{T}\mathbf{X}(\mathbf{I}_T - \mathbf{W}'(\mathbf{W}\mathbf{W}')^{-1}\mathbf{W})\mathbf{X}'$$

Note that these matrices are not needed to estimate the model parameters; they are required only to understand the distribution of the model parameters. If $N = 1$, these expressions are the same as those already established for multivariate regressions. Note that the above estimator of the noise covariance matrix is biased. An unbiased estimator is obtained by multiplying the above by the factor: $T/(T - Np - 1)$.

Estimating Demeaned Processes

In previous sections we assumed that the VAR(p) model had a constant intercept and the process variables had, in general, a nonzero mean. Note that the mean and the intercept are not the same numbers. In fact, given that the process is assumed to be stationary, we can write

$$E(\mathbf{x}_t) = \mathbf{A}_1 E(\mathbf{x}_{t-1}) + \mathbf{A}_2 E(\mathbf{x}_{t-2}) + \cdots + \mathbf{A}_p E(\mathbf{x}_{t-p}) + \mathbf{v}$$

$$\mu - \mathbf{A}_1\mu - \mathbf{A}_2\mu - \cdots - \mathbf{A}_p\mu = \mathbf{v}$$

$$\mu = (\mathbf{I}_N - \mathbf{A}_1 - \mathbf{A}_2 - \cdots - \mathbf{A}_p)^{-1}\mathbf{v}$$

We can recast the previous reasoning in a different notation, assuming that the process variables are demeaned with a zero intercept. In this case, we can rewrite the VAR process in the following form:

$$(\mathbf{x}_t - \mu) = \mathbf{A}_1(\mathbf{x}_{t-1} - \mu) + \mathbf{A}_2(\mathbf{x}_{t-2} - \mu) + \cdots + \mathbf{A}_p(\mathbf{x}_{t-p} - \mu) + \boldsymbol{\varepsilon}_t$$

If we write $\mathbf{y}_t = \mathbf{x}_t - \mu$, the VAR process becomes

$$\mathbf{y}_t = \mathbf{A}_1\mathbf{y}_{t-1} + \mathbf{A}_2\mathbf{y}_{t-2} + \cdots + \mathbf{A}_p\mathbf{y}_{t-p} + \boldsymbol{\varepsilon}_t$$

This model contains N parameters less than the original model as the intercepts do not appear. If the mean is not known, it can be estimated separately as

$$\hat{\mu} = \sum_{t=1}^{T} \mathbf{x}_t$$

The formulas previously established hold with some obvious changes. We will write down the formulas explicitly, as they will be used in the following sections:

$$\mathbf{Y} = (\mathbf{y}_1, ..., \mathbf{y}_T)$$
$$\mathbf{U} = (\boldsymbol{\varepsilon}_1, ..., \boldsymbol{\varepsilon}_T)$$
$$\mathbf{y} = \text{vec}(\mathbf{Y})$$
$$\mathbf{u} = \text{vec}(\mathbf{U})$$
$$\boldsymbol{\Sigma}_\mathbf{u} = \mathbf{I}_T \otimes \boldsymbol{\Sigma}$$
$$\mathbf{A} = (\mathbf{A}_1, ..., \mathbf{A}_p)$$
$$\alpha = \text{vec}(\mathbf{A})$$

$$Z = \begin{pmatrix} y_0 & \cdots & y_{T-1} \\ \vdots & \ddots & \vdots \\ y_{1-p} & \cdots & y_{T-p} \end{pmatrix}$$

$$z = (Z' \otimes I_N)$$

The model is then written in matrix form as

$$y = z\alpha + u$$

$$Y = AZ + U$$

The LS estimators are then written as follows:

$$\hat{\alpha} = (z'\Sigma_u^{-1}z)^{-1}z'\Sigma_u^{-1}y$$

$$\hat{\alpha} = ((ZZ')^{-1}Z \otimes I_N)y$$

$$\hat{A} = YZ'(ZZ')^{-1}$$

It can be demonstrated that the sample mean,

$$\hat{\mu} = \sum_{t=1}^{T} x_t$$

is a consistent estimator of the process mean and has a normal asymptotic distribution. If the process is not demeaned and has constant estimated intercept $\hat{v}$, the mean can be estimated with the following estimator:

$$\hat{\mu} = (I_N - A_1 - A_2 - \cdots - A_p)^{-1}\hat{v}$$

which is consistent and has an asymptotic normal distribution.

We now turn our attention to the Maximum Likelihood estimation methods.

Maximum Likelihood Estimators

Under the assumption of Gaussian innovations, *Maximum Likelihood* (ML) estimation methods coincide with LS estimation methods. Recall from Chapter 14 that, given a known distribution, ML methods try to find the distribution parameters that maximize the likelihood function (i.e., the joint distribution of the sample computed on the sample itself). In the case of a multivariate mean-adjusted VAR(p) process, the given sample data are T empirical observations of the N-variate variable y_t, $t = 1, \ldots, T$ and a presample of p initial conditions $y_{-p+1}, \ldots, y_0$. If we assume that the process is stationary and that innovations are Gaussian white noise, the variables y_t, $t = 1, \ldots, T$ will also be jointly normally distributed.

One can derive the joint distribution of the sample y_t, $t = 1, \ldots, T$ in function of the sample data and apply ML methods to this distribution. However, it is easier to express the joint distribution of the noise terms in function of the data. As the white noise is assumed to be Gaussian, the noise variables at different times are independent. As observed in Chapter 14, this allows considerable simplifications for computing the likelihood function.

The noise terms $(\varepsilon_1, \ldots, \varepsilon_T)$ are assumed to be independent with constant covariance matrix Σ and, therefore, $u = \text{vec}(U)$ has covariance matrix $\Sigma_u = I_T \otimes \Sigma$. Under the assumption of Gaussian noise, the density $f_u(u)$ of u is the following NT-variate normal density:

$$f_u(u) = \frac{1}{(2\pi)^{\frac{NT}{2}}} |I_T \otimes \Sigma|^{-\frac{1}{2}} \exp\left(-\frac{1}{2} u'(I_T \otimes \Sigma^{-1}) u\right)$$

$$= \frac{1}{(2\pi)^{\frac{NT}{2}}} |\Sigma|^{-\frac{T}{2}} \exp\left(-\frac{1}{2} \sum_{t=1}^{T} \varepsilon_t' \Sigma^{-1} \varepsilon_t\right)$$

This density is expressed in function of the noise terms which are unobserved terms. In order to estimate, we need to express the density in terms of the observations. The density can easily be expressed in terms of observations using the VAR(p) equation:

$$\varepsilon_1 = y_1 - A_1 y_0 - A_2 y_{-1} - \cdots - A_p y_{1-p}$$
$$\varepsilon_2 = y_2 - A_1 y_1 - A_2 y_0 - \cdots - A_p y_{2-p}$$
$$\cdots\cdots\cdots\cdots\cdots\cdots\cdots\cdots\cdots\cdots\cdots\cdots\cdots\cdots$$
$$\varepsilon_p = y_p - A_1 y_0 - A_2 y_{p-2} - \cdots - A_p y_0$$
$$\varepsilon_{p+1} = y_{p+1} - A_1 y_p - A_2 y_{p-2} - \cdots - A_p y_1$$
$$\cdots\cdots\cdots\cdots\cdots\cdots\cdots\cdots\cdots\cdots\cdots\cdots\cdots\cdots$$
$$\varepsilon_{T-1} = y_{T-1} - A_1 y_{T-2} - A_2 y_{T-3} - \cdots - A_p y_{T-p-1}$$
$$\varepsilon_T = y_T - A_1 y_{T-1} - A_2 y_{T-2} - \cdots - A_p y_{T-p}$$

The above can be re-written in matrix form as follows:

$$
\begin{pmatrix} \varepsilon_1 \\ \varepsilon_2 \\ \vdots \\ \varepsilon_p \\ \varepsilon_{p+1} \\ \vdots \\ \varepsilon_{T-1} \\ \varepsilon_T \end{pmatrix} = \begin{pmatrix} \mathbf{I}_N & 0 & \cdots & 0 & 0 & 0 & \cdots & \cdots & 0 & 0 & \cdots & 0 & 0 \\ -\mathbf{A}_1 & \mathbf{I}_N & \cdots & 0 & 0 & 0 & \cdots & \cdots & 0 & 0 & \cdots & 0 & 0 \\ \vdots & \vdots & \ddots & \vdots & \vdots & \vdots & \ddots & \ddots & \vdots & \vdots & \ddots & \vdots & \vdots \\ -\mathbf{A}_p & -\mathbf{A}_{p-1} & \cdots & -\mathbf{A}_1 & \mathbf{I}_N & 0 & \cdots & \cdots & 0 & 0 & \cdots & 0 & 0 & \cdots \\ 0 & -\mathbf{A}_p & \cdots & -\mathbf{A}_2 & -\mathbf{A}_1 & \mathbf{I}_N & \cdots & \cdots & 0 & 0 & \cdots & 0 & 0 \\ \vdots & \vdots & \ddots & \vdots & \vdots & \vdots & \ddots & \ddots & \vdots & \vdots & \ddots & \vdots & \vdots \\ 0 & 0 & \cdots & 0 & 0 & 0 & \cdots & 0 & -\mathbf{A}_p & -\mathbf{A}_{p-1} & \cdots & \mathbf{I}_N & 0 \\ 0 & 0 & \cdots & 0 & 0 & 0 & \cdots & 0 & 0 & -\mathbf{A}_p & \cdots & -\mathbf{A}_1 & \mathbf{I}_N \end{pmatrix}
$$

$$
\begin{pmatrix} \mathbf{y}_1 \\ \mathbf{y}_2 \\ \vdots \\ \mathbf{y}_p \\ \mathbf{y}_{p+1} \\ \vdots \\ \mathbf{y}_{T-p} \\ \vdots \\ \mathbf{y}_{T-1} \\ \mathbf{y}_T \end{pmatrix} + \begin{pmatrix} -\mathbf{A}_p & -\mathbf{A}_{p-1} & \cdots & -\mathbf{A}_1 \\ 0 & -\mathbf{A}_p & \cdots & -\mathbf{A}_2 \\ \vdots & \vdots & \ddots & \vdots \\ 0 & 0 & \cdots & -\mathbf{A}_p \\ \vdots & \vdots & \ddots & \vdots \\ 0 & 0 & \cdots & 0 \end{pmatrix} \begin{pmatrix} \mathbf{y}_{1-p} \\ \mathbf{y}_{2-p} \\ \mathbf{y}_{-1} \\ \mathbf{y}_0 \end{pmatrix}
$$

Using these expressions and the model equation $\mathbf{y} = \mathbf{z}\alpha + \mathbf{u}$, we can now express the density function in terms of the variables

$$
f_y(\mathbf{y}) = \left| \frac{\partial \mathbf{u}}{\partial \mathbf{y}} \right| f_\mathbf{u}(\mathbf{u}) = \frac{1}{(2\pi)^{\frac{NT}{2}}} |\mathbf{I}_T \otimes \Sigma|^{-\frac{1}{2}} \exp\left(-\frac{1}{2}(\mathbf{y} - \mathbf{z}\alpha)'(\mathbf{I}_T \otimes \Sigma^{-1})(\mathbf{y} - \mathbf{z}\alpha) \right)
$$

Using reasoning similar to that we used in the LS case, we can write the log-likelihood as follows:

$$
\begin{aligned}
\log(l) &= -\frac{NT}{2}\log(2\pi) - \frac{T}{2}\log|\Sigma_\mathbf{u}| - \frac{1}{2}\sum_{t=1}^{T} \varepsilon_t'\Sigma^{-1}\varepsilon_t \\
&= -\frac{NT}{2}\log(2\pi) - \frac{T}{2}\log|\Sigma_\mathbf{u}| - \frac{1}{2}(\mathbf{y} - \mathbf{z}\alpha)'(\mathbf{I}_T \otimes \Sigma^{-1})(\mathbf{y} - \mathbf{z}\alpha) \\
&= -\frac{NT}{2}\log(2\pi) - \frac{T}{2}\log|\Sigma_\mathbf{u}| - \frac{1}{2}\text{trace}(\mathbf{U}'\Sigma_\mathbf{u}^{-1}\mathbf{U})
\end{aligned}
$$

$$= -\frac{NT}{2}\log(2\pi) - \frac{T}{2}\log|\mathbf{\Sigma_u}| - \frac{1}{2}\text{trace}((\mathbf{Y} - \mathbf{AZ})'\mathbf{\Sigma_u}^{-1}(\mathbf{Y} - \mathbf{AZ}))$$

Equating the partial derivatives of this expression to zero, we obtain the very same estimators we obtained with the LS method. In the case of Gaussian noise, LS/OLS methods and ML methods yield the same result.

ESTIMATING THE NUMBER OF LAGS

In the previous sections, we assumed that the empirical process is generated by a stable VAR model. This assumption entails that the process is stationary. In both the LS and ML estimation methods, the order p of the model (i.e., the number of lags in the model) is assumed to be known. However, there is nothing in the estimation method that imposes a specific model order. Given an empirical time series, we can fit a VAR(p) model with an arbitrary number of lags.

The objective of this section is to establish criteria that allow determining *a priori* the correct number of lags. This idea has to be made more precise. We assume, as we did in the previous sections on the estimation of the model coefficients, that the true data generation process is a VAR(p) model. In this case, we expect that the correct model order is exactly p, that is, we expect to come out with a consistent estimator of the model order. This is not the same problem as trying to determine the optimal number of lags to fit a VAR model to a process that might not be generated by a linear data generation process. We discuss in Chapter 17 the robustness of a VAR model to misspecification of the type of model; here we assume that the type of model is correctly specified and discuss methods to estimate the model order under this assumption.

As observed, we can fit a model of any order to any set of empirical data. In general, increasing the model order will reduce the size of residuals but reduces the forecasting ability of the model. This phenomenon was discussed in Chapter 13 in the context of learning theory. It is a basic tenet of learning theory that, by increasing the number of parameters, we will improve the in-sample accuracy but worsen the out-of-sample forecasting ability. In this section we consider only linear models under the assumption that the data generation process is linear and autoregressive with unknown parameters.[6]

---

[6] The difference between the two approaches should not be underestimated. In its generality, learning theory deals with finding models of empirical data without any previous knowledge of the true DGP. In this section, however, we assume that a true DGP exists and is a finite VAR.

To see how increasing the number of lags can reduce the forecasting ability of the model, consider that the forecasting ability of a linear VAR model can be estimated. Recall from Chapter 12 that the optimal forecast of a VAR model is the conditional mean. This implies that the optimal one-step forecast given the past p values of the process up to the present moment is

$$x_{t+1} = A_1 x_t + A_2 x_{t-1} + \cdots + A_p x_{t-p+1} + v$$

The forecasting *Mean Square Error* (MSE) can be estimated. It can be demonstrated that an approximate estimate of the one-step MSE is given by the following expression:

$$\Sigma_x(1) = \frac{T + Np + 1}{T} \Sigma(p)$$

where $\Sigma(p)$ is the covariance matrix of a model of order p. The $\Sigma_x(1)$ is a covariance matrix of the forecasting errors. Based on $\Sigma_x(1)$, Akaike suggested a criterion to estimate the model order.[7] First, we have to replace $\Sigma(p)$ with its estimate. In the case of a zero-mean process, we can estimate $\Sigma(p)$ as

$$\hat{\Sigma}(p) = \frac{1}{T} X(I_T - W'(WW')^{-1}W)X'$$

The quantity

$$FPE(p) = \left[\frac{T + Np + 1}{T - Np + 1}\right]^N \det(\hat{\Sigma}(p))$$

is called the *Final Prediction Error* (FPE). In 1969, Akaike proposed to determine the model order by minimizing the FPE.[8] Four years later, he proposed a different criterion based on information theory considerations. The new criterion, commonly called the *Akaike Information Criterion* (AIC), proposes to determine the model order by minimizing the following expression:

[7] Hirotugu Akaike, "Fitting Autoregressive Models for Prediction," *Annals of the Institute of Statistical Mathematics* 21 (1969), pp. 243–247.
[8] Hirotugu Akaike, "Information Theory and an Extension of the Maximum Likelihood Principle," Petrov and Csaki (eds.), *Second International Symposium on Information Theory* (Budapest: Akademiaio Kiado, 1973).

$$\mathrm{AIC}(p) = \log\left|\hat{\Sigma}(p)\right| + \frac{2pN^2}{T}$$

Neither the FPE nor the AIC estimators are consistent estimators in the sense that they determine the correct model order in the limit of an infinite sample. Different but consistent criteria have been proposed. Among them, the *Bayesian Information Criterion* (BIC) is quite popular. Proposed by Schwartz, the BIC chooses the model that minimizes the following expression:[9]

$$\mathrm{AIC}(p) = \log\left|\hat{\Sigma}(p)\right| + \frac{\log T}{T} 2pN^2$$

There is a vast literature on model selection criteria. The justification of each criterion impinges on rather complex considerations of information theory, statistics, and learning theory.[10]

AUTOCORRELATION AND DISTRIBUTIONAL PROPERTIES OF RESIDUALS

The validity of the LS method does not depend on the distribution of innovations provided that their covariance matrix exists. However, the LS method might not be optimal if innovations are not normally distributed. The ML method, in contrast, critically depends on the distributional properties of innovations. Nevertheless, both methods are sensitive to the eventual autocorrelation of innovation terms. Therefore, it is important to check the absence of autocorrelation of residuals and to ascertain eventual deviations from normal distributions.

The estimated VAR model distributional properties are critical in applications such as asset allocation, portfolio management, and risk management. The presence of tails might change optimality conditions and the entire optimization process.

Checking the distributional properties of an estimated VAR model can be done with one of the many available tests of autocorrelation and

---

[9] G. Schwarz, "Estimating the Dimension of a Model," *Annals of Statistics* 6 (1978), pp. 461–464.
[10] See, for example, D. P. Foster and R. A. Stine, "An Information Theoretic Comparison of Model Selection Criteria," Working Paper 1180, 1997, Northwestern University, Center for Mathematical Studies in Economics and Management Science.

normality. After estimating the VAR model parameters and the model order—a process that calls for iterating the estimation process—the residuals of the process are computed. Given the linearity of the model, the normality of the model distributions can be checked by analyzing only the residuals.

The autocorrelation properties of the residuals can be checked using the Dickey-Fuller (DF) or the Augmented Dickey-Fuller (ADF) test discussed earlier in this chapter. Both tests are widely used tests of autocorrelation implemented in most time series computer programs. The DF and ADF tests work by estimating the autoregresssion coefficient of the residuals and comparing it with a table of critical values.

In the case of stationary models, the normality of distributions can be tested with one of the many tests for normality discussed in Chapter 7. These tests are available on most statistical computer packages.

STATIONARY AUTOREGRESSIVE DISTRIBUTED LAG MODELS

An important extension of pure VAR models is given by the family of Autoregressive Distributed Lag (ARDL) models. The ARDL model is essentially the coupling of a regression model and a VAR model. The ARDL model is written as follows:

$$\mathbf{y}_t = \mathbf{v} + \mathbf{\Phi}_1 \mathbf{y}_{t-1} + \cdots + \mathbf{\Phi}_s \mathbf{y}_{t-s} + \mathbf{P}_0 \mathbf{x}_t + \cdots + \mathbf{P}_q \mathbf{x}_{t-q} + \mathbf{\eta}_t$$

$$\mathbf{x}_t = \mathbf{A}_1 \mathbf{x}_{t-1} + \cdots + \mathbf{A}_p \mathbf{x}_{t-p} + \mathbf{\varepsilon}_t$$

In the ARDL model, a variable $\mathbf{y}_t$ is regressed over its own lagged values and over the values of another variable $\mathbf{x}_t$ which follows a VAR(p) model. Both the $\mathbf{\eta}_t$ and the $\mathbf{\varepsilon}_t$ terms are assumed to be white noise with a time-invariant covariance matrix.

The above ARDL model can be rewritten as a VAR(1) model as follows:

$$
\begin{pmatrix}
\mathbf{y}_t \\
\mathbf{y}_{t-1} \\
\vdots \\
\mathbf{y}_{t-s+2} \\
\mathbf{y}_{t-s+1} \\
\mathbf{x}_t \\
\vdots \\
\vdots \\
\mathbf{x}_{t-p}
\end{pmatrix}
=
\begin{pmatrix}
\mathbf{v} \\
0 \\
\vdots \\
0 \\
0 \\
0 \\
0 \\
\vdots \\
0 \\
0
\end{pmatrix}
\begin{pmatrix}
\boldsymbol{\Phi}_1 & \boldsymbol{\Phi}_2 & \cdots & \boldsymbol{\Phi}_{s-1} & \boldsymbol{\Phi}_s & \mathbf{P}_0 & \mathbf{P}_1 & \cdots & \mathbf{P}_q & \cdots & 0 & 0 \\
\mathbf{I} & 0 & \cdots & 0 & 0 & 0 & 0 & \cdots & 0 & \cdots & 0 & 0 \\
\vdots & \vdots & \ddots & \vdots & \vdots & \vdots & \vdots & \ddots & \vdots & \ddots & \vdots & \vdots \\
0 & 0 & \cdots & \mathbf{I} & 0 & 0 & 0 & \cdots & 0 & \cdots & 0 & 0 \\
0 & 0 & \cdots & 0 & \mathbf{I} & 0 & 0 & \cdots & 0 & \cdots & 0 & 0 \\
0 & 0 & \cdots & 0 & 0 & 0 & \mathbf{A}_1 & \cdots & \mathbf{A}_q & \cdots & \mathbf{A}_{p-1} & \mathbf{A}_p \\
0 & 0 & \cdots & 0 & 0 & 0 & \mathbf{I} & \cdots & 0 & \cdots & 0 & 0 \\
\vdots & \vdots & \ddots & \vdots & \vdots & \vdots & \vdots & \ddots & \vdots & \ddots & \vdots & \vdots \\
0 & 0 & \cdots & 0 & 0 & 0 & 0 & \cdots & 0 & \cdots & 0 & 0 \\
0 & 0 & \cdots & 0 & 0 & 0 & 0 & \cdots & 0 & \cdots & \mathbf{I} & 0
\end{pmatrix}
$$

$$
\begin{pmatrix}
\mathbf{y}_{t-1} \\
\mathbf{y}_{t-2} \\
\vdots \\
\mathbf{y}_{t-s+1} \\
\mathbf{y}_{t-s} \\
\mathbf{x}_t \\
\mathbf{x}_{t-1} \\
\vdots \\
\mathbf{x}_{t-q} \\
\vdots \\
\mathbf{x}_{t-p} \\
\mathbf{x}_{t-p-1}
\end{pmatrix}
+
\begin{pmatrix}
\boldsymbol{\eta}_t \\
0 \\
\vdots \\
\vdots \\
0 \\
\boldsymbol{\varepsilon}_t \\
0 \\
\vdots \\
\vdots \\
0
\end{pmatrix}
$$

The estimation of the ARDL model can therefore be done with the methods used for VAR models. Coefficients can be estimated with OLS methods and the number of lags can be determined with the AIC or BIC criteria discussed in a previous section.

The ARDL model is quite important in financial econometrics: many models of stock returns are essentially ARDL models. In particular, all models where stock returns are regressed over a number of state variables that follow a VAR model are ARDL models. We now proceed to discuss some applications of VAR processes.

APPLYING STABLE VAR PROCESSES TO FINANCIAL ECONOMETRICS

The estimation processes described in the previous sections lose their meaningfulness when the number N of variables is large. In this case, we encounter the same problems already encountered in dealing with the estimation of a large covariance matrix. In Chapter 9 where we discuss the estimation of large covariance matrices, we found that only a small number of eigenvalues are significant while most carry no information. In other words, the entries of a large covariance matrix are very noisy. Analogously, estimating a large VAR model results in noisy coefficients. For example, it would be impossible to estimate a meaningful unrestricted VAR model of the returns of all stocks included in the S&P 100 or the S&P 500. Estimated coefficients would be too noisy and would therefore carry no meaningful information. (The section on dynamic factors later in this chapter shows how one can deal with this problem.)

However if the number of variables in the VAR process is small in comparison with the sample size, then the estimation process is meaningful. This is the case with broad aggregates such as indexes. Due to mounting empirical evidence that the returns of broad aggregates do indeed exhibit some forecastability, the 1980s and 1990s witnessed a renewed interest in the predictability of aggregates. Even if single stocks are individually unpredictable, the predictability of aggregates is possible thanks to cross autocorrelations between stocks.

The (albeit limited) predictability of asset returns, together with advances in computer technology, spurred a renewed interest in multiperiod portfolio choice. Brennan, Schwartz, and Lagnado coined the term "strategic asset allocation" to describe the farsighted, as opposed to myopic, asset allocation decision-making process.[11] Strategic asset allocation allocates capital to different asset classes dynamically. At each period, allocation is reevaluated and decisions are made knowing that they will be revised at future dates. This is a distinctive character of farsighted asset allocation procedures. Myopic asset allocation makes decisions based only on returns at the end of the period.

In order to perform strategic asset allocation, forecasts of the relevant rates and returns are needed. A number of studies have proposed VAR models in financial econometrics especially to forecast the returns of indexes. Unrestricted VAR models have been proposed by, among others, Kendal and Stambaugh,[12] Barberis,[13] and Campbell, Chan, and

---

[11] Michael J. Brennan, Eduardo S. Schwartz, and Ronald Lagnado, "Strategic Asset Allocation," *Journal of Economic Dynamics and Control* 21 (1997), pp. 1377–1403.

[12] Shmuel Kandel and Robert F. Stambaugh, "On the Predictability of Stock Returns: An Asset Allocation, Perspective," *Journal of Finance* 51 (1996), pp. 385–424. Donald Keim and Robert F. Stambaugh, "Predicting Returns in the Stock and Bond Markets," *Journal of Financial Economics* 17 (1996), pp. 357–390.

[13] Nicholas C. Barberis, "Investing for the Long Run When Returns are Predictable," *Journal of Finance* 50 (2000), pp. 225–264.

Viceira.[14] For example, Campbell, Chan, and Viceira consider the following VAR(1) model of returns and predictive variables:

$$z_{t+1} = \Phi_0 + \Phi_1 z_t + v_{t+1}$$

The variables z_{t+1} are divided into three categories:

$$z_{t+1} = \begin{pmatrix} r_{1, t+1} \\ x_{t+1} \\ s_{t+1} \end{pmatrix}$$

where $r_{1,t+1}$ is the short rate, x_{t+1} is a vector of asset returns, and s_{t+1} is a vector of state variables such as dividend-price ratios. The authors do not include state variables to represent lagged values of returns or state variables. The choice of a VAR(1) model is motivated by simplicity in the context of an academic study that aims at maximum generality. Practical implementations of this type of modeling would search for the optimal number of lags.

The innovation terms are assumed to be normally distributed independent variables:

$$v_{t+1} \sim N(0, \Sigma_v)$$

$$\Sigma_v = \begin{bmatrix} \sigma_1^2 & \sigma_x' & \sigma_s' \\ \sigma_x & \Sigma_{xx} & \Sigma_{xx}' \\ \sigma_s & \Sigma_{xs} & \Sigma_{ss} \end{bmatrix}$$

The authors explore different choices of state variables. The paper concludes that the above VAR(1) model exhibits a considerable level of return predictability.[15]

The above Campbell-Chan-Viceira model is a VAR model where stock returns and regressors are treated in the same way as a vector autoregression. As already observed, working with a large number of stocks, the dimensionality of this model makes estimates very noisy. Many models of stock returns regress each return over a number of common regressors, eventually adding an idiosyncratic dynamics for

---

[14] John Y. Campbell, Yeung L. Chan, and Luis M. Viceira, "A Multivariate Model of Strategic Asset Allocation," *Journal of Financial Economics* 67 (2003), pp. 41–80.
[15] The major aim of the paper is not to explore asset predictability but to discuss asset allocation policies under asset return predictability.

each stock. For example, the well known Fama-French model of asset returns that couples long-term and short-term dynamics can be cast in this factor analytic framework.[16] Chunseng Zhou provides a comparison of different models of stock returns in various autoregressive and factor analytic settings.[17] He discusses the following three models:

Model I

$$r_t = \mu_{t-1} + \eta_t$$
$$\mu_t = \mu_{t-1} + \varepsilon_t$$

Model II

$$r_t = z_t - z_{t-1} + \varepsilon_t$$
$$z_t = \phi z_{t-1} + \eta_t$$

Model III

$$r_t = z_t - z_{t-1} + \varepsilon_t$$
$$z_t = \phi z_{t-1} + \lambda x_{t-1} + \eta_t$$
$$x_t = \lambda x_{t-1} + \xi_t$$

Models I and II are simple autoregressive models, while model III includes a bivariate VAR(1). Zhou concludes that Model III offers a rather faithful representation of stock returns.

Models of this type with various selections of variables and predictors are currently in use at many asset management firms. The actual selection of variables, the number of lags, and many more adjustments constitute the proprietary contribution.

STATIONARY DYNAMIC FACTOR MODELS

As mentioned in the previous section, using unrestricted VAR models is not feasible if the number of variables is large; this is where factor models come in. They allow one to reduce the dimensionality of models. The idea of factor models is that the process dynamics is fairly represented by a small number of factors whereas all other processes are simple multivariate regressions on the factors.

[16] Eugene F. Fama and Kenneth R. French, "Permanent and Temporary Components of Stock Prices," *Journal of Political Economy* 96 (1988), pp. 246–273
[17] Chunseng Zhou, "Forecasting Long and Short Horizon Stock Returns in a Unified Framework," Working Paper, Federal Reserve, Washington D.C, 1996.

Note that factor analysis responds to two different needs. First, factor analysis tries to identify those factors that are responsible for the process dynamics. In fact, factor analysis originated in the area of social studies, where it is believed important to identify the factors responsible for specific social behavior. In this sense, factor analysis might yield exact models as opposed to mere approximations. Second, factor analysis is a statistical dimensionality reduction technique; it attempts to arrive at an approximate description of a given process. In this sense, factor analysis is similar to what, in physics, is called "mean field approximation." Suppose that a large set of interacting particles is given. The idea of mean field approximation is to replace the myriad individual mutual interactions with a much smaller number of interactions between each particle and some average of all other particles. In economics, the idea is to replace the mutual interactions between a large number of interacting agents with a smaller number of interactions with "factors." In financial econometrics, correlations and cross autocorrelations between pairs of stocks are replaced with correlations and cross autocorrelations with factors.

Early factor models were static models that specified a regression relationship between each individual variable and the factors, without specifying the model dynamics. For example, the APT model is one such static factor model. Dynamic factor models, on the other hand, specify the factor dynamics. Although a dynamic factor model is formally a static factor model with the addition of a factor dynamic, estimation issues are quite different.

A dynamic factor model can be written as follows:

$$\mathbf{x}_t = \mathbf{B}\mathbf{f}_t + \mathbf{v} + \boldsymbol{\eta}_t$$

$$\mathbf{f}_t = \mathbf{A}_1\mathbf{f}_{t-1} + \mathbf{A}_2\mathbf{f}_{t-2} + \cdots + \mathbf{A}_p\mathbf{f}_{t-p} + \boldsymbol{\varepsilon}_t$$

In this model there are N individual variables $x_{j,t}$, $j = 1, 2, \ldots, N$, $t = 1$, $2, \ldots, T$ that form the vector $\mathbf{x}_t = (x_{1,t}, \ldots, x_{N,t})'$; and $m \ll N$ zero-mean factors $\mathbf{f}_t = (f_{1,t}, \ldots, f_{m,t})'$, $t = 1, 2, \ldots, T$, $\mathbf{B}$ is a $N \times m$ matrix of *factor loadings*; and $\mathbf{A}_i = (a'_{s,t})$, $i = 1, 2, \ldots, p$, $s,t = 1, 2, \ldots, m$ are deterministic $m \times m$ matrices that form the VAR model of factors. The noise term $\boldsymbol{\varepsilon}_t = (\varepsilon_{1,t}, \ldots, \varepsilon_{m,t})$ is a multivariate white noise with variance-covariance matrix $\boldsymbol{\Sigma} = (\sigma_1, \ldots, \sigma_m)$; $\mathbf{v} = (v_1, \ldots, v_N)$ is a vector of deterministic terms; and $\boldsymbol{\eta}_t$ is the N-vector of innovations, which are possibly auto-correlated but mutually uncorrelated and also uncorrelated with the factors.

This model can be generalized in different ways, for example by assuming that factors are generated by a VARMA process, that is, by assuming factors have a moving average dynamics in addition to the vector autoregression. However, the above formulation is quite general for financial econometric applications.

The estimation process must determine the number of factors, the factors themselves, and the regression equations. If the variables are assumed to be generated by the above process, then the estimation process will try to discover the true factors. If factor analysis is used as a dimensionality reduction technique, the estimation process will be approximate in a sense that has to be made precise.

Note that the model as specified above is not uniquely determined. In fact, given any nonsingular matrix $\mathbf{H}$, we can write an equivalent model as follows:

$$\mathbf{x}_t = (\mathbf{BH}^{-1})(\mathbf{Hf}_t) + \mathbf{v} + \boldsymbol{\eta}_t$$

$$(\mathbf{Hf}_t) = (\mathbf{HA}_1\mathbf{H}^{-1})(\mathbf{Hf}_{t-1}) + (\mathbf{HA}_2\mathbf{H}^{-1})(\mathbf{Hf}_{t-2}) + \cdots$$
$$+ (\mathbf{HA}_p\mathbf{H}^{-1})(\mathbf{Hf}_{t-p}) + \mathbf{H}\boldsymbol{\varepsilon}_t\mathbf{H}$$

In order to identify the model, we have to place restrictions on the matrix $\mathbf{H}$. For example, we could impose that $\mathbf{H\Sigma H} = \mathbf{I}$ or that $(\mathbf{BH}^{-1})'(\mathbf{BH}^{-1}) = \mathbf{I}$, which still leaves the matrix $\mathbf{H}$ not fully specified as the last condition is invariant to rotations.

To estimate the above dynamic factor model, observe that it is equivalent to a state-space model. The factor model can therefore be estimated with the ML methods used to estimate state-space models. These methods will be discussed in Chapter 16, in the section on state-space models.

Peña and Box[18] proposed a different methodology for factor models where $\boldsymbol{\varepsilon}_t$, $\boldsymbol{\eta}_t$ are both white noise. They consider a stationary model with zero-mean variables. This assumption does not produce any loss of generality as the model is stationary and variables can always be demeaned. Define the k-step covariance matrices as follows:

$$\Gamma_{\mathbf{x}}(k) = E(\mathbf{x}_t'\mathbf{x}_{t-k})$$
$$\Gamma_{\mathbf{f}}(k) = E(\mathbf{f}_t'\mathbf{f}_{t-k})$$

Using the model equation we can write

$$\Gamma_{\mathbf{x}}(0) = \mathbf{B}\Gamma_{\mathbf{f}}(0)\mathbf{B} + \Sigma$$
$$\Gamma_{\mathbf{f}}(k) = \mathbf{B}\Gamma_{\mathbf{f}}(k)\mathbf{B}, \, k > 1$$

---

[18] D. Peña and G. Box, "Identifying a Simplifying Structure in Time Series," *Journal of American Statistical Association* 82 (1987), pp. 836–843.

which implies that the columns of **B** are the eigenvectors of the matrix $\Gamma_f(k)$ for every k. Peña and Box propose to recover the factors using the following procedure. First, compute the eigenvalues and eigenvectors of $\Gamma_f(k)$ for $k \geq 1$. The number of nonzero eigenvalues will stabilize to a value r which is the number of factors. The factor loading matrix will be formed by the nonzero eigenvectors. If we assume the normalization **BB'** = **I**, factors are then computed as

$$\mathbf{f}_t = \mathbf{B}'\mathbf{x}_t + \mathbf{B}'\boldsymbol{\eta}_t$$

Establishing *a priori* the number of factors is a critical task of dynamic factor analysis. In the case of stationary models, Bai and Ng[19] proposed a criterion based on information theory.

ESTIMATION OF NONSTATIONARY VAR MODELS

In the previous sections we assumed that all processes were stationary and all models stable. In this section we drop this restriction and examine the estimation of nonstationary and nonstable processes. In a nonstationary process, the averages, variances and covariances vary with time. A somewhat surprising fact is that least-squares methods can be applied to the nonstationary case although other methods are more efficient.

Consider the following VAR process:

$$\mathbf{x}_t = \mathbf{A}_1\mathbf{x}_{t-1} + \mathbf{A}_2\mathbf{x}_{t-2} + \cdots + \mathbf{A}_p\mathbf{x}_{t-p} + \mathbf{v} + \boldsymbol{\varepsilon}_t$$

$$(\mathbf{I} - \mathbf{A}_1 L - \mathbf{A}_2 L^2 - \cdots - \mathbf{A}_p L^p)\mathbf{x}_t = \mathbf{v} + \boldsymbol{\varepsilon}_t$$

Recall that a VAR process can be rewritten in the following error correction form:

$$\Delta\mathbf{x}_t = \mathbf{D}_1\Delta\mathbf{x}_{t-1} + \mathbf{D}_2\Delta\mathbf{x}_{t-2} + \cdots - \boldsymbol{\Pi}\mathbf{x}_{t-p} + \mathbf{v} + \boldsymbol{\varepsilon}_t$$

$$\mathbf{D}_i = -\mathbf{I} + \sum_{q=1}^{i} \mathbf{A}_i, i = 1, 2, \ldots, p-1, \boldsymbol{\Pi} = \mathbf{I} - \mathbf{A}_1 - \mathbf{A}_2 - \cdots - \mathbf{A}_p$$

In fact, we can write

---

[19] J. Bai and S. Ng, "Determining the Number of Factors in Approximate Factor Models," *Econometrica* 70 (2002), pp. 191–222.

$$\mathbf{x}_t - \mathbf{x}_{t-1} = (\mathbf{A}_1 - \mathbf{I})\mathbf{x}_{t-1} + \mathbf{A}_2\mathbf{x}_{t-2} + \cdots + \mathbf{A}_p\mathbf{x}_{t-p} + \mathbf{v} + \boldsymbol{\varepsilon}_t$$

$$\Delta\mathbf{x}_t = (\mathbf{A}_1 - \mathbf{I})\Delta\mathbf{x}_{t-1} + (\mathbf{A}_2 + \mathbf{A}_1 - \mathbf{I})\Delta\mathbf{x}_{t-2} + \cdots + \mathbf{A}_p\mathbf{x}_{t-p} + \mathbf{v} + \boldsymbol{\varepsilon}_t$$

$$\Delta\mathbf{x}_t = (\mathbf{A}_1 - \mathbf{I})\Delta\mathbf{x}_{t-1} + (\mathbf{A}_2 + \mathbf{A}_1 - \mathbf{I})\Delta\mathbf{x}_{t-2} + \cdots$$
$$- (\mathbf{I} - \mathbf{A}_1 - \mathbf{A}_2 - \cdots - \mathbf{A}_p)\mathbf{x}_{t-p} + \mathbf{v} + \boldsymbol{\varepsilon}_t$$

Alternatively, a VAR process can be rewritten in the following error correction (ECM) form:

$$\Delta\mathbf{x}_t = -\boldsymbol{\Pi}\mathbf{x}_{t-1} + \mathbf{F}_1\Delta\mathbf{x}_{t-1} + \mathbf{F}_2\Delta\mathbf{x}_{t-2} + \cdots + \mathbf{F}_{p-1}\Delta\mathbf{x}_{t-p+1} + \mathbf{v} + \boldsymbol{\varepsilon}_t$$

$$\mathbf{F}_i = -\sum_{q=i+1}^{p} \mathbf{A}_i, \, \boldsymbol{\Pi} = \mathbf{I} - \mathbf{A}_1 - \mathbf{A}_2 - \cdots - \mathbf{A}_p$$

The two formulations are equivalent for our purposes as the error correction term $\boldsymbol{\Pi}$ is the same. The error correction term $\boldsymbol{\Pi}$ could also be placed in any other intermediate position.

The integration and cointegration properties of the VAR model depend on the rank r of the matrix $\boldsymbol{\Pi}$. If $r = 0$, then the VAR model does not exhibit any cointegration relationship and it can be estimated as a stable process in first differences. In this case, the process in first differences can be estimated with LS or MLE techniques for estimation of stable VAR processes as discussed in the previous sections.

If $r = N$, that is, if the matrix $\boldsymbol{\Pi}$ is of full rank, then the VAR model itself is stable and can be estimated as a stable process. If the rank r is intermediate $0 < r < N$, then the VAR process exhibits cointegration. In this case, we can write the matrix $\boldsymbol{\Pi}$ as the product $\boldsymbol{\Pi} = \mathbf{HC}'$ where both $\mathbf{H}$ and $\mathbf{C}$ are $n \times r$ matrices of rank r. The r columns of the matrix $\mathbf{C}$ are the cointegrating vectors of the process.

We next discuss different estimation methods for nonstationary but cointegrated VAR models, starting with the LS estimation method.

Estimation of a Cointegrated VAR with Unrestricted LS Methods

In this section on estimation of nonstationary VAR processes, we assume for simplicity $\mathbf{v} = 0$, that is, we write a VAR process as follows:

$$\mathbf{x}_t = \mathbf{A}_1\mathbf{x}_{t-1} + \mathbf{A}_2\mathbf{x}_{t-2} + \cdots + \mathbf{A}_p\mathbf{x}_{t-p} + \boldsymbol{\varepsilon}_t$$

The cointegration condition places a restriction on the model. In fact, if we assume that the model has r cointegrating relationships, we have to impose the restriction rank$(\boldsymbol{\Pi}) = 0$, where $\boldsymbol{\Pi} = \mathbf{I} - \mathbf{A}_1 - \mathbf{A}_2 - \cdots - \mathbf{A}_p$. This restriction precludes the use of standard LS methods. However, Sims, Stock, and Watson[20] and Park and Phillips[21] demonstrated that, if we estimate the above model as an unconstrained VAR model, the estimators thus obtained are consistent and have the same asymptotic properties as the ML estimators that are discussed in the next section.

This last conclusion might look confusing because we say that we cannot apply LS methods due to constraints—and then apparently make a contradictory statement. To clarify the question, consider the following. We assume that the empirical data are generated by a VAR model with constraints. If we want to estimate that VAR model on a finite sample *enforcing constraints*, then we cannot apply standard LS methods. However, there is no impediment, *per se*, to applying unconstrained LS methods to the same data. Sims, Stock, and Watson and Park and Phillips demonstrated that, if we proceed in this way, we generate consistent estimators that respect constraints asymptotically. The model constraints will not be respected, in general, on any finite sample. Intuitively, it is clear that an unconstrained estimating process, if consistent, should yield estimators that asymptotically respect the constraints. However, the demonstration is far from being obvious as one has to demonstrate that the LS procedures can be applied consistently.

To write down the estimators, we define, as in the case of stable VAR, the following notation:

$$\mathbf{X} = (\mathbf{x}_1, ..., \mathbf{x}_T)$$

$$\mathbf{A} = (\mathbf{A}_1, ..., \mathbf{A}_p)$$

$$\mathbf{Z} = \begin{pmatrix} \mathbf{x}_0 & \cdots & \mathbf{x}_{T-1} \\ \vdots & \ddots & \vdots \\ \mathbf{x}_{1-p} & \cdots & \mathbf{x}_{T-p} \end{pmatrix}$$

Using this notation, we can write the estimators of the cointegrated VAR model as the usual LS estimator of VAR models as discussed in the previous sections, that is, we can write

$$\hat{\mathbf{A}} = \mathbf{X}\mathbf{Z}'(\mathbf{Z}\mathbf{Z}')$$

---

[20] Christopher A. Sims, James H. Stock, and Mark W. Watson. 1990. "Inference in Linear Time Series Models with Some Unit Roots," *Econometrica* 58 (1): pp. 161–82.

[21] J. Y. Park and P. C. B. Phillips, "Statistical Inference in Regressions with Integrated Processes. Part 2," *Econometric Theory* 5 (1989), pp. 95–131.

It has also be demonstrated that this estimator has the same asymptotic properties of the ML estimators that we are now going to discuss.

ML Estimators

The ML estimation procedure has become the state-of-the-art estimation method for systems of relatively small dimensions, where it outperforms other methods. The ML estimation methodology was developed primarily by Søren Johansen,[22] hence it is often referred to as the Johansen method. We will assume, following Johansen, that innovations are Independent Identically Distributed (IID) multivariate, correlated, Gaussian variables. The methodology can be extended to nonnormal distributions for innovations but computations become more complex and depend on the distribution. We will use the ECM formulation of the VAR model, that is, we will write our cointegrated VAR as follows:

$$\Delta \mathbf{x}_t = -\mathbf{\Pi} \mathbf{x}_{t-1} + \mathbf{F}_1 \Delta \mathbf{x}_{t-1} + \mathbf{F}_2 \Delta \mathbf{x}_{t-2} + \cdots + \mathbf{F}_{p-1} \Delta \mathbf{x}_{t-p+1} + \mathbf{\varepsilon}_t$$

We will first describe the ML estimation process for cointegrated processes as introduced by Banerjee and Hendry.[23] We will then make the connection with original *reduced rank regression* method of Johansen.

The method of Banerjee and Hendry is based on the idea of *concentrated likelihood*. Concentrated likelihood is a mathematical technique through which the original likelihood function (LF) is transformed into a function of a smaller number of variables, called the *concentrated likelihood function* (CLF). The CLF is better known in statistics as the *profile likelihood*. To see how CLF works, suppose that the LF is a function of two separate sets of parameters:

$$L = L(\vartheta_1, \vartheta_2)$$

In this case, the MLE principle can be established as follows:

$$\max_{\vartheta_1, \vartheta_2} L(\vartheta_1, \vartheta_2) = \max_{\vartheta_1} \left(\max_{\vartheta_2} L(\vartheta_1, \vartheta_2) \right) = \max_{\vartheta_1} (L^C(\vartheta_1))$$

where $L^C(\vartheta_1)$ is the CLF which is a function of the parameters ϑ_1 only.

---

[22] S. Johansen "Estimation and Hypothesis Testing of Cointegration Vectors in Gaussian Vector Autoregressive Models," *Econometrica* 59 (1991): pp. 1551–1581.
[23] A. Banerjee and D.F. Hendry, "Testing Integration and Cointegration: An Overview," *Oxford Bulletin of Economics and Statistics* 54 (1992), pp. 225–255.

To see how this result can be achieved, recall from Chapter 14 that, assuming usual regularity conditions, the maximum of the LF is attained where the derivatives of the log likelihood function l vanish. In particular:

$$\frac{\partial l(\vartheta_1, \vartheta_2)}{\partial \vartheta_2} = 0$$

If we can solve this system of functional equations, we obtain: $\vartheta_2 = \vartheta_2(\vartheta_1)$. The equivariance property of the ML estimators[24] now allows us to conclude that the following relationship must hold between the two sets of estimated parameters:

$$\hat{\vartheta}_2 = \vartheta_2(\hat{\vartheta}_1)$$

We see that the original likelihood function has been *concentrated* in a function of a smaller set of parameters. We now apply this idea to the ML estimation of cointegrated systems. It is convenient to introduce a notation which parallels that already introduced but is adapted to the special form of the cointegrated VAR model that we are going to use:

$$\Delta x_t = -\Pi x_{t-1} + F_1 \Delta x_{t-1} + F_2 \Delta x_{t-2} + \cdots + F_{p-1} \Delta x_{t-p+1} + \varepsilon_t$$

We define

$$X = (x_0, \ldots, x_{T-1})$$

$$\Delta x_t = \begin{pmatrix} \Delta x_{1,t} \\ \vdots \\ \Delta x_{N,t} \end{pmatrix}$$

$$\Delta X = (\Delta x_1, \ldots, \Delta x_T) = \begin{pmatrix} \Delta x_{1,1} & \cdots & \Delta x_{1,T} \\ \vdots & \ddots & \vdots \\ \Delta x_{N,1} & \cdots & \Delta x_{N,T} \end{pmatrix}$$

$$\Delta Z_t = \begin{pmatrix} \Delta x_t \\ \vdots \\ \Delta x_{t-p+2} \end{pmatrix},$$

---

[24] Recall that the equivariance property of ML estimators says that if parameter a is a function of parameter b then the ML estimator of a is the same function of the ML estimator of b.

$$\Delta Z = \begin{pmatrix} \Delta\mathbf{x}_0 & \cdots & \Delta\mathbf{x}_{T-1} \\ \vdots & \ddots & \vdots \\ \Delta\mathbf{x}_{-p+2} & \cdots & \Delta\mathbf{x}_{T-p+1} \end{pmatrix} = \begin{pmatrix} \Delta x_{1,0} & \cdots & \Delta x_{1,T-1} \\ \vdots & \ddots & \vdots \\ \Delta x_{N,0} & \cdots & \Delta x_{N,T-1} \\ \vdots & \ddots & \vdots \\ \Delta x_{1,-p+2} & \cdots & \Delta x_{1,T} \\ \vdots & \ddots & \vdots \\ \Delta x_{N,-p+2} & \cdots & \Delta x_{N,T} \end{pmatrix}$$

$$\mathbf{F} = (\mathbf{F}_1, \mathbf{F}_2, ..., \mathbf{F}_{p-1})$$

Using the matrix notation, as we assume $\Pi = HC$, we can compactly write our model in the following form:

$$\Delta X = F\Delta Z - HCX + U$$

Reasoning as we did in the case of stable VAR models, we can write the log-likelihood function as follows:

$$
\begin{aligned}
\log(l) &= -\frac{NT}{2}\log(2\pi) - \frac{T}{2}\log|\Sigma_u| - \frac{1}{2}\sum_{t=1}^{T}\varepsilon_t'\Sigma^{-1}\varepsilon_t \\
&= -\frac{NT}{2}\log(2\pi) - \frac{T}{2}\log|\Sigma_u| - \frac{1}{2}\mathrm{trace}(U'\Sigma_u^{-1}U) \\
&= -\frac{NT}{2}\log(2\pi) - \frac{T}{2}\log|\Sigma_u| - \frac{1}{2}\mathrm{trace}(\Sigma_u^{-1}UU') \\
&= -\frac{NT}{2}\log(2\pi) - \frac{T}{2}\log|\Sigma_u| \\
&\quad - \frac{1}{2}\mathrm{trace}((\Delta X - FZ + HCX)'\Sigma_u^{-1}(\Delta X - FZ + HCX))
\end{aligned}
$$

We now concentrate this log-likelihood function, eliminating Σ and F. As explained above, this entails taking partial derivatives, equating them to zero, and expressing Σ and F in terms of the other parameters. By equating to zero the derivatives with respect to Σ, it can be demonstrated that $\Sigma_C = T^{-1}UU'$. Substituting this expression in the log-likelihood, we obtain the concentrated likelihood after removing Σ:

$$
\begin{aligned}
l^{CI} &= K - \frac{T}{2}\log|UU'| \\
&= K - \frac{T}{2}\log|(\Delta X - FZ + HCX)(\Delta X - FZ + HCX)'|
\end{aligned}
$$

where K is a constant that includes all the constant terms left after concentrating.

We next eliminate the **F** terms. This result can be achieved taking derivatives of l with respect to **F**, equating them to zero and evaluating them at Σ_C. Performing all the calculations, it can be demonstrated that the evaluation at Σ_C is irrelevant and that the following formula holds:

$$F_C = (\Delta X + HCX)\Delta Z'(\Delta Z \Delta Z')^{-1}$$

Substituting this expression in the formula for l^{CI}, that is, the log-likelihood after eliminating Σ_C, we obtain:

$$
\begin{aligned}
l^{C\Pi} &= K - \frac{T}{2}\log|((\Delta X - ((\Delta X + HCX)\Delta Z'(\Delta Z \Delta Z')^{-1})\Delta Z + HCX)) \\
&\quad (\Delta X - (\Delta X + HCX)\Delta Z'(\Delta Z \Delta Z')^{-1}\Delta Z + HCX)'| \\
&= K - \frac{T}{2}\log|(\Delta X + HCX - ((\Delta X + HCX)\Delta Z'(\Delta Z \Delta Z')^{-1})\Delta Z) \\
&\quad (\Delta X + HCX - (\Delta X + HCX)\Delta Z'(\Delta Z \Delta Z')^{-1}\Delta Z)'| \\
&= K - \frac{T}{2}\log|((\Delta X + HCX)(I_T - \Delta Z'(\Delta Z \Delta Z')^{-1}\Delta Z)) \\
&\quad ((\Delta X + HCX)(I_T - \Delta Z'(\Delta Z \Delta Z')^{-1}\Delta Z))'| \\
&= K - \frac{T}{2}\log|(\Delta X + HCX)M(\Delta X + HCX)'| \\
&= K - \frac{T}{2}\log|\Delta X M\Delta X' + HCXM\Delta X' + \Delta X M(HCX)' + HCXM(HCX)'|
\end{aligned}
$$

where $M = I_T - \Delta Z'(\Delta Z \Delta Z')^{-1}\Delta Z$. Matrices of the form $A = I - B'(BB')^{-1}B$ are called *projection matrices*. They are idempotent and symmetric, that is $A = A'$ and $AA = A^2 = A$. The latter properties were used in the last three steps of the above derivations.

We will rewrite the CLF as follows. Define $R_0 = \Delta X M$, $R_1 = XM$ and

$$S_{ij} = \frac{R_i R_j}{T}, i, j = 1, 2$$

We can then rewrite the CLF as follows:

$$l^{\mathrm{CП}}(\mathbf{HC}) = K - \frac{T}{2}\log\left|\mathbf{S}_{00} - \mathbf{S}_{10}\mathbf{HC} - \mathbf{S}_{01}(\mathbf{HC})' + \mathbf{HCS}_{11}(\mathbf{HC})'\right|$$

The original analysis of Johansen obtained the same result applying the method of *reduced rank regression*. Reduced rank regressions are multiple regressions where the coefficient matrix is subject to constraints. The Johansen method eliminates the terms $\mathbf{F}$ by regressing $\Delta\mathbf{x}_t$ and $\mathbf{x}_{t-1}$ on $(\Delta\mathbf{x}_{t-1}, \Delta\mathbf{x}_{t-2}, \ldots, \Delta\mathbf{x}_{t-p+1})$ to obtain the following residuals:

$$\mathbf{R}_{0t} = \Delta\mathbf{x}_t + \mathbf{D}_1\Delta\mathbf{x}_{t-1} + \mathbf{D}_2\Delta\mathbf{x}_{t-2} + \cdots + \mathbf{D}_{p-1}\Delta\mathbf{x}_{t-p+1}$$
$$\mathbf{R}_{1t} = \Delta\mathbf{x}_{t-1} + \mathbf{E}_1\Delta\mathbf{x}_{t-1} + \mathbf{E}_2\Delta\mathbf{x}_{t-2} + \cdots + \mathbf{E}_{p-1}\Delta\mathbf{x}_{t-p+1}$$

where

$$\mathbf{D} = (\mathbf{D}_1, \mathbf{D}_2, \ldots, \mathbf{D}_{p-1}) = \Delta\mathbf{X}\Delta\mathbf{Z}'(\Delta\mathbf{Z}\Delta\mathbf{Z}')^{-1}$$

and

$$\mathbf{E} = (\mathbf{E}_1, \mathbf{E}_2, \ldots, \mathbf{E}_{p-1}) = \mathbf{X}\Delta\mathbf{Z}'(\Delta\mathbf{Z}\Delta\mathbf{Z}')^{-1}$$

The original model is therefore reduced to the following "simpler model":

$$\mathbf{R}_{0t} = \mathbf{HCR}_{1t} + \mathbf{u}_t$$

The likelihood function of this model depends only on $\mathbf{R}_{0t}$, $\mathbf{R}_{1t}$. It can be written as follows:

$$l(\mathbf{HC}) = K_1 - \frac{T}{2}\log\left|(\mathbf{R}_0 + \mathbf{R}_1(\mathbf{HC}))'(\mathbf{R}_0 + \mathbf{R}_1(\mathbf{HC}))\right|$$

where we define $\mathbf{R}_0$, $\mathbf{R}_1$ as above. If we also define $\mathbf{S}_{ij}$ as above, we obtain exactly the same form for the CLF:

$$l^{\mathrm{CП}}(\mathbf{HC}) = K - \frac{T}{2}\log\left|\mathbf{S}_{00} - \mathbf{S}_{10}\mathbf{HC} - \mathbf{S}_{01}(\mathbf{HC})' + \mathbf{HCS}_{11}(\mathbf{HC})'\right|$$

We have now to find the maximum of this CLF. Note that this problem is not well identified because, given any solution $\mathbf{H}$, $\mathbf{C}$ and any non-singular matrix $\mathbf{G}$, the following relationships hold:

$$\Pi = HC = HGG^{-1}C = H^*C^*$$

so that the matrices

$$H^* = HG$$

$$C^* = G^{-1}C$$

are also a solution. Additional conditions must therefore be imposed.

If the matrix $\Pi = HC$ were unrestricted, then maximization would yield

$$\Pi = S_{01}S_{11}^{-1}$$

However, our problem now is to find solutions that respect the cointegration condition, that is, the rank r of Π which is the common rank of H, C. To achieve this goal, we can concentrate the CLF with respect to H and thus solve with respect to C. By performing the rather lengthy computations, it can be demonstrated that we obtain a solution by solving the following eigenvalue problem:

$$\left| S_{10}S_{00}^{-1}S_{01} - \lambda S_{11} \right| = 0$$

This eigenvalue problem, together with normalizing conditions, will yield N eigenvalues λ_i and N eigenvectors Λ_i. In order to make this problem well determined, Johansen imposed the normalizing conditions: $\Lambda'S_{11}\Lambda = I$. Order the eigenvalues and choose the r eigenvectors Λ_i corresponding to the largest r eigenvalues. It can be demonstrated that a ML estimator of the matrix C is given by

$$\hat{C} = (\Lambda_1, ..., \Lambda_r)$$

and an estimator of the matrix H by $\hat{H} = S_{00}\hat{C}$. The maximum of the log-likelihood is

$$l_{max} = K - \frac{T}{2}\log|S_{00}| - \frac{T}{2}\sum_{i=1}^{r} \log(1 - \lambda_i)$$

The solutions of the above eigenvalue problem, that is, the eigenvalues λ_i, can be interpreted as the canonical correlations between Δx_t and x_{t-1}. *Canonical correlations* can be interpreted as the maximum correlations between linear combinations of the Δx_t and x_{t-1} (for technical details see Appendix B). We therefore see that the cointegrating relationships are those linear combinations of the levels x_{t-1} that are maximally correlated with linear combinations of the Δx_t after conditioning with the remaining terms.

Different types of normalizing conditions have been studied and are described in the literature. A general theory of long-run modeling that considers general nonlinear constraints on the matrix C was developed by Pesaran and Shin.[25] This theory goes beyond the scope of this book.

Estimating the Number of Cointegrating Relationships

The Johansen ML estimation method and its extensions critically depend on correctly estimating the number r of cointegrating relationships. Two tests, in particular, have been suggested in relationship with the Johansen method: the trace test and the maximum eigenvalue test. The *trace test* tests the hypothesis that there are at most r cointegrating vectors while the *maximum eigenvalue test* tests the hypothesis that there are $r + 1$ cointegrating vectors against the hypothesis that there are r cointegrating vectors. The mathematical details are given in the Johansen paper discussed earlier. Lütkepohl, Saikkonen, and Trenkler[26] provide an extensive discussion of the relative merit and power of the various forms of these tests. Here we provide only a quick overview of these tests which are implemented in many standard statistical packages.

The trace test is immediately suggested by the Johansen procedure. Recall from the discussion earlier in this chapter that with the Johansen method the maximum of the log-likelihood function is

$$l_{max} = K - \frac{T}{2}\log|S_{00}| - \frac{T}{2}\sum_{i=1}^{r}\log(1 - \lambda_i)$$

The likelihood ratio test statistics for the hypothesis of at most r cointegrating vectors is

---

[25] M. Hashem Pesaran and Yongcheol Shin, "Long-Run Structural Modelling," Chapter 11 in S. Strom (ed.), *Econometrics and Economic Theory in the 20th Century: The Ragnar Frisch Centennial Symposium* (Cambridge, Cambridge University Press, 2001).

[26] H. Lütkepohl, P. Saikkonen, and C. Trenkler, "Maximum Eigenvalue Versus Trace Tests for the Cointegrating Rank of a VAR Process," *Econometrics Journal* 4 (2001), pp. 287–310.

$$\lambda_{\text{trace}} = -T \sum_{i = r + 1}^{r} \log(1 - \lambda_i)$$

where the sum is extended to the $n - r$ smallest eigenvalues. The asymptotic distribution of this statistic is not normal. It is given by the trace of a stochastic matrix formed with functionals of a Brownian motion. Its critical values at different confidence levels have been tabulated and are used in most packages.

The likelihood ratio statistics for the maximum eigenvalue test is the following:

$$\lambda_{\text{max}} = -T\log(1 - \lambda_{r + 1})$$

As for the previous test, the asymptotic distribution of this test statistics is not normal. It is given by the maximum eigenvalue of a stochastic matrix formed with functionals of a Brownian motion. Critical values at different confidence levels have been tabulated and are used in many standard statistical packages.

ML Estimators In The Presence of Linear Trends

The above discussion assumed a zero intercept in the model and therefore no linear trends or nonzero intercepts in the process. If we add an intercept to a VAR model, we might obtain a linear trend in the variables. With cointegrated systems there is the additional complication that a linear trend might or might not be present in the cointegrated variables. In other words, the cointegrating vectors transform the I(1) variables into stationary variables or into trend-stationary variables.

The original definition of cointegration in Engle and Granger excluded deterministic trends in the cointegrated variables.[27] Now we distinguish between stochastic cointegration and deterministic cointegration. A set of I(1) variables is said to be stochastically cointegrated if there are linear combinations of these variables that are trend-stationary (i.e., stationary plus a deterministic trend). A set of I(1) variables are said to be deterministically cointegrated if there exist linear combinations which are stationary without any deterministic trend.

Therefore, when considering deterministic terms in a cointegrated VAR model, we cannot consider only constant intercepts but must include linear trends. Adding a constant term and a linear trend to the

<hr>

[27] R. F. Engle and C. W. J. Granger, "Cointegration and Error Correction: Representation, Estimation, and Testing," *Econometrica* 55 (1987), pp. 251–276

model variables as we did in the stable case, the estimation procedure described in the previous section remains valid.

ESTIMATION WITH CANONICAL CORRELATIONS

The use of *canonical correlation analysis* (CCA) was first proposed by Bossaerts in 1988.[28] In 1995, Bewley and Yang provided a more rigorous foundation for CCA-based methodology which they called *level canonical correlation analysis* (LCCA) because the canonical correlations are computed in levels.[29] Cointegration tests based on CCA are based on the idea that canonical correlations should discriminate those linear combinations of variables that are I(1) from those that are I(0). In fact, integrated variables should be more predictable while stationary components should be less predictable.

Bossarts proposed performing CCA and the use of the standard Dickey-Fuller (DF) test to discriminate those canonical variates that are I(1). He considers a model of the type:

$$\Delta x_t = H C x_t + \varepsilon_t$$

After performing the CCA between Δx_t and x_t, the canonical variates are tested for unit roots. Bossaerts conjectured, without proof, that one can use the standard critical values of the DF test.

Bewley and Yang extended the methodology, allowing for deterministic trends and other variables explaining short-run dynamics. They proposed new tests, developed the asymptotic theory, and computed the critical values to determine the number of cointegrating vectors.

Computationally, the LCCA methodology of Bewley and Yang is not very far from that of Johansen. Following Bewley and Yang, the LCCA method proceeds as follows. First, if there are additional variables, they have to be removed performing the regressions of x_t and x_{t-1} on those variables. Call R_{0t}, R_{1t} the residuals of these regressions and form the regression:

$$R_{0t} = B R_{1t} + u_t$$

---

[28] Peter Bossaerts, "Common Non-Stationary Components of Asset Prices," *Journal of Economic Dynamics and Control* 12 (1988), pp. 348–364.

[29] Ronald Bewley and Minxian Yang, "Tests for Cointegration Based on Canonical Correlation Analysis," *Journal of the American Statistical Association* 90 (1995), pp. 990–996.

We have now to determine the canonical correlations between R_{0t} and R_{1t}. This is done formally with the same equation as in the Johansen method, that is, solving the following eigenvalue problem (see Appendix B):

$$\left| S_{10}S_{00}^{-1}S_{01} - \lambda S_{11} \right| = 0$$

where

$$S_{ij} = \frac{R_i R_j}{T}, \, i, j = 1, 2$$

as in the Johansen method. However, the interpretation of these quantities is different: Here we are seeking canonical correlations between variables in levels while in the Johansen methods we correlate both levels and differences. The LCCA method picks the largest eigenvalues as does the Johansen method. Bewley and Yang developed the asymptotic theory as well as four tests for cointegration, two DF-type tests, a trace test, and a maximum eigenvalue test. For each test they determined and tabulated critical values for up to six variables. The tabulated critical values are included in their paper.

The asymptotic theory developed by Bewley and Yang showed that one can indeed use the standard unit root tests such as the Dickey-Fuller and Phillips tests, but the critical values depend on the number of variables and are not standard. Therefore, one cannot use the DF test with standard critical values, as conjectured by Bossaerts.

ESTIMATION WITH PRINCIPAL COMPONENT ANALYSIS

Thus far we have discussed methodologies based on OLS, ML, and CCA. In this section we analyze another important method based on *Principal Component Analysis* (PCA). PCA is a well known statistical methodology that, given a set of multidimensional data, finds the directions of maximum variance. PCA-based methods are used in classical factor analysis of stationary returns.

The use of PCA-based methods for integrated variables was first proposed by Stock and Watson.[30] They were the first to observe that the presence of r cointegrating vectors in n time series implies the presence

---

[30] James H. Stock and Mark W. Watson, "Testing for Common Trends," *Journal of the American Statistical Association* 83 (1988), pp. 1097–1107.

of r common stochastic trends. This means that there are r independent linear combinations of the variables that are I(1) while the remaining n-r are I(0). In addition, it means that each of the n variables can be expressed as a linear combination of the common stochastic trends plus a stationary process. (See Chapter 12 for details.)

Stock and Watson conjectured that those linear combinations that are I(1) must have the largest variance. Therefore, by performing a PCA on the variables in levels, one should be able to determine the cointegrating vectors by picking the largest eigenvalues. The Stock and Watson methodology proceeds as follows.

Suppose the data generation process is our usual VAR(p) model:

$$\mathbf{x}_t = \mathbf{A}_1\mathbf{x}_{t-1} + \mathbf{A}_2\mathbf{x}_{t-2} + \cdots + \mathbf{A}_p\mathbf{x}_{t-p} + \boldsymbol{\varepsilon}_t$$

where we assume for the moment that the intercept term is zero. Suppose also that the number of lags p have been determined independently. Next, perform the PCA of the variables $\mathbf{x}_t$. This entails solving the following eigenvalue problem:

$$\Omega\boldsymbol{\beta} = \mu\boldsymbol{\beta}$$

where Ω is the empirical covariance matrix of the $\mathbf{x}_t$, defined as

$$\Omega = \sum_{t=1}^{T} \mathbf{x}_t\mathbf{x}_t'$$

and μ and $\boldsymbol{\beta}$ are respectively the eigenvalues and the eigenvectors to be determined.

Order the eigenvalues and choose the m largest eigenvalues μ_i, $i = 1$, ..., m. The corresponding eigenvectors $\boldsymbol{\beta}_i$ are the candidate cointegrating vectors. Forming the linear combinations $P_{i,t} = \boldsymbol{\beta}_i\mathbf{x}_t$, we obtain the vector $\mathbf{P}_t = (P_{1,t}, \ldots, P_{m,t})'$ first m principal components. We must now check the hypothesis that these principal components are I(1) series and are not cointegrated among themselves.

In order to do this, the Stock and Watson method estimates the following stable VAR(p) model:

$$\Delta\mathbf{P}_t = \mathbf{A}_1\Delta\mathbf{P}_{t-1} + \cdots + \mathbf{A}_{p-1}\Delta\mathbf{P}_{t-p+1} + \boldsymbol{\varepsilon}_t$$

and then computes

$$\hat{F}_t = P_t - \hat{A}_1 \Delta P_{t-1} - \cdots - \hat{A}_{p-1} \Delta P_{t-p+1}$$

Regress ΔF_t on F_{t-1}, compute the normalized eigenvalues of the regression matrix **B**, and compare with the critical values tabulated in the Stock and Watson paper to test the null of m common trends against $m-q$ common trends.

If the VAR model exhibits a nonzero intercept, then there might be linear trends in the variables. This fact, in turn, raises the question of stochastic versus deterministic cointegration. The details of the computations are actually quite intricate.[31]

A major advantage of the PCA-based methodologies is that critical values depend only on the number of common trends and not on the number of time series involved. Therefore, they can be used to determine a small number of common trends in a large number of time series. This is a significant advantage in financial econometrics; we will come back to this in the section on dynamic factors later.

ESTIMATION WITH THE EIGENVALUES OF THE COMPANION MATRIX

A process is called *integrated of order one* if it can be written as: $x_t = \rho x_{t-1} + \eta_t$ where $\rho = 1$, and η_t is a stationary process. Dickey and Fuller established the asymptotic distribution of ρ and tabulated the critical values that now form the basis of the DF and ADF unit root test. Ahlgren and Nyblom[32] developed an equivalent methodology for multivariate processes. They studied a N-variate, VAR(1) process of the form:

$$x_t = \Pi x_{t-1} + \varepsilon_t$$

The major result of their work is that the number of cointegrating relationships depends on the eigenvalues of the autoregressive matrix. Ahlgren and Nyblom determined the asymptotic distribution of the eigenvalues of the autoregressive matrix estimated with OLS methods and computed critical values. The methodology can be extended to VAR models of any order by transforming the original model into a VAR(1) model and considering the companion matrix.

---

[31] The interested reader should consult the original Stock and Watson paper.
[32] Niklas Ahlgren and Jukka Nyblom, "A General Test for the Cointegrating Rank in Vector Autoregressive Models," Working Paper No 499, 2003, Swedish School of Economics and Business Administration.

ESTIMATION WITH SUBSPACE METHODS AND DYNAMIC FACTOR ANALYSIS

Bauer and Wagner proposed a new methodology for estimating cointegrated systems using subspace methods.[33] We postpone the analysis of these methods as well as the dynamic factor analysis to Chapter 16 where we discuss linear state-space methods as well as other linear and non linear methods based on hidden variables. We will also postpone the discussion of applications of cointegration to financial econometrics after discussing hidden variables models.

APPLICATION OF COINTEGRATION METHODS TO THE ANALYSIS OF PREDICTORS

Barghava and Malhotra analyzed the price-earnings (P/E) ratio to understand if it had an impact on subsequent prices and yields.[34] Their analysis is interesting not only for the conclusions they reached but also because of the advanced econometric methodologies they used, namely cointegration. The use of cointegration allowed Barghava and Malhotra to address many issues typically raised in the literature on the existence of predictors.

The question as to whether the P/E ratio is a good predictor of future returns is an important one for practitioners and has been widely debated. Having surveyed the literature and found no strong consensus on the issue, Barghava and Malhotra analyzed the impact of P/E ratios on indexes. The indexes surveyed were the S&P 500, the MSCI World, the MSCI Europe, and the EAFE. The time frame was the 20-year period 1980–2000. As a first step, they performed a regression of prices or yields on the P/E ratios:

$$(\text{Price or Yield}) = \alpha + \beta(\text{P/E}) + \varepsilon$$

In total they performed eight regressions, regressing prices and yields of each index against the corresponding P/E ratio. The results of the regression showed that high P/E ratios tend to be followed by low yields. Tests of the quality of the regression confirmed that all eight

---

[33] D. Bauer and M. Wagner, "Estimating Cointegrated Systems Using Subspace Algorithms," *Journal of Econometrics* 111 (2002), pp. 47–84.
[34] V. Barghava and D. K. Malhotra, "Do Price-Earnings Ratios Drive Stock Values— Evidence from World Markets," forthcoming *Journal of Portfolio Management*, 2006.

regressions were robust. Regression analysis appeared to confirm the theoretical finding that P/E ratios are predictors of future yields; it also lent support to the belief that P/E ratios are mean-reverting.

However, as pointed out earlier in this chapter, regression analysis of predictors needs further testing. Barghava and Malhotra first analyzed the autocorrelation and heteroskedasticity properties of errors. They performed the analysis using the standard Durbin-Watson statistics, which tests the null hypothesis of zero-autocorrelation coefficient of the residuals, and the White test, which is based on forming an auxiliary regression where the squared residuals are regressed against every possible product of the variables. The tests showed that autocorrelation was present in all eight regressions while heteroskedasticity was present in all but the regression of yields against P/E ratios of the S&P 500. The presence of autocorrelation of residuals suggested verifying if the dependent variables and regressors were integrated variables—a condition that could invalidate regressions. Using a variant of the DF test, they found that all series were integrated.

This finding suggested that, unless variables were cointegrated, the regressions might be spurious. In the following step, they analyzed cointegration among the different series. They did so using the standard Johansen methodology. Only the S&P 500 and the EAFE indexes exhibited cointegration between prices and P/E ratios. No other series were found to be cointegrated.

An ECM model for both the S&P 500 and EAFE indexes was then estimated, using the AIC criterion to find the optimal lag structure. Test of Granger causality showed weak causal relationships between P/E ratios and prices. The final result was that the initial conclusion of a robust regression between P/E ratios and subsequent yields had to be substantially revised. While it remained true that an increase in P/E ratios would be followed by a subsequent price increase and yield decrease, the impact of these movements was found to be smaller than anticipated by a simple regression analysis.

SUMMARY

- It is empirically known that there are exogenous predictor variables for returns; it is possible to write a meaningful regression of future returns on the present and past values of predictors.
- Linear regressions of returns on predictors can be estimated with the estimation methods of regressions; estimated regression coefficients are algebraic functions of the sample data.

■ The ability to predict returns can be enhanced using stable vector autoregressive (VAR) models, where both returns and exogenous variables form the VAR model.

■ It is useful to introduce the vectoring operator and tensor product operator to represent the VAR models in compact vector notation.

■ Stable VAR models can be estimated as standard regressions with Least Squares (LS) methods or Maximum Likelihood (ML) methods.

■ It can be demonstrated that LS methods can be performed equation by equation and that it is therefore possible to use Ordinary Least Squares (OLS) methods.

■ In the case of Gaussian VAR processes, OLS and ML methods yield the same estimators.

■ The key estimation formula for stable VAR models is formally similar to those for simple regressions.

■ The sample distribution of model estimators is asymptotically normal.

■ The number of lags of a VAR model must be estimated a priori; this can be done using criteria such as the Akaike Information Criterion (AIC) or Bayesian Information Criterion (BIC).

■ VAR model estimation is sensitive to the autocorrelation of residuals; the latter can be tested with criteria such as the Dickey-Fuller or Augmented Dickey-Fuller tests.

■ Stable autoregressive distributed lags models combine regression on exogenous variables and autoregression on lagged values of the modeled variables. They can be estimated with standard regression estimation methods.

■ Studies have shown that, using VAR models and predictive variables such as financial ratios, it is possible to improve the accuracy of expected return forecasts over forecasts made using the simple empirical average of past returns as is the case with random walk models of prices.

■ Stationary dynamic factor models of returns can be used to identify factors and/or reduce model dimensionality.

■ Dynamic factor models can be estimated as state-space models (as will be discussed in the next chapter).

■ Nonstationary VAR models require special estimation methods for estimating cointegration relationships. However, it can be demonstrated that estimating nonstationary VAR models with unrestricted LS methods (that is, as standard regressions) yields consistent estimators.

■ Estimators cannot be expressed through simple algebraic formulas; a number of methods have been proposed to estimate cointegrating relationships and cointegrated VAR models.

■ The most widely used methods for estimating relationships and cointegrated VAR models are those proposed by (1) Johansen, (2) Bossaerts and Bewley-Yang, (3) Stock and Watson, (4) Ahlgren and Nyblom method, and (5) Aoki and Bauer and Wagner.

■ The Johansen method is the state-of-the-art estimation method for cointegrated systems and is based on Canonical Correlations between levels and returns.

■ The methods of Bossaerts and Bewley-Yang is based on Canonical Correlations in levels.

■ The PCA-based method of Stock and Watson is based on performing a Principal Component Analysis (PCA) of level variables.

■ Ahlgren and Nyblom's method is based on finding the eigenvalues of the companion matrix, that is, of the coefficient matrix of the model in its VAR(1) representation.

■ The methods introduced by Aoki and Bauer and Wagner are based on subspace algorithms and will be discussed in Chapter 16.

Estimation of Hidden Variable Models

This chapter presents methods for estimating hidden variable models, focusing on linear state-space models and (nonlinear) regime-switching models. *Hidden variable models* differ from both the regressive and autoregressive models discussed in Chapters 14 and 15 insofar as they introduce auxiliary variables that are not directly observable (thus "hidden") to model the system dynamics. Examples of hidden variable models used in financial econometrics include *regime-switching models,* which use hidden variables to represent different economic regimes; the GARCH family of models, which use hidden variables to represent volatility; and credit risk models, which use hidden variables to represent credit worthiness. In all these examples, the hidden variables are not directly measurable but are auxiliary variables used to explain the observables.

The advantage of hidden variable models is their explanatory power. By introducing hidden variables, one gains insight into the dynamics of observables such as prices. For example, it is empirically known that return correlations behave differently in bear and bull markets. A hidden market regime variable allows one to gain better insight into market processes by separating the *data generation process* (DGP) of returns in different markets, for example, bull and bear markets. In some cases, hidden variable models are the only feasible modeling choice. However, it might happen that, due to changes in the availability of data, hidden variable models compete with models where all variables are observed. This is the case, for example, with GARCH models, which now compete with models of realized volatility where—thanks to the availability of high-frequency data—volatility is close to be observable.

The disadvantage of hidden variable models is that they are data-hungry. Though, per se, hidden variable models have greater explanatory power than more traditional models, the estimation process, for a given sample, is more noisy. The increased level of noise in the estimation process is due to the higher number of parameters that must be estimated. For example, on finite samples, regime-switching models do not necessarily perform better than more traditional models.[1] We will come back to this important subject in Chapter 17 on model risk.

ESTIMATION OF STATE-SPACE MODELS

We begin our discussion on estimation methods for hidden variable models with linear state-space models, perhaps the most widely used class of hidden variable models. As discussed in Chapter 12, linear state-space models are equivalent to VARMA models and to linear models described by transfer functions: linear state-space models, VARMA, and linear transfer-function models are all three equivalent formulations of the same econometric reality. Because they make use of hidden variables, state-space models can bring better and more immediate economic insight into price and return processes. In many instances, linear state-space models are also easier to estimate than VAR models with the same number of parameters; this is especially the case when many variables are involved.

Because state-space models have been used now for decades in engineering applications, most time-series software packages offer modules to identify and estimate state-space models. Though portfolio managers and analysts will not have to code these models, an understanding of estimation procedures is necessary to correctly use commercial software and make appropriate decisions on portfolio selection.

Recall that a linear state-space model is a system of simultaneous equations that can be written in the following way:

$$x_t = Az_t + By_t + \varepsilon_t$$
$$z_{t+1} = Cz_t + Dy_t + \eta_t$$

where

---

[1] This statement needs refinements that will become clear later in this chapter. In fact, there is more than one way to take hidden variables into consideration. When adopting a regime-switching model, for example, one might decide to simplify the description of each regime.

- $\mathbf{x}_t$ is the n-dimensional vector of observable output series
- $\mathbf{z}_t$ is the s-dimensional vector of latent (nonobservable) state variables
- $\mathbf{y}_t$ is a m-dimensional vector of deterministic inputs
- $\boldsymbol{\varepsilon}_t$ is the n-dimensional observation white noise
- $\boldsymbol{\eta}_t$ is the m-dimensional transition equation white noise
- A is the $n \times s$ observation matrix
- B is the $n \times m$ input matrix of the observation equation
- C is the $s \times s$ transition matrix
- D is the $s \times m$ input matrix of the transition equation

and where the $\mathbf{x}_t$ and $\mathbf{y}_t$ are observed for $t = 1, 2, \ldots, T$ while the noise terms run for $t = 0, 1, 2, \ldots, T$ from an initial state $\mathbf{z}_0$. In other words, the initial uncertainty propagates throughout the system.

The first equation, called the *observation equation*, is a linear regression of the output variables over the state and input variables; the second equation, called the *(state) transition equation*, is a VAR(1) model that describes the dynamics of the state variables. It is generally assumed that the system starts from a state $\mathbf{z}_0$ and an initial input $\mathbf{y}_0$.

The joint noise process,

$$\begin{bmatrix} \boldsymbol{\varepsilon}_t \\ \boldsymbol{\eta}_t \end{bmatrix}$$

is a zero-mean, independent, identically distributed (IID) sequence with the variance-covariance matrix:

$$\begin{bmatrix} \Omega_\varepsilon & \Omega'_{\varepsilon\eta} \\ \Omega_{\eta\varepsilon} & \Omega_\eta \end{bmatrix}$$

It can be demonstrated[2] that every state-space system can be transformed into the following form, called the *prediction error form*:

$$\mathbf{x}_t = \mathbf{A}\mathbf{z}_t + \mathbf{B}\mathbf{y}_t + \boldsymbol{\varepsilon}_t$$
$$\mathbf{z}_{t+1} = \mathbf{C}\mathbf{z}_t + \mathbf{D}\mathbf{y}_t + \mathbf{K}\boldsymbol{\varepsilon}_t$$
$$t = 1, 2, \ldots, T$$

where K is an $s \times n$ matrix. In this form, the noise term $\boldsymbol{\varepsilon}_t$ is the prediction error of $\mathbf{x}_t$ given $\mathbf{x}_s$, for $s < t$, and $\mathbf{y}_t$. The prediction error is the prediction error in the mean squares sense with respect to the best linear predictor.

---

[2] See E. Hannan and M. Deistler, *The Statistical Theory of Linear Systems* (New York: John Wiley & Son, 1988).

The Kalman Filter

We will discuss two methodologies for estimating state-space systems: maximum likelihood estimation methods and subspace algorithms. First, however, we discuss an estimation technique called the *Kalman filter* which is both a key component of the state-space model estimation process and useful tool in itself. The Kalman filter estimates the states given the observables and the deterministic inputs, *assuming that the model is known*. To better understand Kalman filters, it is perhaps useful to recall how state-space methods originated in the fields of engineering and physics in the late 1950s and 1960s.[3] In fact, while state-space models are presently used as multivariate autoregressive processes in cases where states are considered to be abstract entities that explain the overall dynamics, state-space models originated from the need to extract true signals from multiple noisy measurements.

With the advent of supersonic flights and space program, aircrafts and missiles required advanced flight control mechanisms. Control mechanisms work by comparing actual measurements, for example the position of an aircraft, with the desired values. When differences are detected, the control mechanism automatically brings the aircraft back to the desired trajectory. In the late 1950s and early 1960s, the United States Air Force Office of Scientific Research (AFOSR) sponsored research efforts in the area of control theory, already a mainstream and highly mathematical discipline thanks especially to the pioneering work of the father of cybernetics, the mathematician Norbert Wiener.

A key problem that begged a solution was how to get accurate information out of numerous and continuous data streams that contain inherently imprecise data. Let us return to the example of a flight guidance system which needs to accurately determine the position of an aircraft but which has as raw inputs a stream of imprecise measurements from different measuring devices.

Among the efforts sponsored by the AFOSR, one program involved the development and application of statistical filtering. The directors of this project were the Hungarian-born engineer Rudolph E. Kalman, then at the Research Institute for Advanced Studies in Baltimore, and the American-born mathematician Richard Bucy, then at the Johns Hopkins Applied Physics Laboratory. Kalman developed the filter for discrete systems in 1960 and, a year later, working with Bucy, extended it to continuous systems.[4] Their invention revolutionized the field of estimation and had an enormous impact on the design and development of precise navigation systems. The Kalman–Bucy technique of combining and filtering

---

[3] For a quick overview, see Barry Cipra, "Engineers Look to Kalman Filtering for Guidance," *SIAM News* 26 (August 1993).

information from multiple sensor sources achieved accuracies that clearly constituted a major breakthrough in guidance technology.

The Kalman–Bucy technique, often referred to as the Kalman filter, rapidly became a basic building block of the U.S. space program and was used in the Ranger, Mariner, and Apollo missions of the 1960s.[5] It guided the Apollo 11 lunar module to the moon's surface. Most modern control systems, both military and commercial, use the Kalman filter in applications such as navigational and guidance systems, radar tracking, sonar ranging, and satellite orbit determination. Hexad, the "fault-tolerant" gyro system on the new Boeing 777, uses a Kalman filter.

That the Kalman filter was originally developed in control theory to separate noise from true information in a stream of incoming data is important to our discussion of the estimation theory of state-space models: states carry the true, important information while observations are noisy. The objective is to recover the states from the observations. The Kalman filter does not estimate the model: It estimates states from the observables, assuming that the model is known. In economics, however, states do not always carry the key information. While there are applications of state-space models in finance where the important quantity is the state—an obvious example is a credit risk model, where we observe a number of corporate-specific financial variables, but the quantity of interest is the state of the debtor in terms of its ability to repay the debt—in other cases, the state-space model is a statistical device to forecast observable quantities. For example, if we use a state-space model to represent prices, the important quantities are the prices themselves. The hidden states are only tools that help forecast prices.

Conceptually one can take a different view and argue that, in any case, states are the key drivers of the process and the true reality behind noisy observations. For example, one might argue that the many observations of stock prices are nothing but noisy observations of the true state of the market. This is the argument behind the use of hidden variable models in finance. An example is the Hamilton model (see the discussion later in this chapter on Markov switching models), which uses a hidden variable to model alternatively recession or expansion of the economy.

---

[4] R. E. Kalman, "A New Approach to Linear Filtering and Prediction Problems," *Transactions of the ASME—Journal of Basic Engineering* 82, Series D (1960), pp. 35–45; and R. E. Kalman and R. Bucy, "New Results in Linear Filtering and Prediction Theory," *ASME—Jounal of Basic Engineering* 83, Series D (1961), pp. 95–108.

[5] The Kalman filter is sometimes called the *Kalman-Bucy filter*. Kalman is credited with having made the major contribution and having understood the key role of many other concepts in state-space systems.

At present, however, modeling efforts to reveal economic states are not integrated into a full-fledged economic theory where theoretical constructs and economic laws are generally accepted and validated. Portfolio and asset managers, however, devote a great deal of attention to economic states. Unobservable quantities such as correlations, volatilities, or market sentiment often explicitly enter into the decision-making process of portfolio managers. These unobservable quantities can even be priced and traded.

Maximum Likelihood Estimation

We now go back to the estimation process. The estimation process of linear state-space models based on Maximum Likelihood (ML) principles needs to determine a log-likelihood which is a function of observables and hidden variables plus deterministic inputs. Hidden variables, however, can only be estimated, not observed. Hence the usefulness of the Kalman filter to replace unknown hidden variables with their best estimates. The process is the following:

- Compute the log-likelihood function of the model as usual.
- The log-likelihood function is expressed in terms of both the observables and the state variables.
- Use the Kalman filter to supplement the observations with the estimates of the state variables.
- Optimize with standard optimizers or with methods such as the Expectation Maximization method.

We describe first the Kalman filter and then show how to compute the log-likelihood function and apply the Expected Maximization method.

Estimation of the Kalman Filter

The Kalman filter performs three major computational tasks:

- *Filtering*, which computes the present state conditional to all the observations up to the present time
- *Smoothing*, which computes the state at intermediate dates conditional on all the observations up to the present date
- *Forecasting*, which forecasts the state at a future date conditional on all the observations up to the present date

We first describe the Kalman filter using the state-space model specified above with the additional assumption that the noise terms are normally distributed. The assumption of normality can be relaxed. (We will see later how the filter is modified relaxing the assumption of normality.) We need to introduce the following notation—standard in the Kalman filter literature—to express compactly the various conditional means. We need to define the following four variables:

1. The conditional mean of the state variables at time t given observations up to time t:

$$z_{t|t} = E(z_t|x_1, ..., x_t)$$

2. The conditional mean of the observables and of the state variables at time t given observations up to time $t-1$:

$$z_{t|t-1} = E(z_t|x_1, ..., x_{t-1})$$
$$x_{t|t-1} = E(x_t|x_1, ..., x_{t-1})$$

3. The mean squared errors of forecasts:

$$\Sigma_{t|t} = E((z_t - z_{t|t})(z_t - z_{t|t})')$$
$$\Sigma_{t|t-1} = E((z_t - z_{t|t-1})(z_t - z_{t|t-1})')$$
$$M_{t|t-1} = E((x_t - x_{t|t-1})(x_t - x_{t|t-1})')$$

4. The residuals of the regression of the observable on its own past:

$$\tilde{x} = x_t - x_{t|t-1} = x_t - Az_{t|t-1}$$

As mentioned, the Kalman filter is a recursive methodology for computing past, present, and future states given a set of observables up to the present state. Starting from the initial moment, the filter computes the conditional mean and the conditional covariance matrix of the states step by step. Let us now look at the four steps of the recursive equations of the Kalman filter: the prediction step, the correction step, the forecasting step, and the smoothing step.

The Prediction Step

The *prediction step* predicts the state and the variables one step ahead for every time $1 \le t \le T$ given the present state:

$$z_{t|t-1} = Cz_{t-1|t-1} + Dy_{t-1}$$
$$x_{t|t-1} = Az_{t|t-1} + By_t$$

The prediction step also predicts, one step ahead, the covariance matrix of the states and the variables:

$$\Omega_z(t|t-1) = C\Omega_z(t-1|t-1)C' + \Omega_\eta$$
$$\Omega_x(t|t-1) = A\Omega_z(t|t-1)A' + \Omega_\varepsilon$$

The Correction Step

The *correction step* improves the forecast made in the prediction step, taking into account the covariance matrix. The role played by the conditional covariance matrix in improving forecasts was the key intuition of Kalman. The correction step is written as follows:

$$z_{t|t} = z_{t|t-1} + P_t(x_t - x_{t|t-1})$$
$$\Omega_z(t|t) = \Omega_z(t|t-1) - P_t\Omega_x(t|t-1)P_t'$$

where $P_t = \Omega_z(t|t-1)A'\Omega_x(t|t-1)^{-1}$ is called the *filter gain*.

The Forecasting Step

The *forecasting step* forecasts both the state and the variables s steps ahead for every time $t = T + s > T$ given the present state. It is based on the following recursive relationships:

$$z_{t|T} = Cz_{t-1|T} + Dy_{t-1}$$
$$x_{t|T} = Az_{t|T} + By_t$$

The forecasting step also predicts the covariance matrix of the states and the variables one step ahead:

$$\Omega_z(t|T) = C\Omega_z(t-1|T)C' + \Omega_\eta$$
$$\Omega_x(t|T) = A\Omega_z(t|T)A' + \Omega_\varepsilon$$

The Smoothing Step

The *smoothing step* computes the states at intermediate times $t < T$. It is computed recursively backwards with the following recursive equations:

$$z_{t|T} = z_{t|t} + S_t(z_{t+1|T} - z_{t+1|t})$$
$$\Omega_z(t|T) = \Omega_z(t|t) - S_t[\Omega_z(t+1|t) - \Omega_z(t+1|T)]S_t'$$

where $S_t = \Omega_z(t|t)A'\Omega_z(t+1|t)^{-1}$ is called the *Kalman smoothing matrix*.

The filter is initialized with the initial conditions (i.e., the initial state z_0 and the initial input y_0) and computations are carried out recursively to the desired time. Note that the last computation does not depend on the inputs and can be performed offline. If the system is stable and extends to the infinite past, then states estimated with the Kalman filter coincide with actual states. Hence we can say that the state is determined by the system's past.

If the noise terms are not normally distributed but their second order moment still exists, all of the recursion equations remain valid.

The Log-Likelihood Function

Now compute the log-likelihood function of the model. First arrange all the model parameters, that is the four matrices **A**, **B**, **C**, **D**, and the covariance matrices, in one parameter vector $\boldsymbol{\theta}$. The model likelihood has the following expression:

$$
\begin{aligned}
f(\mathbf{x}_1, ..., \mathbf{x}_T; \boldsymbol{\theta}) &= f(\mathbf{x}_1; \boldsymbol{\theta}) f(\mathbf{x}_2, ..., \mathbf{x}_T | \mathbf{x}_1; \boldsymbol{\theta}) \\
&= f(\mathbf{x}_1; \boldsymbol{\theta}) f(\mathbf{x}_2 | \mathbf{x}_1; \boldsymbol{\theta}) ... (f(\mathbf{x}_T | \mathbf{x}_1, ..., \mathbf{x}_{T-1}; \boldsymbol{\theta}))
\end{aligned}
$$

Assuming that the noise has normal density, the $\mathbf{x}_t$ have the following conditional normal densities:

$$
(\mathbf{x}_t | \mathbf{x}_1, ..., \mathbf{x}_{t-1}; \boldsymbol{\theta}) \sim N(\mathbf{x}_{t|t-1}, \boldsymbol{\Omega}_\mathbf{x}(t|t-1))
$$

Therefore, we can write the log-likelihood as follows:

$$
\begin{aligned}
\log f(\mathbf{x}_1, ..., \mathbf{x}_{t-1}; \boldsymbol{\theta}) = &-\frac{NT}{2}\log(2\pi) - \frac{1}{2}\sum_{t=1}^{T}\log|\boldsymbol{\Omega}_\mathbf{x}(t|t-1)| \\
&-\frac{1}{2}\sum_{t=1}^{T}((\mathbf{x}_t - \mathbf{x}_{t|t-1})'\boldsymbol{\Omega}_\mathbf{x}(t|t-1)^{-1}(\mathbf{x}_t - \mathbf{x}_{t|t-1}))
\end{aligned}
$$

We can see from the above expression that all quantities that appear in the log-likelihood function can be computed, for any given parameter vector, using the Kalman filter. The Kalman filter enables estimation insofar as it allows one to write the log-likelihood function.

The Expectation Maximization Algorithms

In order to determine the model parameters, the previous log-likelihood function needs to be maximized. This is a nonlinear maximization problem that can be solved with one of the optimization methods described in Chapter 6. We can also use the *Expectation Maximization* (EM) algorithm, which is an algorithm for maximizing the log-likelihood function of normal models. The EM algorithm will be described later in this chapter when we describe Markov-switching models.

Asymptotic Behavior of ML Estimators

As for all estimation methods, we need to know the asymptotic behavior of estimators. Collect all model parameters in a parameter vector δ. It can be demonstrated that the ML estimator $\hat{\delta}$ of the true parameter vector δ_0 is consistent. It can also be demonstrated that $\hat{\delta}$ is asymptotically normal with the covariance matrix given by the inverse of the asymptotic information matrix. (See Chapter 14 for a definition of the information matrix and its properties.)

Estimation of State-Space Models with the Subspace Method

Though there is a fundamental equivalence between vector autogressive moving average (VARMA) models and state-space models, the analysis of cointegration has paid little attention to state-space models. Aoki[6] and Aoki and Havenner[7] in 1990 and 1997 respectively, proposed subspace methods to analyze cointegration in the context of state-space systems. However, it was only at the end of the 1990s that the theory of cointegration for state-space models was systematically developed by Bauer and Wagner. In a series of papers, they developed a canonical form to describe cointegration in state-space models.[8] They showed how the subspace method can be extended to integrated systems and developed tests to determine the order and cointegration rank of state-space models.

The subspace method is a widely used estimation method for state-space models. Among the algorithms and software systems that implement subspace methods are CCA developed by Larimore in 1983,[9]

---

[6] M. Aoki, *State Space Modeling of Time Series* (New York: Springer, 1990).
[7] M. Aoki and A. Havenner, "Applications of Computer Aided Time Series Modeling," in *Lecture Notes in Statistics* (New York: Springer, 1997).
[8] Dietmar Bauer, "Order Estimation for Subspace Methods," *Automatica* 37 (2001), pp. 1561–1573; Dietmar Bauer, "Identification of State Space Systems with Conditionally Heteroskedastic Innovations," *Proceedings of the 15th IFAC World Congress*, pp. T–Mo–M02; Dietmar Bauer and Martin Wagner, "Estimating Cointegrated Systems Using Subspace Algorithms," *Journal of Econometrics* 111 (2002), pp. 47–84; and Dietmar Bauer and Martin Wagner, "A Canonical Form For Unit Root Analysis in the State Space Framework," *VWI Diskussionsschrift*, University of Bern, Switzerland.
[9] W. E. Larimore, "System Identification, Reduced Order Filters and Modeling Via Canonical Variate Analysis," *Proceedings: 1983 American Control Conference 2*, H. S. Rao and P. Dorato (eds.) (Piscataway, NJ: ACC, 1983), pp. 445–451.

N4SID developed by Van Overschee and DeMoor in 1994,[10] and MOESP developed by Verhaegen in 1994.[11] The subspace method is now available on software packages such as GAUSS and Matlab. In particular, Bauer and Wagner developed Matlab codes to extend the CCA algorithm to cointegrated systems.

The idea of the subspace method is the following.[12] States contain all the information from the past that is relevant for predicting the future. Conversely, states can be estimated from past observations. The model parameters can therefore be obtained by regressing future data on past data.

To make the concept more precise, consider a state-space model that we write in the prediction error form:

$$\mathbf{x}_t = \mathbf{A}\mathbf{z}_t + \boldsymbol{\varepsilon}_t$$
$$\mathbf{z}_{t+1} = \mathbf{C}\mathbf{z}_t + \mathbf{K}\boldsymbol{\varepsilon}_t$$
$$t = 1, 2, ..., T$$

To simplify, we omit the deterministic input. As we have seen, it can be demonstrated that a state-space model can always be cast in the innovation form.

The *order* of the model is the number s of states. A state-space model is said to be minimal if no other equivalent system has a lower order. Recall that in Chapter 12 we defined the following matrices:

The *observability* matrix: $O \equiv [\mathbf{A}', \mathbf{C}'\mathbf{A}', (\mathbf{C}^2)'\mathbf{A}', ...]$

The *controllability* matrix: $C \equiv [\mathbf{K}, \mathbf{CK}, \mathbf{A}^2\mathbf{K}, ...]$

The *Hankel* matrix: $OC \equiv [\mathbf{CA}^{i+j-2}\mathbf{K}]_{i,j=1,2,...}$

Consider the problem of predicting the observable variables $\mathbf{x}_{t+j}$. $j \geq 0$. From the state equation, we can write the following recursive equations:

---

[10] P. Van Overschee and B. DeMoor, "N4SID: Subspace Algorithms for The Identification of Combined Deterministic-Stochastic Systems," *Automatica* 30 (1994), pp. 75–93.

[11] M. Verhaegen, "Identification of the Deterministic Part of Mimo State-Space Models Given in Innovation Form from Input-Output Data," *Automatica* 30, no. 1 (1994), pp. 61–74.

[12] Subspace methods involve many technical details. Here we can only give an overview of the method. The interested reader should consult the original papers by Bauer and Wagner cited above.

$$
\begin{aligned}
\mathbf{x}_{t+j} &= \mathbf{A}\mathbf{z}_{t+j} + \boldsymbol{\varepsilon}_{t+j} \\
&= \mathbf{A}\mathbf{C}\mathbf{z}_{t+j-1} + \mathbf{A}\mathbf{K}\boldsymbol{\varepsilon}_{t+j-1} + \boldsymbol{\varepsilon}_{t+j} \\
&= \mathbf{A}\mathbf{C}^{j}\mathbf{z}_{t} + \left(\sum_{i=0}^{j-1} \mathbf{A}\mathbf{C}^{j}\mathbf{K}\boldsymbol{\varepsilon}_{t+j-i-1} \right) + \boldsymbol{\varepsilon}_{t+j}
\end{aligned}
$$

which show that future observables can be predicted from the present state.

Now suppose that the past observables and the initial state are known, that is, $\mathbf{x}_{t-1}, \mathbf{x}_{t-2}, \ldots, \mathbf{x}_0, \mathbf{z}_0$ are given. We can write the following recursive equations:

$$
\begin{aligned}
\mathbf{z}_t &= \mathbf{C}^{t}\mathbf{z}_0 + \sum_{i=0}^{t-1} \mathbf{C}^{i}\mathbf{K}\boldsymbol{\varepsilon}_{t-i-1} \\
&= \mathbf{C}^{t}\mathbf{z}_0 + \sum_{i=0}^{t-1} \mathbf{C}^{i}\mathbf{K}(\mathbf{x}_{t-i-1} - \mathbf{A}\mathbf{z}_{t-i-1}) \\
&= (\mathbf{C} - \mathbf{K}\mathbf{A})^{t}\mathbf{z}_0 + \sum_{i=0}^{t-1} (\mathbf{C} - \mathbf{K}\mathbf{A})^{i}\mathbf{K}\mathbf{x}_{t-i-1}
\end{aligned}
$$

Note that, in this context, we assume that at time $t = 0$ both the initial state and the initial value of the observable are given. This assumption entails that the present state is known. If the initial state $\mathbf{z}_0$ is not known, it can be estimated with the Kalman filter.

From the above equations we can write: $\mathbf{x}_{t+j|t} = \mathbf{A}\mathbf{C}^{i}\mathbf{z}_{t}$. In addition, with the notation $\overline{\mathbf{A}} = \mathbf{C} - \mathbf{K}\mathbf{A}$, we can write the following equation in stacked matrix form:

$$
\begin{pmatrix} \mathbf{x}_t \\ \vdots \\ \mathbf{x}_{t+j} \\ \vdots \end{pmatrix} = \begin{pmatrix} \mathbf{A}\mathbf{K} & \mathbf{A}\overline{\mathbf{A}}\mathbf{K} & \cdots & \mathbf{A}\overline{\mathbf{A}}^{t-1}\mathbf{K} \\ \vdots & \vdots & \ddots & \vdots \\ \mathbf{A}\mathbf{C}^{j}\mathbf{K} & \mathbf{A}\mathbf{C}^{j}\overline{\mathbf{A}}\mathbf{K} & \cdots & \mathbf{A}\mathbf{C}^{j}\overline{\mathbf{A}}^{t-1}\mathbf{K} \\ \vdots & \vdots & \ddots & \vdots \end{pmatrix} \begin{pmatrix} \mathbf{x}_{t-1} \\ \mathbf{x}_{t-2} \\ \vdots \\ \mathbf{x}_0 \end{pmatrix} + \begin{pmatrix} \mathbf{A} \\ \vdots \\ \mathbf{A}\mathbf{C}^{j} \\ \vdots \end{pmatrix} \overline{\mathbf{A}}^{t}\mathbf{z}_0
$$

$$
+ \begin{pmatrix} \mathbf{I} & \cdots & \cdots & 0 & 0 & \cdots \\ \vdots & \ddots & \vdots & \ddots & \vdots & \ddots \\ \mathbf{A}\mathbf{C}^{j-1}\mathbf{K} & \cdots & \mathbf{A}\mathbf{K} & \mathbf{I} & 0 & \cdots \\ \vdots & & \ddots & \vdots & \ddots & \ddots \end{pmatrix} \begin{pmatrix} \boldsymbol{\varepsilon}_t \\ \vdots \\ \boldsymbol{\varepsilon}_{t+j} \\ \vdots \end{pmatrix}
$$

The above equation describes the future of the system. Its right side includes three terms: the first term describes the effects of the finite past of the system, the second shows the impact of the initial state, and the third describes the impact of the innovation process.

In principle, the equation describes an infinite number of future observations. Empirically, however, only a finite number of observations are available for estimation. Pick two numbers f, p larger than the order s of the system. Using a stacked matrix notation similar to that used in Chapter 14, we can write the following vectors:

- fn-vector $\mathbf{X}_{t,f}^{+}$ of future f observables

- fn-vector $\mathbf{E}_{t,f}^{+}$ of noise terms

- pn-vector $\mathbf{X}_{t,p}^{-}$ of past observables

Note that the distinction between past and future observables is only conventional: all data are obviously historical data. In this notation, the superscript indicates either the future (+) or the past (−), and the subscript indicates the present time t and the number f, p of samples:

$$\mathbf{X}_{t,f}^{+} = \begin{pmatrix} \mathbf{x}_t \\ \mathbf{x}_{t+1} \\ \vdots \\ \mathbf{x}_{t+f-1} \end{pmatrix}, \ \mathbf{E}_{t,f}^{+} = \begin{pmatrix} \boldsymbol{\varepsilon}_t \\ \boldsymbol{\varepsilon}_{t+1} \\ \vdots \\ \boldsymbol{\varepsilon}_{t+f-1} \end{pmatrix}, \ \mathbf{X}_{t,p}^{-} = \begin{pmatrix} \mathbf{x}_{t-1} \\ \mathbf{x}_{t-2} \\ \vdots \\ \mathbf{x}_{t-p} \end{pmatrix}$$

We also define the following three finite matrices:

1. The truncated observation matrix:

$$O_f = \begin{pmatrix} \mathbf{A}' \\ \mathbf{C}'\mathbf{A}' \\ \vdots \\ (\mathbf{C}^{f-1})'\mathbf{A}' \end{pmatrix}$$

2. The Kalman filter matrix: $K_p = [\mathbf{K}, (\mathbf{C}-\mathbf{KA})\mathbf{K}, ..., (\mathbf{C}-\mathbf{KA})^{p-1}\mathbf{K}]$
3. The matrix

$$E_f = \begin{pmatrix} I & 0 & 0 & \cdots & 0 & 0 \\ AK & I & 0 & \cdots & 0 & 0 \\ ACK & AK & I & \cdots & 0 & 0 \\ \vdots & \vdots & \ddots & \ddots & \vdots & \vdots \\ AC^{f-3}K & AC^{f-4}K & \cdots & AK & I & 0 \\ AC^{f-2}K & AC^{f-3}K & \cdots & ACK & AK & I \end{pmatrix}$$

With this notation, the above equation can be compactly written in the following matrix form:

$$\mathbf{X}_{t,f}^{+} = O_f K_p \mathbf{X}_{t,p}^{-} + O_f (C - KA)^p \mathbf{x}_{t-p} + \mathbf{E}_{t,f}^{+}$$

The above is the fundamental equation of the subspace methods. Based on this equation, all algorithms proposed in the literature perform the following three basic steps:

1. Regress $\mathbf{X}_{t,f}^{+}$ on $\mathbf{X}_{t,p}^{-}$ to obtain an estimate of

$$\beta_{f,p} = O_f K_p$$

2. Approximate the typically full-rank estimated matrix $\hat{\beta}_{f,p}$ with a rank-n matrix expressed as

$$\hat{\beta}_{f,p} = \hat{O}_f \hat{K}_p$$

3. Estimate the state z_t using the equation $\hat{z}_t = \hat{K}_p \mathbf{X}_{t,p}^{-}$ and estimate the system matrices by LS.

This basic structure is common to every subspace algorithm. Note that the above only outlines how the subspace method works: the different steps are rigorously justified in the Bauer and Wagner references cited above. The various algorithms that have been proposed, in particular MOESP, CCA, and N4SID, differ in how the steps are implemented. Given the complexity of the technical details, we refer the interested reader to the original papers also cited above.

Note that the present state $\mathbf{x}_t$ could not have been estimated by the Kalman filter alone as the model parameters are not known. Recall that in the ML method we used the Kalman filter to compute the log-likelihood as a function of the observables. The subspace algorithm uses the Kalman filter relationships to compute the basic regressive equation on which the estimation method hinges.

Model Order Estimation for Subspace Algorithms

The model order (i.e., the minimal number of state variables) is the key parameter to input into estimation procedures for state-space models. Standard methods for order estimation are based on the *singular value decomposition* (SVD) of the matrix $\hat{\beta}_{f,p}$. The model order is equal to number of nonzero eigenvalues of $\hat{\beta}_{f,p}$. Small sample corrections have been proposed, among which those of Bauer and Wagner for integrated systems. Information criteria such as the Akaike Information Criterion and Bayesian Information Criterion can also be used.[13]

Asymptotic Behavior of the Subspace Method Estimators

The estimators of the model matrices obtained with subspace methods are strongly consistent. However, precise statements of consistency depend on the choices made by each algorithm and can be found in the literature specific to each algorithm. In general, the asymptotic distribution of estimators is normal even if noise is not normal. Little is known on asymptotic distributions if noise is colored.[14]

ESTIMATION OF FACTOR ANALYTIC MODELS

Factor analytic models are models where the system dynamics is driven by a (small) number of factors. As we have seen in Chapter 12, a typical factor analytic model has the following form:

$$\mathbf{x}_t = \mathbf{B}\mathbf{f}_t + \mathbf{u}_t$$
$$\mathbf{f}_t = \mathbf{A}_1\mathbf{f}_{t-1} + \mathbf{A}_2\mathbf{f}_{t-2} + \cdots + \mathbf{A}_p\mathbf{f}_{t-p} + \boldsymbol{\varepsilon}_t$$
$$\mathbf{u}_t = \mathbf{C}_1\mathbf{u}_{t-1} + \mathbf{C}_2\mathbf{u}_{t-2} + \cdots + \mathbf{C}_q\mathbf{u}_{t-q} + \boldsymbol{\eta}_t$$

In this model, there are N individual variables $x_{j,t}$, $j = 1, 2, \ldots, N$, $t = 1, 2, \ldots, T$ that form the vector $\mathbf{x}_t = (x_{1,t}, \ldots, x_{N,t})'$ and $m << N$ factors $\mathbf{f}_t = (f_{1,t}, \ldots, f_{m,t})'$, $t = 1, 2, \ldots, T$. $\mathbf{B}$ is an $N \times m$ matrix of *factor loadings*; $\mathbf{A}_i = (a_{s,t}^i)$, $i = 1, 2, \ldots, p$, $s, t = 1, 2, \ldots, m$ are deterministic $m \times m$ matrices that form the VAR model of common factors f; $\mathbf{C}_i = (c_{s,t}^i)$, $i =$

---

[13] Details can be found in the cited references for each specific algorithm.
[14] Again, readers are referred to the references cited for more detail.

$1, 2, \ldots, p, s, t = 1, 2, \ldots, q$ are deterministic diagonal $q \times q$ matrices that form the VAR model of idiosyncratic factors u.

In this chapter we do not assume that the common factors are stationary; they can be either I(0) or I(1) variables. The noise term $\varepsilon_t = (\varepsilon_{1,t}, \cdots, \varepsilon_{m,t})$ is a multivariate white noise with variance-covariance matrix $\Sigma = (\sigma_1, \cdots, \sigma_m)$, and η_t is the N-vector of individual disturbances which are serially uncorrelated, mutually uncorrelated, and uncorrelated with the noise ε_t. Under these assumptions, the correlation structure of the model is due only to common factors. Other forms for the factor analytic models are possible but the above is sufficiently general. It can be demonstrated that this model can be adapted to the case where the model includes lagged factors.[15]

Key issues in estimating dynamic factor models are the estimation of the model parameters and the determination of the model order. If both integrated and stationary factors are allowed, it is also important to determine the number of integrated factors. There is a close connection between factor models and cointegration. In fact, Escribano and Peña[16] demonstrated that the following two statements are equivalent:

1. All individual components of $\mathbf{x}_t$ are I(1) but there are p cointegrating relationships.
2. The DGP of $\mathbf{x}_t$ is a m-p-factor model.

We now discuss specifically how factor models can be estimated. First observe that a factor model can be rewritten as a state-space model. In fact, define the vector

$$
\mathbf{z}_t = \begin{pmatrix} \mathbf{f}_t \\ \vdots \\ \mathbf{f}_{t-p+1} \\ \mathbf{u}_t \\ \vdots \\ \mathbf{u}_{t-q+1} \end{pmatrix}
$$

and write the transition equation

[15] Daniel Peña and Pilar Poncela, "Nonstationary Dynamic Factor Analysis," *Journal of Statistical Planning and Inference* (2004).
[16] A. Escribano and D. Peña, "Cointegration and Common Factors," *Journal of Time Series Analysis* 15 (1994), pp. 577–586.

$$\mathbf{z}_t = \begin{pmatrix} \begin{matrix} \mathbf{A}_1 & \mathbf{A}_2 & \cdots & \mathbf{A}_{p-1} & \mathbf{A}_p \\ \mathbf{I} & 0 & \cdots & 0 & 0 \\ 0 & \mathbf{I} & \cdots & 0 & 0 \\ \vdots & \vdots & \ddots & \vdots & \vdots \\ 0 & 0 & \cdots & \mathbf{I} & 0 \\ \cdots & \cdots & \cdots & \cdots & \cdots \end{matrix} & \begin{matrix} & & 0 & & \\ & & & & \\ \cdots & \cdots & \cdots & \cdots & \cdots \\ \mathbf{C}_1 & \mathbf{C}_2 & \cdots & \mathbf{C}_{q-1} & \mathbf{C}_q \\ \mathbf{I} & 0 & \cdots & 0 & 0 \\ 0 & \mathbf{I} & \cdots & 0 & 0 \\ \vdots & \vdots & \ddots & \vdots & \vdots \\ 0 & 0 & \cdots & \mathbf{I} & 0 \end{matrix} \end{pmatrix} \mathbf{z}_{t-1} + \begin{pmatrix} \boldsymbol{\varepsilon}_t \\ 0 \\ \vdots \\ 0 \\ \boldsymbol{\eta}_t \\ 0 \\ \vdots \\ 0 \end{pmatrix}$$

and the measurement equation

$$\mathbf{x}_t = \mathbf{B}\mathbf{f}_t + \mathbf{u}_t = \begin{bmatrix} \mathbf{B} & 0 & \cdots & 0 & \mathbf{I} & 0 & \cdots & 0 \end{bmatrix} \mathbf{z}_t$$

Because a factor analytic model can be rewritten as a state-space model, it can also be estimated as a state-space model. Thus the methods described above for estimating state-space models can be used to estimate factor analytic models. In fact, in the method originally proposed by Geweke[17] and used subsequently by many, factors are estimated with the Kalman filter and the model is estimated with either ML or subspace methods. Details depend on the specific form of the dynamic factor model.

The crucial point here is how to estimate the number of factors which is, as we have seen in the previous sections, a key input to state-space estimation methods. Bai and Ng proposed using criteria based on information theory; Peña and Poncela proposed a method based on a generalized covariance matrix. These and other methods involve rather complex technical details.[18] Stock and Watson proposed a method based on Principal Component Analysis for estimating both the number of factors and the model parameters.[19]

Expectation-Maximization (EM) Algorithms

The EM algorithm is a numerical optimization procedure for finding the maximum of log-likelihood functions in the presence of missing or hid-

---

[17] J. Geweke, "The Dynamic Factor Analysis of Economic Time Series," in Dennis J. Aigner and Arthur S. Goldberger (eds.), *Latent Variables in Socio-Economic Models* (Amsterdam: North-Holland, 1977).

[18] The interested reader should consult the original papers cited above.

[19] For a description of the Stock and Watson method, see the discussion on estimation of cointegrated systems in Chapter 15.

den variables. Originally proposed in the context of factor models by Dempster, Laird, and Rubin, the EM algorithm is now widely used in estimation methods of many other hidden variable models, including Markov-switching models.[20]

The idea of the EM algorithm is to iterate between the estimate of the best parameters given the missing data and the estimate of the missing data given the best estimate of parameters. Suppose that the hidden variables x^* admit a density $l^*(x^*; \theta)$, which is a function of the parameters θ. Consider the log-likelihood of the hidden variable model: $\log l^*(x^*; \theta)$.

Suppose that the observables x are a function of the hidden variables: $x = g(x^*)$ and that the variables x admit a density $l(x; \theta)$, which is a function of the parameters θ. We assume that the parameters θ are identifiable by the observables and, for that reason, also by the hidden variables.

As the hidden variables are not observed, we cannot perform the optimization process of $\log l^*(x^*; \theta)$. The EM algorithm is an iterative method that works in two steps:

Step 1: The *expectation step* replaces this unobservable likelihood with its best approximation based on the observables, that is the expectation of the hidden likelihood given the observables.

Step 2: The *maximization step* optimizes the parameters given the hidden variables from the previous step.

ESTIMATION METHODS FOR MARKOV-SWITCHING MODELS

The intuitive reality of "states of the market" are well known to asset managers. Trending markets, be they bull or bear, are states of the market when price and return processes have a recognizable behavior. In modeling terms, this means that models of a given state share features which differ from other states of the market. From a modeling perspective, this implies that different statistical models are required to describe the market in different moments. If we add rules that prescribe the switching from one state of the market to another, we arrive at a regime-switching model. A broad class of regime-switching models are the Markov-switching vector autoregressive models (MS-VAR).

---

[20] A. P. Dempster, N. M. Laird, and D. B. Rubin, "Maximum-Likelihood from Incomplete Data via the EM Algorithm," *Journal Royal Statistical Society Series* 39 (1977), pp. 1–38.

Recall that a Markov-switching model is a VAR model whose coefficients are driven by a Markov chain.

$$\mathbf{x}_t = \boldsymbol{\mu}(s) + \left(\sum_{i=1}^{p} \mathbf{A}_i(s) L^i \right) \mathbf{x}_t + \boldsymbol{\varepsilon}_t(s)$$

where the matrices $\mathbf{A}_i(s)$ are the coefficients of the process at lag i in state s and the noise terms $\boldsymbol{\varepsilon}_t(s)$ are independent normal variables $\boldsymbol{\varepsilon}_t(s) \sim N(0, \boldsymbol{\Sigma}(s))$. The process is driven by a k-states Markov chain. A Markov chain is a discrete variable which can assume at each instant one of k possible values with transition probabilities:

$$P(s_t = i | s_{t-1} = j) = p_{ij}, j \rightarrow i$$

The realized state determines the coefficients and the vector of the intercepts of the process at each moment, so that the innovation term of the process is distributed as a mixture of Gaussian distributions. The state variable is a hidden (i.e., not observable) factor.

In the above specification of MS-VAR models, the transition between states is independent of the observables. It is possible to specify endogenous transition probabilities, that is, transition probabilities that depend on the observables.

MS-VAR models have different properties with respect to VAR models. Among the differences with a bearing on estimation, innovation terms, not knowing the state, are generally non-Gaussian and there is no equivalence between an MS-VAR model and its mean-adjusted form. In fact, models in mean-adjusted form experience a jump in the variables when the process mean changes in consequence of a regime switch. This property does not hold for models in standard intercept form.

The estimation process of MS-VAR models involves many technical issues due to the complexity of the process itself and to the vast number of different models. Among the packages now available for estimating MS-VAR processes are the open-source packages MSVAR developed by Hans-Martin Krolzig in the Ox language, MSVARlib developed by Benoit Bellone in Ox and Ox-Gauss, and codes made available by Jim Hamilton at UCSD.

We will limit our discussion of the estimation process for MS-VAR to the ML estimation process. While other methods have been proposed, ML estimation is presently the most widely used approach. The general principles of ML estimation of MS-VAR processes are the same as those used in state-space models discussed above and, more in general, as those used in every hidden variable model. One writes a log-like-lihood function that depends on both observables and hidden variables. In linear state-space models, Kalman filters are used to provide an optimal estimate; in nonlinear MS-VAR models, the EM algorithm is used.

Assume that, conditionally to regime s_t, the error term is normally distributed and that the model is expressed in mean-adjusted form. The estimation process estimates the set of matrices $A_i(s)$, the vector of means $\mu(s)$, the covariance matrices $\Sigma(s)$ of the error terms, and the transition probabilities p_{ij} of the Markov chain. This estimation is quite onerous. If there are S states, one has to estimate S-times the number of parameters of a standard VAR(p) model plus $S(S-1)$ transition probabilities.

For a given regime s_t and lagged variables

$$X_{t-1} = (x'_{t-1}, \ldots, x'_1, x'_0, \ldots, x'_{1-p})'$$

we can write the probability distribution of the error term as follows:

$$p(x_t | s_t = i_m, X_{t-1}) = \frac{1}{(2\pi)^{1/2}} |\Sigma_m|^{-1/2} \exp\left(-\frac{1}{2}(x_t - \bar{x}_{mt})' \Sigma_m^{-1}(x_t - \bar{x}_{mt})\right)$$

where m is the index that identifies the state.

Given the history of the states and the observables up to $t-1$, the distribution of the error term is a mixture of Gaussian distributions. If the entire history of states were known, the likelihood would simply be a product of normal distributions. However, neither the history of the states nor the transition probabilities are known; they must therefore be estimated.

In principle one could write the joint sample density from transition probabilities to be estimated on all possible paths. Computationally speaking, this is not feasible; simplifications are called for. To this end, we use the EM algorithm which provides filtered probabilities. A detailed explanation of how the EM algorithm works involves many technical details and is beyond the scope of this book.

APPLICATIONS

We are now in a position to discuss how the models whose estimation we have just described can be used by asset managers. Asset management requires the ability to forecast returns. Broadly speaking, all the models that we have discussed perform return forecasting in one of the following ways:

■ Regress returns on lagged values of exogenous predictors
■ Regress returns on its own lagged values using autoregressive and vector-autoregressive models
■ Forecast factors using dynamic factor models
■ Forecast higher moments
■ Combine the above methods

Most applications discussed in the literature and currently used at asset management firms fall into one of the above categories. In Chapter 15 we discussed a number of applications that use regressive and autoregressive techniques with exogenous factors. We now discuss some additional applications and, in particular, the following forecasting strategies:

■ Momentum strategies
■ Contrarian strategies
■ Cointegration-based strategies
■ Size-based strategies
■ Context-based strategies

Considerable literature on the above strategies seems to confirm that sources of profitability due to predictability of returns based on their own past are not to be found in single stock returns but in aggregated portfolios. Loosely speaking, if we do not use exogenous predictors this means that returns are individually unpredictable but the returns of selected aggregate portfolios are predictable. Portfolio predictability is due to auto cross-correlations (i.e., correlations between one stock's returns and the lagged returns of other stocks).

This fact, together with considerations developed in the applications section in Chapter 15, is an indication that vector autoregressive models, eventually with exogenous variables, might be a reasonable model choice. However, the difficulty is estimating large autoregressive models underlines the need to employ strategies that somehow reduce the complexity of models.

Momentum Strategies

Jegadeesh and Titman empirically demonstrated the reality of momentum strategies.[21] A momentum strategy, as described by Jegadeesh and Titman, is a strategy based on creating portfolios formed with the best-performing stocks in the previous 8 to 12 months. There are many other

---

[21] Narasimahn Jegadeesh and Sheridan Titman, "Returns to Buying Winners and Selling Losers: Implications for Stock Market Efficiency," *Journal of Finance* 48 (1993), pp. 65–91.

versions of this strategy that basically implement the same principle: best-performing stocks are given higher portfolio weights. Following the return decomposition proposed by Lo and MacKinlay,[22] Lewellen[23] argues that momentum is a consequence of cross autocorrelations.

The autocorrelation functions of individual price processes exhibit fast exponential decay, that is to say, individual price processes are not linearly autocorrelated. However, some portfolios exhibit strong auto-correlation. A rather articulated statement of this fact is to be found in Lo and MacKinlay[24] where the variance ratio test is used to show that price processes are not random walks.

A possible explanation of this fact is the existence of strong cross autocorrelations between return processes. Lo and MacKinlay propose a simple but powerful framework for analyzing this fact and, in particular, the existence of momentum and reversals in price processes. They introduce a trading strategy where portfolios are rebalanced at every period with the rule that each asset's weight $w_{i,t}$ is proportional to the corresponding previous period return $r_{i,t}$:

$$w_{i,t} = -(r_{i,t} - r_{M,t}), \; r_{i,t} = \frac{P_i(t) - P_i(t-1)}{P_i(t-1)}, \; r_{M,t} = \sum_{i=1}^{N} r_{i,t}$$

The existence of cross autocorrelations entails that returns follow a stable vector autoregressive process. However, for large portfolios, estimating this vector autoregressive process would be difficult. Lewellen bypasses the problem by defining a dynamically rebalanced long-short portfolio and computing the returns of this portfolio.

Contrarian Strategies

Contrarian strategies are based on the principle "buy the losers, sell the winners." Prima facie, momentum and contrarian strategies might seem to contradict each other. But the contrary is true. In fact, both momentum and contrarian strategies are based on the fact that returns follow a stable vector autoregressive process. Stated differently, momentum is followed by reversals.

---

[22] Andrew Lo and A. Craig MacKinlay, "When Are Contrarian Profits Due to Stock Market Overreaction?" *Review of Financial Studies* 3 (1990), pp. 175–205.

[23] Jonathan Lewellen, "Temporary Movements in Stock Prices," MIT Working Paper, March 2001.

[24] Lo and MacKinlay, "When are Contrarian Profits Due To Stock Market Overreaction?"

Cointegration-Based Strategies

The idea of exploiting cointegration is not new. One of the earliest forms of portfolio management based on cointegration is a strategy called *pair trading*. Pair trading chooses pairs of stocks that are cointegrated, forms a zero-value long-short portfolio when they are far apart and cashes in the profit when their difference becomes negative.

More sophisticated, more robust versions of cointegration-based strategies look for cointegrated portfolios. Alexander and Dimitriu[25] analyze the performance of a cointegrated portfolio based on stocks in the Dow Jones Index.

Size-Based Strategies

Lo and MacKinlay introduced the notion of a lead-lag effect in size-sorted portfolios. Specifically, by forming portfolios with stocks sorted by the size of the firm, they show that there are significant lead-lag return effects. Kanas and Kouretas[26] empirically demonstrated the lead-lag effect in size-sorted portfolios using the ARDL framework of Pesaran and Shin.[27]

A different type of investigation on size-sorted portfolio was performed by Guidolin and Nicodano.[28] The starting point of their investigation is the observation that small firms pay higher returns than large firms. For example, Fama and French found that small firms exhibit a return on the average 0.74% higher than large firms.[29] An oft given explanation is the liquidity premium: Small firms are typically less liquid than large firms. One might expect that institutional investors such as pension funds, which have a long time horizon and are not pressed for liquidity, would hold portfolios including a sizable share of small firms. However empirical studies such as that performed by Gompers and Metrick show that this is not the case.[30]

---

[25] Carol Alexander and Anca Dimitriu, "Sources of Outperformance in Equity Markets: Mean Reversion, Common Trends and Herding," *Journal of Portfolio Management*, Special European Issue (2004), pp. 170–185.

[26] Angelos Kanas and Georgios P. Kouretas, "A Cointegration Approach to the Lead-Lag Effect Among Size-Sorted Equity Portfolios," *International Review of Economics and Finance* 14 (2005), pp. 181–201.

[27] M. H. Pesaran and Y. Shin, "An Autoregressive Distributed Lag Modelling Approach to Cointegration Analysis," Chapter 11 in S. Strom (ed), *Econometrics and Economic Theory in the 20th Century: The Ragnar Frisch Centennial Symposium* (Cambridge: Cambridge University Press, 1999).

[28] M. Guidolin and G. Nicodano, "Small Caps in International Equity Portfolios," CeRP Working Paper 41/05 (2005).

[29] Eugene F. Fama and Kenneth French, "Value versus Growth: The International Evidence," *Journal of Finance* 53 (1998), pp. 1975–1999.

[30] P. Gompers and A. Metrick, "Institutional Investors and Equity Prices," *Quarterly Journal of Economics* 116 (2002), pp. 229–260.

Guidolin and Nicodano attempted a novel explanation of this phenomenon based on the economic intuition that large and small firms behave differently in different market regimes. To prove their conjecture, Guidolin and Nicodano modeled stock returns with a three-state Markov switching model estimated with ML principles applying the EM optimization method. The model shows that (1) small firms' returns are low when aggregate volatility is high; and (2) their volatility is high when aggregate returns are low. The authors applied expected utility maximization with power utility functions to solve the asset allocation problem.

Context-Based Strategies

Sorensen, Hua, and Qian propose an asset management strategy based on *contextual factors*.[31] Factors are contextual when their predictive power depends on the context. A context is a subset of securities chosen in function of a given variable that might define a firm's property such as size, or a market situation such as a positive trend.

Return models based on predictive factors are the starting point of the Sorensen, Hua, and Qian approach. If returns are linear regressions on a set of factors, the regression coefficients can be estimated with the formulas discussed in Chapter 14. However Sorensen, Hua, and Qian argue that the predictive power of factors is conditional on the context. The objective is to find optimal factor weights in any given context. Their objective was not achieved using standard LS methods as in ordinary linear regressions, but required maximizing the Information Coefficient. The Information Coefficient is defined as the correlation coefficient between forecasted and actual returns adjusted for various risk parameters. Multiple contexts can be defined and the final weight of each factor is determined with a process of averaging between different contexts.

SUMMARY

- Hidden variable models introduce variables that are not observable, hence "hidden."
- Hidden variable models have greater explanatory power than classical models but, due to the higher number of parameters that need to be estimated, their estimates are more uncertain.

---

[31] Eric H. Sorensen, Ronald Hua, and Edward Qian, "Contextual Fundamentals, Models, and Active Management," *Journal of Portfolio Management* (Fall 2005), pp. 23–26.

- Linear state-space models and Vector Autoregressive Moving Average (VARMA) models are equivalent representations of the same linear systems.
- Estimation methodologies for linear state-space systems include Maximum Likelihood (ML) and Subspace Algorithm methods.
- The Kalman filter is a recursive algorithm used to estimate states from observables assuming the model is known.
- The Kalman filter is based on recursive equations that make use of Bayes' theorem.
- The Kalman filter performs three tasks: (1) filtering, which computes the present state conditional to all the observations up to the present time; (2) smoothing, which computes the state at intermediate dates conditional on all the observations up to the present date; and (3) forecasting, which predicts the state at a future date conditional on all the observations up to the present date.
- The ML method for state-space systems works as follows: (1) compute the log-likelihood function (expressed in terms of both the observables and the state variables) of the model as usual; (2) use the Kalman filter to supplement the observations with the estimates of the state variables; and (3) optimize with standard optimizers.
- Alternatively, one can use methods such as the Expectation Maximization method designed to optimize in the presence of hidden variables.
- The following are key aspects of subspace algorithms: (1) states contain all the information from the past that is relevant for predicting the future; (2) conversely, states can be estimated from past observations; (3) the model parameters can, therefore, be obtained by regressing future data on past data and thus subspace methods segment available empirical data into two segments—the data which are considered the "past segment" and the data which are considered the "future segment"; (4) states are estimated for the past segment using the Kalman filter; and (5) the key equation of subspace methods is a regression equation that regresses observables in the future segment on observables in the past segment, and from regression, the state-space model can be estimated with LS methods.
- Dynamic factor models can be estimated representing these models explicitly as state-space models.
- The key step is determining the number of factors. Methods proposed to determine the number of factors include methods based on Principal Component Analysis (PCA) and Canonical Correlation Analysis (CCA).
- Regime-switching models are nonlinear models where the parameters depend on a state variable.

- In particular, Markov-switching VAR models (MS-VAR) are nonlinear models where the parameters of a VAR model are functions of the states of a Markov chain.
- Their variables and innovation terms are distributed as a mixture of Gaussian distributions.
- VAR and MS-VAR models are currently used at asset management firms to implement momentum strategies, contrarian strategies, and cointegration-based, size-based and context-based strategies.

CHAPTER 17
Model Risk and its Mitigation

The previous chapters described how to select, from a family of models, the model that best represents the true *Data Generation Process* (DGP) of the empirical data. In Chapter 13 on model selection, a distinction was made between the learning and theoretical approaches to model selection. The former assumes that there is indeed a DGP, eventually including hidden variables (if not, modeling would be a futile exercise), but does not restrict the model estimation process to a specific family of models. Rather, the learning approach uses universal families of models able to approximate any true DGP; it assumes that models are only approximate and looks for the best modeling approximation.

In this chapter, however, we assume that errors in choosing and estimating models cannot be avoided. This is because models are inevitably misspecified as they are only an approximation, more or less faithful, of the true DGP. This chapter discusses how to mitigate these errors. We begin by looking at the sources of error leading to model misspecification and then review remedies, in particular methods based on information theory, Bayesian methods, shrinkage, and random coefficient models.

SOURCES OF MODEL RISK

We begin our discussion by introducing the concept of model risk. In simple intuitive terms, *model risk* means that we cannot be certain that the model that we have selected to represent the data is correctly specified. If models are misspecified, forecasting errors might be significant.

To place the notion of model risk in its scientific context, note that the question of model risk is of scant interest in physics. Though at a deep philosophical level the physical sciences are hypothetical and subject to revision, a vast body of scientific knowledge is considered to be validated to a high degree. No scientist expects the laws of physics that govern the behavior of, for example, trains and planes to break down, though changes might occur at a higher conceptual level.

The notion of model risk entered science with the engineering of complex artifacts, the study of complex systems, and the widespread adoption of statistical learning methods. This is because, in tackling large artifacts and complex systems such as the economy, science begins to address problems of a different nature. When modeling complex systems such as financial markets, we might encounter one of the following characteristics:

- The phenomena under study might be very complex and thus only a simplified description is possible; this leaves open the possibility that some critical aspect is overlooked.
- The phenomena under study can be very noisy; as a consequence, the scientific endeavor consists in extracting small amounts of information from highly noisy environments.
- Being not a law of nature but the behavior of an artifact, the object under study is subject to unpredictable changes.

There are many cases of unexpected modeling failure in engineering. For example, the design of the first commercial jet plane, the De Havilland Comet, which started commercial flights in 1952, overlooked the effects of metal fatigue on critical points of the fuselage. The result of this design error led to a series of crashes. The problem was not due to a mistake by the design team, one of the best at that time, but to the effects of metal fatigue under the stress of high-speed, high-altitude flights were simply not known.

In financial econometrics, there are various sources of error that can lead to model misspecification (though our considerations are quite universal and apply to modeling in general, we will restrict our analysis to models of stock prices and stock returns). In particular, sources of error in financial econometrics include the following two:

- The empirical data are nearly random but might seem to exhibit structure.
- The empirical data have been generated by a time-varying or randomly-varying DGP while the model selected is static or subject to a different time dynamics.

The first source of error—random data appearing to have structure—is due to the large amount of noise in financial time series. Thus models capture apparent regularities that are the result of mere chance. The fact that financial time series are so noisy, to the point of being almost completely random, is a weak form of market efficiency. In financial time series, any source of profit that could be easily detectable would be exploited, making it disappear. This is the principle of absence of arbitrage.

It is because of absence of arbitrage that stock price time series seem to meander randomly and stock return time series are close to random noise. The benchmark model for logprices is therefore the random walk. In addition, as return processes are strongly correlated, the benchmark model of multivariate stock logprices is that of correlated random walks. Deviations from this benchmark model allow profitable strategies. Because in the best of cases there is only very little real structure in financial time series (i.e., the data are essentially random), it is possible that we find structure where there is none. Given the sample sizes available, our statistical tests are not powerful enough to yield overwhelming evidence that data are not random.

The sheer fact that we have to filter a large amount of noise renders the filtering process uncertain. For example, we have seen that estimating an unrestricted vector autoregressive (VAR) process of many stock price processes yields an estimated structure of cross autocorrelation that is almost completely spurious: the model coefficients capture noise. We discussed how to reduce the dimensionality of the model, for example with dynamic factor models, in order to capture the true information. We now come back to the same question as an issue in model risk.

The second possible source of error—that the data have some simple structure but are subject to sudden and unpredictable changes (i.e., the data have been generated by a time-varying or randomly-varying DGP) not reflected in our models—is possibly the most serious source of model risk. For example, empirical data might be represented by a DGP that is stable for a given period, but then the economy is subject to change and the DGP changes as a consequence. If we had lots of data and changes were sufficiently frequent, the latter could be detected and estimated. However, as we typically have only a few years of workable homogeneous data, detecting change is problematic.[1] A key source of model risk is the possibility that we estimate models correctly on a past sample of data but then the DGP changes and the change goes undetected.

One way of dealing with a time-varying DGP is by introducing regime-switching models (see Chapter 12). However, regime-switching models do not entirely solve the problem. In fact, any regime-switching

---

[1] In Chapter 13 we discussed practical and theoretical problems in dealing with long series of financial data given that firms are subject to events such as bankruptcy, merger, and acquisitions and change their lines of business and market sectors.

model is a model estimated on a sample of past data. As such, it can detect only those features that are statistically relevant during the sample period. If a regime change occurs once or twice during that period, the model will not detect the change. One could investigate separately the possibility of regime changes, but doing so is complex and uncertain when applied to models that are already regime-switching.

In Chapter 16 on estimating hidden variable models, we discussed contextual modeling as one way of adapting models to their context. For example, we do not estimate one but several linear regressions on a predictor depending on the context, that is, on the cluster of data we are currently working with. Though contextual modeling has achieved results, it is still subject to the problem that small contexts result in a high level of uncertainty.

The above considerations suggest the adoption of techniques to reduce sources of error in model selection and estimation. Possible techniques include the following:

- Information theory, to assess the complexity and the limits of the predictability of time series
- Bayesian modeling, which assumes that models are variations of some *a priori* model
- Shrinkage, a form of averaging between different models
- Random coefficient models, a technique that averages models estimated on clusters of data

We begin our discussion of model risk mitigation techniques with the information theory approach to model risk.

THE INFORMATION THEORY APPROACH TO MODEL RISK

In Chapter 15 we discussed how information theory helps determine the optimal complexity of models. For example, we discussed that the Akaike criterion is used to determine the number of lags in a model. We now take a broader approach and explore how we can use information theory to mitigate model risk without making reference to any specific family of models.

We saw above that an important source of risk is due to the fact that models might mistakenly capture as stable features of the empirical data what is only random structure. To reduce this source of error, the theory of learning prescribes constraining a model's complexity using criteria based on information theory.

Intuitively, if our model shows too much structure (i.e., in the case of financial time series, if the model appears to offer ample opportunity for realizing excess returns), the model is likely to be misspecified and therefore risky. The critical questions are:

- Is it possible to estimate the maximum information extractable from a financial time series?
- Can we prescribe an "information boundary" such that sound robust models are not able to yield information beyond that boundary?
- Is it possible to assess the intrinsic complexity of empirical time series?

We begin our discussion on the role of information theory in mitigating model risk with a definition of the concepts of information and entropy. The concept of information is associated with the name of Claude Shannon, who laid the foundations of information theory in 1948.[2] The concept of a quantitative measure of information had been introduced in the context of communications engineering 20 years before by R.V.L. Hartley.[3]

Consider a probability distribution. Intuitively, it makes a big difference, in terms of information, if the distribution is flat or highly peaked. If one throws a fair dice, each of the six possible outcomes has the same probability and we are totally uncertain about future outcomes; the probability distribution is said to be flat. If the dice is biased, say number 6 has an 80% probability of coming up, we can be pretty confident that the next outcome will be a 6; the distribution is said to be peaked.

In a finite probability scheme,[4] with N outcomes each with probability p_i, $i = 1, 2, \ldots, N$ information is defined as

$$I = \sum_{i=1}^{T} p_i \log(p_i)$$

The quantity I, which is always negative, assumes a minimum

$$I = \log\left(\frac{1}{N}\right)$$

---

[2] Claude Shannon, "The Mathematical Theory of Communication," *Bell System Technical Journal* 27 (1948), pp. 379–423 and 623–656.
[3] R. V. L. Hartley, "Transmission of Information," *Bell System Technical Journal* 7 (1928), pp. 535–564.
[4] The concept of information can be extended to continuous probability schemes, but the extension is not straightforward. For our purposes discrete probability schemes suffice.

if all outcomes have the same probability; it assumes a maximum $I = 0$ if one outcome has probability 1 and all other outcomes probability 0, that is, in the case of certainty of one outcome. From the above formula it is clear that the maximum information is zero but the minimum information of an equiprobable distribution can assume any negative value.

One can add several considerations that make the quantity I a reasonable measure of information.[5] However, what really makes the concept of information so important is that we can construct a theory of information that is meaningful from the point of view of empirical science. In other words, if we associate the quantity of information to physical processes, we can establish laws that make sense empirically.

To appreciate this point, consider first that the quantity I is the opposite of a quantity H well known in physics as entropy: $I = -H$. *Entropy* is a measure of disorder.[6] A fundamental law of physics, the second law of thermodynamics states that in closed systems the global amount of entropy (i.e., disorder) can only grow or remain constant over time. Next consider that a basic result in information theory is the link between the physical characteristics of a communication channel and the rate of information that can be transmitted through that channel. It is because of physical laws such as these that the concept of information has become fundamental in physics and engineering.

We now introduce the concepts of coarse graining and symbolic dynamics. Consider an empirical financial time series. Through a process of coarse graining, we can view this series as a sequence of symbols. In fact, coarse graining means dividing the possible outcome x_t of the series into discrete segments (or partitions) and associating a symbol to each segment. For example the symbol a_i is associated to values x_t in the range $v_{i-1} < x_t < v_i$. In doing so, the original DGP of the time series entails a discrete stochastic dynamics of the corresponding sequence of symbols.

Simulation-based techniques for choosing the optimal partitioning of data have been suggested.[7] In principle, the process of coarse-graining is not restrictive as any real-world financial time series is discrete.

---

[5] For a modern presentation of information theory, see, for example, T. M. Cover and J. A. Thomas, *Elements of Information Theory* (New York: John Wiley & Sons, 1991).

[6] Entropy was first introduced in physics in 1864 by Rudolf Clausius in the context of thermodynamics. It was the genius of the Austrian physicist Ludwig Boltzman that made the connection between entropy as a thermodynamic concept and entropy as a measure of disorder in statistical mechanics. Isolated and poorly understood in his time, Boltzman, was to commit suicide in 1906.

[7] R. Steuer, L. Molgedey, W. Ebeling, and M. A. Jiménez-Montaño, "Entropy and Optimal Partition for Data Analysis," *European Physical Journal B* 19 (2001), pp. 265–269.

For example, stock prices can assume only a discrete set of values. However, given the size of samples, the number of symbols that can be used in practice is much smaller than the number of possible discrete values of a series. A financial time series, for example, can be analyzed as a sequence of three symbols, while stock prices can assume any price spaced by one-tenth of a dollar.

Given the probabilistic dynamics of the symbol sequence, we can associate a probability to any sequence of n symbols $p(i_1, ..., i_n)$. Recall that the entropy H is the opposite of information as defined above, that is to say

$$H = -\sum_{i=1}^{T} p_i \log(p_i)$$

We can therefore define the entropy per block of length n (or block entropy) as follows:

$$H_n = -I_n = -\sum p(i_1, ..., i_n) \log p(i_1, ..., i_n)$$

From the block entropy, we can now define the conditional entropy h_n as the difference of the entropies per blocks of length $n + 1$ and n:

$$h_n = H_{n+1} - H_n = -\sum p(i_{n+1} | i_1, ..., i_n) \log p(i_{n+1} | i_1, ..., i_n)$$

Finally, we can define the Kolmogorov-Sinai entropy, or *entropy of the source*, as the limit for large n of the conditional entropy. The *conditional entropy* is the information on the following step conditional on the knowledge of the previous n steps. The quantity $r_n = 1 - h_n$ is called the predictability of the series.

The concepts of conditional entropy and entropy of the source are fundamental to an understanding of the complexity of a series. They supply a model-free methodology for estimating the basic predictability of a time series. Unfortunately, the concepts of entropy and information are not widely diffused in financial econometrics. Ebeling et al. performed estimations of the basic predictability of financial time series with the methods of symbolic dynamics using a three-letter alphabet, that is to say, they coarse grained a times series into three symbols.[8]

---

[8] Werner Ebeling, Lutz Molgedey, Jürgen Kurths, and Udo Schwarz, "Entropy, Complexity, Predictability and Data Analysis of Time Series and Letter Sequences," Chapter 1 in A. Bunde, J. Kropp, and H. J. Schellnhuber (eds.), *Theories of Disaster: Scaling Laws Governing Weather, Body and Stock Market Dynamics* (Berlin: Springer, 2002).

They found that series such as the returns of the S&P 500 index have a limited level of predictability—in the range of 5% to 8%.

The analysis of the predictability of time series based on information theory is a basic tool for model risk assessment. It establishes a reasonable boundary to the performance of models. Models that seem to exceed by a large measure the predictability level of entropy-based estimation are also likely to exhibit a high level of model risk.

While the conditional entropy and the entropy of the source of coarse-grained models give an assessment of the complexity of a series and its predictability, the recently introduced *transfer entropy*[9] gauges the information flow from one series to another. The transfer entropy is defined as: the information about future observation $I(t + 1)$ gained from past observations of I and J minus the information about future observation $I(t + 1)$ gained from past observations of I only.

This definition already shows the advantage of transfer entropy over other cross correlation statistics: It is an asymmetric measure that takes into account only statistical dependencies, and not those correlations deriving from a common external driver. Expressing the above relationship in terms of conditional entropies yields the following expression:

$$T_{I \to J}(m, l) = \sum p(i_1, ..., i_{m+1}, j_1, ..., j_l) \log \left[\frac{p(i_{m+1} | (i_1, ..., i_m, j_1, ..., j_l))}{p(i_{m+1} | i_1, ..., i_m)} \right]$$

This quantity evaluates the amount of information that flows from one series to another. Transfer entropy can be used to evaluate quantitatively cross autocorrelation in a general setting that does not depend on specific models and that might also consider nonlinear lead-lag effects.[10]

One might well ask if we can use information theory to evaluate the adequacy of specific families of models. James Hamilton introduced a series of specification tests to evaluate the adequacy of Markov switching models.[11] Hamilton's tests are based on the score of the models defined as the derivative of the conditional log-likelihood of the n-th observation with respect to the parameter vector. The approach is quite technical: the interested reader should consult the cited reference.

---

[9] T. Schreiber, "Measuring Information Transfer," *Physical Review Letters* 85, 461 (2000).

[10] Robert Marschinski and Lorenzo Matassini, "Financial Markets as a Complex System: A Short Time Scale Perspective," *Deutsche Bank Research Note in Economics & Statistics* (November 2001).

[11] James D. Hamilton, "Specification Testing in Markov-Switching Time-Series Models," *Journal of Econometrics* 70 (1996), pp. 127–157.

A very general approach to evaluating the limits of learning from finite samples comes from the Russian physicists Vapnik and Chervonenkis (VC), working in the second half of the 20th century. They went beyond the classical information theory in the sense of Shannon, and defined a number of concepts and quantities to characterize the learning process, Vapnik entropy, empirical risk, structural risk, and the VC dimension. The VC theory establishes limits to the ability of given models to learn in a sense made precise by these concepts.[12] Considered a major breakthrough, the VC theory led to the development of the *Vector Support Machine*, a learning approach based on the theory. However, the conceptual difficulty of the VC theory and the practical difficulty in applying it have thus far limited its widespread application to financial modeling.

To summarize, information theory offers a number of tools for evaluating, in a very general context and in a robust framework, limits to the forecastability of a given time series. Information theory is thus a valuable tool for evaluating model risk. Critical to the information-based approach are methods and techniques to coarse-grain time series. A number of practical information-based approaches have been proposed and are widely used in the physical sciences. Thus far, however, the use of information theory in financial econometrics has been limited to applications such as the Akaike criterion.

BAYESIAN MODELING

The Bayesian approach to dynamic modeling is based on Bayesian statistics. Therefore, we will begin our discussion of Bayesian modeling with a brief introduction to Bayesian statistics.

Bayesian Statistics

Bayesian statistics is perhaps the most difficult area in the science of statistics. The difficulty is not mathematical but conceptual: it resides in the Bayesian interpretation of probability. Classical statistics (which is the statistical approach used thus far in this book) adopts a *frequentist* interpretation of probability; that is to say, the probability of an event is essentially the relative frequency of its appearance in large samples. However, it is well known that pure relative frequency is not a tenable basis for probability: One cannot strictly identify probability with relative frequency. What is needed is some *bridging principle* that links prob-

---

[12] The VC theory was exposed by Vapnik in his book *The Nature of Statistical Learning Theory* (Berlin: Springer-Verlag, 1991).

ability, which is an abstract concept, to empirical relative frequency. Bridging principles have been widely discussed in the literature, especially in the philosophical strain of statistical literature but, in practice, classical statistics identifies probability with relative frequency in large samples. When large samples are not available, for example in analyzing tail events, classical statistics adopts theoretical considerations.

The frequentist interpretation is behind most of today's estimation methods. When statisticians compute empirical probability distributions, they effectively equate probability and relative frequency. The concept is also implicit in estimation methods based on likelihood. In fact, maximum likelihood (ML) estimates of distribution parameters can be interpreted as those parameters that align the distribution as close as possible to the empirical distribution. When we compute empirical moments, we also adhere to a frequentist interpretation of probability.

In classical statistics, the probability distributions that embody a given statistical model are not subject to uncertainty. The perspective of classical statistics is that a given population has a *true* distribution: the objective of statistics is to infer the true distribution from a population sample.

Although most mathematical methods are similar to those of classical statistics, Bayesian statistics[13] is based on a different set of concepts. In particular, the following three concepts characterize Bayesian statistics:

■ Statistical models are uncertain and subject to modification when new information is acquired.
■ There is a distinction between prior probability (or prior distribution), which conveys the best estimate of probabilities given initial available information, and the posterior probability, which is the modification of the prior probability consequent to the acquisition of new information.
■ The mathematical link between prior and posterior probabilities is given by Bayes' Theorem.

The main difficulty is in grasping the meaning of these statements. On one side, the first two statements seem mere educated common sense, while the third is a rather simple mathematical statement that we illustrate in the following paragraphs. However, common sense does not

---

[13] For a complete exposition of Bayesian statistics, see: D. A. Berry, *Statistics: A Bayesian Perspective* (Belmont, CA: Wadsworth, 1996); Thomas Leonard and John Hsu, *Bayesian Methods: An Analysis for Statisticians and Interdisciplinary Researchers* (Cambridge: Cambridge University Press, 1999) for a basic discussion; and J. M. Bernardo and A. F. M Smith, *Bayesian Theory* (Chichester: John Wiley & Sons, 2000) for a more advanced discussion.

make science. The usual scientific interpretation is that Bayesian statistics is essentially a rigorous method for making decisions based on the *subjectivistic* interpretation of probability.

In Bayesian statistics, probability is intended as subjective judgment guided by data. While a full exposé of Bayesian statistics is beyond the scope of this book, the crux of the problem can be summarized as follows. Bayesian statistics is rooted in data as probability judgments are updated with new data or information. However, according to Bayesian statistics there is an ineliminable subjective element; the subjective element is given by the initial prior probabilities that cannot be justified within the Bayesian theory.

It would be a mistake to think that Bayesian statistics is only a rigorous way to perform subjective uncertain reasoning while classical statistics is about real data.[14] Bayesian statistics explicitly recognizes that there is some ineliminable subjectivity in probability statements and attempts to reduce such subjectivity by updating probabilities. Classical statistics implicitly recognizes the same subjectivity when setting rules that bridge from data to probabilities.

In a nutshell, the conceptual problem of both classical and Bayesian statistics is that a probability statement does not per se correspond to any empirical reality. One cannot observe probabilities, only events that are interpreted in a probabilistic sense. The real problem, both in classical and Bayesian statistics, is how to link probability statements to empirical data. If mathematically sound and interpretable probability statements are to be constructed, bridging principles are required.

Before leaving the subject of Bayesian statistics, note that in financial econometrics there is a strain of literature and related methodologies based on Empirical Bayesian Statistics. In Empirical Bayesian Statistics, priors are estimated with the usual classical methods and then updated with new information. We will come back to this subject later in this chapter.

Bayes' Theorem

We now discuss Bayes' theorem, for which there are two interpretations. One interpretation is a simple accounting of probabilities in the classical sense. Given two events A and B, the following properties, called *Bayes' theorem*, hold:

---

[14] Bayesian theories of uncertain reasoning are important in machine learning and artificial intelligence. See, for example, J. Pearl, *Probabilistic Reasoning in Intelligent Systems: Networks of Plausible Inference* (San Francisco: Morgan Kaufmann, 1988).

$$P(A|B) = \frac{P(B|A)P(A)}{P(B)}$$

$$P(B|A) = \frac{P(A|B)P(B)}{P(A)}$$

These properties are an elementary consequence of the definitions of conditional probabilities:

$$P(AB) = P(A|B)P(B) = P(B|A)P(A)$$

In the second interpretation of Bayes' theorem, we replace the event A with a statistical hypothesis H and the event B with the data and write

$$P(H|\text{data}) = \frac{P(\text{data}|H)P(H)}{P(\text{data})}$$

This form of Bayes' theorem is the mathematical basis of Bayesian statistics. Given that $P(\text{data})$ is unconditional and does not depend on H, we can write the above as:

$$P(H|\text{data}) \propto P(\text{data}|H)P(H)$$

The probability $P(H)$ is called the *prior probability*, while the probability $P(H|\text{data})$ is called the *posterior probability*. The probability $P(\text{data}|H)$ of the data given H is called the *likelihood*.

Bayes' theorem can be expressed in a different form in terms of odds. The odds of H is the probability that H is false, written as $P(H^C)$. Bayes' theorem is written in terms of odds as follows:

$$\frac{P(H|\text{data})}{P(H^C|\text{data})} = \frac{P(\text{data}|H)P(H)}{P(\text{data}|H^C)P(H^C)}$$

The second interpretation of Bayes' theorem is not a logical consequence of Bayes' theorem in the first interpretation; it is an independent principle that assigns probabilities to statistical assumptions.

When applied to modeling, Bayes' theorem is expressed in terms of distributions, not probabilities. Bayes' theorem can be stated in terms of distributions as follows:

$$p(\vartheta|y) \propto L(y|\vartheta)\pi(\vartheta)$$

In this formulation, y represents the data, ϑ is the parameter set, $p(\vartheta|y)$ is the posterior distribution, $L(y|\vartheta)$ is the likelihood function, and $\pi(\vartheta)$ is the prior distribution.

A key issue in Bayesian statistics is how to determine the prior. Though considered subjective, the prior is not arbitrary; if it were, the estimation exercise would be futile. The prior represents the basic knowledge before specific measurements are taken into account. Two types of priors are often used: diffuse priors and conjugate priors. The *diffuse prior* assumes that we do not have any prior knowledge of the phenomena. A diffuse prior is a uniform distribution over an unspecified range. The *conjugate prior* is a prior such that, for a given likelihood, the prior and the posterior distribution coincide.

Bayesian Approach to Model Risk

The Bayesian handling of model risk is based on *Bayesian dynamic modeling*. Recall that the objective of model risk mitigation is to minimize the possibility of and the effects of error in model choice. In Chapter 16 on estimating dynamic models, we discussed techniques to reduce the dimensionality of models in order to improve their forecasting ability. The idea is that there is a trade-off between the complexity of a model and the possibility of estimating the model on a finite sample. More complex models have more descriptive power but their estimates are characterized by more noise.

The Bayesian approach to model risk assumes that though there is uncertainty as regards the model, we have a good idea of a basic form of the model. Uncertainty is expressed as a prior distribution of the model parameters where the means of the distribution determine the basic model. In other words, in the Bayesian approach to model estimation, the estimation process does not determine the model from the data but uses the data to determine deviations of the actual model from a standard idealized model. We can say that Bayesian modeling is a perturbation theory of fundamental models.

As is typical in Bayesian statistics, the quality of results depends on the priors. It might seem reasonable that those priors that express complete uncertainty lead to the same estimates obtained in the classical framework, but this is not the case. The key issue is just what priors express complete uncertainty.[15] Specifically, there is no agreement on what should be considered an uninformative prior in the case of unit root processes.

Now see how the Bayesian framework mitigates model risk. We observed that financial time series are very noisy and that we can only

[15] G. S. Maddala and In-Moo Kim, *Unit Roots, Cointegration, and Structural Change* (Cambridge: Cambridge University Press, 1998).

extract a small amount of information from all the noise. If a model appears to extract a lot of information, there is always the risk that that information is camouflaged noise.

We have already explored dimensionality reduction as one possible remedy for misspecification. Dimensionality reduction constrains model complexity, rendering effective the estimation process. In large multivariate time series, dimensionality reduction typically takes the form of factor models. The Bayesian approach to model risk assumes that we know, in the form of the prior distribution of parameters, an (idealized) robust model. For example, as we will see below, the Litterman model allows only small perturbations to the random walk. Next we see how the Bayesian approach works in practice.

Bayesian Analysis of an Univariate AR(1) Model

Let us now perform a simple Bayesian analysis of an univariate AR(1) model under the assumption of diffuse priors. Consider the following simple autoregressive model:

$$y_t = \rho y_{t-1} + \varepsilon_t$$

Assume that the above model is Gaussian so that the likelihood is also Gaussian. The model being linear, Gaussian innovations entail Gaussian variables. The likelihood is a given, not a prior. We can write the likelihood, which is a function of the data parameterized by the initial conditions y_0, the autoregressive parameters ρ, and the variance σ of the innovation process as follows:

$$L(y|\rho, \sigma, y_0) = \frac{1}{\sqrt{(2\pi)}^T}\sigma^{-T}\exp\left(-\frac{\displaystyle\sum_{t=1}^{T}\varepsilon_t^2}{2\sigma^2}\right)$$

$$= \frac{1}{\sqrt{(2\pi)}^T}\sigma^{-T}\exp\left(-\frac{\displaystyle\sum_{t=1}^{T}(y_t-\rho y_{t-1})^2}{2\sigma^2}\right)$$

Assume a flat prior for (ρ, σ), that is, assume that

$$\pi(\rho, \sigma) \propto \frac{1}{\sigma}, \, -1 < \rho < 1, \sigma > 0$$

Then the joint posterior distribution is the following:

$$p(\rho, \sigma | y, y_0) \propto = \sigma^{-T-1} \exp\left(-\frac{\sum_{t=1}^{T} \varepsilon_t^2}{2\sigma^2}\right)$$

$$= \frac{1}{\sqrt{(2\pi)^T}} \sigma^{-T} \exp\left(-\frac{\sum_{t=1}^{T} (y_t - \rho y_{t-1})^2}{2\sigma^2}\right)$$

Let

$$\hat{\rho} = \frac{\sum y_t y_{t-1}}{\sum y_{t-1}^2}$$

be the OLS estimator of the regressive parameter and call

$$Q = \sum y_{t-1}^2$$

and

$$R = \sum (y_t - \hat{\rho} y_{t-1})^2$$

By rearranging terms and integrating, it can be demonstrated that the marginal distributions of (ρ, σ) are

$$p(\rho | y, y_0) \propto (R + (\rho - \hat{\rho})^2 Q)^{-0.5T}$$

$$p(\sigma | y, y_0) \propto \sigma^{-T} \exp\left(-\frac{R}{2\sigma^2}\right)$$

From these expressions one can see that the marginal distribution of ρ is a univariate t-distribution symmetrically distributed around the OLS estimator $\hat{\rho}$, while the marginal distribution of σ is an inverted gamma-2 distribution.

Bayesian Analysis of a VAR Model

The *Bayesian VAR* (BVAR) is a Bayesian specification of a VAR model. The BVAR approach is based on defining a prior distribution for the model parameters, similar to what we did above for the univariate AR(1) model. In simple and perhaps more intuitive terms, this means that the estimated VAR model is allowed only "small" deviations from a fundamental model, which is specified as a prior. The specific form of deviations from the fundamental model is prescribed by the prior distribution. For example, the fundamental model for the Litterman BVAR is a random walk. The Litterman model prescribes that the coefficients of the BVAR model be normally distributed around the coefficients of a random walk. In other words, the BVAR approach prescribes that any multivariate model of stock prices cannot differ much from a random walk.

Now see how BVAR models are estimated. Using the same notation of Chapter **GG**, consider the following VAR(p) model:

$$\mathbf{x}_t = \mathbf{A}_1\mathbf{x}_{t-1} + \mathbf{A}_2\mathbf{x}_{t-2} + \cdots + \mathbf{A}_p\mathbf{x}_{t-p} + \mathbf{v} + \boldsymbol{\varepsilon}_t$$

where $\mathbf{x}_t = (x_{1,t}, \ldots, x_{N,t})'$ is a N-dimensional stochastic time series in vector notation; $\mathbf{A}_i = (a_{s,t}^i)$, $i = 1, 2, \ldots, p$, $s,t = 1, 2, \ldots, N$ are deterministic $N \times N$ matrices; $\boldsymbol{\varepsilon}_t = (\varepsilon_{1,t}, \ldots, \varepsilon_{N,t})'$ is a multivariate white noise with variance-covariance matrix $\boldsymbol{\Sigma} = (\sigma_1, \ldots, \sigma_N)$; $\mathbf{v} = (v_1, \ldots, v_N)'$ is a vector of deterministic intercepts. Using the same notation used in Chapter 11, we can compactly write the VAR(p) model as follows:

$$\mathbf{X} = \mathbf{AW} + \mathbf{U}$$
$$\mathbf{x} = \mathbf{w}\boldsymbol{\beta} + \mathbf{u}$$

where

$$\mathbf{X} = (\mathbf{x}_1, \ldots, \mathbf{x}_T) = \begin{pmatrix} x_{1,1} & \cdots & x_{1,T} \\ \vdots & \ddots & \vdots \\ x_{N,1} & \cdots & x_{N,T} \end{pmatrix}, \mathbf{x} = \text{vec}(\mathbf{X})$$

$$
\mathbf{W} = \begin{pmatrix}
1 & 1 & \cdots & 1 & 1 \\
\mathbf{x}_0 & \mathbf{x}_1 & \cdots & \mathbf{x}_{T-2} & \mathbf{x}_{T-1} \\
\mathbf{x}_{-1} & \mathbf{x}_0 & \cdots & \mathbf{x}_{T-3} & \mathbf{x}_{T-2} \\
\vdots & \vdots & \ddots & \vdots & \vdots \\
\mathbf{x}_{-p+1} & \mathbf{x}_{-p+2} & \cdots & \mathbf{x}_{T-p-1} & \mathbf{x}_{T-p}
\end{pmatrix}, \ \mathbf{w} = (\mathbf{W}' \otimes \mathbf{I}_N)
$$

$$
\mathbf{U} = \begin{pmatrix}
\varepsilon_{1,1} & \cdots & \varepsilon_{1,T} \\
\vdots & \ddots & \vdots \\
\varepsilon_{N,1} & \cdots & \varepsilon_{N,T}
\end{pmatrix}, \ \mathbf{u} = \mathrm{vec}(\mathbf{U})
$$

$\boldsymbol{\Sigma} = [\sigma_{i,j}] = E[\varepsilon_{i,t}\varepsilon_{j,t}]$, while $E[\varepsilon_{i,t}\varepsilon_{j,s}] = 0$, $\forall i,j, t \neq s$. The covariance matrix of $\mathbf{u}$, $\boldsymbol{\Sigma}_{\mathbf{u}}$, can therefore be written as

$$
\boldsymbol{\Sigma}_{\mathbf{u}} = \mathbf{I}_T \otimes \boldsymbol{\Sigma} = \begin{pmatrix}
\boldsymbol{\Sigma} & \cdots & 0 \\
\vdots & \ddots & \vdots \\
0 & \cdots & \boldsymbol{\Sigma}
\end{pmatrix}
$$

$$
\mathbf{A} = (\mathbf{v}, \mathbf{A}_1, ..., \mathbf{A}_p) = \begin{pmatrix}
v_1 & a_{11}^1 & \cdots & a_{1N}^1 & \cdots & \cdots & a_{11}^p & \cdots & a_{1N}^p \\
\vdots & \vdots & \ddots & \vdots & \vdots & \ddots & \vdots & \ddots & \vdots \\
v_N & a_{N1}^1 & \cdots & a_{NN}^1 & \cdots & \cdots & a_{N1}^p & \cdots & a_{NN}^p
\end{pmatrix}
$$

and

$$
\boldsymbol{\beta} = \mathrm{vec}(\mathbf{A}) = \begin{pmatrix}
v_1 \\
\vdots \\
v_N \\
a_{11}^1 \\
\vdots \\
a_{N1}^1 \\
\vdots \\
a_{1N}^p \\
\vdots \\
a_{NN}^p
\end{pmatrix}
$$

The likelihood function can be written as in the classical case:

$$l(\mathbf{x}|\boldsymbol{\beta}) = (2\pi)^{-\frac{NT}{2}}|\boldsymbol{\Sigma}|^{-\frac{T}{2}}\exp\left(-\frac{1}{2}(\mathbf{x}-\mathbf{w}\boldsymbol{\beta})'(\mathbf{I}_T\otimes\boldsymbol{\Sigma}^{-1})(\mathbf{x}-\mathbf{w}\boldsymbol{\beta})\right)$$

At this point the Bayesian estimation method departs from the classical one. In fact, in the Bayesian framework we assume that we know *a priori* the joint distribution of the model parameters. Suppose that the parameter vector $\boldsymbol{\beta}$ has a prior multivariate normal distribution with known mean $\boldsymbol{\beta}^*$ and covariance matrix $\mathbf{V}_\beta$; the prior density is written as

$$\pi(\boldsymbol{\beta}) = (2\pi)^{-\frac{N^2p}{2}}|\mathbf{V}_\beta|^{-\frac{1}{2}}\exp\left(-\frac{1}{2}(\boldsymbol{\beta}-\boldsymbol{\beta}^*)'\mathbf{V}_\beta^{-1}(\boldsymbol{\beta}-\boldsymbol{\beta}^*)\right)$$

Now we form the posterior distribution $p(\boldsymbol{\beta}|\mathbf{x}) = l(\mathbf{x}|\boldsymbol{\beta})\pi(\boldsymbol{\beta})$. It can be demonstrated that the following expression holds:

$$p(\boldsymbol{\beta}|\mathbf{x}) \propto \exp\left(-\frac{1}{2}(\boldsymbol{\beta}-\bar{\boldsymbol{\beta}})'\mathbf{V}_\beta^{-1}(\boldsymbol{\beta}-\bar{\boldsymbol{\beta}})\right)$$

where the posterior mean is

$$\bar{\boldsymbol{\beta}} = [\mathbf{V}_\beta^{-1} + \mathbf{W}\mathbf{W}'\otimes\boldsymbol{\Sigma}_u^{-1}]^{-1}[\mathbf{V}_\beta^{-1}\boldsymbol{\beta}^* + (\mathbf{W}\otimes\boldsymbol{\Sigma}_u^{-1})\mathbf{x}]$$

and the posterior covariance matrix is

$$\boldsymbol{\Sigma}_\beta = [\mathbf{V}_\beta^{-1} + \mathbf{W}\mathbf{W}'\otimes\boldsymbol{\Sigma}_u^{-1}]^{-1}$$

In practice, the prior mean $\boldsymbol{\beta}^*$ and the prior covariance matrix $\mathbf{V}_\beta$ need to be specified. Set the prior mean to zero for all parameters that are considered to shrink toward zero. Litterman's choice for the prior distribution, when all variables are believed to be integrated, is such that the BVAR model is a perturbation of a random walk.[16] Litterman priors, also known as "Minnesota" priors, are normally distributed with mean set to 1 for the first lag of each equation while all other coefficients are set to zero The prior variance of the intercept terms is infinite and that of the other coefficients is given by

---

[16] R. B. Litterman, "Forecasting with Bayesian Vector Autoregressions—Five Years of Experience," *Journal of Business & Economic Statistics* 4 (1986), pp. 25–38.

$$\text{mean } v_{ij,l} = \begin{cases} (\lambda/l)^2, & \text{if } i = j \\ (\lambda\vartheta\sigma_i/l\sigma_j)^2, & \text{if } i \neq j \end{cases} \quad \text{and covariance matrix } \mathbf{V}_\beta$$

where $v_{ij,l}$ is the prior variance of the (i,j)th element of $\mathbf{A}_l$, λ is the prior standard deviation of the diagonal elements of $\mathbf{A}_l$, θ is a constant in the interval $(0,1)$, and σ_{ij} is the ith diagonal element of $\mathbf{\Sigma_u}$. The deterministic terms have diffused prior variance.

The Bayesian analysis of VAR models has been extended to cover the case of state-space models in general. West discusses Bayesian analysis of different state-space models.[17]

MODEL AVERAGING AND THE SHRINKAGE APPROACH TO MODEL RISK

Simple model averaging to reduce model risk has been advocated by several authors. Lubos Pastor,[18] for example, recommends averaging return forecasts generated by different models. The intuition behind model averaging is simple. Here is the reasoning. Reliable estimations and forecasts from different models should be highly correlated. When they are not, this means that the estimation and forecasting processes have become dubious and averaging can substantially reduce the forecasting error. Model averaging should have only a marginal impact on forecasting performance, but should help to avoid large forecasting errors. If model averaging has a strong impact on forecasting performance, it is a sign that forecasts are uncorrelated and thus unreliable. One is advised to rethink the modeling strategy.

Averaging estimators obtained from different models can be done using a statistical estimation technique known as *shrinkage*. By averaging, estimators are "shrunk" closer to each other. Averaging weights can be obtained with Bayesian or Empirical Bayesian methods. Models might be based on completely different theoretical assumptions. An example comes from estimations of the covariance matrix that might be

---

[17] As a detailed treatment of Bayesian modeling applied to state-space models is beyond the scope of this book, the interested reader is advised to consult M. West and P. J. Harrison, *Bayesian Forecasting and Dynamic Models* (New York: Springer-Verlag, 1989).

[18] Lubos Pastor, "A Model Weighting Game in Estimating Expected Returns," in *Financial Times, Mastering Investment*, May 21, 2001 and Lubos Pastor and Robert F. Stambaugh, "Comparing Asset Pricing Models: An Investment Perspective," *Journal of Financial Economics* 56 (2000), pp. 335–381.

calculated using different approaches, including the empirical estimation approach, which produces highly noisy covariance matrices, or estimations based on the Capital Asset Pricing Model (CAPM), which yield covariance matrices that are highly constrained by theoretical considerations. Shrinkage "shrinks" one estimate towards the other, averaging with appropriate shrinkage coefficients. The idea can be extended to dynamic models. Different models offer different approximations to the true DGP. By averaging estimations and forecasts, one saves the common robust approximations and limits the damage when the approximations coming from any given model break down. The concepts and techniques of shrinkage were described in Chapter 8.

The method of shrinkage can be generalized to averaging between any number of models. The weighting factors can be determined by Bayesian principles if one has an idea of the relative strength of the models. Shrinkage is averaging between possibly different models. In Bayesian terms this would call for multiple priors.[19]

RANDOM COEFFICIENTS MODELS

We now introduce another technique for model risk mitigation: random coefficient models. *Random coefficient models* are based on the idea of segmenting data in a number of clusters and estimating models on multiple clusters. The concept of random coefficient models was introduced in 1970 by Swamy.[20] Consider an ordinary linear regression. The regression parameters can be estimated with OLS methods using *fully pooled data*. This means that all the available data are pooled together and fed to the OLS estimator. However, this strategy might not be optimal if the regression data come from entities that have slightly different characteristics. For example, consider regressing stock returns on a predictor variable. If the returns come from companies that differ in terms of size and business sector, we might obtain different results in different sectors. We saw in Chapter 12 that if we make predictors contextual, we improve performance.

However, if our objective is to reduce model risk, we might decide to segment data into clusters that reflect different types of firms, estimate regression for each cluster, and combine the estimates. Random coefficient

---

[19] Raman Uppal, Lorenzo Garlappi, and Tan Wang, "Portfolio Selection with Parameter and Model Uncertainty: A Multi-Prior Approach," CEPR Discussion Paper No. 5041 (May 2005), Centre for Economic Policy Research.
[20] A. V. B. Swamy, "Efficient Inference in a Random Coefficient Regression Model," *Econometrica* 38 (1970), pp. 311–323.

modeling techniques perform estimates assuming that clusters are randomly selected from a population of clusters with normal distributions.

To see how random coefficient models work, suppose that data are clustered and that each cluster has its own regression. Using the notation for regressions established in Chapter 11, we write the following regression equation for the j-th cluster:

$$\mathbf{y}_j = \mathbf{X}_j \boldsymbol{\beta}_j + \boldsymbol{\varepsilon}_j$$

where n_j is the number of elements in the j-th cluster and $\boldsymbol{\varepsilon}_j$ are mutually independent, normally distributed vectors,

$$\boldsymbol{\varepsilon}_j \sim N(0_{n_j}, \sigma^2 I_{n_j})$$

If we assume that the regression coefficients $\boldsymbol{\beta}_j$ are a random sample from a multivariate normal distribution,

$$\boldsymbol{\beta}_j \sim N(\boldsymbol{\beta}, \boldsymbol{\Sigma})$$

independent from the $\boldsymbol{\varepsilon}_j$, we can rewrite the regression as follows:

$$\mathbf{y}_j = \mathbf{X}_j \boldsymbol{\beta}_j + \mathbf{X}_j \boldsymbol{\gamma}_j + \boldsymbol{\varepsilon}_j$$

where $\boldsymbol{\gamma}_j$ are the deviations of the regression coefficients from their expectations:

$$\boldsymbol{\gamma}_j = \boldsymbol{\beta}_j - \boldsymbol{\beta} \sim N(0, \boldsymbol{\Sigma})$$

It can be demonstrated that these regressions can be estimated with MLE or LS methods.[21]

SUMMARY

■ Model risk is the risk that models are misspecified. Misspecification leads to errors in forecasts.

---

[21] For more on random coefficient techniques, see Nicholas T. Longford, *Random Coefficient Models* (Oxford: Oxford University Press, 1993).

■ Because empirical samples are small and time series very complex and noisy, all models used in financial econometrics are more or less misspecified and subject to model risk.

■ Model risk mitigation techniques are used to measure and reduce forecast errors due to model misspecification.

■ Model risk mitigation techniques include information theory, Bayesian estimates, and averaging.

■ Information theory provides tools to estimate model risk, constrain model complexity, and estimate the complexity and forecastability of financial time series independent of the model.

■ The key tool in information theory that allows to estimate model complexity and foecastability is coarse graining. By coarse graining financial time series, we recover a symbolic dynamics and the estimate of block and transfer entropies.

■ Bayesian estimates of dynamic models assume that models are uncertain. They estimate perturbations from a robust basic model constructed using *a priori* judgment. The best known example of a Bayesian estimate of dynamic models is the Litterman BVAR model, which estimates VAR models as perturbations of a random walk.

■ Averaging estimators from different models makes the models robust, thereby diversifying model risk. Shrinkage is a technique used to average estimators from different models with Bayesian weights.

■ Random coefficient modeling is a technique for averaging models estimated on different clusters of data. Estimation techniques include ML and OLS.

Appendices

Difference Equations

In this appendix we develop the theory of linear difference equations and compute explicit solutions of different types of equations. Linear difference equations are important in the context of dynamic econometric models. As explained in Chapters 11 and 12, ARMA and VARMA stochastic models are expressed as linear difference equations with random disturbances added. Understanding the behavior of solutions of linear difference equations helps develop intuition for the behavior of these models. We first solve the associated homogeneous difference equations and then successively solve the nonhomogeneous difference equations.

HOMOGENEOUS DIFFERENCE EQUATIONS

Homogeneous difference equations are linear conditions that link the values of variables at different time lags. Using the lag operator L, they can be written as follows:

$$A(L)x_t = (1 - a_1 L - \cdots - a_p L^p)x_t = (1 - \lambda_1 L) \times \cdots \times (1 - \lambda_p L)x_t = 0$$

where the λ_i, $i = 1, 2, \ldots, p$ are the solutions of the characteristic equation:

$$z^p - a_1 z^{p-1} - \cdots - a_{P-1} z - a_P = (z - \lambda_1) \times \cdots \times (z - \lambda_p) = 0$$

Suppose that time extends from $0 \Rightarrow \infty$, $t = 0, 1, 2, \ldots$ and that the initial conditions $(x_{-1}, x_{-2}, \ldots, x_{-P})$ are given.

Real Roots

Consider first the case of *real roots*. In this case, as we see later in this section, solutions are sums of exponentials. First suppose that the roots of the characteristic equation are all real and distinct. It can be verified by substitution that any series of the form

$$x_t = C(\lambda_i)^t$$

where C is a constant, solves the homogeneous difference equation. In fact, we can write

$$(1 - \lambda_i L)(C\lambda_i^t) = C\lambda_i^t - \lambda_i C\lambda_i^{t-1} = 0$$

In addition, given the linearity of the lag operator, any linear combination of solutions of the homogeneous difference equation is another solution. We can therefore state that the following series solves the homogeneous difference equation:

$$x_t = \sum_{i=1}^{p} C_i \lambda_i^t$$

By solving the linear system

$$x_{-1} = \sum_{i=1}^{p} C_i \lambda_i^{-1}$$

$$x_{-p} = \sum_{i=1}^{p} C_i \lambda_i^{-p}$$

that states that the p initial conditions are satisfied, we can determine the p constants Cs.

Suppose now that all m roots of the characteristic equation are real and coincident. In this case, we can represent a difference equation in the following way:

$$A(L) = 1 - a_1 L - \cdots - a_p L^p = (1 - \lambda L)^p$$

It can be demonstrated by substitution that, in this case, the general solution of the process is the following:

$$x_t = C_1(\lambda)^t + C_2 t(\lambda)^t + \ldots + C_p t^{p-1}(\lambda)^t$$

In the most general case, assuming that all roots are real, there will be $m < p$ distinct roots φ_i, $i = 1, 2, \ldots, m$ each of order $n_i \geq 1$,

$$\sum_{i=1}^{m} n_i = p$$

and the general solution of the process will be

$$x_t = C_1^1(\lambda_1)^t + C_2^1 t(\lambda_1)^t + \ldots + C_{n_1}^1 t^{n_1-1}(\lambda_1)^t + \ldots$$
$$+ C_1^m(\lambda_m)^t + C_2^m t(\lambda_m)^t + \ldots + C_{n_m}^m t^{n_m-1}(\lambda_m)^t$$

We can therefore conclude that the solutions of a homogeneous difference equation whose characteristic equation has only real roots is formed by a sum of exponentials. If these roots have modulus greater than unity, then solutions are diverging exponentials; if they have modulus smaller than unity, solutions are exponentials that go to zero. If the roots are unity, solutions are either constants or, if the roots have multiplicity greater than 1, polynomials. Simulations run for 100 time steps.

Exhibit A.1 illustrates the simple equation

$$A(L)x_t = (1 - 0.8L)x_t = 0, \lambda = 0.8, t = 1, 2, \ldots, n, \ldots$$

whose solution, with initial condition $x_1 = 1$, is

$$x_t = 1.25(0.8)^t$$

The behavior of the solution is that of an exponential decay.

Exhibit A.2 illustrates the equation

$$A(L)x_t = (1 + 0.8L)x_t = 0, \lambda = -0.8, t = 1, 2, \ldots, n, \ldots$$

EXHIBIT A.1   Solution of the Equation $(1 - 0.8L)x_t = 0$ with Initial Condition $x_1 = 1$

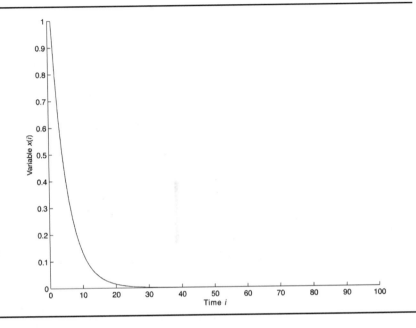

EXHIBIT A.2   Solution of the Equation $(1 + 0.8L)x_t = 0$ with Initial Condition $x_1 = 1$

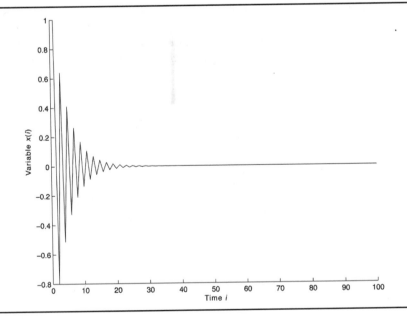

whose solution, with initial condition $x_1 = 1$, is

$$x_t = -1.25(-0.8)^t$$

The behavior of the solution is that of an exponential decay with oscillations at each step. The oscillations are due to the change in sign of the exponential at odd and even time steps.

If the equation has more than one real root, then the solution is a sum of exponentials. Exhibit A.3 illustrates the equation

$$A(L)x_t = (1 - 1.7L + 0.72L^2)x_t = 0, \lambda_1 = 0.8, \lambda_2 = 0.9, t = 1, 2, ..., n, ...$$

whose solution, with initial condition $x_1 = 1$, $x_2 = 1.5$, is

$$x_t = -7.5(0.8)^t + 7.7778(0.9)^t$$

The behavior of the solution is that of an exponential decay after a peak.

EXHIBIT A.3   Solution of the Equation $(1 - 1.7L + 0.72L^2)x_t = 0$ with Initial Conditions $x_1 = 1$, $x_2 = 1.5$

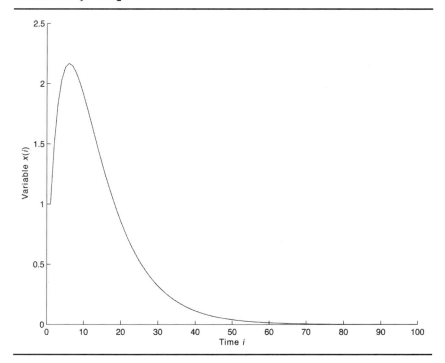

Exhibit A.4 illustrates the equation

$$A(L)x_t = (1 - 1.9L + 0.88L^2)x_t = 0, \lambda_1 = 0.8, \lambda_2 = 1.1, t = 1, 2, ..., n, ...$$

whose solution, with initial condition $x_1 = 1$, $x_2 = 1.5$, is

$$x_t = -1.6667(0.8)^t + 2.1212(1.1)^t$$

The behavior is that of exponential explosion due to the exponential with modulus greater than 1.

Complex Roots

Now suppose that some of the roots are complex. In this case, solutions exhibit an oscillating behavior with a period that depends on the model coefficients. For simplicity, consider initially a second-order homogeneous difference equation:

$$A(L)x_t = (1 - a_1 L - a_2 L^2)x_t$$

EXHIBIT A.4   Solution of the Equation $(1 - 1.9L + 0.88L^2)x_t = 0$ with Initial Conditions $x_1 = 1$, $x_2 = 1.5$

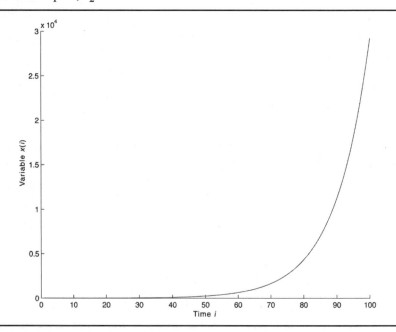

Suppose that its characteristic equation given by

$$A(z) = z^2 - a_1 z - a_s = 0$$

admits the two complex conjugate roots:

$$\lambda_1 = a + ib, \lambda_2 = a - ib$$

Let's write the two roots in polar notation:

$$\lambda_1 = re^{i\omega}, \lambda_1 = re^{-i\omega}$$

$$r = \sqrt{a^2 + b^2}, \omega = \arctan\frac{b}{a}$$

It can be demonstrated that the general solution of the above difference equation has the following form:

$$x_t = r^t(C_1\cos(\omega t) + C_2\sin(\omega t)) = Cr^t\cos(\omega t + \vartheta)$$

where the C_1 and C_2 or C and ϑ are constants to be determined in function of initial conditions. If the imaginary part of the roots vanishes, then ω vanishes and $a = r$, the two complex conjugate roots become a real root, and we find again the expression $x_t = Cr^t$.

Consider now a homogeneous difference equation of order $2n$. Suppose that the characteristic equation has only two distinct complex conjugate roots with multiplicity n. We can write the difference equation as follows:

$$A(L)x_t = (1 - a_1 L - \cdots - a_{2n}L^{2n})x_t = [(1 - \lambda L)^n(1 - \bar{\lambda}L)^n]x_t = 0$$

and its general solution as follows:

$$x_t = r^t(C_1^1\cos(\omega t) + C_2^1\sin(\omega t)) + \ldots + t^n r^t(C_1^n\cos(\omega t) + C_2^n\sin(\omega t))$$

The general solution of a homogeneous difference equation that admits both real and complex roots with different multiplicities is a sum of the different types of solutions. The above formulas show that real roots correspond to a sum of exponentials while complex roots correspond to oscillating series with exponential dumping or explosive behavior. The above formulas confirm that in both the real and the complex case, solutions decay if the modulus of the roots of the inverse characteristic equation is outside the unit circle and explode if it is inside the unit circle.

Exhibit A.5 illustrates the equation

$$A(L)x_t = (1 - 1.2L + 1.0L^2)x_t = 0, t = 1, 2, ..., n, ...$$

which has two complex conjugate roots,

$$\lambda_1 = 0.6 + i0.8, \lambda_2 = 0.6 - i0.8$$

or in polar form,

$$\lambda_1 = e^{i0.9273}, \lambda_2 = e^{-i0.9273}$$

EXHIBIT A.5　Solutions of the Equation $(1 - 1.2L + 1.0L^2)x_t = 0$ with Initial Conditions $x_1 = 1, x_2 = 1.5$

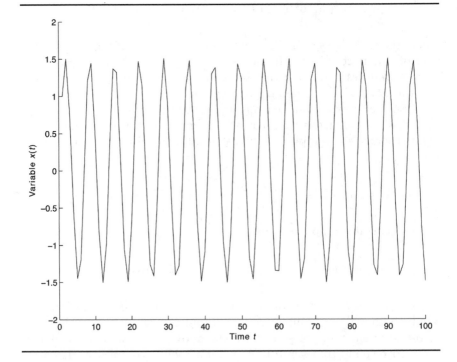

and whose solution, with initial condition $x_1 = 1$, $x_2 = 1.5$, is

$$x_t = -0.3\cos(0.9273t) + 1.475\sin(0.9273t)$$

The behavior of the solutions is that of undamped oscillations with frequency determined by the model.

Exhibits **A.6** illustrates the equation

$$A(L)x_t = (1 - 1.0L + 0.89L^2)x_t = 0, t = 1, 2, ..., n, ...$$

which has two complex conjugate roots,

$$\lambda_1 = 0.5 + i0.8, \lambda_2 = 0.5 - i0.8$$

or in polar form,

$$\lambda_1 = 0.9434e^{i1.0122}, \lambda_2 = 0.9434e^{-i1.0122}$$

EXHIBIT A.6 Solutions of the Equation $(1 - 1.0L + 0.89L^2)x_t = 0$ with Initial Conditions $x_1 = 1$, $x_2 = 1.5$

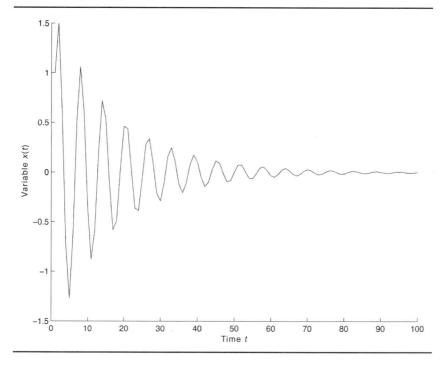

and whose solution, with initial condition $x_1 = 1$, $x_2 = 1.5$, is

$$x_t = 0.9434^t(-0.5618\cos(1.0122t) + 1.6011\sin(1.0122t))$$

The behavior of the solutions is that of damped oscillations with frequency determined by the model.

NONHOMOGENEOUS DIFFERENCE EQUATIONS

Consider now the following n-th order difference equation:

$$A(L)x_t = (1 - a_1 L - \cdots - a_p L^p)x_t = y_t$$

where y_t is a given sequence of real numbers. Recall that we are in a deterministic setting, that is, the y_t are given. The general solution of the above difference equation will be the sum of two solutions $x_{1,t} + x_{2,t}$, where $x_{1,t}$ is the solution of the associated homogeneous equation,

$$A(L)x_t = (1 - a_1 L - \cdots - a_p L^p)x_t = 0$$

and $x_{2,t}$ solves the given nonhomogeneous equation.

Real Roots

To determine the general form of $x_{2,t}$ in the case of real roots, we begin by considering the case of a first order equation:

$$A(L)x_t = (1 - a_1 L)x_t = y_t$$

We can compute the solution as follows:

$$x_{2,t} = \frac{1}{(1 - a_1 L)}y_t = \left(\sum_{j=0}^{\infty}(a_1 L)^j\right)y_t$$

which is meaningful only for $|a_1| < 1$. If, however, y_t starts at $t = -1$, that is, if $y_t = 0$ for $t = -2, -3, \ldots, n$, we can rewrite the above formula as

$$x_{2,t} = \frac{1}{(1-a_1L)}y_t = \left(\sum_{j=0}^{t+1}(a_1L)^j\right)y_t$$

This latter formula, which is valid for any real value of a_1, yields

$$x_{2,0} = y_0 + a_1y_{-1}$$
$$x_{2,1} = y_1 + a_1y_0 + a_1^2y_{-1}$$
$$x_{2,t} = y_t + a_1y_{t-1} + \cdots + a_1^{t+1}y_{-1}$$

and so on. These formulas can be easily verified by direct substitution. If $y_t = y = $ constant, then

$$x_{2,t} = y(1 + a_1^2 + \cdots + a_1^{t+1})$$

Consider now the case of a second-order equation:

$$A(L)x_t = (1 - a_1L - a_2L^2)x_t = (1 - \lambda_1L)(1 - \lambda_2L)x_t = y_t$$

where λ_1, λ_2 are the solutions of the characteristic equation (the reciprocal of the solutions of the inverse characteristic equation). We can write the solution of the above equation as

$$x_{2,t} = \frac{1}{(1 - a_1L - a_2L^2)}y_t = \frac{1}{(1 - \lambda_1L)(1 - \lambda_2L)}y_t$$

Recall that, if $|\lambda_i| < 1$, $i = 1, 2$, we can write:

$$\frac{1}{(1 - \lambda_1L)(1 - \lambda_2L)} = \frac{1}{\lambda_1 - \lambda_2}\left(\frac{\lambda_1}{(1 - \lambda_1L)} - \frac{\lambda_2}{(1 - \lambda_2L)}\right)$$

$$= \frac{\lambda_1}{\lambda_1 - \lambda_2}\left(\sum_{j=0}^{\infty}(\lambda_1L)^j\right) - \frac{\lambda_2}{\lambda_1 - \lambda_2}\left(\sum_{j=0}^{\infty}(\lambda_2L)^j\right)$$

so that the solution can be written as

$$x_{2,t} = \frac{\lambda_1}{\lambda_1 - \lambda_2}\left(\sum_{j=0}^{\infty}(\lambda_1 L)^j\right)y_t - \frac{\lambda_2}{\lambda_1 - \lambda_2}\left(\sum_{j=0}^{\infty}(\lambda_2 L)^j\right)y_t$$

If the two solutions are coincident, reasoning as in the homogeneous case, we can establish that the general solutions can be written as follows:

$$x_{2,t} = \frac{1}{(1 - a_1 L)^2}y_t = \left(\sum_{j=0}^{\infty}(a_1 L)^j\right)y_t + t\left(\sum_{j=0}^{\infty}(a_1 L)^j\right)y_t$$

If y_t starts at $t = -2$, that is, if $y_t = 0$ for $t = -3, -4, \ldots, -n, \ldots$, we can rewrite the above formula respectively as

$$x_{2,t} = \frac{\lambda_1}{\lambda_1 - \lambda_2}\left(\sum_{j=0}^{t+2}(\lambda_1 L)^j\right)y_t - \frac{\lambda_2}{\lambda_1 - \lambda_2}\left(\sum_{j=0}^{t+2}(\lambda_2 L)^j\right)y_t$$

if the solutions are distinct, and as

$$x_{2,t} = \frac{1}{(1 - a_1 L)^2}y_t = \left(\sum_{j=0}^{t+2}(a_1 L)^j\right)y_t + t\left(\sum_{j=0}^{t+2}(a_1 L)^j\right)y_t$$

if the solutions are coincident. These formulas are valid for any real value of λ_1.

The above formulas can be generalized to cover the case of an n-th order difference equation. In the most general case of an n-th order difference equation, assuming that all roots are real, there will be $m < n$ distinct roots λ_i, $i = 1, 2, \ldots, m$, each of order $n_i \geq 1$,

$$\sum_{i=1}^{m} n_i = n$$

and the general solution of the process will be

$$x_{2,t} = \sum_{i=0}^{\infty}((\lambda_1 L)^i + i(\lambda_1 L)^i + \cdots + i^{n_1-1}(\lambda_1 L)^i + \cdots$$

$$+ (\lambda_m L)^i + i(\lambda_m L)^i + \cdots + i^{n_m-1}(\lambda_m L)^i)y_t$$

if $|\lambda_i| < 1$, $i = 1, 2, \ldots, m$, and

$$x_{2,t} = \sum_{i=0}^{t+m} ((\lambda_1 L)^i + i(\lambda_1 L)^i + \cdots + i^{n_1-1}(\lambda_1 L)^i + \cdots$$
$$+ (\lambda_m L)^i + i(\lambda_m L)^i + \cdots + i^{n_m-1}(\lambda_m L)^i)y_t$$

if y_t starts at $t = -n$, i.e., if $y_t = 0$ for $t = -(n + 1), -(n + 2), \ldots$ for any real value of the λ_i.

Therefore, if the roots are all real, the general solution of a difference equation is a sum of exponentials. Exhibit A.7 illustrates the case of the same difference equation as in Exhibit A.3 with the same initial conditions $x_1 = 1$, $x_2 = 1.5$ but with an exogenous forcing sinusoidal variable:

$$(1 - 1.7L + 0.72L^2)x_t = 0.1 \times \sin(0.4 \times t)$$

EXHIBIT A.7   Solutions of the Equation $(1 - 1.7L + 0.72L^2)x_t = 0.1 \times \sin(0.4 \times t)$ with Initial Conditions $x_1 = 1$, $x_2 = 1.5$

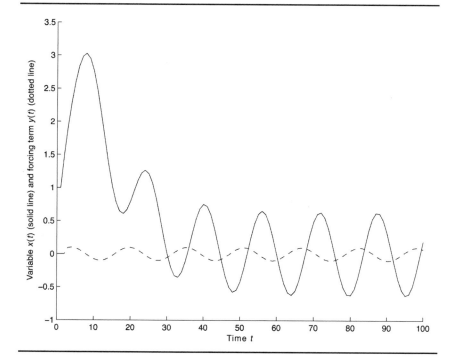

The solution of the equation is the sum of $x_{1,t} = -7.5(0.8)^t + 7.7778(0.9)^t$ plus

$$x_{2,t} = \sum [((0.8)^i + (0.9)^i)0.1 \times \sin(0.4 \times (t-i))]$$

After the initial phase dominated by the solution of the homogeneous equation, the forcing term dictates the shape of the solution.

Complex Roots

Consider now the case of complex roots. For simplicity, consider initially a second-order difference equation:

$$A(L)x_t = (1 - a_1 L - a_2 L^2)x_t = y_t$$

Suppose that its characteristic equation,

$$A(z) = z^2 - a_1 z - a_2 = 0$$

admits the two complex conjugate roots,

$$\lambda_1 = a + ib, \lambda_2 = a - ib$$

We write the two roots in polar notation:

$$\lambda_1 = re^{i\omega}, \lambda_2 = re^{-i\omega}$$

$$r = \sqrt{a^2 + b^2}, \omega = \arctan\frac{b}{a}$$

It can be demonstrated that the general form of the $x_{2,t}$ of the above difference equation has the following form:

$$x_{2,t} = \sum_{i=1}^{\infty} (r^i(\cos(\omega i) + \sin(\omega i))y_{t-i})$$

which is meaningful only if $|r| < 1$. If y_t starts at $t = -2$, that is, if $y_t = 0$ for $t = -3, -4, \ldots, -n, \ldots$ we can rewrite the previous formula as

$$x_{2,t} = \sum_{i=1}^{t+2} (r^i(\cos(\omega i) + \sin(\omega i))) y_{t-i}$$

This latter formula is meaningful for any real value of r. Note that the constant ω is determined by the structure of the model while the constants C_1, C_2 that appear in $x_{1,t}$ need to be determined in function of initial conditions. If the imaginary part of the roots vanishes, then ω vanishes and $a = r$, the two complex conjugate roots become a real root, and we again find the expression $x_t = Cr^t$.

Exhibit A.8 illustrates the case of the same difference equation as in Exhibit A.7 with the same initial conditions $x_1 = 1$, $x_2 = 1.5$ but with an exogenous forcing sinusoidal variable:

$$(1 - 1.2L + 1.0L^2)x_t = 0.5 \times \sin(0.4 \times t)$$

EXHIBIT A.8   Solutions of the Equation $(1 - 1.2L + 1.0L^2)x_t = 0.5 \times \sin(0.4 \times t)$ with Initial Conditions $x_1 = 1$, $x_2 = 1.5$

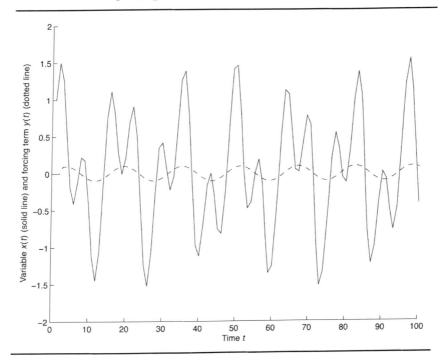

The solution of the equation is the sum of $x_{1,t} = -0.3\cos(0.9273t) + 1.475\sin(0.9273t)$ plus

$$x_{2,t} = \sum_{i=0}^{t-1} [(\cos(0.9273i) + \sin(0.9273i))0.5\sin(0.4 \times (t-i))]$$

After the initial phase dominated by the solution of the homogeneous equation, the forcing term dictates the shape of the solution. Note the model produces amplification and phase shift of the forcing term $0.1 \times \sin(0.4 \times t)$ represented by a dotted line.

SYSTEMS OF LINEAR DIFFERENCE EQUATIONS

In this section we discuss systems of linear difference equations of the type

$$x_{1,t} = a_{11}x_{1,t-1} + \cdots + a_{1k}x_{k,t-1} + y_{1,t}$$

$$x_{k,t} = a_{k1}x_{1,t-1} + \cdots + a_{kk}x_{k,t-1} + y_{k,t}$$

or in vector notation:

$$\mathbf{x}_t = \mathbf{A}\mathbf{x}_{t-1} + \mathbf{y}_t$$

Observe that we need to consider only first-order systems, that is, systems with only one lag. In fact, a system of an arbitrary order can be transformed into a first order system by adding one variable for each additional lag. For example, a second-order system of two difference equations,

$$x_{1,t} = a_{11}x_{1,t-1} + a_{12}x_{2,t-1} + b_{11}x_{1,t-2} + b_{12}x_{2,t-2} + y_{1,t}$$
$$x_{2,t} = a_{21}x_{1,t-1} + a_{22}x_{2,t-1} + b_{21}x_{1,t-2} + b_{22}x_{2,t-2} + y_{2,t}$$

can be transformed in a first order system adding two variables:

$$x_{1,t} = a_{11}x_{1,t-1} + a_{12}x_{2,t-1} + b_{11}x_{1,t-1} + b_{12}x_{2,t-1} + y_{1,t}$$
$$x_{2,t} = a_{21}x_{1,t-1} + a_{22}x_{2,t-1} + b_{21}x_{1,t-1} + b_{22}x_{2,t-1} + y_{2,t}$$
$$z_{1,t} = x_{1,t-1}$$
$$z_{2,t} = x_{2,t-1}$$

Transformations of this type can be generalized to systems of any order and any number of equations.

A system of difference equations is called *homogeneous* if the exogenous variable y_t is zero, that is, if it can be written as

$$x_t = Ax_{t-1}$$

while it is called nonhomogeneous if the exogenous term is present.

There are different ways to solve first-order systems of difference equations. One method consists in eliminating variables as in ordinary algebraic systems. In this way, the original first-order system in k equations is solved by solving a single difference equation of order k with the methods explained above. This observation implies that solutions of systems of linear difference equations are of the same nature as those of difference equations (i.e., that is sums of exponential and/or sinusoidal functions). In the following section we will show a direct method for solving systems of linear difference equations. This method could be used to solve equations of any order, as they are equivalent to first-order systems. In addition, it gives a better insight into vector autoregressive processes.

SYSTEMS OF HOMOGENEOUS LINEAR DIFFERENCE EQUATIONS

Consider a homogeneous system of the following type:

$$x(t) = Ax(t-1), t = 0, 1, ..., n, ...$$

where A is a $k \times k$, real-valued, nonsingular matrix of constant coefficients. Using the lag operator notation, we can also write the above systems in the following form:

$$(I - AL)x_t = 0, t = 1, ..., n, ...$$

If a vector of initial conditions $x(0)$ is given, the above system is called an *initial value problem*.

Through recursive computation, that is, starting at $t = 0$ and computing forward, we can write

$$x(1) = Ax(0)$$
$$x(2) = Ax(1) = A^2x(0)$$
$$x(t) = A^t x(0)$$

The following theorem can be demonstrated: any homogeneous system of the type $x(t) = Ax(t - 1)$, where A is a $k \times k$, real-valued, nonsingular matrix, coupled with given initial conditions $x(0)$ admits one and only one solution.

A set of k solutions $x_i(t)$, $i = 1, ..., k, t = 0, 1, 2, ...$ are said to be linearly independent if

$$\sum_{i=1}^{k} c_i x_i(t) = 0$$

$t = 0, 1, 2, ...$ implies $c_i = 0$, $i = 1, ..., k$. Suppose now that k linearly independent solutions $x_i(t)$, $i = 1, ..., k$ are given. Consider the matrix

$$\Phi(t) = \begin{bmatrix} x_1(t) & \cdots & x_k(t) \end{bmatrix}$$

The following matrix equation is clearly satisfied:

$$\Phi(t) = A\Phi(t-1)$$

The solutions $x_i(t)$, $i = 1, ..., n$ are linearly independent if and only if the matrix $\Phi(t)$ is nonsingular for every value $t \geq 0$, that is, if $\det[\Phi(t)] \neq 0$, $t = 0, 1, ...$ Any nonsingular matrix $\Phi(t)$, $t = 0, 1, ...$ such that the matrix equation

$$\Phi(t) = A\Phi(t-1)$$

is satisfied is called a *fundamental matrix* of the system $x(t) = Ax(t - 1)$, $t = 1, ..., n, ...$ and it satisfies the equation

$$\Phi(t) = A^t\Phi(0)$$

In order to compute an explicit solution of this system, we need an efficient algorithm to compute the matrix sequence A^t. We will discuss one algorithm for this computation.[1] Recall that an eigenvalue of the $k \times k$ real valued matrix $A = (a_{ij})$ is a real or complex number λ that satisfies the matrix equation:

$$(A - \lambda I)\xi = 0$$

---

[1] This discussion of systems of difference equations draws on Saber Elaydi, *An Introduction to Difference Equations* (New York: Springer Verlag, 2002).

where $\xi \in \mathbb{C}^k$ is a k-dimensional complex vector. The above equation has a non-zero solution if and only if

$$|(\mathbf{A} - \lambda\mathbf{I})| = 0$$

or

$$\det\begin{pmatrix} a_{11} - \lambda & \cdots & a_{1k} \\ \vdots & \ddots & \vdots \\ a_{k1} & \cdots & a_{kk} - \lambda \end{pmatrix} = 0$$

The above condition can be expressed by the following algebraic equation:

$$z^k + a_1 z^{k-1} + \cdots + a_{k-1} z + a_k$$

which is called the characteristic equation of the matrix $\mathbf{A} = (a_{ij})$.

To see the relationship of this equation with the characteristic equations of single equations, consider the k-order equation:

$$(1 - a_1 L - \cdots - a_k L^k)x(t) = 0$$
$$x_t = a_1 x(t-1) + \cdots + a_k x(t-k)$$

which is equivalent to the first-order system,

$$x_t = a_1 x_{t-1} + \cdots + a_k z_{t-1}^{k-1}$$
$$z_t^1 = x_{t-1}$$
$$\vdots$$
$$z_{t-1}^{k-1} = x_{t-k}$$

The matrix

$$\mathbf{A} = \begin{bmatrix} a_1 & a_2 & \cdots & a_{k-1} & a_k \\ 1 & 0 & \cdots & 0 & 0 \\ 0 & 1 & \cdots & 0 & 0 \\ \vdots & \vdots & \ddots & \vdots & \vdots \\ 0 & 0 & \cdots & 1 & 0 \end{bmatrix}$$

is called the *companion matrix*. By induction, it can be demonstrated that the characteristic equation of the system $x(t) = Ax(t-1)$, $t = 1, ..., n, ...$ and of the k-order equation above coincide.

Given a system $x(t) = Ax(t-1)$, $t = 1, ..., n, ...$, we now consider separately two cases: (1) All, possibly complex, eigenvalues of the real-valued matrix **A** are distinct, and (2) two or more eigenvalues coincide.

Recall that if λ is a complex eigenvalue with corresponding complex eigenvector ξ, the complex conjugate number $\bar{\lambda}$ is also an eigenvalue with corresponding complex eigenvector $\bar{\xi}$.

If the eigenvalues of the real-valued matrix **A** are all distinct, then the matrix can be diagonalized. This means that **A** is similar to a diagonal matrix, according to the matrix equation

$$A = \Xi \begin{bmatrix} \lambda_1 & \cdots & 0 \\ \vdots & \ddots & \vdots \\ 0 & \cdots & \lambda_n \end{bmatrix} \Xi^{-1}$$

$$\Xi = \begin{bmatrix} \xi_1 & \cdots & \xi_n \end{bmatrix}$$

and

$$A^t = \Xi \begin{bmatrix} \lambda_1^t & \cdots & 0 \\ \vdots & \ddots & \vdots \\ 0 & \cdots & \lambda_n^t \end{bmatrix} \Xi^{-1}$$

We can therefore write the general solution of the system $x(t) = Ax(t-1)$ as follows:

$$x(t) = c_1 \lambda_1^t \xi_1 + \cdots + c_n \lambda_1^n \xi_n$$

The c_i are complex numbers that need to be determined for the solutions to be real and to satisfy initial conditions. We therefore see the parallel between the solutions of first-order systems of difference equations and the solutions of k-order difference equations that we have determined above. In particular, if solutions are all real they exhibit exponential decay if their modulus is less than 1 or exponential growth if their modulus is greater than 1. If the solutions of the characteristic equation are real, they can produce oscillating damped or undamped behavior with period equal to two time steps. If the solutions of the characteristic equation are complex, then solutions might exhibit damped or undamped oscillating behavior with any period.

To illustrate the above, consider the following second-order system:

$$x_{1,t} = 0.6x_{1,t-1} - 0.1x_{2,t-1} - 0.7x_{1,t-2} + 0.15x_{2,t-2}$$
$$x_{2,t} = -0.12x_{1,t-1} + 0.7x_{2,t-1} + 0.22x_{1,t-2} - 0.85x_{2,t-2}$$

This system can be transformed in the following first-order system:

$$x_{1,t} = 0.6x_{1,t-1} - 0.1x_{2,t-1} - 0.7x_{1,t-2} + 0.15x_{2,t-2}$$
$$x_{2,t} = -0.12x_{1,t-1} + 0.7x_{2,t-1} + 0.22x_{1,t-2} - 0.85x_{2,t-2}$$
$$z_{1,t} = x_{1,t-1}$$
$$z_{2,t} = x_{2,t-1}$$

with matrix

$$\mathbf{A} = \begin{bmatrix} 0.6 & -0.1 & -0.7 & 0.15 \\ -0.12 & 0.7 & 0.22 & -0.8 \\ 1 & 0 & 0 & 0 \\ 0 & 1 & 0 & 0 \end{bmatrix}$$

The eigenvalues of the matrix $\mathbf{A}$ are distinct and complex:

$$\lambda_1 = 0.2654 + 0.7011i, \quad \lambda_2 = \overline{\lambda_1} = 0.2654 - 0.7011i$$

$$\lambda_3 = 0.3846 + 0.8887i, \quad \lambda_4 = \overline{\lambda_3} = 0.3846 - 0.8887i$$

The corresponding eigenvector matrix Ξ is

$$\Xi = \begin{bmatrix} 0.1571+0.4150i & 0.1571-0.4150i & -0.1311-0.3436i & -0.1311+0.3436i \\ 0.0924+0.3928i & 0.0924-0.3928i & 0.2346+0.5419i & 0.2346-0.5419i \\ 0.5920 & 0.5920 & -0.3794-0.0167i & -0.3794+0.0167i \\ 0.5337+0.0702i & 0.5337-0.0702i & 0.6098 & 0.6098 \end{bmatrix}$$

Each column of the matrix is an eigenvector.

The solution of the system is given by

$$\mathbf{x}(t) = c_1 \lambda_1^t \xi_1 + c_2 \overline{\lambda_1^t \xi_1} + c_3 \lambda_3^t \xi_3 + c_4 \overline{\lambda_3^t \xi_3}$$

$$= c_1(0.2654 + 0.7011i)^t \begin{pmatrix} 0.1571 + 0.4150i \\ 0.0924 + 0.3928i \\ 0.5920 \\ 0.5337 + 0.0702i \end{pmatrix} \xi_1$$

$$+ c_2(0.2654 - 0.7011i)^t \begin{pmatrix} 0.1571 - 0.4150i \\ 0.0924 - 0.3928i \\ 0.5920 \\ 0.5337 - 0.0702i \end{pmatrix}$$

$$+ c_3(0.3846 + 0.8887i)^t \begin{pmatrix} -0.1311 + 0.3436i \\ 0.2346 + 0.5419i \\ -0.3794 + 0.0167i \\ 0.6098 \end{pmatrix} \xi_3$$

$$+ c_4(0.3846 - 0.8887i)^t \begin{pmatrix} -0.1311 - 0.3436i \\ 0.2346 - 0.5419i \\ -0.3794 - 0.0167i \\ 0.6098 \end{pmatrix}$$

The four constants c can be determined using the initial conditions: $(1) = 1$; $x(2) = 1.2$; $y(1) = 1.5$; $y(2) = -2$. Exhibit A.9 illustrates the behavior of solutions.

Now consider the case in which two or more solutions of the characteristic equation are coincident. In this case, it can be demonstrated that the matrix $\mathbf{A}$ can be diagonalized only if it is normal, that is if

$$\mathbf{A}^T\mathbf{A} = \mathbf{A}\mathbf{A}^T$$

If the matrix $\mathbf{A}$ is not normal it cannot be diagonalized. However, it can be put in *Jordan canonical form*. In fact, it can be demonstrated that any nonsingular real-valued matrix $\mathbf{A}$ is similar to a matrix in Jordan canonical form,

$$\mathbf{A} = \mathbf{P}\mathbf{J}\mathbf{P}^{-1}$$

where the matrix $\mathbf{J}$ has the form $\mathbf{J} = \text{diag}[\mathbf{J}_1, \ldots, \mathbf{J}_k]$, that is, it is formed by *Jordan diagonal blocks*:

$$\mathbf{J} = \begin{bmatrix} \mathbf{J}_1 & \cdots & 0 \\ \vdots & \ddots & \vdots \\ 0 & \cdots & \mathbf{J}_k \end{bmatrix}$$

EXHIBIT A.9   Solution of the System

$$x_{1,t} = 0.6x_{1,t-1} - 0.1x_{2,t-1} - 0.7x_{1,t-2} + 0.15x_{2,t-2}$$

$$x_{2,t} = -0.12x_{1,t-1} + 0.7x_{2,t-1} + 0.22x_{1,t-2} - 0.85x_{2,t-2}$$

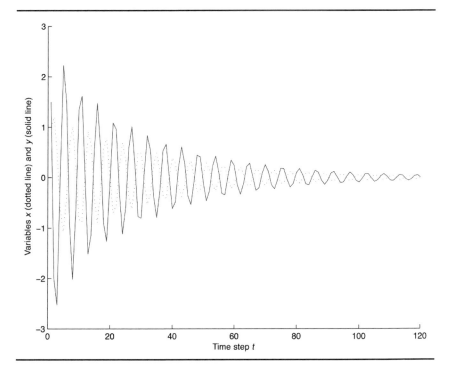

where each Jordan block has the form

$$J_i = \begin{bmatrix} \lambda_i & 1 & \cdots & 0 \\ 0 & \lambda_i & \cdots & \vdots \\ \vdots & \vdots & \ddots & 1 \\ 0 & 0 & \cdots & \lambda_i \end{bmatrix}$$

The Jordan canonical form is characterized by two sets of multiplicity parameters, the *algebraic multiplicity* and the *geometric multiplicity*. The geometric multiplicity of an eigenvalue is the number of Jordan blocks corresponding to that eigenvalue, while the algebraic multiplicity of an eigenvalue is the number of times the eigenvalue is repeated. An eigenvalue that is repeated s times can have from 1 to s Jordan blocks. For example, suppose a matrix has only one eigenvalue $\lambda = 5$ that is repeated three times. There are four possible matrices with the following Jordan representation:

$$\begin{pmatrix} 5 & 0 & 0 \\ 0 & 5 & 0 \\ 0 & 0 & 5 \end{pmatrix}, \begin{pmatrix} 5 & 1 & 0 \\ 0 & 5 & 0 \\ 0 & 0 & 5 \end{pmatrix}, \begin{pmatrix} 5 & 0 & 0 \\ 0 & 5 & 1 \\ 0 & 0 & 5 \end{pmatrix}, \begin{pmatrix} 5 & 1 & 0 \\ 0 & 5 & 1 \\ 0 & 0 & 5 \end{pmatrix}$$

These four matrices have all algebraic multiplicity 3 but geometric multiplicity from left to right 1, 2, 2, 3 respectively.

APPENDIX B

Correlations, Regressions, and Copulas

In this appendix we review three key statistical concepts: correlations, regressions, and copula functions. In our presentation, we assume that the reader is familiar with basic concepts of probability theory.

PROBABILITY DENSITY FUNCTION, MARGINAL DENSITY, AND CONDITIONAL DENSITY

Consider two random variables X_1, X_2 with a joint probability density $f(x_1, x_2)$. Then their marginal probability densities are given as follows:

$$f_{x_1}(x_1) = \int_{-\infty}^{+\infty} f(x_1, x_2)dx_2$$
$$f_{x_2}(x_2) = \int_{-\infty}^{+\infty} f(x_1, x_2)dx_1$$

In plain words, the marginal density of one variable is the density of that variable regardless of the value taken by the other value.

The term *marginal distribution* derives from the margin of tables that give the joint distribution of discrete variables, for example income and age group. Consider a table with 3×3 entries such that each entry of the table gives the percentage, which we can interpret as probability, of persons that have earnings in the Low, Medium, or High range and age in the Young, Mature, or Old range. In order to understand the distribution of income regardless of age or the distribution of age regard-

603

EXHIBIT B.1   Tables and Their Margins

	Low	Medium	High	Age Margin
Young	10	15	5	30
Mature	15	20	5	40
Old	10	15	5	30
Income margin	35	50	15	100

less of income, one creates "margins" with the sum over the age groups or the earnings groups, as illustrated in Exhibit B.1.

The concept of marginal density is not to be confused with the concept of conditional density. The latter is the density of one variable given that the other variable takes a definite value. The conditional density

$$f_{x_1|x_2}(x_1|x_2)$$

is the joint density scaled by the reciprocal of the marginal density:[1]

$$f_{x_1|x_2}(x_1|x_2) = \frac{f(x_1, x_2)}{f_{x_2}(x_2)}$$

$$f_{x_2|x_1}(x_2|x_1) = \frac{f(x_1, x_2)}{f_{x_1}(x_1)}$$

With reference to Exhibit B.1, the conditional density is represented by one row or one column of the table normalized so that probabilities sum to 1.

EXPECTATIONS AND CONDITIONAL EXPECTATIONS

We now define expected values and covariances. The expected value of each of the variables X_1, X_2 is defined as follows:

---

[1] A precise definition of conditional density and conditional expectation involves rather delicate reasoning on the probability space that supports probabilities. We 've not treated these rather complex concepts herein. The interested reader is re- ᵗ to Sergio M. Focardi and Frank J. Fabozzi, *The Mathematics of Financial* ⁰ *and Investment Management* (Hoboken, NJ: John Wiley & Sons, 2004) or ⁿced text on probability theory, for example, P. Billingsley, *Probability* ᵈ ed. (New York: John Wiley & Sons, 1995).

$$\mu_1 = E[X_1] = \int_{-\infty}^{+\infty} u f_{x_1}(u) du$$

$$\mu_2 = E[X_2] = \int_{-\infty}^{+\infty} u f_{x_2}(u) du$$

In the same way we can define an expected value for any function g of the random variables

$$\xi_1 = E[g(X_1)] = \int_{-\infty}^{+\infty} g(u) f_{x_1}(u) du$$

$$\xi_2 = E[g(X_2)] = \int_{-\infty}^{+\infty} g(u) f_{x_2}(u) du$$

Note that we can define the expected value of one variable. If we want to consider jointly the two variables X_1, X_2, we can define the expected value of a function of the two variables. For example, we can define the expected value of the product X_1, X_2 of the two variables as follows:

$$E[X_1 X_2] = \iint_{R^2} uv f(u, v) du dv$$

We can also define the expected value of the linear combination $\alpha X_1 + \beta X_2$ of the two variables, where α, β are constants, as follows:

$$E[\alpha X_1 + \beta X_2] = \iint_{R^2} (\alpha u + \beta v) f(u, v) du dv$$

$$= \iint_{R^2} \alpha u f(u, v) du dv + \iint_{R^2} \beta v f(u, v) du dv$$

$$= \int_{-\infty}^{+\infty} \alpha u \left[\int_{-\infty}^{+\infty} f(u, v) dv \right] du + \int_{-\infty}^{+\infty} \beta v \left[\int_{-\infty}^{+\infty} f(u, v) du \right] dv$$

$$= \int_{-\infty}^{+\infty} \alpha u f_{x_1}(u, v) du + \int_{-\infty}^{+\infty} \beta v f_{x_2}(u, v) dv$$

$$= \alpha E[X_1] + \beta E[X_1]$$

From the above formulas it is clear that the expectation operator is a linear operator as the expectation of a linear combination of variables is the linear combination of the expectations:

$$E[\alpha X_1 + \beta X_2] = \alpha E[X_1] + \beta E[X_2]$$

We can also define the key concept of conditional expectation as the expectation of the conditional density:

$$E[X_1|X_2 = z] = \int_{-\infty}^{+\infty} u f_{x_1|x_2}(u|z)du$$

$$E[X_2|X_1 = w] = \int_{-\infty}^{+\infty} u f_{x_2|x_1}(u|w)du$$

VARIANCES, COVARIANCES, AND CORRELATIONS

We define the variance of each of the two variables as follows:

$$\sigma_{x_1}^2 = E[(X_1 - \mu_1)^2] = \int_{-\infty}^{+\infty} (u - \mu_1)^2 f_{x_1}(u)du$$

$$\sigma_{x_2}^2 = E[(X_2 - \mu_2)^2] = \int_{-\infty}^{+\infty} (u - \mu_2)^2 f_{x_2}(u)du$$

The following relationships hold:

$$\sigma_{x_1}^2 = E[(X_1 - \mu_1)^2] = E[X_1^2] - \mu_1^2$$

$$\sigma_{x_2}^2 = E[(X_2 - \mu_2)^2] = E[X_2^2] - \mu_2^2$$

The standard deviation of a variable is the square root of the corresponding variance. We define the covariance between the two variables as

$$\sigma_{x_1 x_2} = E[(X_1 - \mu_1)(X_2 - \mu_2)] = \iint_{R^2} (u - \mu_1)(v - \mu_1) f(u, v) du dv$$

Clearly the following identity holds: $\sigma_{x_1 x_2} = \sigma_{x_2 x_1}$. Given two random variables X_1, X_2, the variance-covariance matrix is defined as the matrix whose entries are the variances and covariances between the two variables:

$$\Omega = \begin{pmatrix} \sigma_{x_1} & \sigma_{x_1 x_2} \\ \sigma_{x_2 x_1} & \sigma_{x_2} \end{pmatrix}$$

and covariances need not be finite. There are probability den-
ve infinite variance and/or infinite expected value.

We define the correlation coefficient ρ between two variables as the covariance normalized with the product of the standard deviations as follows:

$$\rho = \rho_{x_1 x_2} = \frac{\sigma_{x_1 x_2}}{\sigma_{x_1} \sigma_{x_2}}$$

The correlation matrix is defined as follows:

$$\Theta = \begin{pmatrix} 1 & \rho_{x_1 x_2} \\ \rho_{x_2 x_1} & 1 \end{pmatrix}$$

The correlation coefficient is a measure of the linear dependence between the two variables. It assumes values $-1 \le \rho \le 1$. Two independent variables have correlation coefficient $\rho = 0$, but the inverse is not true as two variables can have $\rho = 0$ but still exhibit nonlinear dependence. However, a correlation coefficient $|\rho| = 1$ entails deterministic proportionality between two variables $X_1 = aX_2 + b$. Deterministic proportionality should not be confused with linear regression, which will be defined next.

Note that the variances of independent or uncorrelated variables have the additive property but are not linear. For example, in the case of two variables, given the linearity of expectations, we can write

$$\sigma_{x_1 + x_2}^2 = E[(X_1 + X_2 - (\mu_1 + \mu_2))^2]$$
$$= E[(X_1 - \mu_1)^2] + E[(X_2 - \mu_2)^2] - 2E[(X_1 - \mu_1)(X_2 - \mu_2)]$$
$$= \sigma_{x_1}^2 + \sigma_{x_2}^2 - 2\sigma_{x_1 x_2}$$

However, the following relationship holds for any variable X with expected value μ and variance σ_x^2:

$$\sigma_{\alpha x}^2 = E[(\alpha X - \alpha \mu)^2] = \alpha^2 E[X^2] - \alpha^2 \mu^2$$

which shows that variance is not linear.

If the variables X_1, X_2 are independent, all the above relationships simplify. The joint density becomes the product of marginal densities

$$f(x_1, x_2) = f_{x_1}(x_1) f_{x_2}(x_2)$$

while the conditional densities do not depend on the conditioning variable and are equal to the marginal densities:

$$f_{x_1|x_2}(x_1|x_2) = \frac{f(x_1, x_2)}{f_{x_2}(x_2)} = \frac{f_{x_1}(x_1)f_{x_2}(x_2)}{f_{x_2}(x_2)} = f_{x_1}(x_1)$$

$$f_{x_2|x_1}(x_2|x_1) = \frac{f(x_1, x_2)}{f_{x_1}(x_1)} = \frac{f_{x_1}(x_1)f_{x_2}(x_2)}{f_{x_1}(x_1)} = f_{x_2}(x_2)$$

The above formulas entail that, if variables are independent, then conditional expectations equal unconditional expectations:

$$E[X_1|X_2 = z] = \int_{-\infty}^{+\infty} u f_{x_1|x_2}(u|z)du = \int_{-\infty}^{+\infty} u f_{x_1}(u)du = \mu_1$$

$$E[X_2|X_1 = w] = \int_{-\infty}^{+\infty} u f_{x_2|x_1}(u|w)du = \int_{-\infty}^{+\infty} u f_{x_2}(u)du = \mu_2$$

NORMAL DISTRIBUTIONS

We can explicitly compute the above formulas in the case of jointly normal variables. It is notationally convenient to arrange expectations and covariances in vector/matrix form as follows:

$$\mu = \begin{pmatrix} \mu_y \\ \mu_x \end{pmatrix}, \text{ the vector of means}$$

$$\Omega = \begin{pmatrix} \sigma_{xx} & \sigma_{xy} \\ \sigma_{yx} & \sigma_{yy} \end{pmatrix}, \sigma_{xy} = \sigma_{yx}, \text{ the covariance matrix of the distribution}$$

$$\rho = \frac{\sigma_{xy}}{\sigma_{xx}\sigma_{yy}}, \text{ the correlation coefficient between } X_1 \text{ and } X_2$$

The joint normal density of the two variables X_1, X_2, indicated as $N(\mu, \Omega)$, can be written as follows:

$$f(x_1, x_2) = \left[\frac{1}{2\pi\sigma_{x_1}\sigma_{x_2}\sqrt{1-\rho^2}}\right]$$

$$\exp\left\{-\frac{1}{2(1-\rho^2)}\left[\frac{(x_1-\mu_{X_1})^2}{\sigma_{x_2}^2} - 2\rho\frac{(x_1-\mu_{X_1})(x_2-\mu_{X_2})}{\sigma_{x_2}\sigma_{x_2}} + \frac{(x_2-\mu_{X_2})^2}{\sigma_{x_2}^2}\right]\right\}$$

while the two marginal distributions are simply $N(\mu_1, \sigma_{X_1})$ and $N(\mu_2, \sigma_{X_2})$ which can be written as follows:

$$N(\mu_1, \sigma_{X_1}) = f(x_1) = \left[\frac{1}{2\pi\sigma_{x_1}}\right]\exp\left\{-\left[\frac{(x_1-\mu_{X_1})^2}{\sigma_{x_1}^2}\right]\right\}$$

$$N(\mu_2, \sigma_{X_2}) = f(x_2) = \left[\frac{1}{2\pi\sigma_{x_2}}\right]\exp\left\{-\left[\frac{(x_1-\mu_{X_2})^2}{\sigma_{x_2}^2}\right]\right\}$$

The two conditional distributions can be written as follows:

$$f_{X_1|X_2}(X_1|X_2 = x_2) = \frac{1}{2\pi\sqrt{\sigma_{X_1}^2 - (\sigma_{X_1X_2})^2/\sigma_{X_2}^2}}$$

$$\exp\left\{-\frac{\left(X_1 - \mu_{X_1} - \dfrac{\sigma_{X_1X_2}}{\sigma_{X_2}^2}(\mu_{X_2} - x_2)\right)^2}{2\left(\sigma_{X_1}^2 - \dfrac{(\sigma_{X_1X_2})^2}{\sigma_{X_2}^2}\right)}\right\}$$

$$f_{X_1|X_2}(X_2|X_1 = x_1) = \cfrac{1}{2\pi\sqrt{\sigma_{X_2}^2 - (\sigma_{X_1X_2})^2/\sigma_{X_1}^2}}$$

$$\exp\left\{-\cfrac{\left(X_2 - \mu_{X_2} - \cfrac{\sigma_{X_1X_2}}{\sigma_{X_1}^2}(\mu_{X_1} - x_1)\right)^2}{2\left(\sigma_{X_2}^2 - \cfrac{(\sigma_{X_1X_2})^2}{\sigma_{X_1}^2}\right)}\right\}$$

It should be clear from the above formulas that uncorrelated normal distributions (i.e., bivariate normal distributions such that $\rho = 0$) are also independent. This is not true in the general case, as observed earlier.

REGRESSION

Given two random variables X_1, X_2 with a joint probability density $f(x_1, x_2)$, the regression functions are the deterministic functions $x_1 = \varphi(x_2)$ and $x_2 = \psi(x_1)$ defined, respectively, as the conditional expectation:

$$\varphi(z) = E[X_1|X_2 = z]$$
$$\psi(w) = E[X_2|X_1 = w]$$

Thus, the regression function is logically determined by the joint probability density function.

There are different classes of joint densities that result in linear regression functions. The best known (and perhaps the most important) of them is the normal joint density. Given a bivariate normal distribution $N(\mu, \Omega)$, its regression function is a linear function $y = ax + b$, which can be written as follows:

$$y \equiv E(X_1|X_2 = x) = \mu_{x_1} + \cfrac{\sigma_{x_1x_2}}{\sigma_{x_2}^2}(x - \mu_{x_2})$$

$$y = \frac{\sigma_{x_1 x_2}}{\sigma_{x_2}^2} x + \left(\mu_{x_1} - \frac{\sigma_{x_1 x_2}}{\sigma_{x_2}^2} \mu_{x_2} \right)$$

Regression equations are often written as a regression equation $y = ax + b + \varepsilon$ where ε is an error term. This relationship between random variables can be interpreted in different ways. One interpretation requires the variable x to be deterministic. For example, the variable x could represent time sampled at fixed intervals. In this case, the regression equation can be written as

$$Y = ax + b + \varepsilon$$

where Y is a random variable.

Suppose ε is a zero-mean, normally distributed variable with variance σ_ε. The random variable Y is then a family of normally distributed random variables parameterized with mean $ax + b$ and variance σ_ε, that is: $Y \sim N(ax + b, \sigma_\varepsilon)$. The relationship $E[Y|x] = ax + b$ holds. Strictly speaking, this relationship is not a regression function as defined above but defines the expectation of Y given a value of x as a parameter.

The regression equation can also be interpreted as a linear relationship between two random variables:

$$Y = aX + b + \varepsilon$$

This regression equation places restrictions on the joint density function $f(x, y)$ insofar as it is not compatible with an arbitrary joint density. If the variables X, Y are jointly normally distributed as $N(\boldsymbol{\mu}, \boldsymbol{\Omega})$, then the linear regression equation holds in the sense that:

- Y and X are both normally distributed.
- The following relationships must hold:

$$a = \frac{\sigma_{xy}}{\sigma_x^2}, \, b = \mu_y - \mu_x$$

- The error term is a zero-mean normal variable: $\varepsilon \sim N(0, \sigma_\varepsilon)$.
- The regression function is $y = E[Y|X = x] = ax + b$.

A linear regression equation $Y = aX + b + \varepsilon$ can hold even if the variables X, Y are not jointly normally distributed.

MULTIVARIATE EXTENSION

The above concepts and formulas can be extended in a generalized setting of N random variables $X_1, ..., X_N$, that is a random vector $\mathbf{X} = (X_1, ..., X_N)'$, with a joint probability density $f(x_1, ..., x_N)$. However, consider that there are many marginal distributions not only because there are N variables but also because any set of variables can be marginalized by integrating with respect to the other variables. Divide the variables $(X_1, ..., X_N)$ into two sets, formed by the variables that are marginalized. The variables in the first set are indexed as follows: $X_{i_1}, ..., X_{i_S}$ and the remaining variables are indexed as follows: $X_{j_1}, ..., X_{j_R}$. Clearly $S + R = N$ must hold. We can then define marginal distributions as

$$f_{x_{i_1}, ..., x_{i_S}}(x_{i_1}, ..., x_{i_S}) = \int f(x_1, ..., x_N)dx_{j_1}, ..., dx_{j_R}$$

where integration is extended to all variables $x_{j_1}, ..., x_{j_R}$. We can define conditional densities of one set of variables given the others as

$$f_{x_{i_1}, ..., x_{i_S}|(x_{j_1}, ..., x_{j_R})}(x_{i_1}, ..., x_{i_S}|x_{j_1}, ..., x_{j_R}) = \frac{f(x_1, ..., x_N)}{f_{x_{j_1}, ..., x_{j_R}}(x_{j_1}, ..., x_{j_R})}$$

Note that marginal distributions are functions of S variables, while conditional distributions are functions of N variables.

The vector of expected values $\boldsymbol{\mu} = (\mu_{x_1}, ..., \mu_{x_N})'$ is defined as

$$\mu_{x_i} = E[X_i] = \int_{-\infty}^{+\infty} u f_{x_i}(u)du$$

and the covariance matrix is defined as

$$\Omega = \begin{pmatrix} \sigma_{x_1} & \cdots & \sigma_{x_1 x_N} \\ \vdots & \ddots & \vdots \\ \sigma_{x_N x_1} & \cdots & \sigma_{x_N} \end{pmatrix}$$

where

$$\sigma_{x_i x_j} = E[(X_i - \mu_{x_i})(X_j - \mu_{x_j})]$$

$$= \iint_{R^2} (u - \mu_{x_i})(v - \mu_{x_j}) f_{x_i x_j}(u, v) du\, dv$$

Correlation coefficients are defined as

$$\rho_{x_i x_j} = \frac{\sigma_{x_i x_j}}{\sigma_{x_j} \sigma_{x_j}}$$

and the correlation matrix is defined as

$$\Theta = \begin{pmatrix} 1 & \cdots & \rho_{x_1 x_N} \\ \vdots & \ddots & \vdots \\ \rho_{x_N x_1} & \cdots & 1 \end{pmatrix}$$

Conditional expectations are defined as

$$E[X_i | X_1 = x_1, ..., X_{i=1} = x_{i-1}, X_{i+1} = x_{i+1}, ..., X_N = x_N]$$

$$= \int_{-\infty}^{+\infty} u f_{x_i | x_1, ..., x_{i-1}, x_{i+1}, ..., x_N}(u | x_1, ..., x_{i-1}, x_{i+1}, ..., x_N) du$$

Formulas for normal variables are conveniently expressed in matrix form. Consider a normally distributed random vector $\mathbf{X} \sim N(\boldsymbol{\mu}, \boldsymbol{\Omega})$, where $\boldsymbol{\mu}$ is the N-vector of expectations and $\boldsymbol{\Omega}$ is the $N \times N$ covariance matrix. The joint density of the elements of $\mathbf{X}$ is

$$f(\mathbf{x}) = [(2\pi)^N |\boldsymbol{\Omega}|]^{-1/2} \exp\left[-\frac{1}{2}(\mathbf{x} - \boldsymbol{\mu})' \boldsymbol{\Omega}^{-1}(\mathbf{x} - \boldsymbol{\mu})\right]$$

where $|\boldsymbol{\Omega}|$ is the determinant of the covariance matrix and $\mathbf{x} = (x_1, ..., x_N)'$ is a vector of real-valued variables.

MULTIPLE AND MULTIVARIATE REGRESSIONS

A multiple regression is a regression of one variable over a vector of regressors. The definition of multiple regression parallels that in the univariate case. Given a random vector $X = (X_1, \ldots, X_N)'$, with a joint probability density $f(x_1, \ldots, x_N)$, we define the regression functions as the conditional expectations of one variables given the other variables. Partition x, μ, and Ω conformably in the following way:

$$X = \begin{pmatrix} Y \\ Z \end{pmatrix}, \; x = \begin{pmatrix} y \\ z \end{pmatrix}, \; \mu = \begin{pmatrix} \mu_y \\ \mu_z \end{pmatrix}, \; \Omega = \begin{pmatrix} \sigma_{yy} & \sigma_{zy} \\ \sigma_{yz} & \Omega_{zz} \end{pmatrix}$$

It can be demonstrated that the conditional density $(Y|Z = z)$ has the following expression:

$$(Y|Z = z) \sim N(\alpha + \beta'z, \sigma)$$

where

$$\beta = \Omega_{zz}^{-1}\sigma_{zy}$$
$$\alpha = \mu_y - \beta'\mu_z$$
$$\sigma = \sigma_{yy} - \sigma_{yz}\Omega_{zz}^{-1}\sigma_{zy}$$

The regression function can be written as follows:

$$y = \alpha + \beta'z$$

A multivariate regression is a regression of a random vector over another random vector, in general of a different dimension. Given a random vector $X = (X_1, \ldots, X_N)'$, with a joint probability density $f(x_1, \ldots, x_N)$, partition X, x, μ, and Ω conformably in the following way:

$$X = \begin{pmatrix} Y \\ Z \end{pmatrix}, \; x = \begin{pmatrix} y \\ z \end{pmatrix}, \; \mu = \begin{pmatrix} \mu_y \\ \mu_z \end{pmatrix}, \; \Omega = \begin{pmatrix} \Omega_{yy} & \sigma_{yz} \\ \Omega_{yz} & \Omega_{zz} \end{pmatrix}$$

We define the regression functions as the conditional expectations of one random vector given the other vector. It can be demonstrated that the regression function is linear, but we omit the rather complex explicit expressions.

CANONICAL CORRELATIONS

The concept of canonical correlations plays an important role in dynamic models. The idea of canonical correlations is the following. Consider, as above, a random vector $X = (X_1, ..., X_N)'$, with a joint probability density $f(x_1, ..., x_N)$, partitioned in two random vectors,

$$X = \begin{pmatrix} Y \\ Z \end{pmatrix}$$

with size S, R respectively. As above, partition X, x, μ, and Ω conformably in the following way:

$$X = \begin{pmatrix} Y \\ Z \end{pmatrix}, \quad x = \begin{pmatrix} y \\ z \end{pmatrix}, \quad \mu = \begin{pmatrix} \mu_y \\ \mu_z \end{pmatrix}, \quad \Omega = \begin{pmatrix} \Omega_{yy} & \sigma_{yz} \\ \Omega_{yz} & \Omega_{zz} \end{pmatrix}$$

The concept of correlation that we defined so far applies only to pairs of random variables. However, we want to extend the notion of correlation to random vectors. Consider two vectors of constants:

$$\alpha = \begin{pmatrix} \alpha_1 \\ \vdots \\ \alpha_S \end{pmatrix}, \quad \beta = \begin{pmatrix} \beta_1 \\ \vdots \\ \beta_R \end{pmatrix}$$

The two scalar products αY, βZ define two random variables as they are two linear combinations of the elements of Y, Z. We want to determine the vectors α, β, which maximize the correlation between the variables αY, βZ, which are called *canonical variates*. The corresponding correlation coefficients are called *canonical correlations*. After determining the two vectors α_1, β_1 that yield two variables $\alpha_1 Y$, $\beta_1 Z$ with the maximum correlation, we can determine a new set of vectors α_2, β_2 that yield maximum correlations and that are orthogonal to α_1, β_1. We can continue in this way forming two matrices whose columns are vectors α, β that yield variates with the highest correlations and that are mutually orthogonal.

To better define this problem, we have to introduce appropriate normalizations. Suppose that we normalize requiring that the vectors α, β have unitary length. Suppose also that the vectors Y, Z have the same dimension, that is $S = R$. It can be demonstrated that the canonical correlations and the canonical variates are obtained by solving the following eigenvalue problems:

$$\Omega_{yy}^{-1}\Omega_{yz}\Omega_{zz}^{-1}\Omega_{zy}\alpha = \rho^2\alpha$$
$$\Omega_{zz}^{-1}\Omega_{zy}\Omega_{yy}^{-1}\Omega_{yz}\beta = \rho^2\beta$$

where the eigenvalues are the squares of the canonical correlation coefficients.

COPULA FUNCTIONS

Covariances and correlation coefficients are fundamental concepts for econometric models. In fact, the coefficients of linear models are generally correlations or covariances between random variables. The correlation coefficient is an exhaustive measure of linear dependence for normal variables. However, it fails to capture nonlinear dependence. Two variables might be linearly uncorrelated though they exhibit important non-linear correlations. This fact is particularly important for those variables that are not normally distributed.

Copula functions have been proposed to capture nonlinear dependence. The concept of a copula function is based on the Theorem of Sklar. Consider a random vector $X = (X_1, ..., X_N)'$, with a joint probability density $f(x_1, ..., x_N)$. The joint cumulative distribution function is defined as the integral of the density as follows:

$$F(x_1, ..., x_N) = \int_{-\infty}^{x_1} \cdots \int_{-\infty}^{x_N} f(u_1, ..., u_n) du_1 \cdots du_N$$

Marginal distribution functions are obtained as

$$F_{x_i}(x_i) = \int_{-\infty}^{+\infty} \int_{-\infty}^{x_i} \cdots \int_{-\infty}^{\infty} f(u_1, ..., u_i, ..., u_n) du_1, ..., du_i, ..., du_N$$

That is, integration limits are $(-\infty, +\infty)$ for all variables except the one that is marginalized.

The Theorem of Sklar states that given any cumulative distribution function $F(x_1, ..., x_N)$, there is a continuous function $C = C(u_1, ..., u_N)$ increasing in each variable that maps the N-dimensional cube $[0,1]^N \to [0,1]$ such that

$$F(x_1, ..., x_N) = C(F_{x_i}(x_i), ..., F_{x_i}(x_i))$$

The copula function expresses the functional link between the variables through a functional link between their distributions. It is able to capture nonlinear dependence and, in particular, dependence in the tail region for nonnormal variables. The N-dimensional copula of a N-dimensional Gaussian variable with correlation matrix R is written as follows:

$$C_R^N(u_1, ..., u_N) = \Phi_R(\Phi^{-1}(u_1), ..., \Phi^{-1}(u_N))$$

where Φ_R is the N-dimensional standard Gaussian cumulative distribution with correlation matrix R and Φ^{-1} are the univariate normal cumulative standard distributions. Normal standard distributions, univariate or multivariate, are zero-mean normal variables with unitary variance.

Capturing the eventually nonlinear dependence structure is important not only in risk management but also for mitigating model risk as outlined in Chapter 17.[2]

---

[2] For a general treatment of the dependence structure of time series, see Victor H. de la Peña, Rustam Ibragimov and Shaturgun Sharakhmetov, "Characterizations of Joint Distributions, Copulas, Information, Dependence and Decoupling, with Applications to Time Series," in J. Rojo (ed.), *Procedings of the Second Erich L. Lehmann Symposium—Optimality, IMS Lecture Notes—Monograph Series*, NSF-CBMS Regional Conference Series in Probability and Statistics (2005).

Data Description

In several chapters, we use the MSCI World Index and its individual constituents (developed market country indices) in some examples. In this appendix we provide some basic statistics and properties of this data set.

We obtained daily levels and returns of the MSCI World Index and all its constituents along with market capitalization weights over the period 1/1/1980 through 5/31/2004 directly from Morgan Stanley Capital International, Inc.[1] The levels and returns are given from the perspective of an investor in the United States.

The MSCI World Index is a free, float-adjusted market capitalization index that is designed to measure global developed market equity performance. As of December 2004, the MSCI World Index consisted of the following 23 constituents (developed market country indices): Australia, Austria, Belgium, Canada, Denmark, Finland, France, Germany, Greece, Hong Kong, Ireland, Italy, Japan, the Netherlands, New Zealand, Norway, Portugal, Singapore, Spain, Sweden, Switzerland, the United Kingdom, and the United States. Other constituents that were part of the index at some point throughout the time period January 1980 through May 2004 were Malaysia, Mexico, and South African Gold Mines.

The different constituents of the index as of January in the years 1985, 1995, and 2004 along with their market capitalization in billions of U.S. dollars and percentage weight, and their ranking (in terms of market capitalization) are displayed in Exhibit C.1. We observe that the relative rankings among the different countries have been relatively stable throughout time. Nevertheless, the total market capitalization of the MSCI World Index has grown from about $1.8 trillion as of January

---

[1] We would like to thank Morgan Stanley Capital International, Inc., http://www.msci.com, for providing us with the data set. In particular, we thank Nicholas G. Keyes for preparing and for answering all our questions in regards to the data set.

619

EXHIBIT C.1 Market Capitalization Weights of the MSCI World Index and its Constituents as of the First Business Day in January in the Years 1985, 1995, and 2004

	1985			1995			2004		
	$US (billion)	Percent	Rank	$US (billion)	Percent	Rank	$US (billion)	Percent	Rank
World	1,765.1	100.00%		7,650.8	100.00%		17,416.4	100.00%	
Australia	27.8	1.57%	6	125.1	1.63%	10	373.6	2.15%	9
Austria	0.8	0.05%	20	18.0	0.23%	20	16.0	0.09%	22
Belgium	7.6	0.43%	15	49.3	0.64%	16	77.5	0.45%	15
Canada	71.7	4.06%	4	171.1	2.24%	7	463.9	2.66%	7
Denmark	3.6	0.20%	17	35.3	0.46%	17	55.5	0.32%	17
Finland	26.7	0.35%	18	122.8	0.71%	13			
France	23.1	1.31%	9	265.6	3.47%	5	727.6	4.18%	4
Germany	49.1	2.78%	5	300.1	3.92%	4	530.8	3.05%	6
Greece							33.3	0.19%	20
Hong Kong	14.7	0.83%	12	136.5	1.78%	9	118.5	0.68%	14
Ireland	12.5	0.16%	23	54.1	0.31%	18			
Italy	15.1	0.85%	10	102.9	1.34%	12	285.3	1.64%	10
Japan	367.5	20.82%	2	2,145.7	28.04%	2	1,576.7	9.05%	3
Malaysia				105.6	1.38%	11			
Mexico	1.7	0.10%	19						
Netherlands	25.7	1.46%	8	167.9	2.19%	8	380.8	2.19%	8

EXHIBIT C.1 (Continued)

	1985			1995			2004		
	$US (billion)	Percent	Rank	$US (billion)	Percent	Rank	$US (billion)	Percent	Rank
New Zealand				17.3	0.23%	21	15.8	0.09%	23
Norway	2.7	0.15%	18	19.9	0.26%	19	35.7	0.20%	19
Portugal							26.5	0.15%	21
Singapore	14.7	0.84%	11	56.8	0.74%	15	60.4	0.35%	16
South African Gold Mines	12.4	0.70%	13	13.6	0.18%	22			
Spain	7.0	0.40%	16	74.3	0.97%	14	271.3	1.56%	11
Sweden	11.8	0.67%	14	76.1	1.00%	13	167.7	0.96%	12
Switzerland	26.4	1.49%	7	215.0	2.81%	6	545.0	3.13%	5
United Kingdom	131.2	7.43%	3	731.1	9.56%	3	1,906.4	10.95%	2
United States	950.4	53.85%	1	2,784.6	36.40%	1	9,571.3	54.96%	1

1985 to $17.4 trillion as of May 2004. Details about how the country indices are constructed are available in the *MSCI Standard Methodology Book*.[2]

In Exhibits C.2, C.3, and C.4 we display some basic statistical properties of the data set. For simplicity, as all of the constituents that were part of the index as of May 2004 also were part of the index in January 1988, we only display statistics calculated over this period. The statistics are calculated over the full period as well as over each half; the first half is January 1988 through December 1994, and the second half is January 1995 through May 2004.

EXHIBIT C.2 Statistics of Daily Returns over the Period January 1988 through May 2004

	Mean	Volatility	Sharpe Ratio	Rank	Skew	Kurtosis	Min	Max
World	6.4%	12.9%	0.49	6	−0.06	6.19	−5.1%	4.9%
Australia	7.3%	17.6%	0.42	15	−0.20	6.02	−8.5%	7.7%
Austria	7.7%	19.1%	0.41	17	−0.17	9.68	−12.6%	9.7%
Belgium	8.3%	18.1%	0.46	8	0.31	9.19	−8.6%	9.1%
Canada	7.2%	16.0%	0.45	9	−0.54	9.73	−9.3%	5.4%
Denmark	11.9%	18.1%	0.65	1	−0.25	6.16	−9.0%	7.0%
Finland	13.7%	33.2%	0.41	16	−0.14	9.76	−18.2%	17.3%
France	10.5%	19.9%	0.53	5	−0.13	5.89	−9.7%	7.6%
Germany	9.4%	22.5%	0.42	14	−0.29	7.87	−12.9%	7.3%
Greece	12.7%	29.9%	0.43	13	0.30	8.54	−11.1%	17.3%
Hong Kong	11.5%	26.3%	0.44	11	−0.47	20.42	−23.0%	17.4%
Ireland	8.7%	19.3%	0.45	10	−0.14	6.94	−7.5%	7.2%
Italy	6.4%	22.3%	0.29	21	−0.12	5.88	−10.5%	6.9%
Japan	1.1%	23.2%	0.05	24	0.41	7.41	−8.1%	13.1%
Netherlands	9.2%	18.7%	0.49	7	−0.14	7.20	−8.1%	6.8%
New Zealand	2.8%	22.1%	0.13	23	−0.14	10.16	−14.6%	11.7%
Norway	9.2%	21.3%	0.43	12	−0.26	8.23	−11.6%	10.3%
Portugal	2.8%	18.6%	0.15	22	−0.03	8.63	−9.6%	9.2%
Singapore	7.6%	21.0%	0.36	20	0.21	11.76	−10.2%	12.6%
Spain	8.4%	21.1%	0.40	19	−0.05	7.02	−10.6%	9.6%
Sweden	13.5%	25.0%	0.54	4	0.07	7.00	−9.3%	12.1%
Switzerland	11.6%	17.9%	0.65	2	−0.14	7.08	−9.0%	7.0%
United Kingdom	6.8%	16.9%	0.40	18	−0.04	5.52	−5.2%	7.5%
United States	10.1%	16.1%	0.62	3	−0.14	7.24	−6.7%	5.8%

Note: The columns Mean, Volatility, and Sharpe Ratio are the annualized mean returns, volatilities, and Sharpe ratios of each country index. Rank is the numerical rank based on each country's Sharpe ratio. Min and Max are the daily minimum and maximum returns, respectively. Skew and Kurtosis are calculated as the third and fourth normalized centered moments.

---

[2] *MSCI Standard Methodology Book*, Morgan Stanley Capital International Inc., May 11 version, 2004.

EXHIBIT C.3 Statistics of Daily Returns over the Period January 1988 through December 1994

	Mean	Volatility	Sharpe Ratio	Rank	Skew	Kurtosis	Min	Max
World	6.4%	11.1%	0.57	12	0.04	7.70	−5.1%	4.9%
Australia	9.0%	17.4%	0.51	14	−0.43	5.98	−8.5%	4.5%
Austria	11.2%	21.2%	0.53	13	−0.08	11.80	−12.6%	9.7%
Belgium	10.2%	15.8%	0.64	7	0.32	12.84	−8.6%	8.5%
Canada	2.7%	10.6%	0.25	19	−0.35	5.08	−3.8%	3.2%
Denmark	13.2%	17.4%	0.76	5	−0.28	7.97	−9.0%	7.0%
Finland	5.7%	21.7%	0.26	18	0.08	5.86	−7.9%	7.3%
France	11.4%	17.8%	0.64	8	−0.30	7.93	−9.7%	7.6%
Germany	12.1%	20.1%	0.61	10	−0.77	14.54	−12.9%	7.3%
Greece	15.7%	31.9%	0.49	16	0.51	10.29	−11.1%	17.3%
Hong Kong	20.3%	24.1%	0.84	3	−2.28	37.08	−23.0%	8.6%
Ireland	10.1%	19.8%	0.51	15	0.01	7.49	−7.5%	7.2%
Italy	3.0%	22.2%	0.14	21	−0.29	7.12	−10.5%	6.9%
Japan	4.3%	22.6%	0.19	20	0.47	8.53	−8.1%	11.4%
Netherlands	11.7%	13.6%	0.87	2	−0.46	6.11	−6.4%	3.4%
New Zealand	2.2%	22.7%	0.10	22	0.02	7.83	−10.0%	8.4%
Norway	13.1%	22.4%	0.59	11	−0.15	9.09	−11.6%	10.3%
Portugal	−3.1%	19.3%	−0.16	24	0.06	12.10	−9.6%	9.2%
Singapore	18.8%	16.2%	1.16	1	−0.52	11.49	−9.1%	5.5%
Spain	1.2%	19.1%	0.06	23	−0.20	11.16	−10.6%	9.6%
Sweden	13.2%	21.0%	0.63	9	0.05	7.59	−9.3%	8.3%
Switzerland	13.4%	17.0%	0.79	4	−0.41	8.47	−9.0%	6.5%
United Kingdom	6.8%	16.1%	0.42	17	0.09	6.13	−5.2%	7.5%
United States	9.0%	12.6%	0.71	6	−0.55	9.30	−6.5%	3.8%

Note: The columns Mean, Volatility, and Sharpe Ratio are the annualized mean returns, volatilities, and Sharpe ratios of each country index. Rank is the numerical rank based on each country's Sharpe ratio. Min and Max are the daily minimum and maximum returns, respectively. Skew and Kurtosis are calculated as the third and fourth normalized centered moments.

We report the mean returns, return volatilities, and Sharpe ratios in annual terms. The minimum return (Min) and the maximum return (Max) are all in daily terms. The skew and kurtosis are calculated as the third and fourth normalized centered moments. The definition of the Sharpe ratio used in this book is the annualized mean return divided by the annualized volatility for the period under consideration.

We observe that the performance of the MSCI World Index as well as for most of its constituents was very good over the period considered. The average annual mean return for the index over the full period was 6.4% with an annual volatility of 12.9%. The average mean return in the first

EXHIBIT C.4   Statistics of Daily Returns over the Period January 1995 through May 2004

	Mean	Volatility	Sharpe Ratio	Rank	Skew	Kurtosis	Min	Max
World	6.3%	14.0%	0.45	9	−0.09	5.39	−4.4%	4.7%
Australia	6.1%	17.7%	0.35	16	−0.03	6.05	−6.8%	7.7%
Austria	5.2%	17.3%	0.30	20	−0.29	5.11	−6.1%	4.0%
Belgium	6.9%	19.7%	0.35	15	0.30	7.57	−6.2%	9.1%
Canada	10.6%	19.0%	0.56	4	−0.54	8.11	−9.3%	5.4%
Denmark	10.9%	18.7%	0.58	3	−0.22	5.10	−6.1%	5.7%
Finland	19.7%	39.7%	0.50	7	−0.17	7.99	−18.2%	17.3%
France	9.8%	21.3%	0.46	8	−0.06	4.93	−6.1%	6.1%
Germany	7.4%	24.1%	0.31	18	−0.08	5.18	−7.5%	7.1%
Greece	10.5%	28.2%	0.37	14	0.07	6.11	−9.4%	8.8%
Hong Kong	4.9%	27.8%	0.18	21	0.42	13.03	−12.9%	17.4%
Ireland	7.6%	19.0%	0.40	11	−0.28	6.44	−7.5%	6.1%
Italy	8.9%	22.3%	0.40	10	0.01	4.97	−6.9%	6.9%
Japan	−1.3%	23.7%	−0.06	24	0.38	6.70	−6.9%	13.1%
Netherlands	7.2%	21.7%	0.33	17	−0.06	6.18	−8.1%	6.8%
New Zealand	3.2%	21.7%	0.15	22	−0.28	12.18	−14.6%	11.7%
Norway	6.3%	20.5%	0.31	19	−0.37	7.20	−9.0%	7.5%
Portugal	7.1%	18.1%	0.39	12	−0.10	5.23	−6.3%	5.2%
Singapore	−0.7%	24.0%	−0.03	23	0.41	10.40	−10.2%	12.6%
Spain	13.7%	22.5%	0.61	1	0.01	5.18	−6.2%	7.3%
Sweden	13.7%	27.6%	0.50	6	0.07	6.32	−9.2%	12.1%
Switzerland	10.2%	18.5%	0.55	5	0.02	6.29	−6.9%	7.0%
United Kingdom	6.8%	17.5%	0.39	13	−0.11	5.15	−5.1%	5.4%
United States	10.8%	18.3%	0.59	2	−0.03	6.05	−6.7%	5.8%

Note: The columns Mean, Volatility, and Sharpe Ratio are the annualized mean returns, volatilities, and Sharpe ratios of each country index. Rank is the numerical rank based on each country's Sharpe ratio. Min and Max are the daily minimum and maximum returns, respectively. Skew and Kurtosis are calculated as the third and fourth normalized centered moments.

and the second halves were virtually the same (6.4% versus 6.3%), but the volatility increased from 11.1% to 14.0%. The individual country returns over the full sample range from 1.1% (Japan) to 13.7% (Finland), whereas volatilities range from 16.0% (Canada) to 33.2% (Finland).

If we rank the performance of individual countries in terms of their Sharpe ratio, Denmark and Switzerland (both with 0.65) come out ahead followed by the United States (0.62). Interestingly enough, comparing the rankings between the two periods based on the Sharpe ratio, we see that there is virtually no persistence at all. Indeed, the Spearman rank correlation coefficient (the correlation between the rankings of the two periods) is −0.07.

EXHIBIT C.5 One-Year Rolling Volatility (Standard Deviation) of the MSCI World Index, Singapore, Spain, Sweden, Switzerland, United Kingdom, and the United States

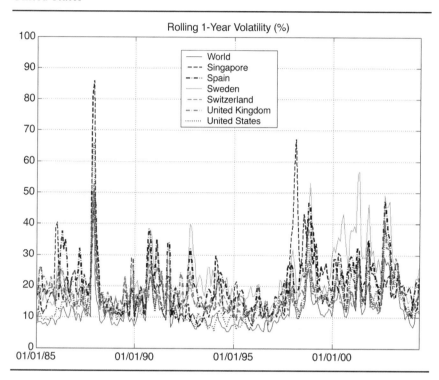

There is significant time-variation in volatilities. Exhibit C.5 demonstrates this fact for some of the countries in the sample, showing the one-year rolling standard deviation for the MSCI World Index, Singapore, Spain, Sweden, Switzerland, the United Kingdom, and the United States.

The correlation matrix for the full period is given in Exhibit C.6. Correlations between the different countries range from 0.01 (United States and Italy) to 0.76 (Canada and the Netherlands). We would therefore expect there to be some benefits of diversification.

Also the correlations exhibit time-variation. For example, in Exhibit C.7 the two year rolling correlations of United States with Germany, Hong Kong, Italy, Japan, and the Netherlands are depicted. Note that while some correlations have increased (United States versus Germany) others have decreased (United States versus Hong Kong). In fact, a further analysis of this data set shows that the correlations between the different countries have actually *decreased* over time whereas the volatilities have *increased*. This result is consistent with several academic

EXHIBIT C.6 Correlation Matrix of the MSCI World Index and the Individual Constituents over the Period 1/5/1988 through 5/31/2004

	1	2	3	4	5	6	7	8	9	10	11	12	13	14	15	16	17	18	19	20	21	22	23	24
1 World	1.00																							
2 Australia	0.29	1.00																						
3 Austria	0.34	0.24	1.00																					
4 Belgium	0.53	0.24	0.48	1.00																				
5 Canada	0.61	0.20	0.14	0.25	1.00																			
6 Denmark	0.41	0.24	0.45	0.53	0.21	1.00																		
7 Finland	0.46	0.22	0.26	0.37	0.33	0.38	1.00																	
8 France	0.65	0.23	0.41	0.62	0.38	0.50	0.51	1.00																
9 Germany	0.65	0.26	0.49	0.63	0.38	0.53	0.48	0.71	1.00															
10 Greece	0.24	0.16	0.28	0.30	0.12	0.29	0.20	0.27	0.29	1.00														
11 Hong Kong	0.31	0.37	0.21	0.18	0.18	0.21	0.24	0.23	0.26	0.15	1.00													
12 Ireland	0.42	0.30	0.42	0.48	0.20	0.46	0.33	0.48	0.49	0.31	0.23	1.00												
13 Italy	0.50	0.22	0.37	0.50	0.28	0.44	0.40	0.60	0.56	0.22	0.19	0.39	1.00											
14 Japan	0.53	0.31	0.26	0.25	0.15	0.23	0.19	0.23	0.23	0.19	0.29	0.26	0.19	1.00										
15 Netherlands	0.64	0.26	0.40	0.65	0.37	0.50	0.50	0.76	0.71	0.26	0.25	0.49	0.56	0.23	1.00									
16 New Zealand	0.19	0.51	0.22	0.18	0.10	0.17	0.16	0.16	0.20	0.14	0.25	0.23	0.16	0.22	0.19	1.00								
17 Norway	0.42	0.31	0.40	0.42	0.25	0.47	0.37	0.48	0.48	0.26	0.25	0.43	0.38	0.24	0.51	0.22	1.00							
18 Portugal	0.37	0.21	0.41	0.47	0.20	0.45	0.34	0.45	0.47	0.30	0.17	0.40	0.39	0.22	0.43	0.18	0.36	1.00						
19 Singapore	0.34	0.36	0.24	0.23	0.18	0.23	0.24	0.25	0.27	0.20	0.54	0.26	0.21	0.35	0.26	0.28	0.29	0.20	1.00					
20 Spain	0.59	0.25	0.43	0.57	0.34	0.49	0.45	0.71	0.64	0.28	0.23	0.44	0.60	0.24	0.65	0.18	0.45	0.48	0.26	1.00				
21 Sweden	0.57	0.29	0.35	0.47	0.36	0.47	0.61	0.63	0.59	0.25	0.27	0.42	0.51	0.26	0.59	0.20	0.49	0.40	0.30	0.58	1.00			
22 Switzerland	0.58	0.24	0.46	0.63	0.29	0.52	0.41	0.68	0.68	0.30	0.21	0.49	0.53	0.25	0.70	0.17	0.48	0.46	0.24	0.62	0.55	1.00		
23 United Kingdom	0.64	0.24	0.34	0.51	0.36	0.43	0.44	0.68	0.58	0.21	0.24	0.50	0.50	0.24	0.70	0.16	0.43	0.36	0.25	0.57	0.54	0.60	1.00	
24 United States	0.78	0.06	0.08	0.24	0.62	0.14	0.24	0.34	0.35	0.07	0.11	0.14	0.24	0.08	0.33	0.01	0.17	0.12	0.13	0.30	0.29	0.26	0.34	1.00

EXHIBIT C.7 Two-Year Rolling Correlations of United States with Germany, Hong Kong, Italy, Japan, and the Netherlands

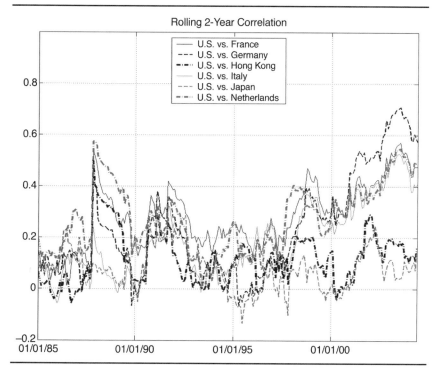

studies.[3] If we perform a decomposition of the correlation throughout the sample, we find that about half the benefits of diversification available today to the international investor are due to the increasing number of available markets, and the other half is due to the lower average correlation among the different markets.

In some examples in this book we use 1-month LIBOR.[4] LIBOR, which stands for the London Interbank Offered Rate, is one of the most widely used benchmarks for short-term interest rates. It is the variable interest rate at which banks can borrow funds from each other in the London interbank market. The 1-month LIBOR is depicted in Exhibit C.8.

---

[3] See, for example, Richard O. Michaud, Gary L. Bergstrom, Ronald D. Frashure, and Brian K. Wolahan, "Twenty Years of International Equity Investing," *Journal of Portfolio Management* 23 (Fall 1996), pp. 9–22; and William N. Goetzmann, Lingfeng Li, and K. Geert Rouwenhorst, "Long-Term Global Market Correlations," Yale ICF Working Paper No. 00-60, Yale International Center for Finance (2002).
[4] British Bankers' Association, http://www.bba.org.uk/bba/jsp/polopoly.jsp?d=103.

EXHIBIT C.8   One-Month LIBOR

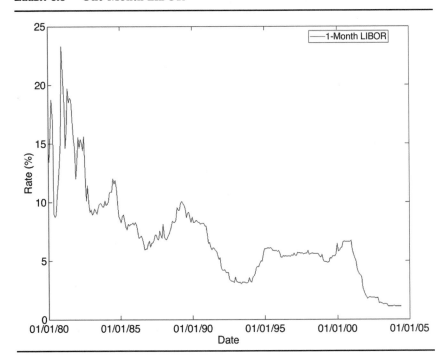

Index